THE ENGLISH
EXPERIENCE

C000132732

PHOENIX
PRESS

HISTORY OF CIVILIZATION

For more than thirty years this distinguished series has provided the general reader with a comprehensive picture of the world's greatest civilizations. The series is free from commitment to any single interpretation of history, and seeks to go beyond the standard works of reference. It presents individual and original evocations, by leading scholars in many countries, of the culture and development of a nation, groups of nations or period of history.

The following books in the series
are all available in Phoenix Press editions:

The Japanese Experience, *W.G. Beasley*
The English Experience, *John Bowle*
The Greek Experience, *C.M. Bowra*
The Chinese Experience, *Raymond Dawson*
The Celtic Realms, *Myles Dillon and Nora Chadwick*
The Golden Age of Persia, *Richard Frye*
The World of Rome, *Michael Grant*
The Climax of Rome, *Michael Grant*
The Medieval World, *Friedrich Heer*
The Age of Revolution 1789–1848, *Eric Hobsbawm*
The Age of Capital 1848–1875, *Eric Hobsbawm*
The Age of Empire 1875–1914, *Eric Hobsbawm*
Ancient American Civilisations, *Freidrich Katz*
The Middle East, *Bernard Lewis*
Byzantium, *Cyril Mango*
Eternal Egypt, *Pierre Montet*
The World of the Phoenicians, *Sabatino Moscati*
The Byzantine Commonwealth, *Dimitri Obolensky*
The African Experience *Roland Oliver*
The Decline of Rome, *Joseph Vogt*

John Bowle taught at Westminster and Eton, and during the Second World War worked in the Air Ministry and the Foreign Office. He taught at many universities around the world, including Wadham College, Oxford; the College of Europe, Bruges and Columbia University, New York.

ALSO BY JOHN BOWLE

Western Political Thought
The Unity of European History
Hobbes and his Critics
Politics and Opinion in the Nineteenth Century
Viscount Samuel
Man Through the Ages
Henry VIII
England, A Portrait
The Concise Encyclopedia of World History (*Editor*)

THE ENGLISH EXPERIENCE

A Survey of English History From
Early Times to the End of Empire

John Bowle

PHOENIX
PRESS

5 UPPER SAINT MARTIN'S LANE
LONDON
WC2H 9EA

A PHOENIX PRESS PAPERBACK

First published in Great Britain
by Weidenfeld & Nicolson in 1971
This paperback edition published in 2000
by Phoenix Press,
a division of The Orion Publishing Group Ltd,
Orion House, 5 Upper St Martin's Lane,
London WC2H 9EA

A CIP catalogue record for this book
is available from the British Library.

Printed and bound in Great Britain by
Clays Ltd, St Ives plc

ISBN 1 84212 013 1

CONTENTS

PREFACE

When narrative history is out of fashion and the analysis of topics preferred, a survey of the entire range of English history may appear unconventional. Yet without a synoptic view it is impossible even for specialists, let alone the ordinary reader, to get a general grasp. We are left with the traditional Whig–Liberal interpretation so attractively expressed by historians from Macaulay to G. M. Trevelyan. It may well be time, therefore, to consider whether the fragmentation following the detailed revision of the old orthodoxy and the shift away from constitutional and political to social and economic themes made during the last two generations, must permanently hold the field; or whether some new and unifying theme may not emerge from the impressive results of so much research.

Inspired by the idea of progress, older historians glorified the rise of English liberties and the prosperity, expansion, and world influence which reached its climax in Victorian times. Indeed, they regarded the two as inseparable. Today the scene has darkened; the loss of Empire, a precarious economy, and disillusionment with the Welfare State have brought in a less hopeful view; we have learnt not to expect too much from politics and to consider the past in a more sober light. But I submit that we can at least discern one realistic and constant theme: that the undoubted historical success of England, so remarkable in relation to its size, has been a triumph not of any commitment to abstract political principles but rather to the absence of it; to a tradition of pragmatism both in the theory and conduct of affairs. It has been a pragmatism maintained through the centuries within a relatively fluid and adaptable social order, which has at each critical juncture enabled a new élite to emerge, unhampered either by the high-minded principles of enlightened despotism or the centralizing doctrines of theoretically inspired revolution. Hence, in spite of a naturally turbulent background, an essential stability and continuity, even beneath political violence and crime.

Such is one main theme of this book: the piecemeal success of a realistic establishment, free from ideological preoccupations, adapting instead of destroying time-honoured institutions, exploiting the advantages to hand and assimilating new men as they achieved representative power. Here perhaps is the reason for the success of a social order which has enabled them to emerge, often in one generation, from provincial obscurity to the leadership of the state, and thus to respond to the pressures created by economic and social change; so showing itself capable of continuous adaptation without violent extremes. Compared with the majestic vision of freedom broadening down and a self-governing people of sturdy individualists making the best of themselves, this prospect may appear banal. The competition for power and afflu-ence, however veneered with the ornaments of title and place, is not a particularly inspiring spectacle; but politics is, after all, not the most enobling aspect of life. The most that can be hoped of political systems is that they are less bad than others in that they prevent the grosser and more direct abuse of power, maintain the rule of law, and provide an administrative framework in which the natural, and more important, variety and vitality of civilization can have their heads.

Such a view of the political facts does not make history less fascinating. It merely puts political life in its place, and allows historians to take account of more creative things: the elaboration of learning, philosophic speculation, religion, social life, science, the arts and literature. Al-though, therefore, it is impossible to understand these aspects of society without the political and administrative framework, I have in general confined the political narrative – and narrative there must be, for it is impossible to know why people did things unless one knows what they did – to essential political events, sometimes viewed in distant perspec-tive, sometimes in close-up. Within a limited space I have also given as full a treatment as practicable to some of the personalities concerned. History is, after all, about people, not abstractions or even things: and I have tried, when the evidence in distant times is limited and contradictory, to bring these people alive and combine a wide sweep with sufficient detail to make the narrative human. In a broad survey, only essentials can be included: but often these essentials are intimate and personal; for, as men of affairs understand and some historians do not, the chances of personality constantly swayed events. In this context I have included many of the famous tales of English history when authentic, and when they have been disproved by modern research, relegated them sympathetically to their proper Valhalla to which they ought now to be confined, though they are still widely believed. The woad-painted Druids who 'built' Stonehenge; probably King Arthur; certainly Alfred and the cakes and Canute and the waves; the political incompetence of Edward the Confessor; Simon de Mont-fort as a fore-runner of democratic parliamentary government; 'corruption' by eighteenth-century ministers by systematic malversation of public funds; the 'tyranny' of a psychopathic George III – all have to go. On the other hand, it has been possible to keep Clarence drowned in a butt of Malmesey wine – or perhaps stifled in a bath; the force and terror of Henry VIII; the great personal ability and magnetism of

Elizabeth 1; James 1 in person sensing the danger of the gunpowder plot; the incredible escape of Charles 11 after Worcester. And all too many of the horrors of medieval history as recorded in the Chronicles are naturally still thought authentic.

In traversing this immense span of time, I have often felt overwhelmed by the richness of the material, by the tantalizing glimpses of topics which have not been followed up; by the fame of the great episodes here so summarily recorded. These events were decisive not only for England but for the English-speaking world, and far too momentous and dramatic to be handed over to sociologists and economists to analyse into dust. It is highly desirable that our understanding of the past should be deepened and widened by elaborate research, particularly in local and economic history; but a specialized fragmentation of the general picture could deprive the past of the reality needed to give perspective and balance to the judgement of current affairs, and impair that sense of the emerging character of England and Great Britain which I have attempted to evoke in these pages, and which is bound to affect the future, however unexpected and strange.

I wish to thank many friends for their help in the writing of this book: particularly Dr Glyn Daniel for reading my chapter on pre-history; Mr J. Q. Davies of H. M. Diplomatic Service for collaboration in the general design and over problems of economic history; Mr Maurice Keen and the Rev. Gervase Mathew for advice on medieval times; Mr Keith Thomas for his counsel on the Tudor and Stuart periods, and Mr Felix Markham for reading my chapter on the Revolutionary and Napoleonic Wars. I am particularly grateful to Mr E. T. Williams, Warden of Rhodes House, who has kindly read the proof.

Mr G. A. Webb of the Codrington library at All Souls and Mr E. V. Quinn, have put their wide knowledge at my disposal, and Mrs Gillian Hughes has taken much trouble in seeing the book through the press. Mrs Barbara Phillips, with her extensive experience of the author's handwriting, has typed the script with her usual alacrity and good sense.

Oxford 1971   *John Bowle*

To John and Penelope Betjeman

PART ONE

THE FOUNDATIONS

PREHISTORIC BRITAIN

In prehistoric times the land that would become Great Britain was part of the Eurasian continent; and even when about 18,000 years ago the Palaeolithic artists of Lascaux near the Vézère in Dordogne were making masterpieces, the country was still not an island. During the vast span of the Ice Ages, with their warm interglacials, sub-arctic conditions alternated slowly with sub-tropical; but this enormous duration of time was of importance only for the physical setting of British history. Earlier still, the decay of sub-tropical forests had laid down the coal seams which would give the British industrial supremacy in the nineteenth century; the expansion and recession of the heavy ice ground out the gravels and boulder clays; and the ebb and flow of the sea created the chalk downs on which flourished the vast flocks of sheep whose wool was England's main export before the development of great industry. And through cumulative geological events the whole area tilted very gradually away from the old rocks of the western moors and mountains across to the downs of the middle west and the south, and so to the East Anglian lowlands, akin to their opposite shores in Denmark and the Netherlands, setting a contrast in environment which would be decisive.

These regions were sparsely inhabited. Swanscombe woman, for example, who lived during a sub-tropical phase of the Lower Palaeolithic in the Thames Valley well over 150,000 years ago, came of that Pithecanthropic-Neanderthaloid stock out of which the specialized Neanderthalers emerged; to be followed, about 40,000 B C, by true men. There were Neanderthalers in Kent's Cavern at Torquay, but the cavemen of the Mendips and of Paviland in Gower were fully human. By 20,000 B C, in the last period of the glaciation, there were Palaeolithic hunters in the Peak District; but their hard world was peripheral to the main area of prehistory in the south: it was snow-and-ice-bound, at best tundra well stocked with game. These hunters, like sub-arctic peoples today, would have lived mainly off reindeer, and they may have been physically akin to their fast-moving contemporaries in the Sahara who lived nearer the original centres of human expansion as recorded in rock-paintings. When, therefore, about 9500 B C, with the slow and tentative experiments in agriculture in the Near East, mankind settled and began to know time in the villages from which the great riparian civilizations of Iraq and Egypt would derive, this far western area was still inhabited by a handful of savages. They had fire and they had flint; but they were still parasitic on the other animals.

About 3000 years later they had become insular: by 6500 BC, 'sudden as the thawing of a frozen pond',[1] came the last recession of the ice and, with the melting of the ice cap perhaps along with a subsidence of the land, the sea flooded into the lowlands between eastern Britain, Scandinavia and the Low Countries, and cut off Ireland in the west. The climate became milder and even wetter than it is today and the vegetation changed. Over ice-fields and tundra, comparable to the Canadian and Siberian north, spread birch and willow; then pine forests. The Palaeolithic men no longer haunted the ice-floes and tundra but became Mesolithic forest hunters like the northern Amerindians, with an environment which was less specialized and more rewarding. At Star Carr in Yorkshire, remnants of canoes and paddles, bows and axes, have survived.

The country lay too far to the north for powerful sunshine; but the Gulf Stream coming from the Caribbean made the climate much milder than that of comparable latitudes in North America or the interior of the continent. The island being canted over to the north-west, the farther north it extended the more it met the warm water; western Scotland is warmer, if wetter, than East Anglia.

So the open tundra, in winter frozen stiff, receded and the forest took root; the glitter of glaciers and ice-fields, the sheen of sun on snow, the air that, as in North America, caught men's breath, gave place to drenched or fog-bound pine forest and to the soft 'bright intervals' which still redeem the climate as the clouds pile up over the Atlantic to sweep over Britain. The crackle of ice and the squelch of thawing bog gave place to the shift of pine needles underfoot and to shafts of sunshine through timber.

The Mesolithic forest peoples hunted deer and wild pig as well as smaller game. They could fell timber and gather sea-food; and if in winter only the blazing logs still enabled them to survive, during the summers the climate grew milder, to reach, in the Bronze Age of the second millennium, a drier and warmer phase than it has since.

Thus, about 6500 BC, the land which had linked the country to the continent from east Yorkshire to the chalk downs of Dover and Beachy Head had broken down before the erosion of the sea; as by the first millennium the land connecting the Isle of Wight and Dorset would also subside, leaving the 'Needles' which still give the sea-borne Atlantic visitor his first close sight of the chalk. The sea had made the Channel:

the north-western extremity of the Eurasian continent had become the British Isles.

The country was never, of course, really isolated from the mainland, for the primitive Mesolithic canoes could have made the Channel passage and the Atlantic sea routes from Brittany and Ireland are prehistoric, but it was now a world of its own. In decisive aspects it would remain so. This geographical revolution, coincident with the village cultures in the Middle East, made the British Isles the place where successive migrants ended up and blended; the rich miniature variety of the scenery paralleled by a cumulative mixture of population. Until the discovery of the Americas, Europeans could go no farther: the insular society became more concentrated.

2

During the early fourth millennium B C, well before Sumerian Mesopotamia and archaic Egypt and contemporary with the pre-dynastic Ubaidani and Fayumi, Neolithic stockbreeders and agriculturists had come north into the Rhineland, the Meuse valley and the Netherlands. Their best-known settlement is near Köln. Along with other Neolithic settlers from Spain and north-western France, they had begun to penetrate eastern and southern Britain, bringing with them a new, more settled, way of life. They were the peripheral and belated exponents of the so-called Neolithic revolution long before made in the Near East and the Balkans. Their camps or 'rings' are fairly numerous on the downs: the one at Windmill Hill (c. 3600 B C) near Avebury in Wiltshire has been most systematically examined: it would seem to have been neither a fort nor even a cattle-kraal, for no one would round up cattle on a hilltop.[2] Probably it was a centre for barter and for cattle and sheep fairs, such as those held within living memory at Yarnbury camp near Wylye. As the debris in the ditch testifies, it was certainly used for feasting and sacrifice.

This centre was in occupation several centuries earlier than the Old Kingdom in Egypt (c. 3000–2200 B C) and the early Sumerian cities. The way of life of these Neolithic people was still primitive compared to that novel and exotic process called civilization, beginning to develop under the Middle Eastern sun amid the clumped date palms of Iraq and the lush fertility of the Nile valley; but they were not cut off from southern ideas. The long barrow at neighbouring West Kennet, made up of sarsen stones and chalk rubble dug out by antler picks and nearly 350 feet long, is a collective tomb, with a forecourt comparable to those which elaborately commemorate the cult of the earth-mother and the dead which are found in Anatolia, Malta, and round Spain, Portugal

5

and Brittany to the Baltic. Earlier than the pyramids and much earlier than the splendid tombs at Ur, this British memorial is one of many such barrows often commanding great views on the crest of the downs; as Wayland's Smithy in Berkshire or Belas (wolf's) Knap high up in the Cotswolds. The peasant pastoralists who made them would have lived in squalor, but they would have exploited the resilient turf, their main subsistence depending on cattle and sheep, supplemented by shallow hoe and mattock cultivation of primitive wheat and barley. They had lean hogs and whippet-like terriers; they made female figurines and chalk phalli and modelled their crude dark pottery on leather receptacles. At the seasonal round-up and cattle-killing in the autumn they would have gathered in their 'camps'; and they were not on occasion above ritual cannibalism.*

The Wiltshire Neolithic pastoralists were now in contact with a related 'Peterborough' folk on the borders of East Anglia, and on this basis of settlement over the island a trade began in livestock, hides and flints. These were no longer just gathered, they were mined: at Grime's Graves in Norfolk the pits are fifty feet deep, excavated by antler picks down to the basic flint layer, still visible. And there were now mines – a more modern version of Grime's – with galleries in Sussex and in Wales. Along the upland trackways the flints were traded as far as Cornwall; both the 'Neolithic revolution' and rudimentary trade had come to Britain.

The most impressive monument from this archaic world is the vast stone circle of huge upright undressed sarsen stones at Avebury. Though Avebury may have been completed in the early Bronze Age, its basic design is Neolithic, closely related to the 'forecourts' of the long barrows, with a central obelisk or phallus in place of the burials, for 'the current system of beliefs may well have embraced the concept of a close relationship between death and fertility.'[3] It may well be part of a cult best exemplified by the well-wrought Neolithic temple at Tarxien in Malta and it has close affinities with the great avenues at Carnac in Brittany. It covers nearly thirty acres and today, looking west from the Marlborough escarpment, one can observe that most of the modern village is inside the circumvallation. South towards the upper Kennet is a long 'avenue' of similar standing stones. Beyond that, to the south-west, Silbury Hill, the largest prehistoric artificial mound

---

* In the first small Neolithic camp at Maiden Castle in Dorset Sir Mortimer Wheeler found the skeleton of a youth; he had been 'systematically dismembered immediately after death . . . the bones bore many axe marks and the whole body had been cut up as by a butcher for the stew-pot. The skull had been hacked into pieces as though to extract the brain . . . the impression given at the time of the discovery was that the body had been cooked and eaten'. Quoted by J. F. S. Stone, *Wessex Before the Celts*. London 1963. p. 29. The original lies in Dorchester Museum.

in western Europe, still defies classification. Such are the mysterious and the most immense of the relics of the Mega religions.

3

While Avebury is the most gigantic of the British Megalithic monuments, Stonehenge, although also of Neolithic origin, is the early Bronze Age masterpiece, completed at latest about 2250 BC. It has a much more sophisticated culture behind it and is technically a great deal more advanced. Here we 'seem to have a product peculiarly British; related to some set of beliefs involving the concept of a sky-directed open temple, rather than the deities of another world beneath the ground'.[4] And this 'Wessex' culture, of which the complete Stonehenge is the culminating religious expression, was created by a new people. They were bronze-bearing warriors originally from the Iberian peninsula, whose first migrations had taken them into central Europe, whence a backwash had come into the lower Rhineland and the regions of the lower Elbe. For want of a better name, they are known as Beaker folk from their well turned drinking mugs, already in a proto-Germanic tradition. A round-headed, thickset people with rugged features, they had bronze daggers, leaf-shaped swords, spears like assegais, and wristguards, as they were bowmen. By about 2500 BC some of them had come to Britain, perhaps under pressure from the peoples of the steppe who had overrun much of Europe and the Levant, and afterwards had created their richest culture at Mycenae out of the decline of the Minoan world. In contrast to the long-headed Neolithic farmers, they were a formidable warlike people who buried their chieftains not in communal family vaults, but alone in round barrows, with their finery about them. At Normanton barrow in Wiltshire, a warrior 'possessed an axe and two massive daggers, one of which had a hilt sparkling with an intricate gold inlay and was hooked to his belt from a finely chiselled gold plate'.[5] They prized maces and discs of amber bound with gold, and they developed a European trade in gold, copper and tin, exploiting the position of Wessex as a natural focus of a commerce in bronze metallurgy extending from central Europe to Cornwall, Wales and Ireland. Copper is not plentiful in continental Europe and tin is rare; the new bronze armaments demanded both. These warriors and merchants brought the first real wealth to Britain, and brought the south of the island into a close relation with Brittany and central Europe. By 1500 BC evidence for trade with the Levant is also apparent: an axe from Naxos has turned up at Calne in north Wiltshire; at Topsham a double axe of the Minoan-Mycenaean style has been discovered, and a

Mycenaean cup was found in Rillaton in Cornwall as well as Baltic amber and beads from Egypt.

These bronze-bearing Indo-European lords or 'rustic princelings' exploited the aboriginal people, though at length they were absorbed by them, for the British are still mainly long-headed. They did not improve the traditional agriculture, and it was not until the late Bronze Age that rudimentary ploughs came into use; but they used textiles and woollen caps similar to those which have survived in Denmark, cut to imitate leather and fur. They have left many barrows in Yorkshire, in the Cotswolds and in Lincolnshire, as well as in the south, and by the time Stonehenge was completed they were well established. They were still predominant during the centuries that saw the fall of Mycenae and the wars against Troy in the thirteenth-century B C, and their decline coincided with the age of King David in Palestine. The first phase of British barbarian Bronze Age culture is thus the result of a near monopoly of bronze metallurgy in the North and connected with the trade routes which spanned the continent from the Iberian peninsula to the Baltic.

Stonehenge, its most elaborate monument, therefore demands further attention. It is a shrine of a European cult, dedicated mainly to the worship of the sun, if reminiscent, like Avebury, of the Maltese temples. It was begun about 2800 B C with a timbered circle, then later enlarged with another circle of sacred 'blue' stones from Wales, presumably brought up the Bristol Channel hung between dug-out canoes to spread the weight, and then transported by mass labour on sledges or forked trunks. Finally, the Megalithic sarsen stones of the trilithons were dragged from the Marlborough downs, pounded smooth and up-ended in pits. The sacred blue stones were then replanted within the new Megalithic circle. It had, perhaps, by now been adapted to the cult of the sun, for the two biggest trilithons frame the mid-winter sunset when the sun god died, and the more ancient 'heel stone' is orientated on the midsummer sunrise. 'If we regard these alignments as intentional, and they seem so intimately connected that they must be . . . it seems that the chief purpose of Stonehenge was to celebrate some great festival at the winter solstice.'[6] There is an astonishing refinement of the stonemason's technique in the proportion of the design and in the tenons which hold the great transverse stones, themselves slightly curved to the circular design. The monument may even have served as a kind of astronomical computer to predict eclipses, so enhancing the prestige of the cult.

Stonehenge commemorates a Bronze Age aristocracy whose barrows are all about the sacred area. What was originally a late Neolithic temple was transformed by 2250 B C into this highly sophisticated shrine, the grandest of many expressions of the earliest wealth in Britain. There are many stone circles from Cornwall through Wales and the west of Scotland, and minor circles in southern Britain, but Stonehenge is the finest of them all – the climax of this mysterious cult in the far west.

Under the clouded sky in winter or the downland summer sun these megaliths still dominate the litter of modernity. Within living memory they were unencumbered, the turf running right up to them; like the beech trees which were introduced during the Bronze Age, they are still an integral part of the ancient landscape. They were old when the Romans took over the island; older when the Anglo-Saxons noticed them as the 'hanging' stones, not in the sense that civilized people named the 'hanging' gardens of Babylon; venerable when, in the thirteenth century, a chronicler drew their picture as the 'Giant's Dance', saying that Merlin had brought them, airborne, from Wales; and romantic when Aubrey in the seventeenth century and Stukely in the eighteenth theorized about them, the latter attributing them to the Druids, a Celtic Iron Age priesthood who were to flourish two thousand years later. With Celtic imagination, the Druids may well have claimed to have built the already venerable shrine; a claim still admitted by the amateur archaeologists of the nineteenth century, but now entirely discredited.

The significance of Stonehenge is more interesting. Its climax marks the rise of the first aristocracy in Britain and the first industrial enterprise in the island – the exploitation of the copper and tin deposits to make bronze and export it to the continent. Many centuries before the rise of Mycenae and long before the great Aryan invasion of India or the consolidation of the Shang régime in China, considerable wealth had already come to southern Britain.*

So, with a better climate and over many generations, by the end of the third millennium the population of the island had increased; contacts with continental cultures had been established and a foundation consolidated for the third phase of prehistoric Britain – the successive settlements of the Iron Age Celts.

4

The Bronze Age culture had depended upon a far-flung seaborne commerce from the Black Sea round the Iberian peninsula and Brittany up to the Orkneys and the Baltic; and landwise across the continent to Bohemia, northern Germany and northern France, and through the Carcassonne gap to the Loire valley. With the collapse of the Bronze

* The dates established by Carbon 14 analysis are not the same as calendar years, and in the first half of the second millennium BC in western Europe they vary by 300 to 500 years.

Age overlordships and the use of cheaper iron weapons, this trade declined and new warlike immigrants came to dominate the island.

These Celtic tribesmen, tall Indo-Europeans originally out of the steppe, whose main settlement was in central Europe, were led by swordsmen who made a cult of war; dashing predators, whose wildly exaggerated exploits – principally cattle raids and vendettas – were to be commemorated in the Celtic epics which have come down in Wales and Ireland. 'The men wore cloaks or plaids fastened at the shoulder with safety-pin brooches, sometimes studded with coral. . . . The chief's weapons were of the finest.'[7] This new aristocracy, widespread in Europe from the Balkans to the far west, made a vivid impression on Mediterranean observers, who thought them picturesque and barbarous with their 'combination of lavish personal display with graceless living'.[8] They were now superimposed on the Neolithic and Bronze Age stock; and their turbulent way of life went on long after Roman times in Wales and the Scottish Highlands; and most vigorously of all in Ireland, where Giraldus Cambrensis describes it in the twelfth century and where it was still recognizable even in Elizabethan times. This prehistoric world of the farthest west was never subdued by the Romans or swamped by the Anglo-Saxons, while even in England the place names of the West country bear witness to its tenacity.

The Celts spoke a language ancestral to Gaelic and to Welsh; and the Christian descendants of these tribesmen and of earlier prehistoric peoples would make their come-back during the Dark Ages, when Irish and Scottish monks would bring Christianity into Anglian Northumberland.

The Celts came, roughly speaking, in three migrations. First, as early as 650 BC, when in the Late Bronze Age, Alpine lake dwellers, some perhaps flooded out by the wetter climate, brought in the primitive ploughs which made the small Celtic fields, later more fully developed in Wessex and Sussex. Then, in the fifth-century BC, when Athens was at its climax, came more formidable tribesmen called after the Hallstatt culture in upper Austria, with iron weapons and implements and superior methods of storing grain and making pottery.* After about 250 BC other Celts followed, equipped with the more elaborate La Tène culture on Lake Neuchâtel in north-western Switzerland. Their relatives had sacked Rome in the previous century and long traded with Etruscan Italy. Some came into Britain from north-eastern France, some from the Seine valley and others from Brittany. They settled in

---

* Their storage pits, as on Martinsell Hill near Marlborough, were lined with wicker-work and tolerably efficient for holding dried wheat and barley. The odd notion that people lived in them, widely accepted, was put about by nineteenth-century antiquarians and is now, like the idea that the Druids 'built' Stonehenge, discredited.

Lincolnshire and Yorkshire as well as in the south. At Mere and Glastonbury in Somerset they made settlements in the willow thickets of the marshes where game and fish were to be found: a version, it may be, of their ancestral way of life in Switzerland. Others from the west of France, moved into the Severn and the Wye valleys and Wales.

This last infiltration cumulatively militarized the island. The invaders built strongholds themselves and provoked the already established tribes into constructing the Iron Age hill forts which remain so spectacular a relic of that time. The biggest of all, Maiden Castle in Dorset, was now greatly enlarged from its Neolithic original by Iron Age warriors who may have come from Brittany. In its original naked chalk, stone and timber, with its elaborate, cunningly designed, defences, it would then have looked even more formidable, if less mysterious, than it does today, couchant on its hill. Hambledon and Hod hills and Eggardun in Dorset, Bredon in Shropshire, and Barbury Camp in Wiltshire, are other examples of these forts. Though the Romans subdued them, so strong a grip did these tribesmen and their following get on the West Country that the Anglo-Saxon supremacy was not confirmed until the time of Athelstan in the tenth century, and the hill forts still dominate the landscape. Their chieftains imported wine and pottery, and struck copper and silver coins stamped with human profiles and horses, or designs recalling them, based on Hellenistic models.*

In our ignorance of their shadowy power struggles we do not miss much. In eastern England other Celts, the ferocious Belgic Catuvellauni, were paramount already, refugees from the Romans. Their main stronghold was in Hertfordshire near the modern St Albans, and their chieftain, Cassivellaunus, was to rally the resistance against Julius Caesar's reconnaissance in 55-4 BC, postponing the Roman occupation for nearly a century. The other most formidable people were the Belgae of Hampshire and south Wiltshire, also from north-eastern France; their tribal stronghold was known to the Romans as Venta Belgarum, later as Winchester, the capital of Anglo-Saxon England. With the Durotriges of Dorset and Somerset, they proved the most implacable enemies of Rome, to be systematically warred down. Devon was held by the Dumnonii, the Cotswolds by the Dobuni; Yorkshire by the Celtic rulers of the more aboriginal Brigantes, still a predominantly Bronze Age

* The Iron Age white horse above Uffington on the northern face of the Berkshire downs is just such an animal, conveying a sense of movement in a few symbolic lines far better than the more pedestrian designs of historic times in other parts of Wessex. 'It seems reasonable to assume that it was related to the cult of some Celtic horse goddess or god . . . The goddess Epona, Divine Horse, was also popular with the mounted section of the Roman Army.' Anne Ross. *Pagan Celtic Britain*. London and New York, 1967. p. 322. One of the great pleasures of the Celtic future life, they believed, would be horse racing.

people, while the Parisi from the Seine had settled in the Vale of York. But the Silures, a pre-Celtic Iberian people, still held the Black Mountains in South Wales and the kindred Ordovices defied everyone in North Wales until they were massacred by the Romans. The traditions of Welsh resistance are Iberian as well as Celtic: if Tacitus, describing the Roman campaigns in the late first century, would exaggerate the difference between the tall Celtic barbarians of central European origin, and the agile swarthy Silures, with their black curly locks.

There was thus great variety both in the population and economy of pre-Roman Britain. The south-eastern tribes, as described by Strabo, whose information was based on the now lost account of Posidonius, a Greek who travelled in southern Gaul, were not dissimilar to the continental Celts: 'Taller than the Celts [of Gaul] and not so yellow haired. The following is an indication of their size: I myself, in Rome, saw more lads towering by as much as half a foot above the tallest peoples in the City, although they were bandy-legged and presented no fair lines anywhere else in the figure.'* The British Celts were probably like those in Gaul, 'insufferable when victorious' and 'scared out of their wits when worsted'; and they would possibly nail up the heads of the enemies over the door, or 'embalm' them and 'exhibit' them 'to strangers'.[9] Perhaps they, too, liked to keep their figures and 'tried not to grow fat or pot-bellied', so that 'any young man who exceeded the standard measure was punished'.

They still live most vividly in popular memory through their Druidic religion; and although we have very little direct evidence about them, it is known that the British Druids were closely in touch with their colleagues in Gaul, whose principal place of assembly, according to Caesar, was on the plains around Chartres. The Druid stronghold on Mona (Anglesey) off the coast of north Wales, beyond the mountains, was apparently their most sacred centre of all.

The cult was elaborate, and influential. The name Druid is probably related to the Greek word for an oak tree, *drus*. The second syllable is cognate with the Indo-European root *wid*, to know.[10] The Druids are typical of the Indo-European world out of which the Celts had come, part of a social pattern apparent from Indo-European invaders of India to the tribal society of pre-Christian Ireland. They were the priests and bards of an 'historic' society with secret rites and signs, though they may also have had Neolithic affinities – they would still kill a child, for example,

---

* *The Geography of Strabo*. trans. H. L. Jones. Loeb. Vol. II. pp. 253–9. q.v. Strabo was a Hellenistic geographer whose survey of the then known world still makes excellent reading. It was written *c.* 7–5 BC and revised in AD 18, so it describes the Celts as they were after Caesar's campaigns. When Strabo is ignorant he admits it, as of Ireland: 'Here,' he writes, 'there is nothing certain except that the inhabitants are more savage than the Britons since they are man-eaters.'

to bury in the foundation of a building in the old Neolithic way. They reckoned time by nights and the passage of the year by moons, and they had lucky and unlucky days: they were the only repositories of an oral social and legal tradition; magicians and witchdoctors who probably possessed the sort of influence held by comparable secret societies and priesthoods in Africa and Polynesia in recent times. But even if 'several of the classical writers credit the Druids with being philosophers . . . it is hard to find convincing evidence that they indulged in any original or speculative thought'; they were perhaps more akin to Shamans and priests of Baal; they believed not in transmigration of souls but in 'shape shifting', and 'their predilection for human sacrifice is incontestable'.* Strabo, in a notorious passage, says that in Gaul they would strike a man in the back with a sabre and divine from his death struggle, or shoot people to death with arrows or impale them; and, most notoriously of all, 'having devised a colossus of straw and wood, throw into it cattle and wild animals of all sorts and human beings, and then make a burnt offering of the whole thing'.† Judging from Tacitus's description of the fanatics on Mona, the British Druids probably did the same, their sacrifices representing to them a necessary propitiation of dangerous gods and an expiation of collective guilt. Yet perhaps this itinerant hierarchy, with its widespread influence and freedom to travel beyond tribal boundaries, may have foreshadowed in the Celtic-Atlantic world the remarkable influence of the itinerant Christian Celtic missionaries in the Dark Ages.

Other classical writers have described the loose morals of Celtic society;‡ but the British Celtic aristocracy had excellent taste. Their shields, weapons and horse trappings were superbly designed and their drinking vessels are revealing;[11] like the Marlborough 'vat' twenty-one and a half inches high and nearly two feet in diameter, 'originally used to hold alcoholic liquid for feasts of a ritual nature, an important feature of Celtic life' (one chieftain had a supply equivalent to seven dozen bottles); and the Aylesford bucket, where 'clean-shaven mask-like faces are surmounted by great helmets with flamboyant plumed crests'. They prized enamelled ornaments, brooches and arm-rings, and their chariot warfare, obsolescent by continental standards and perhaps

* Ross, *op. cit.* pp. 54–6. Piggott concurs, attributing their 'undeserved' reputation as 'noble savages' to the conventions of classical writers, and their supposed political power to Caesar's evocation of a 'Celtic peril'.

† Strabo. *op. cit.* p. 249. 'It is hardly realistic,' writes Piggott, 'to exculpate the Druids from participation, probably active, in both the beliefs and practices involved in human sacrifice. . . . It is sheer romanticism . . . to imagine that they stood by the sacrifices in duty bound, but with disapproval on their faces and elevated thoughts in their minds.' *op. cit.* p. 117.

‡ Notably Athenaeus of Naucratis on the eastern continental Celts in his *Deipnosophistae* (Loeb. Vol. VI. xiii); a book, as Lecky wrote, of 'very painful interest in the history of morals', and 'replete', says Lemprière, 'with very curious and interesting remarks'.

THE FOUNDATIONS

adopted from the pastoral pre-Celtic Brigantes in the north, implies
much skill in the training and breeding of ponies; with its remount
depots and horse fairs 'no haphazard affair'.[12] The tradition was to
persist; there is still a greater variety of breeds of horses in Britain than
in any other country in Western Europe – Dales and Fells in Yorkshire
and Cleveland Bays; Suffolk Punch, Clydesdale; Welsh Cobs, Highlands and Shetlands, and the ponies of Dartmoor, Exmoor and the New
Forest.

The Celtic-aboriginal economy, on which the more elaborate barbaric
pre-Roman culture was based and which the Romans would exploit,
was most advanced in the south. Indeed, the main Celtic field system,
worked by rudimentary ox-drawn ploughs, extends only from the
Wantage downs in Berkshire in a broad belt south-west across Wiltshire
to the Dorset coast; then from Lulworth and Portland along to Bridport
and Lyme Regis, and south-east past Winchester into Sussex. In
Somerset, Devon and Cornwall the cultivation is sparse and patchy.
The storage pits for dried grain follow much the same pattern, which
would considerably determine the distribution of the Romano-British
villa estates. Kent, always the most fertile area, already produced
enough grain to feed Caesar's army, but the north and west were still
pastoral country, where the Celtic cowboys and shepherds, 'footloose
and unpredictable', would 'never adopt the Roman way of life in the
manner of the settled farmers of the South'.[13] Indeed, the Yorkshire
Brigantes were long a client kingdom, and northern Britain would never
become a civil Province but remain a military area. The poorer York-
shiremen were still eating foxes and otters at the end of the third
century AD: the grain surplus, on which the Roman army would
depend, could only be produced in the south.

5

In late Iron Age Britain there was thus a barbarian aristocratic or
'heroic' culture deriving in part from the continent, but long indigenous
from Bronze Age and Neolithic times. In a brief survey our knowledge
of it must appear less tentative than in fact it is. But the veneer of
Roman occupation would be based on an ancient and considerable
culture, and today 'the destruction', as Professor Piggott points out, 'of
the endearing myth of the naked woad-bedaubed savage waving his
flint-headed axe at the resolute Romans on some Kentish beach has, and
with some justice, been noted as something of an achievement in
British archaeology and its popularization'.[14] Yet much remains
mysterious in this background; there are no native literary sources, and
if archaeology has advanced in the last half century, considerable areas

14

remain unexplored. At least we do know that, anthropologically speaking, the Beaker folk and Celtic aristocrats were in due course assimilated into the basic long-headed Neolithic populace, though they survived better in Scotland and Ireland. In their heyday they flourished, large, noisy and temperamental. So, though Caesar observed only the south-eastern area of a varied economy, he found numerous and warlike tribes with a predilection for chariot fighting and guerrilla warfare, if not for sustained battle; a dangerous people in the woods and morasses of the tousled rainy island and difficult to catch.

This last prehistoric Celtic culture was a blend of Gallic tradition with the older Neolithic-Bronze Age way of life, and it was in total contrast with the Graeco-Roman civilization of the south; with its swarming sophisticated cities, its elaborate art and literature, and its relatively enormous wealth, amid the stone-pines and olive trees, the oleanders and cicadas under a Mediterranean light. The clash of these disparate worlds and the inevitable, and characteristic, Celtic defeat following the last resistance in Boudicca's revolt in the middle of the first century AD, form the first grim chapter of British recorded history. It is more important that for well over three and a half thousand years – much longer than the time-span between the present century and the first Roman reconnaissance – agricultural and pastoral peoples had been settled in Britain; and that on this basis successive invaders – Saxon, Scandinavian and Norman – would blend to give the British their character.

PAX ROMANA

'For Governmental purposes', wrote Strabo about Britain between the reconnaissances of Julius Caesar and the Claudian conquest, 'there are no advantages in knowing such countries and their inhabitants . . . particularly if the people live on islands', so the Romans had 'scorned' to occupy the country.[1] In fact, the two expeditions of Julius Caesar in 55–4 BC had brought it well within the Roman sphere of influence, and occupation was already only a matter of time.

By 56 BC, completing the conquest of Gaul, Caesar had broken the sea power of the Breton Veneti and had now turned his attention to Britain. He was popular with his legions,* had a victorious fleet at his command and, ambitious for supreme power, aimed at bringing off another *coup*; that is to say he would take a quick look at a mysterious and potentially dangerous country, subdue the natives and astound Rome. For the Romans were still strangely ignorant of northern Europe: vague about the interior of Germany, vaguer still about the Baltic and Scandinavia and afraid of the islands in the far west. To them it was 'a new world of awesome . . . risk'.† 'Nobody except traders [went] there without good cause',[2] and they naturally kept their knowledge to themselves.

So, by the current calendar on a late August evening in 55 BC, Caesar embarked at Boulogne with two legions (about 8000 men) in eighty ships; but his cavalry, scheduled to embark north of the town, were prevented from landing by the weather. Warned of his intention, the Belgic tribesmen were alert: so that Caesar could not, writes Cassius Dio, 'select the best landing places, for the Britons . . . had secured all the landings on the coast opposite . . .'‡ Checked outside Dubris (Dover), the fleet stood off from the cliffs, later to be crowned with a Roman lighthouse which can still be seen, while yelling barbarians

---

* *Urbani, servate uxores, moechum calvum adducimus* (citizens, look to your wives, we bring the bald lecher), they would sing as they slogged into another town.

† I. A. Richmond, *Roman Britain*, Penguin Books, Harmondsworth, 1955 p. 9. q.v. for the best short account.

‡ Dio's *Roman History* trans. E. Carey, Loeb, 1914. Vol. III, p. 387. Cassius Dio was a Hellenistic Bithynian who wrote a history of Rome which survives abridged. He writes in a rather bogus style, modelled on Thucydides, with set speeches and battles, but afterwards esteemed by the Byzantines. He wrote much later than Strabo, *c.* 200–22 AD

lined the downs: then at midday the fleet moved slowly east past a
forbidding coast with the Celtic hordes keeping pace. 'It is notorious,'
Cicero would write the year after, 'that the approaches to the island are
ramparted with astonishing masses of cliff – *muratos magnificis molibus*.'[3]
Caesar himself writes of the same 'steep heights – *montibus angustis*'.

So the Romans fetched up, casually enough, on the shingle near
Walmer, where a brisk fight developed on the beach, the British wading
out into the sea and riding horses into it. The big Roman transports,
good sea boats but clumsy, could not come ashore, and the legionaries
were 'afraid of the depth of the sea'. They were shamed by a standard-
bearer who shouted 'jump to it, if you don't want them to get the
eagle';* and while they engaged the enemy, the light war-galleys landed
on the Celtic flank and enfiladed the beach. Already alarmed at the size
of the transports, the British now panicked; the legionaries secured
their landing and so ended the first battle of Britain recorded by an eye
witness.

The invaders had got ashore and consolidated their position: but
Caesar, whose combined operations seem oddly amateurish, had taken
a dangerous risk. Soon the weather broke with a north-easterly gale, for
'it chanced', he admits, 'that the moon was full, the day of the month
which usually makes the highest tides in the ocean – a fact unknown to
our men'. As a result, he goes on to tell us, 'the tide was found to have
filled'[4] the beached warships; the transports were buffeted, and the
legionaries, who had travelled light, could not repair them.

Meanwhile, inland, the Romans had encountered the Celtic chariots;
these old-fashioned vehicles dashed into battle creating panic 'through
the terror inspired by the horses and the noise of the wheels – *strepitu
rotarum*'.[5] But by tactics so obvious as to deceive only barbarians, the
Romans trapped them by sending troops to forage and then catching
the Celts when they attacked; moreover, the enemy never managed to
storm the Roman base.

The object of the reconnaissance had been achieved. But there was
now trouble in Gaul; so on about 21 September, the legionaries fired the
crops, burnt the farms and were then safely re-embarked. Caesar had
sized up the enemy and been lucky to get out without disaster. He had
no proper harbour and no reserve fleet; but the gamble had paid off,
and he decided to return again.

What had he learnt? That the south-eastern part of the island was
thickly populated (*hominum est infinita multitudo*) and raised cattle and
crops that could support an invader; that the British were a formidable
enemy, and that to penetrate the interior he would need a very much

* He is also alleged to have added, pompously, 'I at least will do my duty to the republic
and the *Imperator*' – a remark suspiciously *ben trovato*.

larger expedition. The Gauls could have told him as much, but his own troops had to learn it.

The second and more prolonged reconnaissance was mounted with greater care and on a much larger scale. By 54 BC Caesar had about 800 ships and 35,000 men, including more cavalry. Coming up the Channel with the tide in the summer dawn, the expedition rounded the south foreland and landed unopposed on a wider shore near Sandwich; and that very night Caesar struck inland, making due west for the Stour south of Durovernum (now Canterbury) and bypassing the chalk country between Canterbury and Dover. The ships were now beached well above the tide and guarded by deep entrenchments, so that when the inevitable foul weather blew up they were not crippled, though forty vessels were damaged.

The tribesmen retreated into the woods – 'their forests', writes Strabo, 'are their cities'[6]– and the Romans had to storm their hill fort through its defences of felled trees. Moreover the threat of the invasion had at last induced the Kentish tribes to submit to a leader: Cassivellaunus, 'King' of the dreaded Catuvellauni, whose stronghold was at Wheathampstead near Verulamium (St Albans), had even devised a coherent strategy, and the tribesmen retreated north over the Thames, devastating the country. But Caesar crossed the river at Brentford; the Trinovantes of Essex, who detested the Catuvellauni, came in; Cassivellaunus's stockade was found and destroyed and the barbarians sued for peace.

The expedition had not penetrated very far; and the Midlands, the North and the West country remained unknown; but Caesar had again attained his object and so saved face. With autumn coming on, he decided to evacuate the island with a haul of prisoners of rather poor quality ('no loot except slaves', wrote Cicero, 'and I don't expect any of them to be a scholar or a musician'). He also obtained promises of hostages from the tribes, but all but two of these pledges were broken. He had tried in vain to take Britain before he had subdued Gaul where Vercingetorix's rebellion was now coming to a head, but he had proved that, with a sufficient force, Britain could be won. More immediately, he had won 'glory' in terms of political warfare at Rome; the adventurous sideshow had paid off, 'seeing that the formerly unknown had become certain and the previously unheard of accessible'.[7] A triumph lasting for twenty days was accorded him.

So concluded the first historical invasions of the island. For nearly a century it was left to itself: but the British leaders probably understood that conquest was inevitable. Romanization went on; the tribal feuds were now conducted with one eye on the continent and refugees even fled to Rome. When, in the time of Augustus, Cassivellaunus's successor,

Cunobelin (Cymbeline), overlord from Essex to the Severn Valley and south to the Channel, dominated the island from Camulodunum (Colchester), so-called after the Belgic war god, he ruled only on sufferance in what was already a sphere of Roman economic influence.

The island, of course, remained self-sufficient; able to export wheat and hides, honey and 'clever hunting dogs', while the Belgic tribes were now elaborating a more sophisticated barbaric culture. The bulk of the people that Caesar, for his own ends, had misrepresented as savages – 'the Britons', he had written, 'all paint themselves with woad which produces a blue colour, and gives them a most horrid appearance in battle'* – may have been little more prosperous than their Bronze Age forebears, yet, as their remarkable pre-Roman art implies, the Celtic aristocracy still flourished. Their battle techniques however were obsolescent and, strategically, they were at the mercy of the huge continental Roman power.

2

The real Roman occupation of Britain began in 43 AD. Though crippled in 367 by a *conspiratio barbarica*, a concerted attack from the Picts, the Irish and the German pirates, it lasted for over three and a half centuries until about 410, and it proved a good investment. Indeed, the decision to occupy the island was taken for sound political and economic reasons. The bane of Roman politics was the unbridled power of the armies, but Augustus had established a fine balance at the summit of the western world. If a sea-frontier were established in northern France the new legions might be a menace: isolated in Britain and self-supporting, they would not upset the balance and a new field of exploitation could be opened up. With the death of Cunobelin and the outbreak of feuds between his sons, military, economic and political motives combined to impel the Emperor Claudius, who was himself in need of prestige, to mount a massive invasion.

This time the entire island was to be subdued. Though the legionaries complained that they were expected to campaign 'outside the limits of the known world', a three-pronged landing was made at Lympne, Dover and Richborough north of Sandwich, and broad bridgeheads secured. After a two-day battle, the Romans defeated Caratacus, (Caradoc) crossed the Medway and advanced on Camulodunum. Even Claudius himself ventured on to the island for sixteen days, accompanied

---

* Caesar, *op. cit.* IV, 252, *Horridiores sunt in pugna aspectu.* The stress on skins and warpaint gave rise to a legend long accepted that the 'Ancient Britons' were not much different from cave men; a view which, as already emphasized, on the evidence of archaeology has now gone the way of the 'pit dwellings' and the Druids who built Stonehenge.

by an incongruous circus of courtiers, freedmen, eunuchs and business contractors as well as fourteen state elephants, for ornament, not battle. He entered Camulodunum in triumph and was awarded the title *Britannicus* 'because he was the first to bring barbarian peoples across the ocean under the sway of the Roman people'.* The strength of western and Mediterranean Europe had been mobilized to overwhelm Britain.

Having mastered the stronghold of the Catuvellauni, the Romans struck west; and here, Vespasian, afterwards emperor and founder of the Flavian line, got his chance. Based at first in Sussex, the territory of the princely chieftain Cogidumnus, afterwards promoted *rex et legatus*, he subdued Vectis, now the Isle of Wight; then, with Portchester harbour clear, he took Poole harbour. Thence, from an advanced base which was probably at Hamworthy, he struck into Dorset, and in successive swift assaults broke the power of the warlike Durotriges and Belgae of Wiltshire. He took the hill fort at Maiden Castle, where excavation has revealed grim evidence; the bodies of the defenders – women as well as men – hastily interred and one tribesman with a Roman bolt in his back. At Cadbury rings, commanding the plain of Somerset, there is also evidence of Roman attack and, at Spettisbury, a mass grave yields further traces of massacre. At Hod Hill, Dorset, they put in a garrison, commanding wide prospects; other hill forts probably followed the same pattern. The Durotriges were broken, and soon the Romans were able to secure the strategic site of Isca Dumnoniorum (Exeter) as the southern outpost of their western frontier, dominating the approach to Devon and Cornwall, as Ilchester also consolidated the approach to Somerset. Out in Wessex, that summer, the smoke of destruction and the hammering of builders must have cowed the peasantry, while over the chalk downs the word went out that these invincible foreigners were there to stay.

But the defeat of the Catuvellauni and their confederates had not been decisive. After the campaigns of Claudius and Vespasian, the Romans had to deal with a formidable resistance on the Welsh border, for Caradoc had fled with his Belgic war band to the west, where the Silures in the mountains remained unsubdued. Ostorius Scapula, during the campaigns of AD 47–51, advanced across the Cotswolds to Glevum (Gloucester), where he established a strategic base, and then another north of Exeter, commanding the lower valley of the Severn.[8] As warships were brought round into the Bristol Channel, 'the precise

---

* His wife, the notorious Messalina, who had diverted him from her own infidelities by 'taking care of him by giving him sundry slave girls to lie with' (Dio. *op. cit.* p. 415), was allowed to ride in a covered carriage, a privilege she shared with the vestal virgins.

rhythm of the oars gave the shore watchers cause for alarm'. Near Newtown in central Wales, Caradoc was brought to battle and the last resistance destroyed. He fled to Cartimandua of the Brigantes in Yorkshire, who handed him over to the Romans in chains, and they exhibited the outlandish prince and his family in Rome, *urbi et orbi*, to the city and to the world. His life was spared and Tacitus could attribute to him a speech which shamed the conquerors.

Thus, nine years after the invasion, with the parallel consolidation of what would be Lincoln in the north-east, ended the first phase of the conquest. Then the new Emperor Nero decided to subdue the whole island: he appointed Suetonius Paulinus, a veteran of grim Moroccan campaigns, to lead the legions into north Wales to secure the mountains and extirpate the Druid stronghold on Mona. The lurid scene on the beach has been described by Tacitus in a famous set piece depicting the wild women who flitted between the ranks 'in the style of Furies, in robes of deathly black' brandishing torches, while the Druids 'showered' the invaders with proto-Welsh imprecations. 'Scorning to flinch before females and fanatics', the legionaries cut them down and enveloped them in their own flames, while the sacred groves 'consecrated to savage cults' were demolished.[9]

This cleaning-up process was now interrupted. Preoccupied in Wales, the invaders had left what would be East Anglia lightly held. Already Camulodunum had become a centre for tax-gatherers; the virtuous Seneca had 'lent the islanders forty million sesterces which they did not want', and moneylenders were laying out – and calling in – their loans. Indeed, such was the raw haste for Romanization that a temple to the deified Claudius had been built before the *Colonia Victricensis* had been fortified, for the thoughts of the commander, says Tacitus, had 'run more on the agreeable than on the useful'.[10] Already the veterans had settled in, 'acting as if they had received a free gift of the whole country', and they vied with the legionaries in pillaging the natives. A mounting hatred, fanned by the Druids with their ramifications throughout the tribes, eventually produced a dangerous revolt: *conspiratio* became *defectio*.

It broke first in Norfolk among the Iceni, who had tried in vain to conciliate the Romans. Boudicca,* wife of Prasutages, their paramount chief, had been flogged and her daughters raped; she now took an atrocious revenge. From her fastness near Thetford, protected westward by the fenland and southward by the forest, she broke out. 'In stature,'

* Not Boadicea, a version derived from a faulty manuscript, or Boudouika, Dio's misspelling. (Tacitus writes Boudicca.) The name means *victorious*, from the Celtic *bouda*, victory, so the first 'queen' in British history bore, essentially, the same name as Queen Victoria, though not R and I. See Donald R. Dudley and Graham Webster, *The Rebellion of Boudicca and the Roman Conquest of Britain*, Batsford, 1965, for a good detailed account.

writes Dio, 'she was very tall, in appearance most terrifying', with 'fierce eyes and a harsh voice'; 'great masses of the tawniest hair fell to her hips, about her neck was a large golden necklace and she wore a tunic of diverse colours over which a thick mantle was fastened with a brooch. This was her invariable attire.'[11] Boudicca had consulted her gods and paid attention to omens: gripping a hare under her mantle, she had let it loose; it had bolted on the propitious side and the tribesmen had roared their approbation.* 'Show [the Romans]', she is reported to have yelled, 'that they are hares and foxes trying to rule dogs and wolves'; a contemptible lot, with their oil and wine, their warm baths and unguents, who 'sleep on soft couches with boys as bedfellows and boys past their prime at that; slaves to a lyre-player (Nero), and a poor one too'.

This choice invective, or its equivalent in the local idiom, further inflamed the Iceni. The Trinovantes of Essex joined in the revolt, driving the Roman troops into the fenland, while the rest took refuge in Lindum (Lincoln): the combined hordes then swept down on Camulodunum. Here they wrought havoc and committed the usual atrocities of Celtic warfare; most of the ninth legion, coming to the rescue, were destroyed. The tribesmen then wrecked Verulamium and got into London; though gutted, it survived and its authorities would come to commemorate the 'patriot Queen' with a statue on the London embankment, still riding in a chariot which 'has the appearance of an armoured milk float'.[12] To her own people she must have seemed the embodiment of the Belgic war goddess, Andrasta the Unconquerable, Female Battle-Raven and Nightmare Queen.†

The sequel was to be expected. The Romans wisely reckoned Verulamium and London to be expendable, and retired to the west. Their main armies then regrouped at Gloucester and combined to destroy Boudicca's hordes near what would be Towcester in the Midlands. Thus, according to Milton (a mysogynist sympathetic to

---

* These animals were already thought mysterious and the Celts would never eat them. (Dio. *op. cit.* VII, p. 250.)

† The picture of the

> British Warrior Queen,
> Bleeding from the Roman rods

was popularized by Cowper when he wrote,

> Regions Caesar never knew
> Thy posterity shall sway,
> Where his eagles never flew,
> None invincible as they.

The cult derives not from the old Welsh tradition (Gildas, their sixth-century pseudo-historian, disapproved of rebellion against Rome), but from the romantic Geoffrey of Monmouth in the twelfth century. A partisan of the Empress Matilda, he wrote up this Iron Age heroine in his *Historia Regum.*

Latin culture) ended 'the wild hurry of a distracted woman with a mad crew at her heels'. Considered more objectively in its reckless courage, her revolt was the last blind protest of the tribal Iron Age society against an alien and exploiting Mediterranean power.

The Celts were hopelessly outclassed. The Belgic war chariot, 'a vehicle subject to much stupid antiquarian speculation resulting in an entirely false picture which survives in school history books',[13] was neither armed with impracticable scythes on the axle nor could it charge home. As Caesar's account had implied, it was a morale-boosting weapon, charging about the battlefield making an appalling noise with iron tyres, as well as acting as a platform for hit-and-run attacks; a light wicker-screened curricle, it was manœuvrable only by an expert (so that its drivers had the greater prestige). The Celtic onslaughts were thus based on fluid and fast-moving tactics, the swift ponies taking advantage of the lie of the ground; but if the enemy had time to plant stakes and ropes, the chariots were useless; nor could they withstand heavy cavalry.

Roman tactics, on the other hand, were systematic. In close formation and wearing flexible body-armour, fronted by oblong, bossed, shields, the legionaries would hurl their seven-foot javelins at a distance of about thirty yards. These would either transfix the enemy or, being designed with soft iron behind the points, stick in their shields, rendering them useless. Whereupon, with a harsh sustained blare, the trumpets signalled the assault and the heavy infantry would trot forward, thrusting with their shield bosses, stabbing and flicking with their short swords, while the cavalry surrounded the barbarians. Such were the tactics that routed Boudicca's tribesmen near Towcester. And behind the Roman tactical superiority, discipline and eye for country, was an unprecedented organization: systematic encampment, good supply lines, proper communications, even a medical corps. In Britain, as elsewhere, the outcome was not in doubt.

So the cosmopolitan empire – the legionaries came from the Balkans, the Rhineland, Hungary, Friesia and Spain as well as Italy – had overwhelmed half the island and within twenty years ended the first phase of conquest; invasion, revolt, consolidation.

3

Historians tend to minimize the effect of the long if socially superficial Roman occupation, which reflected the changing fortunes of the Empire and waned with the Empire's decline. But the Romans created much of the framework of British history, if only in the cities they founded or enlarged from tribal strongholds. Canterbury and York, for example;

Winchester and Gloucester, Leicester and Lincoln, Chester and Exeter, Rochester, Cirencester and London itself, would all become strategic power points and nodes of economic life, and give their titles to the greatest ecclesiastic and secular magnates of the realm. If, save for the continuance of Celtic Christianity in the west, the cultural aspect of the occupation would be ephemeral, the material aspect would prove more lasting; linking such cities were the roads whose course still determines that of many modern highways. Yet, unlike Spain or France, Britain never became a Latin-speaking country; the peasants went on speaking Celtic, and the language, like the tradition of government, would eventually become mainly Teutonic and Scandinavian. For – and here is the point – the Romans never subdued the entire British Isles: in Scotland and Ireland great reservoirs of barbarism remained, and as the Empire weakened, these swarming western barbarians combined with the Germans to bring it down. For there was a vital strategic failure in Britain; and, like the failure to extend the Empire to the Elbe and properly secure the Danube, it was to prove decisive in the end. In Britain the turning point came earlier, in fact within fifty years of the conquest.

The first consolidation had stopped short at North Wales and with the mastering of the Brigantes at Eboracum (York). Now, under Domitian, Agricola was sent to complete Nero's original design.* By 78 he had crushed the north Welsh, completed the conquest of Anglesey and secured the Roman hold on Yorkshire and Lancashire. Then, in 79, he advanced far into Scotland (Caledonia), and three years later he built a line of forts from the Forth (Bodotria) to the Clyde (Clota); in spite of the shocking climate, says Tacitus, he planned to make the limits of Britain itself a frontier'.[14] He then crossed into Argyll, where 'the sea steals into the heart of the hills', and brought the clans to battle. At Mons Graupius, a site now unknown but which was in hill country and near the sea, the Caledonians had mustered under a chieftain called 'Calgacus'. Tacitus attributes to him a famous denunciation of the Empire, that 'world-wide, age-old, slave-gang', which would 'make a desolation and call it peace';† whereupon he then tells us, 'the Caledonians made uproar of various kinds'. There followed *atrox spectaculum* – literally 'gory drama' – when the clansmen, with their long swords and

---

* Gnaeus Julius Agricola, a native of Provence, had won promotion in Britain under Justinius Paulinus. His son-in-law, Tacitus, wrote his *éloge*, a masterpiece of condensed rhetoric, which secured and perhaps exaggerated his fame. He was a very able soldier and administrator.

† *Solitudinem faciunt, et pacem appellant. op. cit.* p. 220. The whole speech, one of Tacitus' earliest set pieces, is magnificent and moving, if less complex and far-ranging than the famous description of Nero's atrocities (in *Annals* IV, Loeb edition, *op. cit.* pp. 271 ff.), into the texture of which Tacitus worked his worst venom.

round targes, were broken by Batavian (Dutch) legionaries. In a chaos of struggling chariots and driverless horses, they were massacred 'until night and satiety ended the pursuit' and there fell 'the dismal silence of the lonely hills, houses smoking to heaven'.[15] It seemed a decisive conquest: there were 'no other tribes to come, nothing but sea and cliffs before them and victory'; and it seemed all the more so when the fleet circumnavigated Scotland and proved that Britain was an island 'explored and subdued' – *inventa Britannia et subjecta*.

But this victory was not exploited and the north remained untamed. Agricola had meant to subdue Ireland, even thinking he could take and hold it with 'one legion and a fair contingent of irregulars', so rounding off the conquest of the entire north and west;* but Ireland was never taken, and, more important, Mons Graupius was never followed up.

High policy determined otherwise, and the Emperor Domitian now took a strategically unsound decision. It would need four legions to hold the entire island, but he could only spare three; other much more important frontiers had to be considered. 'These formidable shock troops, at once the crack fighters and the skilled technicians of the Roman army, were carefully balanced pieces on the chess-board of the Empire . . . The very conception of a balance of power between the different quarters of the Empire dictated, too, that there should be no mobile reserve of legions to disturb it.'[16] So Britain was stripped of the second *Adiutrix* from Chester, which was sent to guard the Danube in Pannonia while Agricola's best legion, the twentieth, was withdrawn to Gloucester, that strategic base, thus abandoning the north to itself. Agricola was recalled: '*Perdomita Britannia*,' wrote Tacitus bitterly, '*et statim omissa*'.† And he was right: the reservoirs of barbarism remained, in the end with devastating results.

So, by 127, the Emperor Hadrian, 'taking an engineer's view of the problem', would abandon the Lowlands of Scotland, and construct a massive wall which still in part survives, running the seventy-three miles from Solway to Tyne. For more than half its length this immense work was 'ten Roman feet thick and twenty feet high, including its parapet, built of stone with a rubble and mortar core, and protected in front by a thirty-foot ditch'.[17] It was continued westward as a rampart of clay and turf, and furnished throughout its length with forts and signal towers, thus rendering it far more formidable than the equivalent *limes* on the Rhine. Yet it was not, as often believed, built to resist assault and siege,

* Considering the fortunes of later invaders of the island, he was probably well out of an attempt to subdue the Irish. Tacitus, writes his editor, 'never made it clear whether Agricola, before the Sassanachs, ever placed sacrilegious feet on the sacred shores'. He concludes that he never did.

† 'Britain was utterly subdued and immediately lost.'

and visions of barbarian hordes being beaten back from it are unrealistic. 'A wall-top 7 or 8 ft. broad, to which access was provided only by ladders every 500 yards and narrow stairways a mile apart, lacking artillery, lacking bastions, and above all, garrisoned only with an average of 150 men to the .. mile, it was never intended by Roman engineers for a fighting platform. Like the German palisade, it was meant to be an obstacle to raiding and plundering and doubtless also for smuggling.'[18] Its function was not to withstand an assault, but to prevent one from developing, and as far as is known, Hadrian's Wall never fell before direct assault: it was overrun only when there were neither men nor the will to hold it. And if, as on the Rhine and Danube, its very existence was a confession of lost initiative, the resources of even this gigantic Empire could admit only a policy of defence.

Thus the more prosperous areas of Roman Britain were protected but limited. Under Antonius Pius in 143 the barbarians were pushed up again to the Forth–Clyde frontier, and strongholds left by Agricola were made into the Antonine wall; but this shoddy structure, improvised more to keep people in than others out, was abandoned by 183. Massively restored by Septimius Severus, who mounted a punitive expedition in Scotland, but never occupied the country, Hadrian's Wall would remain the frontier of Roman Britain. So guarded and limited, Roman Britain enjoyed considerable prosperity, which lasted longer than in many parts of the Empire. After the reconstruction under Diocletian in the late third century, when the Empire was ruled by two Augusti with subordinate Caesars, the Praetorian prefect of Trier controlled the civilian administration of the west, of which Britain became a diocese. A *magister militum* commanded the armies, responsible direct to the Augusti, with a *Dux* (Duke) *Britanniarum* at York, and a *Comes* (Count) of the Saxon shore. Under Constantius Chlorus, massive forts were completed at Burgh Castle, Suffolk, at Pevensey and at Portchester in Kent. The great monument to the original Claudian conquest at Richborough was so adapted. When in 306 Constantine the Great – Constantius' son by a Balkan concubine* – set out from York to conquer the Empire, he moved from a secure base. Not a barbarian moved.

Well into the middle of the fourth century, the country remained one of the most productive areas of the Empire, and relatively safe. In 359 British grain was still being exported to the Rhineland, for the Emperor Julian rebuilt the granaries to receive it. But the barbarian *conspiratio* of 367 proved to be the beginning of the end. Theodosius sent a force to round up the war bands, 'a mob of various natives and savages . . .

---

* Not, in spite of ancient Christian traditions and Anglo-Saxon legends, and of Evelyn Waugh's brilliant evocation in *Helena*, a British princess.

ranging about laden with heavy packs, and driving along prisoners and cattle'[19]; and London, now termed Augusta, was rescued. But there was trouble on the Rhine with the Germans, roused to 'rage and war'; in North Africa; and in the east. It could be only a matter of time before the Empire would disintegrate, and by 383 Hadrian's Wall was finally abandoned. Nor were the British provincials, forced into hereditary callings and taxed almost to ruin by the coarsening imperial officials, fit to defend the country. German mercenaries began to settle in eastern England; while Romanized Britons began to go over to barbarians who might in the end offer them greater freedom. It was the same tale over most of the Roman world: long in decline, the Western Empire was staggering to collapse and Roman Britain with it.

4

Such in broad outline is the political and military framework within which the Romano-British civilization developed and subsided. Its economic and cultural aspects may now be considered. After the suppression of Boudicca's revolt, the Celtic aristocracy, says Tacitus, were 'seduced to the lounge, the bath and the well-appointed dinner table. The simple natives gave the name "culture" to this factor in their slavery'. *Humanitas* they called it, and their sons began to learn rhetoric, a subject congenial to Celts. Richmond even writes of a 'vigorous and lively response to imperial opportunity': they had long aspired to belong to the Roman world and most of the famous villas were not built by immigrant Romans, but by the Romanized–Celtic landowners, now diverted from battle and head hunting to the amenities of life.

The villas ('estates' or 'country houses' would perhaps be more accurate)* are clustered most thickly in Kent, Hampshire and Somerset. The earliest and most splendid is at Fishbourne, near Chichester in Sussex, where a great palace was already in being fifty years after the conquest, with elaborate tessellated pavements, colonnades and gardens. Here were 'hedge-lined paths and higher banks of climbing vegetation', Corinthian capitals in the Tuscan style, and 'a magnificent formal arrangement as yet unparalleled in Western Europe outside Italy'.[20] Many villas were also established in Oxfordshire, the Cotswolds, the Severn Valley, and even in the Vale of York; but few in East Anglia. These estates, as at Ditchley near Oxford, were often large, and many of them, as at Chedworth in the Cotswolds, developed local industries.

* The term is at its most misleading when applied to Hadrian's vast palace and administrative buildings near Tivoli, but it is inappropriate even in Britain.

Naturally the pre-Roman contrast, already described, between the south with its cereal crops, and the mainly pastoral north, where cattle and horse-breeding predominated, still determined the Romano-British economy. London early developed into an important centre, already by Hadrian's time covering well over three hundred acres; then the tribal centres, Camulodunum with its big restored temple to Claudius in the style of the Maison Carré at Nimes; Winchester; Dorchester; Exeter; Chichester, the main city of the royal principality of Regnum in Sussex; Cirencester, the main centre of the Cotswolds; Venta Silurum (Caerwent) in South Wales; Venta Icenorum (Caistor) in Norfolk; Durovernum Cantiacorum (Canterbury), together with the garrison towns – Gloucester, Lincoln, Chester and York – were cumulatively established. At Aquae Sulis (Bath) with its hot springs, the largest spa in western Europe was early developed; the main buildings are still intact, as also, wreathed in Celtic tresses, a magnificent head of Sul-Minerva.[21] At Buxton, too, in the Peak district, a spa was established. By modern standards none of these towns, except London, was at all considerable; at most their populations would not have been more than 4000, and there were no aqueducts in the Italian or Gallic style; perhaps, in view of the climate, they were not so much needed. Some of these towns were artificial creations which, in times of insecurity or paralysis of overseas trade, fell into decline; others, with an old tribal background, survived in ruined sub-Roman guise. But the continuity of London's life was never entirely disrupted; its position was too favourable.

The Romans early exploited the metals of the island: the Mendips were being mined for lead six years after the Claudian invasion and lead mines in Derbyshire and Yorkshire were rapidly developed, for silver could be refined from lead. Even in the middle of the fourth century the British coinage remained better than any other in the west. Iron was mined in the Weald of Sussex and the Forest of Dean, west of Gloucester, and Purbeck marble was quarried, its grey well suited to tablets with vermilion Roman lettering; while even the unrewarding shale of Kimmeridge on the Dorset coast was made into bracelets, panels and dishes. Tin mines in Cornwall were developed in the fourth century and so were small copper mines in north Wales; Yorkshire jet from Whitby, too, was in demand.* But coal, the great British asset, was neglected; there was too much cheap timber. Pottery was manufactured in quantity; it was sometimes decorated with hunting and racing scenes, or by 'phallic emblems of good luck. The human scenes are seldom successful by classical standards'.[22]

* Richmond. *op. cit.* p. 161. It was made into finger rings and bracelets and 'elaborately carved pendants and medallions, including family groups executed to order, and teddy bears'.

As already emphasized, southern Britain produced much grain, and the Wessex field system was now exploited; at Cranborne Chase in Dorset 30,000 acres became an imperial estate for the army, later, it seems, being turned over to sheep farming; while from the newly drained fenland in East Anglia grain was shipped north to York. Grain was also exported, but already the wool trade was more important. By Diocletian's time in the late third century, British cloaks were already both sought after and expensive. Leather goods were produced in Yorkshire by the pastoral Brigantes, and the prehistoric export of the 'clever hunting dogs' went on, now including bulldogs and spaniels. Again in Diocletian's time bears were being exported, 'mostly . . . for lacerating criminals',[23] including presumably Christians. Furs and seal skins were also in demand. Britannia, as Claudian would describe her in the early fifth century, was still 'clad in the skin of some Caledonian beast, her cheeks tattooed, and an azure cloak, rivalling the swell of the ocean, sweeping to her feet'.[24] Oyster bars were popular, 'the Romano-British equivalent of the . . . fried fish shop',[25] but oysters can hardly then have been exported in quantity.

Such were the urban and market economies of Roman Britain. Most estates, as will be apparent, were run as businesses, though their owners in the more prosperous times had all the Mediterranean amenities they could contrive. They laid down tessellated pavements most of which followed continental patterns – as near Stonesfield, Oxfordshire, where Bacchus rides a panther, framed in acanthus leaves, and at Woodchester in Gloucestershire, where Neptune appears with lobster-claws instead of wings – though some show the Celtic flair for non-representational design and subtler colouring. The Romano-British landowners put up porticoes and loggias facing south, as at Ditchley where a timber-framed barn-like structure was converted in the second century into a stone house with a veranda and a tiled roof. At Wheatley, near Oxford, the complete sequence of Roman baths was installed; hot room, tepid room (*sudatorium*) and cold plunge, though central heating was less common than has been formerly supposed when hypocausts, used for drying grain, were misinterpreted. The Romans also introduced flowers, vegetables and fruit trees new to the island: roses, violets and lilies, cabbages and broad beans; cherries, walnuts, sweet chestnuts and vines, as well as box and laurel. On the more luxurious estates, selected British slave girls and boys were trained to serve elaborate Mediterranean meals, enlarged with a northern plenty of game. The Romano-British landowners had wine and music and good talk, entertaining their neighbours at more or less decorous feasts. Beneath this Romanized class and its dependants, the life of the peasants remained as nasty and brutish as it had been in Celtic times: the idea of improvement was foreign to the Roman mind. To keep the peace and to exploit the populace was enough. Infanticide was common among the people.

5

The native aristocracy, meanwhile, adjusted their religion to the imperial cult of Jupiter and the Eagles, and of the deified *Imperator* himself. But at all social levels they retained the old Celtic and pre-Celtic gods; for example Naponus, the god of fun and music, who was typically Celtic, 'a youthful god of wild aspect with hair so thick and tousled as to suggest a bear-skin, and a torque round his neck'. They worshipped Cernunnos, god of the animals; there were serpent gods who guarded treasure; horned gods of fertility and malevolent or beneficent birds. There were the three Mother Goddesses, a sometimes sinister trinity, coming down perhaps from Neolithic times, who were widely worshipped; and also Condatis, the god of the waters, Sylvanus, the god of the woods, and Colonus, the god of the meadows. There were owl and bull gods, and gods of hunting; garden gods of fertility and love; there was even a godling of the water-borne leaves. All these cults were pre-Roman: but no one attempted to put them down; instead, in accordance with the usual policy, they were assimilated into the Roman pantheon.

Apart from the Imperial cult, sophisticated continental religions did not take root until the third century: Mithraism, with its exacting ordeals and austerities, was mainly confined to army officers and richer businessmen. Indeed, Mithras was hardly congenial to Celts; he was a god of order, who controlled the blind force of nature symbolized by the bull he slew.

Though Christianity had taken strong roots by the fifth century, it cannot, on the archaeological evidence, have been widespread; though after Constantine it was an official religion and, by the time of Theodosius and Honorius at the turn of the fourth century, it had become the official cult. But St Alban and Pelagius, protomartyr and heresiarch, are both authentic: though we know little of the saint. His companion St Amphibalus owes his name – though not his existence – to Geoffrey of Monmouth.* About the time of Diocletian's persecution of the Christians (303), 'a man Albanus did die', and even though the persecution may not have extended to Britain, he 'need not be consigned to the realm of myth'. He was a Roman soldier who sheltered a Christian priest, and, converted, volunteered to die instead. The tradition lived on; and in

---

* St Amphibalus owes his name to a misreading of Gildas by Geoffrey of Monmouth though 'the earliest accounts tell of Albanus sheltering a Christian missionary'. See W. R. L. Lowe & E. F. Jacob, *Illustrations to the Life of St Alban*, with a description of the illustrations

the eighth century the Mercian king Offa would endow the rich monastery of St Albans, one of the greatest early foundations.

Pelagius was more important – a European figure. His name was probably a Greek version of Morgan, 'the man from the sea', and he attacked the doctrine of original sin. Since, he argued, 'perfection is possible to man, it [was] obligatory' to strive for it; being 'free and well created'; i.e. not enslaved and predestinate, man had no excuse to tolerate the evils around him. 'Heroic individuality, not detachment from the world, was the mission of the sons of God.'[26] So Pelagius, who had left his island for the frenetic theological debates of Rome, Carthage and Jerusalem, boldly discussed infant baptism, the fall, free will, predestination and grace. Intrinsic corruption not being inherited, infants he argued, even if unbaptized, did not necessarily go to hell; they had a chance of eternal life. This genial Romano-Celtic heretic and his risky doctrine were fiercely condemned by St Augustine, and in 415 by the Council of Jerusalem: Pelagius, banished from Rome, died in Syria. But his ideas took root in his own land; and by 430 St Germanus of Auxerre would come over to confute them, and incidentally to head the Romano-British against the Picts and Scots whom he defeated in a resounding 'Halleluia victory'.

Despite these early evidences of Christianity, late Roman Britain was predominantly pagan, as it had been during its highest prosperity in the third century. The ruling class had cultivated *humanitas* and *romanitas* in their provincial setting after their lights, and felt themselves to be part of the Graeco-Roman world. Now with the gradual establishment of Christianity as the sole official cult at the centre and with savagery closing in, it was Christianity that inspired the civilization that the sub-Roman Britons were trying to defend. And the memory of these gallant times would be preserved in Welsh legends; of the Spanish-born *Imperator* Magnus Maximus, who married the Welsh princess Ellen of the Hosts and who 'killed the King of the Romans', and who, as the Cornish Myrten Massen, even set out to conquer Rome.[27] Other names would survive, now outlandish in what had been a Celtic-speaking country; for soon the Romano-Britons would become '*Welsh*', from Wealas, which is Anglo-Saxon for foreigners.

by M. R. James, Oxford, 1924, p. 13. Gildas wrote that King Constantine of Damnonia 'killed a certain young man in a church under the mantle (*amphibalo*) of the Holy Abbot himself'; Geoffrey garbled the phrase into 'he fled into the Church of St Amphibalus'. See L. F. Rushbrook Williams; 'St Alban: History and Legend', *Bulletin of History*, No. 11, Queen's University, Ontario, April 1914.

SUB-ROMAN BRITAIN AND
THE SAXON SETTLEMENT

'As when a herd of cattle has been scattered through some vast forest by a storm's violence', wrote Claudian in 402, and 'the beasts eagerly make for the sound of the oxherd's song or whistle', so the legions returned to Rome. He was writing a panegyric on Stilicho, the Vandal *Magister Militum* who had reorganized the defences of Britain and was now defending Rome against the Visigoths. Among the legions withdrawn was the one 'left to guard Britain; the legion that had kept the Scots in check, whose men had scanned the strange devices tattooed on the faces of the dying Picts'.[1]

After the death of Theodosius in 395, his young sons Arcadius and Honorius, brothers of that Galla Placidia whose mosaic tomb at Ravenna is still celebrated, had succeeded him as joint *Augusti*; the latter, aged eleven, now nominally ruled the west. They were confronted by Alaric, the new King of the Visigoths, who had routed the Emperor Valens at Adrianople and was now ravaging Italy. In 403 Stilicho, whose army may have included the British contingent, defeated him; but five years later he was himself murdered. Then, in 410, Alaric sacked Rome; an event which, though by then tactically unimportant, shook morale.

In Britain, meanwhile, a local adventurer had been hailed as *Imperator*. He called himself Constantine III, and, setting out to conquer the Rhineland and Spain, he had denuded the island of most of the remaining garrison. When in 410, the Romano-British turned against this adventurer, Honorius recognized their government; but, in a famous 'rescript', he told them to shift for themselves until better times. Whether or not they received further help, the connection was now tenuous. A *Notitia Dignitatum* or list of officials drawn up in 428 still includes a British civilian and military establishment, but it may well have described a set-up no longer there. The restored fortifications of Hadrian's wall were now primitive, and camp-followers lived in the guardrooms: by the early fifth century the north was barbarized. Probably by 410, and certainly by 420–30, the Romano-British were on their own. But they put up a long resistance to converging infiltrations and attack.

The grim prospect was nothing new: the attrition was now merely intensified and prolonged. Since the north and west had never been subdued, Romano-British civilization had always been precarious and confined mainly to the south: now town life and the villa economy were breaking down. As piracy and brigandage increased, markets for the produce of the estates diminished, purchasing power fell off among the sub-Roman Celtic-speaking *coloni* and there was little vigour left in the bankrupt civic *curiales*.

London, of course, was never destroyed; nor was the economic breakdown as sudden and complete as the laments of the Welsh historians imply; if the Anglo-Saxons had little enough to keep them in their own land, Britain must still have been attractive enough to tempt them to risk migration. They looked with stupid wonder at the sub-Roman cities, *eald enta geweorc*, the old work of giants, and set about colonizing the best areas they could find. Naturally the heavy taxation which paid the armies, whose leaders spent the money on their own adventures, the compulsion on the *curiales* to supply public services from their own incomes until ruined, and the sporadically ferocious enforcement of hereditary callings, must have made the government of the falling Empire widely detested in Britain. Just as in the seventh century the Byzantine government was so disliked in North Africa that the Arabs who overran it were often preferred, a parallel was perhaps provided in Britain by the barbarians from the Scottish Lowlands and Yorkshire with a tinge of Celtic civilization. This was not so with their most dangerous enemy, the Anglo-Saxon savages from the eastern sea, now beginning to come in, as Claudian put it, on 'whatever wind might blow'.[2]

2

The way the Germans settled in is hard to assess: so sparse is the literary evidence that, as Trevelyan remarked, 'the most important page in our national annals is a blank'.[3] Since he wrote, archaeologists have thrown more light on the dim prospect, but not much. We know a good deal about Anglo-Saxon burial places, but little of their habitations: the best one can say is that 'the picture of Anglo-Saxon settlement may grow clearer as the spade grows more proficient. Indeed the certainty that the next decade will bring more knowledge relating to the fifth and sixth centuries from archaeological sources makes all discussion of the nature of settlement very much an interim and adventurous judgement'.[4] We still do not know, for example, if they had heavy ploughs.

From the Anglo-Saxons themselves there is no direct contemporary written evidence at all, and Bede's *History of the English Church and People*, completed about three centuries later in 731, leaves the most crucial decades unexplored. *The Anglo-Saxon Chronicle*, compiled under Alfred in the late ninth century, was based mainly upon oral 'heroic' traditions, as is apparent from its mnemonic genealogies and suspiciously precise dates, glorifying the West Saxon Cerdinga house. At best it may have drawn upon eighth-century *Annals*, since lost.

The Celtic evidence is earlier but unreliable. In the mid-sixth century the sub-Roman Gildas wrote *Of the Ruin of Britain* within living memory of much of the invasion and long before Bede; but as Mommsen remarked, he is a 'preacher', with an elaborate, inflated style and parrot-quotations, and though he can evoke the flowers in the cattle pastures, and the 'clear streams and shining waters of Wales', he is much too well up in the theological controversies of the Romano-Christian world.* As for the other writer, Nennius, or whoever wrote the work attributed to him, he is more barbarous than sub-Roman. Though he used earlier material, he did not write his *History of the Britons* until early in the ninth century; and it is on this writer, and on him alone, that the evidence for the existence of 'King Arthur' depends. Where the early *Anglo-Saxon Chronicle* is unimaginative and laconic, the Welsh writers were all too imaginative, and reflect 'the emotional intensity which was, and is, characteristic of the Celtic race'.[5] Educated at Llantwit, Glamorgan, Gildas writes in waves of loquacious Latin, laced with quotations from the Old Testament; Nennius, in the self-conscious idiom of the Dark Ages untouched by the Carolingian revival. Indeed his disarming preface recalls that of Gregory of Tours to his *History of Merovingian Gaul*: 'I ask all readers who read this book,' he says, 'to pardon me who have dared to write so much after such great writers, like a garrulous bird or some incompetent critic.'† The simile was apt.

Fortunately we have a good deal of information from place names. As already emphasized, Germanic mercenaries had been settled in Roman Britain for at least a century before the major incursion: in Essex and the south-east occupation by permission had become occupation by right. Further, the Picts had settled into the North and the Irish (Scots) into the West Country and north Wales. The Irish heroic age of cattle raids and chariot warfare celebrated in the sagas of Cuchulain, was still

---

* *Gildae de excidio Britanniae. Fragmenta. Liber de Paenitentia accedit et Lorica Gildae*, ed. H. Williams, London, 1899. 'To my mind,' writes his editor, 'it is a grave mistake to call Gildas an "historian" . . . he is a preacher, a revivalist' (p. *vii*). W. P. Ker agrees that 'the great part of his work is not history but denunciation', and considers him 'one of the masters of an enthusiastic sort of Latin prose . . . inflated but not unintelligible'. *The Dark Ages* 1904, reprinted London, 1955, p. 131.

† See F. Lot. *Nennius et l'histoire Brittonum*. Paris, 1934. '*Rogo ut omnis lector qui legevit hunc librum det veniam mihi qui ausus sum post tantos tanta scribere, quasi garrula avis vel quasi quidam invalidus arbiter.*' The book, says Lot, is 'a compilation which has the ill-justified claim to give a survey of the Isle of Britain from Caesar's landing until the end of the VIIth century . . . as for the Latin it is execrable, as an historian he is the lowest of the low – *dessous de tout*'.

going on during the reign of Niall of the Nine Hostages, High King of Ireland (AD 389–405), who perished raiding the Isle of Wight in the 'classical age of Irish piracy'.[6] Many of the Cornish, indeed, must have been driven into Brittany not by the Anglo-Saxons but by the Irish; 'shameless Irish assassins', Gildas calls them, with their skin boats. He writes also of terrible hordes of Picts and Scots, 'alike in covering their faces with hair, and leaving other, more coverable areas, uncovered'.[7]

Sub-Roman Britain was thus attacked from both sides; but the economic decline was patchy. Many villas were falling into a subsistence economy and, with the collapse of the currency, barter would have been common; but if some Romano-British were going native and occupying old hill forts, at Verulamium buildings were being restored in the mid-fifth century. Ruin never overtook the south and east, and the wealth of the mid-seventh century Sutton Hoo ship burial points to recovery. And Celtic art, freed from the often vulgar conventions of Rome, revived by the fifth century.

The Anglo-Saxons thus started off as mercenaries and prospectors in what was still a relatively rich country; they ended as colonizers and settlers. They came mainly from Schleswig-Holstein, from Lower Saxony and Friesland, and some by way of the Lower Rhine. They were in part pushed aside into Britain by the Franks, now a power in Gaul; and they came not, like the Franks, Goths and Burgundians, under tribal kings, but in bands under war-leaders, who, for all their stress on being 'Woden-born', owed their authority to the sword. They all came out of the vast continental world of Germania and shared the oral literature that recalled ancient conflicts in Scandinavia and around the Baltic, on the eastern marches of Europe, and even around the Caucasus.

The equipment of these marauders was primitive: very few had mail or even helmets. Only the leaders had La Tène type swords, the precious *spathas*, their wood and bone grips bound with leather beneath triangular pommels. The *spatha* was clumsy, two-edged, and about two and a half feet long, in a fleece-lined scabbard of leather and wood. The *scramasax* was more handy and homely; a weapon which looks as if designed to hit below the belt or the chin; a knife fifteen to twenty inches long, sometimes, like the grander *spatha*, with runes cut on it. Shields were generally of leather and lime-wood, round, with an iron boss; and Anglo-Saxon archery was primitive. The most common weapon was the seven-foot long ashen spear, tipped with iron. A drawing in the ninth-century Utrecht psalter recalls the rudimentary style. By the eighth century the *spatha* would be superseded by the longer and heavier Frankish sword; the blade sometimes signed by the maker, as at Exeter: '*Leofric mefe [cit]*', 'Leofric made me.'

When therefore, in the mid-fifth century, 'those wild Saxons', as Gildas puts it, 'in three ships of war under full sail first fixed their talons (*ungues*) in the East' and spread their 'virulent plantation', they in fact merely tightened their grip. They now came to settle in the whole eastern side of the island from the Scottish Lowlands down to Kent; and in their own minds they divided the land at the Humber, into *Nordanhumbre* and *Suthenhumbre*, as Alfred would still divide it.

3

With the gradual abdication of the Roman officials, the British had lapsed into more primitive forms of government. The most powerful ruler was now a Romanized tribal king in Wales, whose sketchy authority extended over Kent, for the Kentish Britons, unable to get help from Rome, had put themselves under a semi-barbarian 'overlord', a *vertegernas* or 'high king' – a *Wyrtgeorn* in Anglo-Saxon, a title, not a name. Gildas calls him '*Vortigern, superbus tyrannus*' (a proud tyrant), perhaps because he claimed an *Imperator*'s power, for he had married a daughter of Magnus Maximus.

However, he miscalculated. When he hired Hengist and Horsa, barbarian mercenaries who were meant to settle as *foederati* and protect the land, they terrorized it instead. Nennius, for what his evidence is worth, describes a situation with many parallels in the declining Empire. As the number of Germans increased, so did their demands: 'When they demanded food and clothing as promised, the Britons replied we cannot give you food and clothing because there are so many more of you.'* On being refused, the mercenaries took what they could get.

If its dates are more symbolic than accurate, the *Anglo-Saxon Chronicle* is more practical than Nennius: 'And in these days Vortigern invited the English hither . . . to fight the Picts. Then they sent to Angeln bidding them send more help and . . . informed them of the cowardice of the Britons and the excellence of the land.'[8] By about 473, when, says the *Chronicle*, 'the Britons fled from the English like fire', the Jutish Aelle was 'King' in Sussex. Other Jutes worked up the Sussex coast and took the big Roman fort at Andredescester (Pevensey); while, from Portsmutha, Stuf and Wihtgar occupied Vectis, which became the Isle

---

* *Illos cum postulerent cibum et vestimentum sicut promissum erat illis, dixerunt Britones non possumus dare vobis cibum et vestimentum quia numerus vester multiplicatus est.* Lot. *op. cit.* p. 36. What was worse, says Nennius, Hengest made a feast for 'Quorthigern' and laid on so much wine that his guests got drunk: '*et inebriati sunt et saturati sunt nimis.*' 'Quorthigern', then he alleges, fell, as designed, for his host's daughter, a 'girl with a pretty face', and offered 'half his kingdom' to get her. This story was elaborated by William of Malmesbury in the twelfth century and so passed into the mythology of English history.

of Wiht (Wight): by the late fifth century the Saxons had mastered the main harbours in the south.

But it was an obscure adventurer, with the Celtic name of Cerdic (Caretic) – perhaps his mother was British – who founded the Cerdinga monarchy of Wessex, which united the country and from whom the royal line of England descends. Landing at Southampton Water, he worked up the Test Valley, across to the Avon, then over Wiltshire; perhaps he made contact with the much more substantial Saxon settlements on the upper Thames. For the main infiltration had come from the east; East Anglia had early been overrun, and by the end of the fifth century the Germans had settled well above Dorchester-on-Thames. Here was the best basis for permanent expansion.

The Romano-British now checked the invaders. In 502 at Mount Baden, probably near Bath – 'near the warm pools', writes Gildas, 'where the baths are'[9] – they inflicted 'almost the last great slaughter on the rascally crew'. And here, declares Nennius long after, 'King Arthur' got the victory, a claim later to be considered. The respite did not last. About 556 it seems that the midland and southern invaders combined. Ceawlin from the Thames Valley and Cynric from Wiltshire defeated the Romano-British on the north Wiltshire downs at Barbury Camp, north-west of Marlborough, above Swindon. Even if the part played by Cerdic and his descendants is exaggerated in the *Chronicle*, the dynasty may have come from the south and the main man-power from the Thames Valley.[10]

Meanwhile, by the time of Cerdic, in the hinterland of the Humber in the north, other, Anglian, invaders had settled the land. The *Deifr*, or 'riverside folk' the British called them; in Anglo-Saxon *Dere*, Latinized to *Deire*. They were the subject of Pope Gregory the Great's notorious remark after seeing some 'Angelic' Anglian youths in Rome that they ought to be 'saved *de ira dei*' (from God's wrath). Beyond them the *Bernice* based on Bamburgh overran the north, spreading into the Scottish Lowlands and attacking the Welsh in Strathclyde. We hear much of these ferocious invaders from the Welsh, but out of that settlement and its later interaction with the Celtic Church from Iona would come Christian Northumbria.

The fighting recorded in the *Chronicle*, if by continental standards insignificant, thus marked a widespread, cumulative infiltration, to which the defeat at Mount Baden was merely a setback. Who, then, was 'Arthur' who is said to have inflicted it? He was not the Ambrosius Aurelianus, in Welsh *Emrys Wledig*, 'a Roman' of 'kind disposition and unassuming manners', who, says Gildas, 'alone of the Roman race chanced to survive the shock of such a storm (as his parents, people undoubtedly clad in the purple, had been killed in it),'[11] and who led some sort of resistance in the south, perhaps based on Amesbury in Wiltshire. Nor was 'Arthur' any of the Welsh princes whom Gildas scarifies; not Constantine of Devon and Cornwall, that 'tyrannical whelp' who 'had planted the bitter vine of Sodom in his heart'; not Vortipor of Dyfed, the 'incestuous pard'; not Malcolm Maelgwn, *Machlo Cunas*, 'top dog', who 'wallowed in filth'; not even the 'tawny butcher' (Cuneglas), who Gildas calls the 'Bear' (*Ursa*), 'rider of many, and driver of a chariot belonging to a Bear's den (*receptaculi ursi*)'.* In all his denunciation of Welsh crime, Gildas does not mention 'Arthur' at all.

So we must fall back on Nennius in the early ninth century: and here, as might be expected, the evidence is confused. 'Then', he writes, making the first mention of the hero extant, 'Arthur along with several British Kings fought against them in those days, but he was himself (only) *Dux Bellorum*' – Commander or Captain of mercenaries.[12] Naturally we are told he was an effective one: true to heroic form, he cut down 960 men in one charge himself, and 'no one prostrated them but he alone'. 'Arthur' thus arrives, in Nennius's account, out of the blue. We still do not know where he came from, and what became of him. '*Silence*,' comments Lot, '*et silence intentionel*.'[13] And why was 'Arthur' made by Nennius to fight at Mount Baden or Bath in the south when all his other victories are recorded as in the north – near Dunkeld and Dumbarton and in Ayrshire and in Glendale in Northumberland? Chester is the one furthest south. Perhaps Nennius dragged Mount Baden into the narrative, since Gildas, without mentioning 'Arthur', records that victory.† If it was so inserted, then 'Arthur' can be discerned only in western Scotland and northern England. Both his connection with Amesbury, Cadbury Rings, and Tintagel, and the still more surprising claim that he was a 'cavalry leader with a mobile field army',[14] must surely go. 'Arthur' probably existed; but only as a petty chieftain in south-western Scotland: if not, perhaps he was a Celtic war god. The last seems an attractive hypothesis[15] for one who became such a protean figure in romance.

'Arthur' or no 'Arthur', by the mid-sixth century the West Saxons, '*erumpens grex catulorum*' (a litter of cubs breaking out), had joined with the settlers on the Thames after the victory at Barbury Camp to spread

---

* The word 'Ursa' (the feminine form here used poetically for bears in general) was misguidedly equated with Arthur in the thirteenth century, through *Arcturus* or the Welsh *Artos*, a bear. But Gildas is merely using it as an epithet along with the other animal names, and stresses the bear's den to indicate the sordid background of the prince he is denouncing.

† Nor are we helped by Nennius's only other reference, when he speaks of the dog Clavell, 'the dog of the warrior Arthur', who, when hunting the great Boar Troynt, drove his hind paw so deep into a stone that the mark is there still. For the animal is taken from the Welsh *Mabinogion* or '*Instruction to Young Bards*'.

over the Cotswolds and the Severn Valley, where, according to Gildas, there were still to be found walled towns and imported luxuries. Further, north of the Berkshire downs and the Thames Valley, the *Mierce* or people of the *mark* (frontier) below the Peak District, had settled into the forested Midlands, whence, under Penda and later Offa, they would achieve a brief ascendancy. But the most decisive settlement was made in the west, beyond Selwood (Celtic *Coit Maur*, the great wood), which extended beyond the Blackmore Vale in Dorset and west of Chippenham. Here, in the rich polders of Somerset would flourish Glastonbury (Glestingaburg) and in north Dorset, Sherborne (Sciraburna), in the main centre of gravity of Wessex. Alfred would fall back there before the Danes, when the more vulnerable chalk country had been overrun, and organize his counter-attack.

Thus, very slowly, generations of Anglo-Saxons settled in. Their place-names are thickest in Kent, Hampshire, Wiltshire, Berkshire and the Thames and Severn valleys, but extremely sparse in Devon and Cornwall and all the west. In the north they are thickest in the Vale of York and on the coast, past Tinamutha (Tynemouth) and the Scottish Lowlands up to Bamburgh and Lindisfarne. The Celtic names would last for woods and streams: *Guilou* for the Wylye, for example, which would give Wilton and Wiltshire their names. There was still plenty of room, with vast areas of primeval woodland and swamp. In the Middle Ages the 'steward' of the beech thickets of the Chiltern Hundreds was still appointed to take care of robbers; a 'post of emolument under the Crown' for which Members of Parliament who want release can still apply. It would be long before the country would be at all fully exploited, and the entire Romano-British population had been at most something over a million: but the Anglo-Saxon settlement was the turning-point in the slow mastery of the land.

Compared with this cumulative mastery, the struggle between barbarian princelings of the so-called Heptarchy, an Elizabethan term now well discarded, are not significant. First Northumbria under the converted Edwin would be paramount; then Mercia under the midland heathen Penda, commemorated by the penny (*pending*) – midland 'brass'; then, after a reassertion of Northumbrian power, Mercia again under Offa 'the Great', *Rex Anglorum*. He became paramount in the eighth century and married one of Charlemagne's numerous daughters. Finally the Cerdingas of Wessex came to dominate the whole country. But it is the slow colonization of the land that counts most; that, and the second and more lasting Roman conquest by the Christian Church.

4

It was in Kent, always the most civilized area, that Christianity came to the Old English when in 596, as Alfred would write, 'Gregory sent us baptism from over the sea'. Here by the mid-sixth century, not more than a hundred years after the first major settlement, the Jutish royal house was already taken seriously abroad. For Æthelbert of Kent had married Bertha, the niece of Merovingian Chilperic, and she was a Christian. Her important relations now backed the Roman mission. Of course the heathen habit proved tenacious; and in Sussex, Wessex and Mercia it fought back, religious beliefs combining, as usual, with the power struggles. Even in Kent there was not much for the Christians to build on: a tiny dilapidated sub-Roman church dedicated to St Martin of Tours had survived in Canterbury, to be refurbished by the Merovingian queen.

The Romano-Britons had no interest in the detested heathen, and the background of St Augustine of Canterbury's mission was entirely Roman. Ordered to proceed to Britain from his monastery in Rome, he had asked to be let off the assignment and lingered in the south of Gaul. And his reception, though correct, was cool; Æthelbert, who received him in the open for fear of magic, at first declared that he could not abandon the faith of his forefathers and his subjects. But he gave him permission to convert as many of his people as he could by preaching. Queen Bertha now exerted her influence and in due course king and people were tamed; perhaps, as a sensible ruler, Æthelbert had waited on public opinion.

So Augustine was consecrated 'Bishop of the English' at Arles in Provence, and set about building a Benedictine monastery at Canterbury, the basis of the metropolitan see of all England. Early in the seventh century Gregory the Great, who had advised Augustine to adapt the heathen festivals to the Christian year and not expect too much, had already devised dioceses for England, centred on Canterbury and York, and urged a reconciliation with the Welsh church. So Augustine had to set off across country through the Chilterns, the Thames Valley and the Cotswolds down to Aust in the Severn Estuary; an expedition still commemorated a century later in Bede's day by St Augustine's Oak.

But the Welsh proved touchy and intransigent; they insisted on their archaic date for Easter (much too early), and were furious when Augustine failed to get up to receive them. 'If the Britons do not wish to have peace with us', remarked the saint, 'they shall perish at the hands of the Saxons'; wounding words since the Saxons had recently massacred two hundred Welsh clergy, who, like the Druids on *Mona*, had been 'praying against them'. The mission was a failure.[16]

Yet, as befitted the founder of the Church of England, Augustine, no great enthusiast or diplomat, was a good organizer. He carried out the main papal policy which was to strengthen the whole Church against the Lombards in north Italy and the Visigoths in Spain by recovering an old province of the Empire, as well as saving 'Angelic' boys from the wrath of God.

St Augustine had come from Rome, and the other missionaries were also highly civilized continentals: St Birinus, who baptized Cynegils of Wessex at Dorchester-on-Thames in 635, only about a century after 'Arthur's' supposed death, was from northern Italy; the Merovingian Agilbert of Winchester (fl. 650), was probably, on the evidence of his tomb in France, a man of some taste; and Bishop Felix of Dunwich in East Anglia also came from Frankish Gaul. Theodore of Tarsus, 'the last known pupil of the schools at Athens', an older contemporary of Bede, who consolidated St Augustine's work as Archbishop of Canterbury (668–90) and began to organize parishes, was a Byzantine Greek. His collaborator, Abbot Adrian, came from North Africa.

So, within a century of the first Roman mission, the Church of England became rooted in the land. Already the parish churches were supported by '*tythes*' (tenths) paid in money or in kind, supplemented by 'plough arms',* *soulscot* (burial fees), *lightscot* (candle wax) and food rents in wheat and barley, in cheese and bacon and lard, honey and hens, eggs and fish. Great and lasting as would be the prestige of the early Saints, as St Cuthbert's in the north into Tudor times, the solid parochial foundation of churches and clergy was more decisive. From head 'minster' – cathedral – through minster (*monasterium*) to '*field church*' and local '*cross*', the august cosmopolitan institution took root, and kings and nobles endowed it; an after-life insurance, a temporal investment and 'the done thing'. The lay patron, indeed, with his interest in his endowment, would make for continuity and order. The Church of England would through him become very rich.

The influence of the Celtic Church was also decisive; for some of the energy of the 'classical age of Irish piracy' had now been diverted into missionary zeal, probably reinforced by a desire to see the world. Though the Welsh, whose conversion had been consolidated by St David, had repudiated the Anglo-Saxons and the Roman mission, the Irish evangelized Scotland and helped convert the Northumbrian English. So, in the end, the two streams of Christianity from Iona and from Canterbury converged: with the death of Penda in 654, and the

* A penny for every plough yoked between Easter and Pentecost.

patched-up agreement at the Synod of Whitby in 664, all Anglo-Saxon England would become officially Christian and acknowledge the authority of Rome.

The background of these Celtic missions demands attention. St Patrick who reorganized the existing Christian communities in Ireland, converted many of the pagans of the West and brought that island fully into Roman Christendom. He probably lived from 389 to 461, a contemporary of Vortigern and Hengist. While the Anglo-Saxon mercenaries were turning on their hosts, he was spreading the gospel and the art of writing Latin in that primitive society. He was a Romanized Britain, kidnapped into Ireland at the age of fifteen, who had escaped to the continent and returned as a missionary. His full name was Patricius Magonus Sucat.[17] Patrick, it must be understood, did not go to Ireland to introduce Christianity, but to encourage and discipline the Christians already there, perhaps already affected by the Pelagian heresy.* He made his headquarters at Armagh, and worked mainly in the north and north-west. Determined to protect his people to the end, he is said to have made a bargain with the Almighty that he should judge the Irish on Doomsday himself.

Thus Ireland came out of prehistory, with a vigorous Christian culture in direct contact with the continent. Its leaders, in a tribal society, inherited the prestige and social mobility of the Druids and bards, as well as an outlandish tonsure perhaps adapted from them, for the Christian Irish clergy shaved their heads in front, as their predecessors had cut throats, from ear to ear. Soon Irish missions would go out to Frankish Gaul and the Germanies, leaving their mark at St Gall in Switzerland and at Insel Reichenau on the western arm of the Bodensee.

For in this Celtic tribal society Christianity had developed in an original way, well adapted to the Atlantic environment which had seen the rise of the Megalithic culture and the Celtic heroic age of Cuchulain. Instead of Niall of the Nine Hostages raiding Vectis, now, while Cerdic was getting a grip on Wessex, Irish monks would establish themselves at Tintagel in Cornwall. Northwards, too, and more decisively, St Columba (521–97) would evangelize western Scotland from the isle of Iona (563), off the western Highlands. As abbot and clan chieftain, he

---

* After being captured from his father's farm, probably on the estuary of the Severn, Patrick had been sold into slavery in Northern Ireland. Six years later he absconded to Wicklow and got passage to the mouth of the Loire on a vessel whose cargo included a leash of wolfhounds which in return for his passage he had the experience to handle. He made his way to Arles and perhaps to Italy, then joined the monastery on the isle of Lerins, near Cannes. Having studied at Auxerre under St Germanus, he returned to Ireland as a bishop. For the sources of his life see J. B. Bury, *The Life of St Patrick, op. cit.,* Appendix A.

had complete authority, and imposed his high-strung, ascetic religion in a forceful if humane way.*

This originally Celtic Christianity soon spread south; by the mid-seventh century St Cuthbert, whose banner would become the battle standard of the northern English, was minding sheep on the Lammermoor hills. By then, too, St Aidan, a kinsman of St Columba, had established a monastery at Lindisfarne off the Bernician coast, the eastern equivalent of Iona. The Celtic Church, indeed, had had much to bring to the Synod of Whitby, convened by Oswin of Northumbria, even if he had decided for Rome, because, he remarked, 'St Peter had the keys'.

Thus, though the Welsh clergy would long be irreconcilable and need severe discipline,† and St Aldhelm of Sherborne in the eighth century would still be persuading them to conform, and not until the reign of Athelstan in the tenth century would a Cornish Canon of Bodmin accept a bishopric under Canterbury, the decision had been made.

The old heathenism, of course, went on among the people whose Christianity would long have a pre-Christian tinge; most days of the week, for example, would never be Christianized: Tius-day and Woden's-day, both dedicated to war gods; Thor's-day to the thunder god; Frey's-day to the god of love. But the months, longer time spans, vague to the peasants, were Latinized; August superseding 'weed-month'; and November 'blood-month', when they killed the cattle, though Yule (*Giulu*) survived for the orgies around Christmas.

6

This vigorous hybrid culture now proliferated. As Feiling puts it, 'the fire of Northumbrian religion caught all England'.[18] Its most famous exponent was *Baeda* – the Venerable Bede. Against a background of savage vendettas, it proved the most creative influence of its time, radiating back into heathen Germania in a missionary drive unparalleled until the other great English missionary effort in the nineteenth

* He is said to have come of an aristocratic family in Donegal; a tall man with a habit of command and hospitality. He loved animals, and remarked even of a whale, 'I and that beast are both under God'. See Adamnan's *Life of St Columba*. ed. A. O. and M. O. Anderson, Edinburgh, 1961.

† Gildas is illuminating on the penalties for their sins. 'What can you expect,' he writes, 'from such belly-beasts?' So a presbyter or a deacon committing fornication of any kind had to live for three years on biscuit, cabbage, a few eggs and British cheese, washed down by half a pint of milk and some whey. And he was not to have his bed furnished with too much straw. If anyone was too drunk to sing the psalms, he forfeited his dinner. Other, worse, sins were fully catered for, reflecting the obverse of Celtic asceticism. (*Penitential of Gildas*, Williams, *op. cit.* p. 277.) In another penitentiary a bishop – whose position was not, of course, so grand as a Roman equivalent – committing voluntary homicide gets a penance of twelve years, but only three years if it was done 'in sudden anger'.

century. The Anglo-Saxon clergy still felt a duty to preach salvation to their kin, and the latest western converts would become the agents whereby their heathen cousins in Germany, to whom they could still speak in a common tongue, were themselves brought in to Christendom.

Bede (673–735) was far the best historian in the Europe of his time. This may not be saying much, but his standards were high. 'Allow me', he writes, in the manner of all sound academics, 'briefly to state the authorities on whom I chiefly depend': he apologizes, as would many good men after him, for his failings, and obliquely but disarmingly calls attention to his own diligence; he asks, indeed, to be prayed for, an invocation now out of fashion. If one compares Bede with Isidore of Seville, a century before,[19] aptly likened to a man searching for broken china in a dark room and putting the pieces together wrong, Bede is vastly superior. He is accurate as far as he can be; he has human insight; his Latin is clear and wide ranging, and he has a sense of literary design. Though 'venerable', not 'sainted', he is in effect the patron saint of any professional historians who still require one. And Bede, unlike Gildas, could be tolerant; as of the followers of St Columba on Iona, who went on keeping Easter until 715 on Sunday of the wrong week, for 'they had not lost the fervent grace of charity and were therefore worthy to learn the full truth'.[20] Miracles, tedious in the ordinary hagiographies, glow with Bede's charm;* and the violence of power politics gets short shrift, as when the Northumbrians sent an army into Ireland and 'brutally harassed these inoffensive people who had always been so friendly to the English'.[21] Bede's account of St Cuthbert's 'masterly authority' recalls the burning faith which converted the northern peasantry, whose barbarity and squalor daunted other teachers'.[22] Out of that distant time Bede's personality comes through clearly, the first historian of a long and humane tradition; magnanimous, wise and fair, he made a particularly edifying end, his pupils about him. His original tomb was at Jarrow, but such was the competition for the relics of holy men in the north, that in Knut's time his remains were stolen and placed near the shrine of St Cuthbert at Durham. There, when Henry VIII despoiled the cathedral, Bede's relics were hidden away, to be rediscovered in the nineteenth century, and the inscription of his tomb today reads:

Hac sunt in fossa, Bedae Venerabilis Ossa
(In this grave lie the bones of the Venerable Bede)

The Northumbrian culture was paralleled in the south. St Aldhelm, for example, best remembered for St Aldhelm's Head which confronts

---

* See 'the dumb youth healed' (p. 267) and how brother Badudegn was cured of paralysis by St Cuthbert, seeming to feel 'a great broad hand rest on the seat of the pain in his head'. *A History of the English Church and People op. cit.* (p. 262).

the waves on the iron-bound coast of Purbeck, was a Cerdinga, kinsman to King Ine, the first really important ruler of Wessex. At Malmesbury Abbey, where Irish monks had helped to create a centre of learning, he was taught by Adrian, a Byzantine Greek: he visited Rome in 687 and 701, and wrote poems on virginity in over-alembicated verse, widely popular. He persuaded King Ine to rebuild Glastonbury, and founded churches at Wareham, Bruton and Bradford-on-Avon, where the church remains. In 705 he became first Bishop of Sherborne beyond *Westan wuda*, and he died near Wells. He wrote popular riddles and attracted congregations by singing, as well as visiting his diocese on foot with an ashen staff.

St Aldhelm was an intimate of Winfrith, famous as St Boniface, (675–755) the most important of the Anglo-Saxon missionaries to convert the Germans. Born near Exeter (*aet Axcancastre*) of a substantial family, he went with the blessing of Gregory II (who wanted to bring the Germans into the faith, to counterpoise the losses inflicted by the Muslims in Spain), into Thuringia and Franconia, and settled in Hesse, where he hewed down the Holy Oak of Gaismar, sacred to Thor. By 732, three years before Bede's demise, he was reorganizing the diocese of Bavaria in collaboration with a Frankish drive to the south-east; in the next year he became Archbishop of Mainz, where he ruled for a decade; he founded the abbey of Fulda and he anointed Pepin, founder of the Carolingian dynasty. In old age he retired, went again to convert the heathen; and was martyred amid the polders at Dokkum in East Friesland – *in loco qui Docking dicetur*.*

St Willibrord, too, was an Anglo-Saxon. Though the old Saxons had torn one of his collaborators limb from limb and sworded another and thrown his remains into the Rhine, he converted West Friesland. Willibrord became the first Bishop of Utrecht, ending his days among the vineyards of Echternach on the Mosel. St Willibald, Bishop of Eichstadt, came from Bishop's Waltham (Waldheim) in Hampshire. He sailed from the Hamble river for Rome, and travelled widely in the Levant and lived at Monte Cassino. His brother, St Wunnibald, became Abbot of Heidenheim, and his sister, St Walpurgis, was brought up at Wimborne by a sister of King Ine, Abbess of the joint nunnery. But her association with the licence of *Walpurgisnacht* was not through any

---

* Crediton is only mentioned as his birthplace in the fourteenth century. Young Winfrith ignored the temptations of wealth, and overcame those of the flesh (*infestas diabolicae sugges-tionis persecutiones*) by working at his books all night. His last action was to shield his head with the Gospels: *sacrum ewangelium codicem capiti suo imposuit*: 'He placed the sacred gospels on his head according to a certain old woman who had witnessed the occasion.' *Vita Bonifatii auctore Willibaldo.* ed. W. Levison. S. R. G. Hannover, 1905, p. 5. For a short account of Anglo-Saxon missionaries on the Continent see S. J. Crawford. *Anglo-Saxon Influence on Western Christendom, 600–800*, pp. 32–71, Oxford, 1933.

breakdown of intermonastic discipline: she happened to be canonized on the first of May, already a pagan festival.

Not that all feeling was excluded in such joint establishments: St Boniface himself had a romantic friendship with Abbess Leoba of Bischopsheim, and planned to share a grave with her at Fulda, an intention not apparently frustrated by his demise at Dokkum; and Abbes Bucge, who gave him needlework, sent him a book on the deaths of the martyrs, which may have encouraged him to seek such an end.

In England itself the influence of the church was now pervasive, and with long settlement and renewed prosperity, there was a growing sophistication in the arts. The early Kentish pagan ornaments had been remarkable, and the polychrome jewellery of the mid-seventh century ship memorial at Sutton Hoo was already better than anything of its kind in contemporary western Europe. Great garnets are illuminated by gold foil beneath *cloisonné* settings of filigree gold. The brooches are in mushroom, curvilinear, and animal shapes; the colours subtly juxta-posed.

With the coming of Christianity in Ireland and northern Britain, 'in primitive conditions that would seem to render mental exertion impos-sible, a vivid Latin Culture sprang up and a still more remarkable artistic achievement that has put Celtic monastic illumination and metal work among the masterpieces of art history'.[23] The resultant crossing of Celtic, Northumbrian and Mediterranean styles early produced magnificently illuminated manuscripts. Designed during Bede's lifetime, the Northumbrian Book of Jarrow has a bold splendour of yellow and reds, while the better-known Lindisfarne Gospels show a more Italianate influence. However politically ferocious it might have been,* an age which could produce such art, was not 'Dark'. In this remote north-western corner of Europe dynamic Christian culture was beginning to flourish.

7

The basis of this advance had been the slow and steady colonization of the land, which could now produce a surplus to support a creative minority culture; in fact, 'there is nothing in European history closely parallel to this sudden development of a civilization by one of the most primitive peoples established within the ancient Roman Empire'.[24] It is indeed extraordinary that these barbarians, who had the reputation in the fifth century for outstanding savagery and whose political conflicts continued to be hideous, should have produced so much learning,

* Ceolwulf, to whom Bede dedicated his history, had to abdicate and his son Aldfrith was murdered.

poetry and missionary zeal. Their influence was decisive in Germany and Scandinavia and on the Carolingian revival; and the Old English poetry, later to be described, is the best, both heathen and Christian, of the surviving Germanic literature. Anglo-Saxon England, by the eighth century, had become a power-house of civilization, the result of a blend of Mediterranean and Celtic influences with the Germanic temperament. And this culture was so deeply rooted that it survived the Danish invasions and settlements, as in the time of Æthelred II, when much of it, already archaic, was deliberately preserved in the surviving manuscripts.

The price, as usual in history, had been paid by the vanquished; by the Romano-British inhabitants of the island. They had clung steadfastly to the Romano-British culture, as witness the survival of so many Latin words in Welsh: the words for anchor, wall, gate and window; for pitch-fork, bridle, saddle, mill and well: not least for washing, for soap (*sebon*) and sponge (ysbwyng), as well as for platter and knife.

But the 'Welsh' were now either assimilated by their conquerors, or a free people only in the far west; for whom, a generation before Alfred, their bard Heledd would still speak, keening from the hills above Shrewsbury, devastated by the Anglo-Saxons:

> *Grey-headed eagle of Pengwern*
> *Tonight his claw hangs poised*
> *Greedy for the flesh I loved.*

THE WEST SAXON KINGDOM

The basic achievement of the Old English, from which all else would follow, had been the taming of the land by generations of colonizing farmers, their free dependants and their slaves. Contrary to former opinion, the Romano-British villa estates had not substantially survived; in south and central Gaul townships would 'trace unbroken descent from their eponymous Gallo-Roman estate owners; in England, in violent contrast, there is not a single instance of a villa name surviving the period of conquest'.[1] The settlers had a good eye for country and would have taken over many fields under cultivation; but generally 'the land-hungry Saxons settled anew on land that suited them'.[2] They were a 'valley-seeking people, less pastoral than the British, more concerned with heavy arable'.[3]

Their place-names, many later transferred to North America, reflect the work of 'generations of these forest clearers' who 'laid the pattern of *hams* and *-tuns* which may still be traced so clearly on the map of England'.[4] Rea*ding*, Lan*cing*, Trump*ington*, Hast*ings*, for example, mark the settlements of kindreds (*-ingas*); others the names of people; Idmiston, (Eadmar's *tun*) in Wiltshire; Faversham (Febre's *ham*) in Kent; Cookham (Cocc *ham*) -on-Thames; Rendles*ham* in Suffolk and Eynsham (Egone's *ham*) near Oxford: while the endings *-burgh* and *-ford* speak for themselves.

Whatever the fluctuations of European trade during the crucial eighth and early ninth centuries, in Anglo-Saxon England the market towns and defensive burghs had a healthier rural basis than many of the relatively artificial Romano-British *civitates*, even if the better placed of these survived, such as (York) *Eboracum civitas*. and (London) *Londoniensis civitas*, Lundenwic. Thus directly and indirectly the Anglo-Saxons slowly mastered the land, in a cumulative effort more important than the Roman occupation or the Norman Conquest.

By the ninth century the power of Wessex, now more broadly based on the expansion into Somerset and Devon, had superseded the overlordships of Northumbria and Mercia. Under Alfred (871–99) Wessex would survive terrible Danish wars; under Athelstan it would dominate northern England and become one of the most famous monarchies in Europe; and Edgar (959–75) would call himself 'King of England and Ruler of the Islands and of the Sea Kings' in the climax of the Old English monarchy. Then, under Ethelred II *Unred*, mistranslated 'the Unready', whose real epithet is an ironic joke since his name means literally 'noble counsel' and 'unred' 'no counsel at all',[5] it would collapse before the second Danish onslaught. It would then, after the death of Edmund *Ireneside*, be brought by Knut and his short-lived sons into a Scandinavian empire. It would finally, under Ethelred's son, Edward the Confessor, half-brother of *Ireneside*, revert to the Cerdinga line, still politically coherent in spite of the over-mighty Anglo-Danish earls of the house of Godwin, and with its basic economy and institutions intact.

The main theme of English history now appears. Not so much the emergence of self-governing democracy, as the rise and continuity of an able and flexible establishment based on centralized government in a manageable area. For Anglo-Saxon society was always hierarchical; indeed Stenton writes, 'there is little that can properly be called democratic in their conception of society . . . like their descendants in every age, the English peasants of the earliest time were very sensitive to diversities of rank'.* They always loved a lord. And Loyn insists that anyone who expects to find 'primitive democracy is fated to receive a rude shock'.[6] The Normans and Angevins would exploit this habit of deference and the considerable centralization; they would tighten up and rationalize institutions already there, and in turn would themselves be affected by the wealth and relative security of Anglo-Saxon England.

Thus the supremacy of Wessex was confirmed under Alfred the Great, then the most versatile and intelligent ruler in Europe, whose personality has been described by a contemporary in the first biography of an English layman.† The *gesta* or 'deeds' of kings are today played down and social and economic studies preferred, while statisticians and anthropologists study the 'masses' on tantalizingly meagre evidence, but Alfred's personality was in fact as decisive as tradition makes it.

* Stenton, *op. cit.* p. 310. Slavery persisted in England long after it had died out in most of the west, and slaves were exported to Iceland and even to Muslim Spain.

† Asser's *Life of Alfred* (*de rebus gestis Aelfridi*), *together with the annals of St Neots erroneously ascribed to Asser*. Ed. W. H. Stevenson, Oxford, 1904. Only one copy survived and that was burnt in the eighteenth century, so we know it only through Archbishop Parker's edition, 1574, 'a work which has to bear not only the weight of its own sins but that of the author's, of the interpolators and of the editors'. Parker was probably so busy that he gave his assistants free hands, but the book is not a forgery. Asser was a Welsh monk from St David's invited to Alfred's court in 885. He became Bishop of Sherborne, and died in 909. The authenticity of his biography has been questioned but recently vindicated.

2

When in 825 Egbert of Wessex broke the Mercians at Wroughton on the northern fringe of the Wiltshire downs, he had settled an ancient and gruelling contest. Ine of Wessex (688–726), a contemporary of Bede, had already founded Taunton in Somerset and conquered Devon before he retired to Rome, 'commending his kingdom to younger men'. His laws, in Alfred's recension, provide our richest evidence for his times. During the later eighth century Offa of Mercia may even have called himself 'Bretwalda', a barbarian honorific coined to compete with the Welsh Vertegernas, and meaning 'Ruler of Britain'. He had negotiated with Charlemagne on equal terms, and his silver pennies, more negotiable than the traditional gold now very rare in the west, encouraged an already widespread money economy which would come to full fruition in the thirteenth century. He also built the *Offedicke*, Offa's Dyke, against the Welsh, running south from around Chester for seventy miles, and he controlled London. But the broader-based power of Wessex now began to tell. The feuds of its royal house were ferocious and the Cerdingas had assassinated the heirs of the Jutish Wihtgar in the Isle of Wight; the worst Cerdinga internecine feuds were contemporaneous with the missionary saints. But despite their vendettas, Egbert, 'the eighth king who was [officially] Bretwalda',[7] had by 829 mastered all the land south of the Humber and defeated the Cornish at Hingston Down, above the Tamar, so far had he penetrated to the west.

He had consolidated Wessex only just in time, for in Scandinavia and along the Baltic a storm was building up which was to harass England for generations. The enterprising Scandinavian Vikings, ruthless marauders and splendid seamen, had begun to swarm over the ocean. They came first to plunder; then, as in eastern and central England and Normandy, to settle in. Their raids were 'committed on a massive and extensive scale, and embraced the whole of Europe: in the east they thrust down the great rivers of Russia to the Black Sea, and in the west along the Atlantic coasts, past Arab Spain, through the Straits of Gibraltar and on to the distant Mediterranean. They reached out across the Atlantic to the Faroe Islands, Iceland, Greenland and even to America.'[8] Their name means either a pirate from a *vik*, 'a pirate who lays hidden in a fiord, creek, or bay, waiting to pounce upon passing vessels', or the 'camp-folk', from the Anglo-Saxon *Wic* – Latin *vicus*; or, most intriguingly, from *vikja*, to 'deviate' or escape with the loot.*

* Johannes Brøndsteed, *The Vikings*, pp. 34–7. The rival theories of Sophus Bugge, the Norwegian etymologist; of Wadstein and Steenstrup are described: *vik* commands most support.

In 793 they had first struck at England when Norwegian pirates, stealing up in winter, had sacked holy Lindisfarne itself; 'a resounding and bloody deed which served as a prelude to Viking aggression in the west'. It is commemorated by the Lindisfarne stone, carved on one side with the symbols of Christianity, and on the other with 'the violators of the shrine dressed outlandishly in rough jerkins and narrow trousers, swinging their swords and battle axes as they advanced . . . a poignant monument fashioned perhaps by some Anglo-Saxon monk who witnessed this early example of Viking pillage'.[9]

Down in Wessex, four years earlier, a less spectacular but equally significant episode had occurred. The royal reeve, Beaduheard, had ridden down from Dorchester to the shore near Portland, then an island, where three ships, probably Norwegian, had put in. He had tried to 'force them to the King's residence (at Wareham), for he did not know what they were; and they slew him'.[10] Well they might, for they were professional killers out of Scandinavian prehistory, with horizons which made provincials of the Anglo-Saxons.

For the king's earldormen and thegns of Wessex, they portended disaster: as the attack developed there was no regular fleet and no permanent war bands or militia to resist what the Anglo-Saxons would call the 'Army'. In 835, the year of Egbert's victory at Wroughton, they had come into the Isle of Sheppey in the Thames Estuary; in 851 'for the first time heathen men'[11] wintered in Thanet off the coast of Kent.

For all their panache, these pirates were far more brutish than the sagas, written down generations later and then romanticized by the Victorians, suggest.* Their contemporaries called them thieves and heathen and, when they caught them, killed them, like vermin, out-of-hand. The long-drawn misery of the later ninth century is apparent from the *Anglo-Saxon Chronicle*; from 865 to 878 the very fabric of society was threatened; first by the 'Great Army' led by that sinister ruffian, Ivar the Boneless,† son of Ragnar Lodbrog (Hairy Breeks). In 866 they took York, the strategic centre of the north; then, three years later, they mastered East Anglia and shot to death their prisoner Edmund, the young Wulfinga king, afterwards commemorated at Bury St Edmunds. By 870 they had seized the strategic point of *Raedingan* (Reading) at the junction of the Thames and Kennet, deep in England. Then, in January 871, at Ashdown (*Æscandun*)‡ they were checked by Ethelred I of Wessex and his brother Alfred the Atheling, 'the most belligerent and

---

* Even the romantic view of their ships sailing the seas, with their shields glinting along the bulwarks is false: as might be expected, they only hung out the shields when in harbour.

† Born, supposedly, as the result of a rape when his mother's condition should have precluded conception, and so under-developed.

‡ *Latine mons fraxini*, the hill of the ash, *unica spinoza arbor*, a single spiky tree. Asser, *op. cit.* p. 38.

lucky of the royal youths'. For though Ethelred refused to engage the enemy until he had finished hearing mass, Alfred risked cutting the service and charged the enemy uphill 'in a manly way, like a wild boar'.

That spring Alfred succeeded his brother, and he planned a war of attrition, making the pirates pay an increasing price so that they would turn away to easier countries or come to terms and settle down. With ravaged crops and burning farms, the war went on. Returning from Wimborne from his brother's obsequies, Alfred was worsted by the Danes at Wilton and had to buy them off – immense tribute was taken by the 'heathen', for they broke all the rules and fought in the winter. With their command of the sea, they continued an enveloping double attack beyond East Anglia through the south Midlands and round the south coast. By 875 one 'Army' was in Wareham, as far as they could get into Dorset from Poole harbour, and the English brought them to a parley. They swore on their 'holy bracelet' to be off, only to break out and 'steal' into Exeter, with another estuary behind them. In 877, they took Gloucester, thus commanding the Severn and the Bristol Channel. In 878 came the crisis: wintering in Chippenham in north Wiltshire, 'the Army' again struck in mid-winter, and Alfred fled beyond Selwood to Athelney in the Somerset marshes.* But the turning point had come: Alfred rallied his war-band in Selwood and routed the pirates on the down above Edington, a western bastion of the Wiltshire downs overlooking the wooded west country. The Danes had to come to terms; at Aller near Athelney a truce was patched up, and the Danish leader

---

* *Op. cit.* p. 41. *Per sylvestra et gronnosa Summurtunensis pagae.* But there he did not, it seems, burn the cakes. The story was dragged into Asser's *Life* by Parker or his assistants in 1574, and derives from the *Annals of St Neots* and a homily on the Saint's life, neither compiled until the twelfth century. St Neot in fact lived at least two generations after Alfred, in Cornwall; and when his relics were translated to Huntingdonshire, probably in the reign of Knut, his name may have been linked to Alfred's to enhance his prestige. For it was now, and only now, alleged that, as the monarch's kinsmen, St Neot had prophesied that he would suffer humiliations for neglecting his royal duties when a young man. These penalties included defeat by the Danes, skulking in a swineherd's hut, and 'turning' – not yet burning – bread. St Neot, now with God, then appeared anachronistically to Alfred, and declared that, having purged his sins, he would now gain victory. In a later version, adopted by Parker, the swineherd becomes a cowherd and the 'cakes' are burnt. Though quite unhistorical, the famous tale deserves recapitulation.

Attending to his arrows and other instruments of war, Alfred did not observe that the 'cakes' ('*panes*' – bannocks or loaves), were burning; whereat the cowherd's wife ran and removed them: (*currit et amovit eos*). 'Wretched fellow,' she said, in verse, 'you cannot bother to turn the "cakes" when you see them burning, though you are glad enough to bolt them hot . . .'

> . . . *Heus homo,*
> *Urere, quos cernis, panes gyrare moraris*
> *Cum nimium gaudes hos manducare calentes.*

'Little did the unfortunate woman realize that the man was King Alfred, who had warred so much on the pagans and had won so many victories over them.' *ibidem.*

Gudrum, hard-pressed, even became a Christian. The strategy of attrition was working out: some of the army had already moved into Yorkshire and settled down; Gudrum now retreated into East Anglia where some of his pirates turned farmers.

The worst crisis for Wessex was over: by 886 the West Saxons took London and Alfred deputed his Mercian son-in-law to take care of it. 'Alfred and Gudrum's peace' now secured all England south-west of a line from London to Chester, leaving the 'Danelaw' less of a threat than a problem of assimilation. For the settled Danes of Yorkshire were already fighting the Norwegians who had overrun the Lake District and Lancashire. Further major attack from overseas was beaten off: still on the defensive, the English had proved inexpugnable.

Alfred's son Edward and his warlike daughter Ethelfleda (who, it is alleged, after her first child refused to live with her husband, saying it was 'unbecoming to a King's daughter to give way to a delight which after a time produced such painful consequences'), now launched an attack; and by Athelstan's accession in 924 the Wessex power extended to the Humber. In 937 Athelstan's famous victory at Brunanburg over a coalition of Scots and Irish Vikings gave him command of the north, even over the Scottish Lowlands. The laconic and pedestrian *Chronicle* breaks into eloquence:

There also the aged Constantine (of Scotland), the hoary-headed warrior, came north to his own land by flight. . . . The grey-haired warrior, the old and wily one, had no cause to vaunt of that sword clash.[12]

Martial and Germanic, the *Chronicle* depicts Athelstan's triumphant return to Wessex, leaving his enemies 'to the black raven with its horned beak, to share the corpses, and the dun-coated white-tailed eagle, the greedy war-hawk, to enjoy the carrion, and that grey beast, the wolf of the forest'.

Athelstan also made great marriages for his dynasty; giving Edith, his sister, 'over the sea to the son of the king of the Old Saxons', afterwards Otto the Great; another married Charles the Simple, King of France; another, Louis of Provence, and another Hugh Capet, Count of Paris. Athelstan was prodigal of bracelets and gold; 'a dispenser of treasure to men', the most powerful ruler in all the north. So far, in less than a century, had come the Cerdingas of Wessex. The political framework of an all-English monarchy had been made.

Alfred, from whose stubborn defence this dominion had derived, was not only a soldier. He had little time, he complained, for reading, what with the Danes and hunting and ruling his kingdom and ill health; but in later life he himself construed Orosius' *World History against the Pagans*, translating '*Anno urbis Condita MVIII*', '*Æfter thaem the Romeburg getimbred*

*waes M Wintra VIII'.** Unlike Charlemagne, he could write; 'an individual author struggling with a refractory language'.† He even added
to Orosius and contributed a systematic survey of the Baltic and
beyond, based on the talk of the merchant adventurers he encouraged.
He also wrote an English version of St Augustine's *Soliquies*:
'collecting timber', he wrote, 'in a great wood'; and he translated
Boethius' *Consolations of Philosophy*, a work then much admired,
as well as Gregory the Great's *Pastoral Care*: 'a boc that is genemned
Cura Pastoralis and on Englisc Hirdeboc': 'The message,' he called it,
'that St Augustine brought to the islanders from the south, across the
salt sea, as the Lord's Champion the Pope of Rome had formerly
composed it.' He also had Bede's *Ecclesiastical History* translated and
probably caused the *Anglo-Saxon Chronicle* to be compiled. For he wanted
to give his people a good background for hard times: 'It has often come
to my mind', he wrote, 'what wise men there were in former times
throughout England': but now 'very few men this side Humber . . .
could translate Latin into English and not many beyond'. He would
provide books in English they could understand and he sent copies of
the *Hirdeboc* to all the bishops, for 'some of them', he wrote, 'who knew
least Latin needed it'. But when he ordered his judges to learn to read
or resign, he told those too old to try to get someone to read for them.
Who among the cruel Normans and Angevins would have made such a
proviso?

Alfred was determined not merely that the clergy should be literate,
but 'all the youth of England born of free men who had the means'.
Unless too useful in other ways, they should be set to their books 'until
they could read English'. Where Carolingian learning had been self-
conscious, Alcuin elaborately discussing grammar with Charlemagne
and signing 'your Flaccus', Alfred's similes are homely. 'Load your
wagons,' he writes, 'with fine rods so that you can plait many a fine wall';
or, paraphrasing Boethius, that kings need 'tools for ruling with' – clergy,
soldiers and labourers, and 'land' for them 'to live on' and 'gifts' and
'food and ale, and clothes'.[13]

Such was the versatile and attractive personality of the greatest king
of the Old English. Unhappily after the robust Edward and Athelstan
his descendants proved short-lived. Athelstan's brother, Edmund
(939–46), succeeded him at eighteen: he, too, was a great warrior who
won back the Five Towns of the Danelaw from the Norse and subdued
Cumberland, their base, and all Northumbria. He appointed as Abbot
of Glastonbury Dunstan, who under Edgar, came to dominate the

---

* 'one thousand and eight winters after Rome was built'. See Alfred's *Orosius*, E.E.T.S., ed.
H. L. Sweet, 1883.
† See Loyn, *op. cit.*, pp. 281–3, '*the kaseres nama*', he could write, '*was Agammemnon*'.

English Church;* but he was stabbed at Pucklechurch in Gloucester-shire by an outlaw during a 'carouse'. The youngest brother, Eadred (946–55), defeated Eric Bloodaxe, the son of Harald Fairhair of Norway, who had tried to carve out a Viking kingdom at York, and he brought Yorkshire again under control: but Eadred, too, died young at Frome in Somerset. He was succeeded by his nephew, Edmund's son Eadwig Allfair, *Eall-faeger* (955–9), so-called for his looks, who was seventeen when elected King of Wessex while his younger brother Edgar took over Mercia. But the Allfair quarrelled with Dunstan: bored apparently by the 'fitting' conversation at his accession banquet, the boy retired to the company of his 'uncanonical wife' and her mother, where Dunstan found him sitting on the floor with the crown beside him, clapped it on his head and dragged him back. Furious, the king exiled him to the Low Countries.

The Allfair died at twenty-one and Edgar took over both kingdoms: in his day, says the *Chronicle*, 'things improved greatly' and 'God granted him...peace as long as he lived'. Succeeding at sixteen, he made Dunstan Archbishop of Canterbury and worked closely with the church to enhance the royal prestige and administration, so that he 'improved the peace of the people more than the kings who were before him in the memory of man', for, 'without battle, he brought under his sway all that he wished'.[14]

In 973 Edgar was crowned, perhaps in a ceremonial re-coronation, at Bath with the first recorded ritual after the Frankish custom, followed in its essentials ever since. His brief grandeur, the political climax of the West Saxon monarchy, was symbolized when he was rowed on the Dee near Chester by a crew of outlandish kings: the King of Scots, Iago of Gwynneth, Howell of South Wales, the 'Sea-King' Maccus of Man, Malcolm of Cumbria and the 'King' of Strathclyde. For, we are told 'on a certain day he went on board a boat ... with them at the oars and himself seizing the helm, he steered it skilfully on the course of the river Dee, proceeding from the palace to the monastery of St John the Baptist, attended by all the crowd of ealdormen and nobles also by boat ...' He returned with the same pomp ... [and] As he entered he is reported to have said that any of his successors might indeed pride himself on being king of the English ... when he might have the glory of such honours, with so many kings subservient to him.[15] Nor, says the *Chronicle*, was there 'the

---

* St Dunstan (925–88) came of aristocratic lineage and studied at Glastonbury, where, 'like a clever bee' he had 'darted through' the sacred books, as well as learning 'the art of writing ...' and 'harp playing and skill in painting'. After a chequered residence at court, he was made abbot and entrusted with part of the royal treasure. He was to be the greatest architect of the tenth-century reform of the church 'so that all this English land was filled with his holy teaching'. See translation from *Memorials of St Dunstan*. Ed. Stubbs, pp. 3–52. Cited in E.H.D., I, p. 826 ff.

fleet so proud nor the host so strong that it got itself prey in England so long as this noble King held the throne, who styled himself "Emperor of Britain"'. But in 975 the 'young man Edgar' died: there followed political collapse, Danish domination; then, after a disturbed Indian summer of the Cerdingas under Edward the Confessor, the Norman Conquest.

3

Over what sort of society did Alfred and his tenth-century successors have to rule and what institutions did they find to hand? Our answers must be provisional. Here are quagmires haunted by defunct authorities, some apt to revive at a draught of confirmatory research, others fading, if still articulate.

The Anglo-Saxons had been at once marauders and colonists; their leaders, with or without cause, had stressed their high descent; as the war bands settled down they still retained their prestige, 'proud workers of war' who 'overcame the Welshmen'. The earliest Laws or 'Dooms' of Æthelbert of Kent, who had tolerated St Augustine, already show a strictly graded society; from the high-born *eorls* and *gesiths* through plain *ceorls* or free farmers down to the slaves – *theows*, distinguished by cropped hair. It was an insult, punishable by fine, to give a free man a crew cut.

The 'dooms' of Ine of Wessex in the version transmitted by Alfred show a similar hierarchy, including various grades of Welsh assessed at half the blood-price of the English. At the apex was the Woden-born king, with his sacred prestige, heathen and Christian, and with his intermittent council or *Witenagemot* – literally 'assembly of the wise'. These archaic regional gatherings included the king's more important relations, the local bishops and abbots, and the great ealdormen and lesser magnates. There was no division of Church and State and a contemporary drawing depicts the establishment combining to string up a malefactor. These assemblies were vaguely important, for there was still a flavour of tribal election about kingship, and the king had to carry his magnates with him as repositories of the custom of the folk. But the Witans normally confirmed rather than initiated. The king's household, on the other hand, was always an active force; even in Ine's day there was already a writing office which issued *diplomas* and *landbocs* approved by the Witan for 'bookland' secured by charter, a custom paralleled among the Franks. Alfred already sent out sealed writs, an Anglo-Saxon invention, and the first Great Seal of England would be struck for Edward the Confessor. Thus, though the Witans were intermittent and the household moved about, living off the royal estates, there was continuity: in the worst times of Ethelred II the rudimentary bureaucracy could work well enough to buy off the Danes. On great occasions the king was expected to convene the 'assembly of the wise', but his household was a continuing fact: out of both would come that conciliar government which would be the backbone of medieval and even of Tudor administration.

Below Witan and household came the shire moots. They do not all descend from original tribal assemblies; some are tribal, as Somerset or Devon, some territorial, named from a river or the chief town of the shire, as Wiltshire, after the Wylye, and Hampshire, after (South) Hampton. In Wessex they were already in being under Ine; Alfred's descendants imposed them on the Midlands and the Danelaw. While Norfolk and Suffolk, Essex, Sussex and Kent remained in name tribal divisions, the shire pattern also applied to them. Though the border-lands, Cumberland and Northumberland, were not shired, the well-proved ancient system would be applied by Edward i and Henry viii to Wales.

The shire courts were presided over by *shire-reeves* (sheriffs) deputizing for the ealdormen. These sheriffs are first heard of in the tenth century, and would have an important future in Norman times.

Below the shires, and parallel with them, the 'hundreds' had developed. This hoary institution emerges as a problem from antique mists: it comprised a hundred *hides*, originally units of measurement based on the area which could support a farming household, *terra unius familiae*: naturally the holdings varied, from 120 acres in the more prosperous East Anglia to 40 acres in the west. These original divisions had perhaps been grouped to provide the *feorm* (food rents) in kind for the itinerant royal household or as a basis for service in the *fyrd*; then by the time of Edgar, with an obscure shift of responsibility, they became part of local government. The hundreds appear under various names: in Sussex as *rapes* from the ropes that enclosed the meeting; in Kent as *lathes*, family holdings of great antiquity; in Yorkshire as *ridings*. In the Danelaw they are *wapentakes* from the Danish *vapnatak*, the noise made by warriors who clashed their weapons, presumably to show goodwill. The areas of land measurement varied: but along with the shires, the hundreds came to link up with the central administration in rudimentary self-government, one of the achievements of Anglo-Saxon and medieval England, long after reflected overseas.

Parallel with these public institutions went the private hall moots or manor courts, also of immense antiquity. The origin of the manor has occasioned vast controversy; in England, as on the continent, it is very old, the social and economic basis of the barbarian elites as they encroached on the tribal land held by folkright. And the manor and its lord may have benefited as open fields became more productive than formerly supposed, and 'by concentrating crops on either one or two big fields at any given moment, made the whole sweep of the fallow available for browsing, and at the same time provided maximum protection against cattle'.[16] And where the folk were content with subsistence farming, the manorial lords aimed at higher returns: the standard ceased to be the needs of a family, and with the introduction of the heavy eight-ox plough (probably not until the ninth century), it 'became the ability of a power engine to till the soil'. The old picture of relative stagnation must give place to one of greater productivity.

The term manor derives from the *mansio*, the principal house or hall, with its *heall gemot* or manor court; the term 'lord' from *hlaford*, contracted from *hlaf-weard*, or 'loaf-guarder' who took care of the *hlafeaters* – 'loaf eaters' (hence presumably 'loafers'). The lord took the profits of jurisdiction: *toll*, a sales tax, and *team*, fines on cattle thieves. Manors could be big royal or church estates, or the lordships of noble retainers. Offa's minister, Dudda, for example already had the Windrush estate in the Cotswolds in the eighth century. The king, as Alfred observed, needed to provide 'land' and 'gifts'; he at once both rewarded his war band and his household ministers in the best way he could and recognized accomplished facts of pioneer settlement.

Thus the soldiers, officials and churchmen were provided for and made responsible for their dependants. The system supplemented the waning responsibility of the kin, and the vaguer general obligations of the folk. It was not yet a feudal arrangement, but it was potentially feudal, and it made for better farming and greater order. As in many primitive but settled societies, a habit of responsibility went deep. Time out of mind lawful men of the *vill* or *tun* had 'declared' what local custom had been; now, as crown and magnates compelled the people to manage their local affairs, these lawful men came to reinforce hundred or manor court. Thus, from the centre to the periphery, public and private authority worked together; from the royal household and the Witan down through the shires and hundreds, the hall moots and manor courts, the *vills* and *tuns*, turning ancient obligations to new purposes. The English tradition of self-government under law has primeval roots.

So from Ethelbert and Ine to Alfred and beyond, the Old English laws dealt with crime, accident and muddle. The heaviest fines were for breaking the king's peace in or near his own residence, and for violating the peace of the Church. The main remedy for endemic violence was still the *wergild* or blood-price, steeply graded according to the rank of the victim; it was the alternative to the blood feud.[17] Compensation had to be paid at once; twenty shillings down at the open grave and the rest within forty days. Next to murder came theft: they called up to seven men 'thieves', seven to thirty-five become a 'band'; above that they become an 'army' – the regular term for the Danes. Repeated theft was punished first by mutilation and then by hanging: even a boy of ten was held to be responsible if he had connived at it.

These countrymen were wary people; a traveller off the rudimentary track who did not shout or blow his horn could be killed or held until redeemed by his kin. Sex crimes were elaborately graded. Anyone who bought a wife, but failed to marry her, repaid her price to her kin twice over: if anyone lay with a nobleman's 'girl-cupbearer' he had to pay twenty shillings. If a betrothed maiden of free peasant stock committed fornication, sixty shillings had to be paid; if in kind, in valuable cattle, not just with 'any slave'. There were tariffs for adultery according to rank, but a slave raping a slave girl was castrated. A free man, of course, who found another with his wife, even 'behind closed doors', let alone 'under the same blanket', could kill her without incurring blood feud with her kin; and heavy fines were exacted for abducting nuns. If anybody 'in lewd fashion', for example, seized a nun 'either by her clothes or by her breast without her leave', he had to pay twice as much as he would have for making up to a laywoman. Living in sin with lapsed nuns was discouraged, and any children of the union had no right of inheritance. A considerable fine was set for 'pulling a free woman's hair'.

Slavery was taken for granted; but anyone selling his own country-man, bond or free, overseas paid the full *wergild*, as if he had killed him. There were stiff fines for felling trees without permission; sixty shillings for a tree 'under which thirty swine could stand'. The owner of strayed cattle was liable to find them slaughtered, and then he could only claim the flesh and the hide, with the horns and bones, liver and lights going to the owners of the invaded field. Free peasants were expected to fence in their share of the village holdings, and anyone who so neglected his share of a meadow that stray cattle got in had to compensate the others. By Alfred's time even more elaborate contingencies were provided for; if, when felling a tree, a man let it fall on another, the kinsmen of the victim got the tree, and within thirty days. There were fines for stealing bees, stud horses, and slaves – all considerable crimes; but the owners of savage dogs were lightly penalized: even if a dog has 'bitten and rent' a man to death, the owner paid only six shillings.

Such were some representative provisions of this rural society – no paradise for simple rustics. In collaboration with the folk, the laws and customs were enforced by royal and lordly authority, and they were supplemented by the spontaneous growth of 'Peace Guilds' to keep order and catch robbers. At first much depended on the kin, responsible for *wergilds* and for 'compurgation', swearing to a man's character; an often unconvincing procedure supplemented by the ordeal, whereby the decision was handed over to the Almighty. Under Athelstan this procedure was defined. For three days the accused must live on bread and water, salt and vegetables: if tested by water, he must sink 'one and half ells' on the rope, to be dragged out half drowned but innocent: if by hot iron, his hand must be bound up for three days. If by then it had festered, he was guilty. Trial by battle was a Norman innovation, much resented.

Such, in broad outline, were the complex and rather haphazard arrangements that had emerged out of the original settlements. The society was much richer, officially Christian, and still militarized. The king was now the focus of a much wider power; *Rex Anglorum*, if not yet, as Edgar would claim, overlord of the whole island. Immense difficulties were being met defending the land and maintaining rudimentary order and communications. They would not have been met if the people had not shown enough goodwill, docility and good sense to collaborate with government.

4

Anglo-Saxon civilization was also outstanding in literature and the arts. And here the minds of these people are directly revealed: only a small proportion of the literature has survived, but it is excellent and our own is rooted in it. The beat and swing of alliterative verse, declaimed to the harp with the pause in mid-line, would re-emerge in the late fourteenth century with *Piers Plowman*, and be revived by modern poets. Nearly all that survives comes down from manuscripts of the late tenth or early eleventh centuries, and even *Beowulf*, the best of the Germanic epics to survive anywhere, is thought to have been set down from oral traditions at earliest by the time of Offa. The first notable poet was Caedmon, (*fl. c.* 680) a cowherd who became a monk at Whitby and, after ruminating over the scriptures, could 'quickly turn whatever passages were read to him into delightful and moving poetry in his own English tongue',[18] singing of the creation and the redemption of mankind.

Cynewulf, in the eighth century, wrote long and brisk accounts of St Helena's finding of the true cross, very revealing of the military turn of their minds, for the mother of Constantine, that 'battle prince', travelled 'the road to the Jews' with a 'war band over the sea of the Vandals'. This 'stately war-like queen' took a high line with the Jews who tried to conceal the 'Tree': they could not, they protested, after so long remember where it had been put away. Undaunted, Helena replied, 'Well, the Trojan war was much further back, but you re-

60

membered that.' Then she shut Judas, their leader, into a dry cistern for a week, until, under divine guidance, he found the cross twenty feet down under a steep cliff. Finally, she ferreted out the nails, and convening a synod of bishops, had the site glorified.[19]

Beowulf, a heathen poem with Christian overtones, gives an incomparable description of the hero's barrow burial after they had 'shoved the dragon . . . over the cliff' and 'let the wave take him'. It might have occurred at any time since the Bronze Age, when the 'wood reek' of the cremation 'mounted up dark above the smoking glow', and the companions rode chanting round the 'mound . . . lofty and broad, on the edge of the headland', leaving the 'gold in the ground where it yet lies, as useless to men as it was before'.*

The old poets admired diversity of gifts:

One can steer the prow on the dark waves know the currents, pilot the company over the wild ocean, where bold seamen ply the oars. . . . One is a spry servant in the mead hall. One is well versed in horses, wise in the manage of a steed. One is quick at the dice. One is witty at the wine drinking a great dispenser of beer . . . one is skilled with the hawk . . . one is lovable, his mind and speech are pleasant to men.[20]

The *Seafarer* expresses both the attraction and the bitterness of the ocean: 'My heart's desire,' says the young sailor, 'urges my spirit to travel, that I may see the land of foreigners afar off. . . .' He 'has no mind for anything but the tossing of the waves'. The note would become familiar. But the old sailor sees the other side; he evokes the roar of the ice-cold sea in contrast to the hearty joys of great houses, where men sit 'proud' and 'flushed with wine', forgetful of 'sickness or age or the sword's hate'. And in *The Wanderer* the poet sings of the menace of the north, when snowstorms bind the earth and of 'the terror of winter when the dark shadows of night comes lowering'.[21]

In contrast to this gloom, most familiarly expressed in the romantic lament over the ruins of Bath, there is a lyrical touch, and as well a note of hearty enjoyment, though the more roisterous songs have not survived, probably censored by the Church. Intimate love of animals is early apparent, as in the *Riddle of the Badger* who walks 'on his toes in the green grass', rescues his cubs through the tunnels of his set, and so 'dreads not at all the battle with the death whelp'. 'Fast with my forefeet,' says the badger, 'I must take a path through the steep hill.' Swans and cuckoos provide the subject of riddles, and inanimate objects are made to speak. As the plough: 'I tear with my teeth if he who is my

* *The Epic of Beowulf the Geat* describes many real early sixth-century characters, though it includes many ancient myths; a blend of realism and 'Jack the Giant Killer'. See Gordon, *op. cit.*, pp. 69–70.

lord serves me rightly from behind'; or the barley, 'polished, turned, dried, bound, twisted, bleached, softened' to make beer: or the mead-honey 'from the dales and the downs'; and the oyster – 'men quickly eat me uncooked also'.* Medical spells have a pagan touch:

> *Forget not, Mugwort, what thou disd't reveal . . .*
> *Thou hast strength against the foe who stalks through the land.*

Or *This is the herb Wergulu,*
> *The seal sent thee over the back of the ocean.*

Or the spell when cattle stray:

> *Garmund servant of God*
> *Find those cattle and fetch those cattle.*
> *. . . And bring home those cattle.*

And they pray for

> *Fields growing and flourishing:*
> *Store of gleaming millet-harvest,*
> *And broad barley crops*
> *And white wheat crops*
> *And all the crops of the Earth. . . .*
> *Crescite grow et multiplicamini.*

The finest Anglo-Saxon battle piece is the fragmentary *Song of Maldon*, recalling the first celebrated English defeat. It tells of the death of the ealdorman Byrhtnoth in the Blackwater estuary, Essex, in 991. Provoked by the blackmail of Danish pirates, 'calling over the cold water "give us money for peace",' he rashly allowed 'the slaughterous wolves' to 'pass west over Panta' to the attack. Sending back the horses, and 'letting the loved hawk fly to the wood', he led the main battle line of the East Saxons against the 'ship army'. Then, though some 'turned from the fight and sought the wood . . . which was not right', he fought to the death, thanking God for 'all the joys I have known in the world'. The speech of his old companion, 'heart the keener, mood the more as our might lessens', has become a classic.

And if the moralizing clichés of the religious poems can be tedious, and the allegorical and amiable panther and the whale Fastitocolon, a bore, many of them show great dramatic power; as when the Holy Guthlac defies the demons, or the poet contrasts the fates of the saved and damned on Doomsday, when the poor and rich shall have one law, and 'all the wicked host shall stand, stiffened like stone, awaiting

---

* Making riddles occupied the most eminent minds; as St Aldhelm, Tatwine, Archbishop of Canterbury and Eusebius of Wearmouth. The merits of the riddles vary. See Gordon, *op. cit.*, p. 320.

misery',[22] in flaming vapours and grievous ice. In contrast, the blessed in heaven never know gloom or hail or snow, poverty or sloth; but amid masses of red roses shall 'shine for ever'.

In the visual arts, the Anglo-Saxons were also remarkable. Out of the pagan tradition of Sutton Hoo, from which the Alfred Jewel of crystal and cloisonné enamel still derives, they had developed more complex designs, with Celtic, Byzantine and even Scythian motifs. Their craftsmen in Rome, making chalices for St Peter's with animals and foliage interlaced, won European renown, and English embroidery – opus anglicanum (English work) – was also celebrated. Faded but intact at Durham, the stole of St Cuthbert shows subtle designs in blues and greens, browns and gold.

Contrary to long-received opinion – for the Normans, like the mid-Victorians, intent on the latest style, destroyed many admirable buildings – the Anglo-Saxons built extensively in stone. The complex of buildings lately unearthed at Winchester must have rivalled the Carolingian palaces; while at Bradford-on-Avon, Earls Barton near Northampton, Breamore in Hampshire and Studland in Dorset their skill is still evident.

The Northumbrian art of illuminating manuscripts was revived in Kent and at Winchester, now the main centre of royal patronage. Here, even before the first Danish attack, fine psalters and gospels were produced. There is a superb charter of King Edgar of 966, with gold letters on a purple ground in the Byzantine style, while the Utrecht psalter, taken from an original in Rheims, shows how the Old English artists could depict rapid gestures and flickering draperies, giving a new liveliness to the original.

The Vikings, often starkly destructive, set more colourful fashions, which caught on with their opponents. They wore their hair cropped at the back and long in front, and English conservatives denounced this 'Danizing' style, 'with bared necks and blinded eyes'. But most free men held to the Old English custom of flowing locks, moustaches and beards: indeed, both these northern peoples retained the hairiness of their barbaric origins. As we see from the Bayeux tapestry, it was only with the Conquest that the fashion for clean shaving would come in.

The basic form of dress, going back in its essentials to the Bronze Age, remained constant; light or heavy woollen tunics, cross-gartered leggings and bare knees (as in a vivid drawing of Knut), with mantles fastened by a great brooch for the well-born. The peasants are depicted in duller versions of the same style; the clumsy trousers of the old Germanic barbarians described by Tacitus seem to have gone out of fashion, and it was not until the nineteenth century that these unhygienic garments came back. The high-born women, who had the elevated standing usual in Germanic societies, wore long-skirted tunics, mantles and hoods over linen undergarments.

5

This slow-moving, basically peasant, society had settled in a half-tamed countryside with wide expanses of woodland, marsh and moor; transport was by horses, pack horses and leather-hooded carts trundling over remains of the Roman roads and over the ancient trackways through the forest and over the downs. Under the West Saxon kings the country had been united in a considerable prosperity and the coinage was one of the best in Europe. The set-back caused by the Viking invasions had been surmounted by Alfred and his descendants, and the second and more formidable Danish attack did not, as the first had threatened to do, destroy this deep-rooted and now mainly Christian civilization.

With the Church playing such an integral part, lay society was more developed in England than on the continent; it had rudimentary law courts, laws in English and a remarkable vernacular literature. And the Danish invaders had an ancient, elaborate, and technologically rather advanced prehistoric culture of their own. They were gradually tamed and assimilated; for at least a century before the Norman Conquest East Anglia and most of the Midlands and the north had been Anglo-Danish or Anglo-Norse. Thus, with a broader-based agriculture and rudimentary central and local government, to which the Scandinavians contributed, as they did particularly to the development of towns, England was drawn together by its institutions and its economy. Both would be exploited to build a strong centralized state. And in England, as in the rest of early medieval western Europe, the ninth and tenth centuries saw an economic revival which would culminate in the prosperity of the high Middle Ages.

ANGLO-DANISH ENGLAND

On a March evening in 978 a boy of seventeen rode into Corfe Gate in Dorset in the gap in the Purbeck hills, escorted by a few retainers; but as he 'sat undaunted on his horse' in the press of a formal reception, 'venomous' thegns laid hands on him. One drew him to the right, as if for a kiss; another seized his left hand. '"What are you doing," he shouted as far as he could, "breaking my right arm?"' Then he was stabbed, 'leapt from his horse and died'.* He was Edward, son of Edgar, of the right line of Cerdic and King of England. Never, records the *Chronicle*, was worse deed done since the English came to Britain; and that was saying much. Of the short reign of this hot-tempered youth little good is recorded;† but the crime, committed not by his stepmother but by the partisans of his more amenable stepbrother, Ethelred, marked the decline of the Cerdinga house. The rule of Ethelred ii, the *Redeless* or 'No Counsel' (978–1016) proved 'cruel in its beginnings, wretched in the middle, and disgraceful at the end'. Despite the fierce resistance of his son Edmund Ireneside, by 1017 following a second, overwhelming Scandinavian attack, England would be ruled by a Dane. But as already observed, this outcome, traditionally deplored, was technologically not without benefit, and Scandinavian traditions of independence and local self-government took root in East Anglia, the east Midlands and northern England. Moreover, they brought the English into the orbit of a far-flung trading empire and themselves adopted at least a veneer of Christianity.

Meanwhile, they were still heathen pirates and marauders, and their second great attack on England was on a much larger scale than in

* E.H.D., I, *op cit.*, pp. 841–2, from the *Anonymous Life of St Oswald, Archbishop of York*, probably by a monk of Ramsey Abbey; a florid work, but written 995–1005, only a generation after the crime. William of Malmesbury, on the other hand, a far better historian, but writing in the twelfth century, has it that Edward rode in alone from hunting, for his companions were following the deerhounds, and then called informally for a drink. As he drank 'avidly', he was knifed, spurred his horse, then collapsed and was dragged by the stirrup till he died. *Gesta Regum Anglorum*, ed. W. Stubbs, *Rolls*, 1887, vol. 1, p. 183. Both concur that he was buried without ceremony: 'No Gregorian harmony or funeral dirge was heard', says the *Anonymous Life of St Oswald*.

† His body, transferred from Wareham to Shaftesbury, became the centre of a cult of St Edward the Martyr; a public school in Oxford bears his name; and a representation of him still looks down in injured innocence on the square of Corfe Castle, accompanied by a hound of uncertain pedigree.

Alfred's day; it was the climax of an onslaught made at the height of the Viking power, when they had constructed their elaborate strongholds at Trelleborg, Odense and Jomsborg, and built the great *Danework* across their peninsula against the Germans; hence the professionals who in 991 cut down Ealdorman Byrthnoth at Maldon. Three years later, Sweyn Forkbeard, son of Harold Bluetooth of Denmark, led the worst assault for fifty years, and by 997–8 a huge 'Army' was plundering Wessex. By 1002 they were taking a tribute of 24,000 pounds of silver and gold; the 'Danegeld', *Exactio pecuniae publicae piratis danda*, an exaction of public wealth to be given to the pirates, the first systematic taxation.

So when, that year, Ethelred married Emma, a Norman princess, he was trying to bring the Norse, settled in Normandy by Rollo in the early tenth century, against the Danish host; and on St Brice's day he followed up this diplomacy by slaughtering all the Danes in England that he could, including Sweyn's sister Gunhilde, beheaded after she had seen her son speared. In revenge, Sweyn harried both the West Country and Norwich, such was the mobility of his fleet and army. By the winter of 1006–7 the pirates had marched from Reading along the Ridgeway past Wantage down to Avebury, 'lighting beacons as they went', and defeated the Wiltshire thegns; they then turned south-east with their loot past Winchester to the coast, 'proudly, with no one to stop them'. That year, they were bought off with 36,000 pounds of coin. But in 1009 the biggest host sacked Oxford, and, next year, Ipswich. They held Ælfheah, Bishop of Canterbury to ransom, and getting out of hand on 'wine from the south', pelted him with bones and oxheads, until one, Thrum, seeing him unable to die and moved by 'impious piety', knocked him on the head with the back of an axe to put him out of his misery.[1] Until St Thomas eclipsed him, Ælfheah was Canterbury's principal saint.

The English were now outclassed and derided by the 'Army', which took another enormous tribute of 48,000 pounds. When in 1013 Sweyn, based on Gainsborough and the Danelaw, took Oxford and Winchester and besieged London, Ethelred fled to Normandy. Next year Sweyn, proclaimed King of England, died on the road to Bury St Edmunds; killed, it was said, by the saint.

But London had held out; Ethelred 'promised to do better' in the first-recorded pact between an English king and his subjects, and even ventured back; Knut, Sweyn's second son, had to draw off. But only to return: this time to Poole harbour, where, in 1015, he ravaged Dorset, including the new and out-of-the-way monastery at Cerne Abbas, while Ethelred lay ill at Corsham. On Ethelred's demise, Knut was recognized as king by a Witan at Southampton, and again tried to take

London. In October 1016 Edmund Ireneside, *strenuissimus in armis*, Ethelred's son by his first wife, brought the Danes to battle at Ashington (Assendun) in Essex; but the ealdorman of Mercia, Edric Streona, shouting '*Flet Engle, flet Engle, ded is Edmund!*' deserted to the Danes. Encouraged by the propitious fluttering of their raven standard,* they routed the 'flower of the English'. That autumn, Edmund conceded all England beyond the Thames, including London. And at the end of November he was killed at the age of twenty-two; apparently murdered (perhaps at Oxford) with an iron hook; and *sic periit Edmundus rex fortis* – 'so perished Edmund the brave king'.†

Knut the Mighty (1017–35), 'ruler and Basileus over the noble and fair race of the English', proved the ablest ruler since Alfred. He was Polish through his mother, daughter of Duke Miesceslas, and his ambitions were far-flung. At twenty-two he had been 'chosen' by the fleet, King of England – if he could take it – 'Never younger than you did prince set out to war . . . in your rage you mustered the red shields at sea . . . you turned all your prows westward'.‡ An astute politician as well as a warrior, he at once married Ethelred II's Norman widow Emma, who would support Harthaknut, their offspring, against the Athelings, Alfred and Edward, her Cerdinga sons. He also at once dispatched Edmund Ireneside's children to his uncle in Poland with no good intent. He was also soon received into the Roman Church. Thus Knut and Emma could appear jointly in the first authentic drawing of English royalties; the king crowned by an angel as he places a large cross on the altar, though grasping his sword hilt firmly with his left hand. By 1019 he had won Denmark, and by 1030, after the defeat of St Olav of Norway, he also commanded the southern shores of the Baltic, and he was also overlord of Ireland. Knut was indeed the first Viking leader powerful enough to be admitted to the fraternity of the greatest Christian kings. He exploited the full political and social prestige of his conversion, made a lavish pilgrimage to Rome for the coronation of the Emperor Conrad II, and piously presented a pallium 'coloured like a peacock's tail' to the tomb of Edmund Ireneside at Canterbury.

Despite his Christian veneer and immense benefactions, this able opportunist retained the cunning and violence of a leader of a war band.

---

* It was of white silk on which, when its side was to be victorious, 'a raven seemed to be opening its beak, flapping its wings and dancing with its feet'. *Cnutonis Regis Gesta Sive Encomium Emmae, Auctore Monacho Sancti Bertini*, Ed. S. H. Pertz, S.R.G., p. 18.

† William of Malmesbury writes that his assassin is said 'to have applied an iron hook to his posterior when he was sitting down for the needs of nature' (*ferreum uncum, ad naturae requisita sedenti, in locis posterioribus adegisse*), *Gesta Regum Anglorum. op. cit.*, p. 217. This probably authentic tragedy has been discreetly veiled by nineteenth-century historians.

‡ *Knutsdrapa* (*The Praises of Knut*), by Ottar the Black. Quoted E.H.D., I, *op. cit.*, p. 308. Canute is about the only spelling that is wrong: the correct Latin is Cnuto; the Danish now Knud, the Norse Cnutr. When converted, he was baptized Lambert.

He at once had Edric Streona, who had betrayed Edmund, his lord, beheaded – 'so that by his example the soldiers should learn to be faithful to their kings, not unfaithful'. But the tale of his bidding the waves recede rings false: out of character both for the king and his retainers, just the story easily attributed, three generations after, to a famous ruler by a moralizing monk.*

2

Beneath the personalities of this power struggle, now often played down, but which determined the political framework and decisions of Anglo-Danish England, deeper changes had been going on, both economic, social and administrative.

The basic and laborious taming of the land, which had been proceeding for five centuries, had now created the wealth for which the overlords fought, and Danish settlers had been assimilated in the most productive areas of the island. Eleventh-century England was relatively rich; rich enough for Knut to make it the centre of his empire and for the Normans to covet and conquer. But the type of cultivation varied: 'despite all that has been written about it, the agrarian organization of the Anglo-Saxon community remains a topic full of hazards, controversies and uncertainties'; the evidence 'uneven both in time and place'.[2]

As already remarked, the heavy plough, a barbarian invention alien to the Roman economy, suited for the north and already used by the Slavs in the sixth century, does not, on archaeological or philological evidence appear in England until the ninth. The Anglo-Saxon word for a plough was *sulh*, not yet *ploh*, probably from the old Norse *plogr*; and it was the Danes who measured land, not in hides – the subsistence area for one family – but in ploughlands (*bols*) and *attingars* (oxgangs), units of production. Indeed, the *plogr* may have been 'a novelty introduced by Danish invaders of the later ninth or early tenth centuries'.† The heavy plough which since Carolingian times had opened up vast areas

* The Latin tale runs thus: 'When he had mounted his chair on the sea shore he caused it to be set up there. Then he said to the rising tide "You are under my orders (*Tu meae ditionis es*) and the land on which I am sitting is mine, and no one has ever with impunity resisted my commands. I therefore order you not to rise over my land or presume to wet the clothes or limbs of your lord.' (*Impero igitur tibi ne in terram meam ascendas, nec vestes nec membra dominatoris tui madefacere praesumas.*) 'But the sea, rising in the usual way, soaked the king's feet and his thighs as well without any respect at all. So the king, jumping down again, remarked "Let all the world know that the power of Kings is vain and frivolous, nor is any King of whatever name worthy to compare with Him at whose nod heaven and earth and the sea obey eternal laws".' Translated from *Henry of Huntington, Historia Anglorum*, p. 189. Ed. T. Arnold, *Rolls*, 1879.

† See Lynn White, *Medieval Technology and Social Change, op. cit.*, pp. 50 and 55. The word *plug, pflug* or *plough* is not Slav, Teutonic, Celtic or Romanic, but derives, this authority maintains, from a peasant northern culture not yet identified.

of the continent, may thus have come to England via Scandinavia. However this may be, by the eleventh century, England was far better cultivated than in Romano-British times, with the open field system predominant in most of the south and much of the Midlands.

Barley (*bere*) continued to be a major crop; as Maitland remarked, their barley fields had to be wide 'for their thirst (was) unquenchable and households large'.[3] Hence *bere-tun* (Barton) and Bere Regis, and *Brewern silver* would be the licence to conduct a brewery. *Hweat* made the *hweaten hlaf* and the more sophisticated *cleane hlaf* of sifted flour; so early is the English prejudice for 'white' bread. Manorial obligations included keeping the crows from the crops, later commuted to *Craueselver*. Since the eighth century hand mills had often been superseded by water mills, and time out of mind *mylen brocs* (brooks) had fallen into *mylen puls*: the mill at Grantchester near Cambridge was already at work. The great timber and thatched barns followed the designs that they still do over the northern European plain, and the Danes brought in new skills in handling timber, their metier since the Bronze Age. The old Celtic ranch farming and horse breeding survived and developed, particularly in Yorkshire, whose stallions were especially prized.

And the land was now more productive: when famine came, it was localized, though for lack of transport irremediable. The overall picture is relatively prosperous: the hard toil on the land, doubtless in part evaded, redeemed by bouts of rustic festival. There were *scotales*; drinking parties by subscription – *plena* (full) *scot ella*, lasted three days – as well as harvest ales and malting ales and Michaelmas ales and scythe ales after the mowing. At the rich foundations at Winchester and Glastonbury the young labourers 'below the settle' had free drink on Monday nights.

Fisheries were essential and eels particularly valued: 'the eel bulked large in the fisherman's economy, and was far and away the most frequently mentioned of his prizes. At times it was expressly stated that the render should be of *large* eels. Salmon and herring, though not ignored, received fitful treatment by the side of the eel. . . .'[4] Doddington (in the Cambridge fenland) 'rendered the fearsome cargo of 27,150 eels a year'. There were elaborate fisheries down the 'eminently fishable east bank of the Severn'; here Archbishop Stigand was very particular over his right to every other fish caught and to all 'rare' ones. 'Wye salmon no doubt helped to make Fridays tolerable for the good men of eleventh-century Gloucestershire',[5] and vast quantities of herring were netted round the coast, particularly off Sussex, Kent and East Anglia.

The forests were vast and greatly valued by the Anglo-Saxon kings; the Confessor would often hunt round Clarendon from Wilton and Britford; in Cranborne Chase and Savernake. There were not yet the ferocious forest laws so intensely resented after the Conquest: Knut, for example, decreed 'it is my will that every man is entitled to his hunting in wood and field on his own land', and merely insisted that 'every one is to avoid trespassing on my hunting'. Though the wills of magnates endowing the church often except the deer enclosures, game was plentiful and widely taken, supplementing the produce of the farm. There were also windfalls by the sea: 'I, Edward,' writes the Confessor, 'greet Bishop Alfwold and my thegns in Dorset friendly. I give you to know that Urk my house carl may have his strand, all in front of his own land ... up from sea and out to sea and all that is driven on his strand.'[6]

Anglo-Saxon industries were less advanced, without the pace of Roman exploitation. Iron remained in demand, but there was not now much mined in the Sussex Weald or the Forest of Dean, though it was mined in Northamptonshire and Yorkshire. Lead was still mined for itself and for silver, as in Roman times, particularly in the Mendips and Derbyshire: 'the tinker,' says Loyn, 'has a long and honorable ancestry'; but 'there is no reason for supposing ... that there was anything like a large-scale metallurgical industry', and 'the status of a smith in England does not seem to have been particularly exalted'.[7] The grand swords, the elaborate jewellery and metalwork were made by a few specialists for royal patrons, magnates and great churchmen in this aristocratic society.

Salt was mined at Lyme in Dorset for curing the fish; and at Droitwich to supply the Midlands. Wood largely replaced the mass-produced Roman ware, though pottery was already made at Stamford. If, by Dunstan's time, glass was made in Somerset on a small scale, most of it was still imported. On the big estates the peasant women would have woven cloth, but there is little evidence for expansion of the exports of the eighth century: no major textile industry, for all the large-scale production of wool. Probably slaves remained the most important export.

Coinage, already good under Offa and Alfred, was greatly improved during the tenth century; the coins of Athelstan, who declared that there should be one currency throughout the realm, are remarkably well made; those of Edgar excellent. Ethelred II struck particularly fine ones with the Lamb of God on one side and the Dove of Peace on the other – doubtless appreciated by the Danes.[8] In Knut's day the currency was so good that it served as a model for the coins introduced into Scandinavia.

So, in the overall picture, industry was not much developed; but the internal trade in crops and animals and dairy produce was considerable; enough for the king and magnates to take the tolls and the profits of widespread mints rented by the townsmen. Yet so rudimentary were the roads and trackways that trade must have been chancy and seasonal, and overseas trade was always fraught with risk.

Against this background (only one person in ten would have lived in any sort of town) the cities remained rudimentary; but by Alfred's time, market towns, *ports* – not necessarily by the sea – and military *burghs* (strong points) are common, the latter a strategic answer to the Danes. London continued to be by far the greatest city, with its folk-moot and aldermen, and Knut was known in the north as 'King of London': already there was a stone bridge, for a witch was thrown from it. London imported fish from Normandy and wine from Bordeaux, and harboured Frisians (Dutch) and Flemings and 'men of the Emperor' (Germans), Scandinavians and traders from the Baltic. But Winchester was the political capital so far as there was one; already by Knut's day 'that famous and populous city'.[9] York may have had about 8000 inhabitants; Norwich, 6000; Oxford, about 3500. Such are the representative figures.

Alfred's *burghs*, old and new, showed a broad strategic design, sweeping along the south coast from Hastinge-cestra and Laws (Hastings and Lewes) by Chichester and Portchester and Hamptona to Wincestre; and then up to Wilton, Tysanbyring (Tisbury), and Shaftesbury;* and west along to Wareham and Brydian (Bridport or Bredy) and so by Axanbridge to Exeter and up to Bath and Malmesbury; then by Cricklade, Oxford, Wallingford and Buckingham to Southwark (Suthringa Geweorc). Further, as already recorded, by 942 Edmund, Athelstan's brother, had 'redeemed' from the Norsemen the five boroughs in the Danelaw, the *burga fife*: Ligora Ceaster (Leicester); Lyndcylene (Lincoln); Snotingaham (Nottingham) Stamford and Deora-by (Derby).† Not that the Norse and Irish were ever eradicated from the Midlands and the north-east; witness the Norman*tons* and Norman*bys*, Ire*ton* and Ir*by* in that area: and the Lake District was always Norwegian and British, not Anglo-Saxon.

3

What was the social structure of this society? It had derived from war bands or *foederati* who had plundered or protected the land while their kin began to settle in; it had always been hierarchical and military and, with the Anglo-Danish wars, it became more so. A new class of professional fighting men had grown up; at the summit, along with the

---

* Spelt Soraflesbyring, Soraflesburieg or Sceaftesbyrig; no wonder in the local speech it became Shaston for short.

† An exploit commemorated by the first political poem in English: *Daene wearen aer under Northmannum* . . . E.H.R., *xxxviii*, 551–7.

royalties and bishops, the king's thegns now attested Knut's Laws. A nobility of service, as against the old nobility of descent, real or assumed, they had come to supersede the old *gesiths*; while, beneath them, the originally free peasants tended to sink into greater dependence, even if some went up in the world as a richer and more complex hierarchy sorted itself out – a theme which goes on far into the Middle Ages and beyond.

For in spite of the horrors of the second Danish onslaught, there was much wealth at the summit of society. When Ethelred II's elder son, Athelstan Atheling, made his rather appealing will, he had much to dispose of: 'To my brother Edmund (Ireneside) . . . the sword which belonged to King Offa; and the sword with the "pitted" hilt; and a blade and a silver-coated trumpet: and the estates which I obtained in East Anglia; and the estate in the Peak valley.' To the younger brother Eadwig, afterwards murdered by Knut, he left a 'silver-hilted sword', and to Bishop Ælfsige a black stallion; to his militant chaplain an inlaid sword; to his seneschal a pied stallion and 'my round shield'; to the thegn Sigeferth the estate at Hockliffe, a sword and 'my curved shield'; while Godwine 'the Driveller' got three *hides* of land at Lurgershall, Wiltshire, and 'my staghuntsman the stud . . . at Coldridge'.[10]

Consider, also, the splendour of the ship presented to Knut's short-lived son, Harthaknut, perhaps in 1040:

a skilfully made galley, having a gilded prow, and furnished with the best tackle, handsomely equipped with suitable weapons and eighty picked soldiers, each of whom had on his arms two gold armlets weighing sixteen ounces, [and wore] a triple mail shirt, a partly gilded helmet on his head, and had a sword with a gilded hilt fastened round his loins, and a Danish battle-axe rimmed with gold and silver hanging from his left shoulder, and in his left hand a shield, whose boss and studs were gilded, in his right hand a spear, which in the English language is called *aetgar*, [a sort of javelin],[11]

thus making the best of both worlds. The Danes had clearly set new standards of equipment and display.

This kind of thing required organization. As the king's still itinerant household developed, the power of government had now increased. Through the local officials it pressed both lords and folk to collaborate in doing justice, maintaining order, and providing the rudiments of defence. These duties extended from the archaic threefold obligations of *Bricg-bot*, *burh-bot*, and *fyrd-faring* (service with the host) to the quasi-feudal obligations of the thegns; bound, in honour, like Byrthnoth's companions at Maldon, not to leave the field alive if their lord had fallen, and subject to the death penalty if they betrayed him: 'if a man who in his cowardice deserts his lord or his comrades', Knut commands sea or on land, he must forfeit all his own and his life'.

Some of these king's thegns rose to be over-mighty; as Edric Streon one of the last of the old ealdormen, whose treacheries determined the shifts of power. But by Knut's day they had been superseded by Anglo-Danish earls, appointed as Knut's dominions became so vast. Earl Godwin's family overshadowed the whole country under the Confessor, and even briefly attained the throne. These martial magnates ruled great districts of many shires, and their feuds came to disrupt the state, contributing to the ease of the Norman Conquest.

Beneath this increasingly military establishment and supporting it, were the manorial retainers, the villeins, the cottagers and the slaves. By the eleventh century an elaborate document depicts them on a humanely conducted estate. The *Ranks and Rights of People* is the first social analysis of England, declaring custom 'wherever it is known to us'.* First came the thegns by 'bookright', holding by armed service and the old threefold obligations, supplemented by fencing in the deer, guarding the coast, and sometimes equipping a guard ship. Though the fleet was now also maintained by a national system of taxation, by the Confessor's time the hundreds are grouped to provide a ship, and inland shires – Warwickshire for example – provide *sipesocha* – the origin of 'ship money', revived for Charles I.† Beneath the thegn came the *geneat*, originally a 'companion' and still of some standing; he must ride errands for his lord, 'furnish means of carriage', and on occasion entertain him, as well as help with the hay and corn harvests and 'keep up the places from which deer may be shot'. Like the original *ceorl*, with his 200 shilling *wergild*, he is a free man and, like the thegn, he pays church dues direct. Beneath the *geneat* came the *kotsetlas* or cottagers, who retained a conditional right to their holdings in return for service; but with time the all-important line between freedom and servility became blurred, in particular in the old West Saxon territories of the south and west. In the Danelaw, on the other hand, a peasant aristocracy survived better. Even the free *sokemen* holding about forty acres attended their own soke court, 'commended' to the leaders of their original war bands or their heirs, poor but independent. Some kept their

---

* *Rectitudines Singularum Personarum*, E.H.D., II, ed. D. C. Douglas and G. W. Greenaway, pp. 813–6. Such estates had long been bound to support the lord's *feorm* in kind; already by Ine's time as much as 10 vats of honey, 300 loaves . . . 10 wethers, 10 geese, 20 hams, 10 cheeses, 5 salmon, quantities of ale, butter and fodder and a hundred eels were expected from 500 acres. (Loyn. *op. cit.*, p. 195.) By the eleventh century the lord and his entourage had become even more expensive.

† The Confessor paid off the crews of nine ships to economize, and disbanded the other five, so that 'the dispersal of the King's own naval forces left a gap in the national defences which had a grave and perhaps a decisive effect on the course of events in 1066'. Stenton, *op. cit.*, p. 426.

Scandinavian nicknames: Ase the grim; Ofram, the sluggard; Mole the dull; all in the tradition of the big predators, Ragnar 'hairy breeks', or Torgil Skarthi 'hare lip', or 'boneless' Ivar.

Beneath the cottagers came the *geburs*, the 'boors' (German *bauer*), their deportment as they went down in the world is commemorated in the word 'boorish'. They had very varied obligations, but their standing was low. Even their animals and implements were supplied by the lord and reverted to him as death duties: and 'every pair of boors must maintain a hunting dog', while each boor must provide 'six loaves to the swineherd when he drives the swine to the mast pasture'. As for the swineherd, he keeps a small percentage of his drove, and if 'after slaughter he prepares the hogs properly and singes them', he will get the perquisites. Later many duties came to be commuted; *fos silver* was aid for not digging ditches, a *ward penny* for not keeping watch.

Beneath the boors were the *theows* – the slaves most numerous by far in the old Wessex territory and West Country: they could be sold, and were classed in value with the beasts, though they get their 'provisioning', for all slaves who belong to the estate ought to have 'food at Christmas and Easter and a strip of land for ploughing'.

Yet, bond or free, all had certain rights. The cowherd, for example, ought to have an 'old cow's milk for a week after she has newly calved'; the goatherd gets the milk after Martinmas and a portion of whey before that, and one yearling kid 'if he looks after his herd properly'. The man who keeps the granary gets any corn 'spilt at the barn door' and the woodward any trees 'blown down'. For the sowers and the oxherds there are 'harvest handfuls' and shoes and gloves. There are harvest feasts for the reapers, drinking feasts for the ploughman, 'rewards' for haymaking and 'making the rick'; a log for the woodman for each load. Here we observe a relatively humane exploitation, and many wills granted freedom to slaves on estates bequeathed to the Church, which particularly denounced the sale of slaves overseas.

4

That ramified institution, the Church, was now immensely rich. Anglo-Saxon piety had laid the foundation of the huge estates which Henry VIII would confiscate: one-sixth at least of England south of the Humber belonged to the Church in the eleventh century and in the sixteenth it would be one-third. For since the earliest settlements the Church had been increasingly endowed, and before the Conquest the great ecclesiastics worked together with the lay magnates as a matter of course: the kind of conflict provoked by Becket with Henry II would have been unthinkable. The Church was manned at the top mainly by men of high birth, and royal women were abbesses of Shaftesbury, Wilton and Wimborne. Glastonbury was the richest of the great abbeys; Malmesbury in Wiltshire and Cerne in Dorset were well-endowed. Over in the fenland and East Anglia, Peterborough, founded originally in the seventh century, Ely and Bury St Edmunds, were all very rich. Abingdon and Eynsham, like Cerne, are tenth-century foundations, part of the Dunstanian Benedictine revival. The greatest cathedrals were all connected with monasteries; Canterbury and Westminster, Winchester and St Albans. The wealth of bishops' sees, greatly varied: from rich Winchester and Worcester to York and Rochester, both poorly endowed. But large as were their estates, the great abbeys and bishoprics, like the smaller minsters and field churches, depended on dues and tithes in money and kind. The 'tenth' was a considerable impost and defaulters were heavily punished. Indeed, a church was a good investment, sometimes hired out or sold outright by laymen who had kept a preponderant interest in their foundations.

The intellectual revival attempted by Alfred had now been realized. The formidable Archbishop Dunstan and Athelwold of Abingdon and Winchester, both backed by Edgar, were closely connected with Benedictine houses in Flanders and on the Loire. In spite of the second Danish onslaught, the classical learning coming down from the Carolingian revival, which itself had owed much to the English, had now been assimilated. There was 'an enormous activity in manuscript production, which continued for the rest of the Saxon period . . . in Latin and in English . . . before 1066 the libraries must have again become as full as ever they were before the Viking ravages'. Yet the high-strung ideals of Celtic ascetics and Cluniac reformers never caught on widely before the Conquest; and 'there is no reason to suppose that the rule of celibacy was applied with any vigour in Anglo-Saxon England'.[12] Indeed, the Church was not particularly austere: 'mass thegns', substantial incumbents with a high *wergild*, lived openly, 'like *ceorls*', with unofficial wives and some even had to be forbidden to change them. As for the poorer parish priests, living off a few acres and the 'great tithes' of wheat and barley and the lesser tithes of eggs, fruit, poultry and the occasional hog or lamb, they were in no position to live without some 'helpmeet', a *focaria* or 'hearthgirl', recognized or not.

The best livings were often held in plurality by the great churchmen, closely enmeshed in administration and high politics. The Anglo-Saxon clergy pulled their weight right through society, from the great bishops negotiating treaties and cajoling and taming the Viking leaders, denouncing the evils of the day, and writing the homilies which would become standard pulpit texts, through the minor bishops in the shire courts to the local priests in the hundred courts and the *vills*. It was they who had to conduct the ordeals; Knut, dealing with Northumbria, laid down penalties if they got the procedure wrong, or indeed, failed to shave or cut their hair. Often they would help supervise the rudimentary *juries* (sworn men) of oath helpers who testified to the integrity of the accused, or in the Danelaw the already formed *juries* of presentment of the twelve leading thegns of each *wapentak*, following Scandinavian practice. And not only did the churchmen at the top give government a memory, witness the declaration of customary laws and transfers of property; they controlled the making and ratification of wills. Thus in England, as over most of western Europe, the Church fostered civiliz- ation right through the fabric of society.

Not least in learning. 'It was always a pleasure for him,' writes Ælfric (*c*. 1000) of Cerne and Eynsham, of his master, the venerable Athelwold of Winchester, 'to teach young men and boys and to explain books to them in English, and with kindly exhortation to encourage them to better things.'[13] 'Men particularly need good teaching in this age', he wrote, because it is 'the end of the world', and 'anti-Christ, . . . human man and true devil' could now be expected – 'the visible devil' who 'will say that he himself is God'.[14] Consider, he wrote, God's concern about Lent, and what happened to the Wiltshireman who refused to 'go to the ashes' on Ash Wednesday as other men, and, worse, said he would 'use his wife' at that forbidden time. Some dogs attacked him very violently and, as he fended them off, his horse started forward so that he was transfixed with his own spear. And consider that other who 'drank what he liked in Lent', and when 'by chance a bull was being baited outside' it killed him.[15] Even the Danish ravaging, like the famine and pestilence, expressed 'God's manifest contempt'; they should reflect how well things had gone under Edgar and the resolute Dunstan, when monasteries had been reverenced and laymen were 'ready against the enemy', so that 'our reputation spread widely throughout the earth' and no one heard of fleets except our own. And now 'a heathen army holds us to scorn'.

The traditional duty of denunciation was even better discharged in the rousing sermon of Wulfstan, Archbishop of York; the *Sermon of the Wolf to the English when the Danes persecuted them most: Sermo Lupi ad Anglos* . . . (*c*. 1014). Things, he insists, are going from bad to worse; the devil is abroad, 'evil piled on evil'. There is malice, hate and spoliation; above all treachery, so that 'everyone wrongly stabs another in the back'. Men will buy a woman and 'share her between them, just like dogs'; they are killers and they sell their countrymen overseas to foreigners. The very slaves run off and become Vikings and slay their masters on equal terms. And monstrous taxes crush the land, while 'wizards and sorceresses' exploit the people – an evidence of pagan survival. Even children in the cradle are 'enslaved for petty theft', a situation lately remedied by Knut. Because of these appalling crimes and the withholding of church dues, the *Wolf* insists, God has punished the English, 'the pirates driving them in droves from sea to sea'. There has been, as an Alfredian phrase has it, 'a great breach which will require much repair'.[16]

So, in a wide range of duties, from all-essential prayer, through diplomacy, administration major and minor, teaching and admonition, the Anglo-Saxon clergy showed their mettle; and they now greatly helped in the conversion of Scandinavia. In spite of the allegations of Norman apologists, long accepted, 'the English church was neither decadent nor corrupt when the Normans came'.[17]

5

The treachery denounced by the *Wolf* had full scope after the death of Knut, who was not yet forty, in 1035. His son Sweyn, called after his grandfather, tried to keep Norway; Harthaknut ('swift' or 'deadly' Knut) tried to master Denmark before taking over England; and Harold, Knut's son by Ælfgifu, a daughter of a Northumbrian jarl, set himself up in the Danelaw. Then Alfred Atheling, Ethelred II's son by Emma and brother to Edward, afterwards Confessor, landed from Normandy, making for his mother's court at Winchester, seeking what he might find. He was sidetracked by Earl Godwin and handed over to Harold; they 'butchered his men at Guildford with spears, bound like swine', and Harold dispatched him to Ely, where a man sat on each arm, another on his chest and a fourth on his legs and he was blinded. From these injuries he died: 'my pen itself trembles', writes the author of *Encomium Emmae* 'at what the youth suffered'. But by 1040 Harold, too, was dead. Harthaknut returned, had Harold's body dug up and thrown into the Thames and England became the prey of murderous Scandinavian adventurers. But in 1142, at a wedding feast in Lambeth, 'while he stood drinking with the aforesaid bride and certain men', Harthaknut, King of the English, 'fell suddenly to the ground and expired on Tuesday, 8th June'.

Knut's son, Sweyn, who had secured Denmark, and Magnus of Norway were both now in the offing, and so the English magnates and the leaders of the settled Danes in the Danelaw combined to elect the obvious candidate for kingship, Edward Atheling, Ethelred's second son by Emma. He still had the prestige of the old monarchy, and proved a not unsuccessful king. His only major political crime – perhaps involuntary – was to get no heir. Indeed, Edward the Confessor (1042–66) is an intriguing, probably maligned, figure. He was no incompetent *dévot*, but an astute politician,* determined, after years of indigent exile, not to repeat the experience. He came of martial stock on both sides, English and Norman; he was brought up not, as alleged, in a monastery, but as a knight; and his passion for hunting lasted into old age. 'King Edward,' writes his near contemporary biographer, 'spent much of his time in the glades and woods and his pleasures of hunting: he loved hawks and birds of that kind, and was really delighted at the baying and scrambling of hounds.' When roused, moreover, he was 'of passionate temper . . . leonine in his anger'. Affable and dignified, he carried himself as 'true king and lord', and 'when the festive lords held court', could well 'display the pomp of royal finery'.[18]

Freeman, that tendentious Victorian, depicts him as senile, and alleges, on no good evidence, that he was impotent, when, perhaps, he was merely faithful to his wife. He even suggests, on less evidence, that he was an albino. But Edward's hair, as Barlow remarks, 'was not always snowy white, nor his hands emaciated'. Even Maitland calls him an 'imbecile'; yet he was fully capable of commanding armies, taking swift decisions and handling a fleet. And though he was a great patron of the Church, he may well have been depicted as a passive saint in order to exonerate him from the catastrophe of the Norman Conquest. He was not, indeed, canonized until 1161, and then it was to enhance the prestige of the Angevin Henry II, who played up his own descent from the Old English monarchs through his mother Matilda, daughter of Henry I and Edith of Scotland.

The Confessor played a difficult hand with some skill, and though the Danish earls who had superseded the great eorldermen had now become provincial viceroys with vast estates, as the upstart house of Godwin, the monarchy was never seriously jeopardized. It worked with the local thegns, sometimes in a semi-feudal relationship; retained its jurisdiction through the shire and hundred courts, authorized coinage and controlled the Church. It had, indeed, a great thaumaturgic prestige; hence, in part, the stress on the Confessor's sanctity, of which he himself was sceptical.† Widely experienced in the power relationships on the

* *The Life of King Edward who rests at Westminster: Vita Edwardi Regis*, attributed to a monk of St Bertin at St Omer, edited and translated by Professor Frank Barlow, London, 1962, p. 40. Edward was called Confessor to distinguish him from St Edward, the Martyr of Corfe. He was born at Islip, near Oxford in 1002, and removed to the ducal court at Normandy in 1013: after his mother's marriage to Knut, his prospects were dim, and from 1013–35 he was a dependant upon the rough baronial courts of northern France and Flanders, keeping his head above water as best he could; apparently mocked by his own mother for his 'seedy condition'. But he was 'half a Viking', and a seasoned politician, who seized his chance and kept it. See F. Barlow, *Edward the Confessor's Early Life Character and Attitudes*, E.H.R., 1965.

† When a blind man was cured through the water in the royal wash-basin, Edward, thrusting out his own fingers, asked him what he could see. The man saw the gesture and drew back: the magic had worked. *Op. cit.*, p. 12.

continent, Edward played up the Normans against the Flemings and Scandinavians: indeed 'his political adroitness is impressive, if there is no evidence that he searched for work'.[19] So, in spite of the disruptive Godwin earls, there was no break in the central administration, which remained far more comprehensive, systematic and elaborate than anything the dukes of Normandy could command; as already remarked, the first Great Seal of England was struck by the Confessor. The Normans would further centralize and exploit this system.

The early death of Knut and the brief confusion under his sons had proved of advantage to Earl Godwin, who had abandoned Harthaknut for Harold, organized the murder of Alfred Atheling, and switched to Harthaknut again; Edward had owed the throne to his support. His queen, Edith, was Godwin's daughter. Godwin's son Sweyn controlled huge estates in the west Midlands and Somerset; his son Harold, East Anglia; Godwin himself most of Wessex. It had been through them that Edward had emancipated himself from Emma, the queen dowager, and until 1050 he had to work with them. The political crisis of that year came about through the clash of Norman interests fostered by the king in an attempt to counterbalance their overwhelming power.

Godwin was briefly exiled, but he returned; and when in 1053 he died, his sons fought it out for the family power. The exile of another son, Tostig and the piracies of Harold, form a lurid background to the maintenance of the king's peace if also to considerable prosperity. Harried by ambitious Danish earls, it may well have seemed realistic to the Confessor to arrange the succession of the ablest available ruler, William of Normandy.* Nor would such a decision have been regarded as extraordinary. Perhaps the king's complex motives will never be unravelled: perhaps he was past caring,[20] for he is said to have prophesied that nothing would go right in England until a green tree, cut down in mid-trunk, and replanted three furlongs away, had put out leaves – in other words, never.

But Edward's most permanent achievement proved impervious to the ruin of the native English. He had always been preoccupied with the Church, over which he had exercised a detailed and sometimes arbitrary control; and, with his continental background, he was familiar with the superb romanesque cathedrals now being built abroad. Outside the walls of London was a monastery dedicated to St Peter, though slenderly endowed. Surrounded by fertile fields and meadows and near the Thames, it seemed just the site for a splendid foundation. So, inspired

---

* In 1057 he sent for Irenesides' son, Edward Atheling, relegated to Poland by Knut, for he had survived in Hungary. Edward died on arrival and his son, Edgar Atheling, submitted to the Conqueror. But the old royal line would continue through Edgar's sister, St Margaret of Scotland, through whom the English royal house descends from Cerdic.

by the great Notre Dame de Jumièges in Normandy and without counting the cost, Edward commanded a mighty abbey to be built; a whole complex of huge Romanesque buildings.[21] 'Noble was its most lofty vaulting and the dressed stone evenly joined.' He endowed it with broad and rich estates, and, when William of Normandy won England, the Conqueror would be crowned, as were the English monarchs after him, in Westminster Abbey, the foundation of the last Cerdinga king.

6

THE NORMAN YOKE

'This was a fatal day for England,' wrote William of Malmesbury two generations after the Norman Conquest, 'a melancholy havoc for our dear country brought about by its passing under the dominion of new lords.'* The event had brought most of the Anglo-Saxon aristocracy to ruin and led to ferocious exploitation. Norman propaganda and Victorian bias would depict the Conquest as the rout of a degenerate nation, 'a gluttonous race of Jutes and Angles', as Carlyle would put it, 'lumbering about in pot-bellied equanimity' on the fringe of civilization, overcome by abler men, who imposed more efficient government and launched England into the beginnings of greatness. The facts are different; Anglo-Saxon civilization was older, better established, more sophisticated and much richer than anything Norman. Nor were the Norman kings radical innovators: they were able, improvising, realists, using institutions already to hand with new vigour; combining the advantages of the old monarchy with their new standing as feudal overlords of the whole land by conquest. As feudal lord of the whole country, at the apex of a new hierarchy of 'honours' held by his tenants-in-chief, the Conqueror ordered the great Domesday Book to be compiled; an unprecedented and shocking inventory, so that 'there was not one *hide* in England but he did not know who owned it'; for it was not, as even Maitland thought, a mere geld book but concerned with all sources of exploitation.[1]

2

The Conquest was only part of a movement of European scope which gave rise to the crusades in Spain and the Levant and to the Norman kingdom of Sicily, their other great exploit. The Normans thus had wide horizons and fleeced their subjects for wars in Normandy and

* E.H.D., *op. cit.*, II, p. 290 from *Gesta Regum Anglorum*. William (c. 1095–1143) was the best historian since Bede, whose successor he set himself to become. He was a Wessex man, librarian and precentor of the rich abbey of Malmesbury which had produced St Aldhelm, and of which the elaborate Norman porch is still intact. His book is full of entertaining anecdote and very well constructed. He also wrote a *History of the Popes* and an *Historia Novella* covering the early years of Stephen.

on the Loire, and in the process three terrible kings laid the foundations of an efficient state. The old regionalism of Anglo-Saxon England was crushed out, save along the northern and Welsh marches; William would even devastate his own territory in the north to cow the people and deprive potential Scandinavian invaders of supplies.

The conquerors were French-speaking foreigners, with the swagger and aplomb of a cosmopolitan world extending to Spain, Sicily and the East. Upon that world Norman and Angevin eyes were fixed, and they used England as a spring-board. The Angevin Henry II would be a continental-minded 'Emperor', with a passion not so much for justice as for gain, concerned to lick the realm into shape as a basis for wider designs. Though an innovator of genius, it is unlikely that he had the humane objectives long attributed to him, and his sons, Richard I and John, certainly lacked them. It was largely as a by-product of their continental ambitions that these rulers and their administrators built a stronger realm. Their minds were set on objectives outside the island, symbolized by a fashionable literature of European range; the *Song of Roland*, for example, which Matilda ordered to be translated into German. Astutely, Welsh Geoffrey of Monmouth would adapt his Celtic romances for a more sophisticated court.

The Normans and Angevins were not, like the heathen Knut, respectful to the insular culture; they regarded the Anglo-Saxons with contempt. They were, after all, concerned to compete with the greatest potentates in Europe. Basically the Conqueror and his sons continued to regard themselves as lords of Normandy, and the Angevins to be concerned with the rich valley of the Loire and the broad lands of Aquitaine; territories naturally more attractive than the misty island, for all its actual and potential wealth and the regal title it brought them. This *damnosa hereditas* of continental ambition, which created good government almost as a by-product, would make the English kings the best hated of their kind in their own land; for, as the English establishment became more insular, its interests increasingly diverged from those of the crown. That is the key to the crisis which led to *Magna Carta* and the troubles of Henry III.

The Conqueror was a ferocious character. William, Duke of Normandy since 1035, was the bastard son of Duke Robert I and Herleve, probably the daughter of a tanner of Falaise, where tanneries flourished. Duke since he was eight, William had survived frightful risks and humiliations: by 1066 he was 'a burly warrior with a harsh guttural voice' who swore 'By God's resurrection'; very strong, a good bowman, 'a large man with notably long arms and legs'. He was probably 'repellent as a man', but 'a master of men's wills ... an enigma, admirable, unlovable, dominant, distinct'.* Certainly he had an ironic sense of humour; when his soothsayer got killed at Hastings, the Duke remarked that he could not have been a good one as he had not foreseen his own fate. But tne Conqueror was not, says his latest biographer, just a 'crude ruffian' or 'simply a sanguinary brute'.[2]

His adversary, Harold, was also a formidable warrior; son of Earl Godwin by a Danish wife, sister-in-law to Knut. As already observed, Godwin had been a kingmaker who had dominated the Confessor, and, when expelled, had returned in greater strength: his sons had ruled most of southern England. Harold had no claim to the throne save by election and coronation, but he had defeated the mighty Harald Hardrada of Norway at Stamford Bridge and, told of William's landing and of a suggested compromise, remarked 'we march at once: we march to battle'.[3] To one chronicler he was a 'good man who laboured in his own person by sea and by land for the protection of the realm'; but to the Normans he was 'this insensate Englishman'. He certainly made a strategic mistake in concentrating his inferior force within striking distance of a dangerous enemy, for William, in the old Viking way, had seized the nearest thing he could to a peninsular base, and Harold, furious at the ravaging of his own estates, had tried to shut him in. He had probably planned to repeat the surprise which had beaten the Norwegians, and 'reeking from battle' hurried south with insufficient force, instead of making the invaders live off the country, leave their base and risk campaigning in the interior. The English, free from the Norse threat, might then have mobilized an army of overwhelming strength. Harold may have estimated that the English were too disunited for a long campaign, but in attempting surprise he was caught himself.

The famous occasion is familiar. How the duke, after immense preparation, waited long for the wind, and how in mid-Channel he outsailed his fleet and his look-out 'saw nothing but sea and sky'; how he commanded a good meal and a bumper of spiced wine to put a good face on it till the others caught up; how they made landfall at Pevensey and his reconnoitring knights foundered their horses because of the rough ground. Then how, in the October dawn, the armies faced one another; the English blocking the way to London in a well-chosen

* D. C. Douglas, *William the Conqueror and the Norman Impact on England*, London, 1964, p. 376. William's tomb at Caen was opened in 1522 and the findings described (p. 369). Although the Calvinists afterwards destroyed the relics, a femur is extant which indicates that he was about five foot ten; tall for a medieval man, but not, as suggested, comparable to Henry VIII, who was over six foot and fifty-seven inches round the chest, with a high voice to William's deep one. William's queen, Matilda of Flanders, was exceptionally short: hence, probably, the small stature of their eldest son, Robert *Curthose*, 'short boots' or *gambaron* (fat-legs), and the middling stature of Rufus and Henry I. John, too, was a short stout man.

position taken up late the night before, so that they had not time or supplies for the drunken revels Norman accounts ascribe to them, while the crusading Normans supposedly prayed; and how the duke told his knights 'you fight not merely for victory but survival'.* To the Normans the conflict was *La Bataille*; *the* battle, or *bellum Hastingense*, the battle of Hastings: the English called the abbey built on the site *'thaet mynster aet thaer Bataille'*. Senlac is a bogus name, foisted on his readers by Freeman from *Ordericus Vitalis*, who wrote forty years after and alone used it.[4] In fact, as Round puts it, 'the truth is that the site of the battle had no name at all'.

The *Anglo-Saxon Chronicle* is characteristically laconic; limited but reliable. After 'Count' William's landing, it runs,

> King Harold was informed of this and he assembled a large army and came against him at the hoary apple tree. And William came against him by surprise before his army was drawn up in battle array. But the King neverthe-less fought hard against him, with those men who were willing to support him, and there were heavy casualties on both sides. There King Harold was killed and Earl Leofwine his brother, and Earl Gyrth his brother, and many good men, and the French remained masters of the field . . .[5]

They had done so after the day-long battle, not because they were knights skilled in new shock tactics, charging home *en masse* against the old-fashioned shield wall of Anglo-Danish axemen, but through luck and the personality of the leader who dominated the event. Hastings, it has been well said, was Waterloo without the Prussians, and with less disciplined men. Whether or not the Anglo-Saxons broke line in a piecemeal pursuit or in a counter-attack which failed, and whether or not the retreat of the Norman knights was their old and difficult trick of feigned flight, are questions still in dispute.

* The best Norman account is *Gesta Wilhelmi Ducis, The Deeds of Duke William*, by that militant archdeacon, William of Poitiers; vivid, detailed and partisan: see E.H.D. II, pp. 217–31. Gefrei Gaimar in *l'estorie des Engles* (c. 1135, ed. Sir T. Hardy and C. T. Martin, *Rolls*, 2 vols., 1889) describes how Taillefer the *joculator* rode before the host and perished.

> He took his lance by the butt
> As if it had been a truncheon.
> Up high he threw it
> And by the head he caught it.
> Three times thus he threw his lance,
> The fourth time he advanced quite near
> Among the English he hurled it . . .
> That was an enchantment
> Which he did before the folk . . .
> The horse with open mouth
> Went bounding towards the English . . .
> So the English killed him
> With javelins and darts.

(Translation, Vol. II, lines 5271 ff.)

In that superb work of art, the Bayeux tapestry, we have a vivid picture of the battle.* The great Norman war horses, transported with elaborate care, at least enabled the knights to ride down their enemies once they could get at them, and the Norman archers were superior. But the battle was a slogging match, a near thing: William had to threaten some knights with his spear and shout 'Look at me well, I am still alive'.[6] Suffice it that the English, 'these people, descended from the ancient Saxons (the fiercest of men')[7] and the Anglo-Danes, fought as though 'rooted to the ground', and the housecarls died under the battle standard of Wessex round their lord, as they were bound to do. It is uncertain whether the Conqueror had Harold shovelled away by the sea-shore – 'he who had guarded the coast with such insensate zeal'[8] – a sarcasm, not a compliment; or if, as William of Malmesbury writes, he sent the body unransomed to Harold's mother at Waltham Abbey; but the remark of a knight when William had fallen on landing, 'you hold England, my lord', had been justified.

After a bout of dysentery at Canterbury, William moved slowly westward round London. Winchester submitted and at Berkhamstead he took the surrender of London, for the English had been given time to fall out among themselves. He thus achieved his coronation at Westminster and, with it, as the Confessor's heir, all the rights and prestige of the old dynasty: if the Normans outside, jumpy at roars of Anglo-Saxon loyalty within, fired the houses round Edward's abbey, Duke William was now king of the English who would date the regnal numbers of their monarchs from his accession. By 1067 he felt secure enough to parade Edgar Atheling, 'a gentle boy without guile', with other notabilities round Normandy, half guests, half hostages; 'youths of the north, long-haired, lovely as girls'.† The grand English robes and regalia were much admired.

For England the political and social sequel was grim. Under an alien yoke, a social order more centralized and specialized than any approximation to feudalism apparent in Anglo-Saxon times was

---

* The best account to date is by R. Glover, 'English Warfare in 1066', E.H.R., lxvii, pp. 1–18. At least the 'palisade' which occasioned the entertaining old controversy between J. H. Round and Freeman (see *Mr. Freeman and the Battle of Hastings* in *Feudal England, op. cit.*, pp. 332–420) has joined the Druids who built Stonehenge, the 'woad-painted savages' of 55 BC, Alfred's cakes and Knut's reproof of the sea: but the tactical details are still being mulled over by military experts, and a case has been made against Glover on the grounds that the tapestry is more conventionalized than realistic, an argument not very convincing in view of its accuracy on other subjects.

†   *Crinigeros alumnos plagae*
             Aquilonalis, nec enim puellari
             Venustati cedebant:

William of Poitiers, quoted by R. L. Graeme Ritchie in *The Normans in Scotland*, Edinburgh, 1954, p. 21.

imposed on the land.* The Norman magnates were vassals holding their lands by feudal service from their overlord, their titles defined in a practical way. Vassalage had, of course, been known in Anglo-Saxon and Anglo-Danish times, but it had not been the essential relationship, applied over the whole land and made permanent by hereditary tenure from the king by the eldest son or the husband of the heiress. For the feudal tie as developed by the Normans by 'Knight Service' was designed to provide the specialized force of heavy-armed cavalry on which the power of both king and magnates was based. These feudal levies were always supplemented by professional mercenaries, and infantry played a larger part in battle than often understood; but in the mid-eleventh century the heavy-armed knights were decisive in battle and, with their expensive supporting entourages, could only be sustained by large estates whose productivity, though relatively high by the standards of the time, was still limited.

Thus important tenurial changes, if hardly a tenurial revolution, coincided with the Norman take-over from the Confessor. Military tenures in England, as on the continent, had been common for centuries, but the ties had been ill-defined; now, from the king at the summit down through the great tenants-in-chief to the sub-tenants and their men, military service was more regularly tied to land. And when the feudal host became obsolescent, military obligations were more often commuted for cash.[9]

As the magnates settled in on their immense 'honours', holdings scattered like diversified investments so that if one was devastated or famine-stricken others would escape, they had more to lose: they would accept an overlord for protection if he could give it, as, under Stephen, they changed sides to get the backing of the more effective power.

This more precisely militarized social order had to be rapidly imposed; without it the Conquest could not have been consolidated. Within three years of the invasion the west and north were subdued, and it was only in the fenland that Hereward the Wake – for the historicity of Hereward is beyond doubt – prolonged an Anglo-Saxon resistance until 1071.†

---

* 'It is essential', writes Sayles, 'that we state a truism: we do not find Norman feudalism in England before the Normans came. But we do find a social system cognate to it and cognate still more to the feudalism of other parts of France, noticeably Brittany.' G. O. Sayles, *The Medieval Foundations of England*, London, 1966, p. 211.

† Maurice Keen, *The Outlaws of Medieval Legend*, London, 1961, p. 12. The Hereward story, he points out, smacks more of old Saxon epic than the narratives of Norman feudal society or the late medieval ballads of Robin Hood. The earliest source is the *Gesta Herewardi incliti exulis et militis. The Deeds of Hereward the distinguished exile and knight*, written by one who knew some of the survivors and included in Gaimar, *op. cit.*, Vol. II, pp. 339–404. The hero was very good-looking; small and agile, with large grey eyes, but so pugnacious at eighteen that his father had turned him out. He then killed a Norwegian talking bear, rescued a Cornish

Though in 1075 a baronial rebellion had to be crushed, by 1086 all considerable freeholders had sworn direct fealty to the king at Salisbury (Old Sarum); and, in the year after, the Domesday inquest showed how the Normans had learned to exploit the administrative system of their Anglo-Saxon predecessors, when it employed Norman method. Commissioned after William 'had very deep speech with the Witan about this land and how it was peopled and with what sort of men', it was known to the natives as *Domesday*, the book by which all men will be judged, a detailed record of the wealth of crown and magnates. It was a handsome and well-executed work with initials and numerals in red in an excellent if abbreviated post-Carolingian script.* The survey was probably completed before the king's death in 1087, when, ruptured at the age of fifty-eight when his horse stumbled on embers at the siege of Mantes, the Conqueror woke in the September dawn to hear the great bell of Rouen tolling, asked what it was for and died.

Though the richer bystanders bolted to secure their property and the poorer ones stripped the body and left it half-naked on the floor, William I had changed history as no king of England had ever done, and brought his new realm into the orbit of Latinized continental Europe out of the maritime Scandinavian north. William could not write, though his cross, if he made it himself, is neater than the baronial ones; but he had taken over and reinforced an administration which no baronial anarchy or foreign invader would wreck. England would no longer, as in Anglo-Saxon times, be on the defensive; it became, first, part of a continental

---

* See V. H. Galbraith *The Making of Domesday Book, op. cit.* The first volume of about eight hundred pages is fifteen inches long by eleven broad, and it surveys all the royal demesne and the lands of the tenants-in-chief save those in East Anglia. These are dealt with in the 'Little Domesday', of about five hundred pages, eleven inches by eight.

princess by hitting a giant well below the belt, and was shipwrecked in Flanders. After the Conquest he came home to find some Normans in possession, who had stuck his brother's head over the gate. So he stalked them when they were drunk in the arms of their women and applauding a *joculator* imitating 'the clumsy dances of the English': he then replaced his brother's head by theirs. He took part in the Scandinavian sack of Peterborough, established a formidable resistance from Ely in the fenland, and visited the Norman camp disguised as a potter, calling out '*Ollae ollae, bonae ollae et urnae! Pots, pots, good pots and mugs*'. He then led a raiding party under cover of 'flags and rushes' in a fisherman's boat and, says Gaimar, whose account written a generation later is the next earliest source (lines 5469–5690), killed twenty-six Normans. His party escaped through the woods, led by a large white wolf running in front of them 'like a domestic dog'. According to the *Gesta*, Hereward ended up as King William's man and, though he had to be imprisoned at Bedford for attacking a Norman knight, died in the king's favour. Gaimer writes

> A Noble man was this lord
> Who was named Hereward
> One of the best in the country
> The Norman had disinherited him
> . . . a harder man was never seen.

But Hereward was slain, he believes, by treachery.

power, then with a growing sense of nationality, an insular base for attack.

William's sons who succeeded him were both strong men: William II, Rufus, a famous and ferocious soldier in whose reign the Normans mastered Cumberland, Westmorland and part of the Welsh marches and established the frontier with Scotland; Henry I, an able politician, methodical, literate and far-seeing. In 1106 he won back Normandy at Tinchebrai, for the Conqueror had left it to his eldest son, Robert 'Curthose', an inconsequent character who had mortgaged the duchy to Rufus to go on crusade and then, having got it back for nothing after Rufus's death, attempted to win England. Duke Robert, who lived to be at least eighty, spent twenty years in prison at Wareham, Devizes, Bristol and Cardiff, where he learned enough Welsh to apostrophize a stunted oak, symbolizing himself, on the promontory of Penarth 'facing the Severn Sea'.

> *Oak that hath grown up in the storms . . .*
> *Woe to him who is not old enough to die.*
> *(Gwae! wr na bei digon hen*
> *Gwae! a wyl na bo Angau.)*[10]

William Rufus, *le Rus* (1087–1100), so-called from his complexion, was a famous knight, thick-set and strong with queer glittering eyes; lavish and magnanimous, he loved furs and luxury and was apt to stammer when enraged. He at once quelled a feudal rebellion and would even defy the sea: told at Brockenhurst that his garrison at Le Mans was in peril, he rode for Southampton, and when, writes Gaimar,

> *The steersman asked*
> *If he could go with a contrary wind . . .*
> *'Brother,' he said, 'hold your peace*
> *You never saw a king drowned,*
> *Nor shall I be the first'.*

Following a rather widespread Norman fashion, he was homosexual, surrounded by handsome young men who wore their hair according to his taste. For when a magnate brought a clutch of them to be knighted and, kept waiting for weeks, had their tresses cropped to show his rage, the king preferred them that way and the fashion changed.* 'The

---

* 'It is hard to think,' writes Professor R. W. Southern, in his study of Anselm, 'that the disreputable stories about Rufus have greatly falsified his character.' A. Lane Poole, in his own idiom, grasps the nettle: 'It is tolerably certain,' he writes, 'that he indulged in unnatural vice.' (*Domesday Book to Magna Carta*, O.U.P., 1951, p. 99.) There is a story against Rufus in William of Malmesbury's *Gesta Regum*. Putting on some new shoes, he asked their price and they were cheap: 'You whoreson,' he shouted, 'since when has a king worn shoes at such a price? Go and bring me a pair for a silver mark.' So they brought some which were even less expensive, and he approved them; 'These,' he said, 'are suitable to the royal dignity.'

Emperor of Lombardy did not lead such a company' and 'water in pool or pond was not easier to draw than were his drink and food'; but Rufus was as ruthless as his father: when the Count of Eu lost a trial by battle, he had him blinded and castrated and his stewards hung. He was also extremely arrogant: on the eve of his death he scorned the warning of a monk who had dreamt he was in danger, saying 'he is a monk and has dreamt like one; give him a hundred shillings'; and he was shot, by accident or design, in the New Forest.

> *In the Forest was the King,*
> *He wanted to shoot at a stag*
> *Which he saw pass with the herd:*
> *Near a tree he dismounted,*
> *He bent his bow himself.*
> *Walter Tirrell dismounted*
> *Very near the King, close to an elder,*
> *Against an aspen he leaned,*
> *As the herd passed*
> *And the great hart came in the midst*
> *He drew his bow . . . ,*
> *Now it befell that he missed the hart*
> *And to the heart he struck the King . . .*

William asked for the sacrament, so a huntsman

> *Took some herbs with all their flowering,*
> *He made the King eat a little*
> *Thus he thought to communicate him.*[11]

The dead king was taken to Winchester on a litter of boughs and fern; according to William of Malmesbury, on a charcoal burner's cart, meeting the devil on the way in guise of a big black goat.

It is not known if the accident was arranged; but his successor Henry I at once rode hard for Winchester to seize the royal treasure. Whether or not Rufus 'never got up in the morning nor went to bed at night without being every time a worse man than when he last went to bed or last got up', and was overthrown by 'the just judgement of God',[12] he left a lasting memorial in his 'New Hall' at Westminster, which, restored and embellished by Richard II, remains intact.

Henry I (1100–35) had to fight hard for his throne. He quickly married Edith-Matilda, daughter of Malcolm Canmore of Scotland and the sainted Queen Margaret, sister of Edgar Atheling, a highly cultivated character brought up in Hungary. Margaret had sent Rufus furs as well as attempting to civilize the Scots.* The queen was thus a descendant of the Old English kings, and at the expense of some baronial sneers at 'Godric' and 'Godgifu', Henry had conciliated the English. Towards the Normans he used patronage as well as force – an early architect of the establishment.

The new king was literate and called *Beauclerc*, but not in admiration, for, as a contemporary wrote, 'the highborn in our country disdain letters',† and he became respected among the English for his 'good peace'. He was notorious for lechery and acknowledged nineteen illegitimate children, but he was far the most intelligent of the Conqueror's sons; the first educated king since Alfred. It is, writes Galbraith, 'probably kinder to draw a veil over his Latin learning', but he was bilingual in English and French. Like Rufus, he was thickset, but with thinning black hair; a methodical man who planned his journeys ahead when many medieval rulers acted on impulse. 'For his own peace', it was reported, he allowed no young men 'to see him before dinner'; they would waste time: and 'no old ones after'; they would bore him. He assigned specific duties and salaries to his household and, as will be apparent, tried to impose a far more efficient form of government.

But his plans were curtailed by ill luck: in 1120 William Atheling, his only legitimate son, was drowned in the late November dark off Barfleur near Cherbourg, when his 'White Ship', the 'latest thing', says Lane Poole, 'in marine transport', was run on the rocks.‡ The prince got away, but returned to save his half-sister, the Countess of Perche, and perished.

But Henry had another dynastic card. In 1114 his daughter Matilda had made a grand marriage with the Salian Holy Roman Emperor, Henry v, at Mainz; while the king himself, now a widower, had further strengthened an eastern alliance against the French by marrying Adeliza of Louvain. In 1125 the emperor died and the widowed empress, aged twenty-eight, was married off to Geoffrey, son of Fulk of Anjou, aged fourteen. The two quarrelled savagely, but by 1133 Henry i had a grandson, Henry Plantagenet.§ This boy was destined to be the greatest legal and administrative genius among the English kings, and

* Edith had been brought up at Romsey and Wilton, and made to wear a black cloak of monastic cut to keep away suitors, so that it was alleged that she had taken the veil. In fact, she proved that she had publicly objected even to the cloak and had trampled it underfoot; dynastic marriage could take place.

† V. H. Galbraith, 'The Literacy of the Medieval Kings', *Proceedings of the British Academy*, 1935, pp. 201–7. Rufus probably could not read, for an urgent dispatch had to be read to him.

‡ 'The sailors too,' writes William of Malmesbury, 'who had drunk overmuch cried out with true seamen's hilarity that they must overtake the King's ship.' E.H.D., II, *op. cit.*, p. 297.

§ From *Planta Genestas*, the broom, planted by Geoffrey of Anjou to improve his hunting coverts. For Henry I see. R. W. Southern. *Medieval Humanism and other Studies*. London 1970. pp. 208 ff.

the first Angevin monarch, whose arms became the lions or 'leopards' of England.

Matilda, *mulier de genere tyrannorum*, that 'woman of masculine spirit', was a great German royalty who had left Germany with reluctance, for 'she had been accustomed to the lands into which she had been married and had many possessions in them', and had been invited to be Lady of Lombardy and of Lorraine.[13] Indeed she had only given up the regalia of the Empire under pressure and promises from Archbishop Albrecht of Mainz,[14] and she now plotted with the Angevins against her own father. But Henry I told his magnates that 'she alone had the succession, since her grandfather, uncle and father had been kings',[15] while, on her mother's side, her lineage went back through fourteen kings to Egbert of Wessex.

But the plan failed when, in 1135, Henry I died in a hunting lodge near Rouen at the age of sixty-six – for he ate lampreys once too often, a dish that always made him ill (*eum semper nocebant*) – and Stephen of Blois, grandson of the Conqueror through his mother, jumped Matilda's claim. The ambitious aims of Henry I thus provoked a reaction, but the central administration was never destroyed. The famed 'anarchy' was patchy and intermittent; mainly in the south and parts of East Anglia – as at Devizes, where one ogre used to 'smear his prisoners with honey and expose them in the sun to be bitten by insects' until himself strung up by the king's men;[16] or as it was described in the *Anglo-Saxon Chronicle's* well-known account of the devastation round Peterborough. Even the notorious Geoffrey de Mandeville, pilloried by Round and accused by Lane Poole of 'fiendish atrocities', has found a defender.[17] Moreover the upheaval coincided with the full tide of twelfth-century economic and intellectual advance. Successful barons and mercenary captains compounded for their sins by endowments in compensation for damage done *tempore werrae*, in time of war.

But set-back there was. Stephen (1135–54), the only Norman king who could be considered a gentleman, was lavish but unreliable under his knightly charm;* neither he nor the arrogant Empress Matilda could supply the good lordship or the tenacious purpose of Henry I. If the great barons were not all turncoats, they had no one at the apex of

* See R. H. C. Davis, *King Stephen 1135–54*, London, 1966. Though double-crossed by his father, the castellan of Marlborough, he spared the young William the Marshal, whose career as Regent of England under Henry III will later be considered. The child, a hostage, was being led to execution on a convenient tree when, unaware that he was the cause of the proceedings, he noticed a beautiful javelin in the hands of the Earl of Arundel and said 'Oh Sir, give me that javelin' (*Sire, donez mei cel bozon*). Although, unless child hostages were blinded or hung, the sanction broke down, Stephen intervened. 'I won't have the child hung', he said, 'for all the gold in France', and he was afterwards found playing 'knights' with him, the knights being bunched plantains. See *L'Histoire de Guillaume le Marechal*, ed. P. Meyer, Vol. I., p. 20, Paris, 1891.

the feudal order to trust: it was now every man for himself; 'everything deteriorated through lack of justice'. And when the Archbishop of York rallied the north and repelled the Scots King David, who had supported Matilda with his barbarian host 'roaring round him' at the battle of the Standard (a ship's mast hung with a pyx and the banner of St Peter), Stephen bungled the negotiations that followed.

In 1139, Matilda backed by her illegitimate half-brother Geoffrey of Gloucester, a great power in the west, had landed to claim her dynastic rights and a war of sieges developed. In 1141 Stephen, knocked out by a stone (*ictu lapidis cujusdam*),[18] was captured, and briefly the empress dominated London. She was soon chased out, but the struggle continued until 1147 when, after the death of Gloucester, Matilda retired to Normandy. Then in 1152 Henry Fitz Empress, the young Duke of Normandy and Count of Anjou, Maine and Touraine, brought off a brilliant dynastic coup. At nineteen he married Eleanor of Aquitaine, who had divorced Louis VII, and she brought with her vast dominions: Poitou, Périgord, Angoulême, Limoges and all Gascony including Bordeaux; and, what was more, he survived the consequent attacks. When in 1153 he landed in England, he already had an empire which stretched from Abbeville to the Pyrenees. Stephen came to terms: that year his eldest son had died and, though he kept the throne for life, the Angevin Duke Henry succeeded him. The Plantagenets, even more foreign and more ambitious than the Norman kings, now controlled England.

3

Such were the personalities and main political events which dominated England from the Conquest to the accession of Henry II. The administrative, clerical and social aspects of this expanding society will now briefly be considered.

Far from imposing, as was once thought, a novel and more advanced polity on England, the Normans consolidated their stricter régime with conservative realism. The power of the Norman dukes had been cruder and more uncertain than those of the long-established Anglo-Saxon kings: the duke's entourage, the nucleus of the omnicompetent *curia regis* or King's Court, was informal and fluctuating, if adaptable, and there were few written laws embodying ancient custom, and no writs. Nor could the dukes count on the collaboration of substantial men in local government as the English kings had done. The Normans had fought like tigers over their own land; in England, unless mastered, they would do so again. William needed and took all the powers he could get, and asserted them both as feudal overlord by conquest and as the heir of the Confessor. In Normandy the barons, heirs of Norse pirates, had held their property by right of settlement and waged private wars: in England all men now held their land from William, and his peace and the prerogative power to enforce it pervaded the land. He imposed his feudal rights much more stringently and exploited rebellion to confiscate and redistribute fiefs, to pin men down to their obligations to provide the garrison of the new territory. For such were the Normans, Bretons, and Flemings who had come over with the Conqueror, their power clamped on the country by the crude 'motte and bailey' strongholds, later elaborated into stone keeps, such as the White Tower built by William himself to overawe London. Yet, paradoxically, under the Norman yoke England became less militarized. The great Earldoms were now created which would colour English history: under Rufus, Warwick and Surrey; under Henry I, Gloucester, Leicester and Buckingham; under Matilda, Devon, Somerset, Oxford and Salisbury; under the lavish Stephen, Derby, Hertford, Pembroke, Worcester, Arundel, Essex, Lincoln, Norfolk and Cambridge. But these magnates did not attain the power of the Godwin family, when Godwin had ruled Wessex and Harold East Anglia and overawed the king. Palatine and marcher lords might exploit their position, but by a combination of feudal overlordship and royal administration and prestige the Norman kings had mastered the country. Henry II would restore and decisively extend this government.

The Anglo-Saxon royal household and writing office, well-established under Edgar, were to hand, along with the sheriffs and the shire courts already described. The rudimentary Norman bureaucracy derived from the Anglo-Saxon royal household, galvanized by the more flexible *curia regis*. There had already, in effect, been a treasury at Winchester under Knut; a chamber or royal apartment under a chamberlain, and a wardrobe where documents as well as robes were stored; as well as a secretariat under a chancellor, originally a royal chaplain. 'The Anglo-Saxon chancery [had] exhibited an efficiency to which there was no parallel in Western Europe except in Merovingian and Carolingian Gaul.'[19] It had accumulated formal charters, chirographs, and sealed vernacular writs, so it was taken over and documents were written in English long after the Conquest. And under the Norman kings the household expanded to include the steward who administered the hall, the constable with charge of the stables and the marshals who kept order. If the private and public functions of the monarch were still mixed up, out of them a more impersonal public bureaucracy would emerge.

The Normans naturally took over and exploited the sheriffs and the shire courts. *The Laws of Henry I* declare that shire court pleas are to be held throughout England at the recognized times and no more. Shire moots and borough moots are to be held twice a year; hundred moots and *wapentakes* once a month attended by all free men who are hearth-fast householders. Thus, although many hundred courts would be absorbed into private feudal jurisdiction, the principle was reaffirmed that central government worked with local government, compelling the local courts to help it, and so encouraging responsibility. The sheriff was exploited first as a military official appointed from the magnates by the crown; then, when these baronial sheriffs became a nuisance, Henry I appointed them from his own entourage and controlled them by the new Court of Exchequer.

The Norman kings were concerned to wring all they could out of their subjects on both sides of the Channel, and they could not be in two places at once. Already, under Rufus, Ranulf Flambard, Bishop of the palatinate see of Durham, had wide powers of extortion; under Henry I, Roger, Bishop of Salisbury became the first Justiciar or deputy for the king, with a continuous responsibility. Henry was already ruling not through the magnates but through the representatives of the inner *curia*; and, most important of all, the new Court of Exchequer, using the abacus, was now established.

Under Henry II this institution would be vividly described: it centred on a table shaped like a chessboard, 'quadrangular', about ten feet in length and five in breadth, and around it was 'a raised edge about the height of four fingers, lest anything placed on it should fall off'. On this foundation was 'placed a cloth, purchased at the Easter term – not an ordinary cloth, but a black one marked with stripes' a foot apart.[20] Within this space, counters were placed according to their value, and the cloth was later ruled into black and white squares 'like a draughtboard'. In the regular haggling between the treasurers and sheriffs over their accounts, this business-like invention, like the notched wooden tallies which recorded the obligations discharged, saved much friction. Further the pipe rolls would record these calculations so that accounts could be carried over from year to year. And if the Exchequer was still part of the king's household, its methods were a new departure in bookkeeping and routine; the Justiciar supervised it, and the ancestor of the 'Chancellor of the Exchequer' first appears under Henry II.

Moreover, partly because justice brought in profits, Rufus and Henry I already sent out itinerant justices, 'Justices in Eyre', to invigilate the shire courts, and see to it that the king's rights were exacted, extending the authority of the *curia regis* over the country. Their functions were still limited; but Henry II would extend them to make the king's writ run through the land, superseding other authorities by 'royal justice' and laying the foundation of the English common law. While, therefore, we cannot attribute to any Norman king the creative ideas of Henry II, by 1135 the administration was well enough established to survive a disputed succession and to be the basis of the Angevin achievement.

4

The Norman Conquest changed the social and administrative life of England; the Angevin monarchy would coincide with a change of intellectual climate; with that European twelfth-century renaissance which would be more important than the celebrated antiquarian renaissance of the fifteenth. There would be an expansion of monastic and secular religious orders and new papal claims to a cosmopolitan jurisdiction. The philosophers and theologians would show a more confident and creative outlook, while the clergy, who largely administered government, would show a new initiative. As form superseded chaos and learning became speculative rather than a mere catalogue, there arose a new sense of human dignity; as Professor Southern has put it, St Anselm, Archbishop of Canterbury, could already 'give eternity a more friendly appearance'; and even the terror of the Judgement was assuaged when Christ was worshipped not as an awful judge but as a benevolent incarnate God. A new humanism would win through against the apprehensive form of worship prevalent in the ninth and tenth centuries, as nature was accepted as a cosmic order harmonious for man rather than a demon-haunted darkness from which by prayer or incantation he might escape. This relative optimism stemmed from France and contrasts with the conservative outlook of the Byzantines, concerned, not with harmonizing God and the creation, but with inducing moods whereby a transcendent God could be apprehended. By the twelfth century western Europe began to formulate a creative and dynamic humanism.

In the late eleventh century these tendencies were only beginning to emerge: the prevalent background was still intensely superstitious and the Norman kings apt to alternate between blasphemous violence and terror. Duke William had won England under the banner of a papacy which, with the accession of Gregory VII in 1073, would launch a spiritual and political revolution; but the Conqueror would never admit the papal claims. Instead, he characteristically employed an able. administrator to smooth his own passage to power by keeping the church in line. Lanfranc, an Italian lawyer from Pavia, had become Prior of Bec in Normandy and Abbot of Caen: he was a much-travelled scholar and man of affairs. After 1170, as Archbishop of Canterbury in the tradition of Theodore of Tarsus, he reorganized the Anglo-Saxon

Church, rich, grand, casual and archaic as it had been for many centuries. By 1080 all but one of the prelates were Norman; many dioceses had been reorganized and immense building programmes had been launched. Soon the huge Norman cathedrals dominated the countryside like forts: Ely, towering above the fenland; Norwich and Gloucester with the mighty pillars of their naves; Durham, the most dramatic of all, built high over the river; all of them vivid with white-wash and bold colours and new-cut stone.*

But the changes at the top took a long time to filter down. The Anglo-Saxon church had always been closely integrated with lay society and, if the rural parishes were very ancient, the peasant priests were generally dependent on lay patrons, the spiritual servants of their lords. The old lavish endowment of monasteries, the revival under Dunstan, the aristocratic leadership already described, had not altered the basic pattern; the Norman innovations took time. But they were cumulative. By 1080 at least, separate Church courts were in being in each diocese, and the new principle had been asserted that the Church courts administering canon law had a separate jurisdiction, while the cathedral churches had their own deans and chapters.

And behind this drive, separating Church and State, were the new standards set by the ascetic popes in their struggle to permeate a still half-pagan society with their ideals of a truly celibate clergy. In 1102, for example, a Church council in London decreed that no priest should marry or, if married, retain his wife; that priests were 'not to go to drinking parties or drink by the peg', and that their clothes should be of a single colour and their shoes of the prescribed pattern. Those convicted of sodomy were to be deposed from their preferment, and no one was to engage in the slave trade; while the Anglo-Saxon abbots Godric of Peterborough, Hermon of Cerne and Ethelric of Milton Abbas, were to be deposed for simony.[21]

But the unpopularity of these measures was mild compared to the clash of personalities brought about by the question of the investiture of bishops. Lanfranc had been a shrewd politician, committed to the Conqueror's interests; but St Anselm, appointed to Canterbury against his will by Rufus in 1093 in a fit of superstitious terror when he was ill – for the king had long embezzled the revenues of the diocese – proved intransigent.† The first round of a political struggle, which would

* 'By modern standards,' writes Lane Poole, 'the medieval church must have appeared a little garish.' *Domesday Book to Magna Carta, op. cit.*, p. 263.

† Born in 1033 of a noble but declining Burgundian family at Aosta under the southern massif of Mont Blanc, Anselm became a Benedictine monk and Abbot of Bec in Normandy. His first known poem was on a conventional monkish theme, a lament for lost virginity, *deploratio virginitatis amissae per fornicationem*, but he went on to more important themes. He devised the ontological proof that God exists (He was 'that of which nothing greater can be

culminate in the murder of Becket under Henry II and not be finally decided until the reign of Henry VIII, was now fought out. The Norman kings always insisted on all, and indeed more than, their ancient rights, and Rufus declared that he would never endure an equal in his realm: 'no predecessor of yours', he said, 'would have dared to say such things to my father'. The cloistered Anselm, for his part, hated the world and compared himself with 'an owl (*bubo*) happy with her brood in the dim spaces of a barn, too soon to be blinded by the sun's glare and mobbed by the birds without'. He maddened the king by going to sleep while argument raged.[22] He steadily insisted 'that an Archbishop of Canterbury could not be judged or condemned by any human being except only by the Pope nor on any charge whatever be compelled by anyone to make answer to any man except the Pope, unless he chose to do so'.[23] And when the bishops of Winchester and Lincoln, 'encumbered', as they said, 'with their kinsfolk and by manifold worldly interests', explained that they could not rise to the 'sublime height' of Anselm's way of life, the archbishop replied: 'Go then to your lord; I will hold fast to God.'[24] Anselm then went into exile and remained there. Even after Rufus' death, he made heavy weather of a compromise suggested by Henry I. The controversy would flare up again.

The Normans and Angevins, confronted with appalling problems of administration and dependent upon literate clerical bureaucrats who could only be rewarded by preferment in the Church, were thus challenged by a new claim, unprecedented in Anglo-Saxon times; and this high ascetic ideal of a celibate and autonomous Church transcending all political boundaries also challenged the relatively easy-going traditions of the rich old English monasteries. The ancient and august Benedictine houses; Glastonbury, immensely wealthy amid the Somerset meadows, fishponds and pastures; Malmesbury; Bury St Edmunds and St Albans, re-endowed under the Normans who added to the vast benefactions of Knut, also found it hard to adapt themselves to the stark ideas of the reformers. Lanfranc was a man of affairs, but even his *Monastic Constitutions* are severe.[25] In the darkest months penitential psalms were intoned in the small hours in icy and ill-lit vaults, the schedule designed to break up sleep: so exacting was the routine that some of the brothers could seldom have gone out. During the communal shaves, juniors were shaved by seniors and soap provided 'so that who

thought'), and explained why God had to become man: *Cur Deus Homo?* Since, by the Fall, mankind was cut off from God, He could only thus, like a lord with his vassals, resume contact. Anselm also denied that the devil had any 'just power' over humanity by the terms of the Fall. He was considered a theologian of genius; one of the most original minds of his time with a vast reputation, when he came to be yoked, as he said, 'like an old and feeble sheep' with an 'untamed bull'.

wished could wash his head', but during the periodic bleedings which helped to subdue the flesh, absolute silence was observed. Novices, whose masters had to stand by at bedtime to see their charges properly covered up and who were roused at night to accompany them to the privy, had in the daytime to sit apart so as not to touch one another 'with evil intent'. They could not even converse without permission: only the prior and the sub-prior were allowed to 'smile' at them. The dormitories were cleaned out once a year and the straw changed, and both elders and novices were flogged in their respective chapters. Often, of course, natural affections and gusto and the old traditions of hospitality and high living survived; contrary to the rule, monks still dressed fashionably and hunted; always, they said, to provide book-covers and gloves. Scholars could take pride in manuscripts and artists in illuminations.

Meanwhile the country was assimilating many new monks from the continent. In Henry I's reign, the long-established Benedictine houses were supplemented by the Cistercians, whose original foundation at Cîteaux in Burgundy had been reorganized by Stephen Harding, an Englishman from Sherborne, and inspired by St Bernard, Abbot of Clairvaux, who attained European influence. By 1132 they had founded Rievaulx and Fountains, in Yorkshire, in country suited only to the sheep farming which would in time make this ascetic and laborious order extremely rich. The Austinian or 'Black' canons founded St Bartholomew's Hospital in London under Henry I, and the crusading orders, Hospitallers and Templars, were now already established.

But it was still mainly in the great old-established monastic houses that the history of the time was recorded. Such was the background of the Anglo-Norman William of Malmesbury; far the best historian since Bede, whose *History of the Kings of England* and *Historia Novella*, already cited, are still vivid and superior in judgement to the work of Matthew Paris in the thirteenth century. Less reputable but more secular and popular, is the Welsh Geoffrey of Monmouth, whose *History of the British Kings* up to the mid-seventh century, dedicated to Matilda's half-brother, Gloucester, transposed the old Celtic legends and classical stories into an extraordinary mélange of fact and fiction and launched the legends of King Arthur, later elaborated by other writers.*

* See his *Historia Regum Britanniae*. Ed. Acton Griscom, together with a literal translation of the Welsh Mss. *LXI* in Jesus College, Oxford, by R. E. Jones, London, 1929. For 'Arthur' Geoffrey probably used this Welsh document which embodies traditions not transmitted by Gildas, and which may even have some foundation in fact. His 'Arthur' has 'a golden helmet with the likeness of a dragon of fire on it', and a sword called *Kaledrwlch*, the best in all *Ynys Bridain* (the isle of Britain). He was installed as king at York, aged fifteen (p. 432), defeated the *Ssaesson* and conquered Islay in the West of Scotland before crossing to Ireland. He married *Gwenhwyfar*, daughter of Gogren the Giant, and lived in great splendour. Mortally wounded in 'the greatest battle that ever was fought', he went to *Ynys Avalloch* to be healed;

In the scientific field, Muslim learning was being assimilated by Adelard of Bath, who had travelled in Spain and translated Euclid from the Arabic. He was a pioneer of objectivity and critical of dogma in a way which would become one of the most powerful of English traditions. If England could not yet compare with the continental movement pioneered by Abelard, and her universities had not yet developed, in the Norman monasteries and cathedral schools much was already going on.

Nor, in the early twelfth century, was Anglo-Norman lay society as crude as it had been after the Conquest: the cosmopolitan knightly world which extended from the Welsh and Scottish borders to Jerusalem was no longer content with loutish entertainments. The Conqueror's jester had been richly endowed with land, and, by Henry I's time, the disreputable clerics and tumblers who had mimed religious tales were being superseded by less disreputable *jongleurs* who sang epics of chivalry to the rhythm of a primitive violin. Of these epics the *Chanson de Roland* was far the most popular; it was composed after the First Crusade and set in northern Spain, where a more permanent crusade of reconquest was now under way. This epic of militant Christianity, set back in the time of Charlemagne and his peers, celebrating the friendship of the knights Roland and Oliver and telling of Roland's overweening recklessness and fate, is revealing of the feudal mind: the dying hero, his face to Spain and the enemy 'amid the mountains tall and dark', offers his right gauntlet to God, and Gabriel the Archangel accepts it.

> *Sun destres guant a deu en puroffrit*
> *Seint Gabriel de sa man l'ad pris.*

In more subtle and minor idioms, the troubadours of Provence and Poitou were already setting new fashions, and the discomfort of Norman castles was being assuaged by more sophisticated entertainment: the Anglo-Saxon poetry of mead hall and battle was out of fashion. As the Norman kings secured their position and the new masters settled in, a more creative and confident society had begun to develop with a formidable economic and intellectual power behind it.

---

but, dying, commended his Kingdom to *Kystennin* (Constantine) (p. 542). Another Welsh champion, Ythr, was buried at Stonehenge *Cor y kewri*: ('*infra choream gigantum*' – the giant's dance – writes Geoffrey, '*iuxta Aurelium Ambrosium regio more humeraverunt*') (p. 432), thus further confusing the affair.

PART TWO

THE MEDIEVAL REALM

7

THE ANGEVIN ACHIEVEMENT

When in 1153, aged nineteen, 'the illustrious Duke Henry, driven ... by a gale, had reached England, the earth', wrote a contemporary, 'quivered with sudden rumours like reeds shaken by a breeze'. The Angevin Henry II Fitz Empress (1154–89) was a cosmopolitan continental royalty whose ambitions and responsibilities were vast; in prosecuting his far-flung ambitions he used England as his principal base and centralized and exploited the machinery of government developed under Henry I. 'Destined', as John of Salisbury wrote, 'to be the greatest king of the whole age', he was for many years the most formidable power in Western Europe, and had he mastered Flanders and Toulouse, he would have cut off the French monarchs from both the Channel and from northern and western France down to the Pyrenees. Moreover, his reign coincided with a major expansion of agriculture and of internal and external trade, the basis of the high prosperity of the following century, when English Medieval civilization would reach its climax; and with the full tide of the twelfth-century Renaissance, decisive for all Western Europe, and particularly distinguished in England by a confident and perceptive humanism very different from the apprehensive outlook of earlier times.

Henry II controlled far more of France than did the French king, and by his marriage to Eleanor of Aquitaine, the divorced queen of Louis VII, he gained broad, rich and strategically important territories. He also married off their numerous daughters to further his diplomatic designs. One married Henry the Lion, Duke of Saxony and Bavaria, and so enhanced Angevin influence along the Baltic and in southern Germany; another Alfonso of Castile, now the rising power in Spain; another the Count of Savoy, who controlled important Alpine passes, and another William II of Sicily, the predominant power in the central Mediterranean. Further, by the marriage of his son Geoffrey to the heiress of Brittany he rounded off his control of the coast of western France. Henry's main ambition was to compete with the French monarchy, but so wide was the scope of his diplomacy that he may even have had even wider ambitions, though, following his anti-French policy, he was careful to conciliate the formidable Frederick Barbarossa by a nominal submission.* So far did his wealth and power exceed that

* In 1157, prodigal of fine words, he wrote to Frederick 'our ... realm we submit to your

of the French that, according to that observant courtier Walter Map, it was of Henry II that Louis VII made his memorable and unanswerable remark that while the King of England had 'men, horses, gold, silk, gems, fruits, wild beasts and all things else, we in France have nothing but bread, wine and gaiety'.

By the end of his reign, Henry II's ambitions had failed. He fell out with his beautiful and temperamental queen, who 'repaid' his libidinous infidelities by plotting against him 'for the advantage of her children',[2] and his dynastic policy was crippled by the rebellion of his sons, who allied themselves with the French against their father. For the Angevin princes were an even more ferocious brood than the sons of William the Conqueror, and their family feuds were atrocious even by the standards of the time. Moreover, Henry II overreached himself when he attacked the Church, symbolized by the intransigent figure of Thomas Becket, whom Henry had rashly made Archbishop of Canterbury, and whose 'martyrdom' threatened to wreck much of Henry's work. Yet, in spite of the collapse of his continental ambitions, and the set-back following his collision with the Church, Henry II had so ably centralized the government of England and extended its scope through the criminal law and the law of property, that he gave the realm a new impetus which was never lost. For he 'paid due regard to public order and was at great pains to revive the vigour of the laws . . . the ravening wolves were put to flight or turned into sheep, or even if they were not really changed, they were made, through fear of the law, to dwell harmlessly with the sheep'.[3] During his long reign, the results of Stephen's incompetence were soon counteracted, and the fecklessness of the crusading Richard I and the ferocious overdriving of his regal rights by John and the reaction he provoked, would not cripple the work of this indefatigable monarch, whose reign was a turning point in the history of the British Isles. For he made himself overlord of Wales and Scotland and was the first ruler of England to master Ireland, hitherto immune even from the Romans and from all but Scandinavian attack. And he worked in collaboration with the Jews, 'that perfidious nation, on account of the favourable terms he received for their usurious transactions'; he even died solvent by a hundred thousand marks – a most unmedieval achievement.

Henry II was probably less interested in good government for its own sake than for its profits, but in the course of his exploitation he created in England a centralized government unparalleled in the West outside Norman Sicily, and with greater resources and more widespread and

jurisdiction and commit to your power, so that at your nod everything shall be disposed and in all things your imperial will be done'. And he sent the Emperor a tent so magnificent that it had to be put up by 'machines'. (Trans. from *Rahewini Gesta Frederici Imp.*, ed. G. Weitz, Lib III, VII, S.R.G., 1912,) p. 172.

substantial popular support. In spite of conflicts between church and state, king and baronage, within that framework the English realm would develop.

Henry II is one of the most striking and dynamic personalities in English history. His effigy at Fontevrault depicts a stocky man with a big face and thick neck; he cared nothing for ceremony and travelled incessantly over his vast domains 'like a carrier', dragging his household along with him, and he would eat standing up and fidget and talk and draw pictures during mass. He was an unkempt and violent figure, disreputable in his numerous amours,* passionately devoted to hunting, impervious to mud and frost, expert with dogs and birds. Though he spoke little English, he was bilingual in Latin and French; and though a fierce warrior, he preferred diplomacy to war. He was indeed a new type – a literate layman who could read for pleasure, a crude but brilliant and versatile product of the twelfth-century Renaissance.

2

The political landmarks of Henry II's long reign must now be considered. From 1154–73 he consolidated his position, working until 1162 with his able Chancellor, Thomas Becket. Mercenaries were expelled, illegal castles dismantled, royal property resumed, and the administration, disrupted but never destroyed under Stephen, restored. This work was done to exploit England and provide a base for Henry's power on the continent, always his main concern; even after the quarrel with Becket, Archbishop of Canterbury 1162–70, the king was able to subdue Ireland. More important for England, the king's law was enforced, the bureaucracy consolidated, and the Exchequer now permanently established in London. And when, following the murder of the archbishop and rebellion by the king's sons, there was a two-year crisis, the major magnates did not rebel. The Flemish mercenaries brought into East Anglia 'to destroy Henry the old warrior, and have his wool', and singing

> Hoppe, hoppe, Wilekin, hoppe, Wilekin,
> Engelonde is min ant tin,

in what is probably the oldest Flemish jingle extant,[4] were routed by the Suffolk peasantry. For

> There was in the country neither villager nor clown,
> Who did not destroy the Flemings with fork and flail.

* His liaison with 'Fair' Rosamund Clifford is authenticated by an allusion in Giraldus Cambrensis, and he heavily endowed the nunnery at Godstow near Oxford to which she retired. Leland, the early Tudor antiquary, would write *Rosamunde's Tumbe at Godstow was taken up alate. It is a stone with the inscription Tumba Rosamundi.*

With nothing meddled the armed knights,
But only with knocking them down and the villagers with
killing them
... the wool of England they gathered very late.[5]

There followed (1175–82) a second phase of administrative reconstruction; the coinage was restored and an Assize of Arms mobilized the
country's defences. Finally, another Angevin family quarrel was
fomented by the able Philip Augustus of France, who had succeeded
Louis VII in 1180 and would become the architect of the first really
powerful French monarchy. The reign ended in tragedy; hounded
down by his own sons in alliance with the French king, Henry died at
Chinon aged fifty-eight, having 'raised distinguished offspring to his
own ruin'. Yet these vendettas had not destroyed his main work in
England.

Further, by the Inquest of Sheriffs in 1170, Henry had used local
juries to denounce the abuses of royal and baronial officials at all levels
before itinerant justices with the curial authority behind them. Thus
the central government could now not only get at the facts, but enforce its will by more systematic routine. By 1176 itinerant justices held
regular assizes throughout the land; by the end of the century they
would be dealing with a whole range of judicial and fiscal business,
linking the 'central bureaucracy with the communities of the counties as
the administrative system of Henry's choice, and the permanent system
of the Angevin state';[6] the whole centring on a Chief Justiciar, supervised, as occasion served, by the king.

The range of royal justice was also increased by another use of
prerogative: to protect property. The strength of the monarchy, both
feudal and traditional, had always been its control of the land; now the
kings made their authority more popular by creating a new sense of
security of tenure. If a violation of the king's peace was the king's
concern everywhere, arbitrary evictions and estate jumping had also to
be stopped, and the king's obvious move was to 'place the services of the
curia regis itself at the disposal of ordinary men'.[7] Now the aggrieved
party could apply for a writ, his opponent could answer not by violence,
but by counter-attack in the courts, and these writs would run anywhere
in the realm. All dealt with precise situations. Questions of possession,
inheritance, estate jumping and the rights to present livings could thus
be peacefully determined; and the resulting fees went to the royal
Exchequer. So in De legibus et consuetudinibus regni Angliae (Of the laws
and customs of the English realm), Glanville could describe the register
of writs (formulae brevium) available in the Chancery. These 'writs of
entry' cater for disputes over entitlement to land and trespass. For
example, under the Assize of novel disseisin anyone whose land had been

taken from him could sue for a royal writ which would bring the affair before a sworn inquest of local men; and under the Assize of *Mort d'ancester* an heir whose property had been wrongly seized, could obtain his rights. By the mid-thirteenth century these procedures would become normal: litigation was superseding violence.

And from this protection of tenure and property, royal justice would further expand. The royal writs, obtainable by any free plaintiff, commanded the sheriff to summon the accused before the king's justices at a set place and time; hence an elaborate ramification of the English 'common' law, so called, because 'common' to all England in the royal courts. It would gradually supersede the motley collection of feudal and customary courts; a monopoly that would outclass all competitors.

No wonder that it did. Trial by battle, the *judicium Dei*, judgement of God, which lingered on long after compurgation and the ordeal had been abolished, was an expensive and risky affair. As late as 1287, in spite of the papal prohibition, the monks of Bury St Edmunds would hire a champion at twenty marks with another thirty to be paid after the battle; but he had to hang about for six months and his trainer lost ten pounds. Then he got killed, so they lost their claim to the manor of Groton, Suffolk; and although Glastonbury Abbey would hire a champion to fight Wells, by the end of the thirteenth century most people would come to rely on human judgement.

The king's influence thus superseded other jurisdictions in both criminal justice and in property law; as the government used local men in old procedures adapted to new ways, for the juries of presentment were, in principle, no Norman innovation and the writs were Anglo-Saxon. So the monarchy was adapted to become a more public power, with its own initiative, rather than being just the guardian of custom or the supreme feudal lordship; the concept of active sovereignty, though not defined, was in the offing. Nor was it in these respects an arbitrary power, whatever abuses a royal tyrant could commit through his feudal rights, confiscating estates and offices and holding their occupants arbitrarily 'in mercy'. It worked within the law and customs of the realm, in collaboration with responsible local men, from the magnates down to the villagers.

And although rebellion, brigandage, denial of justice and delay went on, the cumulative decisions taken to meet particular problems would build up that body of case-law which would be the basis of the common law of England, and establish a widespread respect for a power that could secure property and avoid the delay and confusion of overlapping local procedures. And at the centre of this network the essential law-courts would develop; basic to all, the Court of Exchequer, already described, which could not only exact but harvest an often massive taxation. So, eventually, the courts of the King's Bench and Common Pleas would also be established: the English law-courts thus came to work according to known rules: moreover, whatever the king might do in his feudal capacity, the common law, in contrast to arbitrary régimes still extant today, did not sanction arbitrary imprisonment for an undefined offence, interrogation of suspects in prison before trial, or delation by witnesses unseen by the accused. Moreover, the judge acted, not as a prosecutor, but as the voice of the law, uttered after a verdict which came to be given by the juries as their functions changed from presentment to judgement. These fundamental liberties which thus slowly evolved, and were decisive not only for England but for English settlements overseas as well. They were developed by Angevin initiative.

3

That achievement, here necessarily over-simplified, was brought about under Henry II's own supervision mainly by a clerical bureaucracy. These early judges and civil servants were rewarded with bishoprics and other clerical offices, and, working with the Crown, proved a constructive and stabilizing influence in the complex power politics of the time, both at home and abroad.

Yet the claims of the cosmopolitan church had long presented an urgent problem. Already considerable under Rufus, it now came to a spectacular crisis. As, with twelfth-century prosperity the church became richer, it had became more litigious; with luxury came debt, and appeals to Rome involved lay tenants and proprietors at a time when the papacy was reaching the zenith of its power. Moreover as the papal bureaucracy improved appeals became easier and cheaper. The separation of church and lay courts made by the Conqueror had struck deep into society, and it is extraordinary how far-reaching the papal claims had become. By Stephen's time even an obscure dispute over the parishes of Letcombe Regis and Fawley on the Berkshire downs, or Robert Winegot's dispute with William of Sturminster, Dorset, meant an appeal to Rome. The moral jurisdiction of the Church also gave rise to many appeals. The Abbess of Barking's notorious conduct with Hugh, her officer, would be referred to the Holy Father, along with routine complaints about the morals of the Welsh. They live like beasts, complained the Bishop of Bangor, sell their nearest and dearest in the slave trade, barter their concubines and commit incest.

Under Henry II the spate of appeals to Rome increased. They were mainly about property, and caused mounting delay and expense; further, within the country, bishops, abbots and minor clergy were involved in constant litigation with townsfolk, tenants and parishioners. And clearly no efficient government could afford to let felonious clergy go unpunished by the law of the land. Hence the notorious dispute between Henry II and his Archbishop which culminated in the 'martyr-dom' of St Thomas Becket of Canterbury, whose shrine became famous over all western Christendom and the most popular centre of pilgrimage in England. But, adverse as its effect would be on Angevin policy, the dispute was not, as often assumed, representative of the normal relation-ship of the great churchmen and the Crown. Most of the bishops tem-porized or sided with the king. Abbot Sampson of Bury St Edmunds for example, another appointment made by Henry II and also an arresting personality, proved a most satisfactory tenant-in-chief; he discharged important diplomatic missions under Richard I, though he did fight hard for the interests of his house and always maintained his spiritual authority.*

Becket's appointment, indeed, was a normal move to promote the collaboration of the king's government with the Church; a natural reward for a brilliantly successful Chancellor who had shown 'an irresistible blend of high spirits and panache joined to solid work and keen foresight'.† Unhappily for all concerned, the dispute raised many old questions of principle, long fought over through most of Christendom since the time of Gregory VII, concerning such weighty matters as the appointments of bishops and the extent of the Pope's universal jurisdic-tion over clergy. The king suffered a spectacular though, in fact, minor defeat; and given the immense power and pretensions of the papacy that would culminate under Innocent III and Innocent IV, and only collapse with the defeat of Boniface VIII by the French at the end of the thirteenth century, this result was to be expected.

The outline of the dispute is simple; its sequel highly illuminating. Nowhere is the medieval mentality better revealed. In 1162 Becket became archbishop, and to the King's surprise threw himself passion-ately into his new role. The question of the punishment of felonious clergy had long been outstanding: by 1164 the royal officials had looked

---

* See *The Chronicle of Jocelin of Brakelond* (written *c.* 1182–8), translated H. E. Butler, London, 1949, a work much superior to Carlyle's exploitation of it in his *Past and Present*. This autocrat, bilingual in French and Latin, could preach 'in the speech of Norfolk where he was born and bred'. When in Richard I's time a gang of young noblemen, intent on a tournament, quartered themselves on the abbey, and 'began to dance and sing, and after sending out to the town for wine, they drank, and after they yelled, robbing the whole convent of their sleep, and doing everything they could to mock the abbot', he excommunicated them all, so that in terror of the 'fury of St Edmund', some of the culprits came to beg absolution. He also excommunicated and flogged rebellious townsfolk, made to grovel outside the gateway.

† See Dom David Knowles, *Archbishop Thomas Becket* in *Proceedings of the British Academy*, vol. XXXV, 1949, for the best account of an elusive character. The very physique of the protagonists contrasted: the thick-set, florid monarch with the 'harsh, cracked' voice, and his former intimate, a careerist charmer turned dévot; slender, dark, aquiline, high-strung.

up the precedents and produced the Constitutions of Clarendon. The customary safeguards on which Henry I had insisted over appeals to Rome and the choice of bishops were set down in black and white. On the matter of felonious clergy the constitutions presented what to modern minds must seem a sensible compromise: clerics accused of felony must answer to the king's courts; they could still appeal to church tribunals, but if convicted, they would revert to the secular arm and suffer the usual penalties – hanging or mutilation. To the archbishop the expedient was anathema. 'You have not the power,' he would write, 'to drag clerks before secular tribunals, nor should a man be punished twice.'

That autumn, after a violent scene at the Council of Northampton, Becket retired to Flanders, then to France, and there he found a ready patron in the king's enemy, Louis VII. It was not until the winter of 1170 that, after a hollow reconciliation with Henry II, the archbishop returned to Canterbury, there to meet his fate. He apparently 'accepted and in a sense desired it; during the last weeks of his life he was fey'.[8] Aware of the political danger, the king at once ordered his protective arrest; but 'even if the four knights had not acted, men and forces were in action which would have borne the archbishop away'.[9] The climax is well known: the clank of armed men, 'head and body in full armour but for their eyes', their great razor-sharp swords out; Fitzurse with an axe, seized from a carpenter; the cry 'Hither to me king's men' and the yells for Becket, 'traitor to the king'. Then the swift butchery; the blood and brains on the pavement and the conclusive remark, 'come away knights, this fellow won't get up again'.

The 'martyrdom', inflicted by Christian men, was even more dramatic than that of St Ælfheah, killed by drunken heathen, and the sequel was much more spectacular. The Canterbury clergy now possessed a priceless asset and one of European scope. The townsfolk, too, were already flocking to smear their eyes with the magic blood; indeed they brought 'bottles' and 'carried off secretly as much as they could'. But the clergy kept the body, though someone gave the precious pallium and rich outer vestment to some beggars, who promptly sold them for what they could get, which was 'very foolish because', wrote a contemporary, 'they would have fetched so much more later'.

Then, to add to the blood cult, came the final evidence of sanctity. The archbishop's hairshirt was found to be so full of lice that 'anyone would have thought that the martyrdom of the day was less grievous than that which these small enemies had continually inflicted', and the clergy gazed at one another in astonishment at 'this proof of hidden piety'.

No wonder the cult of the martyr spread so fast. Canterbury now had a second, more glorious, saint: soon in Germany and Italy, in Spain, Scandinavia and Iceland the legend flourished. Not only were miracles performed at Canterbury; they began to occur at other places too. A boy pinned to a wall by a baited bull was freed when his mother called on the saint: the animal calmed down; the dogs stopped barking at the mere name.* A lay brother, his face disfigured by the venom of a huge toad (*bufo mirae magnitudinis*), was immediately cured at Soissons; a knight who had spiked his hand on a thorn boar-hunting in Cheshire, was healed at once; a lady's hawk, moribund, was restored to life; lost anchors were recovered; a man with 'noises in the head like the sound of large trumpets' was relieved; a drowned girl revived; lepers and paralytics were cured; a 'mad Frenchman' made sane. And, significantly, almost at the instant of the outrage, a boy walking from Salisbury to Marlborough had met three huge men carrying a skinful of blood. 'What are you carrying, sir?' he had asked. 'The blood of St Thomas', one of them had answered, and they had all vanished.[10]

Such portents could not be denied. By 1220 the Martyr's body would be transferred to an elaborate shrine, and over the centuries an immense treasure would accumulate at Canterbury, now one of the most popular places of pilgrimage in Europe. Indeed, long after, when Henry VIII, deliberately revenging his Angevin ancestor, smashed and plundered the shrine of St Thomas with an added relish, eight wagons were needed to cart the vast treasure away.

The retrospective rage of Henry VIII was justified, for the sequel had been a set-back, though not a disaster, for government. Henry II still kept *de facto* control of appointments to bishoprics, but the clergy remained impervious to royal justice, though on occasion informally hanged. Well into the nineteenth century, *Benefit of Clergy* would protect all who could read the 'neck verse', *Miserere mei Deus* (Psalm 1, i), though, if twice convicted, they would suffer the normal penalty.

4

These major political, administrative and ecclesiastical developments were naturally to most men remote. The vast majority of peasants, of whom we can never directly know much, led rustic and illiterate lives which no amount of modern statistical method or computer techniques are likely to illuminate; nor is their mentality easy to assess, since the Old English oral literature had been so much driven underground,

* *Materials for the life of Becket* (on which this account is based) ed. E. D. J. Robertson, Rolls Series 1872, Vol. I, p. 293, *de Puero quem taurus cornibus ventilavit*. The bull was rampaging through the streets, after some dogs had been deliberately loosed at him (*educti sunt canes ad vexendum taurum*).

surviving mainly in religious forms. The ancient distinctions among the peasantry were now increasingly ironed out, and though the Normans abolished Anglo-Saxon slavery, the distinction between the free men and the lower peasantry increased. What we do know directly is the effect of the colonization which went on; spreading more widely in the twelfth century, forming the basis of much greater prosperity, and still marking the landscape. The predominant open field villages were now supplemented by new clearings in the woods and out on the moors, particularly in the West Country. These colonial conditions, in which vast areas would remain unexploited, continued until well into Tudor times; but, already by the crucial twelfth century, the woodland had much diminished, both by the expansion of the nucleated village fields, and by the foundation of new settlements. By modern standards productivity was low and cattle were wretched animals; but methods of drainage improved, and dykes were built to reclaim land from the sea.

Here the monastic landlords were often pioneers. Glastonbury had been dyking-in rich polders since the tenth century, and in Lincolnshire, Sussex and Kent rich sheep pastures had been developed, as in Romney marshes, exploited since Roman times. Eastern England was the most prosperous and thickly populated area, but the sheep runs of Yorkshire and the Cotswolds, of Berkshire, and Wiltshire, where the bishop of Winchester had huge flocks at Downton, were flourishing. The peasants as well as the big landowners had many sheep which provided not only wool but manure, cheese and mutton, though pork and bacon were the main standby. This comparative prosperity went on from the twelfth century through the thirteenth, and formed the basis of the climax of medieval English civilization. Then, after the Black Death in the fourteenth century, there was recession, and the economy did not fully recover until Elizabethan and Jacobean times.

Apart from a still mainly subsistence agriculture, the most important industry was now the wool trade and its derivatives, and the main centre of the economy was London, far the largest city with its tidal river, fisheries, and water mills 'turning with jolly sound'.* The square fortress of the Tower built by the Conqueror and 'cemented with animal blood', dominated the city; and Rufus had built the great New Hall at Westminster in the meadows by the Confessor's abbey. In Becket's time, indeed, the rich citizens 'seemed like barons', and took their ease and their hunting in the adjacent woods. The Jews, who had often done well since the Conquest, now built in stone for security, though most houses were still of timber, and glass remained a luxury. The London boys would stage water sports on the Thames, the populace applauding or

---

* '*Molinorum versatiles rotae citantur cum murmure jocosa.*' *Vita sancti Thomae* by William Fitz-stephen, in *Materials for the History of Thomas Becket*, Vol. III, *op. cit.*, pp. 3 ff.

deriding from the banks, and in winter glide on bone skates* on the wide frozen river, their shouts echoing in the frost. There was already a night life of 'actors, jesters . . . pretty boys, dancing girls, belly dancers and buffoons'. Horse fairs and horse racing were held at Smithfield (smoothfield), and the life of the city was then, as always, touched with a sense of the sea; for London had been a major port long before the Conquest, and now, with the expansion of trade in the twelfth century, it had become even more prosperous, closely linked with the Low Countries and Gascony. As in Roman times, the exports were mainly raw materials: hides, cheese, herrings, lead and tin; and above all, raw wool was exported, to be made up into cloth in the great cities of Flanders. In return a vast amount of wine was imported, mainly from Gascony, as well as furs, timber and cordage from the Baltic: the 'steel-yard' of the German Hansa merchants had long been established, rather as in the seventeenth century English factories would be set up in the East. Armour and weapons and wine were imported from the Rhine-land; dyes, spices and luxury goods from the south. And though London was already the centre of governmental, social and economic life, many other cities took part in this expansion. The East Anglian ports were already prosperous; King's Lynn, mainly concerned with exporting wool; Boston, closely connected with Lincoln and its hinterland. Southampton was the main southern port; Bristol the biggest port in the west, and Chester traded with Gascony and Ireland. Besides these major cities, many lesser ports throve off the coastal trade and fisheries: the Cinque Ports commanding the Channel; Poole and Bridport; Fowey and Falmouth.

Inland many of the old *civitates* of Roman times, some now cathedral cities, had also fully revived; and the *burghs* founded or refortified by Alfred and his successors were now supplemented by new market towns, founded as an investment by the Crown or by local magnates. Stratford-on-Avon, for example, was founded by the late twelfth century, and in the thirteenth 'New Sarum', Salisbury, would be well planned and rapidly developed. Here Bishop Poore would build a new cathedral to supersede the Norman building on its exposed site at Old Sarum.

These cities were anomalous in a feudal society, and they bought themselves out of it. Henry II was chary of creating independent com-munes; in 1155 he granted London a charter, but not self-government. No burgess, he promised, should undergo trial by battle, or pay *childwyte* if his daughter had an illegitimate child; nor were soldiers to be billeted on the citizens, who were free of tolls throughout the land. It was not until the reigns of Richard I and John, both avid for money, that charters were widely granted: Richard said that he would sell London

* '*Ossa scilicet animalium*', *op. cit.*, Vol. III, p. 11.

itself if he got a good offer, and in 1193 the Londoners obtained a commune, with sheriffs and a permanent mayor. This privilege was confirmed by John on the eve of the sealing of *Magna Carta*, and the mayor, now annually elected, became more dependent on the citizens. John also granted a charter to Bristol.

The collieries of the north were now exploited, if only in a small way. Newcastle-upon-Tyne was already exporting coal to London, and though the Anglo-Saxons had tended to neglect their mineral resources, for they 'did not take easily to industrial life',[11] *'carbon de roche'* was already exported to Bruges, now linked to London by a commercial treaty in 1197 which regularized a *'Hansa Flamande'*. Richard I's government appointed a Warden of the Stannaries to develop the Cornish tin mines and lead mining was further developed because of its use both for silver and for plumbing – for, contrary to widespread belief, people in the thirteenth century were cleaner than in Tudor, Stuart, or even early Hanoverian times.

Thus an expanding trade went along with a more creative and professional kind of government; and if, by later standards, medieval agriculture remained technically elementary, the acreage under cultivation steadily increased. By the late thirteenth and early fourteenth centuries the long colonization of the land would reach its climax, while the sheep on the downs, wolds, and polders now throve in a climate which produced rich pastures.

The resulting wealth of the towns had now created a merchant oligarchy, later challenged by the lesser townsfolk, but now solidly established; an oligarchy which, in the English tradition, was already buying itself into the land-owning establishment, and breaking down the class barriers between the feudal barons and the urban magnates, still so rigid in most areas of the continent. Yet the English townsfolk were not able to acquire the disruptive independence common in larger areas and more difficult for government to control; they remained instead restive, but not anarchic, in a close relationship with the central government in its manageable, insular, setting.

5

It has been well said that the twelfth century was the early summer of the Middle Ages and that the thirteenth century saw the harvest; and this freshness is particularly apparent in the intellectual life of the time, from the speculations of the philosophers and political theorists to the Latin songs of the students and the romances of the courtly world. The culture was of course cosmopolitan, part of the new confidence and deeper learning already prevalent in Western Europe by the time of

Anselm and Abelard; and it expanded in a society bilingual in Latin and Norman French. The historians, if not so attractive as William of Malmesbury, or so vivid and many-sided as Matthew Paris in the thirteenth century, showed a new sense of order and impartial judgement. The author of the *Gesta* of Henry II and Richard I, long attributed to Abbot Benedict of Peterborough, was probably a civil servant; Roger of Hovedon was a judge; Roger Fitzneal, the author of the *Dialogue of the Exchequer*, was himself Treasurer, while the author of the *Treatise of the Laws and Customs of England* attributed to Ranulf Glanville, was an experienced official, well-versed in the discipline of Roman law, as revived in the schools of Bologna, which he brought to bear on the practice of government. From 1156 the Pipe Rolls of the Exchequer are extant; by Richard I's time, with the systematic recording of pleas, 'legal memory' begins; and by John's the Close Rolls of the Chancery record the issue of and payments for writs, giving a wide picture of this litigious society.

The twelfth century saw only the beginnings of the English universities; fully established only in the thirteenth; but it had already produced men of humane learning. This humanism, later to be discouraged by the new techniques of scholastic disputation and by the elaborate attempt to fit Aristotle's knowledge into a medieval world-outlook, was based on sound discipline and wide reading. Its exponents wrote on parchment or vellum in the clear post-Carolingian minuscule which had coincided with Romanesque building, and which would be ousted by the angular, difficult and much abbreviated Gothic script, which would come in with the 'Early English' Gothic architecture. Handwriting would then deteriorate in form until the Roman script was revived in the Italian renaissance.[12] John of Salisbury,* the best known of these humanists, had studied at the cathedral schools at Paris and Chartres. His tutor, Bernard, ('the old man of Chartres', *senex Carnotensis*) had 'taught' he says 'the art of writing and speaking', and 'named Wisdom's keys in a few lines': for he had expounded 'the linking of words and the elegant ending of passages', and advised his pupils 'to avoid the superfluous. . . . For . . . to follow out what every contemptible person has said is irksome'.[13]

The range of John's learning is already remarkable: in the *Policraticus*, a shrewd and realistic book based on first-hand observation of Henry II's court, he quotes not only the obvious authors, but Terence and Petronius, Juvenal, Plutarch and Pliny. He is steeped in classical

---

* John of Salisbury (*c.* 1119–80). Born at Old Sarum, Wiltshire, he was one of the erudite *familiares* of Archbishop Theobald's secretariat, and frequently visited and worked for the papal court. In 1176 he became Bishop of Chartres, where a modern plaque commemorates him. He was a close friend of Becket, to whom the *Policraticus* is dedicated: his *Metalogicus* reveals a remarkable power of thought, and his *Historia Pontificalis* covers the years 1148–52.

learning, and admired the *urbanity* of Roman civilization compared with the still predominantly rustic society of his own times; an *urbanity* also admired by Peter of Blois, one of Henry II's secretaries, who read Livy and Tacitus and scorned the new scholastic technicians, intent on useful results rather than the enrichment of the mind. 'Dogs may bark,' he writes, 'and pigs may grunt; I shall always pattern on the writings of the ancients . . . nor ever, while I am able, shall the sun find me idle.'

The background to this attractive learning was provided by the cathedral and church schools. Grammar schools must also have been numerous, though concerned as much with teaching the rudiments of French as of Latin. In London St Paul's, Holy Trinity, and St Martin's already had famous schools, whose boys so bandied Latin epigrams that 'their hearers wrinkled up their noses in applause'. And after Henry II, during his quarrel with Becket, forbade the English to study in France, scholars flocked to hear the lecturers at Northampton and Lincoln and Oxford – 'sophists who speak paradoxes and are praised for their torrent of words' – forerunners of the regular faculties and colleges of the thirteenth century and indeed of today.

The new individuality and sense of character is also expressed in memorable form by Giraldus de Barri (1147–*c*. 1220), called *Cambrensis*, the Welshman, and by his critics *Sylvester*, 'the wild man', a term then widely used for his countrymen. He came of Norman nobility on his father's side, but was related to the Welsh princes through his mother, and he has left 'a treasure unique for medieval England – a full auto-biography of his eccentric and adventurous life'.* His *de rebus a se gestis* 'deeds done by himself', is the first full self-revelation in British writing. It centres on his attempt to secure the bishopric of St David's, to which he was twice elected; an election quashed by the authorities who were unwilling to have so fiery an individualist in the See. Archbishop Hubert Walter's letter, commending him for following the ways of Mary and not those of Martha, is already a masterpiece of smooth bureau-cratic style. Giraldus appealed to Innocent III, attended the papal court (1199–1203), and fully describes the pope and his entourage. Among his other voluminous works his *Topography of Ireland* is the most interesting, for he accompanied Prince John there in 1185–6, and set himself to be the first historian of the Celtic fringes. Giraldus is one of the most entertaining of British historians; the academic characteristics are

* H. E. Butler, *The Autobiography of Giraldus Cambrensis*, London, 1937, p. 22; an excellent account. He was born at Manorbier castle on the south-western shore of Pembrokeshire, and his family had played a major part in Strongbow's conquest of Ireland. Early known as 'the little bishop', owing to his intellectual interests incongruous in a martial family, he studied in Paris; in 1175 became Archdeacon of Brecknock, and in 1184 a chaplain to Henry II, of whom, in his *On the Instruction of a Prince*, he took a less favourable view than later historians. His works are edited in seven volumes of the Rolls Series by J. S. Brewer, London, 1861.

already apparent – not least his pleasure at reading his works aloud to large audiences; as when in 1188 he first feasted the doctors of the Oxford faculties and then read his *Topography* to them, 'a very grand event'.

Among more amiable and sheltered personalities than Giraldus, the new learning fostered friendship; a new subtlety and playfulness, curiosity and confidence. There was now a new interest in character, and the twelfth century produced the courtier, Walter Map, the first English gossip and wit.

Map was a born story-teller, even if his 'tales are not framed in the bright sunshine of Fiesole, but belong rather to the dark rooms of a Norman castle, or the narrow cell of a monk, with the rain and wind noisy without'.* Well travelled and widely read, he begins with a famous passage from St Augustine 'I am in time, and I speak of time . . . and I know not what time is'; while to his readers he remarks 'I am your huntsman, I bring you the game. Dress the dishes for yourselves.' So he recounts dreams and folk-tales and tall stories; as when a man saw a 'Pan with the feet of a kid, a hairy belly, and on its breast a dappled fawnskin. Moreover, with a glowing face and a bearded chin and horns upright'. He writes of the youth Eudo in the Demon's Snare, and of the Patarines who will suffer anything and kiss the behind of a black cat of marvellous size in the dark; and of Nicolas Pipe the merman who, without breathing, would dwell on the floor of the ocean and could not live far from water, or 'at least from the smell of the sea'.

Walter, like John of Salisbury, disliked the king's court; 'If not hell, it is as like it as a horse's shoe to a mare's. . . . I languish,' he wrote, 'in this wretched prying court, sacrificing my wishes to please other men.' And he mocks, as would Chaucer, at the way the English speak French; there is 'a spring at Marlborough of which, if one tastes it, they say he talks barbarous French; hence if one is faulty in the use of that tongue they say "he speaketh the French of Marlborough"'.†

Latin student songs, like *Carmina Burana*, also proliferated before the lyrics and ballads, written in vernacular French and English, had become the natural medium, and before the frost of scholasticism and the influence of the early Italian Renaissance brought self-consciousness. The wandering scholars, the *vagabunduli*, little vagabonds, have left poignant lyrics and biting satire, coming down from the later twelfth

* See his *De nugis curialium*, of *Courtier's Trifles* (c. 1181–93) translated and edited F. Tupper and M. B. Ogle, London, 1924. Walter came of a well-established Norman family from the Welsh marches, studied in Paris, and became an official in the royal household and a Justice in Eyre. He travelled in Italy and was at Saumur when Henry II died at Chinon near by. In 1197 he became Archdeacon of Oxford. This determined bachelor wrote a *Dissuasion from Matrimony*. 'May the omnipotent God,' he wrote to a friend, 'grant thee power not to be deceived by the omnipotent female.'

† Map, *op. cit.*, p. 310. Many Marlburians have done their best to maintain this ancient tradition.

century and the first quarter of the thirteenth, in 'the good brief moment before the bourgeois shoulders himself into literature'.[14] And to this cosmopolitan literature the English greatly contributed; not least, as Serlon of Wilton, in satire; though it was an Irishman who best caught the feel of the twelfth-century renaissance, 'in those first days when youth in me was happy and life was swift in doing, and I wandering in the divers cities of sweet France, for the desire I had of learning'.[15]

Here is a new note, struck in north-western Europe; different from the Virgilian contentment with olive groves and the sea and the Mediterranean environment, more questing and romantic. And this feel for nature, '*Quan li jors sont lonc en mai*', is apparent in the lyrics: the vernacular poetry, Provençal and Northern French, which now set the Court fashion in England.

For in lay society the martial values of the *Song of Roland* were now touched with a new fantasy; the cult of courtly love in the romantic tales of 'Arthur' and his Round Table, originally devised so that there should be no quarrels over precedence. This cult of the *matière de Bretagne*, much of it already familiar through Geoffrey of Monmouth, is Welsh and Breton and French, and it was expressed around 1160–75 by Chrétien de Troyes in his tales of Tristan, Lancelot and the *Conte du Graal*. It elaborated the cult of knighthood coming down from the *Chanson de Roland*. When the archbishop '*fist Artu Chevalier*' (made 'Arthur' a knight), he tells him: '*Allez querre l'espee et la justice dont vos devez defendre saincte Eglise et la Crestiante sauver.*'[16] The chivalric code was now also enriched with a transformation of love into something unknown to Ovid or Petronius, if not, in principle, to Plato; the cult of the *Lady Blanchfleur of Tintajoel*, sister of the king of Cornwall, and of the fate of Tristan and Iseult. In medieval life marriage was a contract; and highborn women, often with little to do, found emotional fulfilment outside it with lovers who were even, like the poet, *enamoret de la Comtessa de Tripol sans vezer* – in love without seeing her. Hence something new in western civilization; the elaborate cult of chivalry towards women; of their precedence and glamour; a strain of literature which, in the later medieval romances satirized by Cervantes, could become intolerably prolix and tedious, but which contributed to civilize a society still politically often barbaric. This paradox in various forms pervades medieval civilization; not least the creative and forceful twelfth-century Renaissance in which the foundations of the English realm were consolidated.

8

MAGNA CARTA AND THE
CURBING OF MONARCHY; SCOTLAND;
THE CELTIC FRINGES

Richard I (1189–99), whose galley put in at Portofino in August, 1190, *en route* for Sicily and the Palestinian crusade, was the first monarch since the Conquest to be popular. King of England, lord of Ireland, Scotland and Wales; Duke of Normandy and Aquitaine; Count of Maine, Anjou and Poitou; overlord of Brittany and Auvergne and King of Arles, he was a famous European figure. He cared nothing for the English and they idolized him.* His coronation in September 1189, had been magnificent, based on the old Anglo-Saxon ceremonial, followed in essentials ever since. He was the tallest of the Angevins, with red-gold hair and blue eyes; 'his limbs straight and flexible, his arms somewhat long, and, for this very reason, better fitted than most men to draw or wield the sword. . . . Moreover, he had long legs', matching the character of his whole body. At thirty-two he was still a lithe warrior, though already 'shaky'[1] with ague, a 'tremor as continual as that in which he kept the rest of the world'.[2] By modern standards madly improvident, he was then widely considered a splendid feudal king. Though born at Beaumont Palace in Oxford, he had grown up on the continent and had ruled Aquitaine since he was fourteen: his effigy at Fontevrault is neat and martial and French. He composed verses in the current fashion and, in 1187, the very day after he had heard that Jerusalem had fallen to the Saracens, 'he flew to avenge Christ's injuries'.

He was also a ferocious Angevin. When crossed by Greek-speaking Sicilians, who called all Englishmen tailed, he became '*Leo ille teterrimus*, that utterly terrifying lion . . . who roared horribly burning with rage worthy of such a beast', and who had 'the terrible dragon standard carried before him unfurled'.† Though, like Rufus, he had peculiar moral standards, he was a versatile warrior 'in as good fettle and as nimble and

---

* His equestrian statue at Westminster, brandishing a sword, commemorates this enthusiasm, shared by the Victorians.

† *The Chronicle of Richard of Devizes*, ed. J. T. Appleby, London, 1965, p. 20. The author was a caustic north Wiltshire monk at the old Minster at Winchester, who, writes his editor, 'combines information and entertainment to a degree not to be found in any of (his) contemporaries'. The king's appellation 'lion' was first made in Sicily to contrast him with Louis VIII, 'the lamb'. The king's heart, '*Cor Richardi Regis . . . Cor Leonis dicti*', was interred at Rouen in 1199.

THE MEDIEVAL REALM

agile on shipboard as on land'; he swore 'Ho ho! by God's throat!' and once, in rage, 'chewed up the pine staff that he carried in his hand into small bits'.[3] In captivity at Trifels in Bavaria, he teased his German warders with rough jokes and 'enjoyed making sport of them when they were drunk and trying out his own strength on their big bodies'. This born champion of Christendom also had a taste for splendid clothes; glittering on occasion with sunbursts on silk in fantastic and subtle blends of colour, set off by a 'scarlet cap embroidered in gold with beasts and birds' and slippers of cloth of gold.

This lavish and extrovert monarch at once dismissed his father's able Justiciar, Glanville, ousted many of the sheriffs and put all the offices he could up for sale.* He also recklessly gave John an independent principality over the whole south-west of England, then made his bastard brother, Geoffrey, Archbishop of York, and appointed William Longchamp, Bishop of Ely, a detested Frenchman, as Chancellor. Such was this hero whose ransom, after he had been captured in Germany when returning from the Crusade, cost the country a quarter of its income, and who, after being recrowned at Winchester in 1194 at the request of his subjects to decontaminate him from the taint of imprisonment, never set foot in the island again. He has come down in popular tradition as a very splendid king.

John (1199–1216), on the other hand, has left an appalling reputation; 'alone of his brothers he was "temperamentally *mauvais sire*"'.[4] He mocked the conventions of chivalry, despised and blackmailed the baronage, and tried to establish an overwhelming power through the 'new men' of his household and through mercenaries. Yet this paranoiac was a better ruler than his brother: 'his peace', he declared, should be inviolable 'even if granted to a dog'; he judged many cases himself and he had a shrewd eye for trade. He was popular in London and the big ports and was the best supporter of the navy since Alfred.

A short bustling man who cared nothing for glamour, John possessed a small library, took eight baths in five months in 1209, collected jewellery and liked to eat well. From his castles at Marlborough and Corfe he hunted over Wessex, still commemorated by King John's hunting lodge in Cranborne Chase. He afforested all Purbeck 'which ought not to be forest except for the warren of hares purtaining to Corfe Castle';[5] fished in the Kennet at Marlborough, and had his gyrfalcons – the 'noblest' hawks – fed on doves, pork and 'chicken once a week'. Indeed he 'loved fishing, and hunting; pointers, greyhounds and hawks and to take his ease'

– *ama l bordir e l cassar.*

e bracs e lebriers et austers e sojorn.[6]

* '*Omnia erant venalia.*' *Gesta Regis Richardi*, ed. W. Stubbs, Rolls, Vol. II, p. 90.

But he carefully observed the forms of religion; hounded some Byzantine Orthodox clergy from the court, had an Albigensian who turned up in London burnt at once, and founded Beaulieu Abbey. He married Isabel of Gloucester; then divorced her for Isabel of Angoulême. He also kept a girl called Suzanne (*'amica Domini Regis'*) and another one called Clementina, and sired various bastards – among them Geoffrey, John and Oliver. His version of Angevin sadism was more cold-blooded than his brother's; he would starve victims to death in Windsor and Corfe, and probably murdered his nephew Arthur, aged sixteen, with his own hands when drunk, though the boy may have died from being castrated. John would have judicial combats postponed so as to watch them, and in his reign a Jew of Bristol had a molar extracted daily, until, after seven had gone, he paid up the huge sum of 10,000 marks. Such, in vivid contrast to his elegant and spectacular brother, was the able and temperamental egoist, brought to bay in 1215 at Runnymede and forced to seal *Magna Carta*, the most important act in either reign.

2

But before this famous episode is assessed, the reign of Richard I must be considered. The work of Henry II's officials had been so lasting that, even in the absence of the king, the household government carried on by its own momentum, took over more responsibility and actually obtained wider support.

Coeur de Lion's exploits on the Third Crusade (1190–2) are familiar: how, having captured the 'Griffon' emperor, he seized Cyprus as a base; how he married there Berengaria of Navarre, 'a maiden more prudent than pretty', brought out by his mother, Eleanor of Aquitaine, revisiting the scenes of her own adventurous crusading youth. Then, at the siege of Acre, he set up his tower 'Kill Greek', imported from Sicily; and Saladin sent him snow and apples when he was ill, though Richard massacred 2500 Saracen prisoners, and Saladin himself, among other curious habits, was not above poisoning wells.* Then, from the eminence of Nebi Samwil in those barren hills, Richard refused to look upon Jerusalem because he could not come at it. But all these events are outside the main stream of English history here surveyed. Moreover, unlike their equivalent in the Iberian peninsula, the Palestinian crusades were ephemeral. The high Muslim civilization was now coming to its climax, before the Mongol attacks in the next century, and when 'the

---

* Salah-al-din (1171–93) was a Kurdish prince who had taken over Egypt from the Fatimid descendants of Ali, the Prophet's son-in-law, and his court was the centre of a brilliant culture, of which Moses Maimonides was an exponent. The Arab world from Bokhara to Marrakesh and Cordova was then much more sophisticated than that of western Europe.

motley hordes of Christendom made their way into Syria . . .' they were only writing 'the medieval chapter in the long story of interaction between east and west, of which the Trojan and Persian wars of Antiquity were the prelude and the imperialistic expansion of modern Western Europe, [and the reaction to it], the latest chapter.'[7]

In England, meanwhile, the household officials and the magnates came to terms; the more so since the growing power of the Chancery and Exchequer made the great barons, who now had much to lose, want to participate in government rather than, as in Stephen's time, to wreck it. The new centralization was being reconciled with the habit of local responsibility, and a course set between a tyrannical monarchy and the paralysis of government by the assertion of the traditional baronial rights.

In Richard's time the absentee king governed first through Long-champ, deposed without major disruption, by common consent; then through the abler Hubert Walter, Archbishop of Canterbury 1193–1205, Papal Legate and Justiciar 1195, and still Chancellor, 1199–1205, under John. A Bologna-trained lawyer, this realistic archbishop, who would smoke offenders out of sanctuary and hang them, inaugurated permanent records of Chancery business, reorganized the Justices in Eyre and set up coroners elected by the local knights to look after the pleas of the Crown: forerunners of the Justices of the Peace. In a time of prosperity, rising prices and heavy taxation, the more intelligent magnates would now collaborate with the great men of the household to form an establishment with its roots in England. In a feudal society, with its right of 'defiance', Richard, being mercifully absent, presented no problems; John, however, would be all too omnipresent.

In April 1194 Richard returned from captivity, fetched from Antwerp by his own fast galley from Southampton; but he was now further enmeshed in continental politics on an international scale, and he was off again almost at once, having quickly collected more money by again using his prerogative power to make his officials repurchase their offices, an expense they then had to recoup. In 1196 he was already building his enormous Chateau Gaillard, of which the ruins, strategically placed above Les Andelys on a bend of the Seine, still survive; and in 1198 he routed the French at Gisors. Through vast expenditure, he then arranged the election of the Welf Otto IV, his nephew, to the Empire, after the death of the Emperor Henry VI; a major move against Philip Augustus of France. Had he not perished besieging a minor castle at Chaluz near Angoulême in pursuit of alleged treasure trove which the finder refused to give up, he would have continued to play continental power politics. But he was shot by a common soldier, 'to the indignation', as Professor Southern has put it, 'of all right-minded men'.

Richard tried to pull out the cross-bow bolt in his shoulder himself, and medieval surgery did the rest; he died, having ordered all the garrison except his killer to be hanged. And although, with a final contemptuous gesture of chivalry, he dismissed the man with a bag of gold, according to Hoveden saying 'live, even if you don't want to, and on my bounty',* Mercadier, Richard's mercenary captain, spoilt the impression by flaying the culprit alive – *'excoriatum suspendit'*.

3

Richard had designated his nephew, Arthur of Brittany, son of his brother Geoffrey, as his heir. But by May 1199 Hubert Walter and his colleagues, to avoid a disputed succession, had backed John. Obsessed, like his brother, with continental lordships, John at first was little in England, though he soon travelled from one end of it to the other. Government carried on; and when in 1203 he lost Normandy and invasion threatened, a fleet was assembled, taxes levied, and all able-bodied men mustered under constables of counties, hundreds and boroughs. The king then counter-attacked from La Rochelle, deep into Gascony; moved north and took the great stronghold of Angers, securing the Loire valley and the south.

He also defied Innocent III, refusing to accept the new archbishop, Cardinal Stephen Langton, Hubert Walter's successor; quarrelled with his own half-brother, Geoffrey of York and, with both archbishops out of England, impounded their revenues. So in 1207 Innocent III put the realm under interdict and in 1209 excommunicated the king, whereupon he plundered church plate and robbed the rich Cistercians.

John spent the next two years subduing Scotland, Ireland and Wales. He revived the Flemish-Rhineland coalition against the French; then in 1212 he wisely capitulated to the Pope, received Langton and did homage for England and Ireland with a token yearly tribute of a thousand marks. It was a clever manœuvre, lifting interdict and excommunication without imposing any humiliation, so that the powerful Innocent III, further mollified when in 1215 John took the cross, became the king's overlord and trump card and would annul the Great Charter itself. His position thus strengthened, John took his final gamble in a continental campaign in which nascent national loyalties cut across feudal obligations.

---

* '*Vive, licet nolis, et nostro munere, dixit.*' *Chronica magistri Rogeri de Houedene*, ed. W. Stubbs, Rolls, 1868–71, vol. IV, p. 83. Hoveden also quotes scathing couplets on Richard's

> *Virus, avaritia, scelus, enormisque libido,*
> *Foeda fames, atrox elatio, et caeca cupido.*

but admits that neither sea, mountains or tempest could stop him (p. 84).

A strategic attack along the Loire was synchronized with a German-Flemish assault from Flanders; it was an able design, but in 1214 all came to ruin when the German-Flemish coalition was routed at Bouvines between Lille and Tournai. Otto IV escaped, to be ousted by his Hohenstaufen rival, young Frederick II, *Stupor mundi*, and Philip Augustus consolidated the Capet throne with the first recognizable surge of French patriotism behind him. John abandoned all his lands in France, save for La Rochelle and Aquitaine, and now faced the accumulated wrath of the baronage against the exactions of the new Justiciar, Peter des Roches, Bishop of Winchester; indeed, against the whole continental commitment which these taxes were financing.

Such was the background to the Great Charter, with the insurgent barons, mainly from the north (*Boriales*) and from Essex, exploiting the predicament of the king, *Al rei Joan que pert sa gen* – 'King John who lost his subjects'. By the spring of 1215 they had assembled at Stamford whence they moved by Northampton and Bedford to London. They were all in league with the French, and were mostly young men – two already outlawed for treason. The Victorian picture of the barons, guardians of popular liberty and already English to the core, standing in reprobation like Landseer Newfoundlands over a dissolute, shifty and foreign king is long superseded. 'Experience and political sagacity were unquestionably on the side of the crown. It gives therefore a false picture to speak of the Charter forced on a king deserted by the nation and alone except for a mere handful of mercenary captains.'[8]

The king however had been overdriving the power of the household and abusing his feudal rights, and the responsible churchmen and administrators now tried to obtain a compromise and turn the crisis to better account. In the short run they failed; in the long run, following conventional medieval theory, they succeeded in asserting the authority of the politically articulate community of the whole realm, *communitas regni*, against a potential tyrant; a move which formed the precedent for wider claims against the Crown.

So, in 15 June 1215, checked in his course, but with the authority of Innocent III behind him, the king with a small escort and accompanied by the papal legate and the archbishop, rode over from Windsor in the summer morning to the 'meadow called Runnymede' by the Thames: and here the *Articles of the Barons* were sealed, to be finally drafted four days later.*

---

* The king could probably have signed the document, for he could read Pliny in Latin and romances in French, but would have thought it beneath him to do so; 'if John did not sign Magna Carta it is more probably because it was not done than because he could not do it'. Galbraith, *The Literacy of the Medieval English Kings, op. cit.*

Magna Carta, originally so-called only to distinguish it from the *Charter of the Forest* afterwards amplified from it, is an intricately feudal document, concerned with immediate grievances, and 'it contains little that cannot be paralleled in the contemporary laws and even contemporary charters of France and Spain or Hungary'.[9] After a preamble about the salvation of the king's soul, the good of Holy Church and the amendment (*emendacionem*) of the realm, it confirms the liberties of the Church and the free election of bishops – that perennial theme. It then concentrates on feudal wrongs; taking for granted the legal reforms of Henry II, and indeed insisting that the royal justice should be available in a fixed place and without delays; but, within this framework, mainly concerned with class interests.[10] Reliefs on inheritance are to be at the old rates, and heirs in wardship are not to pay them on coming of age; nor are their lands so held to be 'plundered to destruction and waste': while mills and fishponds, livestock and implements, are to be handed over in good condition. Further, wards of the crown shall not be married beneath them or without consent of next of kin: hitherto 'only two expedients were open to those who objected to mate for life with those men to whom John had sold them'[11] – to enter nunneries or buy themselves off. Indeed one did so, after offering the king two hundred marks, three palfreys and two hawks. The dowers of widows are now also to be promptly paid, while 'if one who has borrowed from the Jews any sum, great or small, die before the loan be repaid, the debt shall not bear interest *while the heir is under age*'.[12] For the king's Jews were like sponges, mopping up money at anything between $43\frac{1}{2}\%$ and $86\frac{2}{3}\%$ (and as such periodically squeezed), and many estates were ruined or crippled before the heir came to age. This situation was now assuaged; at the expense of the creditors.

Such were the remedies for the main grievances of the barons. And it is in this strictly feudal context the famous clause appears that 'no scutage or aid shall be imposed except by common consent of our Kingdom', later interpreted in England and America to mean 'no taxation without representation'. In fact, it merely limited the king's feudal rights to the normal obligations; to payments for ransom for his body, for knighting his eldest son and for the marriage of his eldest daughter. As a concession to the Londoners who had backed the barons, the 'aids' taken from them are also limited. But all these provisions are quite specific and limited. Taxation in the modern sense did not exist; they implied no general principle. Nor, of course, does the promise to summon a common council of magnates to assess an 'aid' foreshadow, as alleged, a 'representative parliament': it was an assembly of tenants-in-chief, anxious now to have their say, but no more. The clause, moreover, that no free man, merchant or villein who has 'fallen into the king's mercy', shall be so disproportionately fined that his means of livelihood is gone, does not, as supposed, include the mass of the people; the villeins are cared for merely as the useful chattels of their lords.

Such are the limitations of the celebrated document. But it was of clause thirty-nine that the most useful misrepresentation would be made. No free man, it said, should be imprisoned, outlawed or banished, 'save by the lawful judgement of his peers and by the law of the land'.[13] The provision was later misread as a guarantee of trial by jury, a procedure that did not then exist. In fact it merely provided that tenants-in-chief shall be judged in the full *curia regis* by other magnates. The under-tenants would be judged in the relevant manorial courts, and in the revised version of 1217 this famous *judicium parium* is further limited. In this context, too, probably even the *lex terrae*, the law of the land, only means the archaic trial by compurgation or battle. Paradoxically this reactionary clause would be misinterpreted in the seventeenth century to guarantee freedom from arbitrary arrest, speedy trial and the right to bail.

So limited, in its most crucial aspects, was *Magna Carta*. Other provisions were, indeed, of more general concern: for example, the removal of fish weirs that impeded navigation; the restraint of the king from paralysing hunting and hawking over whole districts when he had a mind to go out himself; the privileges accorded, at the expense of the native merchants, to foreign traders bringing luxuries for the magnates; the expulsion of foreign mercenaries and familiars and 'their whole brood', and the concessions over the forest laws. John's more revolting habit of blackmail through hostages was also checked, to the advantage of the barons' Welsh and Scots allies.

Such, in its essentials is this realistic document. It conceded very little to the towns, merely confirming privileges bought already, and nothing to the peasantry; the clauses which would be so powerful in political warfare are precisely the ones most misinterpreted.

But *Magna Carta* remains a statesmanlike document in the context of its time: it accepts the *fait accompli* of household government as created by Henry II, and in its own feudal idiom, it curbs the feudal monarchy, heading it off from the arbitrary power on which it was set, reasserting the classic difference between *princeps* and *tyrannus* and the ancient dictum of the revered Isidore: '*Rex eris si recte facias; si non facias, non eris* – you will be King if you do right; if you don't you won't.' In principle, *mutatis mutandis*, those patriots who in England and America would later appeal to it were not so far out.

The immediate sequel was failure. The Charter could only be enforced by a packed committee of magnates who remained in arms, and although, under Langton's influence, the king tried to abide by it, he had a strategic answer in reserve; for the whole case was under judgement by Innocent III, now the feudal overlord of England. In August the pope quashed the Charter and, in spite of Langton's protest, excommunicated the insurgents. The hostile barons, who had probably never meant the Charter to succeed, now offered the crown of England to Prince Louis of France, and war broke out again.

After sealing the Charter, the king had put a good face on his defeat: congratulated everybody *familiaritur et jocose*, saying that he had 'fortunately consummated everything', when, in fact, as the sequel showed, 'he was thinking just the opposite'.[14] He took himself off for three months to the Isle of Wight, where he 'led the life of a pirate among the sailors and fisherman'.[15] Then, that autumn, he took the offensive.

He marched into Kent, secured Dover and besieged Rochester to prevent the French invasion: by November he had taken the town, and in the depth of winter moved north to attack the Scots, for 'by God's teeth', he said of King Alexander of Scotland, 'we will chase the red fox-cub from his earths'. Then, having mastered the north, he returned to subdue East Anglia, the other focus of disaffection. That autumn we have a glimpse of the ferocious little man firing the crops of the Abbot of Croyland, 'dashing hither and thither' (*huc illucque decurrens*) amid the smoke. Then, having lost part of his treasure, records, robes and regalia sent by a short cut across the Nene estuary – a loss probably much exaggerated – he arrived at Swineshead Abbey ill with dysentery aggravated by a surfeit of peaches and new cider* – *tristis valde*, very depressed. Jolted by an improvised litter that he complained was 'breaking all his bones and nearly killing him', he was carried into Newark Castle, and there, a true Angevin, he 'raged terribly'; indeed, perhaps, 'since, says the Philosopher, anger is an ascension of blood to the heart', his anger killed him. He found it hard, he complained, to forgive his enemies 'who had tried to take his realm from him'. But he came round in the end, since he could 'get salvation no other way'; still shrewdly insisting that his boy Henry should forgive them too, in case the boy's sins should affect his own prospects. Then he gave up his soul to God and St Wulfstan. He is buried in Worcester Cathedral in the main choir: when, in the eighteenth century his body was examined, he was found to have perfect teeth.

---

* '*Nocte illa de fructu persicorum, et novi pomacii, quod vulgaritur cicera appellatur, nimis repletus.* 'That night too full up with peaches and new pomace, commonly called "cider".' Paris *op. cit.*, p. 191.

4

The Normans and Angevins had not only established in England the strongest monarchy in western Europe, but extended their authority over the rest of the British Isles in a new way. The predominantly Celtic peoples now became more closely linked with the English, and the often contrasting development of Scotland, Wales and Ireland must now be related to the main theme of this survey. With the Conquest, England, mastered by abler predators, had ceased to be a prey to Irish, Scots and Scandinavians; the shadowy overlordships of Athelstan and Edgar were revived and reinforced. Since the Confessor's time, Norman adventurers had penetrated the Scottish Lowlands, and the originally Celtic Scots monarchy was being Normanized. The conquerors had also pushed deep into Wales: Chepstow, Ludlow and Monmouth castles were already founded by the eleventh century, and Pembroke became a springboard whence Earl Richard de Clare (called 'Strongbow') conquered part of Ireland.

The eastern Scottish Lowlands had long been part of the Northumbrian-Anglian civilization described by Bede, but the monarchy had come from the western Highlands and that had been its strength. For Scotland, as the Romans had discovered and many would after them, could not be mastered if the Highlands remained unsubdued. The original Scots had been Gaels from Ireland, whose kingdom, Dalriada, had centred physically on the rock of Dunnad which overlooks the great moss at Crinan. For its religion it had looked to Iona. In the generation before Alfred, their ruler, Kenneth MacAlpin, had been acknowledged by the aboriginal Picts and by the sub-kings of Moray and the northeast as 'High King of all Alban', and he had re-established his capital at Dunkeld, strategically well placed for incursions to the south. Then soon after the death of Knut, Macbeth of Moray had displaced the MacAlpin Duncan. Far from being the brutal tyrant that Shakespeare depicts, he had governed Scotland with such ability and success that 'the comparative prosperity of his seventeen years' reign illumines the bleak annals of her early history with a ray of pale sunshine'.*

But in 1054 Macbeth had been defeated at Dunsinane; and, three years later, he was killed at Lumphanan, Aberdeenshire, by Duncan's son, Malcolm III *Canmore* (Bighead) (1057–93), who had fled to England and done homage to Edward the Confessor. This formidable warrior, bilingual in Gaelic and English, had married the cosmopolitan and afterwards sainted Margaret, sister of Edgar Atheling, and niece of the

---

* R. L. Graeme-Ritchie, *The Normans in Scotland*, *op. cit.*, p. 3, q.v. for a perceptive account to which this survey is indebted. 'Lady Macbeth' had the Celtic name Gruoch.

German emperor Henry II. Like her attractive brother, she had grown up at the Hungarian court and introduced a new sense of sophistication and piety to Scotland. Malcolm III and his four sons, Duncan II, Edgar, Alexander I, and David I, were through her all Normanized and continentalized, and the marriage of Canmore's daughter, Edith Matilda, to Henry I had further linked the two crowns, for the upstart Norman monarchy set much store by the Old English royalty, and played up the memory of the Confessor.

David I (1124–53), as Earl of Huntingdon one of the greatest feudatories of England, had been the most successful of Canmore's sons, and under him the Scots-Norman magnates and knights had consolidated their position.* From this Normanized aristocracy the most famous families of Scots history would emerge: 'From the Normans settled in before 1153 sprang the Bruces, the Balliols, the Stewarts who were Kings; the Comyns, who were hardly less; the Grahams or Graemes, the Lindsays, the Melvilles, the Oliphants, the Somervilles . . . whereas in England the great Norman families went not merely out of power, but out of existence, in Scotland they flourished exceedingly . . . (and) when surnames, long used only by the gentry, were assumed by everyone, those of the great Norman families were generally adopted'.† Norman feudality had thus been firmly entrenched; as in England, primogeniture had consolidated great estates, in contrast to the Celtic equal division of lands. The younger sons had merged into the lesser gentry and even the peasantry, who were not, as often in southern England, reduced to near-serfdom.

The first popular Scots leader, William Wallace (*de Valeys*), would come of this lesser gentry, and the famous Robert Bruce (*de Brus*) would descend from a great Norman magnate whose family came originally from Brix in the Contentin. So in Scotland, in contrast to Wales and Ireland, a powerful dynasty and a Norman-Scots nobility consolidated their hold. Malcolm IV (1153–60), called the 'Maiden' from his appearance and reputation for chastity, had been an ardent knight who, at sixteen had campaigned with Henry II against Toulouse. His

* As Graeme Ritchie puts it. 'David's continual reference to lands which "I myself perambulated" with various personages, mostly Normans . . . bring clearly before us the little party making its way along the ploughed field and down by the burnside stopping to consider the lie of the land. To give ear to "the older and wiser inhabitants and decide on soul and conscience before God whether the boundary is on this side of the rowan tree or the other", starting off again, possibly in the rain, calculating distances, measuring up, with the King of Scots stepping out in front', *op. cit.*, p. 220.

† *Op. cit.*, pp. 293–4. The ancestor of the Stuart kings was a Breton knight, Alain, standard bearer to the Bishop of Dol near Mont St Michel, who held lands in Shropshire, and whose son became standard bearer to David I, an hereditary office. So the 'fitzAlans' became Stewarts, or *Dapifers*. The Balliols came from Picardy, near Abbeville. The Comyns started as door-wards to David's son William the Lion and, it is alleged, would exclaim on appropriate occasions, 'cum in, cum in' (pp. 280–2.)

successor and brother, William the Lion or the Brawny (*Garbh*), also had continental horizons, and even adumbrated what would become the 'auld alliance' with the French; a theme of Scots-English history till the time of James VI of Scotland and I of England. William had soon so increased his nuisance value that 'when a courtier . . . spoke favourably of the king of Scotland, Henry (II) flew into a passion, tore off his clothes, stripped the coverings from his bed and began to gnaw the straw from the mattress'.[16] And when in 1174, having left off his helmet because of the heat, William had been stalked and captured by Henry's knights at Alnwick,* Henry had imprisoned him at Falaise; then, turning to conciliation, married him at Woodstock to one of the greatest heiresses of England. So the Scots monarchy became closely involved with England. William the Lion freed himself from all obligation to Richard I for 10,000 marks, but he was forced to pay tribute and give his daughters as hostages to John, a provision cancelled in *Magna Carta*. Hence, in 1215, the adventures of his son Alexander, 'the little red fox-cub' whom John swore to chase to his earth when, in vain, he had joined with Louis of France.

Thus the MacAlpin dynasty, originating in the Celtic background of Argyll, consolidated Scotland; they came to rule the Lowlands roughly down to the Northumberland border, and played their part in English high politics of the twelfth century during the climax of their political and social influence. The Crown was here part of a Scots-Norman feudal establishment; now mainly un-Celtic, and looking to the south; and if the feuds of this baronage over the succession would enable Edward I the 'Hammer of the Scots', to mount his massive attempts to master Scotland, Scots nationality would by then be too well grounded for him to succeed.

5

While Scotland, as a Normanized monarchy and part of the cosmopolitan feudal world, became involved in English power politics, and the Scots barons proved strong enough to preserve their feudal liberties, the fate of Wales and Ireland had been very different. Since sub-Roman times the Welsh had prided themselves on being Christians, part of a civilization superior to the Saxons; heirs they believed, of Trojan 'Brute' and of 'Arthur'. But they had never remained united for long. As for the Irish, they were overrun by Norman conquerors; and though

---

* They had '*cried the war signal of Vesci*
And Glanville and Balliol likewise'.
The king's horse was slain and fell on him, so that he surrendered to Ranulf Glanville, and when Henry II in London got the news, he 'was so glad that he went to his knights and awoke them all'. See Fantosme, *op. cit.*, lines 1710 ff.

the Normans intermarried with the tribal aristocracy and 'went native', so that their descendants would resist the more systematic Tudor 'plantations', English power was to dominate Ireland till the twentieth century.

The main centre of Welsh resistance had always been Snowdonia; here, in conjunction with Magnus Barefoot of Norway – so-called as an early royal wearer of the kilt – Gruffydd ap Cynan, prince of Gwynedd, had defeated Rufus's Normans when 'the French (had) dared not penetrate the rocks and the woods, but hovered about the level plains'.[17] Though Gruffydd had done homage to Henry I, his successor, Owain Gwynedd, had been able to threaten Chester. Moreover, in Henry II's time, in collaboration with Owain, Rhys ap Gruffydd, grandson of Rhys ap Tewder, had launched a formidable revolt: indeed, he had been 'the head and shield and strength of the south of all Wales, and the hope and defence of all the tribes of the Britons; that man who descended from the noblest line of Kings . . . combatant upon the walls . . . as a bear or a lion'.[18] In 1156 young Henry II, 'proceeding to Rhuddlan in a rage', had failed to subject the north, and he had won no more success in the south. Rhys, indeed, had been so strengthened by the departure of the de Clare Earl of Pembroke to Ireland that Henry had to make him Lord Rhys – *yr Arglwydd Rhys*, with a court at Cardigan Castle, where in 1176 the first recorded Eisteddfod had been celebrated. The Normanizing of the Welsh Church, subjected to Canterbury since the time of Henry I, had been less popular.

Whereas, for the Scots, Richard I's crusade had meant emancipation, for the Welsh it had been an occasion of ferocious rebellion. Lord Rhys (d. 1197) had spent a splendid old age in blazing revolt; handing on the torch to that other Welsh hero, Llywelyn the Great, a grandson of Owain Gwynedd of north Wales. This clever and ruthless prince had gained much by violence and diplomacy. John, indeed in the winter of 1210, had burnt Bangor, held the bishop to ransom for 'two hundred hawks', taken a vast number of cattle and horses, established a castle at Aberystwyth and had seized hostages. But Llywelyn, profiting, like the 'fox-cub' of Scotland from 'the disturbance between King John and the English of the North', retrieved them under a clause in *Magna Carta* which restored all that John had taken from the Welsh. Llywelyn then captured Shrewsbury, and during the English wars against Louis of France, overran all south Wales, save for an enclave in Pembroke. For these conquests, which long remained secure, he did homage to the young Henry III in 1218. Thus, for over one and a half centuries, the indomitable Welsh beat back the English marcher lords and even kings, and retained their independence and their language. Under Llywelyn ap Gruffyd, they would exploit the war between Henry III and Simon de

Montfort; but, unlike the Scots-Norman realm, their political cohesion would not prove sufficient to defy Edward I on their day of reckoning at the end of the thirteenth century.

The strength and the weakness of the Welsh polity and temperament were reflected in their setting. In his *Itinerarium* (1191) and *Descriptio Kambriae* (1194)[19] Giraldus Cambrensis has left a vivid account; he followed Gildas – *Gildas itaque Giraldus sequitur* – but wrote much better. Giraldus had accompanied Archbishop Baldwin of Canterbury on a progress to recruit crusaders and assert his metropolitan authority. He presents a warlike people, agile and fierce; pastoralists, living mainly on milk, cheese, butter and meat; barefooted and hardy, accustomed from youth to the hills and mountains at all seasons. Their frugal meals were enlivened by girl harpists; but they wore their hair over their 'ears and eyes', and slept hugger mugger in one room in their clothes. But they were careful, he notices, to clean their fine teeth.* All classes, he observed, argued incessantly; for claiming to be Trojan southerners, like the Romans and the French, and unlike the English, with their northern apathy, they prided themselves on their verbal skill. And they already sang part-songs 'in crowds', all coming together in conclusion on B flat.† They lived not in towns, but in woods and hills in wattle huts, and calculated genealogies with zest,‡ living sparely, though 'wolfish' in plenty.

But these resilient and gallant people had serious defects: they were treacherous and thievish, even to each other; though they would rally, they ran away as fast as they attacked. They were also unwilling to 'submit to the burdens of marriage' (*matrimonium autem onera*) without trying out the girl first, and bought girls for the purpose; nor were they, as Gildas has stressed, without a taint of their Trojan ancestry.§

After observations on greyhounds and harriers, greyling (*umbra* – the shadow) and one-eyed Scotch mullets, eyed right on the east coast and left on the west, Giraldus concludes, impartially, for he was Welsh-Norman himself, by weighing up the best ways to conquer the Welsh and for them to resist invaders. Their political division, he recommends, must be fostered by diplomacy and bribes, while they are blockaded by land and sea; they should then be attacked by light-armed infantry in the spring, and their limited manpower worn down, for 'we can hire

* 'Which, by assiduous friction with green bark, and by rubbing with cloth, they made like ivory': *quos assidua coryli viridis confricatione, laneique panni purgatione, tanquam eburneos reddunt,* Dimock *op. cit.*, p. 185.

† Only in the north of England, says Giraldus, did he find similar part-singing, and that came from the Scandinavians.

‡   'Rhys ap Griffith ap Rhys
              Rhys ap Theodore, *et sic dienceps* – so on again.'

§ Constantine, says Giraldus, had been deflected from re-building Troy by a voice telling him he would only rebuild Sodom, and so made his capital at Byzantium instead.

plenty of mercenaries'. And it is best to use troops from the marches, trained for this kind of warfare and able to live hard. Having occupied the strategic points, the English should then build castles and roads, and remain constantly vigilant. Above all, in spite of appearances, they should never trust the Welsh.

The Welsh, on the other hand, have the advantage of their mountains, of mobility, hardihood and morale. For they have never forgotten that they once ruled all Britain, and while the Normans and English fight for plunder and pay, these people fight for liberty, *iste pro patria*. Indeed, if they would submit to a single ruler, they could defy the world; as one of them told Henry II to his face, they will never, save by God's displeasure, be destroyed, and they will answer for themselves and their land in Welsh on the day of judgement.

So while political disunion made the Welsh more vulnerable than the Scots, they remained a formidable people able for centuries to take advantage of any weakness in English government. They would only be fully pacified under Welsh Tudors, and then with their own language and culture intact.

6

The fate of the Irish was sadly different. The Norman occupation had been made by independent adventurers, taking advantage of the vendettas within the island. Since the time of Niall of the Nine Hostages, drowned, it will be recalled, off *Vectis*, the Isle of Wight, when raiding the Romano-British in 405, there had been a high king, *ard ri*, in Ireland. But his authority had been vague and fluctuating; a king 'with opposition', as the Irish put it. From the fifth to the early ninth centuries, following the mission of St Patrick, Irish Christian civilization had flourished. John *Scotus Eriugena*, the Irishman, who knew Greek, had won fame in the later Carolingian 'renaissance' a generation before Alfred. As early as the seventh century, the Brehon Laws* and Irish Epics had been written down, and the vivid Celtic literature preserved. But Ireland, like England, had been savagely harried by the Vikings or Ostmen; the Norse *Fin-Gall*, the fair foreigners, and the Danish *Dubh-Gall*, the dark ones. They had founded the first Irish towns; Dublin and Waterford, Wexford, Wicklow and Arklow; Cork in the south and Limerick in the west. In 1014, the *ard ri* Brian Boru had perished when the Vikings had been defeated at Clontarf near Dublin.

But the Viking defeat had not brought peace. The MacMurragh of

* These laws, of a pastoral tribal society, throw much light on chieftainship and cattle-raiding. See Maine's *Early Institutions*, London, 1874, on the primitive forms of legal remedies, pp. 250 ff. – still valuable.

Leinster in the south-east had fought the O'Rourke of Meath, who, in alliance with Rory O'Connor of Dublin, the last *ard ri*, had driven MacMurragh to seek help in 1154 at the court of Henry II in Aquitaine. Adrian IV, the only English pope, who claimed that all islands belonged to the Holy See through the (forged) donation of Constantine, had even sent Henry a Bull authorizing the conquest of Ireland, along with an emerald ring; and the king had permitted Earl Richard of Pembroke ('Strongbow') to act. By 1170 'Strongbow' had landed at Waterford with a well-found force, defeated O'Connor and established himself in Dublin.

Confronted with this *coup*, Henry II had himself crossed to Dublin in 1171, where he spent the winter entertaining the chieftains there, well away from the aftermath of Becket's 'martyrdom'. He was the first king of England to set foot in Ireland. 'Strongbow', who had married the heiress of MacMurragh, was installed as Lord of Leinster and Vice-regent in Wicklow castle from 1173 until his death in 1176. Not only the eastern chieftains, but the McCarthy of Desmond and the O'Brien of Thomond from the western hinterlands of Cork and Limerick, had come in. Henry became Lord of Ireland, *Dominus Hiberniae*; a title held by his successors until 1540, when Henry VIII would be proclaimed King. Rory O'Connor, the last *ard ri*, died in retirement in 1198.

Such, in essentials, had been the background to Prince John's visit to Ireland in 1185. He brought with him John Butler (*pincerna*), ancestor of the Butlers of Ormonde, and the de Burgh ancestor of the Burkes of Connaught and Ulster. But John and his young courtiers annoyed the Irish by laughing at their beards and saffron kilts, and the mission failed. The expedition of 1210 was more business-like: after 'a marvellous example of daemonic energy[20] John thoroughly Normanized the eastern and central areas, imposing sheriffs, justiciars and a coinage stamped with a harp; and he left the renowned William the Marshal, who had married the heiress of 'Strongbow', in charge. So, at least in the Anglo-Norman territories, the Irish were put under a strict feudal régime, and 'in 1215 when England was seething with rebellion, Ireland was at peace'.[21]

The price of this pacification would be heavy. Although the Norman–Irish families would intermarry with the native aristocracy and be absorbed into their way of life, the new lords were at first alien; and the church, as reorganized, was now Norman. Giraldus Cambrensis, here as in Wales, has left a vivid picture of the country, coloured this time by Norman prejudice.* For the wild Irish, he says, are *gens silvestris bestialiter vivens* – a savage people, living like animals,[22] who neglect their

---

*See *Opera, op. cit.*, vol. V. The *Topography of Ireland*, written *c.* 1185–6, was recited at Oxford in 1188. His *Expugnatio* is an account of the Norman conquest of the island.

fertile land. They go about in saffron and black woollens, with long hair and beards, and 'always have an axe ready in hand'. They are a particularly 'jealous' people, and the clergy, though surprisingly chaste, are addicted to drink. The women, who wail terribly for the dead, ride astride; in battle the men make a fearful din with trumpets, though on peaceful occasions they are good musicians, their melodies much more quick and cheerful than 'our slow and morose tunes'. Since as children they are left to run wild, with no enervating baths, they grow up fine men, very handsome by nature but often shocking in behaviour. They have no saddles, and no armour; only spears, swords and axes.

The country, on the other hand, is attractive, though it rains most of the time, and the trees grow eastward because of the prevalent Atlantic winds. There is a great wealth of cattle, game and fish, so that the Irish can import much wine from Poitou in exchange for leather; it is a land of fat pastures (*glebae perpingues*), soft (*mollis*) and watery; of hills and marshes, lakes and islands. Giraldus's sharp eyes notice even the difference between the English and the Irish hare, which is smaller; and he alleges that Irish grasshoppers, like Christian martyrs, sing best when their heads are cut off. He swallows other tall stories; of an 'ox-man' with big round eyes in Wicklow, and of phantom red pigs and witches who take the form of hares; the Irish badger, he observes, is a filthy animal that bites, and he describes the fine salmon – so-called because of their leap – *saltu*. In Ireland, he goes on, there are, of course, no moles or poisonous reptiles, though many kingfishers and barnacle geese, generated from the resin of fir trees steeped in water, as well as convenient beavers. As people do in Germany, you can eat their tails on fast days, for they count as fish.

7

Such were the Scottish, Welsh and Irish backgrounds to the Norman-Angevin monarchy in England, which had made a formidable and various impact upon them all, bringing the whole British Isles for the first time into one sphere of influence. At home it had mastered England, and so far tamed the baronage that, following their own now more insular interests, they opposed the Crown in a more lawful way, and, influenced by the churchmen and the great household officials, set precedents for the assertion of broader liberties. In the rest of the islands the Crown had to deal with a well-established Scottish realm; Celtic in origins, but now Normanized and backed by a Scots-Norman aristocracy and knighthood, which would combine with the populace to assert a separate Scots nationality, under a kingship destined, by the chance of dynastic fortune, to take over England itself. In Wales, the English monarchs had to contend with a persistent pre-Saxon tradition and language, never entirely subdued, until, by another dynastic chance, a Welsh dynasty – the ablest of all her rulers, – would briefly take over England. In Ireland, the English kings long had a source of some strength, even on occasion a refuge; but the régime was not secure, and, outside the areas dominated by the Norman–Irish aristocracy, the native Irish went their own wild Celtic-Iberian way. The Tudor English then set about a more systematic and ruthless exploitation; another chapter in the misfortunes of an island that had been a beacon of civilization in the Dark Ages and the home of a people of singular, if inconsequent, charm.

9

THIRTEENTH-CENTURY CLIMAX

There was once a king, runs a medieval story, whose falcon won wild applause when it killed an eagle; but, despite his courtiers, he had it hung for *Lèse majesté*. The main theme of thirteenth-century history in England, as in much of Christendom, is the emergence of a strong national realm. In face of the conflict of Pope and Emperor, the old cosmopolitan institutions were breaking down, and Louis IX of France, not the Pope or the Emperor, had to fill the role of moral arbiter of the west. In England the perennial rumblings of baronial discontent gave rise in 1258–65 to civil war, but the old feudal order was now obsolescent. The conciliar government had developed a regular household bureaucracy now working through the royal wardrobe as well as through the old Exchequer and Chancery, and manned by clerks who were not feudal magnates in their own right, but regular officials, their acts authenticated by a 'Privy Seal'. Going behind the baronial councillors, John's household clerks had already financed campaigns; now, after a phase of collaboration with the magnates during the minority of Henry III while the realm was being rid of the French and John's mercenaries brought to order, the young king tried to revert to and develop the household government of his father. This move developed renewed conflict with the magnates, who claimed to be *Le Commun de Engleterre*, and were exasperated by the king's expensive cosmopolitan tastes and entourage. Hence also the mounting conflict in which Simon de Montfort, Earl of Leicester, with some popular support against the hated foreigners and rich churchmen, tried to control and purge the administration, not to destroy it. And when he failed to hold the baronage together and was killed at Evesham and the Crown triumphed, the 'original nobility of the Conquest which had been the mainstay of the rebellions of two centuries was destroyed as a distinctive force and left the field to the newer and for a time weaker nobility of the North and Wales'.[1]

The conflict of Crown and baronage, conducted within the political conventions of the day, had also promoted another important change, which at the time seemed insignificant. The *Colloquia* or *Parlemenz* of the Great Council were now part of the routine of government, supposed by 1255 to meet three times a year – 'the end of a prolonged and gradual evolution of public life'.[2] With the growing prosperity of the thirteenth century, not only the land-owning knights, ancestors of the 'gentry', but the merchants of the developing towns, were playing a greater part in local government: with Crown and barons looking for all the support they could find, the knights of the shire and the burgesses came to be included in national affairs. Thus the periodical meetings of the Great Council came to be more representative of the community of the whole realm, as well as of the magnates, to whom the 'community' had been simply that of the great feudal tenants-in-chief controlling enormous 'honours', their estates scattered over many counties. *Magna Carta*, limiting the old feudal powers of the Crown could now be adapted to a wider non-feudal context. So strong government grew up: but as parliamentary monarchy emerged out of feudal kingship, its prerogative was still limited by medieval law and institutions.

The thirteenth century was an age of the definition of law; in England of Bracton's *De legibus et Consuetudinibus Angliae* (*c.* 1258), in Germany of the *Sachenspiegel*, in Rome of Gregory ix's *Decretals* defining canon law. In spite of the masterful ambition of Edward i, the English realm would not go the way of the Sicilian *Regno*, which derived from the other great Norman insular conquest in Sicily. Here Roger ii had established an elaborate and despotic government in the Byzantine-Arab style, with *catapans, strategoi, cadis* and *emirs*, to be restored and exploited by Emperor Frederick ii, and had already stepped up the taxation and excise behind the splendours of the Cathedral at Monreale. In England the Norman consolidation and the Angevin achievement were confirmed by a strengthening of central government; but the king remained *princeps*, responsible to the law, not *tyrannus*; subject to the will of the community of the realm regularly assembled and even becoming more representative. This political development, though accompanied by civil wars, reflects the growing prosperity and sophistication of the climax of medieval civilization 'in that good thirteenth century when all was new'.

For if the creative twelfth century represented the adolescence of the medieval realm, the thirteenth and early fourteenth saw its cultural and economic maturity. It was now that a recognizable English establishment was consolidated, with its familiar realism in coming to terms with new kinds of power and assimilating new men. In spite of the shifts of power among the highest aristocracy and the princes of the blood, after the reign of Edward i the framework of English society would remain relatively unchanged; an adaptable hierarchy would hold its own. There is also a new splendour and luxury for the magnates, and a new comfort and even affluence for the gentry and leading townsfolk. It was an age of more varied pastimes and entertainment, of a more elaborate cult of the chase with its complicated ritual and terminology; under Edward i of more strictly regulated and spectacular tournaments. It is commemorated by a new kind of Gothic as opposed to Romanesque architecture; as at Salisbury and Lincoln and Westminster Abbey as rebuilt by Henry III. The castles in Wales built during Edward's reign were then the last word in insular military architecture, vastly expensive and highly efficient.

It was also a time of vivid and complicated intellectual life, when the scholastic philosophers of the school of St Thomas Aquinas tried to assimilate Aristotle and create a complete synthesis of learning, comparable to the creation of a Gothic cathedral. It saw the establishment of the universities at Oxford and Cambridge and, not least, of bizarre but significant speculation about the world, for the age of Aquinas was also that of Grosseteste and Roger Bacon.

2

Henry III, the nine-year-old son of John and Isabel of Angoulême, was crowned at Gloucester in October, 1216 and reigned until 1272. He turned out to be a temperamental cosmopolitan with much restless and misguided energy and 'the tongue of an asp'.[3] He was a lavish patron of the arts, with a passion for building, jewellery and decoration; more at home with continentals than with insular English barons. Concerned with far-flung dynastic ambitions in the age of the Capet and Hohenstaufen, he pursued a foreign policy of 'grandiose incoherence'. Mathew Paris calls him 'our Proteus'.* In the tide of thirteenth-century prosperity he expected to share in it; but, unlike his son, Edward I, he was no warrior and, despite the efforts of the household administration, he failed to control the magnates and was perennially insolvent. He grew up 'compact of body', of middling stature, the first of his line with the long well-cut Plantagenet profile and with 'one eyelid drooping to hide some of the dark part of the eye'. His effigy shows a strained sensitive face, in contrast to his thick-set Angevin and Norman ancestors; wounded at Evesham, he would cry out 'I am Henry of Winchester,

* Mathew Paris (c. 1200–59) already cited for the events of John's reign, is the most voluminous and readable historian since William of Malmesbury. He was a Benedictine monk of St Albans, with its stream of visitors from the great world, and he was already famous in his lifetime. Henry III knew him quite well, and once remarked 'Have you noticed these things and are they firmly impressed on your mind?'. Mathew diligently recorded the deeds of magnates both lay and ecclesiastical, as well as 'various and wonderful events', for he was naïvely eager for news. He was also a good artist with a fine bold line, who illustrated some of his own works in miniature, though his map of England is appalling, putting East Anglia and East Kent facing south across the Channel. He is partisan and colourful, a better narrator than judge. See Richard Vaughan, *Mathew Paris*, C.U.P., 1958, and A. L. Smith, *Ford Lectures*, 1913. In addition to the *Historia Anglorum* or *Historia Minor*, ed. F. Madden, 3 vols, Rolls, 1866–9, Mathew wrote the *Chronica Majora*, ed. H. R. Luard. Six volumes, Rolls, 1872–83. See also J. A. Giles' translation, Mathew Paris, *English History*, 1235–73, Bohn, 3 vols., London, 1852–4.

your King; do not harm me!' – a remark inconceivable from any of these forebears. Indeed, he was happier helping to consecrate the superb new cathedral at Salisbury; enhancing the cult of St Thomas at Canterbury; or, at Westminster, transferring the body of Edward the Confessor, with whom he felt an affinity, to a new shrine of gold; happiest, probably, meeting Louis ix at Chartres, and inspecting the Sainte Chapelle while the Parisian students received him with 'branches and flowers'. Like the other English monarchs with artistic flair, Richard ii and Charles i, he was not a political success.

His reign divides naturally into four phases, the political setting of the rich economic, social and intellectual life of the century, the climax of the Middle Ages. In the first (1216–32) the aged William the Marshal, long ago spared as a hostage by Stephen, ruled with a vast prestige as *Rector Regis et Regni*. After his death in 1219, Hubert de Burgh, who had risen as a household knight under John, became *Vice-Regent* and chief Justiciar. Between them they evicted the French, put down disorder and preserved the king's inheritance. Then, from 1232–58, Henry iii took over a personal household government, ruling mainly through foreign administrators, of whom the ablest were Peter des Roches, Bishop of Winchester, and his nephew, Peter de Rivaux. In spite of the growing competence of the officials, this personal regime ended in bankruptcy and conflict, aggravated by the hatred between Simon de Montfort, the king's brother-in-law, and the monarch. By 1258 there was open defiance; by 1261 civil war. After the king had been defeated at Lewes in 1264, Simon de Montfort briefly dominated the realm, until his defeat and death at Evesham in 1265. Finally, the Lord Edward, the king's eldest son, restored the monarchy so ably that he could even go on crusade, to return after the death of his father in 1272, to consolidate a more powerful régime, and assert his authority in Wales and Scotland as no English king had ever done.

John had committed his son to the magnate who then possessed the greatest prestige. William the Marshal, now Earl of Pembroke, had made his way by military prowess and a great marriage to the heiress of Richard de Clare, Earl of Pembroke, that 'Strongbow' who had conquered vast estates in Ireland. The now aged Marshal was thought so handsome that he 'ought to be a Roman Emperor':

> *Resemblent il asez haut home*
> *Por estre Emperere de Rome . . .* *

---

* *L'Histoire de Guillaume le Maréchal, op. cit.*, vol. I, lines 731–2 and 3567–8. When he had been a young man on tournament in France, and the judges had come to tell him that he was 'the best knight there', they had found him with his head on an anvil – (*sor l'anclume sa teste*) while the blacksmith tried to extricate his head – a circumstance that added to his prestige (vol. I, 3102). For a good modern study, see Sidney Painter, *William Marshall*, Baltimore, 1937.

Not Arthur nor Alexander himself, it was said, had surpassed him. He was considered valiant, resourceful and loyal. In 1217 with the support of the papal legate, and the backing of the English church and even of John's mercenary captains, he soon defeated Prince Louis, the French claimant to the throne, at Lincoln. And in the same year the fleet improvised by John and now commanded by Hubert de Burgh, destroyed the French reinforcements under the Flemish Eustace the [renegade] Monk in the Thames estuary in the first major medieval English naval victory. Further, to conciliate the magnates and Londoners, *Magna Carta* and the Charter of the Forest were confirmed.

When Hubert de Burgh took over in 1219, the new régime was thus relatively secure. The Marshal had represented the ideal traditional twelfth-century knighthood; de Burgh stood for the new lay bureaucracy of the household. He came of the minor gentry,* and had been Chamberlain to John, custodian of Falaise (when he had tried to protect Arthur), and had held Chinon and Dover against the French. By 1224 he had mined and battered Bedford Castle into surrender† and so destroyed the power of Faulkes de Bréauté, John's most dangerous mercenary captain. Though Henry III resented this self-made magnate's predominance, it had been under his leadership and through the collaboration of the great barons, the church and the household that the authority of the Crown had been preserved.

This harmony would not last long. When, at the age of twenty-five, the king took control, he was not only determined to develop the household to free himself from the magnates' control, but obsessed with the idea of recovering the Angevin possessions in France. Aquitaine was still in hand, a base of attack, and in 1236 he married Eleanor of Provence, whose relatives, like his Lusignan half-brothers by his mother's second marriage, swarmed around the court and battened on English appointments. Further, the indomitable Gregory IX (1227–41), who became pope at eighty-six and died a centenarian, was now in full

* Hubert de Burgh (*c.* 1175–1232), probably came from Aylsham in Norfolk; for he held Runton, Beeston and Rougham 'by inheritance'. He accumulated fantastic possessions: estates at Rayleigh in Essex, at Tichfield in Hampshire and at Cranborne, Corfe Mullen; Moreton and Charmouth in Dorset; at Fittleton in Wiltshire and at Banstead and Sheen in Surrey; in Bedfordshire and Northants, as well as in Somerset and on the Welsh border. These estates helped to sustain vast official commitments: the castles at Rochester, Canterbury and Dover, controlling most of Kent; strategic castles in Cardigan, Carmarthen and Gower, and strongholds in Ireland, as well as Knaresborough in Yorkshire and Odiham near Winchester. At the height of his power, he even held Windsor and the Tower of London, along with a palace at Westminster, afterwards to be Wolsey's headquarters, and as 'York House' handed over to Henry VIII to become the nucleus of Whitehall. This vast accumulation led to his unpopularity and fall, though he was never ruined; he is an early example of a layman rising through the household to great power.

† Ropes for the latest *Trébuchet* siege-engines were brought from Bridport, already a centre for their manufacture.

conflict with Frederick II (1197–1250), and in this European convulsion, demanding from England all and more than he could get.[4] Henry III thus succeeded in rousing what looks like a national opposition among the baronage, the knights and even the towns, particularly London. The theme that the king ought to 'live of his own', which would continue for centuries, was already being reiterated, and most of the feudal magnates, rooted in England for nearly two centuries since the Conquest, were now less interested in adventure abroad. They resented the Poitivins and Provencals who surrounded the king, and the demands of a wildly impracticable dynastic policy. Moreover, the thirteenth century had seen growing popular resentment against the dignitaries of the Church, whose enormous wealth was now denounced by the Franciscan and Dominican friars; while the more confident outlook which had developed since the twelfth century had made the laity less in awe of the Church than they had been in the days of Anselm and even Becket.

Indeed, since John had made England a papal fief, the exactions of the Roman Curia had provoked widespread resistance. This now increased. Representatively, in 1245 the great baron Fulk Fitzwarren, asked by the papal commissioner by what right he had ordered him out of England, replied, 'you are ordered to do so through me by the community of armed knights who lately met at Luton and Dunstable. If you listen to prudent counsel you will get out in three days or be cut to pieces.' And the populace, too, was now becoming hostile to the old and rich monkish orders. Apart from routine student mockery, the clergy were now widely satirized as *Le Ordre del Bel-eyse*; the Black Monks as *Chescun jour yvre* – drunk every day; the secular canons as expert in *le giw d'amour* – the game of love, and the abbots and priors, with their 'pages and boyes with boste', as frauds who '*riden wid hauk and hounds and contrefetan knites*' They should leave 'swich pride', writes a satirist, 'and be religious', for '*orgoyl en pays est urtille en herber*[5] – pride in the land is like nettles in the grass'. Already an insular anti-clericalism, to be developed by Wycliffe and the Lollards, by the Tudor Reformation and the Puritan Independents, was beginning to be heard.

Henry III, like most medieval monarchs, ignored his financial difficulties. Although one year he 'owed so much to continental merchants, wine merchants and others . . . for the necessities of life . . . that he could scarcely show himself among the people', the next year, undeterred, he was rebuilding Westminster Abbey, his best memorial; 'ordering the old walls with the tower on the eastern side to be pulled down and new and handsome ones to be erected by clever architects at his own expense'.[6] And he was expected to be lavish: when in 1250 he tried to economize, Mathew Paris writes vindictively: 'The king, shamefully deviating from the track of his ancestors, ordered the expenses of the court and the amusements of hospitality to be lessened; an execrable act, and bringing on him the charge of avarice.' He was caught both ways. No wonder, when forced to sell his plate and jewels by the weight to finance a Welsh war, 'for the Welsh had been swarming from their lurking hiding places like bees', he hated the Londoners. 'I know, I know,' he said, 'that if the treasure of Octavian were for sale the City of London would purchase and suck it up; for these ill-bred Londoners, who call themselves barons, possess abundance even to a surfeit.' And in 1255 he complained in a 'querulous tone', 'it is no wonder that I covet money for it is dreadful to think of the debts in which I am involved. By God's head, they amount to a sum of 200,000 marks. . . . I am deceived on all sides. I am a mutilated and diminished King'.[7]

Yet, in 1257 he deliberately worsened his predicament. His brother, Richard of Cornwall, was crowned King of the Romans at Aachen at vast expense, as an 'instalment or guarantee' of the Empire; a kingship he held till 1272 in the uncertain phase between the Hohenstaufen and the Habsburgs. Finally, when in 1258, Henry III also paraded his son Edmund before a parliament, 'dressed in the Apulian fashion' to press his claim to the rich but turbulent kingdom of Sicily (a project which even Richard of Cornwall had turned down, saying 'you might as well say I will sell or give you the moon. Climb up and take it'), the gesture led to the end of personal government.

3

The third, and constitutionally most important phase of the reign was therefore brought about not by the incompetence of the household officials, but by the feckless yet typically medieval aspirations of the king. And the most ambitious and formidable of the magnates, who now tried to rehabilitate the bankrupt régime, was the king's own brother-in-law, the formidable, pious and predatory Simon de Montfort, Earl of Leicester.* This imperious magnate detested the king's Poitivin relations,

* Simon de Montfort, Earl of Leicester by inheritance through his grandmother Amicia, daughter of Robert, fourth Earl of Leicester since the Conquest, was a Frenchman born at Montfort d'Amauri near Paris; the fourth son of Simon IV de Montfort, who had led the crusade against the Albigensian heretics in southern France and become Viscount of Beziers and Carcassonne. Simon secured the earldom of Leicester, forfeited under John, from Henry III, and in 1238 married the king's sister Eleanor. He now held vast estates, including Hungerford and Collingbourne in Wiltshire and the great castles at Odiham and Kenilworth – his main stronghold. In 1248 he was made Viceroy of Gascony where his high-handed methods evoked protest. Even before the civil war he quarrelled intermittently with Henry III, who said that he 'frightened him more than thunder and lightning'. But he was well regarded by the Franciscans, who thought him 'a high souled leader marked out for the salvation of men', and he made Richard Grosseteste, Chancellor of Oxford and Bishop of Lincoln, an executor of his will – *Mon Chier pere Richart evesque de Nicole*. The definitive biography is still Charles Bémont, *Simon de Montfort, Earl of Leicester, 1208–1265*, trans. E. F. Jacob, O.U.P., 1930. See also M. W. Labarge, *Simon de Montfort*, London, 1962.

and would have killed Henry's half-brother, William de Valence, on the spot had not the monarch himself intervened; he also remarked that the king should be 'kept under guard like Charles the Simple', and that there were *maisons barées de fer a Windesore* where he could be shut up.

This clash of unbridled personalities at the court and among the magnates exacerbated the power struggle from 1258–65. The rebels, led by Simon de Montfort, were determined to remedy accumulated grievances; not to destroy the form of government, but to get it out of the hands of the foreign courtiers and the officials of the household. The king, on the other hand, declared that he could 'not tolerate that those of the Council should say "*nous volons qe issy soit* – we will that this should be" and "*autre reson ne mettent* – give no other reason"'.[8]

But it was the mounting grievance against the foreign courtiers which produced 'a revolutionary impulse such as had not been seen for forty years';[9] and 'country gentlemen dismissed their cooks for fear of Poitivin poison'. These events now provoked the crisis. Leicester, Gloucester, Hereford and Norfolk, in full armour, personally cornered the king at Oxford in May 1258 and in June the *Provisions of Oxford* were accepted by the king and a *parlemenz*. The *Provisions* placed government in the hands of a baronial oligarchy, working through a council of magnates which in effect put the royal authority in commission. They had the usual grievances; that castles were given to foreigners, heiresses married to them, wardship abused. A Council of Fifteen was to be chosen by four electors representing both sides. Three *parlemenz* were to be held a year and these were to send twelve representatives to consult with the Council. The great offices of state of Justiciar and Chancellor were now to be held not by household officials but by magnates responsible to the Council. Such, in essentials, was this elaborate scheme, guaranteed by the handing over of fifteen royal castles and by the barons' right to nominate the sheriffs in the counties. Its work with the most lasting consequences was to appoint four knights in each county to enquire into the grievances of the populace and bring them before the Council of Fifteen.

Naturally the arrangement failed. Since the king now had no real authority, government itself depended on the shifting alliances among the barons, who could think of no better sanction than those who opposed the Council should be declared mortal enemies. Moreover, the magnates soon lost the support of the undertenants, 'the community of the knights bachelor'; and their interests did not coincide with those of the towns. When, in 1261, the pope absolved the king from keeping the *Provisions*, his support would prove decisive. In despair of an effective settlement, Simon de Montfort himself left England – which he termed a 'coward country'.

In 1263 he returned, determined to impose the full *Provisions* by force and, in conjunction with the Welsh under their Prince Llewelyn ap Gruffyd, raised open war. He was not widely supported by the magnates, but he was followed by many knights bachelor and lower clergy; above all by the Londoners who shared his hatred of the Jews, whom they now proceeded to attack. But the king outmanœuvred him: he had appealed to Louis IX, now his feudal overlord, as in 1259 he had done homage for Aquitaine. In January 1264 at the *Mise of Amiens*, Louis gave judgement for the king; he quashed the entire *Provisions of Oxford* while maintaining the baronial rights under *Magna Carta*; he insisted that the king could choose his own advisers and officials. The initiative not only of Simon de Montfort, but of the more conservative magnates, had failed.

This decision Simon de Montfort refused to accept. The war was renewed, and at the battle of Lewes on 14 May 1264, he captured the king, with the ancient dragon standard of England, his brother Richard of Cornwall, and Prince Edward, the heir. Determined to legitimize a régime of the sword, he now convened a *Parlemenz* to which knights of the shire were summoned; they accepted a *Forma Regiminis* and a Council of Regency was set up. This Council was chosen by de Montfort, Gilbert de Clare, Earl of Gloucester and their adherent Stephen de Berksted, Bishop of Chichester. Under this protectorate another *Parlemenz* was summoned, which has won an undeserved fame; for to this partisan assembly, which contained only five of the magnates and twenty tenants-in-chief, Simon de Montfort summoned not only the knights of the shire, but, for the first time, burgesses from selected towns. He was getting all the support he could; and no one then thought them important. If the move, restrospectively considered, marks a decisive innovation, 'to contemporary eyes it was no far-reaching event'.[10] It was an opportunist measure; the writs for the burgesses sent, not through the sheriffs, but through the mayors on whom the illegal régime could count.

Meanwhile law and order was breaking down. The government commanded so little authority that Simon de Montfort had now to make a more formal alliance with the Welsh, to the fury of the marcher lords of the west. The Earl of Gloucester, one of these magnates, now turned against him. The pope was implacable; the Lord Edward escaped his guards; and in alliance with Gloucester he advanced on Kenilworth. Simon de Montfort, returning from Wales, was trapped at Evesham in August 1265. Fighting to the last, he was cut down, and his head, obscenely adorned, sent to a baronial wife, 'by way of compliment'.

> *Or est ocys,*

wrote a partisan,

la fleur de pris que tant savoit de guere . . .
*Molt fust pyr, que demembrir firent le prudhomme.**

Thus ended a brief and violent bid for power by a masterful and able magnate who alienated most of his peers, but whose evidently magnetic personality won wide support as a popular champion against the foreign entourage and political incompetence of the king. The populace even thought him a martyr, like St Thomas of Canterbury. And these sentiments have had their modern echoes. Although, as Powicke writes, 'Simon had no roots in England and left none behind him', Trevelyan has it that his French origins 'did not prevent him becoming an Englishman at heart . . . dying for freedom on the field of Evesham'.[11] In fact, though he became an English 'worthy', he is 'one of the loneliest and most disconcerting figures in our history';[12] and he 'was making no deliberate contribution to the development of parliament as an institution, and has no claim to be regarded as one of its founders'.[13]

As one might expect, it is the contemporary *Song of Lewes* that best explains the conflict. The king, it laments, wanted everything 'of his own will' (*suomet arbitrio*) and to choose his advisers from any origin (*natio*). And the barons, far from 'diminishing the king's honour', only wanted to take their rightful share in so 'reforming' government as to set it back to an irrelevant past.

Quod honori regio nichil machinatur
quaerit contrario immo reformare.[14]

But they had nothing constructive to contribute. The ancient feudal grievance that the king must 'live of his own' on the old feudal basis was as obsolescent as the old feudal order. It would be the task of Edward i to adapt the monarchy to the new facts. Yet the danger of the rapacious tyranny threatened by John or Henry iii, had he been an abler man, had been evaded by the increasing and widespread resistance of the mid-thirteenth century community of the realm. At least 'Earl Simon [and his supporters had] underlined the length to which the community of the realm would go to ensure the recognition of their stake in good and just government. Ironically, the peace of England and the solution of the problems they raised were best served by their tragic ends.'[15]

4

Beneath the politically conscious minority, the bulk of the English peasantry, who formed the basis of its colourful civilization, had been

---

* Now is slain the precious flower who knew so much of war, but it was much worse that they dismembered this noble man.

sinking into greater dependence; but with the economic expansion of the twelfth and thirteenth centuries, many freeholders and even some villeins had become more prosperous, following production for a market. Indeed, lords now often preferred a money rent to services in kind, and peasants bought their freedom; although on ecclesiastical estates, conducted with a sharp eye, they were often still bound to labour service, and the landless class, the descendants of the old slaves and the lowest ranks of serfdom, was increasingly exploited for its labour. But the luckier and more enterprising peasants were making their way, and many of their descendants would become 'yeomen', destined through the opportunities of local office management and marketing to merge into the lesser gentry.

Meanwhile, above the weather-beaten peasant life, thirteenth-century society was becoming more civilized; for the rich even outwardly splendid. Their castles dominated the landscape, and the magnates moved from one stronghold to another to consume their rents. No longer the log-built strongpoints of Norman times, but stone-built and massive, the castles, whitewashed and painted outside as well as in, reached their climax of military efficiency and expense under Edward I. They were business centres as well as forts, towering above a huddle of courtyard buildings, sheep, cattle, wagons and packhorses. But though carpets were beginning to replace the rushes gnawed by Normans and Angevins in rage, the castles were draughty and cold; a chair was still a sign of state, and trestle tables had to be set up for meals. Candles were expensive, cressets and rushlights inadequate, so households got up with the dawn and settled down at dusk, with the main meal served early, between ten and eleven. The rich consumed vast quantities of meat, game, poultry, eggs, fish and eels: Henry III, taking after his Norman ancestor, thought lampreys 'made all other fish seem insipid'. Meat, often 'high', was spiced with cloves and saffron, pepper and cinnamon, as well as by the more homely onions and garlic, sage and mint; and the crusaders who had 'encountered sugar in Tripoli loved to suck it'.[16] Rice was now imported from Spain. Vegetables, other than beans, were not much eaten, though medlars, quinces, peaches, pears and figs were plentiful in season. Gardens were mainly herbal; but they could include roses and lilies, daffodils and poppies, violets and heliotrope. All classes ate vast amounts of bread; its quality was the concern of government, as in the *Assize of Bread* (1266). Food was served on trenchers (*tranches*) and everyone brought their personal knife. In the great households there was already a wealth of crystal, plate and silver.

Following French custom, huge amounts of claret were consumed, as well as wines from the Rhineland and the Levant. There were now no vintage wines as in Graeco-Roman times, and quantity more than quality was prized. Wine was rightly thought of as a disinfectant; one abbot, it is recorded, got ill from eating too many eels 'without any wine'. Ale was the universal drink from dawn to dusk. It was cheap, and made without hops by local 'ale wives'. As already observed, a vast acreage had always been under barley, but mead and cider were now thought rustic. Most people lived on coarse bread, beans, cheese, garlic and onions; on any pork and bacon they could come by or on what game they could poach.

Dress for the wealthy was gaudy and elaborate. But it was still cut on simple lines; a tunic and super-tunic over a linen shirt with a sweeping over-mantle. Colour and style were related to rank; as were the furs from squirrel down through rabbit – an animal first imported around 1175 with no word for it in English – to sheepskin and deerskin for the poor. Silk was imported from Baghdad, damask from Damascus: already camel hair (*camlet*) was used for coats.

In winter huge log fires blazed on open hearths, but passages were icy, and draughts stirred the cloth hangings that were carted about and put up as the magnates moved around. The tedium of winter evenings was now relieved not merely by *jongleurs* reciting epics, but by resident *joculators*, and a jester (*stultus* or *fatuus*) was often on the strength. *Scurri vagi*, travelling players (hence 'scurrilous'), would bring new repertoires. There were now also actors, *histriones non habentes certum domicilium* – 'of no fixed abode'. And acrobats and contortionists were popular, as well as performing monkeys. These diversions gave scope to those for whom fighting, hunting, praying and farming, the serious business of medieval life, were uncongenial, and they also supplemented the household orchestras which played during formal meals and for the elaborate dances of the knights and their women. Some of the tunes played at John's court had been of eastern origin with a thumping dervish rhythm.

Draughts and backgammon, which John had enjoyed, now supplemented chess; invented, it was thought, by Ulysses, and played by the Vikings. Knut, who cheated, had ordered one of his magnates to be killed after a dispute; and, as early as the tenth century, Louis the Fat, when overtaken in battle, had remarked 'Begone you ill-taught knight, don't you know it's unlawful to take a King even on a chessboard?'. Edward I himself possessed two sets of chess men, one of jasper and crystal, the other of ivory.* Apart from the perennial cult of the horse among the upper classes, and the habit of constant riding for all those not bound to the soil, medieval people prized exotic animals. Henry I had kept lions, lynx, camels and a porcupine at Woodstock: Henry II had a travelling bear, and Henry III accepted three leopards from

* There were no card games till the fifteenth century; the traditional costumes on cards are early Tudor.

Frederick II, in an allusion to his coat of arms, as well as an elephant from St Louis. Bulls, as in the legend of St Thomas, might be baited anywhere, and bear baiting with dogs would remain popular into Stuart times: '*Ursus est animal cholericum*', says a twelfth-century naturalist, '*et calidum*', choleric and hot. It was fashionable and expensive to keep falcons, carried elegantly on the wrist or perched in the room, for the owner had to train his bird himself. The domestic ape was a favourite; it has a natural talent, says Alexander of Neckham, for imitating the actions of mankind; lap-dogs were fashionable, and cats ubiquitous as mousers and pets.*

Though plate armour had not yet come in, chain armour was now more complete, with stockings and mittens of mail; it was worn over padding or leather; and by Richard I's time a flat-topped 'barrel' helmet had been in vogue which must have half-blinded the warrior. All had to be oiled and scoured against rust with vinegar and bran. Indeed, along with the now triangular shield, the long heavy lance and the great swords swung up and over in a downward cut with the full weight behind them, this chain mail was an expensive and cumbrous attribute of knighthood. The Welsh long-bow, first exploited by Edward I, had not yet spoiled the battle for mounted knights.

Next in importance to war and hunting – 'the pleasant bark of the hounds (was) more delightful to the ears of our nobles than the sweet harmony of musical instruments' – came the tournament; by the later thirteenth century better regulated, though still hazardous. Under Edward I, the general battle game, *conflictus gallicus*, was still fashionable. But this mêlée, so much detested by Abbot Sampson, if later better disciplined, had now become obsolescent before jousting over a course in 'lists' or enclosures; a more elegant affair, fought with blunted weapons and watched by high-born ladies. Stiff entrance fees, graded to social status, were exacted. Fashionable knights, such as William the Marshal, would make rounds of tournaments at home and abroad; the young Lord Edward's great renown was won in this way as well as in battle, and he enjoyed drawing up the rules. Henry III on the other hand, an aesthete never liked by the baronage, was less enthusiastic about tournaments.†

Originally a device to distinguish one side from the other, heraldry had been so far developed by the twelfth century that the arms of Geoffrey Plantagenet had borne six golden lions, which have come down on a famous enamel; and though no arms are recorded for Henry II, who cared little for *elegantia*, Richard I had already borne the Angevin three

* In Wales, according to the Laws of Howel Dhu, they were worth as much as threepence.
† Not all people admired them: one entertainer made a hit by taking two apes to watch and copy one, and training two dogs as horses for them.

lions or leopards *passant gardant*, the royal coat of England. Indeed, the conventions and terms of the art of heraldry were now becoming accepted, and some of the magnates already bore the arms and crests which would become fantastically elaborate and complicated in the later Middle Ages and in Tudor times.

Such, in a setting of increasingly splendid lay and ecclesiastical architecture, was the turbulent and colourful society of thirteenth-century feudal England. The politically fading feudal order now reached its social climax sustained by a growing prosperity, before pestilence, economic recession and dynastic vendetta blighted the achievements of a brilliant age. This civilization, like the elaborate culture of the Church and universities, was the concern of a small élite and its dependants; the vast majority of the people, speaking their English patois, was outside it, though it was sustained by their labour in field, pasture and wood.

5

The most hated of the Conqueror's innovations had been his creation of great royal forests in the Carolingian way. They were so-called because they were outside (*foris*) common law and custom, and subject to the arbitrary laws of *vert* and *venison* which preserved the woods and the hunting. Under Henry II, these game preserves had extended over nearly a third of the country, and the Assize of Woodstock in 1184 had reinforced his monopoly. Though the Charter of the Forest of 1217 curtailed some extensions made by John, in the thirteenth-century forest covered the whole of Essex, a wide belt from the Wash to Shotover near Oxford, another from Windsor through Bagshot and Chute to Savernake, and south-west to the New Forest. Grovely in Wiltshire; Selwood and Blackmore Vale, Bere, and as already observed, all Purbeck were afforested by John. Dean and Wrekin, Cannock and the Peak and large areas of Northumberland and the Lake District were forest. So it would remain, until Edward I reviewed his rights and discarded some outlying areas such as Blackmore. Edward III, however, would prefer continental warfare, and by Richard II's time the forest laws were obsolescent, to be replaced by game laws, more comprehensive if less ferocious, and in full force until the nineteenth century.

In a still colonial society these forests became the haunt of brigands, broken men and outlaws – men with a 'wolf's head' – and the legends of them would long embody the folk memories of Anglo-Saxon resistance, as in the *Gesta* of Hereward the Wake; they also express the resentment of all classes against the Crown; as in the tale of another Fulk Fitzwarren, a border baron, who was said to have kidnapped King John.

'*Vert*' meant the woods which could not be cleared but were left to harbour the game; '*venison*', originally *venatio*, hunting in general. The 'beasts of the forest', as opposed to the 'beasts of warren' (*garreyne*), were the red and fallow deer and wild boar – *cerf et sanglier*: wolves were 'noxious beasts', like foxes, to be destroyed. Even under Edward I, they were still a menace along the Welsh borders, and in Somerset Johannes le Wolfhonte held a bovate *ad capiendos lupos in foresta* – to take wolves in the forest.[17] Within the forests there was an elaborate ritual of the hunt, later described in his *Le Art de Venerie* by Twici, head huntsman to Edward II.

England had been famous for hunting dogs since pre-Roman times, and now, besides the hart hounds, buck hounds and mastiffs for hunting wolves, there were boar hounds (*porkericii*), *brachs*, running hounds and otter hounds (*lutericii*) – one master was called Johannes 'le Oterhunte'. And there were *strakers* – poachers' dogs who 'bolted': the word 'tease' derives from hounds worrying deer, and the dogs of the forest peasants had to be 'lawed' – their right forepaws mutilated.

Among the upper classes the royal maintenance of the *vert* was bitterly resented, while grievances over poaching were widespread among the people; for the King's officials were ubiquitous. The Forest Eyres were regular and 'attachment' courts frequently held: from the Justices of the Forest and the hereditary wardens and the verderers to the 'walking' and riding foresters and their incalculable boys, these officials proliferated; so that '*le puple e le comun de forests en Somerset*' would complain to Edward I of the '*surcharge de foresters et de lur garsons*', and demand the restoration of the ancient boundaries of *le Rey Henry Père, le Rey Richard et le Rey Johan*; for 'good people felt themselves aggrieved at the destruction of their woods'.[18]

To enforce the close seasons in high summer and fall, an army of foresters, rangers, and *wudewards* were needed. They recouped themselves from the villagers: the Charter of 1217 forbids compulsory and contributory scotales (they would plunder the barley, make the ale, and compel the people to buy it), or levying lambs or young pigs and wasting the woods if tribute were withheld. The foresters would summon the peasants to frequent *Swanimotes* and fine them for not turning up. Minor poaching was heavily fined; in Henry III's reign Richard de Baseville of Ketton, taken carrying the fresh skin of a buck, bought, he explained, from 'a certain unknown boy' at Kimbolton, had to pay twenty shillings.

In John's time, when Peter and Richard Gerewold, 'seen in the forest with bows and arrows', had fled, the whole village had been 'in mercy'; and Henry, son of Benselin, found 'under a certain bush' near 'a doe with its throat cut', had been imprisoned on mere suspicion. A boy who had 'found a fawn' was shut up for a year, before it was proved to have been already dead, and he was let off for having taken it 'without evil intent'. Under Henry III a whole village could be fined for not raising the hue and cry. Poachers were hard to catch and convict; as the cleric journeying to Huntingdon with a page and his greyhound – *Clericus itinerans cum uno garcione*, who both got away; or worse, when William Bolle, a 'walking' forester, connived at the taking of two bucks and had to be put in prison himself; or when poachers escaped 'owing to the darkness and the thickness of the woods'. The schoolmaster and under-master of Huntingdon, *familiares* of the Abbot of Croyland, were caught taking wild fowl, which the people of Cambridge went after with nets.

Such, from the legal records, was the life of the forest. For the aristoc-racy, from the king down, hunting was the most constant outdoor pleasure, and necessary to stock the larders of itinerant households. Despite winter hardships, the life must have seemed fine for many young poachers who turned gamekeepers; to ride through the woods in sun and rain, learn the ways of the animals and the tracks of the silent forest, to be free and hardy and illiterate. Much of the vitality which would go into oceanic exploration and settlement must then have been so en-gaged, on one side or the other, in Savernake and Selwood, Grovely and the New Forest. Nor was there any outcry against 'bloodsports'; the more robust clergy poached or hunted with the rest.

Such was the background to the folk-tales of popular outlaws, who, like the late-medieval Robin Hood, redressed the wrongs of the poor, and to the Frenchified romances, where knights-errant encountered wizards, fairy bears and talking wolves. So the pervading forest left its mark on popular and courtly imagination: if, from the cries of the huntsmen, *sa sa, oy; avaunt sohow; swef mon ami, swef, swef*, only *'illo loco* (there) *illoeques* has survived as *'yoicks'*.[19]

6

In some contrast with this rural and sylvan society in castle and village, field and forest, were the growing towns and the trade and commerce which they sustained. In greater contrast still, the vivid intellectual life of the universities, now coming into their own to be the foundation of a world-wide influence. For the universities of western Christendom were different in outlook and organization from those of Athens or even Alexandria in classical antiquity, and they would greatly contribute to civilization in Europe and beyond. Cosmopolitan, with a common Latin speech, they first appear in Italy at Bologna and Salerno; then, by the later twelfth century, in Paris. Oxford, already in being under Henry II, was well established by the thirteenth century. These Oxford 'schoolmen', stimulated by the Dominican and Franciscan friars, now set themselves to assimilate the 'New Aristotle' into the cosmic order of which St Thomas Aquinas would be the greatest architect, as against the materialist and deterministic interpretation of the Muslim Averroes and his followers. As already emphasized, they were now less concerned with humanistic culture than with systematizing knowledge; and indirectly, and often incongruously, they promoted a new analytic method. Their relatively barbarous Latin reflected the technicalities of the new discipline, which Giraldus, who lamented this falling off, had compared to 'a man sitting down to play chess with himself', a simile apt enough for some philosophers. On the other hand, their spectacular displays in public disputations gave them prestige. If Alexander Neckham and Bartholomeus Anglicus are hardly analytic, they had boundless curiosity; while both Grosseteste, the first Chancellor of Oxford, and Roger Bacon were original pioneers of a native scientific bent. Indeed, as Bologna was famed for law and Salerno for medicine, Oxford became renowed for science, with Merton college its earliest centre.

It is widely supposed that the medieval 'schoolmen' were unpractical; in fact they were often as practical as their metaphysical bias allowed. Though Aristotle would seem to Renaissance humanists a dead weight and Duns Scotus a name for Dunce, within their own idiom the schoolmen were strenuous. Adelard of Bath had probably tutored the young Henry II, to whom his treatise on astronomy is dedicated, and he had travelled in Italy, Spain and Palestine; 'I have learned one thing,' he wrote, 'from the Arabs under the guidance of reason; you follow another halter, caught by the appearance of authority.'[20] Nature, he had insisted, was 'not without system'. A 'man of Bath' and 'not a Stoic', he would judge facts for himself; he had translated Euclid, taught trigonometry and been a kind of scientist before Oxford was organized.

Alexander of Neckham in the early thirteenth century, also had a practical bent: 'what craftiness of foe', he wrote, 'does not yield to the precise knowledge of those who have tracked down the elusive subtleties of things?'* When told that a lynx could see through nine walls because it raced after meat concealed behind them, he sensibly pointed out that it could smell; at the same time he attributed the spots on the moon and the noxiousness of insects to the Fall, and continually moralizes about the creatures he describes. He writes of hippopotami as though they were fish, and describes dolphins in the Nile who 'bite the soft underbellies of crocodiles'. Coming nearer home, he thinks that the sparrow, 'a libidinous bird . . . and injurious to the fruits of men's labour', is subject to

* See his *De Natura rerum. Of the Nature of Things*, ed: along with his *Poem in Praise of Divine Wisdom*, with an excellent introduction by Thomas Wright, Rolls, 1863. Alexander (1157–1217), was a monk of St Albans who wrote about 1190, and became Abbot of Cirencester in 1213. His critics called him Alexander *Nequam* (mischievous Alexander).

epilepsy, and that grasshoppers derive from cuckoo-spit; his views on the sex life of hares and partridges are very peculiar. He already shows the English love of dogs, and points out that when they bark to welcome their master home, they also warn their mistress in case she happens to be making love to someone else. But, of course, they are liable to hydrophobia. Lions always sleep with their eyes open, and when rescued by humans from any danger, they are embarrassingly grateful, fawning and wagging their tails. On one important point Alexander is very practical: at the Day of Judgement, he reassures his readers, everyone will wake up aged thirty, 'a good age, at which the Saviour died'. He satirizes the more exhibitionist scholastics, but respects their grammar, dialectic and rhetoric: indeed, this *trivium* is a formidable two-edged 'power' – one can learn to argue either way.

Grosseteste, as Chancellor of Oxford University was the most influential of these pioneers. He was a Suffolk man who had studied at Lincoln, in Paris and at Oxford, and became Bishop of Lincoln (1236–45). He encouraged the attempt to harmonize Aristotle's teaching with Thomist Christianity and, like Newton, concentrated on optics: the Gregorian calendar, he pointed out, was already four days wrong in relation to the moon, a fact obvious to any 'rustic' (nothing would be done about it until the eighteenth century). In the true scientific spirit, he explained the rainbow, which the twelfth-century humanists had merely admired; and Roger Bacon, combining religion and science, even tried to explain the halo. 'The student's business,' wrote the Chancellor, 'should be chosen in useful topics because life is short, and these should be set out with clearness and certitude which is impossible without experiment.' He promoted translations from the Greek and complained of the text of the Vulgate Bible brought in by Lanfranc. His aims were often practical: if the phoenix and the eagle could prolong their lives, why not man? And if scientific armaments would be, as they still are, very expensive, and 'to set on fire at any distance would cost more than a thousand marks before adequate glasses could be prepared', the investment would be 'worth an army against the Turks and Saracens'.

His pupil, Roger Bacon (*c.* 1213–94), was even more original, and he fought the academic establishment where his master commanded it. He was a Franciscan from Ilchester in Somerset and studied at Paris before settling in Oxford in 1233. He was against 'unworthy authority', established custom, the 'ignorant crowd', and pretentious metaphysicians; so naturally, after writing a compendium of philosophy, he soon found himself in prison. 'The study of wisdom,' he wrote, 'must always increase in this life because nothing is perfect in human discoveries, and it is most wretched always to be using what has been attained.'[21] In his view the 'great book of Aristotle on Civil Science' – the *Politics* – 'well agreed with Christian Law'; but he had visions of machinery navigating without rowers, of 'cars', moving without draught animals with inestimable speed (*cum impetu inestimabile*), and of flying machines worked by pilots. This obscure rebel is one of the most interesting of English eccentrics, indomitable, and indefatigable.

On a more popular level, another Franciscan, Bartholomew de Glanville, Anglicus, the Englishman, won vast acclaim.[22] Like Neckham, he perpetuated many of the errors of Isidore of Seville as well as thinking of ingenious new ones: Shakespeare would read him, and in the seventeenth century many of Sir Thomas Browne's list of *Vulgar Errors* would derive from him. For, Bartholomew, in the tradition of Neckham, discourses on everything: of the angelic hierarchy and how they are manifest; of the mind and senses; of food and drink and, as an Englishman, of the spleen. He also points out that *testiculi* derive from *testis*, 'proof', for they are *testi*monials to a complete man. (*Lib: V. xliii.*) He deals with the weather and cats, and with the partridge who flies in a circle while her brood escape (*XII, xxx*), and with the ass who is called *asinus* because men sit on them, '*quia homines super asinos sedebant*'. These animals are slow and stupid and easy to catch, and so got domesticated before horses; and having melancholy humours, they are stolid and naturally 'oneriferous'. But the camel is so called because he kneels *cum humile*, humbly, and the dromedary is a small camel that 'goes much faster'. Elephants with their trunks salute the crescent moon, always wash after mating and never commit adultery (*XVIII, xliii*). The hare, *lepus*, is so called from its light foot, *levipes*, and the wolf, *lupus* from *leopes*, lion-like in the paw, his main strength. Unlike the noble lion, he suffers from a rage of rapacity and kills whatever he finds, while the tiger 'goes like an arrow'. The sheep, on the other hand, is placid, and called *ovis* because so often sacrificed as an *oblation*.

These are only a few examples of Bartholomew's wide range of interests. As a popularizer he belongs rather to the cataloguers of an earlier time than to the strenuous scholastics, now examining nature to prove the harmony of God and creation in the vast synthesis of Thomism, and incidentally pioneering, in their incongruous idiom, the methods of scientific observation which the English would so decisively develop.

7

Such was the intense and original intellectual life of the universities, now, for good and ill, more professionalized; and such the rudimentary beginnings of science in England. Such, against the developing administrative and political institutions of the thirteenth century, and more important to most people than political conflicts, were the worlds of the inarticulate peasantry, of whom we shall always know relatively little, and of the upper classes whose lives centred on the castles and their dependencies.

In the kaleidoscope of this society, which ranges from splendid affluence to appalling poverty, from grandeur and sophistication to a welter of confusion and disease such as still afflicts the poverty-stricken areas of the world, a wide range of personalities had now begun to emerge. They are as remote from us as the Romano-Britons or the early Anglo-Saxons. But England is now a *regnum*; no longer an exploited area of a continental empire: but an expanding society with recognizable national characteristics. Already there is a strong but not tyrannical central government, which, along with the landed interest now fully established, would from now onwards dominate the life of the country, assimilating and coming to terms with other interests as they came to economic and political power.

10

THE EDWARDIAN REALM

In Westminster Abbey, among the monuments of the Plantagenet kings, is a plain black box-tomb with no effigy; only, faintly inscribed, *Edwardus Primus: Scotorum Malleus: Pactum Serva*; Edward the First: Hammer of the Scots: Keep Troth. It commemorates a king who was more powerful than any since the Conqueror, whose legal reforms by statute were the most massive until Tudor times, who greatly extended the scope of the household government developed in the thirteenth century, and who even, by selectively associating the various interests in parliament with government, contributed to the evolution of a parliamentary monarchy.

At his accession Edward I (1272–1307) was thirty-five; a hard, proud man, seasoned in war and politics, at the height of his powers. He inherited crippling debts, increased them in campaigns against the Welsh, the French and the Scots, and left a near bankrupt treasury; but his reign saw the climax of English medieval monarchy in the island. Magnanimous and conventional, 'so handsome that he stood head and shoulders above the rest, with a broad brow and a good symmetrical face, his hair dark in manhood, turning snow white with age', he had won a great reputation on crusade; he was knowledgeable about hawks and hounds and on riding down stags and dispatching them himself. He was also a great authority on tournaments; 'the best lance in the world'; a 'fine fierce creature', who made his household a more flexible centre of government.[1]

His background was cosmopolitan. In a strategic alliance to protect Gascony, he had married Eleanor of Castile; then, after her death, and with the same object, he would marry Margaret, sister of Philip IV of France. When commanding his reluctant physician to bleed Queen Eleanor for measles 'for the bad blood', he could remark 'By God's thigh if she does not recover you shall pay for it'; and his intense religion was direct and practical. 'By the piety of God', he told a priest, 'I would rather speak with God than hear you talking about him'; and when a prized hawk was ill, he had its waxen image placed before the shrine of St Thomas. He was merciless to his enemies; he had Robert the Bruce's sister and the Countess of Buchan shut up in 'cages of timber and iron' as though they were 'beasts in a menagerie';[2] and he ordered Wallace, leader of the first Scots resistance, to be disembowelled; 'heart, liver and lungs and all the interior of the said William out of which such perverse thoughts had proceeded, thrown into the fire and burnt'. When his son, Edward of Carnarvon, wished to assign his inheritance of Ponthieu to his favourite Piers Gaveston, the old king is said to have shouted: 'You base-born whoreson, do *you* want to give away lands now? *You* who never gained any? As the Lord lives, if it was not for the breaking of the kingdom you should never enjoy your inheritance.' Then, seizing the Prince's hair in both hands, 'he tore out as much of it as he could. . .'*

Such was the formidable monarch under whom a permanent Council of State emerged, household government was further consolidated and the laws amplified and defined. Moreover, if 'it was a time of slack water between the dying impulse of feudalism and that political life of parliament which was as yet in the future',[3] we now know better from the description of the assemblies convened in 1295 and 1305 how parliaments were composed. And the drive for legal definition, already apparent in Bracton, who had thought of law as '*recta ratio scripta* – right reason written down', was due to the personal bias of the king, who thought of his high prerogative as something justified by '*pro commune utilitate* – in the general interest'.

So the great statutes of Edward i would be decisive in English legal and social history. This achievement, and not the wars in Wales, Scotland and France, or the mounting friction with the magnates which erupted into war in the reign of Edward ii, stands out as being of lasting importance. But the grim man who died on campaign at Burgh-on-sands near Carlisle, commanding that his bones should be borne before the army until the Scots were crushed, left an inheritance of hatred to his incapable heir.

Edward ii (1307–27) was a psychological misfit.† Though early given a 'painted toy castle' to play with and so bred to arms that at seventeen he 'managed his steed wonderfully well', Edward of Carnarvon never enjoyed war. He even 'undervalued' the society of the magnates; 'failed to conceal his boredom' with state business, did not take kindly to book learning, and enjoyed a long lie in in the morning. He liked 'thatching and ditching and mechanical pursuits'‡ and 'rowing about in various lakes, he and his silly company of swimmers'; indeed, he had to compensate his fool, Robert, for 'injuries done to him in the water'.[4]

---

* Hilda Johnstone. *Edward of Carnarvon*, London, 1956, pp. 123–4. 'Highly coloured though the account may be,' writes the biographer, 'there is little in it that is improbable.'

† Born in 1284, not in the present Carnarvon Castle but in the earlier stronghold, he only became the heir with the death of his elder brother, Alfonso, and was not presented to the Welsh until he was sixteen. The Elizabethan tale that his father promised them a prince who could speak no English and then presented the infant must go the way of King Alfred's cakes.

‡ His enemies alleged that the real prince had been mauled by a sow, and that his nurse, not daring to confess, had changed him for the son of a carter, 'so that he loved boorish things by nature'. Johnstone, *op. cit., passim*.

And, though he enjoyed their music, the first Prince of Wales did not like the Welsh.[5] In 1305, sending 'some of our bandy-legged harriers from Wales who may catch a hare if they find one asleep' to a friend in France, he added, 'we can send you plenty of wild men (*gentz sàuvages*) if you like'. The prince had also long felt 'an inordinate attraction towards a certain Gascon knight, Piers Gaveston', his companion in adolescence; to the fury of the royal family, he made this Béarnais adventurer Duke of Cornwall, and the rumour went out that the king better loved a sorcerer (*hominem magum*) and a 'maleficent' man than his own wife, Isabelle of France, 'a most elegant lady and a beautiful girl too'.[6]

The reign of this wayward and passionate neurotic brought the kingship, though not the household government, to its lowest degradation since the Conquest. In the small hours of a September morning in 1327 Edward II woke in Berkeley Castle, 'crushed by a huge table' and was 'wonder sore adrade (afraid)'. Then his murderers 'put an horn into his fundament as deep as they might and took a spit of burning copper (*copur brenning*) and put it through a horn into his body and oftimes rolled therewith . . . and so they quelled (killed) their lord that nothing was perceived', and 'Sir Edward of Carnarvon, sometime King of England, was put adown of his dignity'.[7]

Such was the anti-climax to the grandeur of Edward I. It foreshadowed the vendettas of the royal house that would lead to the usurpation of Lancaster, and which, after 1399, would erode the mid-fifteenth century monarchy. But the structure of household and Conciliar government was not destroyed, nor was the comparative prosperity of the land yet impaired. Within the framework of political events, now briefly to be considered over both reigns, constitutional and legal developments will be surveyed; then the economic background and the relations of the Crown with Wales and Scotland, decisive for both countries.

2

When in 1274 Edward I returned to take up his inheritance, he ruled through the household and a more permanent and experienced Council of State. As king in Council, he made statute laws which overrode customary and case law, and associated his parliaments, in which knights of the shire and burgesses were often included, with government. Royal policy and administration now went forward with a new momentum and institutions were consolidated within which the life of the country would develop. But the ambitions of Edward I were inordinate: he was determined to master Wales and to dominate Scotland; and to exact all and more than his rights in Gascony against the powerful

French kings. Crushing taxation roused increasing opposition; from the Church, the baronage, the gentry and the towns. Then, under Edward II, the magnates reverted to armed resistance, as they had under Henry III; tried to control the Council and the parliaments and made a novel distinction between the Crown and the person of the king. But out of these conflicts the bureaucracy and even the parliaments emerged enhanced. While the reign of Edward I was on balance a success, and that of his son politically disastrous, even in the latter constructive changes can be discerned.

From 1272–90 Edward I overhauled the administration, defined his regalian rights, and made 'legal reforms accomplished mostly before 1290, in volume greater than that of Henry VIII and in effects as enduring'.[8] In 1277 he also 'opened his mouth towards Wales and made it quake'.[9] By 1284 Welsh resistance, 'to which, God willing' the king had said, 'we mean to put an end', had been crushed, and, following a final revolt in 1294, Edward of Carnarvon was created the first English Prince of Wales in 1301.

During the second phase of the reign, 1290–1307, the English became heavily involved in Scotland and in France. In 1286 the death of Alexander III, the last of the McAlpins, occasioned the rival claims of Edward Balliol and Robert Bruce. As feudal overlord, Edward seized his chance: in 1296, when his nominee, Balliol, had failed to control the country, he took over the throne of Scotland himself, and the numinous Stone of Scone was deported to Westminster. The sequel at Falkirk and Bannockburn will later be described. In spite of initial success, the English had provoked a new kind of national resistance. Further, with the Scots campaign on his hands, Edward I had become deeply committed in France and Flanders. With the full force of the Capetian monarchy behind him, Philip IV, now the greatest prince in Europe, had overrun Gascony. In spite of Edward's second marriage and the betrothal of Edward of Carnarvon to Isabella of France, the expensive conflict, officially begun in 1294, was not concluded until 1303.

Taxation and requisitioning mounted in the overburdened realm. Church, baronage, gentry and burgesses defied the king. He borrowed vast sums from the Frescobaldi, Italian bankers who had superseded the king's Jews, evicted, for reasons to be examined, in 1290. By 1297 the Bohun Earl of Hereford, Constable of England, and the Bigod Earl of Norfolk, the Earl Marshal, were in open resistance. Backed by many of the lesser landowners, they now exacted a confirmation of *Magna Carta*, and attacked the household bureaucracy for encroaching on their rights. Moreover, they were supported by the Londoners and townsfolk, who complained of arbitrary *maltotes* – 'evil taxes' – such as that on wool. In 1301 a parliament at Lincoln came near to asserting that grievances had to be redressed before supply. And though the king dealt cleverly with the Church, by inducing Clement v, in return for substantial annates* which would persist until the Reformation, to suspend the archbishop and quash all concessions made since 1279, he died virtually bankrupt and surrounded by mounting opposition.

Such was the background of the campaigns in Wales and Scotland, which destroyed the last native Prince of Wales, broke Wallace, and made Robert Bruce, grandson of the original claimant of that name, a hunted fugitive on Rathlin Island, Antrim, encouraged, according to tradition, only by 'the persistent efforts of the most celebrated spider known to history'.[10] Such, too, were the commitments bequeathed to Edward of Carnarvon, who had been forbidden by the old king on his death-bed to recall Piers Gaveston 'to make riot' – an instruction at once disobeyed.

Indeed, Edward II's reign opens with an eclipse of the monarchy as the barons attempted to dominate the Council at the expense of the officials of the Household. By 1309 the magnates were in arms, and by 1312 they had accounted for Gaveston, a political lightweight who had given them 'turpia cognomina – disgraceful nicknames', and with whom the king was so infatuated that 'Marlowe's view of their relationship is probably nearer the truth than some modern historians have supposed'.[11] Reacting against the power of the household, twenty-one 'Lords Ordainers' now devised 'Ordinances' to control the king. They even chose his ministers, as he complained, in a phrase reminiscent of his grandfather, 'as if he were a lunatic', and attempted to take over the government by dominating the parliaments. But they had no more constructive ideas than had their ancestors, and their formal submission in 1313 left the situation unresolved. Then, in 1314 the catastrophic defeat at Bannockburn put the king more than ever in their power, for 'the Kynge whent to Scottelonde with grate pryde but he was fowle devicted', and 'alas, the Scots won'.

Thus, during the second phase of the reign, 1314–22, the kingship was at first almost in commission; but such was the incompetence of Thomas of Lancaster, the king's cousin and the leading magnate of the opposition, that Edward II was again able to build up his own party. It was led by Hugh Despencer, a baron of the household and castellan of Marlborough and Devizes, and by his son Hugh, a contemporary and intimate of the king, who had acquired by marriage great estates in south Wales and a claim to the earldom of Gloucester.

The complex clash of interests came to war. Though forced in 1321 by a combination of marcher and border lords to banish the Despencers, the king soon recalled them, and in 1322 at Boroughbridge in Yorkshire

* A proportion of the first year's revenue from an appointment.

actually defeated his enemies. Lancaster was 'put on a lean white palfrey full unseemly, with a mock crown on his head' with 'an horrible noise'; pelted with snowballs, and, clinging to a compassionate friar, decapitated. It was the first major Plantagenet dynastic crime since the murder of Arthur, and it set off blood feuds which would haunt English politics until Tudor times.

But immediately, from 1322–6, the monarchy was rehabilitated. A parliament at York now decreed, comprehensively, that 'all the things ordained by the said Ordainers and contained in the said ordinances shall henceforth and forever cease'. With a 'universal' consent in which the 'commonality of the realm' was included the king imposed a conservative settlement, wiping out the phase of baronial domination. The Despencers won control of vaster estates. These able officials now improved the administration of the household; developed the Wardrobe and royal Chamber, with a secret seal, and moved into inner recesses of government to avoid further baronial control. But they overplayed their hands, and salted away vast sums with the Italian bankers; the relatives of the murdered magnates were thirsting for revenge and the king identified with a bloodstained régime. By 1325 the queen had managed to leave the country, ostensibly to negotiate with Charles IV of France on questions of homage due for Gascony and Ponthieu; there she established herself, along with her lover, Roger Mortimer, a great lord of the Welsh border, and afterwards first Earl of March; and there Prince Edward joined her to do homage. Then she moved to the Low Countries, where Edward was betrothed to Philippa of Hainault, daughter of the Count of Hainault, Holland and Zeeland. In 1327, from Dordrecht, she launched an expedition against East Anglia.

Both Despencers were quickly taken and arraigned: '*vous estes robberes et avetz par vostre cruealte robbe la terre*', said their accusers: meticulously, they were drawn for treason and hung for robbery and beheaded for attacking the Church. The Londoners also butchered Bishop Stapledon, one of the best administrators, and stuck the younger Despencer's head on London Bridge 'to the sound of horns'. The queen hounded the king westward across England, the monarch saying, it is alleged, 'now would to God I were dead, so would God I were'. He was imprisoned at Kenilworth; then at Berkeley in Gloucestershire by the Severn estuary, and there, as already described, after two attempts at rescue, done to death. He was forty-three.

Thus for twenty turbulent years king and magnates had failed to solve the problem raised by the development of prerogative power under Edward I: how to reconcile the king's government, now exploited by rapacious favourites and extended by able administrators, with traditional liberties, and win the consent of the *communitas regni* to the legitimate demands of the Crown. Awed by Edward I, the magnates had been quick, when his successors showed weakness, to revert to a traditional and blind opposition. Resentful of the household officials, who alone could conduct government and sustain it, but themselves incapable of administration, they reiterated that the king should 'live of his own' in a time of inflation, while denying him the means of doing so. Far from being men of 'principle', who anticipated a Victorian vision of responsible self-government, they had no 'desire to broaden the basis of the constitution or to alter the structure of government . . .'[12] But two constructive ideas emerged. First, the readiness of the aristocracy or 'Peers of the Realm' to play a more responsible, if not disinterested, part in parliaments. Secondly the distinction between the person and the function of the monarch; between Edward Plantagenet and what was becoming the King-in-Parliament. 'Homage', the 'Lords Ordainers' had told Edward II in 1311, 'and oath of allegiance relates more to the crown than to the person of the King, and is more tied to it than to the individual'.* Nineteen years after, when they renounce homage, they 'protest collectively and individually that they no longer wish to be in fealty or allegiance to you or to claim to hold anything from you as King, holding you now to be a private person without any kind of dignity'.† In this feudal idiom they anticipate an important device in the constitution as later developed.

So, while the old views of deliberate constitution making must go, out of the power struggles of the thirteenth and fourteenth centuries at least two developments can be discerned, though made by men with their eyes on immediate practical objectives. For gradually precedents were also being set by the increasing part being played in government by the knights and in a lesser degree by the burgesses, and the old principle that a tyrant must be resisted if he breaks the laws, 'for he is not a king', as Bracton had written, 'where will predominates, not law', had led to a distinction being made between the man and his office. A more abstract view of authority thus comes about; feeling towards a concept of sovereignty, though not defining it, so that if a king has to be put away, his killers can have clearer consciences, and the king's government be carried on.

* *Annales Londonienses* in Chronicles, ed. Stubbs, *op. cit.* I, p. 153. *Homage et serment de ligeance est pluis par le reson de la corone qe par le reson du persone du Roi, et pluis se lie a la corone qe a le persone.*

† *Annales Paulini, op. cit.,* p. 324. 'Fas protestacioun en nom de eax tous et de chescun de eux, quex ne violent estre en votre feolte nen votre ligeaunce, ne clayment de vous com de roy ren tenir, eyns tegnent desore prive persone sanz nule manere de dignité.

3

Against this lurid background the other permanent achievements of the age must be set. For the first time we have evidence for the personnel of full parliaments, now long accepted as a device for making government more effective, and called into being by the need for information and control. It derives both from the 'Model' parliament, and the parliament of 1305; the latter here to be examined. It naturally centred on the household, still the core of the Conciliar administration, where policy and petitions were decided, 'sometimes with, but more often without, concurrence of the estates of the realm'.* The household of course centred on the king, the queen, the royal children and the great hereditary officials: Steward, Constable, Marshal, Chamberlain, Chancellor, and Treasurer; then on the professional bureaucrats: the Keeper of the Wardrobe and the Privy Seal, and the king's Secretary and the financial experts, the Chancellor and the barons of the Exchequer; then on the lawyers, the Chief Justices of King's Bench and Common Pleas and the Master of the Rolls. Finally came the Butler, the king's Confessor and the palace chaplain; then the admirals of the Channel and northern fleets, the Constable of the Tower and the Lord Wardens of the Cinque Ports and the Channel Islands.

Such was now the core of government; regal, traditional, bureaucratic, legal and executive. Round it a parliament was occasionally summoned, to sit only for three weeks. The one here described now contained two hundred and fifty clergy, prelates and lesser ecclesiastics; nine earls, ninety-four barons, seventy-four knights of the shires and about two hundred burgesses. Among the magnates were still many old Norman names: Bigod, Bohun and de Vere; Fitzwarren and Fitzpaine Courteney and Berkeley, Lovell and Segrave, Ferrers and Tregoz, still familiar from the countryside. Less is known about the shire knights, the *milites comitatus*, and their antecedents are hard to trace:† but already their functions were responsible; as electing coroners and furthering the

* *Record of Parliament 1305*, ed. with an introduction by F. W. Maitland, *Rolls*, 1893, p. *lxxxviii*. This classic introduction is the starting point of a realistic view of parliaments as associates and auxiliaries of the crown, not as the liberal-minded 'constitutional' experiments depicted by Stubbs, in whom there were two personalities: 'one a cautious experienced scholar interpreting the evidence in the light of a prodigious documentation, and the other [to the misfortune of generations of students] an idealist strongly influenced by the Teutonic past created by German historians in response to Fichte's appeal'. G. T. Lapsley, *Crown Community and Parliament*, ed. Helen Cam and Geoffrey Barraclough, p. 2, Oxford, 1951.
† See Lapsley, *op. cit.*, on *Knights of the Shire in the Parliaments of Edward II*, pp. 111–52. Of a member for Cambridgeshire he writes 'he must have been a person of great obscurity', and describes the two members for Hertfordshire as 'rather dim figures'.

business of the shire courts. Already in 1305 a Walsingham came up from Norfolk and a Turberville from Dorset.

The burgesses were summoned in November, over winter roads, for the parliament in February: William Bonenfaunt from Reading, William de Molendino (of the Mill) from Marlow; Thomas de Madingle from Cambridge, Reginald de Treworsi from Helston in Cornwall, Nicholas de Holte from Blandford and William Sparwe from Wareham. Bridport sent John de Bridport and Roger Godfelaw; Yarmouth, John Falstolf; they came up from Montacute and Langport in Somerset, from Andover and Woodstock; Peter Aubyn of Salisbury and Hugh Coteral of Wilton, Roger de Cleverel of Devizes and Roger Page of Marlborough; Ludgershall sent John Dieu-te-eyde, and York, John de sex Vallibus.

The magnates discussed the state of Scotland and Gascony; questions of the forests; of scutage and tallage; but most time was spent in committees appointed for England, Scotland, Gascony, examining petitions. Wages were in arrears; land wrongly seized; the citizens of Salisbury were in dispute with their bishop over tallage.* And in these discussions the knights of the shire and burgesses had their place. As Maitland writes, 'the representatives of the counties want to air their grievances and the king wants to know what is going on. Official testimony the Council can easily obtain, but it wants unofficial testimony also; it desires to know what men are saying in remote parts of England about the doings of Sheriffs and eschaetors and the like.'[13] Though major decisions and cases were dealt with after the shire knights and the burgesses had gone home, these representatives were developing in the course of business into an accepted if intermittent and auxiliary part of government. It was not of course their representative capacity, so dear to nineteenth-century historians, that was then important; but when, as under Edward II, king and magnates fell out, and the economy developed, they would gradually attain more standing, reflecting the fact of a wider establishment.

Still dominated by the king's Council and managed by the royal officials, the knights and burgesses naturally had no vision of a 'constitutional' monarchy. At best they set an 'accumulation of precedents . . . in different directions'.[14] But if, under Edward I they were convened *ad audiendum et faciendum*, 'to hear and do', by 1313, under Edward II, they were being convened *ad consentiendum*, 'to consent'. Further, the High Court of Parliament, with its intermittently attendant knights and burgesses – the term 'House of Commons' in the modern sense does not

* Henry III had made it a free city, with the citizens free of tolls throughout England, but also ordered the bishop to enclose it with 'competent' walls, with appropriate tallage, from which the citizens petitioned to be exempt. *Charters and Documents Illustrating the Cathedral City and Diocese of Salisbury*, ed. W. R. Jones and W. D. Macray, *Rolls*, 1891, p. 176.

come in until the fifteenth century – would begin to differ from its equivalents on the continent. It would not divide into separate estates, noblesse, clergy and bourgeois, but into 'Lords' and 'Commons', with the lesser nobility and landowners assimilated with the burgesses. And though the great bishops and abbots continued to sit in the 'Lords', the clergy would go their own way in separate 'convocations', so-called by the 1360s.

Such was the background to Edward I's extensive reforms. Already in 1274, the king had launched his enquiry into the rights and the resources of the Crown. In the following year, '*Rex in Consilio*' in '*le primer parlement general apres le courounement*', he formulated the first Statute of Westminster based on these reports, defining rights, rectifying wrongs. Then, having defined his own rights, he turned to the rights and limitations of the old feudal tenures. Following the Statute of Gloucester in 1278, he launched the inquest *quo Warranto* into prescriptive land right, and declared that even 'longest possession' could not stand against the Crown.* Then in 1279 the Statute of Mortmain gave the Crown some control over alienation of land to the clergy. In 1283–5 the statute *De Mercatoribus* made it easier to recover debts, and recognized by implication the economic developments of the thirteenth century. Trade demands credit, and credit the acceptance of obligation. The merchant, often considered a foreigner outside his own area, was subject to blackmail and litigation from debtors of more feudal mind. Now written records of obligation were devised and registered: central government had reached out to protect the merchants throughout the realm.

In 1285 the Statute of Winchester had enforced the king's peace. It reached back to Anglo-Saxon times of hue and cry, brigbot and burgbot, and placed responsibility on the whole neighbourhood. Constables of hundreds were appointed, and *Conservatores Pacis* – ancestral to the Justices of the Peace. Able-bodied men had to attend a 'view of armour' and, during the French war, coastguards were organized, most elabor-ately in rich and vulnerable East Anglia.

Then, also in 1285, under *De Donis Conditionalibus*, the land law on the entail of estates was defined. Heirs in entail could not now alienate land at the expense of their own successors. Along with the custom of primogeniture which had been growing up since the Conquest, this law made for the consolidation of great estates. While it would not be interpreted to make the high aristocracy an ossified and exclusive caste, it prevented a minor and impoverished nobility living on fragmented

---

* Thus, the best authorities now admit, probably giving rise to the memorable remark of Earl Warrenne, who 'producing an old rusty sword (*antiquum et eruginatum*) said, "Look you my lord, and see my warrant, for my ancestors coming with William the Bastard, won their lands by the sword"'.

estates, and made for younger sons moving out into the world, there to prosecute their fortunes by arms, law and trade. In 1297, *Quia emptores*, on the other hand, designed to check sub-infeudation, made it possible to buy and sell land more freely, unencumbered by archaic obligations. For land was no longer a thing apart, the basis of a feudal society, but something that could be sold. The social consequences of such transactions had now been better regularized.

With this extension and codification of the law, went a new professionalism. From the reign of Edward I, Year Books recording proceedings in Norman French began to accumulate. The legal-mindedness of the English, apparent since Anglo-Danish times, is reflected in these documents, preserving the work of lay professionals, who by the next reign would have their own Inns of Court in the quarters of the evicted Templars. Their close corporation would become increasingly important, perhaps too important, in English life; attaining great political influence both directly and through the House of Commons.

So, under Edward I, England finally moved out of being a feudal society into one in which 'the power of the Crown and the rights of the generality are the supreme tests of the pretensions of groups and individuals. The subject, not the franchise, is the unit of Edward's scheme of state, and common law, partnered by a jealously guarded regalian right, outweighs the validity of all other customs in England.'[15] Such, in essentials, was the achievement of the King in Council in Parliament; now the supreme authority of the realm, backed by representatives of the community of the land; fluctuating in attendance, infrequently summoned, and meeting only for brief sessions, but giving their added sanction, if only by tacit consent, to the acts of government.

4

The economic background to these political struggles and constitutional and legal changes was still prosperous. The country probably now carried as big a population as could be supported by the techniques of the day, and if large areas were still forest and waste, the wealth of the great landlords, bishops and abbots was now immense. It was the failure of the Crown, with only rudimentary methods of taxation available, to get its hands on the share of the wealth necessary for government, as well as malversation, at its worst under Edward II, that exacerbated political conflict and drove the kings to temporary expedients. By 1290 the old Norman and early Angevin custom of mulcting the king's Jews had been abandoned. Since the Conquest they had been allowed to accumulate great wealth, of which the Crown had periodically taken heavy toll; but by the mid-thirteenth century they had become a political liability.

Many of the minor gentry were now in their debt, and clerical and lay magnates had bought up the bonds they held on estates to round off their own. Anti-Semitism had contributed to Simon de Montfort's popularity: Edward I's government decided that they must go.[16] For decades the warier Jews had been getting out; now, save for a few doctors and goldsmiths, they were expelled, not officially to return until the Protectorate of Oliver Cromwell.

The Crown now had recourse to the Frescobaldi bankers, a more sophisticated form of finance; but it had to pay high interest to the Italians, to whom in 1309 the entire customs on wool from Scotland and Ireland would be pledged. And this method was also resented, since it made the king more independent of the magnates and gave the Italians political influence, while officials, such as the Despencers, could put their own gains out of reach of their opponents.

Another, but non-recurrent, expedient was to plunder foreign religious orders and 'alien' priories. The Church was still universally accepted, though under critical surveillance, and a root and branch attack was not mounted until the time of Wycliffe; but the Templars, who had already been dissolved by Philip IV of France, were plundered by Edward II. In 1308, following the French example, charges were mounted against them which anticipated Henry VIII's method when dissolving the monasteries. The moral indignation of the lay public was deliberately roused against them, for this order of militant knights had become altogether too sophisticated. One of them, it was alleged, had declared that 'no man after death had a soul any more than a dog'. They were also said to wear the cross in a most unsuitable place and their morals to be such that it was a schoolboy joke to shout in chorus 'beware of the Templars' kiss'.[17]

So the bishops of the southern province were 'persuaded to seek permission to use torture, though the inquisitors subsequently complained that they could find no one to do the work';[18] and, though Edward II seems hardly to have been a monarch to take a high moral line, their possessions were confiscated. As a stop-gap measure, the transaction paid off; for though in theory their property was transferred to the Knights Hospitallers, so much stuck to the fingers of the royal administrators that Edward II was able to provide for his wife's dowry and even recoup much of his expenditure on Gaveston, to whom he had recently given 'velvet suits embellished with pearls for tournaments'.

But such windfalls were not enough; the position of the Crown worsened. For along with a continuing prosperity, still precarious before drought, flood and pestilence, went a rise in prices. In 1314 the government tried in vain to check it: '*magna et quasi intolerabilis*', it was said, '*est caristia in hiis diebus*' – 'the cost of living in these days is great and seems intolerable'. King and magnates combined in vain to fix the price of an ox at twenty-four shillings; of a 'cow alive and fat' at twelve shillings; of a pig at forty pence and eggs at twenty for a penny. Ordinances were promulgated, as in Tudor times, restricting magnates to 'two courses of meat of four kinds', and 'gentlemen', *prod hommes*, to much less. It is unlikely that these restrictions were effectively enforced.

5

For some people the price rise was advantageous. It was based on considerable improvements in farming, for which the landlords reaped the main benefit, but which also advantaged the more enterprising or lucky peasantry. While the technical status of the villein was still going down, in fact some descendants of the twelfth century Godric and Walt and Widsi, Osbern and Orm and Tori the Deaf and Big Hugh and the villeins Alwin and Uctebrand, continued to do well. In Wiltshire, for example, at Alton Priors, at Enford on the upper Avon, and at Stockton in the Wylye valley, the usual vicissitudes of country life had been going on:

sheep get stolen or killed by dogs, cows get drowned in rivers, peacocks fly away to more congenial surroundings and, of course, foxes take toll of poultry . . . sparrow-hawks made a clean sweep of the pigeon house. But although the landlords, the monks of St Swithun's Priory at Winchester, were as well heavily cheated by their bailiffs, productivity was going up.[19]

Some landlords had long been farming not for subsistence but for the market, and the medieval roads were not so bad as they have been thought. Fantosme, surprisingly, in the mid-twelfth century, had written of Henry ii's knights that they 'slacken their reins on the great paved roads',[20] and the numerous Justices in Eyre had long covered great distances. The tracks were at least wide, and provided casual grazing for the horses; and though most of them proved atrocious for wheeled traffic, they were not intolerable for riders. They were now not only '*cynges ferdstreats*' or '*herestreats*', military tracks, but more frequently '*portstreats*' – roads to market.[21] Though apart from the remnants of Roman roads, there was no longer any overall design and many tracks richly deserved their name of 'foul way', the English roads did promote a centralization of government and a development of internal trade better than that achieved elsewhere north of the Alps.

But the climate must now, if we are to believe the Chronicles, have been worse than in Roman times. They constantly complain of downpours, *munditio pluviarum*, sometimes lasting for months; in 1280, London Bridge 'cracked' because of the ice, and in Edward ii's time hares were hunted on the frozen Thames in the light of bonfires. There are running complaints of thunderstorms and steeples struck by lightning. The English obsession with the weather, already detectable in the *Anglo-Saxon Chronicle*, runs on. But although the economy was still 'colonial', with vast areas of forest and waste, the population had probably doubled since the Conquest to around three million and a half or perhaps even four million. And following the use of heavy ploughs, the three-field rotation of crops, and the use of horses instead of oxen, productivity had increased; particularly on the vast scattered estates of the magnates and the Church, run by miniature 'councils' of estate officials and by bailiffs and reeves, whose perquisites would increase if more than the traditional produce could be gleaned.

With the expansion of arable following production for a market, stock farming also flourished; even larger flocks of sheep were pastured on the Cotswolds, on the chalk downs and on the fenlands, than in the twelfth century; their wool still the main export. Indeed since the taxes on it were essential to government, the trade was often given priority even over power politics. And in spite of these exports, the nascent English cloth industry was developing. Fulling was now being mechanized by water power, often available in just the best country for sheep. This development was still limited, but it pointed to an immense future, when cloth would supersede raw wool, and become the export 'staple' of the economy for centuries.

6

If government did not much share in this prosperity, insolvency did not prevent medieval kings going to war; and Edward I's campaigns in Wales and Scotland were decisive for the whole island. While the marcher lordships remained a centre of baronial disturbance, Welsh political independence was now extinguished. That of Scotland was preserved.

Llewellyn ap Gruffydd the last native Prince of Wales, had profited by the de Montfort wars and long evaded his homage. In 1277 Edward I moved the whole might of England against him. The apparatus of professional war was mobilized round a nucleus of heavy armed knights, supplemented by light horsemen (*hobelars*), archers and spearmen, and by sappers and technicians for siege engines and castle building. A systematic combined operation, sustained by sea, was launched to cut off Snowdonia from its main sources of supply in Anglesey and the Welsh border. Already the king was making contracts anticipating the indentured service of the Hundred Years' War for which these insular campaigns proved a rehearsal. In Scotland, indeed, Gascon crossbowmen would be supplemented by archers from South Wales, the English using the techniques of one kind of border warfare in another.

In face of this overwhelming assault, Llewellyn came to terms. By the Treaty of Conway he renounced his claims outside his own northern principality of Gwynedd, and, that Christmas, did homage in London. But when, at Devizes in 1282, Edward heard that he was again up in arms, he resolved to destroy him. When in November Llewellyn was speared in an obscure skirmish near Builth in the Wye Valley, and his head first exhibited to the army in Anglesey and afterwards 'in London, encircled with a crown of ivy in mocking allusion to a prophecy current among the Welsh that he would be crowned there',[22] one of the oldest royal lines in Europe was extinguished. Welsh independence, maintained since sub-Roman times, was crushed. Nor would it revive, save for a brief flare-up under Owain Glyndwr in the early fifteenth century.

The disaster had been predictable. No strong government in London could accept a Welsh principality poised to take advantage of the endemic disorder in the marches and quick to intervene in English civil wars. It was only a question of time before the stronger power would strike. But the final collapse had been completed by the feuds among the Welsh themselves. Llewellyn had incarcerated his elder brother, Owain Goch (the Red); and his younger brother, David, who had betrayed first him and then the English, was hung, drawn and quartered at Shrewsbury in 1283.

The victors now moved in on Wales. Gwynedd was shired into Anglesey, Carnarvon and Merioneth; the southern part of the principality into Cardigan and Carmarthen. Strategically placed castles at Conway, Beaumaris, Carnarvon and Harlech now held down the land, and English settlers were planted in the rudimentary towns. In the Statute of Rhudlan Edward I proclaimed that 'since Divine Providence had now of its favour wholly transfered to our proper dominion the land of Wales and its inhabitants', the English system of sheriffs and coroners would be imposed. Welsh law was now superseded, and women's rights were enhanced, if, in spite of bitter protest when bastards were excluded, estates could still be equally divided among heirs. Minor crimes still came under the native code, but major thefts, manslaughter and 'notorious' robberies came under English law. Further, the Welsh bishops now came more directly under Canterbury.

The new régime would only gradually be assimilated. Henry VIII's officials would still find a welter of conflicting law and custom, but the main decision had been made: while the Welsh language and way of life went on, politically the principality became subordinate to England. For the London government that part of Wales was no longer a threat. The new threat would now come from the marcher lordships which still controlled half the country; from Mortimer of Chirk and Wigmore, from Bohun of Brecon, from Clare of Gloucester and Glamorgan, and Valence of Pembroke in the south-west; in the north from the County Palatine of Chester. Here the king's writ still did not run, and the magnates preserved an independence comparable on its lesser scale to that of their equivalents in France and in the Empire; franchises which in the central and southern part of England had never been permitted by the Crown. These marcher lords would remain, like the lords of the Scottish border, the bane of English politics until the early sixteenth century.

If the English had crushed the native Welsh, in Scotland they were defeated in a conflict which might never have arisen. In March 1286, the elderly Alexander III had dined in state, and perhaps too well, in Edinburgh Castle. Then, in spite of a north-easterly gale, he had set off to meet his youthful second queen who had arrived from France. Yolande de Dreux was waiting at Kinghorn and, though conditions were dangerous, the king had insisted on crossing the firth at Queensferry, and pressed on to his objective in the dark. Next morning he had been found dead on the beach: his horse had lost its foothold along the low cliff, or stumbling in heavy sand, had thrown its rider.

So Edward I had seized his chance. The heiress, Margaret of Norway, lived in Bergen; but a personal union of the two realms, in which Scots customs and liberties would be preserved, had at once been negotiated. Margaret was to marry Edward of Carnarvon. But in 1290, on her way back to her kingdom, she had died in the Orkneys from the hardships of the voyage. Outside the Gaelic-speaking Highlands, the ruling class were Norman-Scots, many with estates in England. Nor was the language among the peasantry much different from Northumbrian English. The marriage could have been a viable solution.

All was now thrown into confusion. Edward I, determined to keep some control, now asserted his feudal rights as overlord through Arthur, Athelstan and *Kinutus* in *souereyne seignurie*. In 1292, he assigned the throne of Scotland to John Balliol, great-grand-nephew of William the Lion through his mother Devorguila, passing over the claims of the older Robert Bruce of Annandale, the great-nephew through her younger sister. Legally it was the correct and politically the convenient decision; but when his puppet king failed to control the country and turned against him, Edward took over the realm himself; administered Scotland through English officials and held it down by castellans in the strategic castles already to hand.

Their exactions soon roused fierce popular ire. In 1297, led by William Wallace, a minor laird from Clydesdale, the Scots pikemen routed the English at Stirling Bridge, murdered the most detested English administrators, and swept south to ravage over the border. Edward I moved north against them with an enormous army, including ten thousand Welsh mercenaries. Berwick-on-Tweed was sacked, and at Falkirk in 1298, the Welsh arrow storm followed up by the heavy armed knights overwhelmed the Scots pikemen and bid fair to rivet the English yoke on Scotland. Most of the Scots-Norman barons did homage, among them Robert Bruce, grandson of the original claimant.

But in March 1306, Bruce seized the throne. Then, to clear the way, he murdered Balliol's nephew, the Red Comyn, in the church at Dumfries, when they had met there, ostensibly to come to terms.* The English then tried hard to destroy him. An outlaw tracked by blood-hounds, Bruce took to the heather and survived. Soon he won control of south-west Scotland: after the death of Edward I in the following year, he consolidated his rule, subduing strategic castles and besieging Stirling. And when at last, in 1314, Edward II came north with an elaborate and expensive army and entourage to relieve it, he suffered the most spectacular defeat in English medieval warfare – so 'discom-forted' at Bannockburn that he was 'wonder sorry' and 'fast fled with his folc that was lefte alive'.

The prelude to the battle is famous. King Robert Bruce rose in the stirrups of his palfrey and clove the helmet of the charging magnate Sir Humphrey de Bohun, and when reproached for his rashness '*answer made them none*',

> But turned about the axe shaft wha
> Was with the stroke broken in twa.[23]

The Scots, who had perhaps 'taken a lesson from the Flemings who at Courtrai (in 1302) had defeated on foot the power of France',† now trapped the English, who had spent the night in 'an evil damp and wet marsh', and drove them towards the burn, 'so direfully were their horses impaled upon the pikes'. Edward II, who lost his temper‡ and laid about him manfully with a mace, was led protesting from the field: 'off he went though much against the grain'. But his escort, Sir Giles d'Argentin, saved his own honour. 'Sire,' he said, 'your rein was

---

* 'Unfortunately the famous story of Bruce's words: "I doubt I've slain the Red Comyn", and of Kirkpatrick's answer, "Doubt ye? I'll mak' siccar, (sure)" is of late date, and he would probably have spoken Norman French not Lowland Scots.' W. C. Dickinson, *Scotland from the Earliest Times*, London, 1961, p. 162.

† *Scalacronica*, trans: Sir H. Maxwell, Glasgow, 1907, p. 54. The '*Ladder Chronicle*', so-called in allusion to the author's crest, was written in Norman-French verse by Sir Thomas Gray when in captivity in Edinburgh (c. 1355). The spirited poem is by a soldier whose father witnessed the battle.

‡ *Rex vero, ruinam suorum, et fugam, amare gestans animo, . . . hausto spiritu acriore, in hostes more lionis . . . irruit truculenter*, Trokelowe, *Annales*, ed. H. T. Riley, *Rolls*, 1866, p. 86. 'But the king, taking bitterly the ruin and flight of his men, and inspired by a fiercer spirit, hurled himself truculently at the enemy like a lion.'

committed to me . . . you are now in safety. I am not accustomed to fly nor am I going to begin now. I commend you to God.' Then, setting spurs to his horse, he returned to the mêlée where he was soon slain.[24]

For the Scots, writes Lang, 'not the least agreeable result of Bannock-burn was an unprecedented abundance of booty: when campaigning, Edward denied himself nothing'. They got enormous ransoms and 'all the jewellery of the young minion knights'.

> *Maydenes of Engelonde,*

wrote a Scots versifier,

> *Sare may ye morne*
> *For tynt (lost) ye have your*
> *Lemmans at Bannockesborn.*

So Scots independence was won, and 'Gud King Robert' stayed King of Scots. The victorious Scots army even advanced into England, took Berwick and came south to York. By the Peace of Northampton in 1328, the year before Bruce's death, the English for a time recognized a *fait accompli*. Although the English soon attacked again, and Bruce's heir, David II (1329–71), was a failure, a Scots realm had been preserved, with a traditional policy of scorched earth (*byrnan the planeland*), harrying the border, and an already old alliance with the French. In spite of a gruelling conflict in which the land had been constantly overrun, wasted and plundered, a separate Scots nation had emerged, with its own institutions and traditions. It would be a poverty-stricken, turbulent country, with a history of political crime; but unlike the Welsh, the Scots had maintained their independence as a separate state, with all the consequences.

11

THE CHIVALROUS PREDATORS

In April 1340, the English ambassador told the Venetian government that since 'Philip (VI) of Valois, styling himself King of France, occupied Normandy, the greater and more fertile part of the Duchy of Aquitaine and the counties of Anjou and Saintonge . . . and of Pontoise in Picardy, all of which from time out of mind belonged to the King of England', his master, Edward III, had 'called upon the said Philip to fight a pitched battle'. To avoid Christian bloodshed, the king had even offered

to settle the dispute by single combat or with a band of six or eight; or that, if he [Philip] be the true King of France as asserted by him, he should stand the test of braving ravenous Lions who in no wise harm a true King, or perform the miracle of touching for the evil; if unable, to be considered unworthy of the Kingdom of France.

All these offers, the ambassador continued, had been rejected: and since by law divine and human the oppressed are entitled to aid, the said Prince Edward now requested the hire of forty or more galleys, paid for in advance for one whole year.

Adroitly the Doge of Venice regretted the quarrel; hoped it would be composed: unfortunately, for his part, since a Turkish armada threatened the Venetian territories, he could hardly help, though he would be grateful for the trading privileges also mentioned.[1]

As here set out, the so-called Hundred Years' War (1337 intermittently to 1453) was a traditional ordeal by battle; but it had a realistic political and economic purpose. As Edward III well understood, the prestige of the Crown was best maintained by successful war which also gave the great magnates scope abroad. And beneath the chivalry and panache, war had now become a business; the English won the equivalent of a quarter of a million pounds in ransom in a decade: *Grandes Sommes d'or q'ont este apportez deinz le Roialme de Ranceons des Roys de France et d'autres Prisoners*. The cult of Arthur and the Round Table was institutionalized by the Order of the Garter, inaugurated by Edward III at Windsor on St George's day 1348 in a general haze of magnanimous popularity:* tournaments were now even more magnificently formal,

* In a romantic gesture towards Joan of Kent, Countess of Salisbury, who afterwards married the Black Prince and became the mother of Richard II, the monarch may well have picked up her garter and bound it about his knee, with the celebrated remark *Honi soit qui mal y pense*. Joshua Barnes, in his *History of that Most Victorious Monarch Edward III'd* (Cambridge,

175

and heraldry more elaborately regulated; but the cult of the loyal heart (*coeur loiall*) and 'magnanimous mind' between 'fair sweet lords' went along with a grim professionalism, out for prisoners and loot.

The feudal host had now long been superseded; service was mainly by indenture* and war expensive and complex; an organized interest shared by all classes. The *chevauchées* throughout France were acclaimed not only by the great lords, the bannerets, knights and esquires, but by the highly paid mounted archers and Welsh infantry. They combined to plague the continent from the opening battles at Cadzand on the Scheldt and Sluys on the Swyn, 'the batayll of Scluse in Flaunders upon the Sea' (1340), through Crécy (1346), to Poitiers (1356) – 'Sir John, Kyng of Ffraunce,y taken'. By 1360 the chivalrous predators had won a third of France, far too much to hold. Then, following set-backs, disasters and an uneasy peace, the Lancastrians launched the second major assault and won Agincourt (1415), with archers each with a 'stake of tre sharpid at both ends a–slope before them', and Henry v commanding '*Avaunt Banner* in the name of Almighty God and St George'. Then would come the slow débâcle before a novel national resistance symbolized by Joan of Arc (1429–30); 'a woman taken y-armed in the feld, that was called *Pucelle de Dieux*; a false witch', said the English, 'for through her power the Dolphin and all our adversaries trusted wholly to have conquered again all France'.[2]

At home the French wars were the political trump card of Edward III and Henry v: Richard II would not play it; and Henry VI could not, and both came to disaster. But if at first the expensive war paid dividends, it dragged on and on, an obsession of all the politically articulate classes, and contributed to the virtual bankruptcy and erosion of monarchy in the mid-fifteenth century.

Since Edward III (1327–77) was exactly what a fourteenth-century monarch was expected to be,† he worked in comparative harmony with

---

* So-called because the duplicated document was divided by a saw-tooth line (*dent de scie*) and each party kept his copy.

† Edward III is the first monarch whose appearance we know directly. His idealized monument in the Abbey is corrected by the funeral effigy now in the cloisters museum at Westminster, which shows a thick-set warrior, his mouth slightly distorted by a stroke.

1688), tried to give the Garter a grander origin: 'It has been a common opinion that Joan Plantagenet . . . by chance letting fall her garter in a dance, the amorous King snatching it up for the sake of the Beautiful owner, contrived thus to make it honourable to all Ages.' But Froissart, 'when he comes to the Order of the Blew Garter takes no notice that it was ever intended as an honour or remembrance of this or any other Ladies Garter' (p. 292). The Early Tudor historian, Polydore Virgil, he points out, citing *fama vulgi* (popular gossip), is the first to start the tale. Barnes evokes all sorts of bogus Arthurian legends to give the Order a longer pedigree. Prof. McKisack, on the other hand, writes 'that recent research gives credit to the tale' that the episode took place at a court ball given to celebrate the capture of Calais'. *op. cit.*, p. 251 ff.

his parliaments in which the bi-cameral division between Lords and Commons was becoming clearer, and on whom he depended to finance the war; indeed, the cost of conflict enhanced the authority of the knights and burgesses of the Commons. Since 1327 the knights and burgesses had been summoned to every Parliament, and had taken more initiative in presenting petitions in the Council, of which legislation came to take account, rather than being simply imposed. Further, they now presented and discussed private petitions as well. Already in 1336, after a prolonged struggle over the export tax on wool, they had claimed that the excess had been imposed without the consent not only of the magnates but of themselves, and by the 'sixties they were able to fix the amount exacted. By the time of 'Good Parliament' of 1376 they had elected their own '*Orator*' or '*Speaker*'. Still dominated by the Council, overshadowed by the magnates, and summoned for short sessions, they were now not merely a means of ascertaining opinion and a sounding board for government policy, but were necessary for raising revenue and dealing with a whole range of business.

Moreover, the Crown had now become even more dependent on the gentry in the countryside. The habits of violence and judicial murder under Edward II and the growing cult of war had militarized society. In the early days of Edward III brigandage was still endemic. Gangs led by rogue gentry and even clergy had to be put down, as that of Lionel, King of the Rout of Robbers, who defied the incompetent local authorities from his 'castle of the North wind'.* Only knights of the shire and their kind could enforce order: in spite of jealousy of the London professionals, they had to be given a closer grip on local government because the gangs were lawless and the judges often ineffective or corrupt. Following the Statute of Winchester, Edward I and Edward II had appointed 'Custodians of the Peace'; by 1362 their Quarter Sessions would be regularized and by 1368 they would become 'Justices'. Hence the unpaid Justices of the Peace, who would become essential to Tudor, Stuart and Hanoverian government. So, both at Westminster and in the counties the gentry became entrenched, and as the demands of the war made the government more dependent on them for taxation, the political influence even of the burgesses also increased. And with the power of the purse came a wider right of petition and debate, the power

* '*Lyonel, roi de la route ravenours*.' Blackmailing a victim, he greeted him with a parody of a royal command: '*a nostre faux et desloiaux Richard de Snoweshill, salutz sans amours . . . Donez a nostre Castiel de Bise, en la tour de vert.*' 'With its allusions drawn at one extreme from romance and at the other from the harsh realities of contemporary politics it is an extraordinary document.' See E. L. G. Stones, *The Folvilles of Ashton Folville and their associates in crime, 1326–47*. Transactions of the Royal Historical Society, 1957, pp. 117–35. One of the Folvilles, a Yorkshire parson, shot his pursuers from his own church before being dragged out and beheaded. 'Come with me to the Green Forest of Belregard, where is no annoyance but wild animals,' sang one brigand, 'for the judges sell justice like cows.'

to criticize the Conciliar government, if not yet on major policy, on finance and specific grievances. The Commons had become an essential part of government.

Thus the parliamentary monarchy, with its household administration, its Council, its Lords spiritual and temporal, their rights of attendance now becoming better defined, and with a Commons of increasing though still subordinate influence, developed not into a centralized, bureaucratic prerogative power, but into what would be a balanced constitution of King, Lords and Commons. And it remained limited, in spite of the Tudor enhancement of prerogative, by the complex medieval institutions that had grown up with it.

All was conditioned by the fluctuations of the economy and the social changes following the Black Death. This form of bubonic plague, carried out of Asia by the black rat, first struck in 1348 at Weymouth in Dorset and spread rapidly to London, East Anglia, the Midlands and the West. And 'the foule dethe of Engelonde', as the Scots called it, killed animals as well; it struck again in the 1360s and became endemic. The population, by the end of the prosperous thirteenth century numbering perhaps three and a half to four million, was now very gravely diminished. In 1369 Edward III's queen, Philippa of Hainault, died from it and the general social dislocation was profound.

Many estates in the thirteenth century had been producing with hired labour for the market instead of for subsistence, and the old static order broke up, the landless 'labourer' became more common. He could now command high wages; the surviving peasants, with more land to go round, scented better things, and in 1381 in the reign of Richard II, they would rise in proletarian revolt, the first clumsy and anti-clerical manifestation of egalitarian radicalism.

Profound intellectual changes were also going on. The synthesis propounded by St Thomas Aquinas was now under radical attack. St Thomas, like Plato, had maintained that universal concepts existed in their own right and were 'real'; now the Franciscan William of Ockham (fl. 1320–47) maintained that they were mere 'names', so asserting a 'nominalist' as against a 'realist' philosophy, and this radical scepticism would become the predominant fashion in England. Then, in the 1370s and 1380s, *Mayster John Wyccleef, a doctor in divenyte and by his openyons an eretyke,* anticipated in his voluminous writings the doctrines of Calvin in theology and Luther in politics. He stated what would become a 'Protestant' Nonconformist position and, encouraged and exploited by lay magnates already avid for church lands, attacked the wealth and grandeur of the Church. The Lollards, who developed and vulgarized these doctrines, would keep popular anti-clericalism alive until the Tudor reformation.

More attractively, the English language, long sinking into various rustic patois, now made its comeback against the upper class Norman-French. William Langland, the most important, if not the earliest, of these writers, revived the old English alliterative verse, while with Geoffrey Chaucer, one of the greatest English writers, the language really comes into its own. English was now the language 'not of a conquered, but of a conquering people'.[3] Here, it would seem, in spite of Edward III's suggestion that his rival should expose himself to 'ravenous Lions', for '*enfant du roi ne peut lion manger*', is a society coming nearer to our own. Its outstanding political, social and intellectual aspects will now be surveyed.

2

Edward III was only fourteen at his accession; but by 1330 he had relegated his mother to Castle Rising in Norfolk, where she lived an elegant and pious life on an enormous income; and he had hanged her lover, the Earl of March. Edward proved a popular monarch, easy-going, open-handed and magnificent. Though, like most medieval kings, financially irresponsible, he was a shrewd diplomatist as well as a warrior, and exploited Flemish, Breton and Norman regionalism against the French king. For half a century he lived in tolerable harmony with his subjects, but he bought it by sacrificing the long-term interests of the Crown. The magnates, who recruited large contingents for the war, would become increasingly hard to control. Moreover, the king married his sons to great baronial heiresses, and these princes of the blood, with vast appanages, would combine with the marcher and border lords to dominate the Council and terrorize parliaments. Hence the problems inherited by his grandson, Richard II, who came to the throne aged ten and perished at thirty-three. He tried to retrieve and enhance the power of the Crown; even, it seems, to impose an early Renaissance despotism – 'like tyrants in Lombardy', writes Chaucer. But his court was the most cosmopolitan, elaborate and splendid in the English late Middle Ages, and he was a great patron of architects, artists and writers, lavish and discriminating. The inventory of the king's treasure suggests that he delighted in the 'improbable combination of costly materials',* and where Edward III lived in the kind of heraldic setting admired by Froissart, Richard II lived in the more modern early Renaissance world of Chaucer.

* Gervase Mathew, *The Court of Richard II*, London, 1968, p. 47. 'Much of this must have had the appeal of Fabergé work, though it was probably more sophisticated' (p. 58).

But where Richard ii was brought down from an apparent peak of power, having alienated all the politically articulate interests in the realm, Edward iii, save in his premature decline, won European prestige. 'When the Noble Edward first gained England in his youth,' wrote the French chronicler Jean le Bel, 'nobody thought much of the English, nobody spoke of their prowess and courage. . . . Now in the time of the Noble Edward who has often put them to the test, they are the finest and most daring warriors known to man.'[4]

But in 1327, England was a miniature realm compared with the wide territories ruled or dominated by the Capet kings, whose prestige and prosperity had been at their height in the thirteenth century. When, in 1328, the accession of the first Valois king, Philip vi, gave the English king his opportunity, he first tried to neutralize the threat to his own realm from Scotland, where David ii, the successor of Robert Bruce, was still a child, and where, once again, an English candidate, Balliol, was briefly installed as Scots King. The Scots defeat in 1333 at Halidon Hill marked the first major victory of the reign. Edward then attacked in Flanders, where his influence was paramount through his control of the English wool exports, and where the Gantois under the pressure of Edward iii's embargo on the export of wool, and led by Jacques van Arteveldt, were in alliance with the English against their pro-French count. In 1340, in the great cathedral at Ghent, Edward iii was proclaimed King of France.

He next struck in Brittany; then in the Norman Cotentin, where there was already a revolt against the French Crown; indeed 'the secret of Edward's success was the discovery of diplomatic and military expedients for waging war on the cheap'.[5]

This intelligent strategy was combined with tactical innovation. The small English armies were highly trained and well-disciplined, and they had learnt from the Welsh the value of a new weapon, the long-bow. The combination of dismounted men-at-arms with archers proved invincible. And when in 1346 Edward captured Caen, then turned north-west in a long *chevauchée* to cross the estuary of the Somme, he won his first spectacular continental victory. The French king fled from the field – struck by an arrow in the face; the blind king of Bohemia perished, though the legend that Edward of Woodstock, the Prince of Wales, then assumed his ostrich feather crest and his motto '*Ich dien* – I serve' – is unsubstantiated; for he had inherited it through his mother, Philippa of Hainault. Many of the greatest French nobles were killed or captured. Then, after a year-long siege, Calais was taken, to remain an English foothold on the continent until 1558.*

* The well-known story of the surrender is authentic. '*Sachez . . . seigniour*', ran an intercepted letter, forwarded to the French king, '*que vous gentz ont mangé leurs chyvals, chens et*

In 1356 another *chevauchée*, this time in south-western France, brought an equally spectacular victory. At Poitiers that September, when the English situation looked desperate, the Black Prince with an Anglo-Gascon army trapped the French among the early autumn hedges and vineyards, and by brilliant and highly 'unchivalrous' tactics captured the French king, John II, himself.

Like David II of Scotland, he was lodged, with elaborate courtesy, in the Tower. By May 1360 under the Treaty of Brétigny, three million livres tournois was exacted for his ransom, though tardily and never fully paid, and the English briefly amputated a third of France. To their original territories around Bordeaux and in Gascony, they now added all Aquitaine, including the rewarding territories of Périgord and Armagnac, as well as Quercy and Rouèrgue. In the north they kept Ponthieu and the strategically vital port of Calais.

It was too great an area to hold or manage. The long conflict had created new national hatreds, '*Ils en arrivent à se haïr mutuellement*'.* Free companies of disbanded mercenaries pillaged the country, and when in 1369 the war flared up again, the French applied tactics of evasion and attrition under professionals of whom Bertrand du Guesclin, Constable of France, won the most renown. The English territories were reduced to less than their original size and the first phase of the war ended in anti-climax.

At home, as the ageing king lost his grip, the 'Good' parliament of 1376 used a new weapon of impeachment to bring the government to book; banished the king's predatory mistress, Lady Alice Perrers, and imposed its nominees on the Council itself. John of Gaunt, Duke of Lancaster on his first marriage and a claimant to the throne of Castile by his second, who was acting for the king in the parliament, was unable to ward off from the courtiers the attack of the Commons, pressed home with a new and fiery independence in political action. Many of the magnates clearly sympathized with the Commons in the parliaments of the next reign, and their competing ambitions would combine with their dissatisfaction with government to turn them against the Crown. Such were the consequences of the short-term policies of Edward III, who had bought popularity by excessive concessions; and such, at home and

---

* See Edouard Perroy, *La Guerre de Cent Ans*, Paris, 1946, p. 10. This brilliant book, written, says its author, 'Grace aux loisirs précaires que laissent à l'auteur une passionante partie de cache-cache avec le Gestapo', remains the best general account.

ratez – your people have devoured their horses, dogs and rats'. *Chronicon, Henrici Knighton*, ed. J. R. Lumby, *Rolls*, 1895, vol. II, p. 48. With halters round their necks and 'crying out loud that they had falsely held the city against him', the burghers surrendered. At the instance of the queen they were accorded mercy, to be sculpted in the act of surrender by Rodin in the nineteenth century, and so petrified near the Victoria Tower at Westminster.

abroad, the lowering background to the accession of Richard of Bordeaux.

The predicament inherited by Richard II (1377–99) was not peculiar to England. By the end of the fourteenth century

for reasons which may be left to the scrutiny of historians of economic and social change, custom and reality no longer coincide. Kings were forced either to attempt to impose their will on particularist elements despite usage, or to witness impotently the disintegration of central authority. Of the rulers like Richard II, Pedro I of Castile, and João I of Portugal who determined to take action, only the Portuguese was successful. Circumstances or dispositions left others like Charles VI of France helpless in the face of aristocratic self-interest.[6]

Richard II's attempt to restore and enhance the monarchy was strategically necessary, if tactically incompetent.

The reign divides into three phases: 1377–88, when the king was too young to be fully independent; 1389–97, his personal rule; and 1397–99, his tyranny and deposition.[7] From 1377–88 the Council staggered through successive crises. The Peasants' Revolt of 1381 when the mob killed Archbishop Sudbury of Canterbury, the Chancellor, and the Treasurer Hales, nearly broke its authority, although, as will later be described, in the crisis the young king saved his throne. Ill-considered expeditions to Flanders, France and Spain further taxed the country, and in 1386 when Gaunt, proclaimed King of Castile, left England with an army for Spain, the most dependable and powerful of the king's uncles was removed. Richard, who had proved his mettle in 1381 and made a grand marriage with Anne of Bohemia, daughter of the Emperor Charles IV the year after, built up a court party round his favourite, Robert de Vere, Earl of Oxford and hereditary Chamberlain, whom he made Marquis of Ireland with palatine powers, and Sir Michael de la Pole, an able official of bourgeois origin, whom he made Chancellor and Earl of Suffolk. By 1386 the conflict between the court and the great aristocracy, led by the king's guardian, Arundel, and by Gloucester, his youngest and most brutal uncle, came to a head. 'The community, noticed these quarrels', writes Froissart, whose casual worldly explanations are often illuminating, 'and dreaded the outcome; the more frivolous laughed at them, and said they were "all owing to the King's uncles, who were jealous because the crown was not on their heads", while others said "the King is young, and puts his trust in youngsters: it would be more to his advantage if he consulted his uncles more than that puppy, the Duke of Ireland, who is ignorant of everything and never saw a battle".'[8] So that year they struck down the nascent power of the household before it destroyed them, threatened the king with the fate of his great-grandfather and put the Crown in commission.

In 1387 Richard left London, got the opinion of the principal judges that his prerogative had been violated and tried to raise forces from Cheshire, Wales and Ireland. But, returning to London, he failed to command support; de Vere, now Duke of Ireland, advancing with an inadequate force on London from the north-west, was trapped at Radcot Bridge, escaped by swimming his horse over the Thames near Oxford and vanished in the December fog.* After passionate farewells to the king, he fled to the Low Countries where he died in a hunting accident near Louvain. Suffolk, too, fled abroad, never to return.

Richard retreated to the Tower. The 'Appellant' Lords, so called because they 'appealed' the king's ministers of treason, now used the 'Merciless' parliament of 1388 as an instrument of judicial murder. They would probably have deposed the king had they been able to agree on his successor. Telling the old tale that the governing clique had exploited the king's 'tender years and innocence to make him hate the lords and lieges by whom he ought by rights have been advised', they made as clean a sweep as they could. They killed the Chief Justice Tresilian and the king's friend and tutor, Sir Simon Burley. When the former Lord Mayor, Nicholas Brembre, offered to defend himself by battle, his accusers threw down their gauntlets against him 'a nombre de CCC gauntz et V'.* After the executions, all concerned swore to preserve the tranquillity of the realm, and Richard, officially exonerated, promised to do better – 'destre bon roy et seigneur a eux, to be a good king and lord to them'. So concluded Richard II's first and amateurish attempt to assert the power of the Crown against the great aristocracy.

From 1389–97 a similar conflict is apparent, save that the king's dispositions were now much abler. He brought back Edward III's old servant William of Wykeham, Bishop of Winchester, and ousted Gloucester and Arundel and their followers; Lancaster returned from Spain and for ten years gave his nephew steady if distant support. But in a time of relative prosperity, the king now became more temperamental. The death of Queen Anne in the summer of 1394 so distracted him with grief that he razed the Palace of Sheen where they had lived together to the ground, and when Arundel arrived late at her funeral in Westminster Abbey, he seized a stick from an attendant and struck him on the head 'with such force that he fell at his feet and the blood ran over the floor'. In September Richard crossed to Ireland, probably to consolidate a base for counter-attack. Here he won much success with the

* 'Immisit se in aquam Thamesie, et sic mirabili ausu evadit ab eis', Knighton, op. cit., vol. II, p. 253.
* 'To the number of three hundred and five.' Polychronicon, Ranulphi Higden, ed. J. R. Lumby, Rolls, 1886, vol. IX, Appendix p. 149.

native Irish, whose leaders, says Froissart, were persuaded to eat separately from their servants and even to wear breeches. His next move was to make a twenty-year truce with France, confirmed in 1396 by his marriage to Isabella, the seven-year-old daughter of Charles VI, who undertook to support his son-in-law against his subjects and accorded the princess a large dowry.

The conclusion of the expensive and now unprofitable war which had long wrought 'enormous mischief' – 'les tres grands meschiefs et destructions de guerre intolerables entre les deux Roialmes' – was widely unpopular; but it strengthened the Crown. The king's objective of supreme power now seemed within reach. Only one thing stood in the way; the still danger-ous magnates who had nearly deposed him in 1388, sullen and alarmed at the growing restoration of his prerogative. So Richard, this time, acted first. 'The king's sudden display of high-handed autocracy has been viewed variously as the climax of years of vengeful planning, as an unpremeditated outburst against those who had humiliated him a decade earlier, and as the action of a madman. The last merits no consideration ... nervous and temperamental he was, perhaps, but not by any standard mad.'* On a realistic assessment his *coup d'état* looks to be a typically Machiavellian stroke, and no accusation of insanity was made at the king's deposition.

So in July 1397 Richard struck: by September the detested Arundel, governor of his youth, was executed after a trial before a cowed parlia-ment: worse, the king's uncle Gloucester was 'violently smothered under feather pillows pressed down for a long time over his face', or 'ffoule mordered at Caleys with tovaylles (towels) made square wyse and putte aboute his nekke'.

The king was now at an apparent apex of power. The irreconcilables had been destroyed, a diplomatic revolution had made the French king his ally and, at a parliament held at Shrewsbury, Richard was given a generous supply of money and the duties on wool and leather for life. He was backed by his own Cheshire archers and men-at-arms who wore his White Hart badge, and he had accumulated 'a strong striking force armed with the most modern weapons ... seventy-three cannon ... and a stock of 4000 lb. of gunpowder', and a whole body of 'paid reservists throughout England, particularly in the west and north'.[9] In these last years of the reign his greatest artistic project came to fruition with the full restoration of Westminster Hall, whose great hammer-beam roof still survives. The king, it seems, now had even wider ambitions to the

---

* R. H. Jones, *The Royal Policy of Richard II, op. cit.*, p. 70. McKisack on the other hand maintains that by 1399 Richard had become 'dangerous, perhaps dangerously mad'. *The Fourteenth Century, op. cit.*, p. 497. Dangerous he certainly was, but the other question is always relative, particularly in politics.

empire in Germany, and lavished subsidies on the Rhineland electors. He was wildly extravagant in his personal largess, living in a round of festive luxury; of

> *Wax and wyn*
> *In Wast all about*
> *With dainties y-doubled*
> *and daunsinge to pipers,*

Thus wrote a cantankerous rhymer, perhaps William Langland;

> *For when was ever Christian King*
> *That ye ever knew*
> *That held such a Household?*[10]

He would sit, it is alleged, on a high throne, 'speaking to no man but overlooking all . . . and if he looked on any man he must kneel'.[11]

But the cost of this early Renaissance style of despotism was beyond the resources of the realm, and Richard was brought down not so much because of his political high-handedness as through his attack on property. For he now raised huge sums in forced loans, particularly from London, his civil servants devised a detestable expedient of fines to be paid to regain the king's favour, and those involved in the magnates' *coup* of 1388 were forced retrospectively to compound. Then, early in 1398, he seized a chance to get reversion of the enormous Lancastrian estates. John of Gaunt, Duke of Lancaster was already ailing. His son, Henry of Derby, Duke of Hereford, was now probably trapped into a charge of treason, having, it was alleged by the king's intimate, Thomas Mowbray, Duke of Norfolk, tried to inveigle him into plotting against the throne. The affair came to trial by battle before the king himself. Norfolk sent to Germany for special armour; Hereford to Milan: in a dramatic scene at Coventry, and probably with an eye on John Gaunt's expected death, Richard banished them both; Norfolk ostensibly for life, Henry for ten years. And when, early in 1399, John of Gaunt died, Richard extended Hereford's sentence for life and seized upon the enormous Lancastrian inheritance.

This violation of right – for in medieval theory every man must have his due – sent a shiver through all landowners great and small. The forced loans had set the merchants against him; now he alienated the landed interest. Perhaps by now paranoic, Richard took a great army to Ireland to consolidate a refuge; for he said he was 'caught between two inevitable evils', and he took the royal treasure with him, along with hostages, among them the future Henry v.

So the new Duke of Lancaster seized his chance. While

Richard that regned
So riche and so noble . . .
Werrid be west
On the wilde Yrisshe,
Henri was entrid
On the est half.[12]

He landed at Ravenspur on the Humber and, with the support of the northern magnates, marched for Cheshire, the centre of Richard's power. Richard, advised by traitors, divided his forces, and appeared with an inadequate army in north Wales. Shut up in Conway Castle, he was tricked into parleys, ambushed, imprisoned at Flint and taken to Chester; then south to London and the Tower.*

Richard II, said his enemies, had claimed an arbitrary power he could not enforce, and worse – he had attacked property: 'no man of substance felt safe either in his goods or his life.'[13] It was alleged, in the articles against him, that he had 'said expressly with a harsh and arrogant countenance that the laws were in his own mouth or at other times in his own breast';[14] and that he had despoiled the people by 'taxes and tallages to fulfil his own cursed ambition and pride',[15] having frequently declared that 'the lives, lands, tenements, goods and cattle of his subjects were his, which was entirely against the laws and customs of the realm', . . . 'which roiaume', said Lancaster, was 'in poynt to ben undon, for defaute of governaunce and the undoyng of the lawes'.[16]

Though 'descendit be ryght lyne of the blode comyng of Kyng Henry',[17] Lancaster's own dynastic claim was weak: but he had arrived as the defender of property and law. So his *coup d'état* was masked by a supposed legality. A commission, appointed by parliament, told Richard 'and so, syre, the wordes and the doyng that we schal say to you is not oneliche owre wurdes bute the wurdes and the doyng of all the states in this lond'. Apparently all the monarch could reply was that 'he loked nought thereafter; but . . . that after al this he hopede that hys cosyn wolde be good lord to hym'.[18]

---

* According to a Welsh eye-witness, deserted even by his pet greyhound. 'Ever by his side . . . until the same King, as before told, fled at midnight by stealth and in craven fear from the army, and then, deserting him . . . led by instinct and by itself and with no guide, it came straight from Carmarthen to Shrewsbury and to the Duke of Lancaster, now King . . . and as I looked on, it crouched before him, whom it had never before seen, and with a submissive but bright and pleased aspect. And when the Duke had heard of its qualities he welcomed the hound right willingly and with joy and let it sleep upon his bed.' Froissart says that 'it put its forefeet on the king's neck and made up to him'. The animal now ignored Richard, 'which he took sorely to heart'. The tale was very convenient for Lancaster, since the greyhound was one of his badges. *Chronicon Adae de Usk*, 1377–1421, ed. with translation by Sir E. M. Thompson, London, 1904, p. 196.

It was the last thing his supplanter could do. Having formally resigned the throne, Richard was hustled off to Greenwich, taken disguised as a forester to Leeds Castle in Kent, then to Pontefract. Soon, after two conspiracies on his behalf, he was dead: starved, it was put about, by his own volition; in fact, probably murdered after frantic resistance, when, seizing a bill from one of them, he slew four of his assailants before, 'chased about the chamber', he was 'felled with a stroke of a pole-axe which Sir Piers (de Exton) gave him upon the head'.*

But, contrary to previous belief, when, in September 1399, 'Sir Harry, now Duke of Lancastre', took his seat upon the vacant throne, and at the coronation banquet told the hereditary royal champion Thomas Dymmoc, '*pugil regis*' as Lord of the Manor of Scrivelsby in Lincolnshire, 'if need be, Sir Thomas, I will in my own person ease thee of this office', he claimed no parliamentary title. There would be no 'Lancastrian constitutional experiment': he was there *de facto*; in part by conquest, in part by a vague hereditary right. He was there because he was needed and because the legitimate king had thwarted the establishment. The usurpation of Lancaster, whitewashed by every religious and political sanction it could command, had been consummated: it would last for three generations, until Henry's grandson, too, was set upon and murdered, this time in the Tower.

4

Such were the dynastic crimes that made the fifteenth-century French remark that the Plantagenets were unfit to be '*rois très Chretiens*, for God was not pleased with treason nor with murder either'.[19] They were the price paid for the destruction of a potentially despotic power which, however necessary it must have seemed to Richard II and his supporters as the alternative to the paralysis of government by men with no constructive alternative, could not be made viable in England. The result was an erosion of the royal government over more than half a century.

But beneath the power politics here briefly described, a new aspect of affairs must be considered. We must revert to the earliest and most creditable episode in the tragic reign of Richard II. For in June 1381 the mass of the people had first become politically articulate in the Peasants' Revolt, and created their own primitive and spontaneous organization. It had not amounted to much; all was over in a month and the ruling classes had sunk their differences to show a united front. But the social depths revealed had set English political history in a new perspective.

* See Holinshed, *Chronicles*, Oxford, 1923, pp. 25–6, on the 'desperate manhood of King Richard'. This Tudor description is based upon Walsingham's contemporary account.

It has already been observed how the Black Death had improved the prospects of the surviving peasantry and how their overlords had combined to thwart their emancipation. The Statute of Labourers of 1351 had tried to prevent the peasants exploiting the labour shortage, imposed the old obligations of manorial service, and fixed wages at an artificially low level. At the same time, the lesser artisans in the towns had also been frustrated by the oligarchies who had come to monopolize the crafts and restrict the rise of apprentices to their own ranks. Hence arose a short-lived alliance between the peasants and the lesser towns-folk.

But in 1381 the immediate cause of the revolt had been savage, inequitable and misapplied taxation to pay for the war in France. As Froissart puts it, the people were saying 'what is now become of our grand enterprises and our valiant captains? Would that our gallant Edward and his son were now alive! We used to invade France . . . where are the knights and princes of England who can do such things now . . . what has become of the immense sums of money that have been raised of late?'[20] The notorious poll tax had hit everyone, the poorest worst, and it had been villainously collected. So the people had cooked the returns by which the taxable population had fallen from 1,355,201 in 1377 to 896,481, with a highly improbable preponderance of men.[21] Since all over fifteen had to pay a shilling, the grievance went deep among the people in a new way, and the peasants spontaneously came together against the 'insupportable burden'. One Thomas the baker of Fobbing, Essex, leaving his 'vocation', began to organize the villagers, and the movement spread, 'others associating others with them' in the 'common need'. According to the best contemporary account,[22] the villagers mishandled the tax-gatherers, who fled, while the people 'took to the woods'. The rising spread; the 'great lords and other people of substance' removed to London and the 'commons' sent letters into Suffolk, Norfolk and Kent so that the other folk should rise with them. There were riots at Dartford and the 'commons' of Kent under Wat Teghler (Tyler) of Maidstone, probably a veteran of the wars, got into Canterbury on Trinity Sunday, threatening to decapitate Archbishop Sudbury the Chancellor – 'and so he was', says the chronicler, 'within five days after'.

That revolt was not, of course, against the throne: it was against the government and the ruling classes. 'With whom haldes yow?' the peasants would demand, and the answer was 'Wyth Kynge Richarde and wyth the trew communes'. But they were out for blood. They asked the townspeople of Canterbury if they had any 'traitors' among them and cut off the heads of those produced. Indeed, following the example of their rulers, the people in general enjoyed a good head-hunt, the grisly trophies borne before them on poles; and when they got into London they looted the houses of the Lombard bankers, *'par tout le jour et la noet ensuent od hidous crye et horrible noyce'*.[23] In London the government had not the forces for street fighting: king and Council took refuge in the Tower, while the Kentish rebels encamped at Blackheath, displaying 'two banners of St George and forty pennons', while the Essex men encamped on the other side of the Thames. Richard, aged fourteen, went down-river by barge to meet them at Greenwich, but, warned that if they once got him, they would 'never let him loose but take him with them all round England', he did not go ashore, and returned to London 'as fast as he could and came to the Tower at the hour of Tierce'.[24] When, with the connivance of the city mob, the rebels got into London, he could only watch the resulting conflagrations from one of the turrets.

In collaboration with the Londoners, the peasants now burnt Lancaster's splendid palace of the Savoy (there was 'nothing like it in England'), and threw 'three barrels of gunpowder on the flames and the powder exploded and set the hall in a greater blaze than before'. Then they got into Lambeth Palace and burnt the archbishop's records, as well as destroying, with puritanical zest, a notorious Flemish house of ill fame, rented from the Lord Mayor. They then wrecked the lawyers' quarters in the Temple, and hunted the occupants 'like rats'.

To give the Chancellor and the Treasurer a chance to escape, Richard now went out to meet the Essex peasants at Mile End. Their demands were revealing: that 'for the future no man should be in serfdom'; land should be rented at the low rate of fourpence an acre and not held by service, and 'no one should serve any man but by his own good will under covenant'. Both tenants and landless labourers would benefit. They also demanded that the game laws should be abrogated. Their demands were practical and not anarchic. But while these parleys were going on, other peasants had got into the Tower, clumsily beheaded Chancellor Sudbury and the Treasurer, and killed any foreigners they could lay hands on; 'and many fllemynges loste their heedes . . . and namely they that koude not say breede and cheese, but *Case* and *Brode*'.[25]

Then, in Smithfield cattle market, came the crisis. The king with a small escort, sitting his horse among the seething mob, was listening to Tyler's demands about the game laws. All preserves, he demanded, in ponds, parks and woods, should be common, and poor men as much as rich should be free to fish and take game and course hares in the fields.[26] But Tyler, in one version, was playing with a naked dagger, then 'rinsed out his mouth in a very rude and disgusting fashion' and 'drank a great draught of beer'. And when he even put his hand on the king's bridle, John Walworth, Mayor of London, *'come homme hardy et vigurus'*, struck him with his 'basilard' in the throat and one of the king's esquires ran him through. As their leader collapsed, the peasants began to bend their bows – *commenceront à tréer lour arkes.*[27]

Then Richard rode towards them. The magic of royalty worked; they had always been for the king. Telling them he was now their leader, he mesmerized the mob, and soon had them following him peacefully off into the open fields. And here they were soon enveloped, 'like sheep within a pen', says the chronicler, by the forces rallied by the Lord Mayor. Tyler's head was now set on a pole; and Richard had it displayed to the rebels, so that 'when the commons saw that their chieftain was dead, they fell to the ground there among the wheat, like beaten men'. Other outbreaks in Norfolk and in the west were put down. The establishment regained control. It was all over before the summer was out.

For the peasants, it seems, had no general plan; 'every district went its own way of tumult'.[28] Their 'conventicles' and bands had queer moralizing slogans – *'if might go before right . . . then is oure mylne mys adight'; 'Lokke that Hobbe robbyour* (the Treasurer Hales) *be well chastysed'; 'Synne fareth as wilde flode, trew love is away that was so gode';* and *'Clerkes for welthe worke hem wo'.* They also wanted to abolish all bishops save one archbishop, who would be John Ball, their 'mad priest', a notorious character in prison at the time of the rising, and to massacre all the literate people they could. Somehow, they felt, these people were in league with the rich.

Such was the first seismic disturbance that briefly shook the English establishment and revealed the mentality of the populace. The Revolt was made, not by starving peasants desperate with disease and famine, but by relatively prosperous men on the way up, who resented the archaic social conventions and economic handicaps with which they were confined.

Like most English radicals after them, they were anxious to claim legality for their demands; their leaders argued that serfdom was not sanctioned in Domesday book. They were no more merciful than their 'betters', but as usual among the English, they made practical and detailed demands. They tried to negotiate, and they were awe-struck by the majesty of the Crown. Revolution was already, it seems, tempered by what continental enthusiasts regard as an incurable deference. And their radical egalitarianism was bound up with religious fervour; with the visions of preaching friars who denounced the vices and luxuries of the rich laity and clergy, and who appealed to that sense of 'unfairness' which can often provoke the English into action. Here, already recognizable, are aspects of the radical movements of later times.

5

The anti-clericalism of the Peasant's Revolt was only the popular aspect of a wider hostility to the wealthier churchmen. While the structure and beliefs of the Church were still taken for granted, the lay magnates were ousting the political bishops from the Council and casting covetous eyes on their immense possessions. In a minor way this long-standing conflict now became ideological; and in Wycliffe, the prophet of the 'reformation that did not come off',* England produced its first major heretic since Pelagius and the first exponent of the Nonconformist conscience.

John Wycliffe (c. 1330–84), unlike that optimistic fifth-century Welshman, was a Yorkshireman with a neo-Augustinian conviction of original sin and of predestination. He was philosophically a conservative realist in the Thomist tradition, but his hatred of priestly power reflects the collapse of the old ideal of a Christendom harmoniously united under Pope and Emperor. He took his stand on the literal interpretation of the Bible, advocated what would have been the disestablishment of the Church into the poverty of its origins, and vindicated the national kingship against the papacy, now discredited by the Avignon captivity and the Great Schism. He was a formidable and angry scholastic. Briefly Master of Balliol, he attained great but ephemeral prestige in Oxford, but his political failure was total. An intellectual in politics, taken up by John of Gaunt in his campaign against the political bishops, he was discarded when his views became heretical, and ended his life, exiled from the university, in his parish at Lutterworth in Leicestershire. But in a spate of arid and generally repellent argument, Wycliffe had stated opinions that would prove ineradicable among the classes who would afterwards provide the independent sects in the seventeenth century, and from whom the tradition of Bunyan and the Nonconformists would derive, with all its consequences for modern radicalism.

Since the earliest times there had been relatively little heresy in England, though continental heresy had long caused the authorities concern. As, for example, long ago when some peasants of 'German race and tongue' had impugned the validity of the sacrament, and Henry II had them branded, beaten and turned out into the winter cold, where they had 'perished miserably'.[29] But during the early fourteenth century the nominalist attack on the Thomist harmony of faith and reason had

* K. B. McFarlane, *John Wycliffe and the Beginnings of English Nonconformity*, London, 1952, p. 188, q.v. for the best account: an impartial biography which succeeds, as its author intended, in freeing the subject 'from a great deal of ignorant repainting and several layers of rich brown Protestant varnish' (p. 10).

found formidable advocates among Englishmen.* Then, as already remarked, William of Ockham in Surrey (1270–1347) had formulated a deeper scepticism. He had discarded all metaphysical arguments and accepted a closer limitation of mind: 'entities', he wrote, 'ought not to be multiplied more than is necessary', thus creating his notorious 'razor' which cut out metaphysics. Though he spent most of his life abroad, he is much the most important English medieval philosopher, and his nominalist scepticism came to dominate late-medieval English philosophy. In spite of the intervening platonism of the Renaissance, it is to be found in Hobbes and it would become the prevalent English tradition.

Ockham had also been a considerable political influence on the Continent. He had championed the Empire against the papacy and became a European figure. For this 'invincible doctor', summoned to Avignon by the aged Pope John XXII and incarcerated for heresy, had escaped to Aigues Morts, and thence by sea to Pisa. Here, in 1329, he had joined the Emperor Ludwig of Bavaria, accompanied him to Munich, and supported his cause in a pamphlet *On Imperial and Pontifical Power*.† Christ, he had argued, had set limits to the papal authority. He had not told St Peter 'Fleece my sheep and make yourself garments of the wool', or 'slaughter my sheep and eat them (*Macta oves meas*)', but 'feed my sheep'. Again, he had argued, temporal lords might exercise tyrannical dominion, but Christ had told the disciples, 'It shall not be so among you (*non ita erit inter vos*).'[30] Indeed, the Avignon papacy had tried to impose a worse servitude than the Mosaic law which the Saviour had come to supersede. With cumulative quotations from St Augustine, St Ambrose and St Chrysostom, from Origen and Gratian, he had denounced the 'enormous injuries' inflicted by John XXII on the Emperor and proclaimed the Pope the worst of heretics. He wished to limit, not to abolish, the papal power; but along with the writings of Marsilio of Padua, his treatise had in fact vindicated the lay power against the Church.

It was with this background, both in philosophy and political theory, that Wycliffe, though no nominalist, now launched his attack: first on the Church establishment; then, to the horror of his political patrons, on the doctrine of transubstantiation, the authenticity of the mass, and,

* See Osborn Taylor, *The Medieval Mind, op. cit.*, vol. II, pp. 539–40, for the contribution of the 'intricate and dizzy dialectic' of Duns Scotus (*c.* 1274–1308).

† See *De Imperatorum and Pontificum Potestate* (1346–7), ed. C. K. Brampton, Oxford, 1927. Ockham also wrote a treatise in favour of the divorce of Margaret Maultasche, Duchess of Tyrol ('The Ugly Duchess'), from John of Moravia, to enable her to marry the emperor's son, Ludwig of Brandenburg, so he was well involved in high politics. The *De Imperatorum* is tedious but lucidly arranged, the angular argument making it the more effective at the time.

reverting to a belief in predestined salvation, grounded Christian belief, not on the authority of the Church, but upon the Bible.

In its essentials Wycliffe's argument against the Church was that 'dominion' could be founded only upon 'grace', and grace was predestinate. God, he maintained, had allotted particular 'fiefs' to Pope and Emperor, neither in full sovereignty, and all Christians also 'held' direct from God.[31] It followed that if a Pope or indeed, a priest, was not in a state of grace, his authority lapsed. Still reckoning the years as had Alfred, Wycliffe could argue that 'holy kyrke (itself) had bene in heresy an hundred wynter', and was convicted of stating that, if the Pope were a limb of Satan (membrum diaboli), he had no power over Christians. Nor could a priest in mortal sin give absolution. It followed – and this was the political point – that 'temporal lords according to their will could carry off the temporal possession of an habitually delinquent church'. This opinion naturally commended itself to John of Gaunt, manœuvring against the political bishops, and when in 1377 Wycliffe was summoned to St Paul's to answer for his opinions before the bishop of London, he came accompanied by the duke himself.

But Wycliffe went further. In 1379–80 he attacked the central mystery of the Eucharist. According to his accusers, whom he never refuted, he taught that, though the sacrament was God's body, it was not the same body that it was in heaven: 'For in heaven it is seven foot in form and figure of flesh and blood. But in the sacrament God's body is by miracle of God in form of bread and is neither of seven foot nor in man's figure.'* Further, he denied that Christ had instituted the mass, and declared that the sacrament profited a man only in so far as his soul was fed by charity, not through an intrinsic power mediated by the priest. Moreover, he advocated that the Scriptures should be translated into English; a policy then widely reprobated. 'And so,' said the orthodox, 'evangelical pearls were cast before the swine who trod them underfoot and what used to be dear to clergy and laymen became a joke for the common minds of both, the jewels of the clergy turned into the common games of laymen.'[32]

No wonder that John of Gaunt, still 'that wise and strenuous knight and faithful son of the Church', is said himself to have descended on Oxford and, though still willing to protect his client, 'told him not to speak of these matters any more'.[33] And when, after the Peasants' Revolt, all forms of heresy had become even more suspect, Wycliffe retired to Lutterworth, where, writing to the end – and reading him is 'not fun'[34] – he suffered a paralytic stroke and died, it is said, at the moment of the

---

* Knighton, op. cit., pp. 157–8 (English modernized). The Latin is neater. 'Quod Christus non est in sacramento altaris idemptice, vere et realiter in propria persona corporali. That Christ is not in the sacrament of the altar, identically, truly and in reality in proper bodily person.'

elevation of the host. Such was the fate of the 'morning star of the Reformation'; the forerunner, not of the Anglican compromise, but of Nonconformity.

His more sophisticated followers at Oxford were quickly silenced or dispersed. Some prudently and realistically admitted that 'the matter passed in height man's understanding'. They would believe, they promised, what mother church did, and in that belief would bear witness on the day of doom. Others, nicknamed Lollards from the Flemish *Loellaerd* – a mumbler, combined perhaps with *lollar*, Middle English for 'loafer' – were never put down; and the Wycliffite translation of the Bible, in which he probably took no part, is due to them. Indefatigably they preached to the people in the vernacular, and appealed to Christ against the authorities. William Sinderby, who had preached in Herefordshire and been summoned before the bishop, appealed, with a recognizably Anglo-Saxon idiom, to the House of Commons. 'Christ', he said, 'the Comforter of all, barks for our love against the fiend. That doughty Duke comforteth us thus: be ye strong in battle He says, and fight ye with the old adder.'[35] The people of the Welsh border took kindly to this evangelism, and it was from Almeley in Herefordshire that Sir John Oldcastle, Lord Cobham, derived. In 1414 he would attempt a disastrous *coup* against Henry v, the only dangerous attempt by the Lollards to obtain political power.

Meanwhile, more iconoclastic than their master, the more homely Lollards denounced figure sculpture ('images'), the cult of saints, the grandeur of the Church; even the universities. In 1395, for example, with what must have been political backing, they affixed a list of conclusions to the doors of St Paul's and of Westminster Hall, where parliament was in session. When, they said, the English Church began to 'go mad with riches', like its 'step-mother' in Rome, it fell into mortal sin; and the priesthood, descending through Rome, was not the same as that instituted by Christ. Further, as experience frequently demonstrated, the morals of the clergy were perverse, and the 'feigned miracle' of the sacrament led man to idolatry. Exorcism and benedictions were alike ineffective, and churchmen ought not to take on secular office. Pilgrimages, oblations and auricular confession, all ought to be abolished and the church live in holy poverty.

So while the peasantry had risen to subvert the order of society, Wycliffe had set off a radical and insular criticism of the Church, of the institution whose great foundations often came down from Anglo-Saxon times, but whose ostentation and luxury looked black to moralizing minds. So far back can be traced the pedigree of both English secular radicalism, asserting egalitarian visions of a just society, yet appealing even in revolution to the law, and of the Nonconformist conscience, with its hatred of what it considered immorality and its distrust of ostentation and the arts. In a long alliance they would do much to shape Anglo-Saxon civilization.

6

This ancient moralizing and religious habit, deep in the people, helped English, long a rustic dialect, to survive as a written language. There had always been a public for that perennial theme, *Handlying Synne* (1303).[36] Based on a French original and much expanded, this work in jog-trot verse by Robert Brunnes had warned a large public against the obvious temptations.

> *Whatever be in my thought,*

he had written,

> *Common woman take thou nought.*

And never stoke up on a Thursday night before the fast day on Friday:

> *Also fall men in plight*
> *That sit up Thursday at night.*[37]

And he had denounced '*men and women*' . . . so wild as

> *To fordo a getting of a child*'.

Deeper meditations had also kept the language flexible in more elaborate verse. By the 1370s *Piers the Plowman*, attributed to William Langland (*c.* 1332–1400), revived the alliterative beat of Anglo-Saxon, again in a moralizing tone, and by the end of the century England had produced her first poet of European stature, unsurpassed in the island till Shakespeare; for 'with Chaucer the English language and English literature grew up'.[38]

Both these writers bring their world vividly alive, Chaucer with astonishing exactness. Already, in the dawn of modern English, they express two lasting aspects of their country's mind. Langland is a minor but authentic poet, rooted in the world of St Aldhelm and of Alfred and the '*Sermon of the Wolf to the English*'. He is concerned not only to describe but to improve, preaching at the people to 'do-well, do-better and do-best'; seeing the world with a visionary eye in terms of a waking dream of a Field Full of Folk, of Holy Church and the idealized Piers Plowman; and all

> *On a May Mornyng, on Maluerne hulles.*[39]

He uses homely allegory; of mice who debate how to bell the cat, appropriate to the political tensions of the time;

mygte we with any witte
his wille wistonde
we might be lordes aloft
and lyven at owre ese,

He can also anticipate Milton in describing Lucifer,

Who fell fro' that fellowship in a fiend's liking,
Into a depe derke helle.
*To dwell there for ever.**

If Langland's English is not everyone's choice, Chaucer's appeal is more direct. He combines a novelist's and a painter's eye, hitting off both the character and the appearance of his subjects. Bilingual in London English – 'the King's English' as it would become – and in French, he had twice visited Italy, and was well versed in fashionable literature as well as in the classical writers. Born of a family long-established as wine merchants in the city of London, 'that is so dear to me and sweet, in which I was forth growen, and more kindly love have I to that place than to any other in yerth', he had become page to the Duke of Clarence and afterwards an esquire at Court; then a diploma-tist and controller of customs on wool, leather and wine. By 1386 he was a knight of the shire for Kent and he survived the eclipse of his patron John of Gaunt and the dynastic feuds under Richard II. From a versatile career he drew rich material for his poetry.

The well-known *Prologue* to the *Canterbury Tales* depicts a wonderful cross-section of English society, while his *Rime of Sir Thopas* inaugurates a tradition of spirited parody. Apart from the more famous characters, the knight, the squire, and the wife of Bath, take, for example, his shipman – brown with weather and sun – who knew all the harbours from Gotland to Finisterre and all the creeks in Brittany and Spain and how to 'reckon wel his tydes'; or the merchant in the Flemish beaver hat, who spoke so sententiously that no one knew he was in debt; or the hospitable franklin;

ful many a fat patrich hadde he in mewe
And many a breme and many a luce (pike) in stew;

or the monk who

When he rood, men mighte his bridel here
Gingling in a whistling wind . . ,

and who refused to labour with head or hands,

As Austin bit (bid),
How shall the world be served?
Let Austin have his swink to him reserved

* Spelling slightly modernized.

Chaucer is a perceptive man of the world, who takes life tolerantly and gets the most he can out of it without rancour or illusions, and who has the genius to use the language with a new subtlety and music. And behind this perceptiveness is a serene 'realist' philosophy, deriving from Plato through Boethius, whose central doctrine Chaucer can admirably translate. 'For the nature of thinges he took nat hir beginninge of thinges . . . imparfit, but it proceedeth of thinges that ben all hoole and absolut'.[40] Indeed, Chaucer's writings are so vivid and perceptive and have such range that in the late fourteenth century, 'England possessed the greatest vernacular literature in Europe'.[41]

12

THE EROSION OF KINGSHIP

The usurpation of Lancaster, though smoothly executed, had baleful consequences. Henry iv's position was always precarious; and after a brief martial flare-up under Henry v, the long reign of Henry vi ended in ruin. It was not until the Yorkist Edward iv and Henry vii of Richmond, the Tudor supplanter of Richard iii, had 'occupied' the throne, that the kingship was rehabilitated. But it was restored; not replanted as a 'new monarchy', a term invented by the historian J. R. Green in the 1870s. The breakdown had been due mainly to the chances of inheritance which had allowed the forces provoked by the usurpation their head; indeed 'the fact that the so-called "new monarchy" succeeded by employing the old methods – by wielding them that is to say, more efficiently – merely emphasizes how accidental the collapse was'.[1]

This late medieval restoration was consolidated and developed by the Tudors with no break in continuity. Following the work of Henry vii, the most methodical of his remarkable line, Henry viii would have the full momentum of ancient institutions behind him and overhaul and modernize them. Thus the medieval household bureaucracy and Council carried on and were further adapted: in spite of the so-called Wars of the Roses, the government built by Normans and Angevins on Anglo-Saxon foundations, reorganized under Edward i, and developed through the fourteenth century household as a parliamentary monarchy, would come through a phase of relatively brief breakdown and insolvency.

It had survived because by the late fourteenth and early fifteenth centuries there was already an adequate executive; the Council working through the secretariat of Signet and Privy Seal, the Chancellor, the Treasurer and the civil servants; even, on occasion, reinforced by new men from the Commons: 'More and more the small continual council acting in closest conjunction with the king had come to be the governing and originating authority in the country. . .'.[2] It dealt with a mass of petitions, and it could still be a final court of appeal against local courts terrorized by over-mighty subjects. If the Council itself was the scene of intense rivalries, and the restless magnates manœuvred beneath it with all their ramified patronage and protection, the central initiative could now only come from the king 'against a background of law, human and divine'. This permanent Conciliar administration, backed by the Crown's prerogative, over-asserted by Richard II but in part maintained *de facto* by his supplanter, would continue in principle up to the collapse of the old monarchy under Charles I.

For the current disorders were different from the feudal 'diffidations' which had confronted Henry III. Military service, once given freely as a feudal obligation, had long been paid, and service by indenture had long been prevalent. It was now mainly divorced from the land; and, if from the king downwards, the great magnates based their households on scattered estates, these were administered by professionals expert in audits and accounts, while the regional power struggles were complicated by the shifting loyalties of lesser men; often upstart soldiers of fortune who pushed their interests as part of a local magnate's following. So different were these fluctuating pressure groups from the old feudal order that the term 'bastard feudalism', coined for them in 1885, has been widely accepted. 'The fifteenth century', wrote C. H. Plummer, 'saw the beginnings of that bastard feudalism which in place of the primitive relation of a lord to his tenants, surrounded the great man with a horde of retainers who wore his livery and fought his battles';[3] men pledged to 'ride and go with the same lord and his part take . . .' 'Get you lordship' was the motto of all these men on the make, and it was lordship of a new kind.

The greatest menace to the Crown were still the huge marcher lordships, which controlled half of Wales, and the great families of the Scottish border; but the parliamentary aspect of the monarchy was now increasingly important. The Commons in particular, though they met only for infrequent sessions to vote money, take the blame, attaint the defeated and legalize dynastic crime, represented an increasingly substantial interest which made for continuity and order. It is significant that membership was no longer something to be shirked, but was now a good way of advancement. The knights of the shire had long been marrying into the nobility and the burgesses had been buying land. Indeed, the Statute of 1421 restricting the franchise to forty shilling freeholders (centuries afterwards a stumbling block to 'reform') was designed, not by the Crown, but local oligarchies anxious to keep a good thing for themselves; while the names of the members for the city of London are already 'a succinct epitome of commercial splendour'.[4] Fifty members of parliament fell in the civil wars, forty were executed and ninety were attainted, so far already had the gentry, enmeshed in the aristocratic establishment, come in sharing the privileges of their betters. Further, where continental parliaments became provincial law courts or powerless states-general seldom convened, the English parliament combined both functions; the Commons collaborated with government, avid for the spoils of office central or provincial, and expressed their grievances in the petitions already customary under Henry III. For if 'the English dislike of Rulers ensured the continued existence of Parliament',[5] these men of substance naturally looked to the throne in a world of estate jumping, exploitation of heirs and widows and general disorder; as when 'in the grey morning three men of my lord of Norfolk with long spears, carried off three good horses'[6] and with no redress; or the retainers of a magnate left their victims knifed on the heath.

Already in the fifteenth, as in the sixteenth century, the Commons could show names with a future. William Russell, shipowner and wine merchant, member for Weymouth and grandfather of the first Earl of Bedford; William Wrythe, ancestor to the Wriothesley Earls of Southhampton; a Strangways of Stinsford in Dorset, member for Bedwyn, buried at Abbotsbury and a forebear of the Earls of Ilchester; a Turberville, Constable of Corfe, and the representative John Hall, wool merchant, Mayor of Salisbury and owner of the *James* of Poole, who led the opposition to the local bishop and wrote himself Esquire. Already from Derbyshire came a Curzon of Kedleston and from Norfolk a Sir Roger Townshend of Rainham. So, in spite of the lurid events of the mid-fifteenth century, long misrepresented as an anarchy in which almost the entire nobility conveniently killed themselves off and let in a 'new' Tudor monarchy,* an able king could take or leave as much of parliament as he thought fit. He could now count on a growing interest in maintaining the king's peace; vocal indeed against taxation and foreign war, but supporting a restoration of Conciliar government and glad of a ruler who pounced on conspiracy and rebellion. At the same time, the aristocratic hierarchy remained entrenched and the prestige of lordship would outlive its disruptive power and assert itself in new ways; far from being killed off, the heirs of the old nobility would draw the successful to themselves and assimilate new men; along with the Crown, they would prove themselves formidably adaptable. Within a frame of royal government, loosely but effectively managing the countryside through the local establishment, an aristocratic hierarchy would dominate England well into the nineteenth century.

2

The ruthless political methods of Henry IV (1399–1413) have already been described. Henry of Bolyngbroke, *Dux herefordie comes derbeie et heres Johannis de Gaunt, nuper Lancastrie*, was a *rusé* and cosmopolitan character

---

* This legend was early extant, when the anonymous author of the *Italian Relation . . . of England* wrote that the nobles had 'molested the Court, their own countries and in the end themselves, for they were all beheaded' (*tutti decapitati*). See *A Relation or rather a True Account of the Island of England about the year 1500*, trans. C. A. Sneyd, Camden Society, 1847, p. 39.

who had seen far more of the world than had the cousin he displaced. He had fought in Prussia and been fêted by the Venetians and by the Visconti of Milan; he enjoyed music and patronized the arts, but he drove himself beyond the limits of a deteriorating physique and died at forty-six.* He was early menaced by widespread conspiracies, and the Welsh rose again in his reign under their last and glamorous leader, Owain Glyndwr.

There was indeed a welter of counter-revolt and regional rebellion. In 1403 the Percies of Northumberland in the northern marches, the king's main supporters in 1399, turned against him, disappointed of their rewards, and marched south through Cheshire, Richard II's country, to join the Welsh. The king defeated them at Shrewsbury, but the Welsh revolt went on. Then in 1405 the combined regional powers of Mortimer in the Welsh marches and Northumberland in the north launched an even more formidable conspiracy, backed even by the Bishop of Durham and the Archbishop of York. These regional rebellions, which exemplify the menace which the marcher and palatine lordships presented to the Crown, were not put down until 1406.

Although Richard II had been deposed without immediate violence or even financial default, and the young queen packed off to France, without her dowry but with magnificent gifts, the Crown debts to Sir Richard Whittington had been honoured, and Richard II's standard-bearer, Sir Simon de Felbrigg, had retained his estates, to live on until 1442, the senior Knight of the Garter,[7] the Lancastrian position still depended on the martial and political prowess of the king. And though the deposition of Richard II had commanded the support of the wealthy and settled areas of the country, the weakness of the Crown before the great regional lordships, exacerbated by the dynastic conflict, would be its bane until Tudor times.

In spite of these mortal dangers, the Conciliar government and household bureaucracy carried on. Henry was 'determined to uphold his own prerogative and govern through the administrators closest to himself. . . . If there was any revolution in 1399, it was not in the central organs of administration.'[8] And, fortunately for the Lancastrians, the young Prince of Wales had formidable qualities; for, as Henry V, Harry of Monmouth, knighted in Ireland by Richard II, and in command against the Welsh at thirteen, had to destroy a dangerous conspiracy of magnates on the eve of his great expedition to France.

---

* He was an astute diplomat and a patron of the Court culture. His elaborate tomb at Canterbury reveals a rather hunched, thick-set, figure with a heavy face; he is said to have repented his usurpation, but to have remarked that his sons would not *suffer the regalye to go out of our lineage*. The later Plantagenets were contemporary with Lucca della Robbia and Donatello and the early Italian Renaissance. They were very different from their Angevin forebears.

This Henry v (1413–22), 'a renowned and lucky warrior', was considered *très fort justicier* even by his enemies. With a doubtful title, he set himself with great tenacity to enforce his rights. Far from being the hearty English extrovert depicted by Shakespeare, he was a well-read Italianate prince, who chose a book of chronicles for his share of the loot of Caen, and liked music as well as hunting. Though he conspired against his father, the tales of his wild youth derive only from the garbled reminiscences of an Irish peer, the seventh Butler Earl of Ormonde. They were belatedly incorporated in a Tudor translation of the official Latin biography, written by an Italian in 1437–8 at the behest of the king's brother, Duke Humphrey of Gloucester, then the greatest patron of literature, whose books would form the nucleus of the great library at Oxford.[9] Far from rioting with 'Falstaff' the dour young prince was early preoccupied with heresy; he early *scried Lollardis and they were shent*. When a tailor called the sacrament 'inanimate' and so 'inferior to a living animal like a toad', and 'bellowed (*mugit*) miserably' amid the flames, the prince had the faggots removed and offered the gasping and blackened heretic his life and a pension if he would repent. But the 'miserable fellow' was now again himself: he refused, and died in the renewed combustion.

Henry v was both litigious and peremptory. He remarked of two northern lords, summoned to Windsor for making private war, 'By the faith I owe to God and St George, if they are not agreed . . . by the time I have eaten my oysters, they will both be hanged ere I have supped.'[10] And when the French sent him tennis balls and a carpet as a 'carpet knight' (the story is contemporary), he is said to have answered: 'If God so wills and my life lasts, I will within a few months play such a game of ball in the Frenchmen's streets that they will lose their jest.' Like Richard i, he was impervious to hardship and sea sickness; returning after the victory at Agincourt in 1415, he 'endured the rage and boistrousness of the see without accombrance . . . of his stomacke, for undoubtedly his stomacke was as good . . . uppon the see as uppon londe'. His recreations were also strenuous: at Kenilworth in 1414 he had a rowing barge sent down to the lake and 'amused his leisure time by clearing a swampy place . . . which was overgrown with briars and formed a cover for foxes'.[11]

In tragic contrast to this masterful but short-lived warrior, his son, Henry vi (1422–61) inherited the madness of his Valois grandfather, Charles vi.

> *Royal braunched, descended from two lynes*
> *Of Seynt Edward and of Seynt Lowys,*
> *Holy Seyntes, translated in their shrines*
> *In their tyme manly, prudent and wyse,*

he was none of these things. The founder of Eton and King's College, Cambridge deserves well of posterity; but, like the other royal aesthetes, Henry III, Richard II and Charles I, he was politically inept. Indeed, with his inheritance and upbringing, he never had much of a chance. Early exposed to publicity and exitement, the child one day, 'schriked and cryed and sprung and wold not be carried ferther, wherefore he was bore ageyn to his Inn' at Staines; but another day, 'blythe and glad', he 'went up on his feet from the west door' of the abbey and was 'set upon a courser and so through Chepe and London'. A Henry VIII might have thriven on this treatment: Henry VI could not take it and at critical moments he collapsed. If 'pride could make a prince like a beast', dazed inconsequence could be worse; Henry VI was despised for his poverty,

> For ye have made the Kyng so pore
> That now he beggeth dore to dore
> Alas, hit shuld not be . . . ;

and lectured for his incompetence,

> Beware Kynge Harre how thou doos . . .
> Let no longer thy traitures so loos;[12]

and urged to

> reign lyke a King Riall.

But all in vain.

The tragedy ended in 1471, with the Yorkist victory at Tewkesbury, and the murder of Henry VI in the Tower. 'I, Harry of Monmouth', his father is reputed to have said, 'shall small time reign and much get and Harry, born at Windsor, shall long reign and all lose'; the 'Duchee of Normandy, Gasgoyn and Guyen, Angoy and Mayn lost . . . our trewe lordes and knyghts, esquyers and good yomen lost and sold'.[13] Nor, in spite of the Yorkist and Tudor restoration, was the poison of these blood feuds, sustained by the 'affinities' which bound great lords and their men, worked out until all serious claimants had been executed by Henry VIII.

Why did they take such risks? The great royal magnates were enormously wealthy with incomes of anything up to three thousand pounds a year, when a lesser knight could live on sixty pounds a year and a forty shilling freeholder was a substantial man.* In their wasp-waisted elegance, padded shoulders and sweeping robes of state, their conical and turbaned hats, these glittering insects circled round a lethal light – the perennial lure of the crown. Bored perhaps without the

---

* Under Henry V wheat was 6/8d a quarter, a mallard cost 2d, a woodcock 1d, oysters 3d, salmon 7d, and, for those who could eat him, 'sea-dog' 1d.

excitement of the French wars, victims of their own touchy pride and the archaic conventions of their class, they went on with the dance until, with the full establishment of the Tudors, the climate would change and the elaborate creatures were swept away in a great bold wind from the sea.

3

The French wars of Henry v have been grossly romanticized from their harsh reality. They were great raids, following on fantastic demands for all Aquitaine, Normandy, Maine, Anjou, Touraine, Poitou and Pon-thieu. Like the expensive continental ventures of Henry viii, the wars, if acclaimed in London, were less popular in the country. When a band from Lancashire halted at Fisherton bridge at Salisbury *en route* for Southampton, there was a savage affray; the great bell of the city tolled, four townsfolk were killed, fourteen thrown into the Avon, and peace was only patched up by a 'Welsh minstrel'. Such were the feelings in Wiltshire for the Lancastrian troops celebrated by Shakespeare.[14] Expensive and unpopular Germans had to be hired for the cast-iron siege guns which, with shattering noise and black smoke, hurled stones blazing with tar and tow. The reticulated plate armour, now weighing up to ninety pounds, was so complex that arming a knight could take hours – Henry of Derby, it will be recalled, had sent all the way to Milan for armour for his combat with Norfolk, cancelled by Richard ii. The cost of war was now immense. Archers still dominated battles with their thick six-foot yew bows and their long arrows, accurate up to 250 yards in a sleet of silent death; but they, too, as Fortescue emphasizes, were 'very expensive'. About 1500 ships were assembled at Southampton in 1415 and 25,000 horses against the 'Adversary of France';[15] and besides the 2000 'lances' and 8000 archers, there was a vast supply train, with carters, victuallers, tentmakers, bowyers and cooks. No wonder that the king had to pawn most of the Crown Jewels and all the vestments of the Chapel Royal. And when, in a hot August, the English settled down to besiege Harfleur, about 2000 died of dysentery.

So the famous *chevauchée* of Agincourt was made, with a mere 900 men-at-arms and 5000 archers; a poor substitute for a great march on Paris and Bordeaux. For Henry v, who could not afford failure, risked the march to Calais as a defiance 'in the most foolhardy and reckless adventure that ever an unreasoning pietist devised'.[16]

With wagons bearing the crown and royal seals, the sword of state and a piece of the True Cross, the English marched north-east. Faced on the Somme by an enormous French array, Henry moved up-river to Nesle, where the peasants, to get rid of him, showed him a ford. Once on the other side, he made the best of his situation: 'God,' he sanctimoniously remarked, 'would not be pleased if I should turn back now, for I am wearing my *côte d'armes*.' He even encouraged the archers by telling them that the French would cut off the fingers of their right hands. Then, as usual, the wild indiscipline of the French lords, yelling '*Montjoie!*' and jostling to be in at the kill, gave the deadly English professionals their chance. Fought on 25 October, on the feast of the martyred French cobblers, St Crispin and St Crispinian, on whom some inappropriate sentiment has been lavished, Agincourt was a staggering victory. Stuck in the mud, heads down against the arrow-storm, the highest French nobility were massacred by the 'quick clever long-bowmen', who could hit an oyster shell at two hundred yards. They had the field to themselves, since the French bloods had told their own Flemish and Breton archers to get out of the way. Then, into the panting mass of French knights, the English leapt with their hatchets and 'butchered them like sheep and hammered them like anvils':[17] the king himself and his brother fought deep in the mêlée, 'Duke Umfry of Gloucester . . . sore wounded in the hammes with a swerde'.[18]

At a false alarm a host of valuable prisoners had their throats cut by the king's command, but Henry v returned to an elaborate welcome in London, feeling that God had looked after his own. And perhaps the English deserved their victory. Their discipline, when enforced, was firm; 'every man obeissant to his Captaine to keep his waache and warde . . . and all that belongeth to a souldeour to doo'.[19] Anyone that took the faith of a prisoner in surrender was to have him, and all complaints to be made to the Constable so that 'no riot ne debate be in ooste'. All loot was to be handed over to the captain, and no one was to make forays on their own, 'ne brenne (burn), upon payn of death'. And, in contrast to the French tactics that brought them to ruin in the autumn mud, 'slaine and beten and wounded by the bows of Englonde', no man must 'move him in disarray of the bataille'.

In the long sequel, Henry's grand design naturally proved impracticable. An Anglo-French realm could hardly have come about; and after Henry V's death of 'camp fever', the English ascendancy slowly waned. In 1429, the raising of the siege of Orleans was inspired by Joan of Arc.* The coronation of Charles vii at Rheims – an occasion which

---

* *Jehanne la bonne Lorraine'*, as Villon called her, '*qu' Englois brulèrent à Rouen*', died before she was twenty and achieved her main exploits at eighteen (1428–30). She had won immediate European fame, so that her captors were *moult joyeux, plus que d'avoir pris cinq cens combatans*. She was then discreetly forgotten after her apparent failure, until officially rehabilitated by the victorious French in 1456. It is doubtful if she was a mere shepherdess; she came of a substantial peasant family and was brought up to ride the farm horses, for she 'rode horses so ill-tempered that no one would dare to ride them. . . . Her whole career displays her strength, and we can hardly doubt, despite the illusions which countless painters have sought to create, that her visage was rustic.' (See Charles Wayland Lightbody, *The Judgements of Joan*, London,

the conviction of Joan as a witch and her burning at Rouen in 1431 were designed retrospectively to discredit – revived French morale and French resources began to tell. By 1435 the Anglo-Burgundian alliance, the strategic basis of the war, had broken down. With the Treaty of Arras, Charles VII came to terms with the Duke of Burgundy, and, two years later, the French king entered Paris in triumph. By 1444 a truce was patched up; confirmed in the next year by the marriage of Henry VI to Margaret of Anjou, that *femme fatale*, destined to play her part in the civil wars in England, when many of the English professionals, driven out of France, would plague their own land. By 1450 Normandy had been lost and by 1451 Bordeaux; with the loss of Gascony following the battle of Chastillon in 1453, the year of the fall of Constantinople to the Turks, the so-called Hundred Years' War petered out. Only Calais would remain to the English, commanding the Straits of Dover; a useful asset in diplomacy, if a lure to impracticable ambitions.

4

Despite the set-back caused by the Black Death, the England depicted by Chaucer had been prosperous and full of vigour, and in spite of failure in France and civil war, the fifteenth century carried on the trend; it was a great age of corporate institutions, clerical and lay, and of the build-up of considerable capital. If, following the Black Death, productivity had fallen off from the intensive farming of the late thirteenth century and many outlying villages had been abandoned, there were fewer mouths to feed. The Peasants' Revolt had not been against poverty but against archaic social disabilities. If exports of raw wool were down, the cloth industry was now much more flourishing, and though governments tried to keep them in their station, the abler peasants were making their own way.

The sequel to this change has already been observed – the presence of new men in parliament. On the vast scattered estates of king, magnates and the Church, more managers were now needed, and this pattern of great households served as a means of advancement to many able men well into the seventeenth century. Moreover, the great lords

1961, p. 93, for the best account of the evidence, and of the rise of a great popular myth, still influential). Both the trial and the rehabilitation were conducted with elaborate skill and throw much light on the medieval mind. Her male dress deeply shocked the clergy, though it was argued from St Thomas that such a garb was legitimate in cases of practical necessity. There is no evidence of popular protest at her execution: 'the news of her death was received in a kind of stunned silence succeeded by oblivion' (p. 99), save for the folk memories which gave rise to a 'false Joan'; a pretender acknowledged by her own brothers, anxious to keep the legend alive. After the rehabilitation, they made good careers; the eldest becoming Bailly of Vermandois and Captain of Chartres, and her mother was pensioned by the city of Orléans.

were expected to be lavish and to forward the likely children of their dependants. Revenues derived now more from leases and rents than directly from farming, and the endowments of the Church and the colleges at Oxford and Cambridge were more flexible. With villeins and their descendants absconding to the towns, society was taking on a more modern aspect; and as the feuds of the magnates broke up estates, lawyers of enterprising peasant stock, such as the Pastons in Norfolk, could even exploit the law in local power struggles, swift jackals to the contending lords.

In the cities the richer merchants, the *potentiores*, had now won greater control. Though no town could rival London – the only one in the island comparable to the great cities of the continent – Bristol was now the greatest port in the west; York and Coventry were flourishing, and Salisbury and Winchester had become centres for the cloth industry based on the flocks of Wessex and the Cotswolds. The early fifteenth-century merchants were now competing with the Hansa cities for the Baltic and even the Muscovite cloth markets, and 'vent of cloth' would become the main economic motive of Tudor policy and exploration. And though England remained predominantly rural, Durham coal had now long been mined and sent south from Newcastle; iron was more systematically mined in Sussex and the Forest of Dean, and the Cornish tin mines further exploited.

Amid this relative prosperity the Crown was poor; perennially in debt, yet still expected to 'live of its own'. 'Daily many warantis come in to me of paiementz,' said a spokesman of the government to parliament in 1433, 'of much more than all your revenue wold come to, [even] thowe they were not assigned afore.'[20] The customs on wool, the mainstay of Edwardian finances, had diminished, and parliaments were loathe to grant the equivalent revenue. As the Crown alienated more estates, the magnates battened on the Crown lands. It was not until Edward iv and Henry vii were strong enough to rescue the Crown lands, enforce the king's peace and pursue business-like objectives that this imbalance of power could be redressed: and the relative poverty of the Crown would still haunt the governments of Henry viii and Elizabeth i.

The failure of Henry vi's régime also provoked discontent in the City, accustomed to look to government to promote their interests. Already in 1436 the *Libelle* (booklet) *of Englysche Polycie*[21] depicts a far-flung commerce and urges government to support it – even citing the old tale of King Edgar's sea power and how he was rowed by eight kings:

> *. . . and down they did sit*
> *And each of them an oare took in hande.*

After describing the salt fish of Zeeland, the otter skins of Ireland; the figs, wine, hides and dates of Spain; the bacon, bow-strings and beer of 'Pruce', and saying that the English could do without the superfluous luxury of Italian *'apes and japes and murmusetts tayled'*, the pamphlet concludes with a famous exhortation:

> *Cheryshe Marchandyse, kepe thamyralté*
> *That we bee maysters of the narowe see.*
> *For if this see be kept in tyme of warre*
> *Who cane here pass without danger and woo?*
> *What marchandyse may for by it agoo?*
> *For iiii thygnes our noble (the coin) sheweth to me*
> *Kyng; shype; and swerde, and power of the see.*

Yet, the author complains, government does not exploit them.

> *Where bene oure shippes, where bene our swerdes become?*

This supine policy will *'make fade the flower of the English State'*; as, indeed, under Henry vi it did.

Yet, as the *Libelle* testifies, a great business interest was already growing up. There was mercantile capital from the wool and cloth trades long before Calvinist men of business supposedly set the pace. 'The ultimate future lay with capitalist employers . . . of the Industrial Revolution. But the cloth manufacturers had brought him into existence four hundred years before he swallowed industry whole.'[22] The long wars in France had also given contractors, purveyors and speculators their opportunity. As many memorials testify, there was no contradiction between late-medieval Catholic piety and wealth. And already in the City there was resentment against the more martial and lavish nobles, with their *short gownys thiftless* and their *longe peked schone*. All the warmer would be the welcome for a restoration of monarchy after the final victorious

> *Comyng of Kynge Edward (IV) and his good spede*
> *Owte of Dochelande into Englonde over the Salte sea.*[23]

5

The splendour of the English cathedrals had reached its climax by the time of Chaucer. During the fifteenth century wealth was channelled more into colleges, chantries and elaborate parish churches with superbly carved screens and roofs and glowing glass. The great political prelates were immensely rich and many were lavish in their endowments. William of Wykeham had founded Winchester and New College;

Archbishop Chichele, All Souls' College; William Waynflete, Magdalen College, Oxford; and their cathedrals were centres of elaborately organized dioceses. Lay patrons now also endowed chantries and chapels for intercession for their own and their families' salvation: their marble and alabaster effigies are still extant. The complicated filigree 'perpendicular' designs of roofs and windows attest in particular to the wealth of East Anglia, the Cotswolds and the West Country, where fortunes made from the cloth trade built churches for a larger population on the land than there is today, and which are still impressive in the detail of designs adapted to the flint of Norfolk or the Ham stone of Somerset.

In spite of the onslaught of Wycliffe and the Lollards, the supposedly decadent late medieval Church was in fact still vigorous: the parish priests, farming their own holdings and collecting their tythes, brought at least the rudiments of civilization to the people. They were literate and they could preach, while frescoes and stained glass pointed the moral and adorned the tale.

Much has been made by Protestant historians of the wealth and pride of the political prelates from Cardinal Beaufort of Winchester, half-brother to Henry IV, who took the place formerly held by foreign bankers as the financial mainstay of the Crown and did better out of it, down to Cardinal Wolsey, that last and gross embodiment of medieval arrogance; much, too, has been made of the exemplary burnings of heretics which disfigure the time. But Christian civilization was still precarious: the rulers, like those of the later Roman Empire, felt weighted with responsibility, the more so for their fear of the wrath of God. Heresy could bring divine vengeance on a whole society; once loosen the bonds of faith and undercurrents of violence and superstition would erupt. In 1450, for example, while Jack Cade's rebellion was distracting the authorities in London, the people of Edington in Wiltshire, scene of Alfred's greatest victory against the Danes, killed William Ascoyne, Bishop of Salisbury on the down above their church: 'there they slew him horribly, their father and bishop, and spoiled him to the naked skin . . . and made boast of their wickedness'.[24] And six years later the men of Portland in Dorset, not easily scared, were terrified when a horrible bird came out of the sea 'with a great crest' and legs half a yard long, and stood in the water and crewe three times . . . he was the colour of a pheasant' and vanished.

This violence and superstition, lurking beneath society, were nothing new, as the Peasants' Revolt of 1381 had demonstrated; and the Lollard movement, already described, was still widespread and now more subversive. The Wycliffite Lollards had been Bible men, who had claimed the authority of God's word: the apostles, they had said, had not been 'graduat men in scholis, but the Holi Goost sodenli enspirid em'. Indeed, they had 'all the marks of a true English sect'.[25] But as the movement sank into greater provincialism, and became ineradicable in the textile areas of the west, among the people of north Wiltshire and Berkshire as well as in East Anglia and Kent, the extremists even denied the Trinity and the divinity of Christ.[26] Among many tavern 'unbelievers', a Wiltshire brewer remarked that there was 'more good in a cask of ale than in all the words of the four Evangelists', and one Herefordshire Lollard, reverting to a pagan past, tried to worship the sun and moon. They were rationalizing a provincial resentment against the rich cosmopolitan churchmen of whom they were no longer in awe, and they appealed to just the small craftsmen and artisans who would become the core of Nonconformist radicalism.

It is not therefore surprising that the English government, hitherto relatively tolerant of what little heresy there was, enacted the terrible statute *De Heretico Comburendo* in 1401; and, indeed, the régime needed reinforcement against heresy used for political subversion, as in the dangerous conspiracy of Sir John Oldcastle. There is a certain desperation about the fifteenth century, following the breakdown of the Papacy and Empire, the emergence of national realms, the criticism of the Church, and the fear felt by the established classes of the people, following the Peasant Revolt and other disturbances. Hence the growing desire for order at almost any price, which would culminate in the cult of the Tudor Prince. Hence, too, the systematic ruthlessness of dynastic politics, the killing off of all accessible rivals, that would last into Tudor times. Like other ages of change and uncertainty, the early and mid-fifteenth century appeared a dark time to conservatives.

Among those drawn to religion some counter-attacked heresy by argument; others took refuge in mysticism. Bishop Reynold Pecock, for example, wrote *The Repressor of Overmuch Blaming of the Clergy*.* Apart from its disarming title, it has been described as 'the earliest piece of good philosophical disquisition of which our English prose can boast'. Pecock declared that heresy could only be eradicated by 'clear wit' rather than by 'fire and sword and hangment'. Like Bentham and J. S. Mill after him, this hopeful philosopher thought that the people could be influenced by 'a short compendious logic . . . devised for all the common people in their mother tongue'. So he wrestled with the East Midland dialect to prove that 'Alle Goddis creatures musten needis obie doom of resoun'. But, when in 1457, he was himself indicted for heresy, and made to assist in burning his own books at St Paul's Cross, the

---

* Ed. Churchill Babington, *Rolls*, 2 vols. 1860, p. xxx. After a distinguished academic career in Oxford and London, Pecock became Bishop of St Asaph and in 1450 Bishop of Chichester. See E. F. Jacob, 'Reynold Pecock Bishop of Chichester', *Proc. B. Acad.*, xxxviii, 1951, pp. 121–53, for a sympathetic account.

populace tried to burn him as well. At Oxford, too, his university burnt his works at Carfax, though not before he had set new standards of English exposition.

Among the mystics in the later fifteenth century, England produced Margery Kempe, the uncompromising East Anglian pietist, who tried to 'make her soul dead to all the joys of the world and quick and greedy to the contemplation of god'.* And the *Cloud of Unknowing*, its author also unknown, is still regarded as very illuminating. 'Whilst that the soule is worying in this deedly flesh,' he wrote, 'it shall evermore se and feel this combros cloude of unknowying betwix him and God.' Hence the need to 'Tread down' the world and not welter in it 'as a swine in the mire'.[27]

On the other hand, the more worldly and confident humanism of the Italian Renaissance was now coming in; spreading from the Court and the households of both secular magnates and some of the great church-men. Froissart, after all, was a contemporary of Petrarch, and Italian and Flemish artists were already creating masterpieces in the time of Joan of Arc. Jan van Eyck, for example was painting for the Burgundian Court in the twenties, and Ghiberti designing the doors of the baptistry at Florence, where the brilliant Medici court would flourish during the worst phases of English dynastic strife. And although, following endemic plague and pillage, much late medieval art and popular religious writing is obsessed with death, there was a growing cult of a new secular learning, exemplified by the libraries already collected by the royalties and magnates, and by the elaborate and vastly expensive illuminated manuscript histories and romances which they commissioned. Paper had been manufactured in Italy as early as the late thirteenth century, and by the early fifteenth there were paper mills in England. It now became the basis of the block-printing which was the precursor of the movable type invented in Germany in the 1450s.

For the well-to-do houses were already becoming more spacious as brick was increasingly replacing stone; timbered houses with spacious halls, elaborately carved screens and by Henry v's time big windows were being built for amenity, not defence. Glass was imported, mainly from Flanders and the Rhineland, and some of the most superb windows still surviving date from this bellicose time. Though the English early and mid-fifteenth century saw extreme political tension and even collapse, and much religious and social conflict, it was a time of

---

* See *The Book of Margery Kempe*, ed. S. B. Meech, E.E.T.S., 1940, vol. I, p. 253. This mystic told her husband that she would rather he were slain than that they should continue living together (p. 23). But her enemies alleged that she had not subdued all carnal appetites. 'For sittyng at the mete on a fisch-day . . . [and] served with diners of fyschys as reed heryng and good pyke and swech other . . . she sett away the red herring and ate the good pyke,' p. 253.

increasing and more widespread civilization. A mid-fifteenth century rhymer might well lament that there was no need for Englishmen to read of the falls of princes recorded by the Romans or by 'Bockes' (Boccaccio), for in their own land they had seen

> As wonder changes . . . before our eye
> As ever I trowe before thys any were.

But the amelioration of manners apparent by the time of Chaucer went on. 'The noble Edward' (III), the 'first setter of certainties among domestical men, upon a grounded rule', had long ago set the example; but Lydgate (1370–1451) author of *Troy Book* and *Falls of Princes*' still had to lament the conduct of the young:

> Loth to rise, lother to bed at eve
> With unwashen handys ready to dynner,
> Wilful, reckless mad, starting as a hare
> To follow my lust for no man would I spare.[28]

So books on deportment or 'urbanity', originating in Italy and France, were now common in England. For example, *The Boke of Nurture*, 'by me John Russell sum-tyme servannte wit Duk Umfrey of Gloucester'.[29] Boys, it says, must be presentable at table and not guzzle.

> Pare' clene thy nailes,

they are admonished,

> Thyne handes wasshe also.
> . . . Be not too hasty on brede to byte
> With full mouth speke not lest thou do offense
> Drope not thy breste with sawce ne with potage.[30]

Even in the thirteenth century it had been bad form to stroke cats and dogs at meals. The young are now warned

> Pyke not thi teethe with thy knyfe
> Ne spitte thow not over the tabylle.

> Lay not thyne elbow,

advises another work,

> nor thy fyst
> Upon the tabyll whylis thow etest.
> Byte not thy meat but carve it clean,
> When thou etest gape not to wyde.

And it is better not to 'skratch' oneself at table or 'cast thy bones unto the flore': indeed, if you refrain from these actions, people will say 'that a gentleman was here'.

A Frenchified carving ritual had long been elaborated and a complex upper-class jargon of the table was now Anglicized:

> *'Splatte that pyke,*
> *Tayme that crabbe,*
> *Barbe that lobster,*
> *Wynge that partrich,*
> *unbrace that malarde'.*

Calm deportment is recommended: young people should look their seniors in the face (*lumpischli caste not thine heed a-doun*); 'and make honest cheer with soft speech to strangers sitting at thy lord's board'.[31] Fifteenth-century aristocrats were better washed than those of the seventeenth and eighteenth centuries, for the medieval steam bath was still popular:

> *'If your sovereign will to the bathe his body to wash clean,*

runs a paper on how to conduct a 'Bathe or Stewe',

> *Hang sheets round about the roof, do thus as I mean,*
> *Every sheet full of flowers and herbs sweet and green,*
> *And look ye have sponges V or VI thereon to sit or lean.*

And, of course, always '*be sure of the door and see that he be shut*'. This precaution observed, the lord is sponged and finished off with rose water '*then let him go to bed but first set on his socks*; and be sure to draw the curtains and drive out any dogs or cats, or at least 'give them a clout'.[32]

In another important, if painful, aspect life was now slightly less grim. The Hundred Years' War had at least improved surgery. As already emphasized, *Chevauchées* were not so romantic as Froissart assumed, and both long hours in damp saddles in heavy armour and the sedentary gluttonous habits of civilian life often induced piles or even fistulas. So, in the fourteenth century, the first articulate English army surgeon had written a treatise on these ills, along with some general prescriptions and advice.* His surgical instruments had been crude, but some patients had recovered, for he had dressed their wounds with rose water, not caustics; 'unexpert men', he writes, 'be well ware for the use of arsenic sublimed'. He had used nettle juice to stop bleeding, but had pointed out that bleeding 'emeroids' at least prevent mania, leprosy and hydrophobia, for they get rid of 'melancholicius blode'. Ardernes had appealed to patients to be docile: 'if ye be unobedient and unpatient . . . you may fall into grete perill'; and he advised 'surgeons of the long robe' to keep calm and have a stock of comfortable sayings and merry tales to make

---

* John Ardernes, *Treatises on Surgery* (1349–70), ed. D'arcy Power, 1910. Ardernes was born near Newark in 1307, educated at Montpéllier, and probably served in the household of John of Gaunt.

the patients laugh. It is best of course, too, not to drink or kiss the ladies in great men's houses; one should get on well with the servants, and not breathe garlic and onions over a patient's wounds. Sleep is very important, for then 'nature worketh better about digestion'.* And fees should be charged according to social status: one must not expect much from the poor, but the better off will often give you presents of 'fishes and ducks'; and really high officials should be cured as rapidly as possible as they are notoriously lax at settling their bills. Magnates, of course, should be charged very high fees, for, while the patient comes first, the fee is 'not unimportant'. And it is best to dress soberly; not like a 'minstrel' but more like a clergyman. This sensible advice is backed by much shrewd observation of an empirical kind.

For those who had no need of a doctor, there was now a greater range of sports, though the government tried to discourage them as they took men's minds off archery. Besides the elaborate upper-class cult of stylized jousting and riding at the ring, and the universally popular legitimate and illegitimate pursuit of the chase, golf, which originated in Flanders, had been taken up by the Scots. James IV would play the royal and ancient game, and put down the cost of clubs and balls to the public expense. Pall mall, a kind of croquet, was now becoming popular; and tennis, originally a royal game with elaborate courts and technique, was now played in vulgarized form in the streets, if suitable surroundings were available. One of the constant concerns of government into Tudor times would be to prevent such games from taking the place of archery. Already a recognizable kind of football and hockey were emerging out of the rough and tumble games of medieval times, though 'perhaps the most satisfying pastime was carousing'.[33]

6

Though suffering a phase of political decline, early and mid-fifteenth century England was full of vigour: 'the outstanding merit of the fifteenth-century constitution was that it did not die'.[34] Conciliar government survived, and the landed and civic establishment, already apparent by the time of Edward I, and strong enough under Richard II to oust the monarch himself when he attacked the law and property, had been consolidated with new wealth and ramified alliances. Though the overall power of parliaments had now diminished, the standing of the Commons had increased; and if the surface of society was often disturbed, lawlessness rampant in the countryside, and the great lords of the northern and western marches still dangerous, there was never

* Pillules for to provoke slepe. Recipe *amides zi croci*. 'Make them with water of roses, . . . and he that taketh them schal slepe for certain', *op. cit.*, p. 101.

anarchy. The prosperity and population of the high Middle Ages would not be regained until late Tudor times, but the country had apparently recovered from the consequences of the Black Death, and the volume of internal and external trade had increased. The richer classes, clerical and lay, remained prosperous, and if the Lollard undercurrent of resistance and insularity continued to run, the social influence of the cosmopolitan church remained powerful; showing itself directly in the foundation of rich and splendid colleges, and indirectly when laymen lavished their wealth on elaborate parish churches and stained glass, or founded grammar schools to train laymen for business and administration.

English was now the official language of politics and parliament, and even in the lower ranks of society surnames were coming in. They had been, at first, mainly place names, for the landed classes took theirs from their estates; but now they were often names of occupation: as Salter, Shepherd, Brewer or Tanner, or patronymic Christian names, as Tom*son* or Jenkin*son*. Common nicknames, as Fox or Coney, did not so often stick. We are now beginning to get closer to some understanding of these people; and familiar Elizabethan and Jacobean characters are already seen to be rooted in this chequered, sanguinary, but creative and many-sided time.

PART THREE

EARLY MODERN
ENGLAND

13

THE REVIVAL OF ROYAL GOVERNMENT

In the dynastic vendetta long afterwards termed by Sir Walter Scott the Wars of the Roses, the Lancastrian usurpation worked itself out. Edward IV (1461–83), Earl of March and Duke of York, inherited the claims of Lionel of Clarence and Edmund of Langley, sons of Edward III; at nineteen he was already a capable and lucky soldier. He also had method and foresight: a Renaissance magnifico rather than a chivalrous predator, and he managed to bring the ship of state – 'that noble ship made of good tree' – back to a safer course, which his death at forty did not seriously deflect. After the Yorkist house had committed suicide through the ambition of Richard III (1483–85), the Tudor outsider – 'Henry Tydder', as Richard III called him, 'an unknown Welshman whose father I never knew nor him personally saw' – could take over the realm; and having resumed the huge Lancastrian and Yorkist estates to the Crown, gradually consolidate a restored monarchy, still based upon the old Conciliar government, but now solvent and better organized. For what the conventional division is worth, the England of Henry VI is more medieval than modern; but the England of Edward IV and Henry VII more modern than medieval. As already emphasized, there was no revolutionary 'new monarchy'; the very concept is a nineteenth-century term; rather we find what any medievalist would expect, a restoration and adaptation of old ways, with the existing establishment now broadened and more alert to new chances.

Henry VII (1485–1509), whose tight mouth and wary eyes are depicted in a fine portrait, and whose high competence is caught in Torregiano's superb sculpture, was not only a warrior but a methodical man of business. He was fairly tall, says a contemporary, with small blue eyes and a few black-stained teeth. Experienced in penury and exile, he understood money and he laboriously annotated accounts; but Francis Bacon's famous biography over-estimates his avarice. He was as much a Renaissance figure as his flamboyant son. He extended the Crown's monopoly of force to secure the king's peace, and he used calculated splendour, money, and far-ranging diplomacy to put his dynasty on the European map. He was a patron of letters and the arts, and the Renaissance scholars who are associated with the court of Henry VIII had already been attracted by Henry VII. He died with about two years' revenue in plate, jewels and coin in hand: but, contrary to long-received opinion, he had spent too heavily to leave much capital. Nor did the restored monarchy put down the nobles and exalt a 'rising bourgeoisie': the bureaucracy was too rudimentary and the magnates too strong. Henry VII still mainly depended on provincial magnates and gentry, who would bring up 'tall men with lances' in emergency at the king's command and call out the local militia. The professionals of the French wars had now been killed off, emigrated or faded away; and, though the king had a new personal guard in the green and white Tudor colours and the only artillery train in the country, he had no standing army. Using the new facilities of print, he appealed to what there then was of educated and responsible opinion, and exploited not only the central Conciliar government but the Council of the North – formally established by Richard III – and the Council of the Marches of Wales. He developed the restored Yorkist monarchy into the more powerful government of the Tudors, which under Henry VIII would exalt the Crown and change the basis of religious sovereignty; when the monarch, still orthodox in his own eyes, became his own Pope in the independent 'empire' of his realm; an achievement no medieval king could have compassed.

2

Edward IV looks a chilling blend of charm, cunning and sensuality. Like his grandson Henry VIII, who took after him, he was *faux bonhomme* and would 'lay a kindly hand on people's shoulders'; he was apparently a great gourmandizer, and he, too, would pass on his mistresses to deserving courtiers. He married Elizabeth Woodville, the widow of a mere county knight, and thereby 'affronted' his royal relatives and their faction. Even Edward, himself born out of England at Rouen, was falsely alleged to be the son of an archer; and his brother-in-law, Charles the Bold of Burgundy, once in rage called him 'Blayborgne' after his supposed father.[1] But along with a streak of self-indulgence, went outstanding military and political flair; as already emphasized, Edward's restoration of the monarchy proved decisive, a substantial achievement on which the Tudor take-over was based.

The civil wars out of which this early modern restoration emerged had been waged between rival claimants in the power vacuum created by the incompetence of Henry VI. They had been fought out intermittently in three bouts, mainly in the east Midlands and Yorkshire, with less devastation than the wars of Stephen or Edward II; and London had never been fought over. They are thus important only as a background to the re-ordering of the realm. Indeed 'the highly theatrical, twopence-coloured conflation of picturesque fables, bloody battles, proscriptions and attainders, quick reversals of fortune, desperate flights and sudden victories is a deceptive guide to the state of the country . . . Most probably England was no more war-ridden in the fifteenth century than in earlier centuries,' and 'these almost miniature campaigns bear no comparison with the scale of warfare in the rest of Europe'.[2]

The first bout opened in 1459, when Henry VI had become insane and the Duke of York – with the most extensive estates in England to support his interest – had taken over the government, and defeated the Beaufort Duke of Somerset at the first battle of St Albans in the following year. But ousted by the intrigues of the warlike queen Margaret of Anjou, York had then retired to Ireland, whence, in alliance with his brother-in-law, the Neville Earl of Warwick who commanded great estates in the north, he had regained power; only to be killed at Wakefield by the Lancastrians, and his head, decorated with a straw and paper crown, stuck over the gates of York. It had been in revenge for this outrage that in 1461 his son Edward, backed by his uncle Warwick, had defeated the Lancastrians at Towton, south-west of York, and occupied London.

It was thus in alliance with the Nevilles that Edward IV had first established his power; and the wars had flared up in a second bout in 1470, when his overmighty collaborator and uncle, Warwick, evicted him to the low countries and briefly restored Henry VI. This second phase of civil war ended in 1471 with the return of Edward IV to the Humber, the slaughter of Warwick at Barnet, the murder of Henry VI in the Tower, and the final defeat of queen Margaret, with the Lancastrian heir, Prince Edward, 'slaine in the felde of Gastum beside Tewkesbury'. Finally, in 1485, in the third and last bout of the civil wars, Henry Tudor, the only Lancastrian claimant left, defeated the usurping Yorkist Richard III at Bosworth Field. Such, in broad outline are the main political facts and they are lurid; but, as Lander observes, 'as the evidence accumulates of former centuries, it beggars credulity to think of any massive deterioration of public order in the fifteenth century'.[3]

Edward IV's victory in the first two bouts of conflict had enabled him to confiscate the Lancaster and Neville estates, and apply the new techniques of estate management employed in his own now huge inheritance to the dilapidated fortunes of the Crown. His household officials thus still dealt with local as well as London business, and his administrators so grouped the counties that they bypassed the now antiquated Exchequer, 'a notable step forward in the efficiency of the central government'.[4] The credit of the Crown, in part secured on

Church revenues, was at last good enough for the king to borrow heavily from Medici bankers. He even employed a converted Portuguese Jew who had made a fortune in 'grains of paradise' for spicing wine, had taken the name of Brampton, and landed and knighted, became Governor of the Channel Islands. At this level, the anti-semitic prejudices of Edward I were already becoming antiquated.

Edward IV thus became very rich as, writes the contemporary Sir John Fortescue, 'a Kynge ought to be', for 'euery raume is bounde to susteyne is Kynge'; and his Council now studied 'how the lawes may be amendet in such thynges as they neden reformation in'.[5] Nor did the feuds between the queen's relatives and the royal kin, in which the king's own brother Clarence perished in 1478, probably drowned in the celebrated butt of malmsey wine for raising rebellion and 'compassing the king's death by spells',* shake the régime. So, when in the English spring of 1483 the king allowed a damp cold to strike his vitals, 'when . . . taken in a small boat . . . to go fishing,' he had 'watched their sport too eagerly', or else had succumbed *'en buvant du bon vin du creu de Challueau duquel il but en si grande habundance qu'il en mourut'*,† he died in an unmedieval solvency.

The Yorkists then destroyed themselves. The king's brother, Richard of Gloucester, soon ousted his nephew, Edward V, and 'occupied' the throne, as Richard III. He then appealed to 'legitimate right and public acclaim' for his 'sure and true title'; this claim, he alleged, 'harmonized with the good law, reason, concord and assent of the lords and commons of the realm . . . whereupon the king's good highness, notably assisted by well-nigh all the lords . . . went and took possession'.[6] Though he was depicted by Sir Thomas More as the classic wicked uncle in the first readable royal biography in English,[7] Richard III's reputation has since been heavily whitewashed. He was clearly an able soldier, popular in his own northern estates, a good administrator and a pillar of his brother's régime; but it cannot be denied that he used the 'ignobility' of his nephews' Woodville descent to bastardize them. And once bastardized, they had obviously to go: by October 1483 Edward V and the

* 'Mise et bouté tout vif dedens une queue de Malevoisye defensée par l'un des boutz, la teste en bas: (bottled alive head down in a barrel of Malmesey wine with one end removed).' Armstrong, (ed), De Occupatione Regni Angliae, op. cit., p. 135. Mancini writes in translation, 'The mode of execution preferred in this case was that he should die by being plunged into a jar of sweet wine' (p. 77), and Armstrong considers 'There seems little reason to doubt that he was put to death in a barrel of wine' (p. 134). Jacob, on the other hand, following a French Chronicle, thinks he was probably drowned in a bath, *'en ung baine, comme l'on distoit'*, The Fifteenth Century, op. cit., p. 581. Perhaps the venerable story, unlike the Druids of Stonehenge or King Alfred's cakes, may be preserved. He was fished out, from either barrel or bath, and buried at Tewksbury.

† Armstrong, (ed) De Occupatione Regni Anglie, by Dominic Mancini, op. cit., p. 73, 'from drinking the good wine of Challueau of which he drank so heavily that he died of it'.

Duke of York had vanished, 'last seen shooting and playing in the garden of the Tower, then appearing less and less until at length they ceased to appear altogether'.[8] They disappeared, there is no doubt, when their uncle was king, and he 'never took effective steps to counteract the rumours that they had been disposed of'.[9] More, who described the usurper as the traditional Shakespearian fiend in human shape, 'little of stature, ill-fetured of limmes, croke backed, hard favored of visage', declares that they were 'smothered'. 'Certayn it is,' he declares, 'that hee contrived theyr destruccion with the usurpation of the regal dignitee uppon himself'.* And Sir Thomas More, for all his political pro-Tudor bias, wrote not without evidence; even Richard's most thorough and admiring biographer writes that it is 'very possible that King Richard was guilty of the crime'.[10] Further, the contemporary rumour already ran that he had 'put to deth the ij childer of kyng Edward, for which cawse he lost the hertes of the people';[11] and if it was sheer misfortune that his own ambitions were thwarted by the death of his wife and son, Buckingham, his main supporter, turned against him and had to be executed. So when, in August 1485, in a second attempt, Henry Tudor of Richmond landed at Milford Haven in south Wales with his dubious claim through the Beauforts, the arbiter was again the sword.

Unlike the Yorkist *occupatio*, the Tudor take-over was to endure. When the body of the last Yorkist king, who 'might (as the fame went) a saued hymself if he would a fled awae',[12] was slung over a horse and carried naked from Bosworth Field, and the crown of ornament, salvaged from the battlefield, placed on Henry of Richmond's head, the event would not prove just one more turn in a dynastic game: it would give England a strong monarchy and a brief Welsh dynasty of royal rulers, three of them abler than any before or since.

3

Henry VII was descended from Welsh adventurers whose banner was a dun cow on a tartan field – hence the joke, when Henry VIII married Anne Boleyn, that 'cow doth ride bull'. One Meredith ap Theodore, steward to the Bishop of Bangor, had a son Owain, who had fled out of Wales for murder and fetched up as Clerk of the Wardrobe to Catherine of France, queen dowager of Henry V. He had soon secretly married her; fought for the Lancastrians, and had been executed by the Yorkists. But their sons, Edmund and Jasper, had been made Earl of Richmond and Earl of Pembroke by their half-brother, Henry VI; always 'my uncle' to

---

* For the surely conclusive evidence of the remains of two children, discovered in the Tower in the reign of Charles II and examined in 1933, see Lawrence E. Tanner and Prof. W. Wright. *Recent Investigations regarding the fate of the Princes in the Tower. Archaeologia, LXXXIV.*

the Tudor king. And Edmund had married Margaret Beaufort, through whom their son, Henry of Richmond, had inherited the shadowy Beaufort claim through descent from John of Gaunt. Though they boasted descent from Welsh princes, the Tudors were undisputedly royal only through their Valois blood.

But, like Edward IV, Henry had ability and luck. As Feiling puts it, 'his reign began in treason and a lucky skirmish'; but he would last, 'saved by events in Europe' and a queer power at once to rule and conciliate, for 'a blend of kindliness and contempt enabled him to conjure enmities away'.[13] The power game on the continent had indeed taken a new turn. The French had invaded Italy and renewed and extended the long contest with the vast Habsburg power, now, through fortunate marriages, threatening France through its control of the Low Countries and Spain. The French were thus opportunely diverted from revenge for the English invasions, and the nuisance value the English possessed through their command of the Channel could be exploited in a new way. The two great adversaries could be played off against one another, with a predominant bias towards Spain; and in this policy Henry VII succeeded. Henry VIII, on the other hand, in a less favourable situation, would take greater risks, culminating in 1545 in the most serious threat of French invasion since 1066, and waste vast amounts of treasure in wars in France.

Having consolidated his position at home by his marriage to Elizabeth of York, the heiress to the Yorkist claims, Henry VII quickly embarked on his ambitious and expensive policies abroad. In 1489 they achieved the trade Treaty of Medina del Campo, and they culminated in the grand dynastic match of his son Arthur to Catherine of Aragon, daughter of Ferdinand and Isabella who had rounded off the Spanish *Reconquista* by the final expulsion of the Moors. This alliance with Spain would long be the key to Tudor policy, leading to the marriage of Mary I to Philip II, until the accession of Elizabeth I disrupted the understanding. Later it would even be ineffectively revived by James I. Further, by marrying his daughter Margaret to James IV, king of Scots, Henry VII tried to counter the old Scots-French alliance; it was from that marriage the Stuart kings of England would descend. The dynastic background of the Tudors was thus grander and more far-flung than that of Edward IV, and set the stage for decisive political and economic developments.

Meanwhile Henry VII at once struck a firm note. Only two days after Bosworth Field he proclaimed the king's peace; commanding his subjects 'to pick no quarrels for old or new matters, but keep the peace upon pain of hanging'.[14] In the new age of print, he was reinforcing the ancient Conciliar executive, still manned in the medieval way by great magnates, great bishops and a few 'new men'; and meeting anywhere in the king's presence or, more regularly, in the old Star Chamber, so-called from the thirteenth-century decoration of its ceiling. These proclamations, made, nominally with the advice of Council, by the king as the 'source of law', were a formidable new series of 'public commands' made 'on the grounds of the common good' and 'psychologically gauged to elicit from the subject an obedient response'.[15] They became a powerful weapon of Tudor government, made by writ and transmitted under the Great Seal by the sheriffs throughout the land; a new expression of sovereign power, re-enforcing the ancient king's peace. Henry VII was careful to appear a saviour of society; stressing his 'tender zeal for the wealth, security and defence of his subjects', so that they could live 'in surety of their bodies according to his laws'.[16] Henry VIII's proclamations would become more ferocious: behind the cumulative elaboration of Tudor English there would be a heavier menace.

So 'entirely desiring amongst all earthly things the prosperity and restfulness of his land', the new king, who had been careful to obtain the recognition of the Pope, asserted the Crown's monopoly of force and his many-sided concern for good government. He forbade the employment of retainers with liveries, tokens, cognizances and badges, and enforced statutes against murder, decay of husbandry, beggars and unlawful games. Two years after Bosworth, he forbade his subjects to carry 'bows, arrows, swords and weapons of invasion', save when they should 'journey or ride', and empowered mayors, constables and bailiffs to seek out and confiscate illicit arms. Men were to make 'no manner of affray within host or without'; refrain from robbing churches or the ravishing of nuns, and from taking 'horse meat' (provender) without payment. It is significant that even rumour-mongers were to be pilloried. And the king straitly commanded all the local Justices of the Peace and coroners to enforce the law.

He also began the Tudor attack on a new problem. Since the Peasants' Revolt governments had been trying to maintain the old social order against an incomprehensible economic change, devising laws against extravagance in food and dress, restricting nascent capitalist enterprise. Both Tudors and early Stuarts would still long pursue this negative policy; indeed it would not be until the breakdown of the old monarchy that economic enterprise would be extensively let loose. In this field Henry VII set the tone: merchants were forbidden to export bullion or other treasure out of the realm, and the public told to accept clipped coins at their face value: enterprising sheep farmers were forbidden to add field to field, and even the statutes of Richard II were invoked against the unemployed. As far as the government could arrange it, the populace were to stay put. Vagabonds were set in the stocks on bread and water for three days and nights, then expelled from the towns; if unable to work, 'sent back to their own hundreds'. Even 'vagabond' scholars had to produce a letter from the Chancellor of their university and soldiers one from their captain.* This attempt to hold back forces making for higher productivity may appear misguided to modern minds; but it also reflects the concern for social justice which would give rise to the Elizabethan Poor Law; a system primitive enough, but in providing remedies for the worst distress, to be unique in Europe at the time. In spite of mounting inflation, the idea of the 'just price' died hard. Young Edward vi, trying to devalue his coinage in the hope that prices would fall as 'by natural reason and equity they necessarily ought and should', would still be shocked when they rose; but, after all, the policy of governments often runs contrary to the economic tide.

Thus Henry vii's reinforced Conciliar régime faced domestic, political, social and economic problems according to its lights; taking local corruption, disorder and major rebellion in its stride, and abroad making far-ranging decisions in diplomacy and dynastic alliances on a new scale.

Against this background, the Yorkist conspiracies, based on the relatively lawless north and west, were briskly put down. In 1487 Lambert Simnel, the son of an Oxford tradesman and coached for his part by an enterprising friar, had a run for his money as a pretender in Ireland; but the German mercenaries supplied by the implacable Margaret of York, Dowager of Burgundy, were defeated, and the boy assigned to the king's kitchen, later to be promoted to the more healthy occupation of minding the king's hawks. Then, from 1491 to 1499 Perkin Warbeck, a handsome Fleming from Tournai, had a longer run but a worse end.† Acting in league with the Burgundians and the Empire, he landed in Kent; then returned to Ireland and Scotland, where he married Lady Catherine Gordon. Then, in league with the Cornish who were enraged by the king's taxes, he landed in the west. But he failed to take Exeter, fled to Beaulieu Abbey near Southampton, and was imprisoned in the Tower. Only when he was probably trapped into trying to escape, did he come to the rope. Neither of these pretenders proved important; but their escapades indicate a dormant lawlessness, the legacy of endemic war at home and abroad. The Wars of the

* Under Henry viii a vagabond who had been flogged would be given a certificate. 'A.B., taken at C. in the county of D . . . without token of scourging and therefore whipped at C. aforesaid . . . in the presence of P. C. Constable.' *Tudor Royal Proclamations 1485–1553, op. cit.*, p. 193.

† Born in humble circumstances at Tournai, he had early travelled to Antwerp, Middleburgh and Portugal, then fetched up in Cork in the employ of a Breton merchant; 'And when we were there arrived' he declared in his confession '. . . they of the town, because I was arrayed in some cloths of silk of my master's, came upon me and threped (imposed) upon me that I should be the Duke of Clarence's son.' See Kingsford, *op. cit.*, pp. 219–21.

Roses and conditions that had produced them did not come magically to an end at Bosworth Field in 1485. The new order remained precarious, by no means necessarily final. Its consolidation required the untiring efforts of Henry VII throughout his reign, and that Henry VIII should kill off all the potential claimants that he could. Indeed, the final establishment of domestic peace and harmony took a century of intermittent plots, risings and revolts, and stands as the great achievement of the Tudor dynasty.

Henry VII even knew how to turn such conspiracies to his advantage, pardoning the rebels but exacting heavy fines; and his success in mastering a notoriously turbulent island increased his prestige abroad. After the death of the queen, he tried in succession to marry Margaret, the Habsburg Regent of the Netherlands, and even Juana, the insane heiress of Castile, widow of the Habsburg Philip the Fair and mother of Charles of Ghent, afterwards the emperor Charles v. None of these projects succeeded; but on the death of the heir, Arthur, Prince of Wales, his wife, Catherine of Aragon, was transferred after some vicissitudes to his next son, Henry, and the Spanish alliance thereby confirmed.

Nor was Henry VII blind to the new prospects of oceanic discovery and Levantine trade. The naval weakness which he inherited and which had enabled the pretenders to land, was remedied in the latter part of his reign, for he built the nucleus of the regular navy developed by Henry VIII. His new ships, the *Regent* and the *Sovereign*, were warships, not converted merchantmen, and by threatening the communications of Spain with the Low Countries he could exact a new consideration from allies and enemies alike. By the end of his reign the foundations of a fighting navy had been laid. Thus at a time when the economic and colonizing prospects of Western Europe were being transformed, following the Portuguese contact with the East and Columbus's epoch-making voyages, the English were adapting themselves to oceanic opportunities that would dwarf all their previous enterprise. They would come late to this exploitation, far behind the Portuguese and Spaniards, the Dutch and the French; but eventually their oceanic trade and colonial empire would surpass all the others. Even now, English merchants were well established at Seville, and the alliance with Spain was destined to open opportunities unforeseen in the Treaty of Medina del Campo, if developing from it. For the earlier Tudor adventurers worked not against but, if they could, in collaboration with the Spanish authorities; and it was not until religious warfare and piracy had embittered relations, that their traditional enemies gradually became the Spaniards rather than the French.

4

The relative prosperity of England, based upon a self-sufficient if still 'colonial' economy with large outlying areas undeveloped, and upon the massive export of cloth made from cheap wool of high quality, was enough, by the time of Edward IV, to support a sumptuous royal court, as well as the lavish households of the great magnates and the civic pomp of London.

As might be expected, the entourage of Edward IV had been well-ordered and well found.[17] The king himself fared sumptuously. He was assigned as much as half a gallon of ale for breakfast, and two for dinner and supper, along with 'sufficient wine' and eight loaves. He also had half a gallon of wine by his bedside at night. A baron at court made do with two gallons of ale a day, and a page with half a gallon, though the senior physician got three, while the master surgeon ranked with a knight, with a quart of wine and a gallon of ale daily. Water being regarded a dangerous drink, and coffee and tea unknown, the amount of these assignments can be understood. Meanwhile, his doctor advised the king on diet, evidently not very well, and devised menus suited for the time of the year. The barber for the 'King's most high and dread person' was well paid, but a knight or esquire of the body had to be present when he shaved the king in case he cut his throat. Already the whole entourage was enormous and entertainment incessant: forty squires of the household attended the king in relays 'to keep him company after their cunning in talking . . . or in piping, harping and singing'. Minstrels would blow or pipe at meals, but were forbidden to be familiar with visitors or 'take rewards from lords'.[18] Six royal 'hench-men' or pages of honour were also expected to sing, pipe and dance, and they learned to ride 'cleanly and surely' as well as 'civil courtesy and languages'. They were assisted by pages of the wardrobe, 'clean limbed, personable and virtuously disposed'; and the wardrobe had a cart or wagon with six horses which could also carry such books as the king wished to read.

At his public appearances sergeants-at-arms – 'proud men of conduct and honour' – now kept the press of the people from the king: they were the forerunners of the Tudor yeomen of the guard, 'straight persons, cleanly and strong archers'. Swearing and drunkenness were discouraged: indeed anyone swearing by God's body or any of His other parts was deprived of wine, and a cellarer 'comyn dayly drunkyn', deprived of his keys. 'The Butler of Ynglond Capitall', who had forty pounds a year, had to visit the yeomen of ale 'suddenly' to see there was no 'riot'. There is now much stress on clean linen, and an elaborate office of spicery and fruit. The 'childer clere voysed' of the royal chapel were assigned to the royal colleges at Oxford and Cambridge when they grew up.

Such a household is a world away from the primitive arrangements of the Angevins. It symbolizes the development of a far more sophisticated and urban society; and its complex royal hierarchy, based upon the court of Edward III but now elaborated after the sumptuous Burgundian fashion, was imitated by the great magnates. This competitive ostentation set standards for lesser households and brought a horde of servants at least out of the routine of peasant toil. Indeed, 'urbanity', so much aspired to in the earlier fifteenth century, would become a cult. This amelioration of manners, if not of morals, would culminate in the elaborate Italianate courtesies of Elizabethan times.

Meanwhile, about 1500, England and its inhabitants were observed by an acute Italian eye. The country, says the Venetian diplomat who wrote the *Italian Relation of England*, was rich, but its potential far greater.[19] 'Agriculture is not practised', he points out, 'beyond what is required for the consumption of the people'; if they were to plough and sow all the good land, they could export grain. But this negligence was atoned for by the 'immense profusion of every comestible animal': apart from the vast flocks of sheep, there were many massive oxen 'with much longer horns than ours', and a huge head of game – deer, hares, partridges and pheasants. The tame swans on the Thames were a fine spectacle – *bella cosa vedere 1000 et 2000 cigni mansueti e domestici nel fiume Tamisa.*

Though to an Italian, accustomed to the swarming populace and intensive cultivation of the Lombard-Venetian plain, the country appeared sparsely inhabited, it was a land of pleasant undulating hills, lush valleys and broad meadows, supporting a people who are 'great lovers of themselves and who think there is no other world than England'.[20] They were, of course, suspicious of foreigners; and if they admired anyone said, 'he looks like an Englishman'. But, after a few drinks, they would accept a stranger, being greatly addicted to ale which they often preferred to wine; and the language, though derived from the German, had lost its original harshness. They would stand you a meal, but not lend you money for, in spite of their geniality, they were very close. Indeed, the Venetian was the first-known author to ask the perennial question 'the English, are they human?' He thought that sometimes they were not, having never noticed any of them to be really in love in the exuberant Italian manner; also they kept a glum silence at official feasts. They also sent their children away to better themselves in noble households at a sadly tender age, or bound them as apprentices on hard terms. Family life was thus sacrificed in the race to get on through patronage, for the English were already intensely class-conscious and concerned with advancement. They were, of course, outwardly pious; this was natural, for the country was dominated not only by the showy households of the nobility, but by the even vaster estates of the Church. Indeed, the rich monasteries were like baronial palaces and the treasures of the Church beyond belief.

So already, by the end of the fifteenth century, salient and permanent English characteristics had become apparent; but the English were now contending with economic forces which had long nonplussed the government. Naturally, as already observed, no vision of the economic potential of the country had crossed the official mind. Government was still restrictive, concerned with 'How the money gooeth out of the realm? How to get it in again?' If you 'set your money at double the value that it gooeth', foreigners will buy it and hot money will come in; and 'keep the woll and Fell in the realm', so that we can make our own cloth and compel the foreigners to buy it. Turn out the Lombards and the Easterlings. Prohibit the export of grain. Fix prices. Keep up quality, rather than expand production. That was the tradition, and it would continue. But in one important aspect government was more constructive. Henry VII, like Edward IV, tried to stimulate prospecting and mining; 'considering that the mines within the realm, gold, silver, tin, lead and other metals for lack of diligent labour be left unsought and unwrought', he ordered a staple of metals to be established at Southampton.

So, despite the dynastic wars, which in fact occupied a restricted area and lasted for a relatively short time, there emerged a more modern England; still predominantly rustic and technologically conservative; with little thought of increasing productivity, but being pushed by economic changes towards a more enterprising and profitable economy. In ruling circles the old idea of martial glory and plunder were giving way to a greater concern with practical affairs.

5

With this relative prosperity, the later fifteenth and early sixteenth centuries saw a great flowering of architecture, of which St George's Chapel at Windsor, Henry VII's Chapel at Westminster and the complete King's College Chapel at Cambridge, begun in 1446 and only finished on the orders of Henry VII and his son by 1516, are the most famous examples. There was still a wealth of timber, and wood carving became even more elaborate, as witness the magnificent roofs and rood-screens of East Anglia and Somerset, which mainly reflect the prosperity derived from the cloth trade.

But the most original and momentous change to come about was the introduction of printing from Germany and the Low Countries. William Caxton (1422–91) was a successful merchant, whose affairs had taken him to Bruges and Cologne; under the patronage of Edward IV, he brought in and set up the first printing press at Westminster (1475). And he was not only a printer; he was also a translator. 'I sitting in my study,' he wrote (and I have modernized his spelling), 'where, as lay many diverse pamphlets and books, happened that to my hand came a little book in French, which later was translated out of Latin by some noble Clerk of France, which book is named *Eneydos* made in Latin by that noble poet and great clerk Virgil'. He determined that his translation should be intelligible, and 'reduced' it into 'our' English – that is the 'London' English which since Chaucer's time had come to supersede the various dialects as a common literary form – 'in such terms as shall be understanden'. This London or court English would become the language of Shakespeare and the Jacobean Bible. Caxton's anthology of the *Dictes and Sayings of the Philosophers* (1477) was the first book to be printed in England, and the new medium, as already remarked, had important political results in the printed proclamations of the first Tudor. But romances and theology most interested the public. In 1485 Caxton printed the *Morte Arthur* by Sir Thomas Malory, 'who appears to have been a mid-fifteenth century knight of lawless behaviour who wrote his stories in prison':[21] he had condensed a whole range of legendary tales popularized by Geoffrey of Monmouth and elaborated in France, stressing chivalry and prowess more than mystic sentiment, following the cult of feudal honour and pageantry, still fashionable when political feudalism had long been undermined.

In more serious vein, print gave a new scope to humanist writing for a lay public. Erasmus won a European fame, anticipating the kind of influence of Voltaire. But the humanists aimed at reforming the old Catholic order, not at abolishing it, and the Erasmian moderates, who were later swamped by the contending ideologists of Reformation and Counter-Reformation, naturally worked within the existing framework of the Court and the universities and were sustained by their support. A false distinction between late-medieval and Renaissance culture has obscured the way in which they are bound up together; the old scholastic discipline went on. Henry VIII, though a Renaissance figure and a patron of the new learning, was grounded in Thomism and expert in the arguments of Duns Scotus, afterwards rather unjustly traduced.

The late fifteenth century had already been a great age of patronage; royal ladies, their minds perhaps all the more set on piety and learning by the fates of so many of their relations, had been particularly munificent. Even Queen Margaret of Anjou, with much else to think of, had founded Queen's College at Cambridge 'to the laud and honneure of sexe feminine', and the foundation had been further encouraged by Queen Elizabeth Woodville, perhaps to symbolize the hoped-for reconciliation between Lancaster and York.[22] Then, in 1505, Henry VII's mother, Lady Margaret Beaufort, Countess of Richmond and Derby, founded Christ's College, Cambridge, and, in 1511, St John's College as well, which would be the greatest contributor to Tudor learning and statesmanship in either university. On the advice of the Cambridge Chancellor, John Fisher, Bishop of Rochester and briefly Cardinal before being executed by Henry VIII, the Lady Margaret had also endowed a Chair of Divinity; and Bishop Alcock of Ely had founded Jesus College, displacing the nuns of St Radegunde's, who were thought 'unfit'. Though still provincial in its fenland, late fifteenth-century Cambridge was 'unobtrusively preparing for the supremacy which the following century was to bring, and even by 1500 nine out of twenty bishoprics in England and Wales were already held by Cambridge men'.[23]

Oxford was already heavily endowed; and there Foxe of Winchester had now founded Corpus Christi College. It produced most of the early humanists; men who had travelled in France, Italy and the Levant. By 1490 William Grocyn was lecturing there on Greek, and by 1500 John Colet, who became Dean of St Paul's and founder of St Paul's School, was elucidating the New Testament. Frowned upon by conservatives as new-fangled and subversive, St Paul's under its first high master William Lily, who had travelled as far as Palestine, aimed to teach 'wisdom joined with chaste eloquence' and good manners as well. Lily's own Latin grammar would be a discipline or a torment to generations. Thomas Linacre of All Souls, humanist and doctor, founded the Royal College of Physicians. Erasmus himself frequented Oxford before he taught Greek in Cambridge, where in 1511 he settled with high but frustrated hopes of profit and preferment. He detested the East Anglian climate, complained of the discomforts and the boorishness of his conservative colleagues, and sent for Greek wine, which arrived in poor condition. Sir Thomas More, the most attractive of the humanists, came from Oxford. His most famous work, *Utopia*, published in 1516, shows up the futility of power politics and advocates a saner distribution of wealth: holding up a *Nowhere* in the classical convention to criticize what exists.

If More's satire is urbane, and his ideal rather pedantic, a much less polite figure, the poet John Skelton (*c.* 1460–1529), found his feet at the Court of the first Tudor.* He continued the old tradition of Lydgate and

* He was either from Cumberland or East Anglia, and detested the Scots as well as Wolsey. By 1490, on the strength of his translation of Diodorus Siculus' history, he was asked by Caxton

Gower with a difference. The nearest English equivalent to Rabelais, he bawled and bludgeoned his way into a rank kind of fame. Indeed, as his editor remarks, he is 'an extraordinary mixture of medieval and modern; English above everything else'; at once in the Goliardic tradition and exuberant with the new learning by way of parody and satire. He writes of 'back-chat, characters from pubs, strange birds talking in a multiplicity of tongues, strident with jokes and abuse, then again and most unexpectedly lyrically tender and exquisite'.[24] Skelton in fact invented a new idiom, which reaches its climax in *Speak Parrot*; an original satire in which a great medieval tradition culminates, too little appreciated in the eighteenth and nineteenth centuries with their obsessive cult of the Italian Renaissance. The beat of the opening lines is medieval:

> *My name is Parrot, a bird of Paradise,*
> *By nature devised of a wondrous kind . . .*
> *With my beke bent, my little wanton eye*
> *My feathers fresh as is the emerald green.*

Yet soon the verse is opening up into classical and modern languages:

> *Douce French of Paris Parrot can learne . . .*
> *Parrot Sabe hablan Castiliano*
> *With fidarsi di se stesso in Turkey and in Thrace . . .*
> *Taisez vous, Parrot, tenez vous coy.**

In contrast with this gay poem, the satires are more pointed, as

> *Saint Dunstan,*
> *What was he?*
> *Nothing, he saith, like to me.*
> *There is a diversity*
> *Between him and me.*

Skelton evidently detested foreigners, and Rutherkin, the Fleming who can speak no English, is written off:

> *His tongue runneth on buttered fish.*

---

* Parrot can speak Castilian, trust himself, and shut up. See *op. cit.*, pp. 288–307.

to vet his translation of the *Aeneid*. By 1499 he was 'laureate' of Cambridge and tutor to the Duke of York, afterwards Henry VIII. Disillusioned with the Court, he retired to his living at Diss in Norfolk, where he wrote much vernacular verse. Told by his bishop to turn his wench out of doors, he took her back through the window and displayed their son in the pulpit. His poem, *The Tunning of Eleanor Rumming*, commemorates the ale wife of the *Running Horse* at Leatherhead; an authentic character, for she was fined in 1525. Recalled to Court by Henry VIII as *Orator Regius*, with a green and white robe in the Tudor colours, he soon fell foul of Wolsey who put him in prison. But the licensed buffoon fell at the Cardinal's feet exclaiming 'I pray you let me lie down and wallow', and was soon released. Much of Skelton's work is lost, including *The Grunting Swine, A Devout Prayer to Moses' Horns, Rosamund's Bower* and *The Ballad of the Mustard Tart*. See *The Complete Poems of John Skelton, Laureate*, ed. Philip Henderson, London, 1948.

As for

> *This Dundas*
> *This Scottish Ass,*
> *He rhymes and rails*
> *That Englishmen have tails.*

So

> *Skeltonus Laureatus*
> *Anglicus natus,*
> *Provocat Musas*
> *Contra Dundas.*

Then, lapsing into the vernacular

> *Tut Scot, I say,*
> *Go shake thee, dog, hey!*

Typically, this broad rhymester is best known for his grosser descriptions; but he could write delicately enough about young girls. So, beneath the conventional humanists, with their new antiquarian interests, and their escape from the elaborate scholastic effort to probe the universe by metaphysical argument, the old popular undercurrent would run on, emerging in the comic aspects of Shakespeare and, less transmuted, in the lumbering satire of Samuel Butler's *Hudibras* in the later seventeenth century, as well as contributing in spirit to some baroque convolutions in Burton's *Anatomy of Melancholy*.

Thus printing popularized a wide range of vernacular literature; old chivalric romances, humanist scholarship and criticism, and broad farce and satire in the old English style. Already these three reflect important facets of early Tudor civilization. The first was expressed in the flamboyant cult of an overblown chivalry; late medieval splendour being interpreted with a new and often vulgar exuberance of cloth of gold, jewellery, slashed sleeves and hose in the Swiss and German fashion. Jewelled and feathered caps are set at a jaunty angle, as in the portraits of Henry VIII and Francis I; and complicated pavilions and lavish display would culminate in the Field of Cloth of Gold. All is depicted by artists of new power, who would make Henry VIII and Mary I alive for posterity, as in the portraits that hang today in the hall of Trinity College, Cambridge. The humanist influence would also gradually alter the aims of scholarship. First by means of the critical examination of Hebrew and Greek texts, and later, by opening the way for a more radical and secular rationalism that would become the modern scientific movement of the seventeenth century, no longer antiquarian, but looking forward to a new power over nature. The scholastic discipline still remained entrenched in the universities in a way now seldom realized, but the spirit of the moderns would prevail; the limitations of metaphysical mind would be accepted and thought concentrated on the human condition.

Finally the undercurrent of mockery and sheer fun, never far absent from English writing, had been given a new turn. The quiet humour of More's *Utopia*, shows up the horrors of power politics by understatement. Skelton, on the other hand, sums up generations of rumbustious medieval satire, now spiced with Renaissance learning. Both probably express the sceptical outlook of the populace, on whose broad backs the minority culture here described was sustained, and about whom, since they could not write, little can directly be known.

14

THE EARLY TUDOR STATE

The long reign of Henry VIII (1509–47) marks a great change in the prospects of England. Though the English were slow to realize it and came late to exploit it, their economic position was being transformed. From an outlying island off a continent centred on the Mediterranean, the country became strategically placed to exploit the sea-routes of the oceanic world. Following the enterprise of the Portuguese and Spaniards, contacts were now being made with the Far East and the Americas: western Europeans were outflanking the land powers of Asia and would come to dominate the massive civilizations of India and the Far East; while the Russians, having shifted their base from their western water-ways to Moscow, were consolidating a potentially Eurasian power. For the Atlantic nations enormous territories, first in Mexico and Peru and the West Indies, and then in Virginia, New England and eastern Canada, would be open for settlement; a process disastrous for the Amerindians, but which gave rise to a civilization so dynamic that by the twentieth century America would be the greatest world power.

The Mediterranean economy was not, of course, superseded: but it was dwarfed by an oceanic expansion. The traditional view that the Ottoman Turks blocked all trade with the East has long had to go, for the East still coveted the gold and silver it had long received from Europe; the more so now that a gradual but cumulative supply of these metals would pour in from Central and South America. The Europeans still tried their best to expand the Eastern markets, the English in particular for 'vent of cloth' – indeed their western explorations were directed towards the Far East. By the mid-sixteenth century they were getting at Iran and India through Muscovy and would actually increase their trade with the Levant. Yet the slow shift to an oceanic Atlantic economy would be decisive, and already the greatest days of Venice and Genoa were over. Following the Iberian expansion, the French, English and Dutch built empires of trade and settlement overseas, and their commerce would contribute to the capital which was eventually to finance great industry and transform the environment of man.

Such is the broad picture. But Henry VIII was little concerned with it: in spite of his Renaissance panache and versatility, confirmed by the Germanized change of fashion, depicted by Holbein, of slashed sleeves, broad-cut swaggering coats and flat-topped caps, which makes the early Tudor English look rather misleadingly different from their late medieval forebears, he is more medieval than he seems, looking back to an old ideal of kingship. Fluent in Latin and French, with some Spanish and Italian; a composer and patron of learning and the greatest builder of the English kings, he had a powerful, rather than an original mind. A cold *politique* from youth upwards, with a deft political touch, yet a man of immense passions and rages, he was an able business-like opportunist whose greatness was due to an implacable will. Developing the work of his father, he strengthened the parvenu dynasty and the still relatively small-scale early Tudor state, and he was the main founder of the Royal Navy. He commissioned the ocean-going ships and sanctioned new ship-smashing tactics, which would revolutionize warfare by the cannonade of ranked guns that would defeat the Spanish Armada; while in the Gulf of Corinth, Lepanto would still be won by galleys using the old tactics of ram, grapple and board. And he developed the dockyards and built the foreign-designed forts which gave the navy its bases. This work, though designed for as conventional and unrewarding a foreign policy as had inspired Henry v, in fact proved preliminary to the Elizabethan mastery of the North Atlantic; and if Henry viii was concerned mainly with the 'entire Empire' of the British Isles, he turned out to be one of the founding fathers of a wider British Empire.

He was not much aware of these horizons. His attention was naturally fixed on the continent; like his father, he depended on the turn of events abroad. He could compete neither with Habsburg nor Valois, but he could sometimes exploit their laborious power struggles and manoeuvre to prevent their coalition. The Tudors imposed the king's peace, restored the battered prestige of the Crown, reorganized Wales and dominated Scotland and Ireland, and fended off conspiracy and invasion. Though this success owed as much to what now appears the main trend of events as to far-sighted direction, the late Elizabethans, emerging from great danger, could rightly feel they had 'come through'. Historians keen to give history an analytic look and to deprecate obvious enthusiasms, have belittled the 'heroic' aspect of the Elizabethan age; but the English at the time felt the danger and the promise; nor does new evidence diminish the achievement, with all its momentous consequences.

The other passionately contested change was the separation of the Church of England from Rome under a monarch who proclaimed himself Supreme under God. The English, long resentful of a cosmopolitan hierarchy and its demands, had come a long way from the simple faith of the Anglo-Saxons, and they would now become more self-contained and insular towards the continent of Europe just when their economic interests were becoming oceanic. If the Anglican Church preserved much more that was medieval than did the Protestant Churches of the continent, and maintained a tradition of Erasmian humanism strong enough to survive extremists of both camps, English learning, literature and arts became centred on a northern Renaissance Court. It would remain the major source of patronage until Charles I, the greatest art collector of his age, was beheaded by the more fanatical and philistine of his subjects, outraged by a now archaic Conciliar government and by the economic and ecclesiastical supervision it had tried to perpetuate.

Though he imposed Erasmian reform on the universities, Henry VIII encouraged them to stand their ground against the depredations of the courtiers, and lavishly supplemented their medieval endowments. In the last year of his life he 'diligently perused' a report on them, and 'in a certain admiration said to certain of his lords that stood by that he thought he had not in his realm so many persons so honestly maintained in living by so little land and rent'. He promised to continue them in their possessions, such as they were; and, to the predatory courtiers' disgust, bade the universities hold their own. Which they did, with a salutary independence.

The strategy and tactics whereby Henry VIII wrenched England away from Roman Catholic Christendom, while remaining in his own eyes orthodox, much affected government. The prerogative power was reinforced, and parliament, long divided into Lords and Commons but tending under Henry VII towards eclipse, now became more important. The king had to include it in making statutes, and since he was alert to public opinion, which he deliberately whipped up to support his takeover of the monastic lands, he committed the most powerful interests in the country to the new deal, the result of economic necessity. For the Crown was heading for bankruptcy and, divorce or no divorce, the move would probably have had to be made; nor did the Crown do very well out of what was in effect a forced sale. Then, as now, economic theory and the facts singularly contradicted each other, and government, caught in a wave of inflation and enhanced administrative and military expense, had to sell off most of the great capital of confiscated estates and treasure that came in, and spend it as income for the 'maintenance of the King's estate and wars', so that it did not become the basis of a potentially absolute monarchy. Indeed, though government seems generally to have got the best terms of the sale it could, such were the encumbrances of debt, prior charges, alienated property, founder's kin and corruption that the Crown did not make as much profit as it might have. Rather the Church lands came to reinforce an even more widely and deeply rooted landed and commercial interest, which would become more powerful than the Crown. In particular the new nobility – Russells, Herberts, Cecils – were based upon a vast accumulation of Church lands. The English establishment, recognizable since the thirteenth century, had grown up under relatively strong kings in a manageable area; now it would come to tame the Crown itself, first into a 'mixed' and then into a 'constitutional' monarchy. Such, in retrospect, the gradual and complex process appears; but it came about gradually and it must have been largely unforeseen.

2

Some historians, in particular those who think naturally in terms of continental revolutions or of dated doctrines of inevitable class conflict, have discerned a Tudor 'revolution' in government, following the defeat of the old feudal order by the 'bourgeois'-controlled sovereign state. Others, better attuned to the late medieval and English mentality, and unable to discover this traumatic experience, have stressed the continuity of the late-medieval restoration of a realm already regarded, under Richard II, as an 'empire'.[1]

The early Tudor administrative innovations were formidable: but Henry VIII was a very conventional king: he tried to subdue Scotland in the medieval way, extended his power over Wales and, as far as he could, over Ireland in an attempt to create an 'entire empire'. All these objectives were traditional. He would have roared with rage at being thought a revolutionary; nor was he the man to let go of personal power. A good judge of men, he knew how to delegate responsibility, but he discarded his servants with cold ingratitude; an aloof royalty, the fate of upstart commoners, as that of treasonable aristocrats, hardly concerned him. And whatever the expansion and overhaul of the administration demanded by the increasing responsibilities of government, policy was still, as in medieval times, under the king's personal authority, delegated or direct. When, under Edward VI and Mary I, that authority faltered, late medieval vendettas at once broke out. High policy remained personal, and though administration improved, the day of the faceless civil servant had not dawned.

Three clear phases of the reign illustrate this personal quality of government. From 1509–29 it was still typically Conciliar, even if, from 1514, dominated by Wolsey, the last medieval prelate to hold sway in England. He had risen, like William of Wykeham, through good practical service; in organizing the supplies for the young king's flamboyant and traditional adventures against the French in Picardy and Flanders, and for the resounding victory against the Scots at Flodden in 1513, when the Scots king, James IV, was slain and his tartan displayed by Henry VIII to the Emperor Maximilian.

239

By 1515 this probably odious but immensely able man was Lord Chancellor and Cardinal of York; by 1518 Papal Legate with a fantastic plurality of appointments, up to his neck in continental high politics and with an eye on the papacy itself. But, though bored with 'London business' and living in a lavish round of hunting, jousting and court masques, Henry VIII, as Feiling puts it, was 'from first to last . . . supreme when he took the trouble . . . until in the end he became his own law'.[2] Already in a *Remembrance* drawn up in 1519, 'Henry the King pleasured is' to demand quarterly reports on the state of the realm; to lay down policy on Ireland, on internal and external trade, unemployment, defence and the navy. And, in a *Privy Remembrance* he is significantly concerned to 'put his self in strength for the succession'; a phase which could mean anything from executing potential claimants to an annulment of his marriage, eight years before this idea is supposed to have been put into his head.[3]

This concern about the succession, so vital to the dynasty, runs through the entire reign and it broke Wolsey; for here the king would mix up passion and policy. Royal marriages, and, indeed, most others of the time, were made for policy, not love; and an annulment in favour of another royalty could well have been contrived. But Henry was set on marrying Anne Boleyn, the vivacious sister of one of his mistresses; known to foreign ambassadors as, at best, 'the Lady', and to her numerous enemies among the populace as 'one common stued huer'. The letters that the monarch wrote her show a passion strangely romantic for one of his position and age, an impression confirmed by the rapid disillusionment that followed.[*] But Henry VIII, whoever he wished to marry, had good political reasons for an annulment; and before the Legatine Court held in England by Wolsey and the Papal Legate Campeggio he reiterated the concern to 'put himself in strength for the succession' he had shown eleven years before.

All suche issue males, as I have receyved of the quene died incontynent after they ware borne, so that I dought the punysshment of God in that behalf. Thus beyng trobled in waves of a scripulos conscience, and partly in dispayer of any Issue male by hir, it drove me at last to consider the state

---

[*] 'Myne awne sweetheart,' he writes, 'this shall be to advertize you of the great ellingness [loneliness] that I have held since your departing . . . me thinketh the time longer than I was wont to do a whole fortnight . . . wishing myself (specially of an evening) in my sweetheart's arms, who pretty duckys [breasts] I trust shortly to kiss.' 'Henry's sentiments towards a young girl in her teens,' comments Dr C. H. Williams primly, 'were not such as should have been entertained by a man sixteen years her senior, with eighteen years of married life behind him.' *English Historical Documents 1485–1558*, vol. V, ed. C. H. Williams, London, 1967, p. 39. But Anne Boleyn was no innocent. She came of a rich merchant family in London; her grandmother was an Ormonde Butler and her mother a Norfolk Howard, so that Elizabeth I inherited a high aristocratic and Irish strain through her mother.

of the Realme, and the daynger it stode in for lake of issue male to succeed me in this emperyall dignyte.*

He felt it his dynastic duty to set aside the queen, if, like other men, he tried to combine duty with pleasure. Thus, when Clement VII, who always thought the king's case unconvincing and who was bound to the interests of the queen's nephew, Charles V, predominant in Europe since the battle of Pavia in 1525, revoked the case to Rome, it was clear that a titanic struggle would ensue.

From 1529–40 Henry VIII made a cumulative bull-headed attack on the whole papal authority in England, and, as he may well have done anyway, confiscated the vast monastic estates of the Church. So the fall of Wolsey and the summoning of the 'Reformation' parliament in 1529 marked a radical change of policy. It was executed by another immensely able instrument, Thomas Cromwell; first allowed, and then deprived of his head. It was concentrated into a decade, and followed after Cromwell's fall by a phase of more directly personal government from 1540–7, marked by mounting inflation and insolvency, but by no means incapable or unsuccessful.

This Thomas Cromwell, a Machiavellian adventurer of 'villein blod',† set himself, as he wrote in his last abject plea to his master for a merciful death, to make him 'the richest prince in Christendom'; and he came, indeed, to act as the first modern Secretary of State.[4] He managed parliament as Wolsey had never done, and he was ingenious in adapting government to a new range of business, elaborating the kind of administration already common in late medieval estates and used by the Yorkists and Henry VII. From an hierarchical late-medieval commonwealth, a more exalted monarchy would emerge; the king's Grace, now styled His Most Royal Majesty, commanding by the later 1530s a more regular and streamlined executive; a Privy Council, developing out of the old one with a similar if smaller blend of great magnates, ecclesiastics and new men. The king, of course, had the last word; and when Cromwell boasted that he was 'sure of' his master (how detestable that any subject, said his accusers, should speak so of his sovereign!) he was wrong. Indeed, as one authority points out, 'because the King was not much addicted to writing – and after all why keep a secretary and write letters yourself? – it is much too easily assumed that he was, if not a mere

* Quoted from Cavendish's Life of Wolsey by G. de C. Parmiter, *The King's Great Matter*, London, 1967, p. 9, n. 2, q.v. for the best analysis of the legal and diplomatic manœuvres of the king. Queen Catherine attributed all to the machinations of Wolsey. 'Of thys trouble I onely may thanke you my Lorde Cardinal of Yorke for because I have wondered at your hygh pride and vainglory and abhorred your volupteous life and abhominable lechery . . . therefore of malice you have kindled this fyre,' p. 4. n. 5.

† He was the son of a brewer and innkeeper at Putney and Oliver Cromwell would descend from his sister.

cipher, at least only in remote control'.* On the contrary, there is reason to 'think that Henry VIII was anything but a novice in Government'.[5] Callous and cruel, but a shrewd tactician and tenacious strategist, whose authority increased with the overhaul and extension of the administration, his tactics, as one would expect, were conservative. Attacking the clergy in 1531, he invoked an ancient writ of Richard II (1393) *Praemunire facias*: a process, wrote a foreign observer, that no one could understand so that the king could make what he would of it. 'Have A.B. forewarned', it ran, that if by applying for bulls from Rome 'you diminish the King's "regality" and put yourself out of the crown's protection, you may forfeit all your goods, perhaps your life.'† Hastily they made submission; without mentioning the writ, they presented the king, spontaneously they said, with a hundred thousand pounds as Defender of the Faith. And in 1529 when the king by a succession of statutes broke from the authority of Rome, he used his father's tone, at once commanding and beneficent, while, like his daughter Elizabeth I, he flattered them as was needful. Never, he would say, did the regality stand so high as when parliaments were in session.‡ He would remedy the vexations and disquiet that too long had diminished the royal prerogative, and, not by his own mere will, but by the advice and consent of Council and parliament. In 1532 he blackmailed the pope by an Act for the Restraint of Annates (a year's revenue from an appointment); in 1533 by the Act of Restraint of Appeals he abolished the papal jurisdiction. In 1534 an Act for the King's Succession forced all subjects to take an oath of loyalty to any male offspring the King might have by the new Queen Anne, and after that to the Princess Elizabeth, born the year before. Even the illiterate had to 'make their schepe mark'. And by 1535 the entire papal power in England was 'entirped, abolished, separated and secluded out of our realm'; and this by the whole assent of the nobles and commons in parliament. Further, to the 'Crown Imperial', a new sanction was added: 'the title dignity and style of Supreme Head on Earth immediately under God of the Church of England, as we be and undoubtedly have hitherto been'.

* See R. B. Wernham's review of G. R. Elton's *Tudor Revolution in Government* in E.H.R., 1956, pp. 92–5, for criticism of Elton's thesis, confirmed by recent research. He stresses the continuity between medieval and Tudor administrators and ideas. 'It is indeed', writes Wernham, 'in his view of the relationship between Henry VIII and Cromwell that Dr. Elton carries least conviction' (p. 95.) See also my *Henry VIII*, London. 1964. pp. 17–19.

† Chancellor Audley, afterwards chaffed Gardiner, Bishop of Winchester: 'We will provide that the *praemunire* shall ever hang over your heads, and so we laymen shall be sure to enjoy our inheritance by the Common Law and Act of Parliament.' *E.H.D.*, V, *op. cit.*, p. 629.

‡ Had not Reginald Pecock, nearly a century before, argued that if the King wrote 'a noble long letter' from Gascony to tell the English to keep their laws, it ought not to be said that the epistle 'grounded' the laws, for their ground had to be 'by acte and decree of the hool Parliament of Englonde'. (Translated from *The Repressor*, *op. cit.*, vol. I, pp. 21–2.)

This retrospectively asserted authority was ruthlessly enforced. 'If you neglect stumble or shirk,' the king thundered, 'we, like a prince of justice will so entirely correct and punish you that the world shall take care of your example and beware'.[6] A complete break with the papacy, dominant in England for over eight centuries, was thus made to seem merely a facet of the Tudor concern for the general public good; as doubtless it so appeared to the king's 'scripulos conscience'. But the Bishop of Lincoln remarked that he would 'rather have been the poorest man in the world than have been the King's Confessor'; and this disruption of Christendom was too much for Sir Thomas More, who invoked the august authority of the Universal Church. 'My lord,' he told his accuser, 'for one bishop of your opinion I have a hundred saints of mine: and for one parliament of yours, and God knows of what kind, I have all the general councils for a thousand years.' No merely national parliament could make laws against the 'union of Christendom'; no temporal lord could be head of the spirituality. For More was not concerned with existentialist introspection: he was afraid of hell, and asserting traditional Catholic doctrine: like Bishop Fisher of Rochester, he would die for it. They were only the most distinguished victims of the purge with which Henry VIII reinforced his success.

Always alive to public opinion, the 'most dreaded Sovereign Lord' also threatened those who 'made and published new-fangled news'; in general he attacked negligent Justices of the Peace who allowed offenders to escape 'with no punishment done'; and he also tried to prevent merchants cornering grain, a perennially unsuccessful purpose of government. Indeed, the changes in religion were made to look only one aspect of a many-sided autocracy – rather old-fashioned and hierarchical, for Henry's 'idea of kingship lay in the past'.[7] And when in 1536 religious innovations and increased centralization provoked risings in Lincolnshire; and, in Yorkshire, the 'Pilgrimage of Grace' aimed both at the hated Thomas Cromwell and the London government, bluff, diplomacy and the Tudor monopoly of artillery put the rebels down. In 1537 the Council of the North under the Bishop of Durham was reinforced by London magnates, resident officials and a Clerk. And in 1540, after the fall of Cromwell, the routine constitution and procedure of the Privy Council were written down. The king's government had also settled Wales, and attempted to settle Ireland, uniting both countries into what the king would call his 'Empire'.

For centuries a scene of lawlessness and a source of political unrest, central and south Wales was now made part of the English realm. Since 1534 a re-enforced Council of the Marches of Wales had imposed the rudiments of order; by 1536 Cromwell had the whole country, save the areas shired by Edward I, divided into shires on the English model.

Welsh knights of the shires and burgesses now attended parliament, and the writ of the Conciliar government ran, at least theoretically, over the whole land. The local gentry were now becoming Anglicized and collaborating as Justices of the Peace with the authorities in London. There was strangely little resistance to the Reformation of the Church, though the mass of the people continued to speak their own language and preserve their own literature and music. They became reconciled to a Welsh dynasty, while the more enterprising English-speaking career-ists emulated the original Owain Tudor by seeking their fortunes in England, where Shakespeare would depict and caricature them.

Ireland, on the other hand, proved much more intractable and would remain so. Here the Protestant Reformation provoked violent protest, giving a new impulse to an irreconcilable division. The English were still trying to rule through the native Anglo-Irish aristocracy, but Henry VIII's continental adventures and diplomacy had made this indirect rule even less satisfactory. The island now presented a strategic threat. In 1534 the Geraldine Earl of Kildare had to be detained in the Tower, and his son Thomas Lord Offaly raised the first Irish rebellion; ostensibly on behalf of the Pope. The English then massacred the garrison of Maynooth Castle, and by 1537 had hanged Offaly and his five uncles. A new policy had become imperative. Under the Council for Ireland the Protestant Reformation was now imposed, and Henry was proclaimed Head of the Church of Ireland. In 1541, in the Irish parliament, he was proclaimed not simply Lord (*Dominus*) of Ireland, a title originally bestowed on Henry II by the pope, but king. Royal rule was now to be direct.

A campaign was started to Anglicize the island. The greatest clan chiefs were conciliated and flattered; brought over to London and made peers. It was hoped that the English system could be imposed on Ireland as on Wales, and that even the Irish outside the areas of medieval English settlement – 'beyond the Pale' – would come round to what the Tudor English termed 'civility'. In 1542, when it was rashly assumed that the native Irish had been brought into better 'obedience', the Scots mercenaries who had long contributed to Irish disorder were supposedly expelled, and the ancient Irish laws abolished. Conciliar government was extended by a Council of the West and a Council of the North. But here Henry VIII and his ministers had miscalculated. Under the veneer of appeasement the native loyalties of the magnates remained; there was no capitalist class to buy up the confiscated Church lands, and the people, incited by the clergy, clung with all the greater tenacity to a tradition of Roman Catholic Christianity that went back to the time of St Patrick, and the days when Ireland had been the centre of a Christian culture and missionary effort which had spread deep into 'Dark Age'

Europe. The island remained a problem which under Elizabeth I would become a menace for the English; for the Irish a tragedy. Unlike the organization of Wales, the pacification of Ireland was never a Tudor success.

So, out of more than a decade of conservative innovation, extending to Wales and attempted in Ireland, the monarchy emerged with greater strength. This strength was needed, for though there was now, at last, a Tudor male heir, the last years of the reign saw the greatest dangers.

Anne Boleyn, executed for alleged adultery, had given place to Jane Seymour, a more dependable character and the queen the king loved best. But she had died in 1537 after giving birth to the future Edward VI. Passionately concerned to preserve the boy's life, the king had all the palaces decontaminated and strangers and dogs kept out. He could not know that his cold clever boy would die at the age of fifteen.

With the death of Jane Seymour, the Bluebeard reputation which has made Henry VIII the most notorious of the English kings and clouded his serious achievements, began to set in. First the King's marriage to Anne of Cleves, designed to consolidate an English alliance with the disaffected princes of Germany and the Baltic Schmalkalden League, cost Cromwell his head. For the 'King's Highness liked not her body . . . and mistrusted her to be no maid'; indeed, 'he could not', he said, 'overcome the loathesomeness of her company . . . tho' he felt himself able to do the act with other than her'. She was handsomely pensioned off, spent a fortune on clothes – she was the best-dressed though the ugliest of Henry VIII's wives – and thankfully played cards at Court with her successor.

The next venture was even more ridiculous: Catherine Howard, flighty, feather-brained and twenty-one to the king's forty-nine, was the most obviously attractive of the six consorts, and she soon cuckolded her husband. Henry wept before the Privy Council, complaining of 'ill-conditioned wives', and had her executed. Finally the rich Catherine, Lady Latimer, a cultivated Erasmian humanist aged thirty-one and the twice-widowed daughter of Sir Thomas Parr, Controller of the House-hold, brought a quieter domesticity to the Court. Save for one crisis, she managed her husband till the end; only to die in childbirth after a fourth marriage, this last for love. Such, and in the broad picture they are not so important, were the matrimonial fortunes of the ageing king. They produced no offspring, but there is no proof that, as widely supposed, he was syphilitic. Neither Mary, Elizabeth nor Edward VI were so tainted; and the king died of a kidney disease, gout and an occluded sinus in the leg, aggravated by the Tudor diet and too much wine and ale.[8]

Such was the personal background to the final phase of his reign; to the preventative harrying of Scotland; to the expedition against Boulogne, perhaps necessary to consolidate the English hold on the Straits, that main card against Charles v; and to the French counter-attack on Portsmouth to control the Channel and cut the British supply-route. This last was beaten off by the new galleasses, which combined oars and sail; though the new flagship *Mary Rose*, overweighted with guns, capsized when turning to catch the wind because her gun ports had not been closed.

Nor was the king's vigilance confined to major policy and defence: in 1540 the government was prohibiting subjects to shoot with the new-fangled hand guns 'in cities, and towns and other unmeet places without having respect where the pellets do fall': they should do their shooting only at the butts. In 1544 it was forbidding players to act in 'dark and inconvenient places, to the encouragement of vice and sin and the high displeasure of Almighty God'. They must only perform in the houses of noblemen, the Lord Mayor, aldermen and substantial commoners and in the Halls of City Companies. Common players and masterless men would be sent 'to serve his Majesty in certain galleys'.[9] People, too, who had been poaching fish in the Thames and stealing hawks' eggs were ordered to desist. Always concerned for his subjects' morals, in the last year of his life the king closed down the brothels of London, for the 'enormities going on in the stews' provoked God's anger and youths were tempted into fleshly lust. 'Bag and baggage' the whores had to go, and the bawds who had kept 'notable and marked houses' too. Nor was bear baiting allowed in the area any more or 'in any place on that side of the Bridge called London Bridge'. Further, in July 1545, the king, though supposedly on his last legs, 'much desired to have the game of hare, partridge, pheasant and heron preserved for his own desert and pastime' from Westminster out to St Giles in the Fields, Islington, Highgate and Hampstead Heath.[10] Surrounded by demoralized sycophants plotting for power after his expected death, Henry VIII went down in awesome regality, thinking his main objective won;* the succession secured to a Tudor prince; the Church subjugated without civil war; Wales reorganized, Ireland subdued, Scotland cowed; the island impregnable.

3

The attack on the monasteries had been cunningly conducted by a régime threatened with bankruptcy. Clumsy abroad, at home Henry

---

* His last days were spent arranging for the execution of his oldest servant Norfolk, whose son, the Earl of Surrey, had shown ambition for the crown. Norfolk survived his master only because the bureaucracy became bogged down over the procedure for executing a duke: Surrey, an earl, was executed in time.

VIII and Cromwell seem to have been masters of psychological warfare. They played up the old anti-clerical feeling most manifest in the later Lollards, and in 1528 put about a venomous pamphlet denouncing 'holy idle thieves' who did no manual work; representing King John as a righteous king, and asking 'who is she that will set her hands to work to get 3d. a day, when she can get at least 20d. a day to sleep an hour with a friar, monk or priest?'[11] If the country people still believed in the magic of relics and the cult of saints, along with prehistoric superstitions, to ward off illness and make the fields and animals fertile, the more articulate classes disliked the clergy, in its higher rank luxurious and foreign. 'And likely,' wrote a typical historian describing the Roman court, 'there is none of their Cardinals and Prelates without *iii* or *iiii* paiges trymmed like younge prynces; for what purpose I wolde be lothe to tell.'[12] And that jolly former Carthusian, Andrew Borde, could write with heavy sarcasm, 'Our Peter's pence was well bestowed in the re-edifying of St Peter's Church, the which did no good but to nourish sin'.[13]

So in 1535 a *Valor Ecclesiasticus*, the first for centuries, assessed the wealth of the clergy. It was immense, about £300,000 a year. In 1535 the king, as Supreme Head, appointed Cromwell Vicar-General with sweeping powers, and that cynical opportunist set about his task, at the same time feathering his own nest. He may, indeed, have consciously taken his cue from the policy of dissolutions already exemplified by the rulers of Germany and Scandinavia.[14]

First the lesser houses were attacked. Cromwell's Visitors used the regular medieval procedure to enquire into morals and finance, and they found what they wanted to find. Many houses were well conducted; but many more casually administered; insolvent, battened on by founder's kin and local gentry and with rain coming through the roofs. Others were more concerned with the varieties of sexual rather than of religious experience; 'corrupt in vices of both sexes'; or 'keeping concubines in the cellars', with priors providing for a horde of illegitimates, nuns with child and so on. The Visitors also made much of the gourmandizing and drinking in which bored celibates often indulged, for monks in the richer houses were now more like Fellows of eighteenth-century colleges than their examplars in the days of Bede and Boniface. Soon it was easy for government to declare that 'manifest sin vicious carnál and abominable living is daily used among the lesser and small abbeys', and to proceed with self-righteous unction to dissolve them. By 1540 even the great historic abbeys, Glastonbury, Malmesbury and St Albans, had been dismantled and sold up. It was a savage destruction; in particular of splendid manuscripts, even if the junk of centuries was also dispersed – such as relics efficacious in child bearing and illness, for the fertility of man and beast, and for better harvests. Jewels and plate by the cart-load came in from famous shrines: from the shrines of St Thomas at Canterbury and St Cuthbert at Durham, from Glastonbury, from Walsingham, to a new Court of Augmentations of the Revenues of the King's Crown.[15]

Too much has been made of the hardships of the religious orders. Most heads of houses were generously pensioned off or appointed to high office in the Anglican Church. Some were glad to escape back into the world: 'Thank God,' said the Abbot of Beaulieu in Hampshire, speaking for many men in authority over the ages, 'I am rid of my lewd monks.' Only the great ones who were implicated in politics and defied government were killed with all the circumstances of cruel publicity – the Abbot of Glastonbury hung on Glastonbury Tor and his quarters distributed round the West Country; the Abbot of Reading judicially murdered.

Some of the wealth was diverted to found six new bishoprics and seven new cathedral chapters. Anxious to bring the universities into line, the king founded Trinity College, Cambridge, expanded from an amalgamation of King's Hall and Michaelhouse and lavishly endowed; at Oxford he re-founded Wolsey's Cardinal College as Christ Church, with a huge endowment, in part from the revenues of Osney Abbey. Both these foundations surpassed anything created by his predecessors. Politically the king had to mobilize and maintain the flow of educated people to conduct the affairs of Church and State: nor was he untouched by the Renaissance ideal of an enlightened Christian prince, whose authority was a trusteeship. And how could that be discharged unless God's word were better set forth and children brought up in learning?

In bringing the universities into line Henry VIII did not forget the schools: 'among the manifold business and most weighty affairs pertaining to our regal authority and office', he wrote in 1543, 'we forget not the tender babes and youth of our realm. We command and straightly charge all you schoolmasters, if ye intend to avoid our displeasure and have our favour' diligently to teach Latin grammar. And he set Visitors to overhaul the whole structure of Oxford and Cambridge, sweeping away much scholastic lumber and promoting the teaching of Greek. The Erasmian influences of his youth were indeed reaffirmed in the court by Catherine Parr, and were still strong in the court of Edward VI, the long-term results contributing to the brilliance of Elizabethan England.[16] Indeed, some of the better traditions of English education stem from this time. The office of the tutor, wrote Sir Thomas Eliot in 1531, 'is first to know the nature of his pupil ... whereto he is most inclined or disposed, and in what thing he setteth his most delectation and appetite' ... for 'by a cruel and irous master the wits of children be dulled ...[17] Continual study exhausteth the spirit vital and hindereth natural decoction'. A summer spent out of doors in the 'service of the wild Gods', as another humanist put it, could even be salutary.

If these views are not representative of the routine to which the young were often subjected, that early master of English prose, Roger Ascham, in 1542 could praise the 'munificence of our best of Kings' who had bestowed, on Cambridge as on Oxford, 'a most noble and immortal aid to all kinds of learning' in Regius professorships of Law, Greek, Hebrew and Medicine. In an idiom still current, he wrote, 'Sophocles and Euripides are better known than Plautus used to be when you were up.'[18]

An immediate concern of government was to define doctrine, for they had loosed forces which had far-reaching effects and were hard to control. In 1536 the *Ten Articles* attempted compromise; the year after appeared the 'Bishops' Book' or *Institutes of the Christian Man*; in 1539 the *Six Articles*, reaffirming mainly Catholic doctrine. Finally the 'King's Book', *A Necessary Doctrine and Erudition for any Christian Man*, with a preface by the monarch himself, reaffirmed orthodoxy. Then, as now, ideas were mixed up with the struggle for power, and the closing years of the reign saw mounting tension between politicians exploiting the Protestant 'left' and those exploiting the Catholic 'right'. As in our own day, the canonical scriptures of Marx and Lenin are reinterpreted and were revised, so then the expedient interpretation made of the sacred texts. In 1524, William Tyndale, before he was laid by the heels and burnt by the Inquisition in the Low Countries, had translated the Bible; but Sir Thomas More had confuted him in venomous controversy, showing a side to himself not now much noticed by his admirers. Tyndale himself had not minced words: the orthodox clergy to him were 'maggots' and 'horse-leeches', and the Pope would 'set all the world together by the ears ... to come hot from blood-letting to a bishopric'.[19] Tyndale also described the Holy Father as a great dry tree that sheltered foxes and deserved to be burnt. But it was Tyndale who suffered – a pity, for his case was reasonable. If, he wrote, from 'one text thou provest hell while another prove purgatory ... and another the assumption of our Lady and ... of the same text that an ape hath a tail', it is wise to clarify the meaning. People may freely read, he argued, of Robin Hood and Bevis of Hampton, Hercules, Hector and Troilus; yet they are not allowed to read God's word.

Then, in 1535, Miles Coverdale had used Tyndale's translation for his edition of the New Testament: an official version was needed, and by 1539 'Cranmer's Bible' had appeared. Considering that one of the counts against the heretic Richard Hunne, hanged in 1515 in mysterious circumstances while awaiting trial by the Church, had been to possess a Bible in English, the authorities had now come a long way; but it was the more urgent to control so incalculable a power. If all men interpreted the Bible according to their lights, where would be the authority of the Supreme Head?

Henry decided on a compromise: while the teaching body of the Church ought to read the scriptures, the taught had no such duty, and should do so only as the prince of the realm should think convenient. Thus caught between the advantages of the appeal to the Scriptures against the Pope and the disadvantages of free opinion, the government did its best. They also stabilized and enriched the language, with incalculable effect.

4

Like the hardships of the religious orders, the social and economic effects of the dissolutions have been exaggerated: they were more a symptom than a cause. Naturally the foundering of archaic and rich foundations sent tremors far and wide, and in the poverty-stricken, still medieval, north the effects were greater and more resented than in the south; but the charity dispensed had been local and limited and the monks had often been hard landlords. The household officials, bailiffs and work-people were generally taken over by new and exacting proprietors – as Lord Russell in the west, who (wounded in the French wars) 'could see more with one eye than most men could with two and who got such a good share of the gold in the shower of Abbey lands that fell into his lap'.*

The economic and social tensions that confronted a government concerned to do rough justice and conserve manpower, went back a long way; the fundamental cause, the gradual and uneven change-over from subsistence farming to producing for a market. Since the Black Death and the Peasants' Revolt the authorities had tried to stem economic forces that were little understood, for economic theory remained highly conservative. In 1509, for example, Edmund Dudley, Henry VII's tax-gatherer, had spent his last weeks in the Tower before being executed by Henry VIII to 'quiet' public opinion, writing *The Tree of Commonwealth*. This financial expert, who wrote, as 'an Englishman born', and who professed a 'hearty good will and love towards the prosperous estate of (his) natural country',[20] had compared society to that particularly immobile object, a 'fair and mighty tree that shelters fat beasts and lean'. It must, he insisted, have strong roots for stability and 'due order'; and the monarch and his magnates must above all give

* Thomas Fuller, *Anglorum Speculum* or *Worthies of England in Church and State*, abridged edition, London, 1684, p. 175. Dr A. L. Rowse estimates the profit at '£1496.18.9½ to[Russell] (multiply by at least 25).' *The England of Elizabeth* London, 1950, p. 80.

employment; they must live lavishly, keep plenteous households and exercise hospitality. For if everyone played their due part in the hierarchy of a conservative commonwealth, there would be employment, 'quietness and surety'.

An ideal to be expected after the disruptions of the fifteenth century, it takes little account of the mounting economic dynamism in the sixteenth. And still, in 1538, when unemployment was becoming more severe and the experts advised government on *How the Common People may be set aworke*, their remedy was to force men 'back to the land' and 'set them to work the earth with ploughs'; to make the cloth workers stay in the old manufacturing cities when it was better business to spread out into the villages and new towns, and to exhort employers to cut down on servants who ought to be working in the fields. In 1517, when the prospering cloth trade made big sheep farming even more profitable and the sheep masters were putting down arable to pasture, the king attributed the 'long-continued scarcity' to 'covetous persons' who had for 'their particular lucre' neglected 'tillage':[21] so, he said, 'grain diminished, poultry decreased, and infinite numbers of the king's subjects for lack of occupation fell into idleness'. Government, naturally concerned to allay discontent and maintain a primitive agriculture, even tried to thwart the expanding production of wool by commanding that anyone who held more than one property should put his other lands back to tillage. In 1529 it misguidedly tried to increase employment by forcing the cloth manufacturers to export 'dressed' cloth instead of 'undressed' cloth to the Low Countries, though the buyers only wanted the latter, which they could then dye themselves to the colours popular in Flemish markets.

The denunciations of preachers against the 'cormorant' sheepmasters and cloth merchants and the sheep which 'devoured' men's houses, have been exploited by sentimental historians or by writers set on discerning a class war between a supposedly 'rising bourgeoisie' and the exploited masses: but there was nothing new in land hunger, and the old Catholic magnates exploited the situation as much as the new men, themselves anxious to conform to the establishment. 'What is not found', writes a good authority (*pace* R. H. Tawney), 'in contemporary literature is any indication of an ideological encouragement of class war between the social orders of the commonwealth'; and 'to read back into the period any such notions is to reveal a complete misunderstanding of the thought and practice of the Early Tudor world.'[22] The contemporary documents reveal more homely grievances; breaking out, as in Kett's rising in Norfolk under Edward vi, into a conservative if fierce protest against the gentry for disrupting the old ways, and a demand, as in 1381, for redress of limited grievances. Often the villagers would agree to change over from the old open-field agriculture to better 'enclosed' methods of farming, and even petition for it. It was the big sheepmasters who mainly provoked protest.

Meanwhile, for the successful, sheep farming offered enormous prizes: when, under Edward VI, Sir Francis Cheney won a great diamond off Henry II of France and the king asked him what he would have done if he had lost the throw, he could answer, 'I have sheeps' tails enough in Kent with their wool to buy a better diamond than this.' The vast Spencer fortunes were founded on wool, and the fine houses and the benefactions of the clothiers were already conspicuous under Henry VIII. But the gap between rich and poor was widening: 'It was never well with poor craftsmen', said the country people, 'since gentlemen became graziers'; or 'these enclosures do undo us all'. And gentlemen would answer the merchants 'we cannot raise our wares as you do yours'.[23] Sporadically, government ordered 'disenclosures'; sometimes within forty days and at the wrong time of the year, and working farmers pointed out that it could not be done. Certainly the sheepmasters destroyed villages: John Baker of Castle Combe in Wiltshire told the king, 'I think there was never more people and fewer habitations.' 'Yea, these schepe', they all said, 'is the cause of all these mischiefs'; hence 'such a dearth of all things as I never knew the like'.

But the Tudor enclosures in fact were small compared with the far bigger changes in the late eighteenth century. They were most widespread in the area from Berkshire through Oxfordshire up to Warwick, and north-east to Buckinghamshire, Northamptonshire, Bedfordshire and Leicestershire, and on balance their agricultural effects were salutary. The countryside was better hedged and ditched. The increased crop of wool meant new textile enterprises; at Burford and Abingdon, and at Malmesbury and Newbury, for example. Outlying areas, abandoned since the Black Death were now re-colonized. There is no simple picture of widespread and brutal Protestant capitalists disrupting society; what was deleterious in one district did good in another.

Far the worst hardship came from inflation. It was fluctuating but cumulative: by 1580 the cost of living appears to have been three times as great as it had been in the late fifteenth century, and by 1600 four times as much.* Contemporaries were bewildered; there was a European

---

* See George Ramsey, *Tudor Economic Problems*, London, 1963, for a good summary. 'An emphatic warning,' writes Ramsey, 'must be given that no sixteenth-century price index has the accuracy of the twentieth-century cost of living index' (pp. 115–16); but the evidence compiled by E. H. Phelps Brown and Sheila V. Hopkins is 'the next best thing'. According to this, taking 100 as the basic index from 1451–75, the inflation began in 1510, and from a basic 100 was at about 150 in the early 1540s. It then rose to 270 in 1555, and to 409 in 1557. Under Elizabeth it at first declined, but rose to 340 by 1586. The biggest rise came in the 1590s following bad harvests, to 685 in 1597. In 1600 it was 459.

'dearth' even after good harvests, and in 1570 the French pioneer economist Bodin would blame it on the influx of bullion from America, a theory long widely popular. Indeed the Bohemian and Austrian silver mines were being exploited, but Peru was only discovered in the 1530s and the 'mountain' of silver at Potosi in 1545. So the sheer volume of money cannot have much increased; and considering the unfavourable English trade balance it is hard to see how enough bullion could have come in to be a major cause of inflation, though under Elizabeth the booty of Drake and Hawkins and the privateers may have had some effect. The root cause would seem to be an increase in population with which agricultural productivity failed to keep pace. This would best explain why the price of food and rents, in elastic demand, rose fastest, while manufactures, in inelastic demand, often hardly rose at all. And there is considerable though imprecise evidence from the growth of towns and from parish records for an increase of population of perhaps forty per cent between the reigns of Henry VII and Charles I. This evidence could account for important aspects of political as well as economic history: inflation, land hunger, agrarian revolt and the deterioration of the relative financial position of the Crown.

The anxious concern of earlier Tudor government to stop the inflation thus had little success. By 1534 it had to admit that it had failed to fix victuals at a 'certain' price and, like a modern prices and incomes board, fall back on exhortation and the redressing of specific complaints. It also reiterated the old rules restricting courses at tables – rules hard to enforce. But the government did manage to mitigate the worst sufferings of those incapable of work: the distinction was made between the 'impotent' and 'lusty' unemployed, and a novel responsibility accepted that the former were a charge on their parishes. The system was rudimentary, but it foreshadows the Elizabethan Poor Law, the first systematic attempt in Europe to deal with the worst aspects of poverty and prevent the kind of brigandage which followed continental famines and wars.

5

The Early Tudor English speak to us much more directly than their fifteenth-century forebears. They spoke in an idiom still current in country districts today, and the divines and officials now used a prose close to the Elizabethan style. A man born in the year of Henry VIII's accession could have lived to hear of the defeat of the Armada, and the prose of More or Ascham is already a limpid and flexible medium, in contrast to the deliberate circumlocutions of bureaucratic and official documents, already skilfully designed to leave no loophole unstopped and several options open. Three developments out of many will here be briefly observed: the new Renaissance style of writing history; the sophisticated Italianate verse of the courtiers Wyatt and Surrey; and, by way of contrast, the new style of travel book which anticipates the more elaborate narratives of the Jacobean traveller Coryat, who developed this very English genre.

The official biographies of both Henry v and Edward iv had been commissioned from an Italian. Now Polydore Vergil of Urbino (1470–1555) inaugurated a new kind of narrative in his *Anglica Historia* published in 1534, and written from a cosmopolitan outlook, more analytic than even that of the best medieval chroniclers. Just the kind of man detested by the anti-clerical Protestants; a deputy collector of the hated Peter's Pence and absentee archdeacon of Wells, he was also a prebendary of St Paul's well able to observe events.[24] He thought all the old chroniclers, save Bede, William of Malmesbury and Mathew Paris, 'uncouth' and 'deceptive'; and he aimed, as an impartial Italian, at the truth – 'a full rehearsall and declaration', as his English translator wrote, 'of things don, not a gesse or divination' – though it was asking too much from him, as a European Catholic, to judge either Wolsey or the Reformation impartially.

Where Polydore Vergil was cosmopolitan, Edward Hall was Protestant and insular. His *The Union of the two noble and Illustre Fameties of Lancastre and Yorke,** first published in 1542, is Tudor propaganda; but it develops the rudimentary picturesqueness of Adam of Usk and the romantic chivalry of Froissart into a great pageant of narrative, the first powerful description written by a layman for laymen, which brings Court and parliament vividly alive. He had Froissart's eye for colour and splendour, but a shrewder political eye; and he was the first historian writing in English to create so comprehensive and detailed a narrative.

If Renaissance analytic power came naturally to Polydore Vergil, the court poets of the later years of Henry viii are conscious imitators of the Italians. Sir Thomas Wyatt and Henry Howard, Earl of Surrey – the earl executed by Henry viii – were courtiers, their poems distributed in manuscript to a small circle. They had both travelled in Italy at the height of the Renaissance; Wyatt had been a hard-worked ambassador to the court of Charles v, and Surrey the intimate of Henry FitzRoy, Earl of Richmond, Henry viii's illegitimate son who had died aged seventeen. Wyatt, in particular, handled Italianate metres with a pleasant skill and with an elegance unknown since Chaucer, and his

* See C. A. Whibley's Selected Edition on *Henry VIII*, London, 1904. Hall was a layman, educated at Eton and King's College, Cambridge, and Gray's Inn. He became the member of parliament for Bridgnorth and so also observed events at first hand.

verse is poignant with a haunting romantic regret. The difference between Wyatt and Skelton, both Court poets, is the measure of a new English sophistication.

But Skelton's rumbustious tradition was carried on by a disreputable and eccentric doctor, so characteristically English that he deserves attention, for he was the first of a long line. Dr Andrew Borde (*Andreas perforatus* he called himself) was a popular physician and won a wide public with his *A Compendyum or a Dietary of Helth*, and his *First Boke of the Introduction to Knowledge*.* 'I cannot,' he wrote, 'away with water, and take myself to good Ale; otherwhyle for Ale I take good Gascon wine.' But though he approved 'wyne of Angeou or Orleance or Renysh', he drew the line at strong Malmesey, 'Greke and Secke'.[25] A good cook, he said, was 'half a physician' and pork was a healthy meat – 'tho' I never did love it'. If 'onyons doth provoke a man to veneryous acts . . . lettyse doth extinct' them; chilblains of the heel and feet could be assuaged by rubbing them with a 'good proper wine', though lice could come originally from the corruption of 'hot humours' with sweat, and if one lay with a lousy person one must expect the consequence.

His description of the continent of Europe was more original. He depicted Cologne 'to the which cometh the fair water of Reene, on both sides of the which water . . . do grow the grapes of the which the good Renysh is made of'; and Lombardy – 'a champion country and fartyle', where 'ther be many vengeful cur dogges, the which will byte a man in the legs'. He described the 'merchants of Venice' who 'go in long gowns like priests with close sleeves', and the speech of Naples, which was 'Italian corrupted'. The Flemings of course are 'buttermouthed', and apt to drink till they piss under the table; while the Germans 'fede grosly' and are 'boystrous in speech', and the refrain of the Roman beggars is *dona, dona me*. In this insular round-up many of his countrymen's prejudices were already enshrined, but he had to admit that 'in all the world there is not such odyble swearing as in Englonde, specially among youth and childer, which is a detestable thing'.

6

On its own level, Borde's prejudiced and robust insularity represents a new confidence. For 'Henry VIII', as a seventeenth-century historian would remark, had 'carried a *mandamus* in his mouth, sufficiently sealed when he put his hand to hilt. He awed all into obedience'. He had

* Made by Andrew Borde, of Phisick Doctor. *E.E.T.S.*, 1870. He was born about 1490 in Sussex and, emancipated from the Carthusian order by Cromwell, acted as one of his spies on the continent. He is last heard of accused of 'keeping whores at Winchester' and imprisoned in the Fleet. He probably died in 1549.

mastered the realm. At the time of his death, moreover, the position of England had been profoundly changed. In spite of immediate insolvency and mounting, if repressed, religious strife, a modernized Conciliar government, reinforced by the wider Tudor claims for the prerogative and by the overhaul of administration made under Thomas Cromwell, was now well in control. Wales had been shired; the Irish problem at least shelved; the power of the navy asserted in a new way. Political plots in the late medieval style would still imperil the dynasty even into the reign of Elizabeth I, and religious policy would swing first towards extreme Calvinism, then back to Catholic reaction, before a comprehensive settlement would be made which commanded a more general confidence. But the economic prospect was now far wider: so long as the island base could be secured by a strong navy, new opportunities were opening out for a people now most advantageously placed to develop a commerce and colonization which would dwarf the medieval concern for territories in France, and even the long predominant concern with Gascony and the Low Countries. An oceanic world had been revealed. Rather belatedly, the English would now begin to exploit it.

And this widening of horizons would coincide with the full assimilation of Renaissance learning and music and a vigorous re-interpretation of both. The crude, if forceful, late medieval and early Tudor English would now be enriched by a new colour and precision; and by the last quarter of the century it would become the flexible instrument of Marlowe's 'sumptuous rhetoric' and of Shakespeare, the greatest English writer, 'perhaps the greatest poet of all time; one who has said more about humanity than any other writer, and has said it better'.[26]

15

PROTESTANT AND CATHOLIC REACTIONS

Long after Henry VIII's death, Bishop Gardiner of Winchester recalled a significant episode. The king had demanded his opinion on the adage *'Quod principi placuit legis habet vigorem*, what has pleased the prince should have the force of law'. Cromwell had at once agreed with it; but Gardiner had pointed out that the English kingship had long been under the law: 'by this form of government', he had warned the king, 'ye be established. I would never advise your Grace to leave a certainty for an uncertainty'. Whereat, characteristically, the monarch had turned his back. But Gardiner was right: it was not by despotism but by political flair and personality, backed by the Renaissance cult of the prince, that Henry VIII had dominated the realm. The measure of his achievement was that the dynasty and the structure of government, local and central, survived almost unimpaired by the uncertainties and disruptions of Edwardian and Marian times.

For when he was succeeded, first by a delicate boy of nine, then by a fanatical *dévote* of thirty-seven, the exalted authority of the prince was diminished and Henry VIII's life-work threatened. But the realism of Elizabeth I and her ministers would retrieve the position. For the reigns of Edward VI (1547–53) and Mary I (1553–8) saw a climax of religious conflict and social unrest, if also the beginnings of a new Oceanic enterprise. All Christendom was torn by ideological warfare and dynastic power politics, and it looked as if England would go the same way. The decisive fact proved to be that under Edward VI the country first went officially Protestant, and that in spite – and in part because of – the Catholic reaction under Mary this decision was modified but never rescinded. Veering first to one extreme, then the other, the country would regain its balance and avoid the atrocious religious wars that would devastate the Continent, and settle into the Anglican Elizabethan compromise, with its Erasmian learning and political conformity.

Nor did the economic dislocation and social discontent disrupt society, though they were severe. As will be apparent, the peasant rebels in East Anglia revived many of the grievances of the Peasant's Revolt, and the still predominantly Catholic peasantry of the west made their belated protest; but the economic forces, let loose under

Henry VIII, made for a more dynamic society. Controversy raged between conservatives, looking back on a half-fictitious golden age when the peasantry had been relatively prosperous, and those who were making new positions for themselves on the ruins of the old system of land tenure; but even the mounting inflation, worsened by the debasement of money under Henry VIII and Edward VI, gave openings to enterprising men among the old and new nobility, the gentry and free-holding yeomen, who were making huge profits out of sheep farming. Hence an unprecedented capital accumulation, and, most significantly for the future, the new capital financed new, oceanic, enterprise; down to the coast of West Africa, to Brazil and the West Indies, and east to the Levant, Muscovy and Iran. In this sense the reigns of Edward and Mary are the prelude to the exploits of the Elizabethans. Moreover, we now have a much better picture of the country; the *Itineraries* of John Leland, the first systematic English antiquary, undertaken at the behest of Henry VIII, provide a detailed and surprisingly recognizable survey.

2

Edward VI died aged only fifteen, but we know a good deal about him. He was the model pupil of the famous Cambridge humanist, Sir John Cheke; he kept a journal and already wrote able state papers himself. This pale, serious boy had an impressive mastery of Latin and Greek and 'a nearly idiomatic command of French'; he wrote 'a bold clear Italianate hand . . . and loved words, savoured them and used them with considerable skill and linguistic daring'. He has long been thought a bigot, but in fact 'showed little evidence of religious warmth, still less of zeal'.[1] He was more interested in administration and economics; no cloistered invalid 'wrapped in doctrinal studies with no eye for the great outlines of Tudor policy, for the broad prospect of England's ploughlands and pastures, thronged marts and manor houses, and England's ships tossing on distant seas'[2], but a typical Tudor, alert, suspicious and practical.

He was concerned, for example, with establishing an overseas market at Southampton, since the trade from Italy had been interrupted by the 'Almains lying on the river Rhine'; with amending the pier at Dover and with strengthening the forts at Falmouth and St Mawes. Brought up a Renaissance royalty, he regarded his kingdom as his personal estate, referring to 'my' coin, and 'my' debts. If he has 'enjoyed an undeserved reputation as a very good boy who founded schools, when in fact the Edwardian schools were only the survivors of those not destroyed to which his name was sycophantically appended', and if 'the legend of the boy benefactor to education must be . . . finally abandoned',[3] he was in fact remarkably able.*

But the short reign of this intelligent prince was a political nightmare. It was out of a welter of religious conflict, rigged trials and liquidations, that Cranmer's second prayer book, substantially the prototype of the modern liturgy, would be launched. Indeed the vocabulary of abuse is all too familiar, save that the terms are more rural; 'false shepherds, shearers and wolves', instead of 'lackeys, deviationists and revisionists'. 'Shameless' then, as now, was a favourite word.

First, the king's uncle, Edward Seymour, by August 1547 Duke of Somerset, took over as Lord Protector. An able soldier and no radical, but embodying a baffling blend of conservative humanity and ruthless avarice, he had little sense of timing or of the realities of power. Faced with the near bankruptcy left behind him by Henry VIII, the government now dissolved the guilds and chantries and their schools; Protestant iconoclasts defaced images, smashed stained glass windows, and whitewashed frescoes and painted texts over them.

Abroad government was equally inept. A victory at Pinkie Clough in Scotland proved a diplomatic defeat, wrecking the projected marriage of Edward to Mary, Queen of Scots. 'I haud wi' the marriage', said a Scots peer, 'but I like not the wooing.' So the young queen was smuggled out to France, there to be affianced to the Dauphin. Faced by revolt at home and unable to pay its mercenaries, the government even abandoned Boulogne to the French and evacuated Scotland. The consequences of this double strategic defeat, confirmed by the loss of Calais in 1557, would confront Elizabeth I.

The peasants in East Anglia and the west, encouraged by the 'good Duke' to resist the landlords, now broke into revolt, 'caring nothing for the Protector nor the king'. 'And what is the cause', wrote a colleague to Somerset, 'but your own levity and softness?'

Kett's rising in Norfolk in 1549 was reminiscent of the Peasants' Revolt in 1381, but the rising in the west was more catholic and conservative; mainly against the new-fangled protestant liturgy which many Cornishmen could not understand; they preferred the equally unintelligible but time-honoured Latin. Both risings were quickly put down, mainly by German and Welsh mercenaries. The new Henrician magnates, Russell and Herbert, became Earls of Bedford and Pembroke for their grim work in the west, thus consolidating their

* See Hester Chapman, *The Last Tudor King: a study of Edward VI*, London, 1958, for a well-grounded portrait, distinguished by much insight into the psychology of boys. The king, who was brought up sensibly with selected contemporaries, records his games as well as business.

families.* In Norfolk the adventurer, John Dudley, Earl of Warwick, the son of Henry VII's tax-collector executed by Henry VIII, soon hanged and quartered the leading rebels; Kett, handed over to Sir Edmund Windham, the High Sheriff, was left swinging in chains from a gallows at Norwich Castle, 'hanged up for wynter store'.

Warwick now used his prestige as a soldier and saviour of society to oust Somerset, 'whose weakness had given evil men boldness to enterprise as they had doone'; and whose position had been further weakened by the treason and execution of Somerset's own brother, the Lord Admiral. For the latter, the widower of queen Catherine Parr, had tried to marry the Princess Elizabeth and shot the king's dog, apparently in an attempt to overawe Edward himself.† By 1552 Somerset had been judicially murdered; Dudley, now Duke of Northumberland, pushed forward with an ultra-Protestant policy, extending and consolidating the interest of the holders of Church lands.

But all his schemes were now jeopardized. By the summer of 1553 Edward VI was dying of a tumour of the lung, aggravated by too much remedial arsenic, for his doctors had forgotten Arderne's caution on 'arsenic sublimed'. Faced with the accession of Mary, Northumberland now grew desperate; playing on the boy's religious fears, he persuaded him to disinherit both his half-sisters in favour of Dudley's own daughter-in-law, Lady Jane Grey, a descendant of Henry VIII's sister Mary, Duchess of Suffolk. This girl, found by the humanist Ascham 'reading (by Jupiter) Plato's *Phaedo* in Greek' at the age of fifteen, had been literally beaten into a marriage with the equally reluctant Guildford Dudley. The Crown, it was planned, would now come to her and her heirs male, and Dudleys would replace Tudors.

This attempted *coup* was too much even for mid-sixteenth century England. On the proclamation of Jane, Mary retired to Norfolk, already a centre of disaffection after Dudley's repression of Kett's rebellion and the stronghold of the Catholic Howards. On a surge of popular loyalty, she returned to be crowned in London. Northumberland was executed – unlike Somerset he did not even die game – and Lady Jane was imprisoned in the Tower, to be beheaded the following

---

* The former, who had come up from Weymouth, where his family had a wine business, as interpreter when Philip the Fair and Juana of Spain had been forced to land at Weymouth by a storm, had made his way so far in the service of Henry VIII that by 1540 he was building a great house at Chenies, Bucks. The latter, 'black Will Herbert', a Welsh soldier of fortune, had married a sister of Queen Catherine Parr and obtained the ancient Abbey of Wilton. Russell's effigy at Chenies shows the injury to his eye; Pembroke's portrait at Wilton the wary resolution of this able man.

† 'As soon as the Admiral and his men started fumbling with the lock, the dog . . . sprang up and started barking furiously. Maddened, desperate, Seymour shot him.' Chapman, *op. cit.*, p. 130.

year after a dangerous rising in Kent led by Sir Thomas Wyatt, in protest against Mary's projected marriage to Philip of Spain. So with the strong hand of Henry VIII removed, Conciliar government lapsed into factions reminiscent of the fifteenth century.

The new Queen, the first in her own right since the ill-famed Matilda, was thirty-seven. Though frequently referred to as 'bloody' Mary, she was in fact the least cruel of the Tudors; domesticated, sincere, fussy and naïve. She belonged to the world of high European royalty through her mother, and saw England as a part of a cosmopolitan Christendom which it was merely her duty to restore to the fold. Short in stature, myopic, with a loud mannish voice, the queen, wrote a Spanish observer, 'was not at all beautiful; small, rather flabby than fat'. Her unhealthy pallor was not helped by regular bleedings prescribed for a feminine irregularity, and her reddish hair was growing sparse. But she played the clavichord and the lute and spoke Spanish, Italian, French and Latin; indeed, 'her very intelligent remarks in that language surprised everybody'. On her dynastic rights she had both her parents' determination, and on questions of doctrine she was stubborn. 'As for your new books,' she told Ridley, the Oxford 'martyr', 'I thank God I never read any of them nor ever will do.'[4] On this firm basis of faith, and on the advice of her confessor and her bishops, she burnt nearly three hundred heretics.

Such was the woman that Philip of Habsburg, Prince of Spain, who was made King of Naples for the occasion, married in Winchester Cathedral in July 1554. At twenty-five Philip was an experienced lover with one marriage and many affairs behind him. 'For the love of God,' Charles V had written, 'see that my son behaves in the right manner.' The Prince did his best; he even appeared to relish English ale as an example to his supercilious entourage, who admired nothing in England save the bold horsemanship of the women. He was horrified at the sight of Mary, and complained of the mendacity of the artist who had painted her; but he was not a man to shirk his political duty.

None the less, in September 1555, following the abdication of his father, he left England, not to return save for a few weeks nearly two years later, to embroil England in his wars in France. And the queen still had no child.

The Spanish alliance, mainly against the French, had always been a cornerstone of Tudor policy; and the Spanish connection would still serve Elizabeth I well at the precarious beginnings of her reign, for the last thing Philip wanted was a Scots-French conquest of England. But protestant nationalism now cut across political and economic interest; what had been possible for Henry VII was now politically disastrous, and the Spanish-Catholic alliance was bitterly unpopular. English interests, it was thought, were being sacrificed for foreign 'Catholic' and dynastic concerns. Parliament soon saw to it, however, that the Church lands were not significantly restored, and a tactless Dean of St Paul's who preached for their restoration was at once reprimanded.

The queen's radical redemption of the heretic island thus proved a failure. The Spanish ambassador warned Philip that 'the haste with which the bishops have proceeded in this matter may well cause a revolt': if the people got 'the upper hand' the throne itself would be in danger, and he advised that further executions should be stopped, 'unless for overwhelmingly strong reasons'. The populace, he wrote, gathered up the ashes and bones and wrapped them up as relics in paper. It was best to proceed slowly. The mob in Henry VI's time had wanted to burn Bishop Pecock as well as his books: now the old laws against heretics appeared an anachronism, and the queen had achieved exactly the opposite of what she set out to do. And when in 1558 the news arrived that Calais had surrendered to the French, the régime reached a nadir of unpopularity.

Thus two short reigns, both in contrasting ways politically disastrous, followed Henry VIII's attempt to secure the dynasty and stabilize the religious conflicts he had let loose. After the neo-medieval chaos under Edward VI, Mary had at least reasserted the crown's authority; but, had she lived, rebellion would probably have succeeded. When late in 1558 the princess Elizabeth, sitting with her ladies-in-waiting at Hatfield under an oak, learnt that she was Queen of England, she came to a precarious throne and a divided and impoverished state, in a European power-balance fraught with menace.

3

Out of this background came the Anglican Church. Its liturgy and ritual were composed under Edward VI, its roots were nourished by the blood of the Marian martyrs, and it was already planted firmly as a vested interest of the dominant classes in the realm.

Henry VIII's attack had been so swift and overwhelming that medieval institutions and ideas long taken for granted had been but lamely defended; and under the Edwardian onslaught they were rapidly and subtly undermined. Renaissance learning had not, as often implied, swept suddenly over England; many fifteenth-century magnates had made a cult of Italianate humanism, and Greek had long been taught at Eton and Winchester. The diffusion of printed books had multiplied an influence already there, and spread it to a wider lay public, well before Cromwell was imposing the new learning on the universities and using translations of Erasmus's *Colloquies*[5] and *Adagia* as propaganda;

for Erasmus's fables and satires had the sort of influence that Orwell's *Animal Farm* has had today.

But against this humanist background, the effects of the translated Bible and the English prayer book were now cumulatively decisive; whatever Cranmer's political defects, he was a master of prose. If most mid-Tudor poetry was nothing to boast of, prose was already superb, and he combined poetic and homely diction with doctrinal compromise. 'Some', he wrote, 'are too slow to need the spur; some too quick and need the bridle . . . in the scriptures are the fat pastures of the soul, therein be no venemous meat; they be dainty and pure feeding.' It was nothing new, either, he said, to translate the Bible; it had already been done into the 'Saxon's tongue'.[6] Moreover the first Edwardian Prayer Book of 1549 was based on the old Catholic Use of Sarum, with new prayers and preparations, and the second was a 'masterpiece of studied ambiguity'.[7] 'Hear what comfortable words our Saviour Christ saith unto all that truly turn to him'; 'Draw near with faith and take this holy sacrament'; the phrases would sink in over the generations. But Cranmer, and he would burn for it, none the less denied transubstantiation, and affirmed Wycliffe's doctrine that the sacrament was a commemoration; efficacious according to the 'hearts' of those who received it, and not, as he said at his trial, 'that corporality that sitteth in heaven'. Here, still, was the crux of the conflict. Catholics might sing:

> *The bread is flesh in our credence*
> *The wine is blood without doubtance,*

affirming the guaranteed reality of the incarnation; but the Anglicans would feed on Christ only 'in their hearts', even if they could still sing 'with Angels and Archangels and with all the company of heaven . . . laud and magnify thy name'. It was the threat to this guarantee, opening vistas of damnation if the incarnation had not been literal, that equated even Cranmer in Catholic eyes with the unspeakable Anabaptists, who declared that physically the Saviour could not have been the Virgin's son, since by taking flesh he would have incurred original sin; and who, by denying baptism to infants, made them risk an eternity in hell. In 1547 the people of Poole threatened to disembowel Thomas Hancock when, after creating uproar in Salisbury and Winchester, he had preached God's word in their church, and other congregations had stoned the innovators: but with time Cranmer's careful ambiguities would come to blur the distinction and make it easier for conservatives to conform.

Further, if the protestant preachers held standing congregations spellbound for hours in performances then unrivalled by other forms of respectable entertainment – and the eloquence of Latimer is still moving – for those who relished coarser controversy there were the representative diatribes of Bale. Appointed Bishop of Ossory, he gave a rousing account of the morals of the Irish clergy ('I see many abhominable ydolatryes mainteined by the epickurysh prestes for their wicked bellies sake'[8]) and anatomized with relish the *Unchaste Examples of the English Votaries* and the *Private Lives of the Popes*. With the old Lollard anti-clericalism ready to light up, there was always tinder to this sort of fire, and government hammered away at the idleness and alleged immorality of the Catholic clergy.

Not that they were any worse than they had been before; but laymen were now more critical. Dr A. L. Rowse, in his classic *Tudor Cornwall*, has pointed out how vigorous was Cornish piety in the early sixteenth century; so many churches completed and decorated until the Reformation 'swooped down on it'.[9] The Bishop of Exeter still had £1500 a year, an enormous revenue based on vast estates, and his influence pervaded the west. The cult of images and pilgrimages was still fervent; of the ashes on Ash Wednesday, of palms on Palm Sunday, and of crawling to the cross, a ceremonial performed – and it could not have come easily to him – by Henry VIII. The Church was still a great European institution, relating its members to cosmopolitan Christendom. And the wills of the substantial classes still observed the Catholic forms. Further, if with inflation and taxation the churches were often decayed and the value of livings diminished, the parochial clergy were now probably better educated. As some laborious research has shown, the usual moral lapses were still the most frequent occasion for episcopal reproof, for 'clerks' 'were apt to find celibacy irksome'.* Parishioners complained, as did Kett's followers in Norfolk, that priests were non-resident or neglected to teach the children; but most people still took such things for granted. And the rector who frequented the local inn because his rectory was falling down, or had to farm his own glebe, was nothing new. The parochial clergy were now, in fact, rather better than their prototypes in the fifteenth century. And, as for the monasteries, 'the picture from the evidence is not the old popular view that they were dens of vice ... but rather antiquated, well-nigh useless corporations faltering to decay: there was a gradual running down'.[10]

But the initiative, political as well as intellectual, was with the

---

* See Margaret Bowker, *The Secular Clergy in the Diocese of Lincoln, 1495–1520*, Cambridge, 1966. Her statistics, compiled with eager scholarship, show that she has, not surprisingly, discovered that over three-quarters of clerical sins were moral. But the incumbent who, as she delicately puts it, 'found in his cook the companion of his solitude', or the curate accused of forcing himself on the wife of William Tailboys, saying 'he needs must have his pleasure of her, by putting a noble (the coin) in his bed', are figures familiar to Chaucer, long tolerated in the general run of rural life.

reformers; and when the Counter-Reformation sent the dedicated Jesuits to England, the Catholic cause had already been substantially lost; not only because there was a great vested economic and social interest established against it, but because the people were bewildered and ready for a new lead. Further, when 'the sparks from Mary's madness lit the countryside with a wild beast glare as of blood',[11] she gave the *coup de grâce* to established Catholicism in England. Apart from the continuing appeal of the English Bible and Liturgy, Foxe's *Book of Martyrs* had all the macabre detail of modern crime fiction. How, in particular, could young readers forget the incredible resolution and fascinating torments of the 'Martyrs' of the Reformation? If, in fact, only about three hundred perished (Henry VIII's victims, more impartially selected, had been as many), and even if the persecutions had been confined mainly to the London area, Kent and East Anglia and had little effect in the north, who could forget John Rogers, the first of them? 'That is what I preached', he had said, 'I will seal it with my blood', and he then 'washed his hands in the flame as though it had been cold water'.* And how memorable was Laurence Saunders of Eton and King's, who refused pardon and, as so often in the English climate, was burned slowly with green wood after a touching farewell to his wife and child. Or John Hooper, Bishop of Gloucester, who, when the reeds were heaped up, embraced them and put bundles under either arm, and when they burnt slowly because the wind was the wrong way, cried out 'For God's sake good people let me have more fire!' and from whose finger ends there dripped 'fat, water and blood'. And who could forget William Hunter, an apprentice of nineteen, in whose formative years protestantism had been compulsory, who, when he lay in irons and his parents came to comfort him, told them, in the idiom of commerce, 'I have cast my count what it will cost me already'; and, who, when the faggots and broom began to flare, 'dived his head into the smothering smoke' to get it all over?[12]

4

For a description of the countryside, in which this strange lunacy took place, we may turn to John Leland, whose vast *Collections* and *Itinerary*† (1534–43) – *perigrinatio laboriosa totius Britanniae* – were commissioned

* *The Acts and Monuments of the Christian Martyrs by John Foxe.* ed. Rev. Josiah Pratt, viii vols, London, 1877, vol. vi, p. 611. The first edition printed in 1563. (The earlier volumes deal with the martyrs of the early church and so through the ages. The topical volumes are vi and viii).

† *The Itinerary* by John Leland, ed. Lucy Toulmin Smith, 5 vols, London, 1906–8. Leland (1506–52), was educated at St Paul's and Christ's College, Cambridge. He then became a fellow of All Souls, and studied in Paris. At first tutor to the Norfolk family, he became

by Henry VIII. This pioneer antiquary was commanded 'to peruse and diligently to search out all the libraries of the monasteries and colleges in your noble realm', and 'bring them out of the dreary darkness into lively light' with an eye on securing treasures for the royal library. 'I trust,' wrote Leland, 'that your reaulme shaul so well be knowen and paynted with his native colours, that the reuaume shal gyve place to the glory of no other region.'

The task was urgent and gigantic. Many Germans had swarmed into England to buy up the monastic books; but Leland added vast topographical projects to the assignment. And if he published little in his lifetime and died insane, this man of genius left an enduring monument. Leland preserves many old legends of monastic foundations; the tale of Edith Forne, for example, the wife of the castellan of Oxford, who used to walk to a certain tree where magpies would come and talk to her, and who, 'somewhat feered by such a wonder', asked her confessor what it meant; and when the astute cleric replied that it meant that she should ask her husband to build Oseney Priory, arranged for it to be done.

But Leland is best remembered because he describes so many towns and villages still familiar today; as Northleach in the Cotswolds 'a praty uplandish town'; Lechlade, 'most apt for grass', or Fairford with its new and splendid church, that 'never flourishea afor the coming of the Tames (wool merchants) unto it'.

Besides the houses of the new rich in Trowbridge and Bradford-on-Avon – 'old Bayllie builded also of late in the town; he was a rich clothier' – Leland observes the 'seats' of the county families. Already in Somerset there are Spekes, Paulets, Lutterels, and Sydenhams at Orchard, whose heiress married a Norfolk Windham of 'Fulbridge' (Felbrigg). Cornish Arundels, Grenvilles, Vyvyans and Killigrews are already established; as are the Seymours of 'Wolphe Hall' in north Wiltshire, who had moved higher up the social scale. And so over the whole country.

The topographical landmarks are also familiar: the Vale of the White Horse in Berkshire; Cadbury Rings in Somerset, and in Dorset the beach of Chesil, 'cast up by the sea'. He observes bridges still familiar, as Fisherton and Crane bridges at Salisbury, and Harnham bridge there, 'a main stately thing'. At Barnstaple, a clothier, who saw a woman drowned by the tide, left money to build one, and the vicar at Wadebridge began one which his parishioners helped to complete; but

librarian and chaplain to Henry VIII, and in 1533 'King's Antiquary'. He also became a Canon of what would be Christ Church, Oxford, and though he was based on London, Prebendary of East and West Knoyle in Wiltshire. Hearne, the eighteenth-century Oxford antiquary, first edited his works.

between Melcombe and Weymouth in Dorset they still used a boat on a rope between the houses.

Lelend also observes the smiths and cutlers of Birmingham and the new ingenious chimneys at Bolton, 'the smoke' strangely conveyed; but his fullest account is of Bath, whose ruins had intrigued a Saxon poet. The common bath was frequented by all and sundry, who suffered from leprosy, pocks, scabs and great aches, but the 'Gents' wisely frequented the larger one with thirty-two arches, wherein the sexes bathed separately. Leland is fascinated by the relics of Rome – 'a greyhound running and the tail of him engraved in great Roman letters' – and two antique Celtic heads with ruffled locks. His sharp eye traversed the whole land, leaving a vivid and detailed picture.

Such was the setting of the restive mid-Tudor society. Its contrasts were sharply emphasized by the grievances of the poor, as against the profusion of the old and new rich. Kett's followers in Norfolk, for example, had complained that they ate 'pease and oats like beasts', and 'shouted out these words in English, "Kill the gentlemen" '.[13] Kett himself, who was a tanner, had proclaimed 'often with a vehement voice' that power and avarice so excessive could not but be hateful to God. Like their forebears under Richard II, his followers had claimed to be 'King's men'; why should they not go to Court and appoint the king new counsellors? The free-born commonalty, they had said, was oppressed by a few gentlemen, who 'glutted themselves with pleasure', while the 'pore commons' were wasted, like packhorses, with daily labour.[14] So they had 'surfeited' and revelled on Mousehold Heath, killing 3000 bullocks and 20,000 of the offending sheep; pulled down park palings and spoiled woods. They had prayed that reedground and meadow and 'copyhold lands that be unreasonable rented' should be priced as they had been under Henry VIII, rivers made free for fishing and passage and poor mariners have the whole profits of their fishing. Gentry should 'pale' their conies – enclose their rabbits – so that they should not be 'noisome' to the commons, and limit their head of bullocks and sheep. 'Comyns' had indeed briefly 'become a kinge'; and when a local squire, Sir Roger Wodehouse, with three carts loaded with beer and provisions, had tried to win them over as 'near neighbours', they had 'tugged' him and cast him in the ditch. Warwick, coming down from London, took more decisive measures: his 'Almain horsemen' and arquebusiers from Calais knew their business, and soon the 'routs and uproars' were put down.

Meanwhile, in contrast, the magnates in their vast overcrowded mansions were flourishing with a more than medieval ostentation; their hectic cookery and profuse banquets, 'seemingly designed for half-starved giants':

Swan, peacock, viande motlee
Venison with fruments
And pheasant full rich.

There were twelve highly spiced dishes to a course, and it was customary to sample them all.* But when Cranmer drew up a *Constitution for moderating the Fare at Bishops' tables,* he limited the prelates to two partridges at a time. But one legacy of episcopal splendour would survive in the Christmas pudding – *viande ardente,* first mentioned at a feast given by the Bishop of Salisbury in 1477.[15] So, in the familiar experience, inflation created new wealth as well as distress; in a more dynamic economy those who were well-placed at Court and in the City heaped up wealth, and some of it found an outlet overseas.

5

Though the religious, economic and social changes here described would be decisive, the most novel aspect of the time, and the one with the greatest future, was oceanic. The reigns of Edward VI and Mary I saw the beginnings of the Elizabethan enterprise and of a *tour de force* of exploration and settlement which would lead to empire. Though the English, with their eyes on France, Flanders and the Baltic, could still show nothing to compare with the vast enterprises of the Spaniards and Portuguese, Henry VII had in fact granted capitulations to Columbus through his brother Bartholomew. But Christopher Columbus had accepted the Spanish commission and already made his discovery. In 1497, five years after Columbus's landfall, the Venetian John Cabota, commissioned 'to sail to all parts under our banner' by Henry VII, had discovered Nova Scotia and Newfoundland and may have reached Florida. His son Sebastian, 'seeking to sail by the west into the east, where spices grow by a way never knowen before',[16] may have entered Hudson's Bay; but save as a basis for later claim to sovereignty, these voyages had not come to much. As already emphasized, the Turks did not stop the old trade with the Levant; they merely made it more risky for a time. And where there had once been a Venetian monopoly, now, from 1511 onwards, 'tall ships of London, Southampton and Bristol' had maintained an 'ordinary and usual' trade with Sicily, Candia, Cyprus and Beirut; exchanging fine Kersey cloth and White Westerns and 'certain cloths called Cardinal Whites' and 'Calvesskins' for silks, Malmesey and Muscadet wines, cotton wool, turkey carpets, pepper and spices. This trade had been a prelude to the Edwardian and Marian expeditions to Muscovy and Iran.

* See Mitchell and Leys, *op. cit.,* p. 195. They ate sea-gulls, oysters with onions, and haddock with garlic.

But it was 'old Mr William Hawkins of Plimmouth', father of Sir John Hawkins, the main organizer of Elizabeth's navy, who in 1530-2, when the Reformation was being launched, had opened up the English trade with West Africa and Brazil; buying up elephant's teeth on the Guinea coast and trafficking with the Amerindians for Brazil wood on the other side of the South Atlantic. He had brought back a Brazilian Cacique, whose bizarre appearance intrigued Henry VIII, though it is not known what the Cacique made of the monarch. The 'savage king' had died on the homeward voyage. This venture would lead to the lucrative slave trade out of Bristol, conveying Negroes to the West Indies and the Spanish Main; an enterprise which now appears horrific but which was long regarded as respectable; for the Negroes, it was said, had the benefits of Christianity and often a better chance of survival than at home. Thus, by the early years of the century, wide horizons had already been opened up; and in 1553 Captain Thomas Windham, 'a Norfolk gentleman born, but dwelling in Somerset', having the year before sold linen and cloth and amber in Morocco, and taken on sugar, almonds and molasses, penetrated, via Madeira, to the highly organized West African state of Benin in search of pepper and gold. But his men 'drank without measure the wine of the palm tree that droppeth in the night'; and though the survivors brought back a profitable cargo, Windham and most of his crew perished.[17]

More important, in that year, was 'the New Navigation and discoverie of the Kingdom of Muscovia in the North East, enterprised by Sir Hugh Willoughby, Knt. and Ric: Chancellor, Pilot Master'. So vague were the English about Muscovy that two 'Tartarians', surprisingly employed in Edward VI's stables, were consulted: but they 'could answer nothing to the purpose, being indeed, more acquainted to toss potts than to learn the states and dispostion of peoples'. On 20 May the ships were towed down river past Greenwich, the sailors 'in Watchet or Skie coloured cloth rowing amaine'. The courtiers came running out and the people crowded along the shore; 'the Privie Council lookt out at the windowes of the Court, and the rest ran up to the toppes of the towers'; the ships saluted with their great guns and it was a 'very triumph'. But 'good King Edward, in respect of whom all this was prepared', lay dying.

North east they sailed, until there was 'no night at all, but continuall light upon the mightie sea', and after severe vicissitudes found themselves off Archangel in 'Muscovy which was the name of Russia the White'. They were in the dominions of 'Ivan Vasiliwich', Ivan the Dread. After maddening delays, Chancellor and his company proceeded by sledge to Moscow: they observed vast plains and forests where bears were 'hunted afoot with wooden forks', and where black wolves were all too abundant. They thought the Kremlin 'almost inexpugnable' and were awed by the majesty of the Tsar. At Novgorod they found flax and hemp, hides, honey and wax; at Yaroslav, wheat, salt fish and skins; there was a wealth of rich furs – sable, marten, ermine – and 'walrus teeth'. The timber houses were heated with stoves and stuffed against the cold with moss, and the people wore caps 'peaked like a diamond, broad beneath and sharp upwards'; taller according to rank. This expedition would be followed up under Elizabeth I by Jenkinson's visit to the Safavid Shah Tamasp of Iran, and in 1568 by Thomas Randolph's embassy to Moscow, when a trade treaty would be signed.

So, for the first time, the English embarked upon a really far-flung commerce: down past the dry Saharan heat to the tropical forests and the mango swamps and red earth of Guinea and Benin; out across the South Atlantic to the strange world of Brazil and the West Indies; north east to the midnight sun and the winter darkness and the ice. The experience, recorded with eager accuracy, would be reflected in a new range of literature; in a wider, un-medieval, awareness. It is this experience, and not the fanaticism and social conflict, that makes the reigns of Edward VI and Mary I most memorable.

16

THE ELIZABETHAN AGE

'To be a king and wear a crown,' Elizabeth I told her parliament in
1601, 'is a thing more glorious to them that see it, than it is pleasant to
them that bear it.' The nineteenth-century legend of a hearty Protestant
'good Queen Bess' is as misleading as the modern one of a vacillating
sex-starved neurotic whose greatness was vicarious. This elaborately
sophisticated monarch was tough as leather, hard as steel; fascinating
and dangerous; her high Plantagenet profile matched by a high
Plantagenet scorn; disillusioned and wary after a lifetime of danger.
'For God's sake regard your surety,' she told James VI, 'against the
wicked suggestions of the Jesuits who make it an acceptable sacrifice to
God . . . that a king not of their profession should be murdered.' After
one of her nobles had been stabbed on the Scots Border, she wrote, 'God
send us better luck . . . after this bloody beginning'; and concluded 'If
you mean, therefore, to reign, I exhort you to show yourself worthy of
your place'.[1] Recent evidence has indeed produced 'a deep and growing
respect for the queen's ability and the part she played in policy both at
home and abroad'.* Unmarried, at a time when this status in a monarch
was considered extraordinary; excommunicated and reviled, she won
by nerve and self-mastery a success which, perhaps just because it was
so obvious and celebrated, modern critics have disparaged, but for
which there is solid evidence.

Elizabeth I had all the versatility of a Renaissance prince. She could
reply to Latin and Greek orations in kind; as when in 1564 she visited
Cambridge, stayed in King's, and attended disputations and plays in the
chapel 'adorned with fresh rushes and a fair turkey carpet'. Having
listened to the question 'Is Monarchy best for a Commonwealth?'

* *Elizabethan Government and Society*, essays presented to Sir John Neale, ed: S. T. Bindoff, J.
Hurstfield and C. H. Williams, London, 1961. Neale, Rowse and Conyers Read all agree with
Pollard's favourable opinion: only Dr G. R. Elton, who calls her oddly 'the most masculine
of female sovereigns', seems to dissent: 'whether queen or minister was responsible for the
great success of the reign is not at present a question we can answer' (*England under the Tudors*,
p. 263). But even he is inspired to a curiously mixed metaphor, admitting that she matched 'a
marvellous capacity for keeping six balls in the air at once for an equal skill in keeping a
dozen strings from getting entangled'. The best authorities thus concur that popular myth is
based on fact. But the minor myth that Sir Walter Ralegh threw down his cloak in the mud to
gain the entrée to the Court is based on no convincing evidence. He would have had his
introduction anyway. See J. E. Neale, *Essays in Elizabethan History*, on the *Sayings of Queen
Elizabeth*, Cape, 1958, pp. 85–112.

being tactfully determined, and the veteran Dr Caius 'make his position' on whether plain food was better than an elaborate diet – *simplex cibus praeferandus multiplici*?, – she rode through the streets 'very merry', talking to her scholars in Latin. And at Oxford, two years later, she stayed in Christ Church and spoke 'so wise and pithie [in Latin] as England may rejoice in such a Prince'; and she pleasantly reproved a Puritan divine with the words 'Mr Doctor, this loose gown becomes you mighty well: I wonder your notions be so narrow'.* 'That Elizabeth,' concludes Neale, 'had an irresistible way with her, the documents of the time prove amply enough.'[2]

The queen also had another and coarser side; as was demonstrated at Kenilworth in 1575, when she was 'hunting the hart'. The stag had taken to water and the waterman 'held him up by the head'; whereat, with a sporting gesture – not, as supposed, in sadism – 'by her Highness' Commandment the quarry lost his ears for ransome and so had pardon for life'. And she loved to watch bear-baiting; as when, we are told, that summer, 'a great sort of Bandogs whear thear tyed in the utter Court, and thyrteen Bearz in the inner ... debated with sharp byting arguments ... skratting and byting, by plain tooth and nayl .... It was a sport very pleazaunt of theeze beastz; to see the Bear with his pink nyez (nose) leering after his enmiez approch, the nimbleness and wayt of the Dog to take his advauntage'. There was a grand 'roring and tossing and tumbling'; and, when the bear was loosed, to see him 'shake his ears twyce or thryce with the blud and slaver aboout his fiznamy, was a matter of goodly releef'.†

In the broad perspective of English history, Elizabeth I's long defensive secured the base from which the first calculated strategy of empire was developed. 'After so many notable things happening ... the alterations in religion, the change in our coins, the turning of troubles into peace done so quietly and quickly', was it not, indeed, 'prodigious that Religion for which all the world made warre should be so chaunged, refound and established into Peace? That our base coins should be turned into Rich Moneys?' So wrote the contemporary biographer of Sir William Cecil, Lord Burghley, the first great modern civil servant who collaborated with the queen for decades and whose cunning and foresight were so unfeudal and realistic.‡ Their joint strategy was far-

---

* *The Public Progresses of Queen Elizabeth*, ed. John Nichols, London, 1788, vol. I, p. 3. She had her father's flair for 'public relations' – 'a brilliant sun' as Nichols puts it, 'to cheer the nation chilled with the horror of more than inquisitorial cruelty'.

† Nichols, *op. cit.*, vol. I, p. 14. Laneham's *Account of the Queen's Entertainment at Killingworth Castle*. The phonetic spelling throws light on the Elizabethan pronunciation.

‡ *The Compleat Statesman*, in Peck's *Desiderata Curiosa*, London, 1732, vol. I, p. 17. William Cecil (1521–98) came of minor Welsh gentry on the Herefordshire border. David Sitsylt, a younger son, became a man-at-arms in Henry VII's guard, and by 1494 he had settled at

sighted and prudent and their tactics flexible; the kind of systematic scheming of the Pastons and their kind, now better informed and writ large. 'Gentility', wrote Burghley, a business-like founder of an aristocratic house, 'is nothing less than ancient riches'; always, he told his son, save a quarter of your income and never trust anyone entirely, not even your best friend. Above all, get a patron, or you will be a 'hop without a pole'; and avoid strong drink, for to have the reputation of a good head is 'a better commendation for a brewer's horse'.

This sort of cunning matched Elizabeth's realism and ruthlessness. She killed as many religious dissidents (who were hung, cut down alive and disembowelled or burnt) as had Mary, though the executions, spread over a longer time, have not made such a sensation in history. Threatened by discord at home and outclassed by mighty enemies abroad, she could take no chances. The Elizabethan exploit was primarily defensive: its literary achievement was brilliant, but, politically and economically, it was a time of promise more than, as often thought, of fulfilment; a time in which the foundations of riches and empire were secured.

2

The political events of the age were heavily determined by the shifts of European power politics. During the first phase, 1558–73, the régime was consolidated, a French-Scots envelopment avoided and the last Catholic rebellion in the north put down. And since the queen put policy before inclination, the political danger caused by Elizabeth's attraction to Sir Robert Dudley, Northumberland's son, whom she

Stamford, Northamptonshire. Here he bought the manor of Burghley, married well and became mayor and member of parliament for the borough. Henry VIII made him Sergeant-at-Arms, and his son, Richard, Yeoman of the Robes and sheriff of Northants. From 1537 Richard bought up extensive Church lands, and it was with substantial backing that in 1535 William went up to St John's College, Cambridge. Here, in spite of his father's opposition, he married the sister of his tutor, John Cheke, whose mother kept a wineshop in Cambridge and from whom the senior (Exeter) branch of the Cecils derive. After her death, he married Mildred Cook, whose sister married Sir Nicholas Bacon, the son of a sheepreeve of the Abbey of Bury St Edmunds, and became the mother of Francis Bacon, Lord Verulam. From the Cook marriage the Cecil Earls of Salisbury descend. William became secretary to the Protector Somerset, then by 1550, Secretary of State to Northumberland and in 1553, Chancellor of the Garter. 'Moving unerringly to the winning side', he skilfully navigated the reign of Mary, and Elizabeth at once appointed him Secretary of State. In 1561 he obtained the lucrative office of Master of the Court of Wards; in 1571 became Baron Burghley and in the year after Lord Treasurer. Burghley was well-established before he came to great office; he built lavishly and had a passion for gardens. His eldest (Cheke) son Thomas disregarded his father's precepts; Burghley even said he was 'a spending sot . . . fit only to keep a tennis court'. But he turned out to be a good soldier and served as Governor of Brill in the Netherlands. Robert, his stepbrother, became as cunning a statesman as his father, and was the main architect of the Stuart succession. For the Welsh origins of the Cecils see A. L. Rowse, 'Alltyrynis and the Cecils', *E.H.R.*, Jan., 1960.

created Lord Leicester, and whose wife, Amy Robsart, had perished all too conveniently, was evaded. A conformist Church settlement was now arranged and the coinage rehabilitated. In spite of assassination plots against the queen, the second phase of events, 1573–88, saw greater internal security and proved the most prosperous time. But the cold war against Spain, which had gradually replaced the old Anglo-Spanish alliance, now hotted up after the assault on the English ships at San Juan de Ulloa in 1568; and would culminate, after the execution of Mary Queen of Scots in 1587, in the defeat of the Spanish Armada in 1588. This famous event, the first great international crisis and major sea battle of modern times, was a strategic turning-point. The island base survived; and though the war went on and the immediate sequel was anti-climax, the Spanish Empire turned to the defensive. But the final phase of Elizabeth's reign, 1588–1603, saw the English bogged down in costly campaigns in Ireland and the Netherlands. The Armada campaign had cost £160,000; but Ireland cost nearly two million, and commitments in the Netherlands a million and a half. Moreover, following bad harvests, the Tudor inflation reached its climax in the 1590s. At the same time the Puritan opposition in parliament became more militant; while the Essex rebellion, when the queen's young favourite attempted a *coup d'état*, was the last belated medieval-style revolt, put down in the medieval way. Though her prestige was enormous, the queen was at last by this time losing grip, and it was fortunate that the accession of James VI and I was smoothly transacted.

In all three phases ideological warfare coincided with official and unofficial war. The English exploited the Calvinist national rebellion in Scotland by the Lords of the Congregation against the Catholic régime of the Regent Mary of Guise; and Elizabeth gave underhand help to the Dutch Protestant resistance against the Spanish Catholic repression. During the first phase the conflict was stepped up when in 1561 Mary Queen of Scots returned as the widow of Francis II of France, to her realm. Then, after conniving at the murder of her next, Catholic, husband, Lord Darnley, (who had helped to kill her favourite, Rizzio)*, she had married Lord Bothwell, one of her husband's mur-

* David Rizzio (1533–66) a musician from Turin, arrived in Scotland, aged twenty-eight, in the entourage of the Ambassador of Savoy, to make up a quartet in the Chapel Royal. He became the queen's *valet de chambre*; in 1564 her French Secretary. He helped arrange her marriage to Darnley, and his promotion marked her attempt at independence. He infuriated the Scots lairds by his 'haughty carriage' and rich clothes, kept a stud of horses and left the huge sum of £11,000 in gold. He also had twenty-two pairs of velvet hose and twenty-two swords. Although Darnley alleged that 'he had a partaker in play and game with him', there is absolutely no evidence that Rizzio was the queen's lover or that the Stuarts descended from him. Considering the dynastic status of a queen, the allegation is wildly improbable. Rizzio played a political game and his murder was a political crime.

derers. He soon deserted her; the Scots queen took refuge in England, 'her grace's attire very mean'; and in 1569 these lurid events gave the pretext for a rebellion of the northern earls, Northumberland and Westmorland.

This still late medieval occasion shows how hard it was for government in London to find out what was going on, and how inadequate were their resources on the spot. Elizabeth complained that she was 'a stranger to her own cause'; out of 189 men mustered at Barnard's Castle, her main stronghold in the north, only. seven were arquebusiers – the rest 'spears' and 'bows'; while her commander, the Earl of Sussex, complained of 'lyyiing upon the cowlde grownde' that had 'driven him into a fevar'.[3] And already a marriage of the Queen of Scots to the Catholic Duke of Norfolk to supplant Elizabeth was being 'muttered'.

With the failure of the rebellion, the dilapidated Catholic feudalism of the north was finally overcome, and Northumberland's extradition from Scotland and execution – his head 'smitten off with a broad carpenter's axe' at York – showed that Elizabeth could be as deadly as her father. Further, the Scots religious feuds were swiftly exploited to break the Scots-French alliance. Then, as the French Catholic interest died out in Scotland, and the civil war subsided in France, England, in fear of Spain, moved to an understanding with the French. This was confirmed by the Treaty of Blois in 1572 which remained unaffected even by the massacre of St Bartholomew in that year – so strong was the common Anglo-French interest against Spain.

Against this background of continental power politics, a religious settlement at home was now even more urgent. In 1559 the Acts of Supremacy and Uniformity had restored the Protestant religion by statute, with the queen 'Governor', if not, like her father, 'Head' of the Church. Despite Elizabeth's own prejudices – 'for Clergymen, *ceteris paribus*, and sometimes *imparibus* too, she preferred the single man'* – the clergy were again allowed to marry. So, against the will of the Catholic bishops and the majority of the Convocation, a compromise settlement was imposed; the Catholics had the predominant interest against them and the Calvinist extremists were divided. In face of both the Catholics and the Calvinist 'Puritans', the structure of medieval Church government was preserved. Most of the clergy acquiesced; since the cult of the prince then made it a political duty to put outward conformity before conscience. Also for the good reason adduced by that

* '*Other things being equal*' and sometimes '*unequal*'. From Sir John Harington, *Nugae Antiquae*, ed. Rev. Henry Harington, London, 1779, vol. I, p. 5. After she had been 'greatly feasted' by Archbishop Parker and his spouse, the queen remarked, 'looking on his Wife, "and you, Madam, I may not call you, and Mrs. I am ashamed to call you, so I know not what to call you, but yet I do thank you"'. (p. 4.)

famous and 'vivacious' vicar, who, living under Henry VIII, Edward VI, Mary I and Elizabeth I, found the martyrs' fire too hot for him, and being taxed for a turncoat said, 'not so, for I always keep my principles, to live and die the Vicar of Bray'.

Elizabeth found in Archbishop Parker a prelate whose bland good sense was fortified by his interest in the Anglo-Saxons, whose amiable Christianity his own personality recalls.* He caused, it will be remembered, Asser's life of Alfred to be edited, if not very well. And it was also said of Whitgift, the other moderate who held office in the later part of the reign, that 'being made Archbishop of *Canterbury*, and of the Privy Council, he carried himself in that mild, and charitable course, that he was not only approved greatly, by all the Clergy of *England*, but even some of those called *Puritans*, of whom he won divers by sweet perswasions to conformity. In the Star Chamber . . . ever leaning to the milder censure, as best became his Calling'.[4]

On the economic front, government also acted swiftly. By 1561, the debased Edwardian coinage had been called in, and a sound silver currency established; further, by 1563 a new Statute of Labourers set new standards – if they were not always observed – in the training and deployment of the skilled and unskilled. The main concern, as always, was to get the 'sturdy' unemployed back on the land in the interests of public security and production. Already in 1536 under Henry VIII the parish had been made the basis of poor relief, and in 1547 London had even instituted a poor rate; now the Elizabethan government enabled the Justices of the Peace to assess and raise compulsory donations. By 1598 a general poor rate would be set up, and beggars more regularly replanted in their own parishes. The system was probably more impressive on paper than in actual performance. Parish accounts suggest that the 'statutory powers of local authorities were rarely invoked in practice, that a poor rate was only levied in times of dire emergency', and even that 'this continued to be true even after 1598'.[5] But if 'the national system, comprehensive and progressive though it was, served only to supplement in emergencies the work of private charitable enterprise', it long served its turn and contributed to better order and some social relief. Government, moreover, as usual in Tudor times, set itself to encourage industry; while heavily protectionist, it welcomed the settlement of skilled refugees from France and the Netherlands, whence many craftsmen had fled from the 'Duke of Alva's long nose and longer sword'.

---

* Matthew Parker (1502–75) was the son of a 'calenderer of stuffs' in Norwich, who became a fellow of Corpus Christi College, Cambridge, chaplain to Anne Boleyn, and, under Edward VI, Dean of Lincoln. Hunted about in the Marian persecutions, for he had connived at the *coup* in favour of Lady Jane Grey, he had been injured by falling from his horse, and lived in poverty till better days. He became Archbishop in 1559.

The second phase of the reign is most interesting for a widening of horizons and the high drama of the conflict with Spain. Philip II had indeed supported Elizabeth through the first and most dangerous vicissitudes of her reign; but following the English understanding with France, whose corsairs had long been harassing the Spanish empire in the Caribbean, where the Spanish colonial régime was now becoming more systematically exclusive, a new conflict was growing up on the other side of the ocean, off coasts hitherto unknown. A romantic, if predatory, note is struck of exotic adventure, and though there was nothing romantic about the sufferings of most of the adventurers, the profits of cold war piracy could be fabulous. Drake's circumnavigation of the globe in 1577–80 – the second after Magellan's in 1525 – won him European renown; and Elizabeth neatly committed the French to approval of the exploit by handing their ambassador the sword to administer Drake's accolade on board the *Golden Hind*. So through the 1570s and 1580s the tension mounted. When in 1586 the Babington Plot to assassinate Elizabeth was ferreted out and Mary Queen of Scots executed in the following year, it became impossible to avoid war. The struggle culminated in the vast crusade of the Armada; an enterprise surely condemned from the first to failure, since the link-up with Parma's forces in the Netherlands, on which the whole strategy depended, was impracticable.

The third phase of the reign, on the other hand, is most interesting for the brilliant flare-up of drama and literature, which carried over into Jacobean times; if its political and social aspects are less attractive than nineteenth-century Protestant historians supposed. For the war dragged on. Compelled for strategic reasons to master Ireland, the English committed and suffered the mounting atrocities which would lead up to those later perpetrated by Oliver Cromwell; in the Netherlands equally dreary and more massive campaigns also took their toll of casualties and disease. In parliament the politically minded Puritans and the many critics of the monopolies granted to the great courtiers, now voiced interests which would undermine the old Conciliar government under Charles I; and though the queen still commanded immense popular loyalty and prestige, her perennial youth became macabre against the bloody tragedy of Essex's amateur rebellion. Yet if Elizabeth's sun went down in a sombre sky, her achievement had been brilliant and decisive; the long defensive strategy had paid off and now promised greater wealth and new oceanic horizons. So the English mourned the old queen, and hailed the outlandish James VI and I only as the lesser of other evils:

What melting words,

wrote one of the fellows of Trinity College, Cambridge,

> *such sorrow can impart?*
> *A dying Queene is tombed in my heart*
> *And such a queen . . .*

Then, turning to make the best of the new prospect, he continued,

> *What means this shining lustre of the aire*
> *As though our Northern Welkin was on fire?*[6]

At least the dangers of a disputed succession had been avoided, and the queen and Robert Cecil had brought in the legitimate Stuart line. They could not know how politically disastrous all but one of them would be.

3

The mainspring of Conciliar government, as in medieval times, was still the personality of the monarch. With the Renaissance cult of the prince, the aloofness and prestige of royalty had increased. Even the design of the English palaces reveals this growing remoteness: 'The sixteenth-century prince, surrounded and to a certain extent besieged by a court traditionally large and on the increase, was forced to regulate the distance between himself and his courtiers in order to obtain any privacy at all. The process culminated in the astonishing epiphanies of queen Elizabeth.'* Even the wise Camden, antiquary and oracle and Clarenceux King of Arms, writing of Henry VIII, takes it for granted that the prince is a law unto him or herself: 'it is the usual practice among Princes to put to death their kindred upon quite slight surmises'. Yet, in spite of theories which would culminate in patriarchal doctrines of Divine Right and passive obedience, reinforced because the family was so much the pivot of Elizabethan and Jacobean society, in England the medieval distinction between the prince who rules by law and gives every man his due, and the tyrant who says that the laws are in his own breast had survived. Medieval law, as in *Magna Carta*, had been designed to protect privileges and property; a franchise was something you were free of, and the duty of the ruler was to protect rights, not override them, for the English common law, product of custom and precedent, had

---

* Hugh Murray Baillie, *Etiquette and the Planning of the State Apartments of Baroque Palaces* Oxford (for the Society of Antiquaries), 1967. p. 178. The English monarchs were now much more remote than the French kings. In France 'no-one knelt, as in England, or bowed as they passed by, but all rank disappeared in his presence, and no-one, not even his heir, received any mark of respect or title . . . and the French have always put the worst construction on any desire for privacy evinced by their royal family'. pp. 183-4.

never been swamped by Roman law with its concept of absolute princely power.*

So, under Mary, the exiled Bishop Ponet of Winchester had as usual appealed, as would Hooker and Locke, to Thomist 'natural reason', and asserted the supremacy of natural law.[7] Political errors, he had maintained, as Pecock had of heresies, came from not following it; for although 'oxen, sheep, goats and such other unreasonable creatures cannot, for lack of reason, rule themselves', man, though handicapped by the Fall, still has a spark of sense. The Greeks, Assyrians and Romans had all been very unreasonable and so perished; but the potential for good (as Pelagius had argued) remained. So legitimate political power, which descends from Noah, cannot be mere will: rulers who would be taken for Gods and use their subjects 'as men do their beasts and lords their villeins and bondmen, getting their goods by hook or crook, with a *sic jubeo, sic volo* (that I command, that I will), and spend to their subjects destruction', are all tyrants, and the representative establishment has a duty 'to God and the world' to 'reform' them. Mary's bigotry, like the romantic egotism of Richard II, had threatened life and property; and it had already provoked a protest which in many ways anticipates that provoked by the Stuarts.

Elizabeth, for all her prestige, had to take account of such opinion; the more so as her courtiers were hard to manage and the influence of parliaments increased. 'The Elizabethan monarchy, outwardly a system of power of majestic simplicity, in fact rested on a curiously complex foundation, its maintenance requiring the most assiduous practice in the arts of political persuasion.'[8] The Court was a potential bear garden; the scene of the desperate competition which, in 1553, had even threatened the dynasty. But it was also the great road to fortune. It could, in Ralegh's words, 'glow like rotten wood', the destructive focus of innumerable ambitions; but its glamour served the queen's turn. The Crown, as in medieval times, was still relatively poor; Elizabeth I had to exact the greatest service she could for the least reward, while deflecting the magnates from conspiracy and treason. Indeed, Elizabeth and Burghley tamed the nobility – 'nobles' now, not 'barons' – out of the gangster habits of the fifteenth century into corrupt but peaceful and absorbing intrigue.

This aim could be achieved in part because the governing class was in fact still very limited – at most it numbered about 2500 persons, of whom not more than sixty were peers; and below them were the richer

* It is remarkable how even the property of convicted rebels could be safeguarded by the law, if previously settled on their wives: after the rebellion of the northern earls, Elizabeth spared a good many insurgents, for she could get at their land if they were alive, but not if they were dead and it had become the property of their widows.

gentry, many also exploiting the Church lands. For these 2500 about 1200 places would have been available, and the scramble for even minor office was so intense, not for the salary, but for the perquisites.[9] Hence a vast black market developed, complicated by the loyalties of family and ramified kinship. At the dizzy heights of favour, the inner ring were often related by politic marriages, and they often secured vast profits, though it was said of Burghley, who did very nicely, that he 'might have had more'. Ralegh, on the other hand, lost a great fortune at home and overseas; and in the end, his life. The lesser men, in particular the lawyers, perhaps did relatively better than the highest flyers.

Beneath the glittering court with its extravagant inhabitants, came the complex and concentrated world of parliament and the law. For 'the Common Law being secure, so necessarily was Parliament, for the inevitable amendments and extensions of this law – other than its judicial interpretations – could only be effected by statute'.[10] Moreover, since any taxation above the normal Crown revenues had to be voted by them, 'the English Parliament would survive when the trend of the age was hostile'. As already observed, since the fifteenth-century seats in parliament had been sought after; in 1543 Ferrers' Case had won Members freedom from arrest. The Commons had, indeed, long ceased to be a collection of minor provincial worthies; they were now mainly the representatives of prosperous county families: the 296 members in 1558 would become 462 by 1603 and 'the gentry were now in occupation of almost the whole representation in the Commons';[11] indeed, only 60 of the burgesses were now in fact townsmen. As the more enterprising gentry became richer, so the power of the Commons would increase; until, along with the great peers who set interest before loyalty, powerful men among them would overcome the Crown in the crisis of confidence that would bring down the Caroline government. While the transition from medieval violence to peaceful political faction had been made, the opposition in the Commons was becoming formidable and often articulate in Puritan eloquence.

As the richer gentry controlled the Commons, so increasingly they controlled the counties. The Crown had to work through them. The new Lords Lieutenant were, of course, great nobles with estates in the counties; appointed by the Crown, they and their Deputies were in close touch with the Council, and concerned mainly with raising forces in emergency. But the local routine business which mattered was in the hands of the unpaid Justices of the Peace, rooted in the counties since the fourteenth century. The judges of Assize had superior authority, and could purge the Commissions of the Peace, but the Justices of the Peace in Quarter Sessions dealt with crime and disorder. If they could settle felonies only after trial by jury on indictment, and local juries were often reluctant to convict, they had power of life and death; in a society not far removed from medieval violence they hanged malefactors in a way then thought necessary for law and order. Apart from criminal jurisdiction, their responsibilities were very wide: the ancient Anglo-Saxon obligations to see after bridges and highways still stood; and if, in the words of Lambarde's *Eirenarcha* (1581), the Justices were mainly concerned to keep the peace and 'do equal right', rather than with compelling people to 'conformity of mind', their many-sided functions gave them a pervasive influence. They were concerned with labour disputes, wage restraint, and poor relief; with licensing ale houses and with making the fathers of bastards support their offspring; and they worked through the constables, borsholders, tything men and churchwardens to manage the whole gamut of local affairs. If their social influence could be stifling, they set the precedent for the strong local self-government inherited and developed by the English-speaking peoples overseas. In a world of widespread illiteracy, intermittent plague and local famine, they brought the influence of government to bear on a vigorous society, where, despite the sufferings of the poor, social mobility was considerable, and in which men of talent and enterprise could go a long way. The problem of liberty and order, that perennial concern of government, was intelligently tackled in Elizabethan England, and in a hierarchical but not a bureaucratic society, a good deal of medieval liberty was preserved.

4

Though the really decisive mercantile economic expansion came in the later seventeenth century, the Elizabethan age was a turning-point in finance, industry and agriculture, even if in the last new methods were slowly adopted. In this way, as in many others, the country now began to catch up with the advances on the continent, most marked in northern Italy and Flanders. On the advice of a new kind of international financier with a wider grasp than the author of the *Tree of Commonwealth*, Wolsey, or even Thomas Cromwell, the monetary blunders of the mid-century were now redeemed. Sir Thomas Gresham, who netted a steady fifteen per cent from his own extensive businesses, and the Italian, Sir Horatio Palavicino, who made a fortune out of papal alum for treating cloth, were both able men. Being men of business and not academic theorists, they did not think competitive debasement of the coinage sound policy. It was better to 'bring the base money into fine'; for 'the exchange' wrote Gresham, 'is the chiefest thing only above all others . . . and is the means that makes all foreign commodities and your own commodities good and cheap'.[12] Further, as Edward VI had foreseen, the continental wars were England's opportunity; when Antwerp, long in decline, was sacked by the Spaniards in 1576 and later blockaded by the rebellious Dutch in the Scheldt, London, where the Royal Exchange had been opened in 1570, drew ahead as the financial capital of northern Europe.

The wool and cloth industry remained far the greatest export; indeed the country was still much too dependent on this speciality. But though, in 1550, there was a glut in the market, and the boom conditions of Henry VIII's reign were over, new fabrics were devised for new markets; for Russia and the Levant and the East. The oligarchic Merchant Adventurers had concentrated on the Antwerp market and suffered from the Henrician and Edwardian debasement of the coinage; but, with the collapse of Antwerp, a new trade was developed with Morocco, regularized by the foundation of the short-lived Barbary Company in 1585. After the defeat of the Turks at Lepanto, the Levant trade began again to open up, and the Levant Company was founded in 1581. In the Baltic the Hanseatic League had been disrupted by the wars between Denmark and Sweden, and in 1579 the Eastland Company was founded, mainly trading cloth for grain. The Edwardian expedition to Muscovy, was followed up by the foundation of the Russia Company, which, though it failed to develop its ambitious contacts with Iran, brought back hemp and cordage and timber for the fleet. But the company with the greatest future was founded in 1600; the East India Company, trading with India and the Far East. None of these enterprises was yet on a great scale; but they had staked claims later to be vastly exploited.

The most thriving cloth manufacturing areas were still in Somerset, Gloucestershire and Wiltshire; in East Anglia, and in Yorkshire. The wool was mainly put out to cottagers in areas where water for fulling mills was plentiful, as in the valley of the Bristol Avon or of the Wylye in Wiltshire, where the drowning of water meadows was first practised; both districts where the peasantry were numerous, but not too much occupied with tillage.[13]

The other great industry, though old-established, was new in scale. The English had always been pioneer coal miners, and by the end of the reign as much shipping was employed in bringing 'sea coal' from Newcastle to London as in the trade with Flanders; this traffic rose from 24,000 tons in 1586 to 74,000 twenty years later. Though it is premature to speak of an industrial revolution in this or any other Elizabethan industry, the Durham, Lancashire and Yorkshire and south-Wales pits were now being rapidly developed. The growing shortage of timber forced Londoners in particular to accept this new and murky fuel, and chimneys now mitigated its effects, repulsive to those accustomed to blazing logs. So, by Jacobean times, England would be far the greatest producer and exporter of coal in Europe, and the exploitation of coal meant the better exploitation of iron in Sussex, south Wales and the Forest of Dean. Since the later years of Henry VIII, England had made its own cannon, and in the 1560s Elizabeth's government set about a systematic rearmament: German experts were brought into Cumberland at high rates of pay to extract copper, and into the Mendips to develop the lead mines, once superficially exploited by the Romans. Leather goods and cutlery and glass were now manufactured, mainly in the Midlands, and industries developed in newly expanding towns unhampered by the regulations of the old-established centres. Textiles were already produced in Lancashire, though their 'cotton' was in fact still a coarse mixture of wool and linen, and it was not until 1610 that true cotton came in from Turkey. Thus, over a wide range of industries, old patterns were adapted and new patterns set in a time of cheap labour and versatile enterprise.

But Elizabethan England remained overwhelmingly rural. As in medieval times, the vast majority lived off the land, and under Elizabeth I, the town market for agricultural products improved, especially around London. By the end of the reign 'the steady growth of farming improvement is a conscious aim',[14] while 'the remedies for the great difficulties of Tudor farming – lack of winter keep and the want of means for restoring the fertility of the soil are beginning to be suggested by Elizabethan writers'.[15] It is likely that the new masters of the Church lands were determined to get value for money, and that their closer attention often set new standards in many great estates. Sheep were prized not only for wool and meat, but for manure – hence more mixed farming and higher productivity: and already by 1577 a treatise translated out of Dutch was in circulation, advocating root crops for winter feed for livestock. Thomas Tusser's *Five Hundred points of Good Husbandry* (1573) went into many editions, its jogtrot verses memorable to rustic minds; though Tusser himself, educated (and, he records, well flogged) at Eton and then, more happily, at Trinity Hall, Cambridge, failed to make a success of farming.

The rich, who were frenetic and competitive builders, creating vast ornate structures of glass and brick, more after the Danish and Flemish style than after the mansions of the French Renaissance, were also great lovers of formal gardens. New fruits and shrubs were acclimatized, for the 'grand tour' was beginning to become fashionable; among them 'apricocks' and the 'curious peach'. Flemish hops for the beer which now competed with ale, were now raised on ground good for little else. Cypress and myrtle now adorned formal parterres of clipped yew and box, and the variety of garden flowers mentioned by Shakespeare is far greater than anything observed by Chaucer. Vineyards, a concession to the cult of Italy in a cold climate, must have produced doubtful wine: bees from whose honey mead was made, as in Anglo-Saxon times, were better value.

In Henry VIII's day, Leland's *Itinerary* depicted a fairly prosperous land, but now Camden's famous *Britannia* shows a richer country. His picture of Wiltshire, for example, is already familiar, though his place names are now often archaic –*Devizis* 'the Vies'; *Euerley* warren of hares; *Edmerston, Gummeldon*; *Martinsall* and *Selbury* hills, and the 'wild structure' of Stonehenge. *Sauernac* is already famous for 'plenty of game and for sweet-smelling fern (*filici gratissimi odoris celebris*'); at *Marleborow* every freeman gives the Mayor a couple of beagles (*duos canes leporarios*) on his admission to office', and *Ramesbury* is already 'delectable' because of its meadows,[16] Camden is also felicitous in describing East Anglia. *Iceni*, (Norfolk) for example, where the German ocean is full of fish and the tide 'beats upon the shore with a great roaring', the country is well stocked with sheep, conies and cattle, and swarming with people 'of a bright clear complexion, not to mention the sharpness of their wit'.[17] At Cambridge they make good malt from a vast acreage of barley, and the fens abound in water fowl and fish, though the fenmen are brutish, call strangers 'upland men' and go about on stilts.

Such, and here only two examples can be cited, was the rural background of Elizabethan England: not yet committed to the systematic cultivation of root crops for winter fodder which would so much enhance prosperity in the following century, but already more productive and diversified than the earlier Tudor countryside.

5

The most spectacular Elizabethan exploit is also the most novel. Where political, religious and economic changes developed gradually from medieval times, the oceanic enterprise of Hawkins and Drake and their kind was in a new dimension. Since the reigns of Richard I and John, the Crown had intermittently fostered the rudiments of a navy; Edward III had won the battle of Sluys and Henry V had assembled a considerable fleet. Already by the early thirteenth century the mariner's compass had been in use: 'an iron needle (which) after having been in contact with a lodestone turns itself always towards the northern star ... very necessary for those who navigate at sea'. The swarming fisheries and coastal trade had long fostered the tradition of seamanship behind the Elizabethan navy. Henry VII had laid down dockyards and the nucleus of royal ships; Henry VIII had set up a permanent Navy

Board, some of its members still in office at the accession of Elizabeth I. He had also commanded that maps be made of the entire south coast, as well as founding new dockyards at Deptford – where Drake's father was chaplain – and at Woolwich, since supplemented under Northumberland by the dockyard at Chatham. And in 1546 Henry VIII had inaugurated the corporation of Trinity House, still in existence today; responsible for lighthouses and buoys round the entire coast. He had thus created a solid background for the Royal Navy.

But the crucial change in the design of ships, then tentatively begun, did not come about until John Hawkins took control, after the attack on the English at San Juan de Ulloa had shown that conflict with Spain would be inevitable. The early Henrician navy had fought in the old way of grapple and board in doubtful contests off the Breton coast; and if by 1541 the *Great Harry* and the *Mary Rose* were high-built carracks of a thousand tons – as big as many of the Armada ships and heavily gunned in a new way – the first never went into action, and the latter had capsized. The fast new galleasses, which combined oars with sail, were more adaptable; but the royal ships, laid up in the winter, were still built of unseasoned oak. Moreover, under Edward and Mary, the Navy Board had become excessively conservative, dilatory and corrupt. It was, as usual, only against entrenched opposition that Hawkins in the 1570s introduced ships in principle of similar design to those of Nelson's navy; more streamlined and heavily gunned, yet manœuvrable. It was due to him that when, in 1588, Lord Howard of Effingham, like Jellicoe at Jutland, could have lost the war in an afternoon, the extremely formidable Armada was confronted with a fighting navy of ocean-going ships, capable of a spoiling attack the year before, and of striking back at Cadiz afterwards. For the Spaniards were outmanœuvred and outgunned. Drake and Hawkins had grasped the essential point, unappreciated by conservatives accustomed to fighting sea battles in the Channel, that the navy had now to operate far from its bases with ships well enough armed and provisioned to fight on the high seas, and even capable of a global strategy, of which Drake's voyage round the world was the most spectacular example.*

But Drake was only the most able of the swarm of adventurers who plundered the Iberian empire. Off the peninsula itself privateering became a well-organized business. After 1585, when the Spaniards

---

* Once in the Pacific, Drake outclassed anything the Spaniards could bring against him and ranged freely as far as California. He was probably in search of the exit from the North-West Passage, thought to run from Hudson's Bay. This transit, politically desirable as outside Spanish jurisdiction, was still thought practicable by navigators and geographers, unaware that the absence of the Gulf Stream and the presence of the Labrador current made the climate of North America much more severe than that of equivalent latitudes in Europe. They estimated that the passage emerged near the latitude of modern Monterey.

arrested all English ships in Iberian ports, letters of reprisal were issued to those who could prove loss: soon these letters became a mere formality, and while Drake was plundering the West Indies in the 1580s, official and unofficial marauders flourished. Some were financed by West Country gentlemen and merchants; others had more substantial backing from syndicates in Bristol and London. Then, as the scale of depredations increased, the syndicated professionals came to supersede the local amateurs; if the game was risky, the profits could be enormous.[18] And there was no shortage of crews. The seamen preferred the chance of major loot and appalling conditions of service to the steadier pay and relative discipline of the queen's ships. They died off from scurvy, typhus and dysentery – 'the bloody flux'; sometimes simply from starvation: but the plunder of a rich prize and the free for all that often followed proved an irresistible lure, and there was a long tradition of piracy in the southern ports. It was hard to prevent up-country men and boys from running away to sea: 'as for the business of pillage', wrote a contemporary, 'there is nothing that more bewitcheth them'.

If the cargoes were less exciting than often supposed – more hides and wine, sugar and fish than jewels and gold – the value of prize goods at the height of the boom ranged from £100,000 to £200,000 a year, when the entire extra-parliamentary revenue of the queen was £300,000: plunder accounted for ten to fifteen per cent of imports. Most of the profits went to London syndicates, but in the West Country the loot helped to establish a good many county families; Pitts and Bonds in Dorset, Treffrys and Killigrews in Cornwall. Further, as the big London syndicates piled up their capital, it was used for legitimate trade, and the risky enterprises of the privateers contributed to less directly predatory expansion.*

This long-term expansion would not have come about if the vast enterprise, planned by Philip II and his advisers in his new-built palace of the Escorial, on the southern slopes of the Guardarramas and commanding great views of the plateau of Castile, had succeeded. If Spanish pikemen had landed in England, the country could have suffered a devastation as great as that of the Low Countries, and its whole future would probably have been different.

But spectacular as had been the English success, when that 'most felicitous fleet' the Armada of Spain, such 'as never the like before saild upon the Ocean Sea', took such a beating, it now looks different from the straight nineteenth-century myth. If the 'deliverance' proved

* In 1589–91 the known value of prizes taken by London privateers was £97,283. Dorset (probably with London backing) took £71,226; Devon and Cornwall £34,330 and Southampton £22,571, Andrews, *Privateering, op. cit., Elizabethan* p. 125.

that the Spanish bid to dominate Europe had failed, to the English at the time this brilliant pay off of calculated risks seemed too good to be true. 'In the spring of 1588,' writes Mattingly,[19] 'none of the naval experts on either side foresaw much of what was to come. The size of the forces involved and the nature of their armament was unprecedented.' As in 1940, 'all Europe watched the battle in the Channel with breathless suspense'.[20]

The result was thought 'miraculous';* a judgement of God in a clash between rival ideas and ways of life, not a mere conflict of economic interest.†

The English were in fact awe-struck by the megalomaniac enterprise. The Armada alone carried well over 27,000 men and over 2,650 great guns, with vast stores and ammunition: it was laden with wagons and with mattocks and baskets for the pioneers; with hides and hemp to stop damage from gunfire, and with cables daubed with pitch to protect the great oaken masts. Nothing, it seemed, had been forgotten. And though women were not allowed with the fleet, they hired four ships and followed the Armada, to fetch up, frustrated, in Normandy. In Flanders, meanwhile, Parma, the most famous commander of the day, had long made massive and complex preparation: canals dug or enlarged from Antwerp and Ypres to Ghent and Bruges; hoys and barges assembled at Sluys, Nieuport and Dunkirk, with Flemish crews reinforced by seamen from Hamburg and Bremen. The crack Spanish infantry were supplemented by whole regiments of Germans, Walloons, Burgundians and Italians; 5,000 cavalry were assembled at Kortrijk, while morale was boosted by the presence of several of the king's own bastards, and Pope Sixtus Quintus had published a *cruzado*, with comprehensive indulgences.[21]

So, far from being full of confidence, the English were profoundly alarmed. And, apart from the Catholics, who thought their excommunicated queen was a heretic, there were appeasers. The Spaniards, they argued, were too canny for so mad an enterprise; they must be out

---

*'The Miraculous Victory atchieved by the English Fleete, under the descreet and happy conduct of the right honorable, right prudent and valiant lord, the L. Charles Howard, high Admirall of England, etc., upon the Spanish huge Armada,' Richard Hakluyt, *Voyages and Documents*. Selected. J. Hampden. Oxford. 1958, pp. 358–98. '*La Felicissima Armada*', was the official term, changed in Lisbon tavern talk into *La Invincible* and afterwards, ironically, so termed in Spain.

† Evelyn Hardy, *Survivors of the Armada*, London, 1966, pp. 27–8. The contrast, as well observed, is symbolized by the names of the ships; 'the English bearing such simple, clipt ones as the *Black Crow*, the *Bear*, the *Bull*, *Cygnet* and *Dolphin*, the *Tiger, Lion, Antelope, Swallow* and *Little Swan* . . . the *Elizabeth, Jonas* or *Mary Rose* . . . the *Charles*, the *George*, the *Edward Bonaventure* . . . the *Rainbow, Sun* and *Moon*. . . . But when we come to the Armada ships, with hardly an exception, they carry religious names . . . The *Holy Spirit*, and the *Crucifixion* . . . *Conception, Assumption* and *Coronation* . . . or the Italian merchantman *La Sancta Maria Rata Incoronada*, known to the English as the *Rat*'.

to attack Holland; or perhaps they could be bought off. Too many English-made guns, sold to Spain, were in the Armada: and when, after the decisive success of the fire ships off Calais, the final attack off Gravelines appeared inconclusive, the admirals were fiercely criticized by the civilians. The Armada was even expected to return, and the parade at Tilbury, when the queen's famous oratory rallied her inadequate forces, was held under this illusion. Only after the Armada had 'vanished in smoake', were the propagandists able to prove that God was Protestant: *Afflavit Deus et dissipati sunt*, said the English; '*Glory to God only*' said the Dutch, '*It came, it went, it was*'.

The contest had in fact been decided by an early and expert strategic decision. A conservative medieval strategy would have stood to fight in the Channel and provoked just the mêlée the enemy desired. Instead, on 30–31 July, the English had warped out of Plymouth, then got a following wind and kept it. The Armada had already been outmanœuvred. But the slow and sinister progress of the great fleet up the Channel had underlined the calculated risk. Though the long-accepted legend that the Spanish galleons dwarfed the queen's fighting ships is untrue,* the English had been impressed by their 'castle-like' crescent maintained by skilled Iberian and Levantine crews. A vast expenditure of shot had produced no major result, and when on 7 August the Armada arrived off Calais, it had carried out Philip's strategic intent.

Unfortunately for the Armada, the strategy was wrong. Parma himself well knew that only if the deep-water harbour of Vlissingen were taken and the Dutch and English fleets neutralized, would the invasion have the remotest chance; indeed, his final preparations appear perfunctory. Further, an unpractical strategy had brought the fleet to dire tactical danger. Experts in Channel winds and tides, the English now struck like lightning. When their fire ships, packed with 'gunpowder, pitch and brimstone and other combustible matter', crackling with flames and thundering with double-shotted cannon, bore down through the darkness on Calais Roads, they decided the campaign. The Spaniards could only cut their cables and stand out to sea. And then, off Gravelines, the English launched the fiercest attack they could. If the gunnery on both sides was wild and the ammunition again ran out, many Spanish ships were crippled, and the fleet twice escaped total disaster; first off Dunkirk, then off Zeeland, only by a last-minute shift of the wind as the muddy olive-green breakers roared along those treacherous sands.

It was, indeed, a remarkable feat that they avoided worse catastrophe.

* 'It must have begun', writes Mattingly, 'when some literary landlubber, watching perhaps from the Isle of Wight, compared the swarm of English pinnaces with the ponderous *urcas* (transports) and neglected to notice the fighting ships'. *op. cit.*, p. 328.

On 9 August Medina Sidonia, by no means the incompetent commander of legend, correctly cut his losses and set course for Spain; 'a tremendously laborious one ... to sail round England, Scotland and Ireland 750 leagues through stormy seas almost unknown to us'. Off Rockall, out in the Atlantic, he told his commanders to avoid Ireland and make for Finisterre and Corunna. And this most of them did: out of the sixty-eight that were off the Lizard on 30 August, by late September forty-four battered typhus-ridden ships had returned. Caught in a succession of equinoctial cyclonic gales, the galleons rolling and pitching in mountainous Atlantic seas, grey or indigo under the rain squalls, waves cascading through scuppers and wind howling through spars, many commanders might have done worse.*

But if the Atlantic gales are authenticated, there is no evidence that the wild Irish massacred the Spaniards and that the survivors made up for it by populating the country. Few of the Irish could swim, and many thought it bad luck to rob the sea god of his due, so they often left the Spaniards to drown; when the survivors came ashore they merely robbed them to the skin. It was the English, a precarious garrison, or Irish bands directly under English orders, who strung up or hacked to pieces any Spaniards they could catch: the peasantry sometimes hid the survivors and even dressed their wounds. Captain Francisco de Cuellar, for example, whose fascinating account survives, escaped to the mountains; then to Scotland, and so, after desperate vicissitudes, to Dunkirk.

Such was the fate of the enormous enterprise and such the relation of legend to fact. Undeterred, Philip II at once set about assembling another fleet; the English *riposte* on Cadiz achieved little; and the war went on. Elizabeth's government, obsessed by the strategic danger from Ireland, sank vast sums putting down the formidable rebellion of Tyrone and on sustaining the resistance of the Dutch. But the dedicated king was now forced to more realistic designs; the defeat of the Armada led the Spaniards to create a more efficient navy and better defences against the English attempt to intercept the treasure fleets; the Azores was secured; and more treasure got through to Spain between 1588 and 1603 than ever before. Yet the long-term consequences of '88 were decisive. Despite the immediate disappointing sequel, the English, like the Dutch, became a first rate maritime power: Parma had been diverted from his proper objectives in Holland and Zeeland; the pro-Spanish party in France would fail, and the bid of Counter-Reformation Spain for European domination was in fact over. The defeat of the Armada had

* The weather was as 'foul as tradition has it': see 'The Wrecks of the Spanish Armada on the Coast of Ireland', by W. Spotswood Green, *Geographical Journal*, vol. xxvii, No. 5, pp. 447-8, cited in Hardy, *op. cit.*, p. 22.

proved that neither side in the vast European religious conflict could win, though it took the Thirty Years' War to confirm that both must compromise. Already, in fact, if not in appearance, the vast Spanish–Portuguese power had passed its peak. Spain had created an empire which ranks among the greatest colonial exploits in world history, with results decisive for Central and South America; but already her vast resources had been overstrained, and the home country would begin its slow decline into what would appear to a cynical eighteenth-century historian as that grand but poverty-stricken 'republic of bewitched beings . . . a republic whose most famous citizen was Don Quixote de la Mancha'.[22]

7

The Elizabethan government's fear of a successful Spanish invasion of Ireland had been the sequel to events already recorded: for it was there that Henry viii had left his least successful legacy. His determined attempt to impose the kind of settlement imposed on Wales had left the island superficially pacified, but the Irish beyond the Pale remained unreconciled. Of all the English attempts at colonization Ireland would be the least successful. After all, the Irish were there already.

The tragedy is hardly remarkable considering the profound discrepancy between the two societies. The one was now militantly Protestant, settled, relatively methodical; the other Catholic, pastoral, underdeveloped, even migratory. In this final phase of their Atlantic prehistory, the Gaelic Irish were still ungovernable: elusive in their woods and bogs. Henry viii had never closed the gap between discrepant centuries. To put it mildly, 'there was a very strong sentiment . . . against government from a distance', and the archaic Brehon Laws which he had failed to put down, still 'operated . . . against positive legislation by the ruler'.[23] Flattered by their panegyrists and itinerant musicians, sustained by their barefoot *kerns* and *gallowglas* mercenaries, the wilder chieftains still lived very much as described by Giraldus in the twelfth century. Their saffron-coloured mantles still had a Bronze Age style, and, if Tudor artists were accurate, their swordsmen did not have so much as a sling but carried their swords separately in their scabbards. With *glibs* of tangled hair over their foreheads – perhaps an echo of Danish fashion in the tenth century – the tall young axemen, who belonged in spirit to the Celtic epics of prehistory, appeared as savage to the Elizabethans as Amerindians or West Africans. They would sleep stark naked on the ground by the dozen round the fire in their wattle and turf 'booley' huts; live off oatcakes instead of bread and think it 'unlucky' to clean the milk pails. The English alleged that they were too lazy even to take the wildfowl and the fish; they lived off cows' blood, butter, milk and raw vegetables – a diet that in fact produced the stature and clear skins admired by Sir John Harrington. Wives were still often kept for a year and a day on probation, and their cooking was only made tolerable by whisky (*uise beathadh* or *usequebaugh*) drunk at all hours. To most of the English they appeared murderous; 'outlandish and reprehensible'.[24]

Such was the stock image presented to the Elizabethans, now settling like vultures in Ireland. Some were taking up vast estates; and most were much too sanguine of their future among a people who found them repulsive heretics. The Irish looked to Rome and Spain for redress, and the few Renaissance-educated magnates looked to Florence and Italy, not to London. The resulting conflict was long and arduous: it lost the English government enormous sums, and landed them in immense difficulties of logistics and supply. Disease took an even greater toll of the English forces in Ireland than in the Low Countries, and during the 1590s the campaign against the O'Neill Earl of Tyrone brought successive defeats – for the Irish tactics were highly intelligent, taking advantage of the country to trap the English columns and isolate their garrisons. And when in 1599 the queen appointed her favourite, Essex, as Lord Lieutenant, she had to send 16,000 foot and 1,300 horse with him, and even then he failed. It was only when Mountjoy succeeded him and used a strategy of attrition, aptly compared to that employed three centuries later by Kitchener in South Africa,[25] that the morale of the troops was at all restored; and when a substantial Spanish expedition tried to land at Cork and was besieged there in Kinsale, Tyrone's relieving army was destroyed. 'His heroic effort for Gaelic Ireland was at an end. . . . He was no longer a danger.'[26]

But even this apparently conclusive English success did not solve the problem. The conflict would smoulder on, and flare up again in the seventeenth century. An Irish rebellion against the Protestant settlers in Ulster would contribute to set off the English civil wars, and lead to Cromwell's notorious campaigns and the legacy of hatred they would create.

8

Looking back over the various aspects of the long reign of Elizabeth I, one must conclude that her strategy and her success had been more negative and defensive in the game of European power politics than is often supposed. Like Henry VIII, she had been outclassed by the manpower and resources of France and Spain; and if, unlike her father, she now had a navy that was second to none, she well knew that the

Spanish empire could not be ruined. Nor did she wish to destroy the Spanish counterweight to the traditional enemy – the French. She had, indeed, been driven reluctantly to break the old Spanish alliance, and her policy long remained improvising and equivocal, limited by slender resources. Indeed, even after 1588, her reign closed in an atmosphere of anxiety.

Yet historians have gone too far in repudiating the nineteenth-century cult of Protestant success: if Shakespeare is politically conservative, typically Tudor in his concern for order and degree, and the brilliance of the late Elizabethan Court cannot be proved to be the result of the 'deliverance' of '88, it reflects a more articulate patriotism and self-confidence; a wider range. The dynasty, after all, had been rehabilitated: in spite of recurrent conspiracy, the queen had survived. The religious conflict, which had convulsed France and would convulse Germany, had been damped down at least to an outward conformity congenial to a realistic establishment, now confirmed in its hold on the Church lands. The debased coinage had been restored, and the grip of the London government on the country reinforced by the Lords Lieutenant and their Deputies and by the steady interest of the substantial gentry in the Tudor peace. In spite of what at times was a roaring inflation which depressed the living standards of the poor below that of the later Middle Ages, the successful on all levels, from sheep farming and industry to privateering, got their heads, creating new enterprise and building up new capital. If there was not yet an industrial revolution, the basis of heavy industry was being secured in coal and iron, and with the advice of continental experts technology in general had improved: even in conservative agriculture, modern methods were beginning to come in, mainly from Holland, while the new trading companies were extending their enterprise into areas hitherto mysterious or unknown. Hence an impression of vigour and promise, but not widespread fulfilment: for that one must turn to the sudden and astonishing late Elizabethan literature and drama which came to its climax in Jacobean times, and which can compare with the greatest achievements of any other people.

This literature, which contrasts vividly with the mainly clumsy and provincial writing of the mid-century, was the result of the assimilation of an originally Italianate Renaissance learning and culture now permeating a wider élite, and which, in spite of vicissitudes, had centred through the reigns of all the Tudors on a brilliant and intelligent, if dangerous, Court. This régime, the climax in England of the Renaissance monarchy which had emerged since the days of Edward IV with the growing cult of the prince, had adapted the old Conciliar government with roots in medieval and even Anglo-Saxon times to new purposes; it still worked through a relatively flimsy bureaucracy and depended on the voluntary, unpaid, collaboration of the magnates and gentry in the counties. But if ever the central administration became incompetent and the court lost the confidence of its natural supporters, the régime would be undermined. It was just such a crisis of confidence that the Stuarts would provoke.

17

JACOBEAN ENGLAND

On the ceiling of Inigo Jones's banqueting hall in Whitehall may be seen the apotheosis of James I; a swirling fantasy by Rubens which gives the homely monarch an unwonted and bewildered grace. It depicts the extravagant ideal of the late north Renaissance prince, soon, on the continent, to change into the more formal and efficient grandeur of the absolute monarchy promoted by Richelieu and realized by Louis XIV and his imitators. In England, on the other hand, after civil war and a republican interval, monarchy would be modified into a something more 'mixed' and informal, shrewdly manipulated by Charles II in what was to be economically and socially a more modern context.

In contrast to Rubens's exuberance, the banqueting hall itself, though a Jacobean structure, reflects the austere taste of Charles I; a prince of remote and elusive mind, at once dedicated and frivolous, the greatest connoisseur and collector of pictures of all the English kings and 'the last English sovereign who discharged in any fullness the function of a literary patron'.[1] In spite of economic recession and political tension, there was now a less harsh way of life for the successful, if not for the mass of the people. This change is apparent not so much in sophisticated Court writers, or in the profound, sometimes baleful writings of genius, but in the idiom of the casual and ordinary world to be depicted retrospectively by John Aubrey, the first perceptive biographer in English, or by many treatises on sport and country life and gardening. The latter was well represented by the *Compleat Angler* or *Contemplative Men's Recreation* (1653) of Isaac Walton, a London merchant who retired to the country during the commotions brought about by conflicts then little understood; aggravated by fanatics and politicians, and perhaps in retrospect even given an exaggerated importance in recent times.

2

Contrary to widespread belief, James VI of Scotland and I of England (1603–25) was no fool. He could be sometimes a shrewd politician in his own right. He was also the first, and so far the last, English monarch to write massive and learned books, and by no means 'the buffoon in purple or the impossible pedant that the scandal-mongers of the court would have us believe'.[2] As the Venetian ambassador told his masters, the new king was 'a man of letters and business', who spoke Latin and French perfectly and understood Italian quite well. But he was also, the Venetian reported, determined 'to enjoy the Papacy' – wilful, lazy and self-indulgent. He had three obsessions; hunting, learning and young men. Riding up to Everleigh on Salisbury Plain from Lord Pembroke's house at Wilton, he enjoyed coursing the hares; at Oxford in 1605, he relished academic disputations; and he was delighted when at St John's College 'three young youths, in habits and attire like nymphs, representing England, Scotland and Ireland, welcomed him at the gate'. The college had struck the right note.

An only child – his father was murdered, his mother imprisoned – he had always longed for affection. Indeed it was said in the idiom of the time that he had long been one for 'quiet purposes'. 'I pray the reader,' writes a discreet bishop, 'to consider the Sweetness of the King's nature (for I ascribe it to that cause) . . . that from the time he was 14 years old and no more . . . when the Lord Aubigny came into Scotland to visit him [from the Court of Henry III of France], even then he began, and with that noble personage, to clasp some-one *gratioso* in the embraces of his great love, above all others.'[3] Further, in an age not over nice in such matters, the monarch's language was appalling –'a florescence of obscenity'.[4] Though he raised a talented family by his empty-headed Danish queen (who shared her husband's taste for the bottle), the emotional life of this weather-beaten, witty and foul-mouthed Scots royalty centred on a succession of favourites, culminating in George Villiers, Duke of Buckingham, for 'that lord was our Alcibiades for Beauty'.[5] Unlike Elizabeth, he put heart before head.

So when at last the first of the Stuarts came into his English kingdom, he declared that he had wished to see the old queen 'neither alive nor dead', and refused even to wear mourning or attend her funeral. Moreover, his Court soon cost more than that of Spain or France. The 'fire' in the Northern Welkin had heralded not the advent of an enlightened prince, but a régime of mounting, if genial, corruption and staggering irresponsibility; all the more lamentable in a time so creative in colonial enterprise, drama and literature and speculative thought.

The political events of the reign fall naturally into three phases. In the first, from 1603–12, government was relatively sound; still mainly conducted by Sir Robert Cecil, since 1604 Earl of Salisbury. Then, with the death of Salisbury, and of Henry Prince of Wales, the promising and able heir, government lapsed into increasing confusion and infirmity of purpose both at home and abroad. For the king casually accorded political power first to Robert Carr, a handsome but brainless young Scot, whom he made Earl of Somerset; then, after 1616, to George Villiers, whom he made Duke of Buckingham and who proved more grandiosely incapable. It was mainly through Buckingham's influence that the third phase, 1620–5, ended in a serious crisis at home and abroad, which carried over into the next reign and first brought Charles I into head-on collision with his parliament. The relatively high standard of the Elizabethan régime had long collapsed.

At his accession James I faced four simultaneous dangers; assassination, religious warfare, bankruptcy and constitutional strife. It is not surprising that he feared the first; William the Silent, Henry III and Henry IV of France had all three been murdered; and, following two minor conspiracies, in 1605 a group of catholic extremists, disappointed of greater toleration, tried to blow up not only the monarch but almost the entire establishment. And they nearly succeeded. The tale that the king himself discovered the Gunpowder plot is suspect, but it has never been disproved.[6] In the November murk the cellar under the Parliament House was searched. Guy Fawkes, a soldier with some routine skill in mining who had been brought over from the Low Countries by the conspirators, was found lurking there with a dark lantern and all the attributes of a cloak-and-dagger conspiracy. At the sight of the instruments of torture he confessed all. A Catholic régime was to be instated and the continental Catholic powers presented with a *fait accompli*. The familiar episode, still celebrated on 5 November in England to this day, is a conclusive example of the chancy aspects of great affairs, putting paid to dogmas of the inevitable course of history. Whoever discovered the plot, it was by a hair's breadth that the design had failed.

James's reaction was in character, if not ignoble. 'Had God,' he said, 'for my sins permitted the execution of the plot, I should have had the satisfaction of dying not in a tavern, nor among the rabble, but on a mighty stage and in honourable company.'[7] It is a remark worthy of one of the more imaginative Roman emperors. The Catholic extremists thus confirmed the popular view of their religion created by the Marian persecutions, Foxe's *Book of Martyrs* and the threat of the Armada.

But James had not only to contend with the more fanatical Catholics; he had also to deal with the Calvinist Puritans. In the Millenary Petition of 1603 they had already demanded that the sign of the Cross be abolished in baptism, and the ring in marriage; indeed, in the view of orthodox Anglicans, they 'aimed at the overthrow of the present Church government and instead thereof at the setting up of a presbytery in every parish'.[8] No wonder that, in view of his experience of the Kirk in Scotland, the king told them at the Hampton Court Conference of 1604, 'I will have one doctrine and one discipline. . . . I will make them conform themselves or I will harry them out of the land or else do worse'. The long-accepted idea that these people could have been brought into the Church is untenable; if James offended a powerful interest, he had no alternative. And he deserves credit for commissioning in that year the famous authorized translation of the Bible. He had never, he said, seen a good translation of it.

His responsibility for the financial vicissitudes of his reign is direct. Within three years he was deep in debt. The expenditure on his wardrobe quadrupled; on building nearly doubled. The cost of court entertainment became fantastic, and fashions even more ostentatious and expensive. The 'great tub farthingale' now came in, and when Lady Wyche, the wife of the ambassador to the Grand Turk, wore one in Constantinople, the ladies in his harem envied her spacious hips. Were all English women, they asked, so well endowed?

Inflation had long threatened the *modus vivendi* between the Elizabethan crown and parliaments, and for decades the crown had been forced to demand extraordinary revenues for ordinary purposes, to the indignation of the Commons. After the relative boom at the beginning of the century the cloth trade would fall on bad times, and in the second decade of the reign the available revenue was even less able to sustain the mounting cost of government.

Salisbury had been the architect not only of the succession, but in 1604 of the peace with Spain, and since 1608 he had also been Lord Treasurer. He had faced, but failed to solve, the problem of 'squaring the circle of inadequate revenue and irresponsible extravagance'.[9] Though far the ablest statesman of the time, he had concentrated excessive power in his own hands, and had himself been exploiting the system too much to be able to improve it. Moreover, for the last two years of his life he had been seriously ill, and he died widely detested. So much so that one of his chaplains wrote an elaborate account of his death at Marlborough to prove that he had made an edifying end.*

The welter of intrigue which now began, increasingly paralysed government, and in 1614 the king quarrelled with the 'Addled' Parliament and dissolved it. The major episodes of the time are notorious;

* Assured that his sufferings did not mark God's wrath and that 'the lord careth for his faithful sheep', Salisbury ingeminated 'that sheep am I!' 'Certified' that he was 'in an estate of salvation . . . then quoth my Lord "You have a power?" I answered "I": he said, "From whence?" I said from the Church by the imposition of hands. He asked from whence the Church had it. I said "From Christ". "Oh", said he, "that is my comfort, then I am happie".' In Peck's *Desiderata Curiosa*, vol. I, p. 8. Written to the Bishop of Bath and Wells by I.B.

the most scandalous the conviction of the Earl and Countess of Somerset of poisoning Sir Thomas Overbury, the Earl's close friend.* Indeed, 'the properer the man', it was said at Court, 'the worse the luck'. In 1618 Ralegh was executed, a sacrifice to the futile attempts of the king to appease Spain; in 1621 Bacon, the ablest man in government, was disgraced on pretence of peculations which, though substantiated, were relatively insignificant compared with the plunder achieved by Somerset or Buckingham. When Lionel Cranfield, Earl of Middlesex, nearly balanced the budget, he was broken by interests who battened on the inadequate revenues. No competent financier could survive.

Then, by the third phase of the reign, the scene was darkened by the effects of the ideologically coloured power struggle that in 1618 had convulsed central Europe. England became indirectly involved in the Thirty Years' War. In 1613, the king had sought to consolidate what was then a rather formidable position as the leader of Protestant Europe, equipped with a battle fleet which, if sent to the Mediterranean, could seriously jeopardize the interests of Spain, by marrying his daughter Elizabeth to the Elector Palatine of the Rhine. Since, it was said, 'she preferred to eat sauerkraut as the wife of a king than roast meat as the wife of an Elector', she encouraged this rash youth to engage in a disastrous adventure. He had attempted to exploit the old Czech-German feud, to defy the Habsburg Emperor in Vienna, and win the crown of Bohemia. By November, 1620, he had been put to the ban of the Empire and driven from the Palatinate. '*Je supplie donc très humblement V.M. d'avoir soing du Roy et de moy*', wrote Elizabeth from Breslau, '*en nous envoyant du secours, autrement nous seront ruinez.*'[10]

Without means of direct military support, James attempted an ambivalent policy, at once threatening and appeasing Spain. And since he was now far too insolvent to mount any serious threat, his diplomacy carried little conviction. And his pro-Spanish policy infuriated the Parliament called and dissolved in 1621. Even, when in 1623, Prince Charles and Buckingham made off incognito, with the king's reluctant consent, to Madrid to prosecute the prince's suit to the hand of the Infanta, the daughter of Philip IV, the Spaniards merely played with this inept *démarche* to neutralize English policy. The English public, still deeply hostile to Spain, were horrified, and the wildest rejoicing marked the safe return of the uncommitted prince. Nothing constructive had come of his venture, save that the greatest patron of Velasquez had set the prince's mind more closely on his favourite hobby – the appreciation

---

* He had incurred the animosity of the countess when, after her contrived divorce from the Earl of Essex, Overbury had opposed her marriage to Somerset. See Selection from Harleian Miscellany, *op. cit. The Five Years of King James; or the Condition of the State of England* by Sir Foulke Greville, late Lord Brooke. pp. 286–314.

of art. And when James I told the Commons 'not to meddle with our dearest son's match with the daughter of Spain', he roused them to claim that an unheard of range of policy, foreign as well as domestic, was their concern.

So religious, economic and foreign affairs combined to aggravate a constitutional crisis which would culminate in the Civil Wars. For the problems damped down by Elizabeth were now worsened by an even more fundamental conflict – the challenge to the accepted Tudor doctrine of the royal prerogative itself. Historians, thinking in terms of nineteenth-century concepts of liberty, have done less than justice to the doctrine of Divine Right and patriarchal power. Confronted with a disconcerting change, conservatives merely reasserted and refurbished a traditional view. Religious fanatics had long been out to kill the sovereigns on whom the social order was considered to depend. Hence a renewed cult of the Prince, of which the *Patriarcha* of Sir Robert Filmer would be the belated but influential English expression. This patriarchal authority, descending from Adam, was taken as an expression of the great 'Chain of Being'. To modern minds it appears grotesque, but it was then taken as seriously as the chronology of the Bible. If James I is called a tactless pedant for defining what was better left unsaid, he was claiming nothing more than all the Tudors had taken for granted.

He roused an equally pedantic resistance. When he claimed the right as supreme judge of the realm to withdraw spiritual and temporal cases from the courts and decide them himself, he got from Chief Justice Coke the old answer out of Bracton *'quod rex non debet esse sub homine, sed sub Deo et lege* – that the king ought not to be under any man but under God – and the law'. Dismissed in 1616, Coke – 'a lawyer', writes Christopher Hill, making an interesting distinction, 'not an intellectual'[11] – was a redoubtable champion of the old Common Law against a prerogative claiming power over life and property. Indeed, this archaic Common Law had now been sorted out by Coke in his new *Reports*; the first since the 'Year Books' of Thomas Cromwell's time. With a splendid misunderstanding, he thought that the Trojan ancestors of the Ancient Britons, who had arrived with Brutus, had laws in Greek; and that parliaments and sheriffs had existed before King Arthur.[12] He also cited ancient liberties infringed by 'Norman Colonels'. 'Nothing,' says Dicey, 'can be more pedantic, nothing more artificial, nothing more unhistorical than the reasoning by which Coke induced or compelled James to forego the attempt to withdraw cases from the courts for his Majesty's personal determination.'

But in political warfare no holds are barred; and 'by his tremendous labours', Sir Edward Coke '. . . gave Englishmen an historical myth of the English constitution parallel to Foxe's myth of the English religion'.[13] The famous phrases are still familiar; *Magna Carta* is 'such a fellow that he will have no sovereign'; 'the house of an Englishman is to him his castle', and the rest. So Coke asserted precise medieval 'liberties'; and 'one of Coke's most quoted passages of eloquence about the Common Law being the best birthright of the subject comes in a section discussing the landlord's right to distrain on unpaid rent'.

It is the old theme. But now the whole structure of prerogative Courts, Star Chamber, High Commission and Requests; even the Councils of the North and of Wales, essential instruments of government, were called in question. They could only be properly sanctioned, Coke argued, in collaboration with parliament. He also invoked the medieval doctrine, cited by Ponet and stated in so many classical and medieval writings, that Natural Reason sanctions good law, so giving the pragmatical Common Law an abstract justification. And in principle, the medieval distinction between the prince who rules according to the laws and a tyrant who claims that they are in his own breast was again mobilized.

Such are the main themes of conflict, economic, religious and constitutional, early apparent under James I. Against the broader background already described, and by the chance of personalities, they would culminate in the Civil Wars. The tragedy of 1649 is already implicit in the tensions of Jacobean times, and only against this background are they intelligible. But before we consider the course of the political conflicts and their sequel, there are other, more important and more attractive aspects of the age that deserve attention – the settlement of the North American colonies and the brilliant cultural achievements of Jacobean and early Caroline times.

3

On the low-lying banks of the James river in Virginia, looking out over a broad estuary, are the remains of a small brick church; and, near by, a swashbuckling statue of Captain John Smith and a sentimental statue of Pocahuntas. Farther up the estuary, past the reed beds of the barren little peninsula selected presumably for defence, there are also thatched replicas of the original houses around Fort James and of the ships that brought the original settlers to tide-water Virginia. The inhabitants were Alconquian Amerindians, whose chief, to the English 'the sable and revengeful Powhatan', had subdued the local tribes into a confederacy of 161 villages of well-placed wigwams; covered, some with mats, some with the bark of trees, and 'all compassed about with small poles stuck thick together instead of wall'.[14] The women practised rudimentary hoe cultivation of corn (maize) and beans, squash, pumpkin, sunflower and tobacco. The men hunted the swarming deer and wild pig for hides and food, still by methods depicted in Palaeolithic paintings in Europe.*

In 1607 into this strange world, 106 assorted English colonists were incongruously planted: 'Being in displeasure of my friends', wrote a Norfolk boy, Henry Spelman, at first befriended but later killed by the Indians, 'and desirous to see other countreys ... after three months sail we come with prosperous winds in sight of Virginia'.[15] The company included a gunsmith, a surgeon and, already, a maker of tobacco pipes; but also, according to Captain Smith, 'footmen' and adventurers 'who did not know what a day's work was; ten times more fit to spoil a commonwealth than either to begin or help maintain one'. The interior teemed with game – 'innumerable hogges ... racoons as good meat as lamb, apossums of the bignesse and likeness of a pigge a month old, wild turkeys and pigeon and perakeriottes'.[16] It was also rich with chestnuts, walnuts and wild vines.

Pent up on the fever-ridden settlement, only forty settlers survived. They were held together by the resourceful Captain Smith, who was capable, when knocked out by a sting-ray, of eating it for dinner; and by Sir Thomas Gates, a soldier of European wars, who had the settlers grow corn in their own three-acre plots instead of in common cultivation, 'where men were apt to steal from their neighbour', and so avoided the 'starving time' of the second winter. The Puritan John Rolfe from Norfolk married Powhatan's daughter Pocahuntas, and so avoided for a time the danger of 'enmity with the naturalls', who at least hated the Spaniards worse than the English. All these episodes have become part of the authentic folk-traditions of the English-speaking world.† By 1619 the first representative assembly in English

* They generally drove the game, but 'if a Powhatan Indian wanted to hunt alone he had an ingenious method of stalking. He disguised himself by covering his body with the entire hide of a deer. By skilfully manipulating the stuffed head, he could easily ... get close enough for an effective shot with his bow and arrow'. McCarey *Indians in Seventeenth Century Virginia, op. cit.*, p. 21.

† Rolfe, who was, in fact, obviously in love with her, was careful to explain that he married the 'unbelieving creature' when he could have had an English girl more pleasing to the eye, 'not from the unbridled desire of carnal affection, but for the good of the plantation and the country and because of her great appearance of love for me'. The frontispiece of the original edition of John Smith's *General History of Virginia*, afterwards incorporated into the *General History of Virginia, New England and the Somers Isles* of 1624, shows Pocahuntas thick-set and swarthy, though dolled up as a Jacobean lady. 'A fine picture' as the suave, observant courtier Chamberlain, remarked, 'of no fair lady ... you might think her and her worshipful husband to be somebody if you did not know that the poor company of Virginia out of their poverty are fain to allow her £4 a week for her maintenance.' The 'Virginian woman', he said, had no wish to go back. See *A Selection of the letters of John Chamberlain. Concerning life in England 1597–1625*, ed. E. M. Thomson with a Preface by A. L. Rowse, Putnam, New York, 1965, p. 216.

America had met in Jamestown church, and the first twenty Negroes had been brought in. In spite of the Indian massacre of 1622, savagely avenged (the Alconquians 'lurked in the woodes and corne' and 'set upon and shotte' the settlers carrying corn to the ships), the tiny colony took root; its main export being tobacco. By 1624 the settlement was a Crown colony and, by the accession of Charles I, there were about 1,200 settlers all told: by 1635 there were about 5,000. From these precarious but cumulative beginnings the well-wooded estates and tobacco plantations of Virginia would derive, the mellow centre of the Old South – 'such a main continent as Virginia, boundless for all we have discovered'. The Indians had told the English that 'they were a people come from under the world to take their world from them', and they were right.

Meanwhile, north of Virginia, equally momentous settlements were being made. Since 1609, in its miniature way, Bermuda had been the most prosperous colony and it would long remain so, exporting hogs, fruit and timber; its parishes still named after the lordly backers of an enterprise intended for Virginia. Here the first Protestant church in the western hemisphere had been built, its interior still scented with cedar and containing a medieval font laboriously saved from the original wreck.

Later, on the main continent, Lord Baltimore would take up vast tracts north of the Potomac and call them Maryland after Henrietta Maria, Charles I's queen. But, most decisive of all, 'New England' was now settled in a harder but spacious environment of lakes and rocks and woods. As early as 1614 the indefatigable Captain Smith, next year 'Admiral of New England', had surveyed the coast and collected £1500 worth of furs: 'this land is only as God made', he wrote, 'when he first created the world . . . worthy is that person to starve here if he cannot live if he hath strength and health'; and 'for gentlemen, what exercises should more delight them than ranging daily these unknown lands?'[17] The fur trade could yield vast profits and the fisheries were 'better than a mine'. Already young Prince Charles had been 'intreated to change the barbarous native names into such as posterity might say Prince Charles was their godfather'. So the broad 'Massachesits' river became the Charles; Accominticum became, more respectably, Boston; Hahanna, Dartmouth, and Ahmoughcawgan, Cambridge, Mass.

In spite of the potential riches of the country, the first settlers had nearly starved. The so-called Pilgrim Fathers were Independent sectaries mainly from Nottinghamshire, Lincolnshire and Yorkshire: not, as often in Virginia, 'gallants packed thither by their friends to escape, ill destinies'. They were serious persons, who had no doubt of theirs. They had already emigrated to Amsterdam and Leyden, but had found it hard to get a living, and what was worse, their morals had been endangered. How in 1620 they had sailed from England for Virginia, and 'pestered for nine weeks in this leaking ship lying wet in their cabins', had first come ashore on Cape Cod in November, just as the North American winter was setting in, is even more well-known than the story of the Virginian settlement. How, too, wading through icy water, they 'went up and down in the frost and snow'; townspeople, singularly ill-equipped to tame the wilderness or to subsist off the game. Having landed at what is now Providence, they crossed Cape Cod Bay and founded Plymouth. In winter they heard the 'hideous cries of wolves and foxes'; in summer they 'could not sleep for the fleas and the musketas'. The settlement survived, although half of them died in the first winter of starvation and scurvy.

But by 1630 John Winthrop of Groton, Suffolk, was already the governor of a better-found Congregationalist settlement, backed by the Massachusetts Bay Company, on the fine harbour at Boston at the mouth of the Charles. They formed a stiff oligarchy under their famous first minister, John Cotton. Rhode Island and New Hampshire were now founded; then the more radical settlers under Roger Williams broke away and colonized the fertile Connecticut valley. By 1642 there were 16,000 settlers in Massachusetts alone. And they were all settlements made by social contract, not Crown colonies. The Civil Wars would secure their independent development.

Among them the old English form of local government naturally took root; the colonists clung tenaciously to their traditions, and while the main body of the farmers exploited corn, cattle and fish, 'comfort, decency and culture were as much part of the scheme of things as congregational churches and responsible government'. In October, 1636, the General Court of Massachusetts agreed to transfer £400 towards a school or college; two years later young John Harvard, now commemorated by a statue in Harvard Yard, left it a legacy and his library. The college was called after him, to become one of the great universities of the world: he turned out, indeed, a 'rare scholar, and he made many more such'.[18]

So from sub-tropical Virginia, north-east to the austere coast of Maine, the English settlements multiplied. They were still small compared with the vast Spanish empire or with the far-flung enterprise of the French in Canada. But they were more compact and they would come to dominate the civilization of North America in language, institutions and culture. Here, rather than in the social conflicts which broke down into the Civil Wars, is to be found the most important achievement of the Jacobean and Caroline English.

4

While these momentous settlements were being made in North America, in England the northern Renaissance had come to fulfilment. Music, architecture, drama, oratory, poetry and prose were no longer provincial, but creative and original in their own right. Within two generations English drama and literature came to a climax never surpassed, decisive for a vast English speaking world.

Yet, while the age in retrospect seems so brilliant and various; extrovert in Marlowe; profound, compassionate and universal in Shakespeare; in Donne and Milton more introspective and severe, and in Bacon confident in the 'betterment of man's estate', to many Jacobean and Caroline minds the outlook seemed dark.[19] The elaborate structure of Thomist philosophy which had provided a complete explanation of a divinely ordered cosmos, had long been undermined by Ockham and his nominalist followers, and while the humanism of More and Colet had been mildly optimistic, the Reformation and Counter Reformation had unloosed the full horrors of religious strife. Looking back on this time, the predominant tendency now seems clear; the victory of the 'Moderns' over the 'Ancients', of the new seventeenth-century cult of knowledge as power over the scholastic and antiquarian Renaissance learning: but to many contemporaries the future was more than usually opaque. There seemed a prospect of a real defeat of mind, and, far from sensing a prospect of progress, many learned men thought they were living in the last degenerate age of the world, or expected the coming of Anti-Christ and the Day of Judgement.

All questions now seemed open. And when, with the collapse of the old Conciliar régime, censorship was modified, a babel of religious, political and economic arguments would break out; pamphlets and newspapers became important, and projects which would have appeared wildly impossible in early Tudor times, would be debated – manhood suffrage, education for all the people, the emancipation of women.

It was out of this welter of old and new that the practical ideas of Ralegh and Bacon, of Harvey and Hobbes began to emerge. The old Pelagian optimism would be asserted in a new way, and man would try to command nature and 'repair the ruin of the Fall'. After 1640 Bacon's more scientific works would become popular.[20] Marlowe's Faust, still climbing after knowledge infinite, now moves down to earth, better equipped.

This climate of doubt and enterprise, and of scepticism and promise, which is expressed in the immense range and power of the literature, in no way impaired the many-sided vigour of the Jacobean and Caroline

304

society: it enhanced it. This is apparent most remarkably in the dramatists and the poets; but in music and architecture a new creativeness is
also apparent.

Henry VIII had himself been musical. He possessed an astonishing
variety of instruments and installed complicated organs in the royal
chapels. Then, with the Reformation, the old Catholic plainsong in
Latin went out of fashion, and new harmonies were developed. Psalm
singing came in, and the congregation took a greater part. In secular
society, in which the Renaissance cult of the complete man had blended
with late medieval good manners, a gentleman was now expected to
take his part in a madrigal or play the lute and guitar; and this fashion
had its roots in the folk music of the villages, for the people had to make
their own music. In Court circles taste in music, as in literature and the
arts, was taken for granted; just as contemporary Japanese warriors,
expert in cut and thrust, competed to arrange chrysanthemums without
anyone making the dangerous mistake of thinking them effete, so
Elizabethan and Jacobean courtiers would be expected to play and
dance with the same elegance with which they transfixed an opponent.
Over the whole land, from court to village, music was made with
natural gaiety and pathos, as an accompaniment to ballads and love
lyrics of varying sophistication. The lyrics of Shakespeare and Campion
reflect an elaborate yet rustic culture, attuned to the seasons, un-
mechanized.

Of the church composers Thomas Tallis (c.1507–85), who served
Henry VIII and Elizabeth I; and William Byrd (1543–1623), organist
to the Chapel Royal, set Latin anthems to music before the Reformation,
and English ones after it. Byrd, though he remained a Catholic, kept
his appointment, and wrote secular as well as church music: he was the
first famous English composer, the Tudor equivalent to Palestrina.
Orlando Gibbons, organist at Westminster Abbey under James I and
Charles I, and Thomas Tomkins, organist at the Chapel Royal, wrote
music for madrigals still unsurpassed. And English keyboard music,
which had owed much to the Netherlands, would in turn contribute to
the Dutch and north German Protestant tradition brought to its
climax by Bach.

Architecture also flourished. English twelfth-century Romanesque and
thirteenth-century Gothic had been magnificent in their austere way;
now the elaborate late-medieval style exemplified in King's College
Chapel at Cambridge and in Henry VII's chapel at Westminster, went
on in the universities, if in less flamboyant form. At Oxford and Cambridge admirable buildings in the old style would be designed into
Caroline times; the superb staircase to Christ Church Hall or Laud's
Quadrangle at St John's College, both in Oxford; or the Great Court

with its fountain at Trinity, Cambridge. In secular building the florid Elizabethan and Jacobean palaces, such as Hardwick, the most extraordinary of these fantasies of glass and light, are as elaborate in their own way as the Portuguese palaces with their hint of the tropical seas. Montacute in Somerset with its mellow colour, or Hatfield, on which the first Earl of Salisbury lavished a great fortune, though he was never to live there, are like great galleons stranded by the ebbing seas of time – an extraordinary blend of late medieval and Renaissance fantasy.

It was Inigo Jones (1573–1650) who became the first British architect of international celebrity. He worked in the full classical tradition and became 'the posthumous sponsor of the Palladian movement of the eighteenth century'.[21] This Welsh genius, originally a joiner's apprentice, early visited Italy. He then made his way as a designer of court masques to Anne of Denmark; afterwards as surveyor to Henry Prince of Wales. In 1612 he again travelled in Italy, this time with Lord Arundel, the pioneer collector, and in the next year he became Surveyor of the King's Works. In 1622 he began the banqueting hall at Whitehall and in the year after designed the Queen's Chapel at St James's Palace. 'Buildings,' he wrote, should be 'solid and proportionable, according to the rules, masculine and unaffected'. These principles are particularly well illustrated by the contrast between the elaborate older east front of Wilton House and the plain new south front, designed by de Caux and John Webb on Jones's recommendations, with its double cube room adorned by the masterpieces of Van Dyck.

But at the time, Jones's main celebrity was won by his flair for designing sets and costumes for the masques in which the royalties themselves took part. These were a more elaborate version of the shows laid on at Henry VIII's court; themselves rooted in medieval convention, much influenced by the Burgundian court. In the Baroque elaboration of these Jacobean and Caroline masques, with their complicated mechanism and vast expense, the exotic and sophisticated court culture is most conspicuously expressed. Above a welter of mass illiteracy, superstition and distress which modern historians are now busy investigating, this exotic court culture now came to its climax, soon to be cut off by bankruptcy and insular Puritanism.

While the court culture was circumscribed, the Elizabethan and Jacobean poetic drama was much more broadly based. It derived in part from shows improvised at the great medieval fairs; from the vernacular 'miracle' plays performed outside the churches; from 'morality' plays which embodied popular fables; from medieval allegories of the virtues and sins, often equally deadly, and from the pageants encouraged by the Guilds. Biblical characters, including God, the Devil, and Adam and Eve – in white leather – had long performed their expected roles, relieved by buffoonery, horseplay and stylized combat. On wagons competitively equipped by the Town Guilds, these allegories had long been popular. In the Wakefield cycle of morality plays, for example, broad farce had been enjoyed on the already well-worn theme of the domestic life of Noah. The old English habit of moralizing about the human condition, which runs on various levels from the pagan Anglo-Saxons to Thomas Hardy and beyond, is apparent in the late fifteenth-century *Everyman*, so laboriously well-intentioned.

But, with the Erasmian humanists, plays had become based on classical models and more secular. Unsubtle domestic comedies were written by the friends of Sir Thomas More; Nicholas Udall, the head-master first of Eton then of Westminster, a more conscientious play-wright than schoolmaster, transposed classical comedy into the homely idiom of *Ralph Roister Doister* for the benefit of his boys; while the rustic comedy *Gammer Gurton's Needle* (1553) with its rousing song *Back and side go bare, go bare*, in praise of *Jolly good ale and old*, reproduced with the accuracy of the Breughels the preoccupations and the dialect of the Cambridge peasantry.

Such, by the mid-century, had been one strain in the development of the Elizabethan drama. But there was a more sophisticated side. Plays now came to be written by lay professionals, often highly educated university 'wits' who would probably before have been provided for in the pre-Reformation Church, but who now lived by their pens. They still led the knockabout life celebrated in the student songs of the Middle Ages, but they were older, more desperate and more versatile. And they now wrote for a more regular public; by the 1570s and 1580s permanent theatres had been built on the south bank of the Thames, outside the jurisdiction of the City. They were modelled on the galleried yards of inns, and audience and players were much mixed up. These supplemented the older private theatres patronized by the Court and the great nobles, who still maintained their own troupes of players in medieval style, and the new playwrights had to cater for both audiences, the popular and the fashionable.

They did so with relish and success: for example in melodrama, with Kyd's *Spanish Tragedy* (1580), and in romantic farce with Greene's *Friar Bacon and Friar Bungay*. Christopher Marlowe was far the best of them. This genius, the first great English playwright, who was 'stabb'd in a tavern and died swearing' aged twenty-nine in 1593, wrote *Tamberlaine* in the winter before the Armada and *Dr Faustus* in the winter after it. There had been nothing like him before; he could evoke a recondite classical mythology and a new exotic romance of the East, taking his characters from Central Asia and the Levant. Yet the 'appealed to the people. He brought blank verse on to the public stage and sent it echoing through the town.'[22] When he depicts the power-mad Tamberlaine or the promethean Dr Faustus, whose agony he transforms into great poetry, he soars into a new pace and splendour of language. Since Chaucer there had been no one in the same class; appropriately, he is a very different character, dying young after a hectic career, involved in secret service for government and in the vendettas of the Elizabethan underworld.

It was into this world of theatre that William Shakespeare (1564–1616), the greatest of all English dramatists and poets, developed his genius. He was better educated than is generally realized, being well grounded in Latin – in particular in Ovid – and well read in Plutarch, steeped in the language of the Protestant Bible, psalms and prayer book, and trained in the current dialectic. Though a countryman who returned to Stratford and bought the best house there by 1597, he was no rustic; and his gifts were such that he crossed the strict social boundaries of the time to become as knowledgeable about aristocratic society as about the people. In contrast to the high-powered but relatively simple outlook of Marlowe, Shakespeare shows a more versatile sympathy, entering into the minds of a vast range of characters, his wonderful verbal memory assimilating and using a wider range of knowledge. 'Shakespeare baffled all imitators by his speed and inexhaustible variety' and 'the Shakespearean drama is an instrument of expression incomparably fuller and richer than the tongs and bones of moralists and metaphysicians'.[23] His personality pervades his work, and the idea that he was too illiterate to have written his plays has of course long been disproved: 'in no case has it been possible to produce a shred of evidence that anyone in Shakespeare's day questioned his authorship. And not one fact has been discovered to prove that anyone but Shakespeare was the author.'* A professional actor and manager, when Marlowe was purely a writer, he dashed off his masterpieces with an unfailing sense of theatre, and however diverse the sources he adopted, set his own stamp on them all. *Hamlet,* for example, combines a Senecan-Renaissance story of revenge with a tale found in the Danish Saxo Grammaticus, written in the twelfth century, in which the heir to the throne

---

* *Life and Letters in Tudor and Stuart England,* ed. Louis B. Wright and Virginia La Mar, Cornell, 1958, p. 89. There is much less mystery about the poet than generally believed. He came of well-established gentry on his mother's side, and the carefully chosen coat of arms, issued for his father by 1596, with its apt motto *Non Sans Droit,* was in the sombre colours then fashionable: *Gold, on a bend sable, a gold spear steeled argent.* He settled for the then very large income of £1,000 for two plays a year, and New Place was the finest house in Stratford. Indeed, the bust of the poet, made before 1623, and accepted as authentic by his family, makes him look more like a successful man of business than the kind of poet the nineteenth-century romantics admired. See A. L. Rowse, *William Shakespeare,* London, 1963, which definitively places him in his social setting, both in the country and in London.

pretends to be insane. *Othello* comes from a collection of Italian stories; *Lear*, originally a Celtic sea god, came to hand through the twelfth-century Geoffrey of Monmouth, and *Macbeth* is drawn from Holinshed on Scottish history. Shakespeare could interpret chronicle-plays, as in *Henry V*, in terms of extrovert patriotism, or, as in Richard II, of tragic introspection. He was equally at home in popular farce and stylized comedies written for the Court. Always alert for the topical, he seized upon current politics and exploration, and while seeing through the hypocrisy and cruelty of public life, he vindicates the hierarchy whereby civilization is precariously maintained. His genius is so widely acknowledged that it here calls for little comment; but any historian must emphasize what an early and extraordinary breakthrough he made, so that he becomes the greatest of all English writers, setting standards unknown before and not attained since.

Shakespeare's greatest plays are Jacobean, part of the harvest of originally Elizabethan genius. The complex and inward-looking poetry of John Donne (1572–1631) shows that, for a later generation, the savour of old learning and excitement of new places were not enough in a world where the cosmic order itself was being questioned, as the globe, and indeed the universe, opened out. The contrast between the basically optimistic Erasmian good sense of Sir Thomas More and Donne's feeling that the closest human relationships are puzzling and dwarfed by death, shows how far the later Jacobean and Caroline English had come to a more melancholy sophistication, haunted by the neo-medieval fears only briefly exorcized by Erasmian optimism. This sense of doom is expressed in a passionate cult of love, and in a high-wrought antithetical pulpit eloquence, of which Donne was only the most skilful exponent, deployed before congregations who were connoisseurs of the art.

Yet, by Jacobean times, there is also a new note. The magnificent prose of Ralegh is not confined to description; he ranges freely into speculative thought, feeling towards the new objectives which Francis Bacon, Lord Verulam, more fully and resoundingly defined. For Bacon was no Renaissance antiquarian or Elizabethan romantic; like More, he looked forward, but in a much more practical way. He realized, as had More in his *Utopia*, that nature could be exploited for the benefit of mankind, and, like Descartes, he tried to discover a method whereby this could be done. Human powers, vitiated by the Fall, could thus be restored to their original scope with man again the master. When Marlowe's Faust, having sold his soul to the devil, won promethean power, he did not know what best to do with it; Bacon, the first great English popularizer of a practical outlook, did know. And if he wrote philosophy like a Lord Chancellor he deserves much credit.

Bacon's prose, with its sententious moralizing, and obviously epi-gramatic touch, is only a deliberately lofty version of the sort of English which ordinary writers were now coming to employ. So wide is the range of the literature that it is hard to select. Much of it is good humoured and merry: on a more pedestrian level, for example, 'topo-graphical' Tom Coryat's *Crudities* deserve attention.* He developed the popular literature of travel, begun in a primitive way by Andrew Borde: 'of all the pleasures in the world', he wrote, 'travel in my opinion is the most delightful'. He wished, he said, 'to encourage gents to undertake journeys beyond seas'. In a jauntily pedantic style with a Rabelaisian undercurrent, he recorded his adventures: 'the mere superscription of a letter from Zurich', wrote Ben Jonson, 'sets him up like a top'. He particularly enjoyed Venice and Mantua, but even in the grip of a perennial wanderlust, he kept a love for home: 'I prefer the very smoke of Odcombe before the fire of all other places in the sun'. After trudging across the continent, he hung up his shoes in Odcombe Church. But in 1612 he set out again; this time for Iran and India, where he died of the flux at Ajmere. His last recorded utterance was 'Sack, sack, is there such a thing as sack? Pray give me sack'. He got it and succumbed.

5

Such, in representative outline, are the main aspects of the late Eliza-bethan and Jacobean culture, in music, architecture, drama and literature. All was set against a background of rising political tension; in part derived, at the deeper level, from a clash of interests long building up between the old Conciliar government, with its late medieval provenance and Tudor prerogative power, and the factions in parlia-ment representing the rich and powerful landowners and City magnates, with their new range of economic enterprise opened up by the discovery of the Americas and the new contacts with the East. And this conflict was exacerbated both by the religious controversies of the time and by the gross incompetence and corruption of the Jacobean régime after 1612, when Salisbury's guiding hand had been removed, and the king, with staggering irresponsibility, handed over the conduct of affairs first to Carr, then to Buckingham, while he sank into a premature dotage that eclipsed even his natural cleverness in manœuvre. Crown and parliament were set on a collision course.

* Coryat's *Crudities*, hastily gobbled up in five moneths travels in France, Savoy, Italy, Raetia, etc., newly digested in the hungry aire of Odcombe in the county of Somerset and now dispersed to the nourishment of the travelling members of the Kingdom by Thomas Coryat, 1611: reprinted, Maclehose, Glasgow, 1905. Coryat was that lasting English type, the rogue Wykehamist, reacting against a sense of duty to the civil service and the Church.

Yet, on a wider view, the time was immensely constructive and important. The first precarious plantations were settled in the American wilderness in Virginia and New England, and in drama and literature the full scope of English genius now appears. The other great English contribution to world history is also now apparent: the application of scientific method to the mastery of the world. The philosophical scepticism of Ockham in the fourteenth century had undermined Thomist metaphysics, and already Hobbes was meditating a radically sceptical and utilitarian theory of politics: but it was Francis Bacon, that great popularizer, who discerned the possibilities of applied science, and who, like Descartes, would understand that it could take a grip on the world in a new way. Further, in Jacobean England we can begin to feel at home: it speaks to us directly in the still recognizable characters of Shakespeare.

18

THE CIVIL WARS AND THE ENGLISH REPUBLIC

In July 1644, as the rival armies mustered, a Yorkshire farmer was warned off Marston Moor; a battle, they told him, was about to begin. 'What,' said he, 'have them two fallen out then?' He was doubtless representative; as Hobbes put it, 'the common people care not what government they live under so they may plough and go to market'. The Civil Wars began as a quarrel within the ruling class – 'fratricide, not class war'.[1] Most of the populace were indifferent 'save for pay and plunder'. Only a minority even of the upper classes were deeply engaged. Apart from some adventurers who established themselves during the Republic and managed to keep their estates, only the shrewd operators, who exploited the biggest market in land speculation since the dissolution of the monasteries, gained by the conflict – as in Dorset, where 'families whose religious hatred of monasticism had founded their estates, augmented them through their devotion to constitutional liberty'.[2] Many families in other counties, as in Norfolk, stayed neutral, trimmed their sails and rounded off their estates; many would have agreed with Fuller's remark of the representative campaign in Berkshire that both sides might be traced by 'a trail of bloody footsteps when the peaceful Cloth Town of Newbury became "New-burying"'.

The Civil Wars, moreover, were fought after the main point had been conceded. By 1641 the increased and now detested prerogative power grafted by the Tudors on to the old Conciliar government and long, as already described, under attack, had already been dismantled; indeed, in 1641, Charles I had offered to accept a 'regulated' or 'mixed' monarchy, though he insisted on retaining the right to choose his ministers and conduct policy. He would never, he said, be 'but the picture, the sign of a King'.

But the cause of the conflict was fundamental. The members of the Long Parliament who in that year had passed the Grand Remonstrance, wanted what we now call sovereignty: full power to appoint the king's ministers, to control the army and transform the Church. The Stuart favourites, they insisted, had been, in the medieval phrase, 'evil counsellors'; picturesquely incompetent as was Buckingham, or potential tyrants as were Strafford and Laud. Nor, probably with some justification, did they trust the king, surrounded by the court influence, to stay 'regulated'. So the crisis came to battle. As the war spread over the entire British Isles, 100,000 men were killed in England alone.

Then, gradually on the Parliamentarian side, the professionals took over. At the end of the struggle, a new and mighty power had emerged – the Cromwellian army. It was mainly officered by 'Independent' sectaries, radically hostile to both Anglican and Presbyterian hierarchies and often out to feather their own nests. It came to replace all other powers, conservative or radical; and a revolution, begun by a clique of moderate men, ended, as revolutions tend to do, in the dictatorship of a military saviour of society.

The relatively mild Caroline régime was replaced by a 'sword government' that judicially murdered the king, set up a Republic, imposed taxation four times heavier than anything the Caroline authorities could exact, and even collected it efficiently. The Commonwealth and Protectorate governments wielded formidable power; and they saved Great Britain from breaking up into a Catholic Ireland, a Presbyterian Scotland and an English Republic. It was the former government which passed the Navigation Act of 1651, the first major move in a mercantilist policy to diminish the excessive dependence on the cloth industry and give English shipping a better deal; English naval power was now first permanently asserted in the Mediterranean and the Caribbean, following wars of aggression against Holland and Spain.

Yet at home the Republic was increasingly detested: the more so when time-honoured festivals and recreations were put down and upstart 'Colonels' got great estates. Not since the legions had left Britain had the country heard the tramp of such massive armoured columns, and so many barked words of command. There were 40,000 troops under arms during the Protectorate; regular forces which dwarfed the old feudal armies or the paid professional gangs of the fifteenth century, and they were used to enforce extraordinary restrictions on private life.

Most of the people never wanted the war, into which 'both parties' had 'slipped by one accident after another'; still less to 'die like a fool in the company of heartless beasts'.[3] The English developed a permanent hatred of 'the military'; the civilian bias of an insular country was confirmed. But at the Restoration the old Conciliar régime was not reimposed, it had long been dismantled. The country reverted not to the 1630s, but to 1641, and the abolition of the prerogative courts was confirmed. Further, for all the political reaction and backlash, a broader social and economic structure had emerged, well symbolized by Professor Stone's comparison of the old Tudor society with the monolithic United Nations building in New York, and the Restoration society with the several smaller towers of medieval San Gimignano in Tuscany.[4] The Levellers and sectarian 'Saints' on whom so much attention has been lavished, thus proved less influential than the lawyers, administrators and professional men who exploited the eclipse of the peerage and the general upheaval. The *bourgeois gentilhomme* in England was never a figure of fun; he was too representative, too formidable; and it has been shrewdly said that 'this singular adaptability to changing circumstances by the forces of the Establishment is a feature that above all others has distinguished the history of England from that of her continental neighbours in recent centuries'.[5]

This fact is naturally conspicuous during the English revolution. Though the Civil Wars coincided with a European economic recession and increased poverty and social discontent, social development was not seriously disrupted. This is evident in the new diversification of the economy, in the roar of political debate, in the new freedom of the Press and in a flourishing education and literature. The country got rid of the archaic Conciliar régime which no longer commanded confidence, and after a phase of political confusion but of administrative advance, the monarchy was conditionally restored, since government could not command assent without it. In contrast to the absolutist régimes on the continent, it would still reflect Fortescue's late medieval distinction between the 'Tyrant' and the 'Prince' who may not 'rule the people bi other lawes than such as thai assenten unto'. If the 'people' would long mean the politically articulate ruling classes, the English now adapted to a new shift of power and shrugged off the threat of anarchy and its antidote, military dictatorship. When, in May 1660, Charles II came ashore at Dover, 'all the people making joyful shouts, the great guns of the ships and castle telling the happy news of his entrance to English ground', an aberrant phase of English history was over.

The mounting crisis of confidence must be briefly considered. As already recorded, after 1612 the relatively high standards of the Elizabethan régime had collapsed, and through the dynastic marriage with the Elector Palatine the country had been involved in an increasingly ambiguous and unprofitable policy towards the continent. After the accession of Charles I (1625–49), the brilliant but incompetent Buckingham still dominated the court. The vicissitudes of the protestant Elector and his 'Lady Bess' in the Thirty Years' War had drawn the normally insular English into an unwonted ideological concern with foreign affairs. The majority of the politically conscious class zealously supported the protestant interest; but James I, though he had tried to further this aim by diplomacy, had been far too wary to commit himself further. Now Charles I and Buckingham, offended by their failure in Madrid, were set on a more adventurous and at the time popular course. The first move was a rapprochement with France; and in May 1625 the king married Henriette-Marie, daughter of Henry IV and Marie de Medici; a consort on whom, after initial misunderstandings, he came much to depend, and who would exercise a malign political influence over him. For the queen had vivacity and charm: 'she is nimble and quick', wrote an observer on her arrival at Dover, 'black eyed, brown haired, and in a word, a Brave Lady, though perhaps a little touched with the green sickness'.* Then, although the first parliament of his reign promptly raised most of the old grievances, attacked Buckingham, and only voted the essential revenues of tonnage and poundage for one year, the king launched the country in a neo-Elizabethan war with Spain. It was disastrously conducted. The Protestant crusade proved a mirage; the allies in Germany and the Low Countries were defeated. An expedition against Cadiz ended in disaster; troops sent against Flushing died of camp fever; the French, faced with a Huguenot revolt, pulled out of the alliance. The hatred of Buckingham increased, though the king insisted that he took all the Duke's responsibility upon himself. Buckingham was impeached and parliament dissolved.

The king and Buckingham, still pursuing their Protestant crusade, now switched to a war in support of the Huguenots against the French government. Richelieu was now bringing massive and well-organized forces against their stronghold in La Rochelle; so in 1627 Buckingham in person followed up the fiasco at Cadiz with a worse one on the Ile de Rhé. These adventures, though they reflected the public demand for a militant Protestant foreign policy, were accompanied by mounting demands for supply, by a political purge of Buckingham's opponents and even critics, and by widespread billeting of soldiers, always a source of grievance. Nor were the troops themselves properly paid. So it was not surprising that, given the security arrangements of the seventeenth century, in August 1628 Buckingham was assassinated with a 'tenpenny knife' at Portsmouth by one John Felton, an obscure lieutenant 'stung with denial of a captain's place'. So ended the fabulous career of the glittering favourite, whose charm and audacity had hypnotized two monarchs into giving him a virtual control of the State which he was entirely unfitted to exercise.†

* Ellis, *op. cit.*, vol. III, p. 197. Characteristically, Charles dispensed with the publicity traditionally attendant on a royal marriage. 'Being entered his bedchamber the first thing he did, he bolted all the doors round about (being seven) with his own hand, letting in but two of the bed-chamber to undress him, which being done, he bolted them out also. The next morning he lay till seven of the clock, and was pleasant with his lords that he had beguiled them; and hath been since very jocund.' *op. cit.*, p. 198.

† 'One thing', wrote Sir Henry Wotton, 'in this enormous accident is . . . beyond our wonder . . . that within the space of not many minutes there was not a living creature in either of the chambers, no more than if it had been in the sands of Ithiopia': Felton was only taken

Meanwhile, in a momentous session of the king's third parliament, a 'Petition of Right', moved in the Commons, had been endorsed by the Lords. In June 1628 on the understanding that it did not prejudice his traditional prerogative, the king had been forced to make it statutory. It declared that no man should be 'compelled to yield any gift, loan, benevolence or tax . . . without common consent by Act of Parliament'; that no free man should be detained in prison without cause shown, and that soldiers and 'warriors' should not be billeted on householders without their consent.

Unreconciled by the removal of Buckingham, and citing this Petition, the Commons early in 1629, tried to limit even tonnage and poundage to a yearly grant; and, infuriated by the high Anglican 'innovations' already sanctioned by the Crown, they attacked the high Churchmen and the queen's catholic entourage. That February, they defied their own Speaker's move to adjourn, and even held him down in his chair by force. They had made it financially impossible for government to carry on, and roused religious passions to white heat. They had rejected the balanced traditional constitution: they were in effect demanding sovereign power. In March Charles 1 dissolved his third parliament: another would not meet for eleven years. He reverted to Conciliar government without parliaments, and backed by the long-accepted but now questioned Tudor style prerogative.

This second phase of the mounting crisis was less abnormal and less unsuccessful than often represented. It was no innovation to regard parliament as merely auxiliary. But the king had 'shelved his problems, not solved them, and the beauty and order with which he had surrounded himself deceived him into the belief that his authority in the Kingdom was as absolute as his authority at Court'.[6] And if the régime nearly became solvent, it was at the price of mounting discontent. The nascent bureaucracy now exploited all the archaic expedients of taxation that ingenuity could devise; the gentry were fined for not taking up the expensive honour of knighthood; landowners were mulcted under obsolete forest laws for enclosing royal lands; above all, the ancient Ship Money – in fact spent on the fleet – was exacted from inland as well as coastal counties and threatened to become permanent. It was not heavy: 'mark the oppression', wrote Hobbes, of John Hampden who refused it . . . 'a Parliament man of 500l a year taxed at 20/–.' Inspired by the obstinate litigiousness of his class and time, Hampden resisted on principle. To the government this rich landowner was simply disclaiming his obligation for the defence of the realm.

Such, in essence, was the political conflict. An old-fashioned régime

because he had lingered about the house 'by very pride of his own deed'. Ellis, *op. cit.*, pp. 255–6 n.

tried to govern without the support of the Commons, who could buy up the Lords, it was said, three times over. And the tension had been worsened by the current 'decay of trade'. The final boom in cloth exports which had produced the florid prosperity of early Jacobean times, had slumped by 1620; and from a peak export of 120,000 cloths it would fall to 45,000 by 1640. The Thirty Years' War and currency manipulation was dislocating markets in the Baltic; the Dutch were becoming more formidable competitors, while the wars with Spain and France had paralysed trade. Despite a revival in the early 1630s, government had to contend with a declining economy; poverty and unemployment would form the background to the Civil Wars and explain in part the surge of popular radical discontent which it would release. And this recession, part of a European crisis, was not yet counterbalanced by major long-term prospects of colonial settlement and enterprise.

The other cause of discontent was the Laudian Counter-Reformation. Backed by the king, William Laud, Bishop of London since 1628, and Archbishop of Canterbury by 1633, now attempted to restore the Anglican Church to what would now be considered decent order. The Calvinist iconoclasts had defaced churches, destroyed medieval glass and smashed up 'images'; Elizabeth I had kept the ceremonial of her own chapels, but the Elizabethan churches had been bare and often dilapidated. In many Jacobean villages the leading parishioners had spontaneously repaired their churches, carefully assigning pews according to the social order; in others, particularly in the cathedrals and colleges, a lamentable decay is revealed. In 1633 for example, Laud told the king that at Rochester the bishop complained that 'the cathedral suffers from want of glass in the windows, etc. . . . the church-yard lay very indecently', and 'the gates are down'. By 1635 the bishop had got the diocese 'in order'.[7] At Cambridge there were 'negligent and unskilfull quires' at Trinity and even at King's, where 'the quiremen cannot sing' and the choristers were 'half mute' and without surplices: at Caius they 'made their chapel a common meeting place for the ordinary disposal of leases', and at Taplow on Christmas Day 1638 worse occurred; 'a very ill accident by reason of not having the communion table railed in'. For 'in sermon time a dog came to the table and took a loaf of bread prepared for the Holy Sacrament in his mouth and ran away with it. Some of the parishioners took the same from the dog but the minister did not see fit to consecrate it'.[8]

It was not unreasonable to rail off communion 'tables', or decree that pews should not be 'over high so they which be in them cannot be seen, how they behave themselves'; even for the archbishop to hope that 'the people must be won by the decency of the thing', or 'if His Majesty thinks, by a quicker way'. 'Try your way for some time. C.R.', the king replied.[9]

In the event the old prejudice nourished by the Marian persecutors and the Gunpowder Plot caused such a panic at 'innovations', 'Popish or Cantuarian', that by 1643 the 'Long' parliament would order all altars of stone, rails, pictures and organs to be demolished; though, being upper-class English, they decreed that coats of arms and 'images of persons not taken or reported for saints' should be preserved.

So, in contradiction to the prevalent course of English history, the resentment of an oligarchical interest, determined, in the medieval way, to assert their own liberties and privileges and extend them, combined with economic distress and religious animosities, to create a rift in the establishment. Both sides muddled themselves into a war occasioned neither, as liberal historians believed, by a concern for the rights of all the people nor, as Marxists assert, by an 'inevitable' economic contradiction, but by a more subtle and complex combination of circumstances, by the chances of personality and the impolitic assertion of abstract principle – by a failure, in short, of pragmatic flair. For there had been no need for the Stuarts to alienate just the interests that the Tudors had known how to handle – the wealthy civilian magnates who during the Tudor peace and after the nationalization of the Church lands had superseded the late-medieval gangster barons, and who were now so strongly entrenched that no government could override them. And as Trevor-Roper conclusively argues, 'the Marxist identification of the seventeenth-century revolution with "bourgeois" capitalist revolutions successful in England, unsuccessful elsewhere, is a mere *a priori* hypothesis'.[10] And G. E. Aylmer concurs; 'Any attempt to classify all landowners as feudal or capitalistic is best abandoned: still less does it appear profitable to think of the English state as having been, before 1640, the instrument of the feudal interest'.[11] The Marxist 'contradiction' between the 'backward' feudal lords and gentry rallying to the king, and a progressive parliamentarian 'bourgeoisie', complete with appropriate *laissez-faire* ideology, shouldering their way into a pre-destined future, is not reflected in the way in which men divided. For two-fifths of the members of the Long parliament, who passed the Grand Remonstrance in 1642 by only eleven votes, became royalists. The lesser gentry, merchants, and lawyers were similarly divided, more by regional and local loyalties than by class, if the more prosperous east and south tended to be for parliament. But few old feudal families survived, and any feudal backwoodsmen around would have settled local scores in a local medieval way.

The conflict cannot be explained either in the liberal or Marxist interpretations. Its ramified causes would have baffled better men than the first two Stuarts and their ministers after 1612. How to adapt the archaic and increasingly insolvent Conciliar government to collaborate with parliament, long regarded as auxiliary and with a tradition of economic grievance and religious complaint? How to assuage the hostility provoked among many country gentry by the glittering extravagant metropolitan Court, whose opportunities and monopolies they could not enjoy and whose magnates and officials were all too apt to insult them? How, also, to provide for the excess of graduates trained up in Tudor fashion for service in Church and state? And such are only the outstanding complications of the problem.

In 1640–1 the crisis blew up; immediately occasioned by the king's quixotic attempt to impose bishops on the Presbyterian Scots. The First and Second Bishops' Wars soon revealed that the régime was insolvent – only £200 had been 'found' in the treasury. It also brought up the crucial question of who was to control the army. For the Scots, nobility as well as people, revived both the fervours of John Knox and the depredations of their ancestors. Having already sworn to a 'National Covenant', they now occupied Northumberland and Durham. Pending a settlement, they demanded £850 a day.

In this crisis Charles I sent for his ablest administrator. Sir Thomas Wentworth, now created Earl of Strafford, though once an opponent of the régime, had been appointed President of the Council of the North in 1628; then, from 1633, Lord Deputy in Ireland. And there he had achieved an extraordinary feat: he had managed the Irish parliament, protected the Irish from English exploitation, doubled the revenues and organized an army. Charles never liked this formidable and rather baleful man, but he took his advice; in April 1640 he summoned the Short Parliament – the first for eleven years. Strafford had reckoned on the traditional dislike of the Scots, now, it was rumoured, in league with France; but within three weeks parliament had to be dissolved. It had raised the accumulated grievances of a decade, and petitioned against the war. There was only one army in being: it was in Ireland, and Strafford now advised that it could be used to reduce 'this Kingdom'. He meant Scotland: the remark, garbled to mean England, would be his death warrant.

That August Charles I marched north, but his inadequate and unpaid army virtually refused to fight. In September a council at York had to accept the Scottish demands and, faced by bankruptcy, the king summoned another parliament. On 3 November 1640 the Long Parliament met at Westminster; it would last until Oliver Cromwell evicted the 'Rump' of it in 1653, and it would inaugurate the English revolution.

Long frustrated, the opposition, organized by John Pym, at once struck hard. They reiterated their old complaints, and within a week Pym was planning to impeach Strafford for high treason. And when in the spring of 1641 this palpably illegal charge failed, the earl was judicially murdered under a Bill of Attainder. There was still no constitutional way of bringing the king's servants to account. In fear for the royal family and intimidated by the London mob, Charles I had betrayed his greatest minister to his enemies. This betrayal would haunt him till his own death.

The parliament had already fallen out over religion. The Lords wished to retain the Anglican ritual; the Puritans in the Commons wanted to impeach Archbishop Laud. But they had already made a momentous political and constitutional decision, accepted by the king: they had abolished the whole apparatus of Conciliar prerogative power. Having passed an act whereby parliament had the right to assembly every three years, whether summoned by the king or not, they had even provided that they should not themselves be dissolved without their own consent. They had then granted tonnage and poundage for only two months instead of a year, and abolished the power of arbitrary imprisonment overriding the law. They had also abolished the ancient Star Chamber, the High Commission Court – the main instrument of Anglican religious discipline; even the Courts of Wales and the North. The old Conciliar government had been dismantled. Parliament had made a profound administrative revolution.

The question of sovereign authority remained unanswered. And it was now more acute, for unbridled passions over religion had been unloosed. In Ireland in the autumn of 1641 there had been a Catholic peasant rising in Ulster against the Protestant settlers; thousands had been massacred. Strafford's Irish government, already undone by his enemies in England, had fallen into ruin. A wave of anti-Catholic feeling swept England, and Pym seized his chance. The Grand Remonstrance was drawn up, an appeal to public opinion against the Lords who had refused to remove the bishops from their House: it demanded that a general synod should set about a Calvinistic reformation of the Church. What was more, it tackled the question that the abolition of the old Conciliar structure had left unresolved. It demanded, on pain that supply be cut off, that the king should appoint 'only those counsellors' as they themselves 'would have cause to confide in'. 'We are earnest', they said, remembering Strafford and Buckingham, 'with his Majesty not to put his affairs in such hands'. Couched in traditional, even medieval, language, here was a bid for sovereign power. Cromwell retrospectively remarked that had it not been carried, he would have sold up his property and emigrated to America. It was carried by only eleven votes.

The king reacted disastrously. Influenced by his French queen, who saw English politics in terms of her own upbringing, and by a belligerent clique about the Court, in January 1642 he had Pym, Hampden, three other members and a peer impeached for high treason. What was worse, he came down to the House, with 300 swordsmen at his back, to arrest the 'Five Members' himself. Forewarned – for the amateurish plot had become common knowledge – they had at once escaped to the City of London. When, supported by the City trained bands, they returned to Westminster on 11 January, Charles had left his capital the day before. He was not to see it again until the winter of 1648, when he was brought back in custody to his death.

Both sides, reluctantly preparing for battle, now set about political warfare. In June, 1642, in *Nineteen Propositions*, the parliamentarians again demanded the supreme power; to appoint the executive, the councillors, the officials, the ambassadors and even the tutors of the king's children; to control the militia and transform the Church. The king and his advisers, probably Hyde and Culpepper, replied in *His Majestie's Answer to the XIX Propositions of Both Houses of Parliament*. It is a strangely neglected document, for it ably put in a nutshell what the moderate royalists considered the long-term consequences of these demands.*

In this revealing manifesto, the king, like his enemies, appeals to precedent; calls God to witness that he will 'never subvert' (though in a 'Parliamentary Way') 'the ancient equall happy well-poised and never-enough-commended constitution of the Government of this Kingdom'. And he defines what he terms an English 'regulated' monarchy. 'The House of Commons,' he writes, '(an excellent Conserver of liberty, but never intended for any share in government or the chusing of them that should govern) is solely intrusted with the first Propositions concerning the leavies of Money.' If the 'power of Preferring (to office) be added', he argues, 'we shall have nothing left for us but to look on'. The Crown would then become 'despicable', and 'so new a power' would 'intoxicate persons not born to it'. Church and Lords would then follow the fate of the monarchy, 'till (all Power being vested in the House of Commons,

* See Corinne Comstock Weston, *English Constitutional Theory and the House of Lords, 1556–1832*, London, 1965, Appendix I, pp. 263–5. 'Until the appearance of this study,' she writes, 'there has been no extensive study of the *Answer* in print. It received either no attention at all or very little from Samuel Rawson Gardiner and Sir Charles Firth and Godfrey Davies in their generally comprehensive accounts of the political and constitutional history of the years from 1603 to 1660. Neither Miss C. V. Wedgwood in *The King's War, 1641–7* ... nor George Macaulay Trevelyan in his standard *England under the Stuarts* shows awareness of the significance of the *Answer*. The comments of Charles I on English Government were as influential in the reign of Charles II and afterwards as they had been earlier, but these are not discussed by Macaulay nor by Sir George Clark nor by David Ogg who have written more recently of England under the later Stuarts.' *op. cit.*, p. 6.

and their number making them incapable of transacting Affairs of State with the necessary secrecy and expedition, those being intrusted to some Close Committee) at last the Common people (who in the mean must be flattered, and to whom license must be given in all their wilde humours how contrary soever to . . . their own reall good) discover this *Arcanum Imperii* (Secret of State) that all this was done by them but not for them'. The populace will then devour the Commons itself, and 'by this means this splendid and excellently distinguished form of government (will) end in a dark equall of chaos and confusion, and the long line of our noble ancestors in a Jack Cade or a Wat Tyler'. 'To all these demands,' the king concludes, 'Our Answer is *Nolumus leges angliae mutari* – we will not have the laws of England changed.'

The royalists later played the *Answer* down: it had given too much away. And liberal historians would not be interested. How far this able defence of a balanced constitution was the king's own opinion we do not know, and he was capable of a concurrent *coup d'état*; but considering his exclamation at his trial, 'I know that I am pleading for the liberties of the people of England more than any of you', and 'For the charge I value it not a rush, it is the liberties of the people of England that I stand for', Charles I deserves the benefit of the doubt.

3

The Civil Wars and the Interregnum divide naturally into three phases. The first (1642–9) includes the campaigns of 1642–6 and of 1648 and the King's execution; the second the Commonwealth (1649–53), the suppression of the radical Levellers, the wars in Ireland (1649–50) and against the Scots (1650–1), and the naval war against the Dutch; the third (1654–60) the Protectorate of Oliver Cromwell (December 1653–8) and its sequel up to the Restoration. In this last phase Cromwell repeatedly tried to legalize an illegal régime, attempting to work with successive versions of a parliament, and to divert attention from home affairs by a neo-Elizabethan war against the Spanish Empire. But in fact he always ruled by the sword and never escaped from his own past. Though his son, Richard Cromwell, succeeded without opposition, he was jostled by ambitious generals, and soon abdicated. Power devolved on General George Monk, who was ruling Scotland, and he restored the monarchy.

On the scale of this survey only the outstanding military and political aspects of the time may be observed; economic developments demand attention and intellectual life remained particularly original and vigorous. There was a spate of pamphleteering by all parties, in which the language reached new levels of invective and little was left undiscussed. As regular newspapers were printed, the first journalists appeared, already much in character. The Puritans closed the London theatres and the king's pictures were dispersed; but Milton was widening his experience, if ruining his eyesight, as Latin secretary to Cromwell, and writing his most reverberating prose; and Thomas Hobbes, the most original and eloquent English political theorist, published his *Leviathan* in 1651, defining the question of sovereignty which had occasioned the conflict and stating his remedy for it.

The Civil War, or as the English characteristically put it, 'The un-happy differences between his Majesty and the Parliament', was fought mainly by amateurs who learnt the hard way. As the best authorities point out, there had been no serious fighting in England for over a century, and the 'four years struggle did nothing to advance the military art'.[12] Though the royalists had something like a unified command, the king was irresolute and inexperienced – and parliament at first tried to run the war by committee. Prince Rupert of the Rhine, the king's nephew, was a first-rate cavalry officer, but he was unpopular, known as the 'German'; and he was often overruled. And he met his match when Cromwell – 'old Ironsides' as Rupert called him – adopted tactics developed by Gustavus Adolphus in the Thirty Years' War, as set out in England by the new manual, Cruso's *The Millitarie Instruction for Cavallrie.**Taught by his observations at Edgehill, the first major battle, Cromwell always insisted on the importance of *morale*: 'Truly,' he later recalled, 'I did represent to him (John Hampden) in this manner conscientiously; and truly I did tell him "You must get men of a spirit; and take it not ill what I say – I know you will not – of a spirit that is likely to go on as far as a gentleman will go, or else you will be beaten still". I told him so, I did truly.'

Parliament indeed controlled London and the more prosperous south-east, but they took a long time to mobilise their resources. And not all the ports were against the king: Falmouth and Exeter, King's Lynn and Newcastle supported him. The royalists captured Bristol, though, in a long war, the weight of London was bound to be financially decisive. If the queen sold the crown jewels in Holland for a million and a quarter guilders to buy arms, the king obtained 1160 lb. of 'White and Gilt plate' from the Oxford colleges, and coined it into money at the Oxford mint, these were wasting assets.†

---

* 'A Cavalryman,' wrote Cruso, 'must be active and nimble and one that loveth (and knoweth what belongeth to) a horse. He (the horse) must also be used to the smell of gun-powder and the sight of fire and armour, and the hearing of shot and drums, etc. Your horse must be accustomed to become bold to approach any object.' F. J. Varley. *The Siege of Oxford*, Oxford 1932. Appendix, p. 142.

† Magdalen and All Souls raised 296 lb. and 253 lb. respectively; prudent Balliol 41 lb.; Exeter even had the hardihood to refuse. Following the theory of one academic expert that

If the royalists were to win, they had to win at once. So when the Earl of Essex, the parliamentary commander, had ineptly allowed the king's army to get between him and his London base, 'the Cavaliers at Edgehill had their best chance to end the war with one swift stroke'.*
But after Edgehill, unnerved, perhaps, by his first experience of battle, Charles I turned aside to Oxford, his base for the rest of the war; he thus gave the parliamentarians time to regroup, and at Turnham Green in the outskirts of London, the king was confronted with 24,000 men and never occupied the capital.

The royalists now fell back on an ill-coordinated pincer movement on London, based upon a conjunction of Newcastle's forces in the north, Hopton's in the west and the king's in the Thames Valley. But parliament muddled through. They defended the perimeter of London; and, even, under Fairfax, their ablest commander, launched a counter offensive in Yorkshire. When in January 1644, they at last got the initiative, it proved the turning point of the war. Pym had long negotiated to bring in the Scots, and his posthumous diplomatic stroke now paid off. In spite of Montrose's diversionary exploits, 20,000 Scots, in alliance with a parliamentary army, routed the royalists in the major battle of Marston Moor in Yorkshire. And when in June 1645, the royalists were again overwhelmed at Naseby near Northampton, and their army in the west mopped up at Langport in Somerset, the war was decided. By June 1646, when offered favourable terms, the king's headquarters at Oxford surrendered, and the garrison marched out with 'Horses, servants and compleat Arms: flying colours, trumpets sounding, drums beating. Matches lighted at both ends, bullets in mouth'.†

But in April the king had already vanished in disguise from the city. He still had immense popular prestige; he was the only legal head of government, and he himself was convinced that God would not 'suffer rebels and traitors to prosper'. Still far too hopeful, he had gone to negotiate with his Scots subjects at Newark, now at loggerheads with parliament over religious questions, as they soon were with him. For an immense sum – £400,000 – they then handed the monarch over to

the bow was still superior to firearms, 'perhaps by way of experiment bows and barbed arrows were provided for a hundred scholars who had volunteered', but they were never used in action. Varley, *op. cit.*, pp. 24, 37. At Cambridge Parliament exempted all clergymen, scholars and students, and in London those studying at the Inns of Court, from being 'pressed'. There was not then a conscripted 'equality in sacrifice' or fair shares in death.

* Burne and Young, *The Great Civil War, op. cit.*, p. 31. Essex, a pompous little man in contrast to his glamorous father, executed by Elizabeth I, was so incompetent that Colonel Burne and Brigadier Young, breaking their usual impartiality, declare in a footnote 'the authors beg to state that neither of them would have liked to serve under this officer'. (p. 227 n.)

† The cavalier gentry were accorded passes to go abroad and allowed to compound for their sequestered estates at only two years' revenue.

parliament, who lodged him in state at Holdenby House in North-amptonshire, hoping to come to terms with him. It now looked as if parliament had all the cards. In fact their position was precarious; they were now fewer and less representative, and they had fallen out with their own army.

Indeed they detested the military to whom they owed their success; nor did they now want a large and expensive army quartered on the land. And they were determined to get rid of the more politically minded and ambitious officers – some, as Cromwell, themselves members of the House. So they tried to disband the army without even settling its large arrears of pay, or even according it an indemnity for Acts of War. The army organized resistance: it set up regimental committees with dele-gates and 'agitators'; many of them radicals hostile to the remaining landowners and men of property in the Commons. Forced to choose, most of the officers sided with their regiments; not least Oliver Cromwell, an 'Independent' in religion and aware of the jealousy of his civilian colleagues.

So the leaders of the army, most of them men of property, decided to seize the king and force a settlement of their own. In June 1647 Cornet Joyce briskly removed him to Newmarket (a scene for him of better days) and in August the army leaders put forward a compromise settlement. Their moderate *Heads of Proposals* envisaged a cooling-off period of ten years. There would be a parliament, biennially elected, which would nominate the king's ministers and control the militia, but the worst controversies would be shelved; all Protestant forms of worship would be tolerated; Lords and Monarchy would remain intact. Crom-well may even have hoped for an earldom; perhaps the viceroyalty of Ireland, where the army would have plenty to do.

He failed to square his parliamentary colleagues. Having risked their popularity with the soldiers, the army leaders had to pull back and conciliate the rank and file – now becoming more violently radical. And when the king, more than ever lost to reality, double-crossed the army, reopened contact with the Scots and retired to Carisbrook in the Isle of Wight, he ceased to be credible as a negotiator to anyone.

Hopefully, he awaited the outcome of his negotiations. It arrived in the form of a second Civil War. It was brief but bitter. In the summer of 1648 the royalists rose in Kent and Essex, in Wales and Ireland. In July part of the fleet came out, and the Scots, still intent on putting down the 'impious toleration' of the *Heads of Proposals*, again invaded the country. As the only faction with real power, the army had to deal with the crisis, and they emerged as the only united and overwhelming force. They at once occupied London. Fairfax contained the rebels at Colchester and forced their surrender. Cromwell in August caught the

Scots army at Preston in Lancashire and routed it. That autumn he advanced in Scotland and entered Edinburgh to dictate his own terms. The royalist commanders at Colchester were not accorded the honours of the Oxford garrison: they were shot. Only the king retained his illusions. 'They must preserve me,' he said, 'for their own sakes.' But he was wrong: to prevent him negotiating with parliament, the army officers seized a sovereign they now regarded as a 'man of blood'. He was conducted from Carisbrook to the thick-walled Tudor fort, part of Henry VIII's coastal defences, called Hurst Castle at the end of the shingle beach opposite Yarmouth. After a farcical 'trial', the monarch was beheaded outside Inigo Jones' banqueting hall at Westminster on a bitter afternoon at the end of January 1649. Given the characters of those concerned, the tragedy seems inevitable: but it was a colossal political blunder. Charles the martyr triumphed where Charles the king had failed. The army leaders had to kill him, but in doing so they sealed the fate of their own ephemeral domination.

4

There was now no power in England but the sword. In December 1648, before the king's murder, Colonel Pride's musketeers had been posted outside the Parliament House: they had excluded over a hundred members of the Long Parliament and arrested fifty. A week after the king had been beheaded, a remnant, later termed contemptuously the 'Rump', had proceeded in collaboration with the army, to abolish the House of Lords. 'The Commons of England,' they asserted, meaning this mere remnant of the Long Parliament, now had 'the supreme power.' In fact, of course, it now lay with the army, and the army was now represented not by the moderate Fairfax but by Oliver Cromwell.

In 1649 he put down the army Levellers, some shot out of hand: he crushed the rebellion in Ireland and left a memory of atrocities which remains alive today; next year routed the Scots in their own land. In short he became an unpredictable and redoubtable general, set on creating a self-sufficient Republic of Great Britain, strong enough to prosecute commercial wars against the Dutch and ideological wars against Spain. A Council of State was set up; new treason laws promulgated; censorship reimposed; and in April 1653 the general would evict even the 'Rump'. But he never legitimized his power.

Oliver Cromwell is the 'opportunity and the despair of the biographer and historian'.* Elusive and contradictory, at once a religious fanatic and a great cavalry general, he would now erupt, briefly, violently, and

---

* Wilbur Cortez Abbott, *The Writings and Speeches of Oliver Cromwell*, IV volumes, Harvard, 1937-44, vol. I, p. 758. 'There is scarcely a man,' he writes, 'who rose to such eminence of

on the whole rather irrelevantly, into the main course of English politics. The Victorian view of him as a champion of popular liberty, symbolized by his brooding statue outside the Houses of Parliament, is quite unwarranted. The magnates who had begun the quarrel had failed, and he came in to fill the power vacuum. He can hardly be blamed for Carlyle's version of him, but G. M. Young's verdict stands that 'in a volcanic hour of anger and disappointment, ambition, impatience and perhaps despair, [he] flung himself against the English tradition at the point where it has always been strongest and most sensitive, its respect for law'.[13] As Clarendon would write, 'He was not a man of blood and totally declined Machiavels' method', (of extirpating all his enemies) and with 'all the wickedness against which damnation is denounced, and for which hell fire is prepared, so he had some virtues which have caused the memory of some men in all ages to be celebrated; and he will be looked upon by posterity as a brave bad man'.

In February 1649 the regicide Council of State faced great danger. They fought themselves out of it. The survivors of a political power struggle and of a long war, these soldiers soon outclassed their enemies and brought a new kind of disciplined power to bear; first on Ireland; then on Scotland; then on foreign affairs. From being a despised and detested régime they became more feared abroad than any previous British government; their fleets making their presence felt in the Mediterranean, their regiments victorious in the Low Countries. They fought the first commercial war with the Dutch and attacked the Spanish Empire in the

---

whose early years so little is known.' He was descended from Morgan Williams, a Welsh brewer of Putney, who married the sister of Thomas Cromwell, Henry VIII's minister; herself the daughter of another, less reputable, brewer and blacksmith. Their son, Richard Williams, took his uncle's name and founded a wealthy, substantial and conservative family out of the spoils of the monastic estates at St Neots, Hinchingbrooke, Ramsey and Huntingdon. Oliver, born in 1599, came of a cadet branch, and his mother from small Norfolk gentry. He was deeply influenced by his schoolmaster, Thomas Bearde, a Puritan 'lecturer' who wrote *The Theatre of God's Judgements*, and he became steeped in the Jacobean Bible. He spent a year at Sidney Sussex College, Cambridge, but left at seventeen; apparently 'an average youth of athletic tendencies with no bent towards books' (p. 37). He may have got a smattering of law at Lincoln's Inn; but 'what evidence there is seems to indicate that he was rude and unmannerly if not worse'; addicted to horseplay and practical jokes, with a strain of violent religious and other melancholy feelings. At twenty-one he married Elizabeth Bourchier, the daughter of a fur dealer in London, who had a house in Essex. Cromwell first entered Parliament in 1628; but from 1631–6 he was a farmer and grazier at St Ives until a legacy from an uncle improved his fortunes. It was not until 1641 that he made his mark in Parliament, and there is no evidence that his colleagues appreciated his outstanding genius until it was proved in war. He was essentially an Elizabethan squire, with not much understanding of the City, and his foreign policy was neo-Elizabethan, predatory and ideological. A great soldier rather than a far-sighted politician, Cromwell was a good judge of horses and farming, who enjoyed music and society; but he was haunted with fears over predestinate grace and interpreted his victories as evidence of God's election. He died, like many Calvinists, terrified that he may have fallen from grace, and clinging to a covenanted salvation. For the most interesting modern assessment, see Christopher Hill, *God's Englishman* London (1970).

Caribbean. But since in the process they imposed crippling taxation and arbitrary fines, they never secured popular support and abroad their *tour de force* proved ephemeral.

The republicans turned first to Ireland. Here the king's Lord Lieutenant, the Butler Marquis of Ormonde, had come to terms with the Catholic 'wild' Irish, proclaimed Charles II, and taken Drogheda. He was now threatening Dublin. In August 1649 Cromwell himself arrived, with a formidable army and artillery. In October he stormed Drogheda, and put the garrison and many inhabitants to the sword; at Wexford in the south east similar atrocities were committed. The policy of terror was traditional, only Cromwell was more ruthless. The Irish had to submit to a settlement which in effect provided an English garrison. The English now made a Protestant plantation of the whole island east of the Shannon: a class of Protestant landlords, reinforced and extended, remained rooted in the land until the late nineteenth century, while the Scots plantation of Ulster was confirmed. Such was the situation created in response to the need for the immediate security of the strategic island.

Cromwell now turned on Scotland. Here the Presbyterian Kirk were irreconcilable; set on their old objective of enforcing their religion on England, they were even negotiating with the exiled Charles II. Determined to forestall them, the republican government ordered their best general north. Following the well-tried strategy of Henry VIII's campaigns, he attempted to capture Leith, the port of Edinburgh. Drawing a blank, he withdrew to Dunbar, and there, on 3 September 1650, he destroyed the Scots army, caught between the Lammermoor hills and the sea. That Christmas he occupied Edinburgh, then advanced on Perth. The Scots factions, now in part reconciled in common fear of the English, replied by crowning Charles II at Scone; and the young monarch, who detested the Kirk, soon resolved on a desperate gamble. With inadequate and divided forces, he did what Cromwell wanted him to do and advanced deep into England in the hope of royalist support. In 1651 at Worcester, again on 3 September, Cromwell routed the Scots-royalist army. Charles II escaped, and after fantastic adventures, took ship from Shoreham to Fécamp in Normandy.*

* This authentic adventure story has become part of English folk-memory. After the battle, the king, aged twenty-one, lurked about disguised as a woodcutter, his hair cropped, his face and hands stained with walnut juice to give him a rustic appearance. He even practised the clumsy gait of a countryman, incongruous to his Stuart elegance. At Boscobel in Shropshire, fortified by bread and cheese, ale and two cushions, he hid in a pollarded oak, whose thick foliage concealed him, while republican soldiers sought him within earshot. He was harboured in country houses and barns until, from Trent in Somerset, he got down to Charmouth in Dorset on the western end of Chesil Beach. Here the skipper who was expected to take him off was locked up by his wife and daughter, who suspected him of the escapade. The king now proceeded to Bridport, where disguised as a servant, he occupied a room in the George Inn

The English now had the mastery of Scotland as well as Ireland. Scotland was at once incorporated into the republican Commonwealth; even the power of the Kirk was curbed, and the Highlands cowed. Instead of breaking up into warring kingdoms, Great Britain had been temporarily united by the sword.

With the battle fleet built with 'Ship Money' and now much expanded, English naval power was now asserted in a new way. The royalist fleet under Rupert had been preying on commerce: by 1650 the Commonwealth turned on the Protestant Dutch for purely commercial objectives. In 1653 in a great naval battle fought off Portland Bill between the two greatest naval powers in the north, Blake was victorious over van Tromp.

But in spite of these successes, the regicide government remained precarious. Following the dramatic eviction of the 'Rump', when Cromwell, in a fit of rage in the Commons, summoned his musketeers and turned out the members, shouting 'you have sat here long enough for all the good you have done', and concluding, 'take away these baubles, so that the soldiers took away the mace and all the House went out', the last remnant of the old structure of King, Lords and Commons had disappeared. Yet the majority of politically responsible opinion in the country wanted to get back to the old relatively harmonious and time-honoured form of government, each part in its place; for the English, then as always, were predominantly conservative and no one could then envisage a new political structure.

So it was necessary to disguise the facts. As a temporary measure in July 1653 a curious assembly had been brought together, nominated by the Congregational churches in the counties and chosen by the Army Council. 'Barebones' Parliament, so-called from a particularly loquacious 'Saint', in fact made important administrative reforms. It made civil marriage legal and it elaborated parish registers; but when it began to attack tithes, now diverted to the support of the supplanters of the Anglican clergy, and threaten property, it had to go. The army leaders arranged that this inconvenient pseudo-Parliament should dissolve itself.

That winter they devised an *Instrument of Government*, and the general was cast as the saviour of society. The moneyed men in the City and the landowners who had done well out of the upheaval would have been happy to settle for a new dynasty. Cromwell became Lord Protector, with a nominated Council of State, empowered to choose his successor,

which was swarming with republican soldiers. He made his way deviously north to Hele House near Amesbury, and after a rendezvous at Stonehenge at two in the morning, across to Sussex. Here, after further vicissitudes, he was taken off in a collier ostensibly bound for Poole, which was diverted, with the consent of the crew, to France. See Hester W. Chapman, *The Tragedy of Charles II, 1630–1660*, London, 1964, pp. 193–217.

and a triennial Parliament was elected on a strict property qualification. The new deal gave the executive sweeping powers: all royalist 'malignants' were disenfranchized. Armed with this authority, Cromwell secured trading privileges for English merchants in the Baltic and with the Portuguese; and he made an alliance with the French against Spain.

At home the royalists and the radical sectarian fanatics remained irreconcilable. Cromwell jailed some enthusiasts; argued with others, whom he accused of being Anabaptists who would cut the throats of all not of their persuasion. But he was more widely than ever detested. 'Lord,' men said in their Old Testament jargon, 'Thou hast suffered us to cut off the head' and 'suffered the tail to set itself up.' They hated 'that great thief there'.

So within a year the first Protectorate Parliament had to be purged, then dissolved. It had demanded to appoint the Council and cut the money for the army on which the régime relied. And the country was now seething with discontent. Disillusioned radicals at odds with the regime; Presbyterians at odds with the various Independent sects; the army magnates jockeying for position. The royalists had formed the 'Sealed Knot', a ramified if inefficient network of conspiracy. Though the Cromwellian spies were efficient and alert, the Cavaliers conspired at race meetings, now illegal, but difficult to disperse. In the spring of 1655 a small party of Wiltshire gentry, assembled by John Penruddock of Compton Chamberlaine and Hugh Grove of Chiseldon, rode into Salisbury and seized the Judges of Assize. Part of a much wider conspiracy, it was an ill co-ordinated venture, already betrayed and soon put down, but it was representative. 'I was never guilty of much rhetoric,' said Grove on the scaffold, 'all that I shall desire of you besides your hearty prayers for my soul, is that you would bear witness that I die a true son of the Church of England and a loyal subject of King Charles II, our undoubted sovereign; and a lover of the good old laws of the land, the just powers of Parliament and the rights and liberties of the people, for the re-establishment of which I undertook this design and for which I am ready to lay down my life . . . God forgive the judge and counsel for perverting the law and God forgive the bloody-minded jury.'[14] Grove's unstudied words put the royalist case in a nutshell.

But, immediately, the rebellion gave Cromwell his chance to strengthen the régime. A new decimation tax was imposed on the royalists; a rigid censorship imposed on the news sheets: and the country was now carved up into districts, each under a major-general, empowered to tighten up security and, for good measure, morals – the most hated aspect of an arbitrary power. In 1657, by a 'humble petition and advice' Cromwell was offered the Crown. He refused it, but he could now nominate his successor. Meanwhile, in 1655, the government had embarked on a war with Spain. It was naturally costing money and a second Protectorate Parliament had to be summoned. Though granted wider powers, it proved as recalcitrant as the first. A new House of Lords, mainly of Cromwellian nominees, disgusted the old peerage and proved a failure. But the war against Spain had been successful. Blake destroyed a Spanish fleet off the Canaries and, after a failure on the island of Hispaniola, an ill-found expedition captured Jamaica, then thought of little account but afterwards strategically important. Though Cromwell's ambitions to lead a great Protestant coalition were not realized, Dunkirk in the Spanish Netherlands was taken by the new 'regular army'. But when, on his day of destiny 3 September, this time in 1658, Cromwell died on the morning after a great gale, so that his enemies said the devil had claimed his own, he left a régime that without his strong hand was no longer viable.

It had been not without success: Cromwell had saved England from anarchy and renewed civil war, effectively imposed the first if brief political union of Great Britain, prevented a Presbyterian take-over of the church and secured an unwonted toleration for the sects. In spite of the recession which reached a nadir in 1649 and exacerbated discontent, the Republic had also begun to diversify the economy by protecting ships and fisheries. 'With the Navigation Act (of 1651) we have arrived at a fully-fashioned conception of economic policy in an essentially national form. Its dynamic was no longer the achievement of social justice through Christian ethics working against private greed and exploitation. It was the welfare of *Leviathan*',[15] the national sovereign state. But the critic who said 'the machine is strong, but I do not deem it durable for it is violent' was right.

5

Against this political background English life went on. As has been well said by the historian of the Civil War in Cornwall,

the economic life of the people, the customs of the manor, the petty life of the borough, and the traditional relation of the landlord and tenant, survived the changes and chances of civil war, for they were the very fibre of which society was constituted and beside them the political conflict appears transient and superficial. So the history of Cornwall in the seventeenth century is but the history of England in miniature, for everywhere is this dualism between the visible political changes at the centre and the unvarying life of the country-side, between the speculations of the few and the inarticulate conservatism of the many.[16]

Indeed, the most lasting achievement of the English Republic was to improve the administration: to raise regular taxation and dispatch business by committees in parliament and outside it, and actively to promote a mercantilist policy. But the most original development of the time was the spate of pamphleteering in which the common people began to dispute 'things not before discovered or written of'.

As usual, their ideas are in the moralizing vein; mainly, even when radical, trying to get back to an imagined past. Conservative and religious, they naturally belong more to the world of the Peasants' Revolt and of late-medieval and early Reformation heresy than to anything else. Others are Christian-Humanist, the product of the old Erasmian learning. The seventeenth century was a great age of English eccentrics, in this aspect second only to the nineteenth century. The most radical were religious enthusiasts, soaked in the Jacobean Bible, obsessed with Calvinist doctrines of predestination or sectarian hopes of free grace. Their greatest popular exponent is John Bunyan, whose *Pilgrim's Progress* (1678) still belongs spiritually to the mid-century and interprets Puritan religion in homely terms which have become classic. Their grandest, most learned and most poetic interpreter is the Christian–Humanist John Milton.

When religious fervour came out of the cloister into the streets it could take strange forms. The Leveller Overton, for example, who wrote with 'raucous derision and blunt irony', attacked the *Ass-Embly* of Presbyterian divines, and called the lice in the government prisons the 'trained bands of Newgate'. It was Walwyn who hopefully preached Christian pacificism to Cromwell; and John Lilburne, with his appetite for martyrdom and unfailing zest for legal argument even under the lash, won a wide following. 'He that kills and he that is killed,' it was rightly said, 'they both cry out it is for God.' Eternal salvation was at stake, and in Old England, unlike New England, there was no frontier.[17] Some took up Utopian projects. Winstanley, for example, who objected to 'pride of life' and 'selfish imagination', held that the Creator had made the earth 'a common treasury', and encouraged his followers to plant communal parsnips and beans on the sandy soil of St George's Hill near Weybridge.

The army radicals were more formidable; they demanded fundamental social and political change. 'If we have not a birthright in the kingdom,' they argued, 'we be mere mercenary soldiers.' 'The poorest hee that is England,' said Colonel Rainsborough, 'hath a life to live as the richest hee' – the hackneyed slogan still deserves quotation. A whole range of questions was raised by these articulate soldiers. Not that they were representative, for the vision of an enlightened Nonconformist Puritan army thrashing out fundamentals of democracy round its camp-fires does not reflect the facts. The 'Saints in Arms' who counted did not believe in democracy so much as the rule of the Elect, sealed by

God's approval through victory. The rank and file were mainly pressed men, and some had changed sides; they enjoyed the usual opportunities for plunder and iconoclasm, and 'it is quite doubtful if [they] were as deeply imbued with religious ideas as their chaplains believed'. Nor could discipline have been maintained in an army which practised self-government in the ranks. The majority, as in any army, were concerned with pay and prospects, and the radical minority were soon disillusioned. They accused their officers and comrades of 'turning war into a trade' and England into a camp; they denounced the Council of War itself. 'Stop not the breathings of God,' wrote one of their chaplains to Fairfax, 'in mean private Christians.'[18]

Beside this pamphleteering, regular newspapers now influenced opinion. Reporters in Amsterdam had early relayed news of the Thirty Years' War and the first English newspapers had been printed in Holland – verbatim translations from the Dutch, 'forraign avisoes'. But by 1642 London – that 'sea of news' – had replaced Amsterdam. *A Diurnall* or *The Heads of the Proceedings weekly in Parliament* appeared in 1641; *Diurnall Occurrences* and *England's Memorable Accidents* in 1642; eight pages in poor type for a penny. They also featured the atrocities in Ireland. Samuel Peake, the first recorded English journalist, had been a stationer 'until he crept into a hole in Westminster Hall'. He was a proper newshawk, a 'bald headed buzzard . . . with long legs', constant it seems, 'at nothing but wenching, lying and drinking'. Such men understood that the public wanted facts, and they wrote to make money: by the late 1640s advertisements were being printed. 'The price of beer,' after all, 'was of more concern than the price of salvation, a fact of which editors were aware.' The Deity was for them a 'slogan rather than a mystery'.[19] Such were the brisk and realistic beginnings of the journalistic profession.

Meanwhile, aloof as far as they could be from the tumult, the old élite schools went on: the leaders of both sides still sent their sons to them. For over a century the ancient medieval foundations, Winchester and Eton, and the Tudor Westminster and St Paul's, had been supplemented by schools endowed by pious commercial magnates: Harrow, Shrewsbury and Rugby; Charterhouse and Merchant Taylors; Blundell's at Tiverton in the west. The humanistic traditions of Richard Mulcaster of St Paul's, of the Jacobean Farnaby and of the perennial and austere Busby at Westminster, carried on and spread. And during the Interregnum a new idea was mooted: the entire population might be educated. Comenius, the Czech master, was called in, but the 'distractions' of the time made the project impracticable.

At the universities, it has been claimed, the revolution advanced science, but there seems to be little evidence for this development.

William Harvey (1578–1657) the greatest doctor of his time and physician to the king – 'Inventor', as Aubrey put it, 'of the Circulation of the
Blood' – had been trained in the old way at Caius College, Cambridge
and at Padua. His papers were plundered by the Puritan soldiery (as
were those of Inigo Jones) and 'he often said that of all the losses he
sustained no grief was so crucifying to him as the losse of these papers
which for love or money he could never retrieve or obtaine'. And when
Charles I made him Warden of Merton College, Oxford, the parliament
men put him out of it: no wonder this benefactor to the human race
'was wont to say that man was but a great mischievous Baboon'.[20] The
rise of experimental science, fundamental to the whole century, already
under way before the conflict, was probably little promoted by the
Puritans, who were concerned more with a Godly life than improving
fallen man: and such interests were not on the face of it likely among
men obsessed with predestination.

The most distinguished scientists and mathematicians, were latitudin-
arians: indeed, 'no less than five of the members of the Wadham College
group at Oxford in the 1650s, the precursor of the Royal Society, became
Anglican bishops at the Restoration. Wilkins and Ward, both of whom
became bishops, defended the role of reason in religion rather than the
"enthusiasm" or revelations of the Holy Spirit that were so characteristic
of the Puritan sects'.* Far from confidently advancing the frontiers of
knowledge, as Bacon, the real pioneer, had wished to do, the Puritans
looked back to the religious fervour of the previous century and clung
to election and grace in a degenerate or apocalyptic world: 'for the most
part these people were looking backward to the corporate ideal of the
medieval period, not ahead to the individualism of the enlightenment'.[21]

But the most characteristic mid-seventeenth century writers were the
late Renaissance Christian Humanists, fascinated with a vast range of
miscellaneous knowledge: not, like Bacon and Descartes, trying to
organize it in a new way. Robert Burton (1557–1640) whose *Anatomy of
Melancholy* had appeared in 1621, compiled an extraordinary work, full
of recondite knowledge and classical quotation, undisciplined by either
Thomist or scientific method; accumulated out of sheer love of learning
for its own sake. He describes at length the symptoms of love – 'at least
it is *suavis amarities*, a bitter-sweet passion';[22] and how the dying Petronius, 'instead of good meditation, he made his friends sing him bawdy
verses, and Scurrile songs';[23] and how there is no cure for the despair
which 'consumes to nought. I am like a Pelican in the wilderness (saith

* Leo F. Solt, *Puritanism, Capitalism, Democracy and the New Science*, American Historical
Review, 1967, vol. *LXXII*, No. 1, p. 21. 'The empirical approach of science,' he writes,
'involves the observation of physical objects and their arrangement in some sort of regularity;
the experimental approach of Puritanism involves the metaphysical confrontation of an
anxious pilgrim with the overwhelming power of God, Holy Spirit or divine grace.' (p. 25.)

David of himself, temporarily afflicted), an owl because of thine indignation. *Psalm* 102, *verse* 6.10. . .'.[24]

Sir Thomas Browne, a generation after him (1605–82), achieves an extraordinary depth of meaning by a similar range of cumulative learning, set out in an oratorical prose. His *Religio Medici* or *Faith of a Doctor*, appeared in 1642, the year of the final breach between king and parliament, so there was one man of genius better engaged than in political controversy. He combines plain English words with elaborate Latin ones, in complex cadences which .glitter with many-faceted implications. This art is at its most sophisticated in the famous *Urn-Burial*, published in 1658, the year of the death of Cromwell. In his famous *Pseudodoxia Epidemica* or *Enquiries into Vulgar and Common Errors*, he examines the behaviour of insects: 'It is generally conceived, an ear wig hath no wings, and is reckoned among impennous insects by many;' and he writes of tigers – 'It may seem too hard to question the swiftness of tigers, which hath given names unto horses, ships and rivers,' but Pliny 'affirmeth that indeed it is a slow and tardigradous animal.'[25] He enquires whether men are lighter after meals than before, 'the addition of spirits obscuring the gross ponderosity of the aliment ingested'; and, in the notoriously intolerant seventeenth century, raises racial questions no one would now dare to ask. That Jews stink naturally he will not agree; particularly because, owing to the Diaspora and Gentile marriages, they have so long been a mixed people, for 'the women often affect Christian carnality above circumcised venery'.[26] How Negroes get to be black is all too intimately discussed;[27] in general 'Things become black by a sooty and fuliginous matter proceeding from the sulphur of bodies torrified'. This extraordinary encyclopaedia of *Vulgar Errors* comes out of the tradition of the medieval writers, Alexander Neckham and Bartholomeus Anglicus. But the range of knowledge is much richer, and common sense constantly breaks through; for where the medieval writers had propagated their errors, Sir Thomas Browne, with immense gusto, pulverizes them. Both these admirable writers, Burton and Sir Thomas Browne, still enrich the mind; unlike the ranting sectaries and 'Levellers' with whom the time has lately been so much identified, they are outside politics.

John Milton (1608–72), on the other hand, a dedicated genius, steeped in Christian-Humanist learning, plunged into the conflict. He felt it his duty to return to England from Italy in 1638, abandoning a tour in Sicily and Greece, 'thinking it base that I should be travelling . . . abroad while my fellow citizens were fighting for their liberty at home'. But the young Milton had been less Puritanical than is generally thought. Grounded at St Paul's and Christ's College, Cambridge, in the fullest Erasmian learning in Latin, Greek and Hebrew, he was well able to turn a sonnet in Italian as well as Latin. His splendid *Ode on the Morning of Christ's Nativity*, written when he was twenty, shows his feeling for the pagan past he denounces, and the formal masque *Comus* (1637) shows him to be something of a Court poet. His grand tour of Italy to Florence, Rome and Venice had enhanced this imaginative grasp. And when he took to ephemeral political warfare, his poetic impulse inspired the best of his prose, though written, as he said, 'only with his left hand'. In his anti-prelatical tracts of 1641–2 Milton is still the political idealist. Like many intellectuals in politics, he hoped for too much – that God, for example 'parting the clouds, amid the plaudits of the Elect, would descend to reward a righteous commonwealth'. But by 1644 he was becoming disillusioned, and writing *Areopagitica* against the new Presbyterian censorship; moving over to the Independents. By 1649, after the king had been beheaded, he had become the main apologist for Cromwell; like many medieval writers, he was defending tyrannicide, and in March of that year he was Latin secretary to the Council of State, commissioned also to vindicate the régime abroad. By 1652 he was blind; not before he had seen the realities of politics from the centre of power.

But this political experience, following the collapse of his hopes at the Restoration, when he reverted to his dedicated mission as an epic poet, bore fruit in the insights of *Paradise Lost*, where, contrary to much opinion, Satan is not the hero at all, but given the false if splendid rhetoric of a deceitful politician. Milton's conviction of original sin had been reinforced by his failure to impose his ideals on politics; he at last withdrew into his dedicated purpose, to write the greatest epic in the English language. More than the tragic blunders, the waste and confusion of the Civil War and the Interregnum, it symbolizes the intellectual force and vision by which this confused but creative age is best remembered.

PART FOUR

COMMERCE, INDUSTRY AND EMPIRE

19

THE LATER STUARTS

When in February 1660, General Monk entered London, the 'loyal English', writes Fuller, 'did rather gaze on than pray for him, as ignorant of his intentions . . . he was an Absolute Riddle'.[1] In fact he had already assessed the tide of opinion as running strong for a Restoration, and 'went into it dextrously to get himself great rewards . . .', for 'enthusiasm was now evaporated, and the nation returning to its wits again'.[2] Following free elections under the old franchise, a 'Convention' parliament at once appointed commissioners to negotiate with Charles II.

That wary cynic, wittiest and most dangerously charming of English kings, was much abler than the lazy lecher of popular belief: early experienced in danger and the shadier side of politics, he was well fitted to deal with the political magnates who now contended for the spoils of office which they considered theirs by right, and to manage his father's enemies who had done well out of the wars. 'Of the four of Pym's pall bearers arrested in Pride's Purge,' writes Hexter, 'one sat in Cromwell's House of Commons and became a Knight of the Bath at the Restoration; a second in Cromwell's House of Lords and became a baronet at the Restoration, and the third fattened off the confiscated estates of the Irish Royalists and became a Viscount at the Restoration.'[3] Politically speaking, in this tricky situation, 'the two ablest men in the country were the restored Monarch himself and his Chief Minister', Edward Hyde, Earl of Clarendon, the master architect of the Restoration settlement.[4]

That settlement, which confirmed the king's financial dependence on parliament, placed the militia under the control of the magnates and the gentry, and allowed the king only two regiments of regular troops, was none the less a genuine Restoration. 'Even though the Prerogative Courts had been abolished, the supremacy of the Crown in executive matters had been reaffirmed: the judicature, too, remained under royal control. The monarchy might have been bullied and battered, yet it emerged victorious in 1660, its powers undefined.'[5] Hence the paradox that just when the responsibilities of government were becoming more elaborate, new standards of centralized administration were being set in France, and England was becoming committed to power politics on a new scale, the politically conscious nation was haunted by the fear of arbitrary power, and the executive was constantly hampered by parliaments riven by faction, which could only be managed by astute political manœuvres. Moreover, the centuries-old tradition of the turbulent assertion of private liberties would now be reinforced by a larger and less responsible electorate. The forty-shilling freehold was no longer a substantial qualification, and elections were becoming party contests in a new way; while the restoration of the Anglican Church with all the apparatus of privilege and intolerance had perpetuated the hatreds of the Interregnum.

These animosities would now be exploited by politicians out for power and place; and they could provide the popular following behind the 'Whig' and 'Tory' parties; the first formed as an attempt to exclude the king's brother, the Catholic convert James, Duke of York, from the succession; the second to defend his dynastic rights. For though Charles II notoriously 'scattered his maker's image through the land', his Portuguese queen, the amiable Catherine of Braganza, twice miscarried and bore him no legitimate heir.*

2

From the Restoration of Charles II (1660–85), through the brief reign of James II (1685–8), English policy towards the continental powers was opportunist in the old Tudor way. After the Revolution of 1688 and the reigns of William III and Mary II (1688–94), of William III (1694–1702), and of Anne (1702–14), Great Britain (united with Scotland in 1707), launched out into nearly a quarter of a century of continental and oceanic wars against France on a scale previously unknown. Concurrently with this new commitment, and making it possible, the American and West Indian colonies were better exploited, and the hold on important areas of India consolidated. The English now had a firm grip on Bombay; on Madras; and on the lucrative trade with Bengal on a scale which dwarfed the original enterprise at Surat.

* Catherine of Braganza was twenty-two when betrothed to Charles II. After a secluded upbringing, she was thought to possess 'an almost angelic innocence' which would be 'an irresistible bait for the royal voluptuary'. Hebe Elsar, *Catherine of Braganza*, London, 1967, p. 13. And though, apart from Bombay and Tangier, she brought over only half the enormous dowry stipulated, she tried hard to adapt herself to the contrasting informality of the English court. Since she could hardly speak English and was surrounded by Portuguese attendants, she was relatively aloof from the court intrigues and provided a placid alternative to the monarch's various and exacting mistresses. But although her extreme devotion to the Catholic faith made her so unpopular that the Whig extremists accused her of trying to poison her husband, and pressed for a divorce, she maintained her position with calm obstinacy. After her departure from England in 1692 she found herself immensely popular in Portugal, to which the English alliance had brought substantial advantage in the struggle for emancipation from Spain, achieved in 1668. She died there as Queen Regent aged sixty-eight. It was Catherine of Braganza who first made tea-drinking fashionable in England.

Following the first, Republican, trade war with the Dutch, Charles II's government fought them again in 1664–7 and 1672–4. The Second Dutch War was supported by shipping and financial interests and fought for world-wide colonial objectives in the West Indies and North America, in West Africa and the Far East. But the great sea battles off Lowestoft and the Thames Estuary produced no decisive result, save that they taxed the more limited resources of the Dutch, and the Treaty of Breda's most memorable consequence was to confirm the English capture of New Amsterdam in America, later renamed New York.

The Third Dutch War was no longer in the interest of the country, for the Dutch were now a waning colonial power and the French the real competitors. It was fought in nominal alliance with the French, for Charles II was now in French pay, at the price of a policy which played into French hands. Sanguinary battles off Southwold and the Dutch coast only weakened the Dutch resistance to the invading armies of France, and under pressure of public opinion, the king's government withdrew from the war. The English then veered towards the Dutch alliance confirmed by the Revolution of 1688–9. For the long colonial rivalry with the Dutch now had to give place to resistance to the French, whose domination of the European continent would have carried oceanic and colonial supremacy with it.

If nearly half the population still lived below what would now be termed the 'poverty line', and if, in spite of advances in manufacturing and agriculture, the country remained what would now be called relatively 'underdeveloped', new wealth was coming in from colonial imports and re-exports, while the enclosures, going on since Tudor times, were giving the countryside its modern aspect of hedged fields and better-kept woodlands. The population was still less than six million, but London became the greatest financial and trading centre in northern Europe and British merchant shipping and the Royal Navy now outclassed the Dutch. All this had been brought about within the fifty-four years since the Restoration. Nothing, not even Divine Right of the monarchy, had been allowed to stand in the way.

The reigns of Charles II and James II saw hectic political warfare. The Settlement of 1660 – a restoration of parliament as much as of the king – had left the initiative and responsibility with the Crown, but it had deliberately shackled the monarch. Granted an inadequate revenue for life, he depended on parliament for the rest. Yet, as Charles II remarked, he 'did not think he was a King so long as a company of fellows were looking into all his actions'. Determined, like his father, to choose his ministers, he exploited his command over foreign policy to extort large sums from Louis XIV. By nature and upbringing a cosmopolitan member of the European dynastic caste, and, in so far as he had any religion, a crypto-Catholic, Charles II had one fixed principle – to stay where he was, maintain his throne, and secure the legitimate succession. And in this he succeeded: a success that the tactless manœuvres and uncompromising convictions of his brother – '*la sottise de mon frère* – my brother's stupidity' as he put it – would quickly throw away.

The 'Cavalier' or 'Pension Parliament' (1661–79) became the more restive the longer it lasted, and since the problem of reconciling the will of the king's government and Parliament had yet to be solved, the harder to manage. Clarendon's* administration (1660–7) thus inherited the problem of sovereignty which had baffled his generation in 1642 – for he was a contemporary of Stafford and Pym. Moreover, the returned Cavaliers, the older men battered and hardened by misfortune, the younger raised in penury and exile, were more brutally class-conscious and self-seeking than the relatively high-minded pre-war politicians of whom Clarendon was a belated representative. Clarendon's régime saw the Restoration Settlement consolidated in a highly realistic way – marred only by the intolerance of the Clarendon Code which did not represent his views, but reflected the vindictiveness of the restored Anglican clergy. But by 1667, after a succession of disasters, the Plague and Fire of London, and a disastrous conclusion of the renewed republican trade war with the Dutch, when the enemy towed the *Royal Charles* out of Chatham Harbour, Clarendon had to go.

There followed a period of frenetic party strife, in which the king tried to govern through successive political cliques which could only manage the Parliament by complicated bribes and manœuvres. A coalition of king's men known as the Cabal governed from 1667–73; but they tended too much towards the Catholic and French interests. Parliament brought in a Test Act which purged the administration of Catholics and

---

* Edward Hyde, Earl of Clarendon (1609–74), was born at Dinton near Salisbury in Wiltshire of a minor county family, descended from Laurence Hyde, an auditor to the Exchequer, and also from the Thynnes of Longleat. Like his uncles, he made his way by the law. Educated at Oxford, he had been a member for Saltash in Devon in both the Short and Long Parliaments, a constitutional royalist who had opposed Pym and Hampden in their attempt to shift the sovereign power to Parliament. He shared the vicissitudes of Charles II's exile, drafted the Declaration of Breda and as Lord Chancellor at the Restoration was largely responsible for the moderation of the Settlement in all aspects but that of religion. But Clarendon was 'apt to talk very imperiously and unmercifully'; he bored Charles II and as the father-in-law of the Duke of York he provoked added hostility from his own kind. Dismissed, he took refuge in France, where he composed the later part of his *True History of the Rebellion and the Civil Wars in England*, begun during his first exile in 1646. He also wrote his own *Life*. These works were published, respectively, in 1702–4 and 1759, and assured Clarendon's reputation not only as a statesman but as a writer of the first rank. But Clarendon's old-world integrity and pomposity must have been incongruous in 'a society perpetually in masquerade; the men padded and flounced like ambulant four-posters, with astute, dissipated faces, patched, powdered, and raddled under flowing periwigs and all that lush femininity, like a show of overblown dahlias...'. Nesca A. Robb, *William of Orange*, London, 1962, vol. I, p. 181.

even forced James, Duke of York, to resign as Lord High Admiral – the one position he ever fulfilled with success.

The king then fell back on Sir Thomas Osborne, later Earl of Danby, the first able party manager since Pym, a parliamentarian who managed his constituency in a new way, and who created the nucleus of what became the Tory party. But, like the Cabal, in 1679, his administration was brought down by a rabid anti-Catholic campaign. It arose out of a bogus Popish Plot, the first major popular political ramp in English history.* Invented by a couple of unscrupulous clergymen, it was exploited by Anthony Ashley Cooper, Earl of Shaftesbury, the leader of the rabidly Protestant or 'Whig' party, in an attempt to exclude York from the succession and to replace him by the Protestant James, Duke of Monmouth, the king's eldest bastard. The Whigs would thus get the spoils of office. Danby's administration collapsed in a welter of political warfare. The king sent him to the Tower to avoid attainder, and in 1679, dissolved his first Parliament.

The subsequent election of his second Parliament, when the country was again on the verge of civil war, saw rudimentary electioneering on party lines; green ribbons for Whigs, red for Tories. Both sides derived popular support from the old divisions of the Civil War, and although they cannot be compared with the organized parties of later times, they mark at least a new convention in politics. Indeed, they came to represent great interests. Though the original Whig tradition came from the small artisans and the dissenters, led by aristocratic politicians, the Whigs in fact became the party of the land-owning magnates and the rich men of the City with wide political-commercial horizons; the Tories that of the lesser gentry and their tenants and of the high-Anglican clergy – the 'country' party who resented the land taxes which a forward foreign policy implied. Behind the Whigs were the Nonconformists and the myth of the 'good old' Parliamentarian 'cause'; behind the Tories, the Cavalier tradition of Divine Right and 'non-resistance' to the legitimate king as well as the social contempt of the gentry for small traders and dissenters. The terms 'Whig' from 'Whiggamore', fanatical Scots covenanters of the 1640s, and 'Tory', derived from Catholic bandits in Ireland, ripe for murder and arson, thus became part of the political scene; and these amiable epithets, accepted

---

* It was concocted by the Rev. Titus Oates and the Rev. Israel Tonge, the first educated at Cambridge and claiming, falsely, to be a Doctor of Divinity of Salamanca; the second, a former fellow of University College, Oxford, who had become an anti-Catholic pamphleteer. They alleged that the king was to be assassinated and York brought in. In a frenzy of suspicion and fear, the public was convinced that the French intended to invade England and Ireland and that the Catholics intended to start another Fire of London. The whole episode is an early example of the power of a rudimentary press, of scare headlines and the deliberate manipulation of a myth known to be false; techniques afterwards much better developed.

by both sides, would long persist; the latter incongruously into our own day. Like all successful political myths, they represented both an interest and a state of mind.

So, in 1679, the king was faced with an overwhelmingly Protestant, or Whig Parliament; it brought in an Exclusion Bill against York and it had to be dissolved. It is memorable only for passing the *Habeas Corpus* Amendment Act, a measure of permanent importance carried apparently in the House of Lords only because Lord Grey, the teller for the occasion, counted a very fat peer for ten votes. For the ancient writ of *Habeas Corpus* – 'you may have the body' – had enabled the Law Courts to bring before them anyone wrongfully imprisoned or detained even by the king's officers, and since this privilege had long been evaded, the writ was now refurbished to stop further abuse. It was now legally impossible even for the Crown to incarcerate anyone against the will of parliament and the courts of law, or hold them indefinitely without trial. The Bill was passed mainly since the leaders of both parties were still liable to find themselves in prison; but this by-product of party warfare would benefit the common man.

The king's third Parliament soon proved equally recalcitrant; and his last, too, was overwhelmingly Whig in composition. In fear that, like the Long Parliament, it would perpetuate itself if protected by the London mob, Charles shrewdly summoned it to meet in Oxford. And here he offered a major concession: William and Mary, he declared, might be Regents, if James were nominally to reign. As he had probably calculated, the triumphant Whigs were set on entire exclusion and on Monmouth. They refused the compromise, and they had been given rope enough to hang themselves. So when, in March 1681, Charles II suddenly dissolved his last Parliament, he recovered much support in the country and ruled for the rest of his reign without one. For what it was worth, he had saved the legitimate succession.

Shaftesbury was politically ruined. He fled to Holland and died there. And soon the reaction against the Whigs was confirmed by another, this time authentic and Protestant plot, hatched by Cromwellian ex-officers, to kidnap, perhaps murder, the king and York on their way back from Newmarket at Rye House at Hogsdown in Hertfordshire. There was another witchhunt; the Whig Lord Essex committed suicide and two Whig aristocrats, Lord William Russell* and Algernon Sidney, were beheaded; the last merely for writing a Whig discourse of government, a martyr for political theory. In fear of another Parliament, Louis XIV continued his secret subsidies; the government carried on, and

---

* Russell stuck to his principles with the independence of his family; he remarked dryly that beheading was so quick that it could not be very painful and that he expected soon to be in better company.

when in 1685 Charles II died after a stroke aggravated by the remedies of his physicians, with a characteristic ironical apology for being an unconscionable time about it, James II succeeded him on a wave of loyalty.

The English establishment which had restored the Stuarts had just managed to live with Charles II: when pushed to it, he had connived with them to keep the throne, though he had also astutely saved his brother's rights. But James II would not so connive. He at once alienated the Anglicans, his best support, for they felt that the toleration he proposed for those they termed respectively 'papists and fanatics' was the thin end of the wedge. The atrocities after Monmouth's rebellion in the West Country in 1685, the last popular rebellion in the old style and put down in the old way, also roused widespread and lasting hatred; and by maintaining an army of 16,000 men with many Catholic officers, the king challenged a fundamental provision of the Restoration Settlement – the control of the militia by the magnates and the gentry. Further, by a freak of fate, the belated birth of a male heir to his second wife, Mary of Modena, opened the prospects of a Catholic royal line and convinced James that he must assert Catholic influence while he could. And by executing the discredited Monmouth, the king had stupidly removed the only protestant alternative to the far more formidable combination of William and Mary.

James II took less than four years to prove, as the Declaration of Rights would state, that it had been 'found inconsistent with the safety and welfare of this Protestant kingdom to be governed by a Popish prince', and, as one politician would put it, that 'it had been an error to let him in to the throne'. The English, it was now apparent, could not have both succession by Divine Right and the rule of Law, and the monarchy had to be saved by changing the monarch. But the so-called 'Glorious' or better, 'Respectable' Revolution of 1688 did not, as Whig historians believed, create a 'constitutional' monarchy. It merely reinforced the decision, in effect made in 1641 and confirmed at the Restoration, that the monarchy should be 'regulated' or 'mixed'. The Commons would vote supply and the gentry control the militia, but initiative in government was still with the Crown in the traditional and balanced collaboration of King, Lords and Commons. The Revolution was made to preserve the monarchy within these conventions; and though it limited the prerogative power, William of Orange insisted upon, and obtained, terms which would not, in his own words, diminish the 'lustre of the crown so long as he wore it'. As in 1399, after the forced abdication of Richard II, the throne was declared 'vacant', and William had enough support to effect 'occupation' by conquest: but he had intervened to prevent a civil war, not to start one.

345

William and Mary thus never recognized any break in legitimate continuity. As next in succession, they 'accepted' the Crown, to protect, as William put it in his Declaration of September 1688, the 'consciences and liberties and properties' of their subjects from 'arbitrary government'. He could thus appear 'the glorious instrument of Almighty God in delivering this kingdom from popery and arbitrary power'. Indeed, in the olympian words of von Ranke, whose account of these transactions remains in essentials unsurpassed, we do not, in contemplating the actions of James II and their sequel need 'to adopt the tone which English historians have borrowed from criminal courts', but observe how he 'sets himself with rash hardiness in opposition to a state of things which is the result of past history . . . under the impulse of religious zeal, he disregards the limitation of his power', attempting in his own words 'to win or lose all'.[6]

So, when James II had thus imperilled the Crown itself, William of Orange, on his own terms, intervened to save it. When, as one magnate put it, William and Mary 'accepted' the throne from 'the hands of the representatives of the most valuable part (of the nation) and all that deserve to share in government', they had consolidated a mutual interest. The compromise brought England into the full tide of the European contest for supremacy and commercial empire and enabled a realistic generation to restore the balance of power in Europe. The great political decision confirmed the limitations on the Crown, and would make it hard for the executive to govern; but it reconciled the monarchy to the establishment, which supported the Crown in the great wars on the continent and the oceans which were the first concern of the new king, and from which England emerged as a first-class power.

Thus both the Whigs and the 'non-resisting' Tories had to recognize that the attempt to make the best of the restored Stuarts had failed, and sacrifice the rights and glamour of the senior royal line for the practical advantages of a monarch whose interests better coincided with their own. When, in December 1688, James II, haunted by his father's fate, lost his nerve and fled the country, England at once felt the hand of a continental professional diplomat and soldier.

'Dutch William', *Sijn Hoogheid de Heer Prins van Orangje*, was no uncouth 'Dutch Bear'.* He was a high cosmopolitan royalty from a country

* William of Orange (1650–1702), great-grandson of William the Silent who had led the Dutch resistance against Spain, was the posthumous son of William II and of Mary Henrietta, daughter of Charles I. A dedicated politician who thwarted the ambitions of Louis XIV, he was of frail physique and acute sensibilities, masked by a cold self-command. Apart from his Stuart-Bourbon descent, he had a French-German ancestry, and took his title from Orange in Southern France. He was brought up in the elaborate court culture of the time, and his Dutch background was rich and elegant: his eyes early 'trained on vistas of stately rooms and gardens whose long prospects of lawns and clipped evergreens were lighted by the glint of water and a changing mosaic of colour . . . in the figured beds'. (Robb, *op. cit.*, p. 68.) But

socially more civilized than England; a rich, relatively well-conducted business Commonwealth, whose atmosphere of religious toleration and intellectual freedom made it the refuge and the admiration of some of the best minds of the age. A new military and political expertise came in with this continental prince, seasoned in war and diplomacy, whose long-calculated ambition was now realized – a move in a greater game, the thwarting of the Bourbon ambition to dominate Europe and the world.

3

When in November 1688 William of Orange entered Exeter, the citizens were impressed by an exotic parade. After a squadron of expensively equipped cavalry in 'headpieces, back and breast, bright armour', marched two hundred Negroes from the Dutch plantations in Central America in embroidered caps lined with white fur, to attend the horse. Then, by way of contrast, came two hundred Finns and Lapps in bearskins and black armour. After this spectacular prelude, came the prince's own banner, inscribed 'For God and the Protestant religion'; and then, behind fifty war horses and their grooms, William of Orange himself on a white palfrey, 'armed cap-a-pie, a plume of white feathers on his head, all in bright armour, and forty-two footmen running by him'. He was followed by two hundred gentlemen and pages. Then came the professionals who could outclass anything in England; 'three thousand Switzers with fuzees' and six hundred of the prince's own troop of armoured guards.[7] And all these were only the vanguard of the considerable army.

Asthmatic but determined, William of Orange marched east in vile weather, though he stopped at Wilton to observe the paintings by Van Dyck. By December, making for Oxford, he had established himself at Littlecote House near Hungerford. Here, in the Bear Inn, (still in existence today) the English negotiators made their propositions. For William had been careful so to manœuvre that 'the responsibility for his

William, unlike his popular uncle Charles II, was an aloof royalty, who preferred retirement at Hampton Court to London, so that 'the face of the (old) court, and the rendezvous in the public rooms were quite broken. This gave an early and general disgust'. (Burnet, *op. cit.*, p. 299). He was deeply attached to his favourites, Hans Willem Bentinck, whom he created Earl of Portland and with whom he had been brought up, and to his page, Joost van Keppel, created Earl of Albermarle. And he greatly relied on them in the conduct of business. Burnet writes that 'the daily diversion of his life was always hunting, and the governing passion of his soul the depression of France. He had no vices but one sort in which he was very cautious and secret'. (*op. cit.*, p. 250.) This remark may in fact have referred to a mistress of the king, but it has been taken as a different sort of innuendo. The king's affection for Keppel, writes his biographer, was natural for a 'childless man who centred his starved affections on a youthful object . . . though the world said that His Majesty had fallen in love with a handsome play boy'. (*op. cit.*, vol. II, p. 406.)

actions was theirs, not his . . . it was up to them to decide the process by which final settlement could be reached'.[8] Since James had violated the laws, the prince declared that he had come to maintain them; not, like Monmouth, as a rebel. Nor did he wish to seize his uncle himself. '"Did they have a mind", asked Lord Halifax of Burnet, "to have the king in their hands?" "By no means", was the answer, "for we would not hurt his person". "What", hinted Halifax, the astute "Trimmer", "if he had a mind to go away?"'[9]

By luck and calculation the king's departure was arranged. On the news that his uncle had fled, William at once marched for London. He checked at Windsor when James, intercepted, returned to Whitehall; then, when the king, guarded with deliberate negligence, again escaped, he occupied the Palace of St James's, the Dutch commands sounding strange to Londoners through the December fog.

Though the government had not yet been turned over to him, the prince at once dealt with essentials. He issued orders to the army, writs for the election of a 'Convention' parliament, and commanded the tax-collectors to carry on. By 28 January 1689, the newly elected Commons passed the resolution that the old monarch had broken the original contract between king and people, violated the fundamental laws, and left the throne vacant. But William stated his own terms: he would either be joint ruler with his wife or 'go back to Holland and meddle no more with their affairs'. He would not, he made it plain, impair the authority of the throne but preserve it.

The Declaration of Rights set out on 13 February and accepted on 23 February by William and Mary, on the day that they accepted the throne, is a conservative and limited document, unlike the American Declaration of Independence or the French proclamation of the Rights of Man. It asserts that the king's power to suspend the laws is illegal, and reasserts that the Crown cannot interfere with the Church or levy money without the consent of Parliament. The raising and keeping of a standing army in times of peace without Parliament's consent is also declared to be against the law. Elections must be free and speeches in Parliament not subject to proceedings from outside it, while excessive bail, fines, and 'cruel and unusual' punishments are disallowed. Parliaments 'ought to be frequently held'. Like the clauses in *Magna Carta* in their now alien feudal context, these rights, on which 'we do claim, demand and insist', are specific and limited. They are not innovations: it had been James II who had been the innovator. They are a declaration of existing law.

The Respectable Revolution was thus highly conservative; a bargain between a continental prince who wanted to harness the force of England to a continental war and prevent the country again becoming paralysed by civil strife, or another belligerent republic, and the

English establishment, determined to protect Anglican Protestantism and property. Yet although the powers of the monarch to govern remained decisive, the will of Parliament had been asserted once and for all. An annual Mutiny Act made the armed forces dependent on Parliament; by 1694 a Triennial Act guaranteed that Parliament would be so summoned; and after, in 1700 the Stuart heir, Princess Anne's son, the Duke of Gloucester, died aged eleven,* in 1701 an Act of Settlement was arranged. The Crown would go to the Electress Sophia, grand-daughter of James I by Elizabeth of Bohemia, and then to her son, Georg Ludwig of Hanover, on even stricter conditions. The sovereign had to be a member of the Church of England, and could not leave the country or make war in defence of his continental territories without parliamentary consent, while stringent restrictions were placed on foreigners taking part in government.

Though still 'mixed' rather than constitutional and retaining formidable powers, with the Respectable Revolution and its sequel the monarchy had been harmonized with the predominant social and economic trend of the times. And like those of *Magna Carta* in its different setting, the negative 'liberties' the takeover had secured would be interpreted in a wider context as more people arrived at political consciousness and power, if immediately it still made for faction and instability of government.

This realistic settlement was paralleled by economic expansion in shipping and finance; by the build-up and exploitation of colonies of settlement in North America and of trade with India and the West Indies. All these things now give a much larger and more modern dimension to English history. The foundation of the Bank of England and the funding of a 'National Debt' reinforced the alliance between government and the moneyed men. And it was on this political and economic foundation that the second-rate power of 1660 became the formidable Great Britain of 1714, whose battle fleets had gained the mastery of the oceans after the defeat of the French at La Hogue in 1692, and which had won great victories on the continent, first at Blenheim in 1704, in southern Germany, and then in the Low Countries, as well as obtaining naval bases in the western Mediterranean at Gibraltar and Minorca.

By Queen Anne's reign the navy consisted of over 200 ships and about 50,000 seamen. Fleets sailed the Baltic, the Mediterranean and the Caribbean; others protected the Channel and blocked Brest and Dunkirk. In addition, the navy had to organize complex convoy arrangements. An army

* The boy died of dropsy on the brain. His mother had contracted a dropsy in her first confinement, transmitted to all her six children, all of whom died young. She also had many miscarriages.

of over 40,000 soldiers was under the command of Marlborough in Flanders, and significant bodies of British troops were also engaged in Spain; the network of alliances was more complicated than any in which Britain had previously been involved.[10]

At the head of a Grand Alliance, Great Britain thus prevented Louis xiv from dominating both Europe and the vast colonial areas which a Franco-Spanish monopoly would have denied to English trade and settlement.

For the European dynastic sovereign states, standing towards each other in a 'posture of war', were now competing to exploit the massive old civilizations of the East and the vast new territories in the Americas. Following the decline of Spain's domination, France and Great Britain had now become the main antagonists in this phase of European domination. If the wars of William iii and Marlborough were not, as in 1588 or 1939–45, wars of sheer survival, far more was at stake than in the medieval depredations of Edward iii and Henry v; nothing less than the creation of a predominant colonial empire and the naval mastery of the world. Such, at the end of the seventeenth century, when 'enthusiasm' was out and business calculation in, were the hard facts of what were now becoming global power politics.

The change-over to a more diversified economy and to a highly aggressive foreign policy was enhanced by the new methods of administration, mainly created during the Civil War and its sequel. Under Henry viii, Thomas Cromwell had done much to improve this aspect of government and Oliver Cromwell's régime had done more. But the wars of William iii and Anne now demanded a much more elaborate bureaucracy and heavier and more regular taxation. The important figures are not now the ephemeral political managers of the Restoration and the crisis of the succession, still exploiting the religious hatreds of the Civil War, but Samuel Pepys at the Admiralty, Sir Josiah Child of the East India Company, Sir William Petty, the surveyor of Ireland and pioneer economist, and their able successors during the Marlborough wars.

Further, after 1688–9, John Locke, the wisest of English political theorists, whose influence would be important in England and even more decisive in America, had adapted his *Second Treatise of Civil Government*, written in 1679–80, and revised in 1681, to 'justify to the world the people of England', and to define the principles behind the Settlement. And his practical and lucid arguments were in harmony with the main intellectual movement of the time, for Isaac Newton, the first great English scientist and a world figure, had now made the cosmos appear rational in a new way. By deducing laws proved by experiment he had demonstrated that the 'Moderns' had beaten the 'Ancients', and that far from all coherence being gone from a degenerate world, coherence had been restored to one in full vigour by his vision of an ordered universe.

The destruction of the last Renaissance court in Europe had diminished the time-honoured Tudor and early Stuart patronage of music, the arts and literature; but after 1660, when the magnates again began to pull ahead, aristocratic patronage revived; and there was now, with the broader establishment already observed, a much wider middle-class public. Purcell, the greatest English composer, and Sir Christopher Wren, the greatest English architect, now reinterpreted continental influences. During the Interregnum the theatres had been closed, though recitative opera had occasionally been permitted, but at the Restoration drama revived. It was inferior to the Elizabethan, urban and exotic, and its values were more social than human; but it was sophisticated and clever and dialogue was witty, natural and brisk. The old baroque prose of the learned and the polemics of sectarian debate, with its homely phrases and abrupt style, now gave way to the pointed couplets of Dryden, the plain irony and racy argument of Swift, and the telling narrative of Defoe. Prose became more accurate and serviceable, appropriate to an age of hard rationality, nicely calculated self-interest and 'good sense'.

4

In the great park at Blenheim, near Woodstock in Oxfordshire, there stands a column topped by the statue of John Churchill, Duke of Marlborough, and bearing a proud inscription at its base; 'a masterpiece', as his descendant Sir Winston Churchill would put it, 'of compact and majestic statement'.* It records victories on a scale no English armies had ever before achieved, in campaigns undertaken in what was a permanent English interest – to keep the Low Countries out of the hands of any potentially or actively hostile power, and to keep command of the sea to prevent invasion and protect commerce and colonies.

The political and military strategy devised by William III and carried to its climax by Marlborough, must be set against a background of complicated political intrigues. Within a few weeks of the coronation of

---

* 'A monument designed to perpetuate the memory of a signal victory obtained over the French and Bavarians near the village of Blenheim on the banks of the Danube by John, Duke of Marlborough, the hero not only of his nation but of his age. Who became . . . the fixed important centre which united in one common cause the Principal States of Europe. Who by military knowledge and irresistible valour in a long series of uninterrupted triumphs broke the power of France when raised to the highest, when exerted to the most, rescued the Empire from desolation, Asserted and confirmed the liberties of Europe.'

William and Mary, England was plunged into major conflict. First the War of the League of Augsburg or Nine Years War against Louis xiv (1689–97) was fought in alliance with the Dutch, the Habsburg Emperor and Spain; then the War of the Spanish Succession (1701–13) in alliance with the Dutch and the Emperor against France, Spain and Bavaria. The range of these wars was vast: on the Danube and the Rhine, in the Netherlands, Catalonia and north Italy; in the Mediterranean, the Channel and the North Atlantic. In an age when war has lost its glamour, the panegyrics of historians may now seem flat; but the waste and suffering were not pointless. They were the price of the survival of the Dutch Commonwealth and of the political and economic development of Great Britain. Without the Marlborough wars, western civilization on both sides of the Atlantic would have assumed a different constitutional, linguistic and cultural aspect. If ever there was a turning-point, these complicated campaigns provided one.

Before the British could intervene on the continent they had to secure their base. James ii had continued a resistance in Ireland; but after the Battle of the Boyne in 1690, William mastered the country, perpetuating the Protestant–Catholic hatreds of Elizabethan and Cromwellian times, and confirming both the Protestant ascendancy and the feud of Ulster with the south. In Scotland, the Highlanders under Claverhouse, who was killed in the action, won the battle of Killiecrankie for James ii, but Edinburgh and the Lowlands accepted the settlement, and in 1692 the Highland clans were forced to take an oath of allegiance; an occasion marked by the notorious massacre when the MacDonalds of Glencoe, whose chief had been slow to take it, were nearly extirpated by soldiers of Argyll's regiment, many of them their hereditary enemies.

After the battle of La Hogue off the Cotentin, 'the Trafalgar', as Churchill puts it, 'of the seventeenth century',[11] the British secured command of the sea. Their armies in the Spanish Netherlands now played their part in capturing Namur, a strategic base for the French assault on the Dutch, and the fleet relieved Barcelona. Checked, Louis xiv failed to overrun the Netherlands and was forced to negotiate the Peace of Ryswick.

But the expensive war was unpopular. An isolationist Tory government under the astute Robert Harley tried to cut the commitment and appease the French. Then a new and worse threat appeared. By 1697 Charles ii, the last degenerate representative of the Spanish Habsburg line, was nearing his end. 'Afflicted with convulsive fits, the wretched monarch was believed to have been bewitched, and the court pullulated with confessors and exorcists and visionary nuns employing every artifice known to the Church to free him from the devil.'[12] In 1700 he died without direct heir. His designated successor, Joseph Ferdinand

of Bavaria, had predeceased him, and he had been persuaded to nominate Philip of Anjou, grandson of Louis xiv. The Bourbons thus secured
the throne of Spain for Philip v; and in 1701, on the death of James ii,
Louis xiv also recognized James's Catholic son, the 'Old Pretender' as
James iii. Apprehensive now of invasion, the English urged William to
retrieve their mistake and reconstitute the Grand Alliance. And even
when the king died in 1702, to be succeeded by Anne (1702–14),
Marlborough had a free hand. But the prospect was bleak, worse than
in 1689. The French were in the Rhineland; Bavaria and Spain were
their allies; the Hungarians in revolt against the Emperor, the Turks
threatening Vienna. But from 1702 to 1708, backed by Godolphin, a
moderate Tory who could manage both parties, Marlborough and the
allies restored the balance of power in Europe. At Blenheim in Bavaria
in 1704 he won a victory so resounding that, as the inscription already
cited justly claims, it transformed the European scene, broke the long-
accepted prestige of French arms and saved Vienna. In the same year an
Anglo-Dutch fleet took Gibraltar, and the British have held on to it ever
since.

The war now shifted to Flanders. At Ramillies, north of Namur,
Marlborough won control of Antwerp and of Brussels; at Oudenard,
south of Ghent, he opened the decisive prospect of an invasion of France,
and in 1708 the frightful slaughter at Malplaquet near Mons forced the
French to accept their strategic failure. Moreover, the Austrians had
now driven the French out of Turin. And when in 1705 the Catalonians
had revolted against the Bourbon Philip v, and proclaimed the Habsburg Archduke Charles of Austria as Charles iii, an English expedition
under Lord Peterborough had exploited a new strategic opening. The
revolt had failed and the Catalonians were left to their fate; but the
British had secured Minorca, which confirmed their command of the
western Mediterranean.

But Marlborough's resounding victories had been followed by his
political downfall. The accession of Queen Anne in 1702 had been
greatly to his advantage; but the new monarch, though she possessed a
placid dignity, was ailing and apprehensive; singularly ill-equipped to
cope with the crises which marked her reign; martyred, almost to her
last gasp when she died at forty-nine, by her duties. Her husband,
Prince George of Denmark, was a less fatuous character than most
historians aver;* and in spite of the fate of their numerous offspring,
their domestic life was not unhappy: but the Queen was apt to feel
guilty at the personal betrayal which her father's policies had forced

* He is recalled in folk memory mainly by Charles ii's remark 'I have tried him drunk and
I have tried him sober, and 'Od's fish, there is nothing in him', and by the sobriquet *'est-il
possible?'* from his exclamations of bewilderment during the crisis of 1688.

upon her, and she was all her life curiously dependent on female confidantes. In fact Marlborough's position was less dependent on Duchess Sarah's ascendancy over the Queen than often supposed; but Anne's reaction against her imperious domination did not help his prospects. And by 1708 the coalition of Whigs and Tories, held together by Godolphin since 1702, was disintegrating. The Tory Robert Harley, later Lord Oxford, was manœuvring to oust what was now a Whig ministry saddled with the responsibility of the war. In 1710 Marlborough's supporter, Godolphin, was dismissed, and that autumn, a Tory ministry under Harley came in. The war was now thoroughly unpopular, and it was represented that Marlborough was prolonging it for his own advantage. In 1712 he retired abroad. So the Tory government, having discarded their best general, now deserted their allies. In 1712 the French overran much of the Flemish territories gained by the Alliance, and an English army under the incapable Duke of Ormonde retreated to Dunkirk.

The terms of the Treaty of Utrecht concluded in 1713 were therefore less favourable to the British than they might earlier have obtained. But the essential objectives of both wars had been secured. The Bourbon Philip v remained upon the Spanish throne; but on the understanding that the French and Spanish crowns should not be united; moreover, the French recognized the Protestant Hanoverian dynasty in England and the exiled Stuarts had to leave France. The Dutch also retained control of the Scheldt and of the forts along the Flanders frontier. The Netherlands and the vital bases of Antwerp and Brussels had not been overrun. Although the Catalans were left to the mercy of their enemies, the British retained Gibraltar and Minorca. At the price of Austrian domination, northern Italy was secured from the French, and in the Americas the British retained Nova Scotia, Newfoundland and large territories round Hudson's Bay, as well as new bases in the Caribbean and a thirty years' monopoly of the slave trade. This highly realistic settlement had checked, if not destroyed, the ambitions of Louis xiv. It set Europe and its dependencies again in a precarious equilibrium, now restored through the military and naval power of the Anglo–Dutch– Austrian alliance designed by William iii. Such were the conflicts whereby the European nation states settled the background to the partition of much of the world between them.

5

'Bankers,' Clarendon had written with a nuance of contempt, were 'a tribe that had risen and grown up in Cromwell's time, and never even heard of before the late troubles.'[13] The wars of William iii and of

Queen Anne greatly enhanced their importance: where scriveners and goldsmiths had accepted deposits of valuables and coin, a new kind of financier now actively supported government. There was now much more capital pressing for investment; hoarded funds were released and passed on to contractors who supplied the armies and the fleet. Since even land taxes at four shillings in the pound and heavy customs and excise could not meet the enormous cost of the wars, a new kind of 'deficit' financing came in; there was now an official 'National Debt', the interest secured on the taxes. This funded debt provided much better security than the precarious loans of Tudor and early Stuart times, on which the Crown had been apt to default. In 1694, following Dutch methods, the Bank of England was founded, paying interest at eight per cent, and government 'annuities' now commanded public confidence. The future Duke of Marlborough wisely invested his first capital (obtained through the affection of one of Charles II's mistresses, Barbara Villiers, Duchess of Cleveland) in this way. The moneyed interests thus profited by the wars, to the indignation of the Tory squires who paid the land tax, now diverted, they complained, to pay 'Dutch' financiers. Further by 1697 clipped and debased coins were called in, and the consequent deflation helped to stabilize prices. In contrast to the Tudor inflation, they would remain pretty constant from the late seventeenth to the mid-eighteenth century.

By 1697 there was even a rudimentary stock exchange, where brokers dealt in East India, Hudson's Bay and Royal Africa stocks. In the City a new nationwide interest was growing up: the possibilities of large-scale credit had been discovered. And if the bursting of the 'South Sea Bubble' would teach the public that investment was a tricky business, the new techniques of investment and exchange redistributed and circulated wealth, financed the armed forces, transmitted money and proved that land or plate was no longer the sole reliable means of accumulating wealth. Government now collaborated with business, instead of trying, with misguided Stuart paternalism, to thwart it; and 'a hierarchical society based on custom and landholding, faded imperceptibly into one based on enterprise, success, luck'.[14]

But the resulting wealth which would be behind the Industrial Revolution and 'take off' in the late eighteenth century, did not represent 'easy profits by the capitalist. Each step forward represented the conquest of a problem. Dutch competition, food shortage, labour shortage, the burden of debt . . . the weapons used in each contest were those of applied intelligence and enterprise'.[15] Although the prosperity of the time must still be set against what now appears a relatively backward countryside, and derives mainly from the vast expansion of colonial and carrying trade, stimulated by investment channelled to

COMMERCE, INDUSTRY AND EMPIRE

limited opportunities, the scale was now quite different from that of the miniature Tudor economy. A wider distribution of wealth among the small propertied class provided for a much less uncomfortable way of life: if civilization was still a veneer over a mass of under-employment and illiterate poverty, it was now more widely spread.

Nor is the traditional picture of ruthless capitalists exploiting their advantage a just one: economic theorists were still much concerned to promote full employment. It has been remarked that,

When R. H. Tawney writes 'Restoration society was dominated by the commercial classes whose temper was a ruthless materialism, determined at all costs to conquer world markets from France and Holland and prepared to sacrifice every other consideration to their economic ambitions', he becomes less convincing in the light of recent evidence concerning the extensive philanthropy of the seventeenth-century merchant class as a whole.[16]

Mercantilist economic theory still retained much of the old concern for rudimentary welfare, and took considerable account of the nation as a commonwealth, if only to use available resources of manpower and intelligence in the sharp competition.

There was now a major change in the tempo and direction of overseas trade. From 1663–1701 imports increased from £4·4 million to £5·8 million; exports from £4·1 to £6·4 million. Whereas in 1640, 80–90% of exports from London had been woollen cloth, by 1699–1701 this accounted for only 47%. The new prosperity now came mainly from the trade in Virginian tobacco, West Indian sugar, and in calico, which led to the commercial revolution of the eighteenth century.[17]

The mounting popular demand also enriched the soap manufacturers and the brewers, who now came to supersede the ale wives, for, as their beer was now preserved by hops, they could produce on a bigger scale. Wood for fuel had long been getting more scarce, and coal now became the basis of the more advanced industries of iron foundries, paper manufacturing and glass-making, and of the further exploitation of tin and lead. There was not yet anything like an 'industrial revolution', but the techniques out of which it would come were being elaborated. In Elizabeth's time Dutch refugees had brought in their skills; now, after the revocation of the Edict of Nantes, Huguenot immigrants also brought in new techniques, while the designers of English ships had learnt much from their Dutch rivals. In the early seventeenth century, the English had been technologically behind the French and the Dutch; now they were abreast of and indeed surpassing them.

The increased prosperity was apparent from the boom in building. Stimulated in London by the Great Fire, and symbolized by Wren's enormous new St Paul's, it was also apparent in country towns and country houses throughout the land. By the turn of the century, spacious windows, built to catch the sun, commanded wide vistas of park and lake, and panelled rooms with wide fireplaces provided the rich with a space and comfort hitherto unknown. For the merely well-to-do, smaller but snug interiors reflected the influence of the Dutch with whom the new régime was much bound up. Solid comfort rather than splendour was the aim of a growing class of merchants and investors, while, following the growing cult of the 'grand tour', the aristocracy competed in a more cosmopolitan ostentation. Security and continuity could now be taken for granted among a wider class. Hence the rather complacent tone of many Augustan writers, when they were not engaged in scarifying each other, but writing for the more prosperous public. And if, outside the propertied and professional minority, the mass of the people continued to live dependent and limited lives, food was now cheaper and in more regular supply. The local famines which had afflicted late medieval and even Tudor England had now no longer to be taken for granted.

What was more, agricultural methods were beginning to improve and pioneer statisticians to find out what was going on. Turnips, brought in from the Netherlands, now provided winter feed for cattle, which no longer had to be slaughtered in the autumn; clover and grasses to restore the land now alternated with wheat and barley, and manuring and marling were better understood. Though in some areas cattle were coming to be a better proposition than sheep, vast flocks still fed on the downs, and there is no evidence that the continuing though still limited enclosures were diminishing the rural population. Moreover, apart from the expanding demands of London, the growing markets in the towns provided a demand for garden produce, fruit and livestock. The great 'improving' landlords of the eighteenth century had not yet emerged, and most squires, farmers and smallholders were doubtless very conservative; but, here, as in manufacturing industries, new methods were coming in.

What is more, governing circles in London now had better information about the state of the economy. The cult of 'the mathematiques', already apparent in Hobbes, was confirmed by Newton's *Principia Mathematica*, published in the year before the Respectable Revolution; and the fellows of the Royal Society patronized by Charles II, were mainly interested in applied mathematics and experimental science. With the example of the Dutch before them, the early economists believed that information could be collected by 'politique arithmetick'. Sir William Petty, the many-sided character, so brilliantly depicted by John Aubrey, who had taken the profitable risk of surveying Ireland for the Commonwealth government when the acknowledged expert had preferred to 'sleep in whole skin', had been the first expert who had systematically tried to determine the wealth of the country;* and Gregory King's *Natural and Political Observations*, published in 1696, two years after the foundation of the Bank of England, provide the first tolerably reliable statistics of population and income. As early as 1664 Thomas Mun's posthumous *England's Treasure by fforaign trade*, had been the first full statement of mercantile economic theory, which carried further the medieval and Tudor concern to keep bullion in the country; in modern terms to create a favourable balance of trade.

Government, indeed, now increasingly set itself to politics designed to increase trade and commerce; the wealth of eighteenth-century England would be built on colonial expansion, and war conducted not for glory but for survival and aggrandizement in a world of mounting competition. Since England's resources were ampler than those of Holland and better organized than those of France, for her taxation was adequate but not crippling, and her social system was not so exclusive as to provoke revolutionary resentment, the adaptable English establishment was able to lay the foundations of world power.

6

The seventeenth century had been an astonishingly creative time for all western Europe, when the intellectual foundations of the modern world were laid. Following the destruction of the time-honoured metaphysical scholastic philosophy and the recognition of the limitations of mind, profound consequences would follow. Thomas Hobbes, whose *Leviathan* had appeared in 1651, had accepted a nominalist sceptical philosophy, and though he regarded fundamental religious questions with awe – for he was no atheist, but merely said the Deity was 'like the sun', too dazzling for direct apprehension – he relegated them to the realm of the unfathomable, and set about putting human political affairs in better order. The profoundest, if not the most practical of English political philosophers, Hobbes was a great artist in prose, so that, in his own phrase, his thought 'bites in'; yet for all his old-fashioned Baroque style and genius for the startling metaphor, his objectives were down to earth. The *Leviathan*, as his contemporaries pointed out, was an artificial and clumsy monster, mechanical and deterministic, if memorably portrayed;

* Challenged.to a duel by one of 'Oliver's Knights', Petty, who was short-sighted, nominated for the place a dark cellar and for the weapon a carpenter's axe, thus ridiculing the affair. In his lighter moments he could be an 'excellent Droll' and 'preach extempore incomparably, either in the Presbyterian way, Independent, Cappucin frier or Jesuit'. Aubrey's *Brief Lives*, ed. Oliver Lawson Dick, London 1950, p. 240. Always adaptable, this capitalist pioneer of the labour theory of value has even come in for some unexpected praise from Marxist historians.

but Hobbes shifted the basis of political speculation to the laws of physics and psychology as he understood them and his objectives were strictly utilitarian.[18] He has long been tendentiously portrayed as a prophet of 'bourgeois' individualism; but he was in fact trying to give the traditional order of society a new sanction, proof against both knaves and fools. His object was peace and order; and if religion disturbed them, then the Church must be subordinated to the State; and if necessary, economic enterprise also be controlled. For in spite of his reputation then and since, Hobbes was aristocratic and hierarchical in his view of society, and dissociated himself from any intention 'to encourage men of low degree to a saucy behaviour towards their betters'.*

If Hobbes had tried to build his political theory on the 'laws of motion' and of human psychology, discarding metaphysical assumptions, Locke, too, banished metaphysics from philosophy; but since he was very well thought of by the establishment of his day, while Hobbes had been regarded as a rebel or, as Charles II had said, 'a bear to be baited', Locke became much more popular and influential. His political theory was set out in the easy colloquial and lucid prose then becoming fashionable, and he achieved great practical importance both on the continent and in America. The essential philosophical point he raised, as it was defined by the critics of his *Essay Concerning Human Understanding*, was whether man was endowed with a 'soul' or 'spirit' whereby he could apprehend the direct revelation of God, or if in the idiom of the time, '. . . this soul were nothing but the contexture of several parts of our Bodies to perform those feats of motion which for an honorable kind of Distinction we call Thoughts'. Locke's influence would stress the limitations of mind, and confirm the empirical trend of English philosophy.

Similarly, Locke's business-like political theory, which affirmed that government ought simply to defend its subjects' persons and property and, if it failed in its trust, forfeit their allegiance, had cut the ground from under the current theory of Divine Right as expressing the order of the 'Chain of Being' which held a cosmic order together. It is now hard to believe that Filmer, the royalist advocate of patriarchal Divine Right descending from Adam, was an opponent worthy of Locke's pen; but he represented widespread and influential opinion. Those who then took their stand with the 'Ancients' against the 'Moderns', and believed that the age was not, as we now feel, creative and promising, but one of

* English Works, II, p. 79 n, quoted by K. V. Thomas, *The Social Origins of Hobbes' Political Thought*, in *Hobbes Studies*, ed. K. C. Brown, Oxford, 1965, p. 200. This article is the best modern appraisal of Hobbes in this context and supersedes the widely accepted picture that Hobbes advocated individual equality before the forces of the free market.

confusion, degeneracy and decay, clung to the idea that the ruler was a link between God and man; and the Elizabethan cult of degree and place long persisted among conservatives into a more dynamic social order. There was also still a Renaissance cult of 'Ruminant' history and of the 'Archives of Ancient Prudence Ransackt', and even the advocates of 'mixed' or 'regulated' monarchy had long appealed mainly to past precedent and ancient laws.

But the tide was against the 'Ancients'. If Hobbes had appeared to be taking a leap in the dark, it was now increasingly accepted that the cosmic system, as apparently revealed by Newton, could be understood by ordinary good sense. The universe and human society were ordered and intelligible; as affirmed by Francis Bacon, reason and applied science could indeed be harnessed to the improvement of the human condition.

Such relative optimism had naturally appealed in a society 'returning to its wits again', in reaction against Baroque 'fanatick' excess, and concerned with the political and economic changes which the English situation on the sea routes of an Oceanic world had now brought about. This predominantly practical bias is also apparent in famous discoveries: in the way in which the Hon. Robert Boyle went to the essentials of physics, or Halley tested the laws of astronomy, or Thomas Sydenham classified illness by clinical observation.

In traditional scholarship, moreover, Richard Bentley, Master of Trinity College, Cambridge, from 1700 to 1742, won European fame and parochial detestation by his rigorous methods of textual criticism; setting an author in his historical context, relating classical literature to life, and giving better than he got in academic warfare. And for the first time medieval chronicles and charters were now adequately edited and arranged; Anglo-Saxon and Scandinavian antiquity investigated. Although, with the Restoration, the universities became more the preserve of the gentry than in Tudor or early Stuart times, and the standard of popular education in the grammar schools fell away, they still drew genius and talent from rustic and provincial origins, supplementing the élite schools, Eton, Winchester, Westminster and St Paul's. Further, the Nonconformist academies, which had grown up to cater for those excluded from the Anglican foundations, now began to offer modern subjects not included in the strict classical curriculum. If the Anglican Church had become more exclusive, the Noncomformists, too, now had their solid tradition; while within the Anglican Church, the Cambridge Platonists were creating a broader and more tolerant philosophy, from which the latitudinarian eighteenth-century orthodoxy would emerge. These people, in contrast to the Puritan fanatics of the Interregnum and their High Tory enemies, enabled the Anglican establishment to come to terms with the increasingly powerful trend towards empirical science, and to reconcile the Moderns with the Ancients in a more tolerant world.

7

It seems extraordinary that the Puritanical bigots of 1642 could have suppressed so vital an aspect of London life as the popular theatre, with its traditions of Shakespeare and Ben Jonson, as well as put down the more exotic performances at the Court. With the Restoration a reaction set in; but drama was no longer so much rooted in the people. The change from boy actors to actresses – made not because the women acted better, but because they were more to the taste of the courtiers off stage – may also, as one critic believed, have impoverished the poetic aspect of the drama.* The Restoration stage itself was more of a picture, more cut off from the audience than in the more intimate and primitive popular theatre of Shakespeare's time. The tone of most of these plays is shallow and often cruel; the characters stock types, the plots ringing the changes on elaborate adulteries and on the contrast between urban sophistication and bucolic simplicity. They are brittle comedies, written for a heartless society, and live not through their insight or sympathy, but through their wit and stage technique. The best of them, even Congreve's *Way of the World*, still in this style though performed in 1700, are vastly inferior to the great Elizabethan and Jacobean plays. Nor are the great ranting tragedies in the French manner now anything but tedious, though Dryden's are relieved by some attractive lyrics.

It was, appropriately, in satire that this age excelled. The lumbering English style of Skelton was picked up and made topical. Samuel Butler (1612–80) in *Hudibras*, had a field day not only against the more self-righteous Puritans, but against a wide range of astrologers and quacks, including the

> *Quacks of government who sate*
> *At th' unregarded helm of state.*

Nor are Butler's more neglected works unrewarding: his satire, for example, on the Royal Society, called *The Elephant on the Moon*, or his gay parody of heroic verse in his *Repartees between Cat and Puss at a Caterwauling*, which begins,

---

* 'It may be doubted whether Shakespeare has not suffered far more than he has gained by the genius of latter-day critics, who bring into his plays a realism and a robust emotion which sometimes obscures the sheer poetic value of the author's conception . . . with the disappearance of the boy players the poetic drama died in England, and it has had no second life.' Raleigh, *op. cit.*, p. 120.

When Puss, wrapt warm in his own native fur
Dreamt soundly of as soft and warm amours,
Of making gallantry on gutter tiles
And sporting in delightful faggot piles . . .
Or bolting out of bushes in the dark
As ladies use at midnight in the park.

Butler uses a homely cudgel, but John Dryden (1631–1700) uses a rapier. The polished invective and irony of *Absalom and Achitophel*, a political satire on the attempt of Shaftesbury to displace the Duke of York by Monmouth following the Popish Plot, appeared in 1681, when Shaftesbury was to be tried for high treason. It is unsurpassed of its kind in the language. Dryden can hit off a character in a brisk line and his racing couplets at once exhilarate and carry the reader along. He could be equally deadly, as in *McFlecknoe*, against literary dullness and pretence;

To die for faction is a common evil
But to be hanged for nonsense is the devil.

His prose style set new standards of lucid and readable exposition, while his kind of satire, expressed in plain and immensely readable prose, is more deadly than Thomas More's *Utopia*, the product of amiable Erasmian humanism.

The dark genius of Jonathan Swift (1667-1745) belongs not to the Restoration but the Augustan age of Queen Anne and the French wars. Like Dryden, a great satirist, his bitterness went deeper than mere political hatred; for he is sometimes livid with disgust at the human condition itself. But the driving force of his savage indignation was not aimless. He at least cared enough for mankind to attack abuses and the evils occasioned by rival fanatics; he was not past caring. His technique is subtle, using utterly commonplace examples to deflate vast hypocrisies, and he uses what is supposedly a children's tale of *Gulliver's Travels*, or *The Voyage to Laputa*, to scarify the fashionable politicians and intellectuals, often types with us still.

Both Swift and Dryden could only have emerged from a society both more mature and more profoundly sceptical than that of the England of Henry VIII; and their easy, conversational prose commanded a wider audience. But the élite of this civilization was still very small. In his *Brief Lives* John Aubrey (1625–97) depicts an intimate society, centred on London, Oxford and Cambridge, in the great country houses of the magnates and lesser houses of the well-to-do. Already Shakespeare had described a whole range of English characters, recognizable today; Aubrey depicts in miniature the finer shades of English eccentricity. He can depict people in a few deft strokes; his criticism marks a new self-consciousness and a new romantic curiosity towards the past. Like all the best biographers, he had an intuitive insight regarding people and revealed it by anecdote. As Thomas Allen, the Oxford astrologer and mathematician, whose servant would tell the undergraduates that 'sometimes he should meet the spirits coming up his stairs like Bees'. Or Edward Davenant who 'could not endure to hear of the *New* (Cartesian) *Philosophy*; for said he, if 'a new philosophy is brought in, a New Divinity will shortly follow'. Or General Monk, who when in command at sea, 'instead of *tack about* he would say *Wheele to the right* or *left*'. Aubrey was no recluse and cobwebbed antiquary, but a knowledgeable and popular man of the great world, with the entrée to a richly diverse society.[19] Out of it, in spite of the harsh political conflicts of the day and the illiterate and poverty-stricken world on which this civilization still depended, had come the thrust and enterprise that transformed the half-crippled England of the Restoration into the great power that it was becoming in the reign of Anne.

20

OLIGARCHY AND FIRST EMPIRE

In the late evening of 30 September 1714, in thick autumnal fog, a small choleric German prince, with prominent china-blue eyes, stepped ashore at Greenwich to be received by the political élite of England in the palace rebuilt by Wren. Georg Ludwig, Elector of Hanover, who came to the throne at fifty-four as George I (1714–27), was a military autocrat long set in his ways. Like his son, the new Prince of Wales, with whom he was on the worst of terms, he distrusted his English subjects; 'looked upon them all as king-killers and republicans, and grudged them their riches as well as their liberty.'[1] He had never troubled to learn English; but since he spoke fluent French he could converse freely with his ministers, and he had a bilingual secretary to hand.* Nor was his entourage confined to the predatory mistresses who appeared so uncouth in English eyes: he brought over able German advisers through whom he often dealt with foreign affairs, naturally his main interest. Though the Prince of Wales, who succeeded as George II (1727–60) spoke English, if with a heavy accent, he, too, was more preoccupied with Hanover than Great Britain, and he was the last English monarch to lead his army on the continent. Both monarchs were shrewd realists, ready to adapt themselves to their position; but they both naturally detested the limitations set on their power by the English oligarchy and spent as much time as they could in their Electorate, where their word was law. It was only with George III (1760–1820), whose father, Frederick, Prince of Wales, had died in 1751, that the new dynasty became fully acclimatized.

Queen Anne had 'pronounced all her speeches with great weight and authority and with a softness of voice and a sweetness of pronunciation that added life to all she spoke',[2] and when she had touched the young Samuel Johnson for the 'King's Evil', had left him with 'somehow a sort of solemn recollection of a lady in diamonds and a long black hood'.[3]

---

* The legend that he spoke dog-Latin with Walpole has had to join the other time-honoured stories now discredited. 'Language', writes Professor Plumb, 'was no barrier. George I wrote and spoke French fluently as his first language. Bernstorff told Lady Cowper that the King understood neither Latin nor English. The English ministers either spoke French fluently . . . or haltingly, as did Walpole . . . further evidence destructive of the old myth that George I and Walpole could only converse in dog-Latin.' Plumb, *op. cit.*, p. 107 n. See also the same author's *The Four Georges*, London 1954, for an appreciation of the characters concerned.

Now the Stuart charm had vanished; and the court, though still the centre of political power lost its old style and distinction. But stability had been achieved. The Whig politicians who had backed the Hanoverians now imposed what was in effect a one-party government, and brought the feverish strife of cliques and parties which had come near to paralysing government even during the great wars of William III and Anne, under better control. The traditional turbulence of the electorate, which produced 'more general elections between 1688 and 1714 than at any other comparable period in the history of parliament, excluding medieval times',[4] would now be mastered. Further the mounting expense of elections put power into the hands of the rich, and the interests of the great Whig landlords and moneyed men came to coalesce with those of the executive whose scope had been greatly expanded during the wars.

. . . The Whig party fused the interests of the aristocracy, high finance and executive government, a process extended by Walpole to embrace the bulk of the landed gentry. By doing so he put the noblemen and gentlemen back at the heart of English political society. This was to be of tremendous importance for England's future development. The seventeenth century had witnessed the beginnings and partial success of a bourgeois revolution that came near to changing the institutions of government. In this, however, it never succeeded. The Revolution of 1688 and all that followed were retrogressive from the point of view of the emergence of the middle class into political power. Socially and economically they continued to thrive, but not politically.[5]

The aristocratic and plutocratic establishment became an oligarchy.

The 'violent and lasting heats and animosities' occasioned by triennial parliaments had long threatened the stability of government; now by the Septennial Act of 1716 parliament prolonged its own powers and, though he disclaimed the title – then one of abuse – Sir Robert Walpole (1721–42) became, in effect, a sort of Prime Minister. And if 'the history of Prime Ministers before 1832 – and perhaps after – is more like that of the Cheshire cat; sometimes there is almost a whole cat, sometimes no more than a grin, and it is not always the same end that appears first',[6] seventeenth century party strife now began to subside into consensus politics; a fact confirmed by the failure of the Jacobite risings in 1715 and 1745.

The Court meanwhile still remained the centre of government and patronage: 'though Walpole has always been painted as a great parliamentarian, something more than a mere minister of the crown . . . he was a great "king's man" . . . a link between two sources of power'.[7] For all their tantrums, the Hanoverians themselves recognized the advantages of the limited monarchy. As Queen Caroline well remarked;

My God! what a figure this poor island would make in Europe if it were not for its free government! It is its excellent free government that makes its inhabitants industrious, as they know that what they get nobody can take from them: it is its free government, too, that makes foreigners send their money hither, because they know it is secure and the prince cannot touch it.[8]

King and ministers thus collaborated in what was still a royal government, if one sustained by adroit management and patronage within a political nation now less restive as 'the rage of party gave way to the pursuit of place'.[9] And since the kind of cabinets evolved since 1688 had become a scene of faction, Walpole, often supposed to have been the creator of cabinet government, in fact bypassed them. He worked mainly through an inner group with the Chancellor, the two Secretaries, the Lord Privy Seal and the President of the Council. And this group collaborated with the monarchs themselves, who, far from withdrawing from politics, both took a close interest in business, in particular in foreign affairs, in which they were well informed.

Besides this inner executive, a much larger bureaucracy was now established. Following their rise during the Interregnum, boards and committees had been further developed and the civil servants had become more professional; first under Charles II and James II; then with much wider scope, during the great wars with France. Both the Treasury and the Customs and Excise Office had now become more elaborate, while the Admiralty and the War Office had expanded; the instruments of government now dwarfed the often ramshackle expedients of the Tudor and early Stuart past. This fact gave government greater security and momentum, and in days before competitive examinations, provided the political nation with the opportunity of securing 'places', though not on the scale that has often been alleged. Hence, as confidence in the solvency and the relative competence of the executive became established, the strength of the oligarchy was enhanced. Crown and ministers were united in a common interest, and the problem was no longer the old one of controlling the arbitrary power of the Crown or preventing faction-ridden parliaments from creating chaos, but how to ensure workable government through the political cliques within the Whig consensus. For though the terms Whig and Tory would last, kept alive by religious prejudices and local interests, and take on new meanings, the Tory party was now in hopeless disarray. Henry St John, Viscount Bolingbroke had wrecked it. Playing upon Queen Anne's preference for her half-brother, the Catholic 'Old Pretender', he had gambled, like the propagandist Swift, on keeping the Elector out, and lost.

But neither Whig nor Tory party had been systematically organized. Now, as peace settled in, the labels became blurred within a prosperous

366

and privileged ruling class, determined to maintain the balance of power which limited government. Great landowners, merchants and a growing body of investors became bound together in this common interest, while they got on with their main business – to exploit Great Britain's position as the greatest commercial country in Europe; and, following this concern, they would even pay for expensive wars to promote trade. Despite the in-fighting among the Whig factions, a political consensus had been building up: it was Walpole's achievement to realize it. Like Baldwin, in a very different context, this adroit political manager aimed to unite the nation for conflicts he did his best to postpone. Revising traditional policy, he even appeased the French; the best way, he thought, to neutralize the Jacobites. And, concentrating on financial and commercial objectives, he long avoided war.

Yet by the 1740s the logic of international power politics asserted itself; the Anglo-French competition for European domination and colonial markets had again become inescapable. By 1739, to Walpole's disgust, the country had drifted into a traditional commercial and colonial war with Spain; then, led by Carteret (in 1744 Lord Granville), who played upon the concern of George II for Hanover, England was edged into a major conflict – the War of the Austrian Succession (1740–8) against France. After an attempt to revert to peace and isolationism under Henry Pelham (1743–54) and his brother the Duke of Newcastle (1754–6), the country then entered a third and much greater conflict with the French in the Seven Years' War (1756–63). A belligerent and ambitious commercial imperialism now got its head, and under the masterful leadership of William Pitt, later Lord Chatham, the British acquired an enormous empire in America and India. In spite of the loss of the American colonies in the 1770s and the reverses signalized by the Treaty of Versailles in 1783, they would retain most of it. They would keep Canada and remain paramount in India, while they retained the most lucrative and important West Indian islands, as well as keeping Gibraltar.

The small and close-knit upper class was now secure; brilliantly articulate and sophisticated. It had long consolidated its hold and it was reaping the harvest. It derived from the landowners and merchants of medieval England, enriched by the Church lands under Henry VIII, and reinforced by generations of able men whom the ruling classes had been realistic enough to assimilate. Few great medieval families now survived; but there had been continuity in leadership – or exploitation – the main theme of English history. In spite of the relative poverty of the mass of the people, they were better off than most of their continental contemporaries; and in spite of frequent wars, which, though decisive, did not much effect civilian life, the main patterns already apparent were drawn together in a society long culturally mature. It was the age of Gibbon and Johnson, of Hume and Burke, with its curious undercurrent in the romantic movement which began in England. It was a small élite culture riding above a mass of poverty and illiteracy and crime, savagely repressed, but one which from top to bottom had tremendous drive. And this insular self-confidence symbolized in the figure of John Bull, first projected at the close of the Marlborough wars, would be inherited by Regency England and the Victorians.

2

Against this long-term prospect, the essentials of domestic and foreign policy must now be considered; then the social and economic developments that, in spite of the poverty and illiteracy of the bulk of the population, meant enhanced prosperity and vigour; finally the intellectual and artistic culture of the high eighteenth century.

Although consensus politics and the pursuit of place made for a new solvency and stability, England even under the Whig oligarchy was still hard to govern. Sir Robert Walpole, a character symbolic of his time,* was essentially a political boss. He aimed at practical objectives, he was a superb man of business, and he knew how to manage men. Contrary to popular belief, his reputation as a prescient financier over the 'South Sea Bubble' is undeserved; indeed, writes his best biographer, 'few reputations have such strange and inaccurate origins as Walpole's. Generations of historians have praised him for restoring the country's ruined finances, yet for this there is no foundation in fact, the finances restored themselves . . . wealth had not been destroyed but bizarrely

---

* Sir Robert Walpole, first Earl of Orford (1676–1745) came of an old-established family in Norfolk; his father was the squire of Houghton, member of parliament for King's Lynn, and principal Whig political manager for the county. Educated at Eton and King's College, Cambridge, which he left young to succeed to his estate, Walpole married the daughter of a rich timber merchant who traded with the Baltic ports. He also kept 'a very pretty young woman . . . whose name was Skerret', to whom he was said to have given £5,000 'by way of entrance money', and whom he married after his wife's death. He rose through the patronage of the Marlboroughs, who needed Whig allies: by 1708 he was Secretary at War, by 1710 Treasurer of the Navy and by 1715–7 Chancellor of the Exchequer. With luck rather than judgement he got out of South Sea stock in time, evaded responsibility, and returned in 1721 to try to deal with the consequences of the financial crash and help to restore confidence. He remained in power till 1742, when he went to the Lords as the Earl of Orford.

Walpole was a great all-rounder, ruthless in politics, but affable to the defeated; a collector of pictures and furniture, a sportsman and *bon viveur*, but capable of intense and swift application to business. He had Baldwin's sense of timing and astute management without being lazy and, like Baldwin, he was insular. He never went abroad. He revelled in luxury and display, but retained the Norfolk accent of his forebears, and his conversation was coarse even by standards of the time. He is the first great parliamentary political manager in English history. Gay's *Beggar's Opera* and *Polly* are satires on Walpole.

redistributed'.[10] Nor did he manage parliament by 'corruption' in the way that former historians believed; 'the limitations of patronage as the sole or even predominant method of parliamentary management are clearly revealed.' The myth that Walpole and later Henry Pelham controlled the House of Commons by virtue of 'every man having his price will not bear close examination'.[11] Indeed, the long-accepted idea is an echo of contemporary political warfare, for the 'legend of "corruption" seeped from the *Craftsman* (an opposition paper) ultimately into "history"'. And, again, 'very little' (even of the secret service funds) 'was spent on elections, and practically none on buying for cash the votes of members of the House of Commons. The analysis in fact bears a striking resemblance to the budget of the *Maison du Roi* under Louis XIV, and "the political" nation . . . at Versailles'.[12] The House of Commons in fact contained fewer 'place' men and holders of sinecures than generally supposed, if some were picturesque.* Many of these offices provided for men who would now be minor ministers or civil servants, the 'men of business' on whose work and ability the security of the government depended; for the rest, it had 'the character of private charity rather than public corruption, and as a constitutional lubricant between executive and legislature it was always of subordinate significance'.[13] There were also many seats long owned by substantial families, who occupied them for their own benefit and whose judgement would be influenced, not by 'corruption', but by their estimate of the personal qualities of the ministers. And these independent members would at most coalesce in shifting groups, determined by fluctuating and often local interests. They could be managed and even led, but neither openly bribed nor coerced. The old independence of the gentry, if no longer whipped up by party passions as in the reign of Anne, was still there; if basic stability had been achieved, the government had to contend with vested interests and conciliate and manage a class often indifferent to office; even as Henry Penruddocke Wyndham put it, with a 'restless aversion to all government'.[14]

There were thus openings for men of ability, and a pocket borough might provide a chance. Within a political élite where 'a wide class of active citizens was raised above the masses; and . . . this high plateau . . . was not overtowered by inaccessible peaks . . . personality, eloquence, debating power, prestige, counted far more in the eighteenth-century House of Commons . . . than it does now, unless the whips are taken off – an exceedingly rare event'.[15] Thus the stability achieved by Walpole did not mean the destruction of liberty, as brought about by the

* As C. FitzRoy-Scudamore, Master of the King's Tennis Courts; inoperative Colonels of regiments, the Deputy Governor of the Scilly Isles, and the Master of the King's Revels in Ireland. Owen, *op. cit.*, p. 51 n.

more efficient, centralized and massive government of eighteenth-century France.

Further, in spite of the preponderance of the oligarchy, the mass of the people possessed certain basic rights. Although they had no votes or substantial property, they had 'freedom from absolutism (the constitutional monarchy), freedom from arbitrary arrest, trial by jury, equality before the law, the freedom of the home from arbitrary entrance and search, some limited liberty of thought, of speech and of conscience, the vicarious participation in liberty (or its semblance) afforded by the right of parliamentary opposition . . . the right to parade, huzza and jeer at the hustings, as well as freedom to travel, trade and sell one's own labour . . . a moral consensus in which authority at times shared and of which at all times it had to take account'.[16] Insular and Protestant, the volatile 'mobs' believed themselves 'freeborn Englishmen'.

Within this setting, Walpole achieved much. He bought time for the Hanoverian settlement. He contributed to restore the finances by developing the 'sinking fund', first established in 1717 to reduce the 'National Debt' and the interest on it; and, in a time of stable prices, he overhauled the archaic system of taxation. The land tax, introduced in 1692, was now reduced from four shillings to a shilling, and excise and customs duties rationalized to bring in more regular returns. So revenue was stabilized and a surplus even deployed to promote a favourable balance of trade and foster employment. Justices of the Peace could still fix wages and prohibit combinations of workmen, and the interests of Ireland and the colonies were sacrificed; but compared with the inept paternalism and monopolies of the old Stuart conciliar government, Walpole's administration moved in a different world. For his objectives, public and private, were practical, obvious, worldly. Devoid of the high purposes of Laud and Strafford or even Clarendon, he piled up a huge fortune and spent it, rebuilt Houghton in lavish style, and entertained his friends and clients at hunting congresses and gargantuan meals; 'up to the chin in beef, venison, geese and turkeys, and generally over the chin in claret, strong beer and punch'.[17] But though, perhaps as part of his political 'image', he opened his bailiff's and huntsman's letters before attending to public business, when he brought himself to do so he despatched it with 'implacable' ability. His régime was a turning point in English history; from now onwards, business interests would come first, with the power of the State behind them.

3

By 1739, probably because of the confidence and stability his cautious régime had secured, Walpole had been undermined by rivals who roused a belligerent public to war; first in a traditional colonial war with Spain, then in the War of the Austrian Succession. And following the consequent stalemate between France and England, the Peace of Aix-la-Chapelle in 1748, proved the prelude to the first global struggle for empire in the Seven Years' War.

That conflict and its sequel, the revolt of the American colonies and British paramountcy in India, must be considered against a colonial and Asian background which dwarfs even the Marlborough wars. We are in a new dimension of ambition, though the struggle was more for trading advantage than for territory and settlement. After Walpole's consolidation, the country launched into much wider enterprise; and though much of the first Empire was lost, what was retained in 1783 after the American colonies had won independence, made Great Britain the most formidable colonial and oceanic power of all the European states that were now exploiting the world. Walpole had long been holding an aggressive nation on leash, and his successors, Henry Pelham and his brother, the Duke of Newcastle, would have similar objectives. But the Spanish colonial war, forced on the government by commercial interests who tried to anticipate the policy, realized by Canning in the early nineteenth century, of breaking the ties between the Spanish colonies and Spain and reaping economic advantage, merged into a continental struggle. The brilliant and cosmopolitan Carteret, Foreign Secretary by 1742, attempted, with the backing of the king, to shift the balance of power against the French, now even more formidable in spite of their setback in the Marlborough wars. Unlike Walpole, Carteret was ready to take a chance on a Jacobite invasion and here he proved right; but his continental alliances were too complex and unstable and British power insufficient to bring about the resounding defeat of France that he projected.

The conflict over the Austrian succession that he tried to exploit was so involved that even historians hardened in political narrative shrink from explaining it in detail.* But the essentials are plain. Carteret was trying to thwart a new and dangerous threat posed by the alliance of Frederick II of Prussia, now the strongest power in north Germany, with France. The object of this alliance was to dismember the Habsburg territories inherited by Maria Theresa, Queen of Hungary, the heiress of the Emperor Charles VI; and it was made in defiance of the Pragmatic Sanction arranged by her father whereby she would inherit his

* 'The war itself . . . has always proved a stumbling block to historians to give a clear account of its kaleidoscopic phases and of the motives of those engaged in it. To Carlyle, for example, it was merely "an unintelligible, huge, English – and foreign – delirium, with its disjointed campaigns in Italy, Silesia, Bohemia, on the Rhine and in the Low Countries, and overseas in India, the West Indies and North America".' Basil Williams, *The Whig Supremacy, 1714–1760*, revised C. H. Stuart, Oxford, 1962, pp. 265 ff, q.v. for the best short account.

dominions. For the English the war was an aspect of the old policy, which went back to Henry VIII, of weighing in on the ancient Habsburg-French conflict, and, in principle, a revival of the Marlborough wars. But in fact this policy no longer made sense; neither the Habsburgs nor the Dutch were now strong enough to be reliable allies, and Frederick II, though concerned only to retain Silesia which he had seized from the Austrians, was not yet to be bought.

The English victory at Dettingen near Frankfurt in 1743, when George II, as Elector of Hanover, led the English-Hanoverian contingent of the Pragmatic (pro-Austrian) army, was offset in the following year, when an English squadron blockading Toulon was driven off at Hyères, and when a French fleet in the Channel threatened invasion. Then, in 1745, after the British defeat at Fontenoy in Flanders, when the king's second son, Cumberland, led the Guards against an impregnable French redoubt, the army was withdrawn to meet the Jacobite rising under Prince Charles Edward, who had landed in the western Highlands that June, and the British, in effect abandoned the continental campaign.

Legendary in Scots and English history, the gallant adventure of the 'Forty-Five never had a chance. But the Hanoverian government showed extraordinary incompetence. The Prince took Edinburgh and even advanced as far south as Derby. The City panicked, and there was a run on the Bank of England; yet the world of clans and mountains, of peat-smoke and heather and romantic loyalties and depredation, now belonged to the past. The Prince simply had not the resources or the following in England to succeed. Driven back to the Highlands, his army was routed at Culloden. After lurking about, a hunted fugitive in the western Highlands and Isles, the prince escaped to France and a permanent and dilapidated exile. For the first time since the Roman attempt to subdue the Highlands, the entire area was now systematically subjugated by garrisons and military roads. Over all Great Britain the Hanoverian stability was now finally confirmed. Long an unsettling influence, the Jacobite threat had been eliminated.

This achievement, along with Commodore Anson's voyage round the world (1740–4), which netted the equivalent of half a million pounds, were the only favourable results of the intervention in the War of the Austrian Succession, an attempt to turn a continental imbroglio to account without the power to do so.

After the inconclusive peace, a Pelham-Newcastle régime reverted with some success to domestic affairs; but it still drifted with inadequate armaments toward the greater and more far-flung conflict which was now predictable. For, reversing the policy of centuries, the French now made a 'diplomatic revolution'. They arranged an alliance with the Habsburgs. The British countered by an alliance with Frederick II; the

372

Prussians were heavily subsidized, and again British regiments would fight on the continent. But for the British the Seven Years' War was fought out mainly in America, the West Indies and India in a global strategy unlike anything undertaken before, and under a new and spectacular kind of leadership.

For William Pitt, the first imperialist statesman in British history, was a new sort of politician; a careerist of extraordinary genius, forced on the king by overwhelming popular demand. If Walpole was the first all-pervading political manager, the Elder Pitt was the first national leader to win power and conduct global campaigns by sheer force of ability combined with theatrical appeal.*

In his first phase of power, 1756–61, he was victorious: in his second, 1766–8, when, as Earl of Chatham, he might have prevented the secession of the American colonies from the Empire, he failed. His meteoric career links climax with anticlimax in a dramatic way, for the first architect of the Empire was the greatest orator of his time. 'His eye,' writes Feiling, 'was compared to a hawk's, and he seems to have scorched up his opponents in debate like fire;'[18] and he is the first statesman to symbolize a popular commercial imperialism, for the 'bent of the people was violent'.[19] Just how he achieved his ends without modern mass communications is mysterious; but his theatrical style of oratory, the political equivalent of Garrick's histrionics, reinforced by a rumble of Latin quotations then widely understood, dominated and swayed the political nation. In Parliament, withering scorn – 'fewer words, my lord, for your words have lost all weight with me', or, of

---

* The Pitts, like the Churchills, came from Dorset. Pitt's great-grandfather was rector of St Mary's, Blandford; his grandfather, the adventurer who became Governor Pitt of Madras, made a great fortune in India, bought the Pitt Golconda diamond (410 ct; 135 ct when cut) for £25,000; sold it to the Regent Orléans of France for £133,000, and purchased large estates, including the pocket borough of Old Sarum. Pitt's parents were the governor's second son, Robert, and Lady Harriet Villiers, who came from the Anglo-Irish aristocracy. Educated at Eton and Trinity College, Oxford, he joined the army as a Cornet of Horse, and became member of parliament for Old Sarum in 1736. He won notoriety by collaborating with the only opposition, the household of Frederick, Prince of Wales, in attacking Walpole; and, when given office as Paymaster General to the forces, he won a useful reputation by refusing the perquisites. At forty-six he married Lady Hester Greville, who was related to powerful Whig political families, and his domestic life was happy. He was wildly extravagant, with all the building mania of the time, rejoicing in the extension and embellishment of a large estate at Burton Pynsent in Somerset, left him by an admirer. In London he took 10 St James's Square, now Chatham House, and he possessed an estate at Hayes in Kent. In contrast to Walpole, Pitt had no sense of humour and took himself with portentous seriousness, appearing always in full dress and presenting a theatrically frigid face to the world. He suffered from kidney disease and gout, aggravated by the large amount of hock, port and madeira which, along with a rich meat diet, the doctors then prescribed for these ailments. He was also liable to fits of manic-depressive insanity at critical moments. Pitt is a most eccentric, even megalomaniac, figure in the humdrum world of Whig domestic political intrigue; an example of the success that would derive from sheer ability within the limited political circles of the day, even when handicapped by extreme arrogance and secretiveness and uncertain health.

Newcastle, 'a child in charge of a go-cart' – would alternate with appalling solemnity and fierce invective.* He called the Red Indians, employed to scalp the American colonists in 1777, 'horrible hell hounds of savage war, hell hounds I say of savage war'; and proclaimed, 'My Lords, if I were an American as I am an Englishman, while a foreign troop was landed in my country I would never lay down my arms – never, never, never!' For good and ill, Pitt's high-flown rhetoric set the fashion of much parliamentary oratory for generations.

At last allowed his head in 1757 in his second year of office, this dynamic genius got spectacular results, for he had an extraordinary grasp of detail and power of rapid decision. There had never been such victories; from panic and a scare of invasion when the county militias had been hastily embodied,† Pitt transformed the prospect, and the landmarks of this transformation are familiar.

In India, at Arcot in 1751, Clive had already become master of the Carnatic; now in 1757 he defeated the pro-French Nawab Suraj-ud-dawla at Plassey; a victory, confirmed in 1764 at Buxar, which won British paramountcy in the sub-continent. In 1759 Wolfe won Canada at Quebec, and with it the command of huge territories in the Middle West beyond the Alleghenies and Appalachians: Fort Duquesne now became Pittsburg and a vast prospect was opened up. In Germany at Minden in 1756 an English-Hanoverian army had checked the French, and Frederick II was supported by huge subsidies, for Pitt's strategy was continental as well as oceanic. And in 1759, in the same year as the capture of Quebec, Hawke, in a great gale off the treacherous Breton coast, destroyed the French fleet in Quiberon Bay. Pitt, moreover, had even brought the American colonies into a colonial war.

The published volumes of his colonial despatches show how he did it, as appeals, orders, instructions flowed out from (his office in) Cleveland Row, backed by the demonstrable reality of the British Navy and battalion after battalion arriving from the motherland. And in some inexplicable way the flame of inspiration from 10, St James's Square leapt the Atlantic to kindle fires, smouldering at best in the gloom of depression and distrust.[20]

What these resulting conquests implied in India will later be de-

---

* Debating a proposed tax on sugar, the West Indian plutocrat Beckford had bored the Commons to 'horse laughs'. Pitt rose to speak. '"Sugar, Mr Speaker", thundered Pitt, and again horse laughs, more hesitantly, were heard, "Sugar" thundered Pitt . . . and in the dead silence that followed, "Sugar, Mr Speaker", he whispered in his most dulcet tones, "who will laugh at sugar now?"' Basil Williams, *William Pitt, Earl of Chatham*, London, 1915, vol. II, p. 53.

† In one of which Gibbon served, so that 'the discipline and evolution of a modern battalion gave me a clearer notion of the phalanx and the legion, and the Captain of Hampshire Grenadiers has not been useless to the historian of the Roman Empire'. For the raising of the Norfolk Militia, see R. W. Ketton-Cremer, *Norfolk Portraits*, London, 1944, pp. 140–58.

scribed; the immediate sequel in England, as well as in the American colonies to whom the victories had brought greater ambitions, must first be considered. Like Walpole, just because of his success, Pitt was widely detested. The 'Great Commoner' who used the Commons as a sounding board to appeal to the political nation, was like a pike in the pond where the Whig magnificos, like lazy carp, took their ample political nourishment. Further, by 1760 all the colonial objectives had been achieved. The commitments to Prussia now seemed expensive and superfluous; taxation was mounting, and apparently only Pitt understood that, unless French power was further checked on the continent, the colonial victories would be precarious. When, that year, George II, who had become a reluctant supporter of Pitt, was succeeded by George III, the backing of the Crown was lost. Spain was now threatening to enter the war; so Pitt determined to attack the Spaniards first and cut them off from their colonies in South America. Thwarted in this policy, in October 1761, he resigned.

Newcastle was in fact forced to carry on Pitt's policy; important Caribbean bases, including Havana, were seized, and even Manila in the Philippines was taken by an expedition from Madras; but in 1762 Newcastle also resigned, and Lord Bute, the new king's nominee, decided to consolidate what gains he could.

So by the Peace of Paris of 1763 the first British Empire was recognized. It was enormous: quite out of scale with the objectives hitherto recorded, and it would have staggered the Elizabethans or even Cromwell. The British gained all Canada, including the strategically vital Cape Breton at the mouth of the St Lawrence; all the Middle West up to the Mississippi and most of Florida. In the West Indies, they obtained Tobago, Dominica and St Vincent, and in West Africa they acquired Senegal. The East India Company were now recognized as predominant in Bengal and the Carnatic; Minorca was restored, and with it the command of the western Mediterranean. From now on, the British would predominate in Canada and India and retain an enormous oceanic empire.

But one thing was lacking, probably because it was impossible. The war had not permanently, as Pitt desired, destroyed the naval power of France; and since they had now ditched Frederick II with a cynical realism equal to his own, and he had only been saved by a change of régime in Russia, the British were left without continental allies. When in the 1770s the war with the American colonists flared up, the French fleet in conjunction with a continental coalition would get their revenge, deprive the British in 1781 of command of the Atlantic and secure the independence of the colonies in America, the basis of the United States.

4

In spite of the loss of the American colonies, the long reign of George III was on balance highly successful. It would see the final and greatest bout of Anglo-French conflict, in what had proved in effect a second Hundred Years' War, decided in favour of the British. They would emerge from the revolutionary and Napoleonic Wars with an even greater empire and with undisputed command of the oceans of the world, the basis of the *Pax Britannica* of the nineteenth century. But we are here concerned with the first and least successful part of the reign, from 1760–84, when the American colonies were lost to the empire, and the British paramountcy in India, jeopardized by incompetence at home, was only saved by the ill-rewarded genius of Warren Hastings. And it was now, also, that the old republican radical tradition of the seventeenth century combined with a new rationalism to attack the eighteenth-century establishment which Walpole had secured.

The new monarch, who came to the throne at the age of twenty-two, has been grossly misrepresented. He never wanted to be a tyrant, and probably never even read Bolingbroke's treatise on a patriot king, supposed to have been his inspiration. He merely wanted to govern as he was expected to do. Backward, segregated, priggish, amiable and shy, he had to deal 'with a generation of politicians who, having run the place for twenty years, had almost ceased to take account of anybody's opinion but their own'.[21] Naturally indolent, he had made himself almost pathologically industrious, and 'his maxims, in mid-career, were those of a conscientious bull in a china shop: "I know that I am doing my duty and therefore can never wish to retract"'.[22] But he was far from being the philistine often depicted; he was intensely musical, interested in antiquities, very widely read and an expert on furniture, gardens and farming. Moreover, he was no psychopath. His intermittent madness was of mainly physical origin and it only overtook him when he was fifty, for his illness in 1765 did not produce it. It probably derived from a now recognizable disease, so that George III did not go out of his mind through any hereditary psychological taint or transmit one; nor, as often supposed, was he engaged in the 'flight from reality' now fashionable; or even crazed with frustration because faithful to a supposedly unattractive wife, by whom he had fifteen children, the royal record for legitimate offspring. For if the King suffered from a defective metabolism which caused intermittent porphyria, this may have been aggravated by a rheumatic condition, so that toxins in his blood-stream produced a widespread nervous and mental disorder in later life. Porphyria derives from chlorophyll, the green pigment in plants which enables them to breathe, and from haemoglobin. If not metabolized, it produces the symptoms of toxaemia recorded in 1788–9, 1801, 1804 and 1810. The king's strong constitution enabled him to recover his sanity after three attacks, though he never recovered from the last, for his condition was worsened by senility and blindness. But his physicians were still obsessed with keeping the four 'humours' in balance. Without thermometers or stethoscopes, handicapped by the formality which surrounded a king even when seriously ill, they could not even make a proper physical examination; so they called his affliction 'fever of the brain', and tried to counteract the symptoms – incessant, often obscene talk, insomnia, acute stomach pains and blurred vision – by constant bleeding, purging and applying agonizing 'blisters' to 'draw out the humour', and making him sick. Dr Wallis, who specialized in lunacy, and put the king in a strait waistcoat and cut him off from his family and familiar surroundings, prided himself on 'breaking his patient in . . . like Horses in a *manège*'. Nor has the monarch had much better treatment from modern psychologists, who, with the best intentions, have misled even the most reputable authorities by their assertions. As the investigations of the medical facts of this tragedy, which have now come to light, clearly conclude, 'George III's psychiatric symptoms [which did not appear until he was fifty] were part and parcel of a widespread bodily disorder. No conclusion can be drawn about his personality in health from the fact that when he was ill he became deranged. . . . The currently accepted image of George III will have to be drastically recast.'*

Politically this fussy, benevolent and conscientious monarch had much to contend with. The need was not so much for legislation; it was for government, so the king had to become a politician. And this he did; 'the first among the borough mongering, electioneering gentlemen of England'; managing the House of Commons, 'that peculiar club, election to which at all times required some expression of consent on behalf of the public'.† Following the manifest incompetence of his

---

* I. Macalpine and R. Hunter, *George III and the Madness Business*, London 1970, p. 362. q.v. for a plausible account of the king's illness, if one less convincing on those of his ancestors. The authors are highly critical of the 'psychological' interpretations, widely accepted and elaborated, which derive from M. Guttmacher's *America's Last King: an Interpretation of the Madness of George III*, New York, 1941.

† Sir Lewis Namier, *England in the Age of the American Revolution*, London, 1930, pp. 3 and 4. The introduction is still the best political and social analysis, superseding the long-accepted Whig liberal interpretation, which often passed judgement on George III for not behaving like Queen Victoria. The legend of this well-meaning monarch as a tyrant and of an organized Whig party protecting 'liberty' must follow the other venerable *idées reçues*, already enumerated, into oblivion. In 1788, the year before the French Revolution, George III could walk about quite unguarded among his subjects at Cheltenham, and in 1801 the King and his entourage

personal friend, Lord Bute, George III rang the changes on the cliques of landed magnates and career politicians; in politics for prestige, habit, perquisites and for 'the due exercise', as Pares put it, 'of the talents God gave them and for fun'.

The blunders of the king's government, indeed, reflect a narrowing of the Crown's field of choice. The party rancour of the late Stuart times had been considerably smothered by Walpole's consensus politics; but the penalty had been monopoly of office by a series of Whig cliques among the plutocratic oligarchy, who commanded a stifling amount of patronage. Any administration had to provide for a horde of their clients and shuffle round posts among the political class. Complacent coteries blandly assumed that their nominees could turn their hands to anything, sinecurists discharged their functions through ill-paid deputies, inept governors outraged colonial assemblies, political generals muddled campaigns; only the fleet, where skill had had to count, was relatively immune. Such was the price of the 'mixed' constitution Blackstone described and admired, and the king had to govern through aristocratic amateurs or career politicians, without Pitt's abilities and often desperately on the make. These generally mediocre representatives of English mid-eighteenth century stability contrast with the much abler leaders of the American revolution, who had better preserved the mid-seventeenth century traditions of independence, now enlarged to a wider appeal by Locke and the French Enlightenment. Indeed, save when the tyrannical genius of Pitt the Elder briefly won power, mid-eighteenth century government was more than usually ill-conducted; often a mere umpire between ramified family interests and corporations who defended their freeholds to the last ditch. Challenged by the revived radicalism of Wilkes, who exploited social and economic unrest in England, and by Tom Paine, who rallied the small farmers and artisans in America, it proved singularly inadequate.

Soon disillusioned with Bute, George III worked first through Grenville, a nominee of the Whig Duke of Bedford (1763–5); then through the Marquis of Rockingham, the Whig patron of Burke; then through the Duke of Grafton (1766–70), who briefly collaborated (1766–8) with Pitt, now Earl of Chatham and soon incapacitated. It was not until 1770 that the king found a less able Walpole in Lord North, who at least stabilized government until 1782. Faced with mounting crises in America and India, all these administrations disastrously bungled the first; and it was only through the ability of Warren Hastings that Lord North even muddled through the second.

were overwhelmed by their popularity at Weymouth, where 'His Majesty . . . had no sooner popped his royal head under water, than a band concealed in a bathing "machine" struck up "God Save Great George Our King".'

378

5

The American colonies, whose origins in Virginia and New England have been described, were now vigorous and self-confident societies. From rock-bound Maine and the forests and lakes of New Hampshire down to the Carolinas and the red earth and cotton fields of Georgia, they covered an area much larger than the British Isles. In New England many descendants of the Puritan settlers were now rich, backed by a self-sufficient agriculture and far-flung commerce. New York, New Jersey, Pennsylvania, Delaware, had all prospered, and in the South great tobacco and cotton estates had been developed. Here, on a basis of slave labour, the landowners had devised a sunnier, lazier and more spacious version of English country life. From the tight-lipped comfortable oligarchy of Boston to the easy-going debt-ridden aristocracy of sub-tropical Charleston,* these people were accustomed to go their own way. To the long established and insular English, separated by three thousand miles of ocean, they were provincials; the scale of America, the stimulus of the climate and environment, were little understood; and now, following the conquest of Canada, a huge swathe of territories which would become Ohio, Illinois, Indiana, Kentucky and Tennessee, lay open for settlement.

Against this background the war of American Independence came about. The home government, burdened with an immense national debt, felt that the colonists who had benefited from the Seven Years' War ought to contribute to local defence; with new responsibilities, they abandoned their old policy of salutary neglect. And since a free-for-all in the wilderness would worsen relations with the Indians and between the colonists themselves, they tried to hinder the colonization of the West. This attempt to shut the door after the horse had been stolen led to an unprecedented tax. In 1765, since the colonists refused to tax themselves, a Stamp Act, normal in England, was imposed to pay the troops deployed to enforce the new policy. In a time of general debt and depression, the stamp duty particularly hit the lawyers, tavern-keepers and journalists – all articulate professions. And it was imposed without American consent; old mercantile restrictions, long thought adverse to the colonies, were now also tightened up. Even when Rockingham repealed the Stamp Act, the government, to save face, passed a Declaration Act asserting Parliament's right to 'bind the colonies in all cases

---

* They now owed English creditors about two million pounds: for the seventeenth-century fashion of taking tobacco had been much displaced by the less profitable snuff, and among the politer classes smoking would be confined to the 'smoking room' till late Victorian times.

whatsoever'. When in 1767 Grafton's administration imposed duties on glass, paper and tea, it was believed in America that this revenue would free the colonial governments from the influence of their legislatures, and all the old distrust of the executive flared up with added force. There had been no Walpole-type 'stability', with its oligarchic establishment, imposed on America.

There was a roar of protest and a boycott of British goods. The principle of 'no taxation without representation' had again been violated. And though North's government repealed the duties, they, too, made the affair one of principle. They retained a diminished duty on tea. So, when, in 1773, the ingenious politicians thought to benefit the near bankrupt East Indian Company by giving it the monopoly of importing tea at a lower price, the American merchants were further infuriated. On a December night the contents of 342 chests were scattered on the icy waters of Boston Harbour; 'In a spirit of a Harvard Commencement, the Sons of Liberty were somewhat casually dressed as Indians: no one interfered with their fun, but what they commenced was a revolution'.[23]

Meanwhile, down in Virginia at Williamsburg, in the panelled Ralegh tavern, the Virginian legislators, though dissolved by the British authorities, had turned themselves into a revolutionary convention. The first centres of resistance had thus been in the two oldest colonies, Massachusetts and Virginia; and in 1774 the first continental congress met at Philadelphia in Pennsylvania.

From 1775–81 the War of Independence was fought out over a huge area; in part a guerrilla war, to which the European parade-ground formations were irrelevant. Suffice it that from the brutish tactics of Gage at Bunker Hill, when the red-coats or 'lobsters', laden with equipment, marched, as at Fontenoy, in line against the American redoubt and lost a third of their strength before the objective was overwhelmed, to the inept strategy whereby Burgoyne advanced from Canada down the Hudson, while Howe, based in New York, marched south on Philadelphia, instead of moving north to join him and destroying Washington's army with their combined force, the campaign in the north was totally mishandled. It concluded in October 1777 with the surrender of Burgoyne's army at Saratoga.

The sequel, in 1778, was an American–French alliance, the turning point of the war. In the south, however, the British, who had advanced from Georgia into the Carolinas, took Charleston and moved up into Virginia. But Cornwallis withdrew into what proved a trap; at Yorktown on the northern bank of York river, not far from the original settlement on the James, he was attacked by an American-French force under Washington and cut off by a French fleet. By October 1781, he, too, had surrendered. American Independence, proclaimed with resounding effect in 1776, had been won; and its principles had been defined in a declaration of historic import that government was responsible to the governed.

For world history the result was decisive. The United States would become not an extension simply of Great Britain, but of Europe; a civilization in which a much wider variety of cultures would be blended and transformed. But they retained a political outlook and framework inherited from the English seventeenth century, with its distrust of executive power and stress on a balanced constitution; still reflecting liberal and individualist ideas, best defined by Locke, but now in a more radical and spacious setting.

For the British the event appeared as a disaster; and, to the Americans, George III became an ogre. Modern historians take a more impartial view. While Chatham and Burke both championed the colonists and denounced the pedantic obstinacy of the king's government, even they were not prepared to concede what would be termed 'Dominion Status', with the monarch as king in America and an American sovereign legislature. Such a separation of king and parliament would then have been unthinkable. By insisting on maintaining sovereignty over the colonies George III was not just imposing his own obstinate will; he was identifying the Crown with parliament in strict accordance with the settlement of 1688. Both sides were reacting to their past; caught up, as often in history, in a clash which their differing outlooks made inevitable, and by social and economic forces which their convictions only unconsciously expressed.

6

The problems of India which at the same time confronted the British government were also without precedent and out of scale with their own society. The East India Company had at first been humble petitioners to the great Mughal and to the Nawabs who governed provinces as big as many countries of Europe; but gradually in the breakdown of the Mughal Empire, 'the Europeans having inserted themselves into the interstices, were pushing their way through the ruined fabric like banyan or peepul trees in a crumbling fort'.[24] And the competition with the French had forced the Company to new commitments. The Mahrattas now dominated the Deccan and Hyderabad; Afghans ruled even in Delhi, and the French and English had long played off puppet rulers against their rivals and each other. In this confused situation, the East India Company merchants who survived the climate and the long and dangerous voyage round the Cape, were fully engaged in making their own fortunes, and reluctant to take over the administration when it broke down.

But some adventurers like Governor Pitt, and now the young Robert Clive, who had raised the siege of Arcot from Madras and crippled French influence in the Carnatic, were particularly unscrupulous and able. Bengal was now the principal objective and area of commerce, its rivers linking it up with the interior. In 1765, the year of the Stamp Act in America, Clive got himself appointed Revenue Minister, nominally under the Mughal, and Viceroy for Bengal, Orissa and Behar. The Directors in England had been 'presented with an Empire at which they looked with the incredulous elation, shot with sharp twinges of doubt, of a village grocer who has inherited a chain of department stores, and is not quite sure whether they will pay him a profit beyond his dreams or drag him down in ruin'.[25]

While the long-term prospects of the Company were still sound, they were not now spectacular; but the expectations of the share-holders in England now became extravagant. The shares boomed far beyond their immediate worth. Following local disorders, famine, almost universal corruption and exorbitant taxes – Clive himself had netted a fortune of quarter of a million – even the prosperity of Bengal began to wilt. The East India Company, long vital to the British economy, had to be loaned nearly a million and a half pounds by the government, and so, in 1773, the ill-judged monopoly of tea which set the Americans by the ears was devised. North's ministers were compelled to pass a Regulating Act, whereby, under a characteristically eighteenth-century arrangement of checks and balances, direct political responsibility for Bengal was at last accepted, with indirect authority over Madras and Bombay.

The Governor-General under these regulations was Warren Hastings (1773–85), the first architect of British administration in India, and the resolute and ruthless defender of British interests during the American–French War. Since his youth he had served in India; first in Bengal, then in Madras, and since 1772 he had been Governor of Bengal. This able son of an impoverished Cotswold clergyman understood the power politics and the civilization of India; he was the man on the spot and he proved the man for the job. But North saddled the Governor-General's Council, on which Hastings had only a casting vote, with two military figureheads and a malicious adventurer. Philip Francis was probably the author of the scarifying *Letters of Junius* (1767–72) which had so vitriolically attacked the government; he may even have been thus bought off. Hastings, long experienced and accustomed to the power-struggles and devious diplomacy of the East, was now fettered. And in 1776, the year of the American Declaration of Independence, the Governor-General was called out by his colleague to a duel. Francis, lightly wounded, returned to England determined to ruin him. But when, in 1778, the French declared war, and the British, already tied up in America, also seemed in jeopardy in India, Hastings and Sir Eyre Coote, an abler soldier than Burgoyne or Cornwallis, emerged victorious from a welter of political manœuvre, bribery, intrigue and battle.

In 1784 Hastings returned to England with a hundred thousand pounds accumulated by the usual methods, and expecting a peerage; he found himself a scapegoat for the politicians. The younger Pitt was now in control, and under his India Act he wanted a fresh start, with a new Governor-General independent of the Company and all for which it stood. Hastings was impeached on charges of conduct which looked black in England, but which at that time in India had been common form, and indeed probably the price of survival. His melodramatic trial, though it aired the eloquence of Sheridan and Burke, lasted from 1788–95 in mounting tedium to all concerned except the lawyers, who relieved Hastings of his fortune. The Company now came to his rescue and he retired to his ancestral Daylesford Manor, where he lived in some affluence until 1818. But the man who had done most to secure the British *raj* in India was given no public recognition.*

7

'Nothing', wrote Francis Hutcheson, the preceptor of the pioneer economist Adam Smith, has 'occasioned more misery in human life than a vain ambition both of princes and popular states of extending their empire'. Against the predominant bouncing complacency of the mid-eighteenth century, there was now widespread discontent. It drew inspiration from seventeenth-century ideas of commonwealth, kept alive mainly among the Nonconformists; from Milton, with his passion for righteous government and freedom of expression; and from the new ideas of humanitarian reform already widespread and expressed by the dissenting Joseph Priestley.[26] The first, republican, tradition, though driven underground at the Restoration, had been kept alive when the original Whigs had still been the party of lower-middle class dissent, and before they had transformed themselves mainly into the interest of the great landowners and moneyed men. Disillusioned with the Respectable Revolution, and excluded from the official establishment, many ramified and now often wealthy dissenting families had organized their

---

* His monument in Daylesford Church, now a Victorian pseudo-Gothic edifice, was preserved when the old church was demolished. In the churchyard he is commemorated by a plain Grecian-style urn on a slightly Indianized pedestal, the sole inscription, *Warren Hastings*. There is a good short biography by Sir Penderel Moon: *Warren Hastings and British India*, London, 1947. The standard biography is Sir Keith Feiling's *Warren Hastings*, London, 1954.

own academies; with growing prosperity, they had also shed some of the narrow intolerance of their origins. The Baptist divine, Isaac Watts, for example, though most renowed as a hymn writer, wrote a *Treatise on the Mind* on self-education, ranging over wide fields of knowledge and designed to encourage those outside the pale of the Anglican universities to make the best of themselves. There was now a solid world of earnest, purposeful piety which went its own way, apart from the florid Hanoverian establishment, the political bishops and the patronage of the great.

But, politically, it was the radical appeal to the traditional liberties of Englishmen that was most effective on both sides of the Atlantic. The established order now came under raucous attack when the agitation fomented by John Wilkes reached its climax, exploiting the traditional turbulence of the London electorate. Then, with the American Revolution, Tom Paine, who won his greatest following in America, began to achieve wide popular influence at home, at its peak during the early days of the French Revolution when the French appeared the prophets of a new order, and not yet, as they would later to the majority of British opinion, architects of ruin.

John Wilkes, like John Lilburne, was a born rebel, though in a much less high-minded way.* The demagogic champion of a vast majority outside the ruling circles, he also came to symbolize an old and legitimate popular resistance to arbitrary power, whether of king or Parliament or both. For the judges had disallowed general warrants issued for reasons of state, and parliament had been made to accept an elected but discountenanced candidate. 'Wilkes and Liberty' became the slogan of radical merchants, shopkeepers and artisans, not merely of the London mob. This sort of protest was volatile and unorganized, and it would climax in the anti-Catholic Gordon riots of 1780, put down by the army:

* The son of a wealthy distiller, Wilkes (1727–97), was anxious to shock the bourgeoisie of his time, and his excesses were notorious. As Member of Parliament for Aylesbury and a client of Lord Temple, he attacked not only Grenville's administration but in 1763, in the *North Briton*, the king himself. Arrested under a general warrant, he was released as being a member of parliament and recovered damages. Whereat the House of Commons, further outraged since he was charged with obscenity for printing an *Essay on Woman*, a poor competitor with the already popular *Fanny Hill*, voted that his privilege did not cover seditious libel and expelled him from the House. In 1768 he returned from France, whither he had fled as an outlaw, and stood for Middlesex. He was elected, expelled again, and re-elected four times. At the fourth try, in 1774, the year when he was also elected Lord Mayor of London, he was allowed to take his seat. But he succeeded less in parliament than outside it, and subsided into insignificance. The episode shows up the ineptitude of government rather than the constructive ability of this pathological rebel. 'No government of ordinary firmness would have allowed such an affair to become a crisis, still less to develop into one of the major events of the history of British liberty. But through sheer incompetence, under the pressure of the king's obstinacy ministers continued to stumble from indiscretion to blunder, from blunder to folly, from folly to illegality and misgovernment.' Edward Lascelles, *The Life of Charles James Fox*, Oxford, 1936, p. 33.

but it foreshadowed the better organized and more widespread radicalism which would be provoked by the hardships of the Industrial Revolution and the French wars, and become a major force in early nineteenth-century politics. [27]

Immediately and politically the attacks of a few brilliant Whig aristocrats and their following cut more ice. In the long run they, too, would prove highly significant, for they created a tradition of liberal aristocratic leadership which would survive the French wars and their sequel, and without which the radical tide might have swept the country into revolution, when in fact it would be contained by the Whig reforms of 1832.

Charles James Fox (1749–1806)*, in particular, made eloquent forays against the often fumbling expedients of government. He only briefly held high office as Secretary of State for Foreign Affairs under Rockingham in 1782, then in coalition with North in 1783; but, following the rejection of his India Bill by the King, not again until 1806, when he would be responsible for the abolition of the African Slave Trade in British territories and shipping. But he was the best debater in the Commons, and he brought something new to politics unthinkable in the less secure times of Harley and Walpole. For, as occasionally occurs among those born to great wealth and privilege, he judged public affairs with directness and even compassion, in terms not so much of power and 'interest' as of life. Although as skilled in smart intrigue and devious manœuvre as most major politicians, he championed the Americans, the Irish, the people of India, the slaves – even, as long as he could – the enemies of his country who had seized power in Revolutionary France. By sheer force and charm of personality, he created and sustained a humane, if sometimes wrong-headed liberal tradition with a long future in British politics. Moreover, Fox's Whig colleague, Edmund Burke (1720–95), though also no mean intriguer and a virulent party man, and who, with greater realism, would early denounce the excesses of the French Revolution, made the most eloquent statement of what would now be termed liberal conservatism. Neither Fox nor Burke were 'democrats' in the modern sense – 'what acquaintance', asked Fox, 'have the people at large with the arcana of political rectitude?'; and Burke would denounce the 'swinish multitude'

* Fox was the third son of the first Lord Holland, who had made a huge fortune out of the perquisites of office, and he was descended through his mother from Charles II. He had a passion for gambling, racing and sport, but also for classical learning. His enormous debts – he called the room assigned to his Jewish creditors the 'Jerusalem Chamber' – did not impair his enjoyments, whether gambling at Brookes's or Almack's till dawn, racing at Newmarket, or 'panting through the stubbles after the partridges'. But when in office he could deal with business with casual and efficient despatch. Lascelles, *op. cit.*, p. 70, q.v. for an interesting biography.

as well as doctrinaire fanatics; but both stood for the independence of Parliament as representing not only the political nation but, through it, the interests of the whole people, and for a more generous outlook towards the empire. Both denounced arbitrary power, whether of monarch, ministry or mob, and both defended a balanced but flexible constitution, giving a theme constant in English history a new and more imaginative interpretation.

The other and more slow-working criticism of the prevalent eighteenth-century complacency had a very different inspiration. Already Jeremy Bentham (1748–1832) had formulated his revolutionary principle of deliberate 'improvement'. Though, like the Foxite tradition, his influence would not become decisive until well into the next century, this wealthy and benevolent eccentric published his *Fragment on Government* in 1776, the year of the American Declaration of Independence. He formulated a new basic principle or '*Felicific Calculus*' – that 'the greatest happiness of the greatest number is the measure of right and wrong'[28], and declared that the 'fabric of felicity' could be 'reared at the hands of Reason and Law'. He applied the test of plain 'utility' to the hoary compromises and irrational abuses of the British Constitution as glorified by Blackstone. For Bentham combined the humanitarian impulse of Hutcheson and Priestley with the confident rationalism then fashionable in France to enormous social problems now at last being recognized, and would prove to be a decisive influence not only in Great Britain but in the world.

Thus, by the second half of the eighteenth century, the very success, power and prosperity of the ruling class – so hard-won during the Respectable Revolution, the Marlborough wars and during the crisis over the Hanoverian succession – had provoked the beginnings of a reaction, radical, Whig-liberal and utilitarian. It was not yet widely representative or politically influential; but it would survive the long period of Tory rule during the second half of the reign of George III and, in time, it would become formidable.

Growing prosperity had also enabled many rich merchants and professional men to mitigate some of the worst sufferings of the majority of the nation by more traditional means.

Since medieval times there had been a long habit of charitable benefaction, unbroken by the destruction of the old Catholic Church. Following Catholic tradition, the Protestant Elizabethan and Stuart magnates had been great personal benefactors. Now, with greater affluence, an even wider range of benefaction had grown up. When, in 1850, the Victorian Charity Commissioners came to view the scene, they found an astonishing variety of complicated trusts; some far gone in corruption, others still of substantial benefit. All rich men did not share the ambitions of Walpole or the elder Pitt for plutocratic display; some even thought charity a 'sort of Restoring that Proportion of wealth which does not belong to you'.[29] Old Puritan piety merged into the new rational humanitarianism. Charity was also thought of as self-interest, and the 'lower orders' were encouraged to remain docile and laborious. Among the Nonconformists, such benefactions were particularly approved, and prosperous provincial merchants liked to leave a substantial memorial. In 1777 John Howard, for example, launched a fully documented attack on the *State of the Prisons*; he 'wanted no statue', remarked George III, for his virtues would live when every statue had crumbled into dust. Rescued from Hogarthian slums, it was hoped that girls would become 'chaste, meek and patient', and 'the poor' more obedient. And how 'can men', wrote one benefactor, 'without doing violence to their own nature, be insensible and untouch'd by the distress and misery of their fellow-creatures?' Thomas Guy, for example, who had made a fortune out of importing Bibles printed in Holland, and increased it by speculating in South Sea stock, sold out in time and left £220,000 to found Guy's Hospital. 'Bart's' Hospital was also now rehabilitated; Thomas Coram, a retired sea-captain, distressed by the spectacle of unmarried girls deserting their offspring, endowed a 'foundling' hospital. These men were representative of many substantial local benefactors; such as Richard Taunton, a maltster and wine merchant, and first cousin of Isaac Watts, who gave away £13,000 for charities and hospitals, and in 1752 left his entire estate to benefit 'my dear town of Southampton'; a bequest cut down by his heirs after a Chancery suit, but out of which came Taunton's School, still flourishing today and originally intended to train boys for the sea.*

And, in spite of the appalling treatment to which the monarch was subjected, medicine was now becoming less lethal. Dr Sloane, who had been trained at Montpéllier, recommended 'Lazaretts' to isolate those stricken with the plague. They were 'made of timber covered with tarpawlings, encompassed with ditches and strong palisadoes'. He was created the first medical baronet and left a large fortune. And Dr Radcliffe's benefaction financed the Radcliffe foundations at Oxford. Surgeons still had less prestige than physicians; but William and John Hunter from Glasgow (1718–83 and 1728–93), basing their techniques on empirical study, now revolutionized comparative anatomy: and James Lind, of Hasler Hospital, established the remedy for scurvy which, in spite of the empirical practice of a few sea-captains, still killed

---

* The fortune of this worthy came in part from financing privateers who captured two French ships laden with silver; and 'even his involvement in two notoriously corrupt parliamentary elections, one of which was investigated and the outcome reversed by the Commons, left Taunton's prestige in Southampton undiminished'. Owen, *op. cit.*, pp. 80-1.

more sailors than did the enemy, though nearly half a century elapsed before the Admiralty accepted his advice. But the obsession with 'letting blood', rampant in the seventeenth century, continued through the eighteenth. Fresh air was still considered dangerous.*

Thus the Hogarthian side of eighteenth-century civilization provoked both a political protest which kept radical seventeenth-century traditions alive, a new urge for rational improvement, and a considerable expansion of traditional charity; though medical science was still retarded by the medieval obsession with the four 'humours' which had so long perverted it.

8

The arts and literature of the eighteenth century reflect an aristocratic civilization, sure of its standards and set in its ways, and the beginnings of the 'romantic' reaction to it. In the early eighteenth century it was only in architecture that the English could then hold their own in Europe, for the tradition of Inigo Jones and Wren, adapting classical architecture to a colder climate, went on. Wren's pupil, Hawksmoor, designed the admirable Clarendon building and the superb Codrington Library, both at Oxford; Gibbs the domed Radcliffe camera at Oxford and the Senate House at Cambridge (1737–49). The Dutch desire for comfort and sunshine had been reflected in the new buildings put up for William of Orange at Hampton Court, and is apparent in the manor houses and town houses of the time, their panelled rooms spacious and convenient; and this admirable domestic architecture would persist in America in frame houses suited to a country where wood was abundant. For the rich, mansions designed on the principles of Palladio, a late Renaissance master influenced by Hadrian's Pantheon, now became fashionable; their massive lines set off by a new 'landscape' gardening, an English invention which adapted rather than formalized nature. In the later years of the century a more austere neo-Roman and neo-Greek style caught on; reflected also in Jefferson's design for Montecello and in the White House itself, even as rebuilt after the English burnt it in 1814.

---

* A representative medical handbook, with a preface by Dr Addington and still in use at the end of the century, recommends what may well have been an originally Anglo-Saxon remedy for 'greensickness' in young women. 'Take Roots of Madder, Smallage, Butcher's Broom and Zedoary, of each four Ounces; leaves of Mother-wort, Penny Royal and Mug-wort, each a Handfull; Thyme and Dittany of Crete, of each a Handfull; three Ounces of Daucus-seed, an Ounce of Grains of Paradise, and half a pound of filings of steel. Hang them in a bag in four gallons of Ale, during the fermentation.' A liberal application of 'blisters' was still a sovereign remedy, 'to draw off the serous liquid in a fever', particularly in smallpox and in 'a nervous fever, when the pulse is low and the eyes dim'. John Theobald, MD, *Medulla Medcinae Universae; or a New Compendious Dispensary*, London, 1761. The owner of the book notes hopefully in the margin, *'a person saved from leprosy by living on green lizards'*.

388

The best sculptors were foreigners; Roubiliac was a Frenchman; Rysbrack from Holland, and they were very good. But the English of Walpole's day were provincial in their taste in all but architecture, and the rich bought up treasures on their 'grand tours' in accordance with strict academic theories of art, often with more of a collector's enthusiasm than a connoisseur's. Nor did they much appreciate native artists. Hogarth (1697–1764) had to circumvent this snobbery by realistic paintings that pointed a moral: reproduced in engravings, they had a wide popular appeal, as in the notorious *Rake's Progress*. But he never won a reputation among the arbiters of taste. Kneller, who died much more esteemed in 1723, had been a German, who had provided the flattering likenesses in vogue during the Marlborough wars.

The first English painter to make a comparable reputation was Sir Joshua Reynolds (1723–92), who came from Devon, and who could catch, at his best, the serenity and charm of country house life and present his sitters without pomp. He had studied the late Renaissance painters in Italy and had as good a sense of composition as of colour; fortunately he was unable to concentrate on the classical, historical and mythological subjects he admired, for he was too busy painting portraits. Like Rubens, he became a popular social figure; he was the first President of the Royal Academy (1769) and his *Discourses*, there delivered, express theories which failed to spoil his native genius. Gainsborough (1727–88), who came from Suffolk, was less worldly; he was a craftsman, with an eye for landscape in the Dutch style, and a passion for the detail of a brocaded coat or a muslin dress. Both these artists were of European calibre, if not of the first rank; and the landscapes of Stubbs and Wilson developed a pleasing and mellow style.

The early and mid-eighteenth century was a musical age, though here, again, the best composers were foreign. The early Hanoverian monarchs loved music, even if not otherwise much aware of the arts. Handel, born in Saxony at Halle, who had settled in England in 1712, was naturalized under George I, for whom he wrote his *Water Music* for a festival on the Thames. His German-Italianate style swamped the simpler native idiom of Purcell, and his oratorio, the *Messiah*, was first performed in London in 1743: he died in 1759, in the 'year of victories' and was buried in Westminster Abbey. The powerful simplicity and strict order of his compositions recalls the admired classical architecture of the time as well as its vigour and confidence.

On a different level, the German Pepusch arranged the catchy melodies of Gay's *Beggar's Opera* (1728) mainly from current popular tunes. It was a parody of Italian opera, and, as already remarked, presented the government in the guise of highwaymen. The sentiment and the tunes are still popular today. In 1740 Thomas Arne set some of

Shakespeare's best lyrics to music and wrote a masque about *Alfred* which included the buoyant strains of *Rule Britannia*. And *God Save the King* first became popular during the 'Forty-Five. British patriotism had now found vigorous musical expression.

Intellectually the age was singularly rich. Following the trend set by Locke, Bishop Berkeley had argued in his *Dialogues* (1713) that there was no proof of anything existing outside the mind and that objects were 'real' only in the mind of God; while the Scots philosopher Hume (1711–76) arrived at an even more total scepticism, elegantly expressed. His *Enquiry Concerning Human Understanding* (1748), affirmed the limitations of mind so conclusively that metaphysical notions could only come back through a cult of faith and will. Meanwhile 'Deist' theologians, rejecting revelation, now tried to equate Christianity with the harmony of a reasonable and benevolent natural order, as argued in Bishop Butler's *Analogy* (1736). The Unitarians even 'ungodded Jesus Christ'. Against this rationalistic and latitudinarian tide, orthodox theologians did battle, and the controversy became as acrimonious as that of the 'Ancients' and 'Moderns' in the previous generation.

The Anglican Church was now as much part of the establishment as the political set-up, and though it still supported many scholars, its lucrative positions mainly provided for more or less deserving members of the ruling class. It served its social purpose of damping down the fanaticism which had disrupted the seventeenth century, and though the 'Methodist' Wesley managed to remain within it, most of the 'enthusiastic' movements which took on during the century were outside it.

It was the dissenters who kept in touch with the flourishing descendants of the sects in America, where already a great variety of creeds proliferated. Further, the Nonconformists sent their sons to Edinburgh and Glasgow universities with their habit of intensive work, and to the Dutch universities which had maintained the tolerance which had attracted Locke. Wesley, whose impact on the mass of the people will later be considered, also wrote memorable hymns. Along with the even finer hymns of Watts, they expressed the original seventeenth-century ardour in more attractive terms, and kept alive the emotional appeal of the Christian religion when the leaders of the Church regarded 'enthusiasm' as a 'horrid thing'.

In richness and variety English eighteenth-century prose can stand comparison with any age; from the lucidity of Berkeley and Hume to the rotund periods of Gibbon and Dr Johnson, with their Latinized sentences proceeding in well-marshalled array to a resounding conclusion, the field is immense. Since Dryden and Swift English had long been flexible and clear, and also *en robe de parade*, could proceed with classical dignity and force. The novel, pioneered by Defoe, now developed: Fielding, whose *Tom Jones* appeared in 1749, and Smollett, his contemporary, depicted their age with racy observation; the former a genial observer of character, the latter writing with a more bitter skill. Richardson, whose *Pamela* appeared in 1740 and 1742, and *Clarissa* in 1748, was more subtle, though for many less readable: he explored the nuances of the social hierarchy and their effect on character in a new way. Compared to the genial and vigorous world of the immortal *Tom Jones*, his values are tame; expressing the middle-class prudence and convention which was beginning to emerge out of the rumbustious world of Fielding and Smollett. He is a forerunner of Jane Austen, and no one else in western Europe had then achieved such subtlety in this form.

But the predominant figure of the high eighteenth century was Samuel Johnson (1709–84). He won his first fame as a lexicographer, for his great *Dictionary* (1755), though not without forerunners, marked an epoch in the definition of the language. It was only after meeting Boswell in 1763, who immortalized him, that he emerged as a moralist and the greatest 'character' of many 'characters' among English writers. He was a man of the people from the Midlands, who spoke with the accent of his origin. Horace Walpole indeed, being uninterested in the deep compassion and practical good sense of one who had to meet the full brunt of life, detested him as a boor. It is this compassion beneath Johnson's realism, as well as his memorable sayings, that has won him lasting renown.

Edward Gibbon belonged to another social world, and proceeded serenely to complete a project no one had dared to attempt on such a scale before. Sir Walter Ralegh had been a genius, but anyone who compares his history of the world with Gibbon's *Decline and Fall of the Roman Empire* (1776–88) will realize how much richer was the range of Gibbon's historical view. He remains the most compulsively readable of all English historians.

Eighteenth-century memoirs were particularly brilliant. Horace Walpole (1717–97), whose published memoirs cover the years 1751–71, and his last journals 1772–83, depicted character with more deliberate virtuosity than John Aubrey. Consider, for example, his bland reference to Bishop Hayter of Norwich, 'a sensible well-bred man, natural son of Blackbourne the jolly old Archbishop of York, who had all the manners of a man of quality, though he had been a buccaneer and was a clergy-man; but he retained nothing of his first profession except his seraglio'.[30] Or the narrative skill of his description of the Hell Fire Club, a parody of the Franciscan order, founded by Sir Francis Dashwood in the restored ruins of Medmenham Abbey near Marlow: 'Whatever their doctrines were, their practice was vigorously pagan: Bacchus and Venus were the deities to whom they almost publicly sacrificed; and the nymphs and hogsheads that were laid in against the festivals of the new church sufficiently informed the neighbourhood of the complexion of these hermits.'[31] Or the celebrated piece on the Countess of Northumberland – 'a jovial heap of contradictions. The blood of all the Percies and Seymours swelled in her veins and in her fancy; while her person was more vulgar than anything but her conversation, which was larded indiscriminately with stories of her ancestors and her footmen. Show, and crowds and junketing were her endless pursuits. She was familiar with the mob, while stifled with diamonds; and yet was attentive to the most minute privileges of her rank, while almost shaking hands with a cobbler. . . . She had revived the drummers and pipers and obsolete minstrels of her family; and her own buxom countenance at the tail of such a procession gave it all the air of an antiquated pageant or mumming.'[32]

How far this highly sophisticated, and often heartless and arrogant, culture had come since the first brilliance of late Elizabethan times is plain. All is based upon the discipline of classical studies going back to Erasmian learning, and it is now stimulated by the superb French civilization which dominated Europe.

Walpole, in a minor way, also had a hand in the romantic movement; largely an English development which was enthusiastically adopted in Germany, and which found its most influential expression in Rousseau's cult of scenery and sensibility. Just why this 'movement' emerged in England has never been really explained; but it evidently derives in part from the old Welsh element in British civilization, long ago expressed in Geoffrey of Monmouth's fantasies, and even perhaps from the Anglo-Saxon feeling for the ruins of time. Obviously it was in part a reaction to the stress on order and comfort by which, after the mid-seventeenth century, the English naturally set store; in part a reaction, like Voltaire's *Candide*, to the brutalities of the age.

Thomas Gray (1716–71) is the most famous poet of the early romantic movement. A meditative genius of great technical skill, he used the Pindaric ode and what he thought to be Celtic and Norse verse forms in an artificial diction still curiously moving, even if it is by the simpler stanzas of the hackneyed but beautiful *Elegy Written in a Country Churchyard* that he is best known. By the 1760s there was so much demand for romantic verse that Macpherson's bogus epics *Fingal* and *The Poems* of *Ossian* (1765) had a European success.

This kind of sensibility could also strike a harsher and more realistic note. The high prosperity and the military and naval victories which have been here described were bought at a price: as that now neglected poet Edward Young wrote,

'War, famine, pest, volcano, storm and fire
Intestine broils, Oppression, with her heart
Wrapped up in triple brass, besiege mankind.
God's image, disinherited of day,
Here plunged in mines, forgets the sun was made . . .

And

Some for hard masters, broken under arms
In battle lopp'd away, with half their limbs,
Beg bitter bread through realms their valour saved.'*

Such are the most representative writers. The harvest was various; novels, criticism, history, memoirs, conventional poetry, and new, and more romantic, verse. The eighteenth century saw the climax of the pre-industrial élite culture, which had liked to compare itself under Queen Anne to the Augustans of the Roman Empire, and whose best historian thought that under Hadrian and the Antonines, in the climax of the Roman Empire, mankind had enjoyed the greatest felicity. But the outstanding quality of the age, in spite of the strict conventions and apparently stifling rationalist orthodoxy, is the freedom for those at the top or near it; and, also, within the bounds of poverty, for the mass of the people in the rough and tumble of unregulated life.

* *Night Thoughts and a Paraphrase of Part of the Book of Job, The Complaint*, Night I, On Life, Death and Immortality, 1812. p. 9. Edward Young D. D. (1681–1765) son of Edward Young, Dean of Salisbury, was educated at Winchester and in 1708 nominated as a fellow of All Souls College, Oxford, where he spoke the Latin oration at the foundation of the Codrington Library in 1716. 'The other boys ' remarked a senior, 'I can always answer, because I have always known whence they have their argument, which I have read a hundred times, but this fellow Young is continually pestering me with *something of his own*.' (Italics mine.) A prolific dramatist and writer, he influenced many continental romantics and is now too little appreciated.

21

THE NAPOLEONIC WARS AND THE INDUSTRIAL REVOLUTION

In the late eighteenth century the British made a technological revolution without precedent in history. By exploiting new inanimate sources of power they broke out of the economic bounds of all previous civilizations and began a gradual 'take-off into self-sustained economic growth'.[1] This radical and apparently irreversible innovation coincided with the political revolution in France, which directly and indirectly destroyed most of the old régimes in continental Europe. But the British, confronted with economic opportunity and political danger, again managed to adapt themselves. In spite of archaic institutions, muddle, miscalculation and virulent party strife, a great war was surmounted, new men assimilated and fresh chances seized: the country rode out the political and social storm into the brief climax of Victorian Empire when the influence of Great Britain would become paramount in the world.

'Although,' as Professor Asa Briggs writes, 'the concept of an industrial revolution has been queried by certain recent economic historians, during these years the beginnings of a total change in English society can be traced to which the label revolution still deserves to be attached.'[2] Why this 'industrial revolution' took place in the island is a problem later to be examined; the framework of power politics in which it took place must first be considered.

The French Revolution had provoked the invasion of Austrian and Prussian armies: counter-attacking in 1792 with the ardour of their own political and social revolution behind them, the French invaded the Low Countries, the Rhineland and Italy; then Napoleon, the last of the enlightened despots and the first modern dictator, harnessed their armies to ambitions of world conquest. The last major bout of the old Anglo-French conflict was the most gruelling and prolonged. During the second phase of the reign of George III (1783–1820, the final period, 1811–20, a Regency), Great Britain was at war for over twenty years. And, under George IV (1820–30), there was an aftermath of severe social and economic distress. The war lasted from 1793 to 1802; then from 1804 to 1814, with a final flare-up in the year after. Like the great battle of Waterloo which ended it, it was a 'damned nice thing –

the nearest run thing you ever saw in your life'.* But in conjunction with three successive continental coalitions, British wealth and sea-power had strangled Napoleon's over-extended empire, the first continental hegemony to be overwhelmed by forces drawing on power from outside Europe.† A 'balance of power' was restored, and major European wars avoided for nearly half a century; for then, as now on a vaster scale, that maligned and precarious expedient was the best option open.

The struggle coincided with the early industrial revolution and with severe class conflict. Confronted with new conditions, some critics of society appealed to seventeenth-century traditions of independence and moral reformation; others to radical ideas from America and France. The mass of the people, whose living standards were on balance improved, were brought into a new self-awareness as they became organized for factory labour, and a new militancy when their standard of living was threatened by sporadic slumps. The rudiments of trade union organization began to emerge, and the ruling classes, fighting a war of survival, struck back with acts of repression. New social forces were at work, and the leaders and the crowds behind them have only lately been properly studied as interest has grown in the mass of the people, hitherto not much the concern of historians save in brief phases of revolt.[3]

But, as social and economic historians are apt to forget, these social changes, which will later be assessed, were all dwarfed by the war. The British had entered it very reluctantly and only when they had to; they were fighting for vital interests, and their contribution, in wealth, land and sea-power, was decisive. The country became united in a long-established fear and hatred of the French, and the great majority of the people were more concerned with beating Bonaparte than with social grievances.

It was only after the war and twenty years of repression and cyclical economic distress, that the main popular tide set in to bring about the inescapable political reforms of 1832 and the 'improving' legislation which followed them. And they were put through at first by the heirs of the eighteenth-century Foxite Whigs, who had kept relatively liberal traditions alive, and then by the more open-minded Tories of the stamp of Canning and Peel; not in the light of general principles, but to meet the facts.

The course of politics and of the great war will therefore first be examined; then the parallel beginnings of economic revolution and its

* *The Creevey Papers*, ed. John Gore, London, 1963, pp. 133–4. 'By God,' added Wellington, 'I don't think it would have done if I had not been there.'

† See Ludwig Dehio, *The Precarious Balance: the Politics of Power in Europe 1494–1945*, London, 1963, for a good perspective. Dehio thinks Europe was already becoming the cage it proved to Wilhelmine and Hitlerite Germany, and that the Napoleonic Wars were the turning point.

social effects; finally the rich intellectual life of the time. In conjunction with their continental allies the British were now to defeat the greatest threat to their independence between the Armada and the Battle of Britain, and emerge from the conflict as the greatest industrial and naval power, with a second Empire, often reluctantly and casually acquired, larger than their first. The scale and prospects of British civilization were to be vastly expanded and, in spite of endemic social conflicts, it shows a creativeness which would come to full expression in Victorian England.

2

In December 1783, and before the election that swept the Fox–North coalition from power, William Pitt became Prime Minister at the age of twenty-four. The king's personal choice and backed by the City, he inaugurated a period of Tory government which would last, with one brief interval, until 1830. It was to be the sequel to the long Whig domination.

Pitt's régime lasted from 1783 to 1801; and, following Addington's ineffective administration, again from 1804 to 1806. Then after a brief and predominantly Whig coalition sarcastically termed 'All the Talents' under Lord Grenville, which included Fox and Grey, the Tories came back under the Duke of Portland (1807–9), Perceval (1809–12) and Lord Liverpool (1812–27). Then, after Canning's short ministry, and its brief sequel under Goderich, the Duke of Wellington took over (1828–30). The government that conducted the Napoleonic Wars was thus still mainly eighteenth century in outlook, though Canning was a new kind of Tory politician who evoked a new popular following.

The younger Pitt had genius, but with none of his father's flamboyance and dramatic flair. He had greater staying power but narrower vision.* By nature a high-powered administrator and financier, he is

* William Pitt (1759–1806), was set on a political career from childhood. At the age of seven he remarked, when his father had been made Earl of Chatham, that he was glad he was the second son as he wished to enter the Commons. Indeed, he was a boy of 'appalling precocity'. (Holland Rose, *William Pitt and the National Revival*, London, 1911, p. 64.) Brought up mainly at Burton Pynsent, at Weymouth and Lyme Regis, he was educated by tutors, and went up to Pembroke College, Cambridge at fourteen. Here he read Adam Smith's *Wealth of Nations* and added a grasp of economics to classical learning. He became a barrister and member of Parliament for the pocket borough of Appleby in Cumberland: at twenty-three he was Chancellor of the Exchequer. Pitt inherited his father's gout and used the same remedy; when stricken in middle age, his 'daily potion of port wine for many years must have further told against recovery'. He never married, and in his later years his niece, Lady Hester Stanhope, kept house for him. He had a patrician aloofness, optimism and self-confidence and worked himself to death at forty-six, already a white-haired wreck. He was careless of his private fortune, and his debts were paid by the State. But this dedicated public man rallied the nation and expressed the defiance of his class and of the majority of countrymen in the French war. See J. Ehrman. *The Younger Pitt. The Years of Acclaim.* London. 1969.

credited with 'some idea of the political and financial machinery which a modern state requires'.[4] He set himself to rehabilitate the country after the American disaster; to reorganize administration and finance, and to deal with the urgent problems of India, Canada and Ireland. He gave the old Tory label a new look, more business-like and metropolitan; a tradition further developed against the more extreme conservatives by Canning and then by Peel, the first modern-style Prime Minister. Still the 'King's servants', the inner cabinets now took a more concerted line, though Pitt, 'a man of marble', writes Pares, did not conciliate colleagues. Within the 'mixed' constitution, governments were now less subservient to the monarch, and the king's bouts of illness in 1788–9, 1801 and 1804 raised the urgent question of a Regency and with it the hopes of the Whig opposition which centred, as usual, upon the Prince of Wales. But when George III finally went out of his mind in 1810, a Tory ministry continued in office under the Prince Regent.

During his first period of power Pitt, though never really interested in 'reform' as such, abolished the more flagrant sinecures; tried to deal with the debt outstanding from the American war, brought the king's Civil List under the control of parliament, and promoted internal and external trade. Vital decisions were also taken for the Empire. The India Act of 1784 set up a new kind of Governor-General under a Board of Control over the East India Company on which two ministers were now included, and in 1786 the armed forces in India were subordinated to him. Moreover, between 1768 and 1779, during the crisis of the American War, Captain Cook, the greatest of all British maritime explorers, had disproved the legend of a great Southern Continent which the European powers might exploit, opened up much of the Pacific to European knowledge, and charted the shores of New Zealand and eastern Australia. If the government could think of nothing better than to use Botany Bay and Sydney for convicts settling in the 1780s, since they could no longer be consigned to North America, the first step in a vast enterprise had been made. Moreover, in 1791 Pitt divided Canada into Upper and Lower Provinces for the English and French-speaking colonists; an arrangement which probably kept the country within the Empire, though it later led to trouble.

But in the following year, as already recorded, the French revolutionary government, under external attack and riding a tiger at home, invaded the Low Countries and the Rhine; they overran Flanders, and by the autumn their ships had entered the Scheldt to join in the attack on Antwerp. Pitt's government had manœuvred to avoid conflict, and turned a cold face towards the *émigrés* and the continental anti-Jacobin crusade: now they had to realize that the revolution could only be contained by war. Tempted by the wealth of the Dutch, the French were out to dominate areas regarded as vital to British interests since the fifteenth century: Pitt, though uninterested in ideological principles and detesting war, reluctantly concluded that war was 'not only unavoidable but absolutely necessary to the existence of Great Britain'. So the country entered the next great bout of conflict among the European states, and the consequences were global.

It was often said that Pitt was a great peacetime Prime Minister, but out of his depth in war; and indeed neither Pitt nor Dundas, his Secretary at War, understood that they were in for an unlimited and prolonged conflict, the first of the ideological wars in which whole peoples would participate. Their original military strategy was deplorable. In 1793 the main force was sent to the West Indies to pick up French colonies; 40,000 men died and as many more were invalided, mainly from yellow fever. An inadequate British expeditionary force was hunted out of Flanders and evacuated from Bremen. Subsidies were poured out to Russia, Prussia and Austria; but these powers were more concerned with partitioning what was left of Poland than with campaigns in the west. By 1796–7 Bonaparte's armies had overrun Italy.

At sea, on the other hand, the British were successful. For Pitt understood naval strategy, picked the right admirals and gave Howe, St Vincent and Nelson their chance.[5] This strategy was soon decisive; by 1794 the French Atlantic fleet had been destroyed by Lord Howe off Brest on the 'Glorious First of June'; in 1797 Sir John Jervis, afterwards Earl St Vincent, defeated a great Spanish fleet off Cape St Vincent in Portugal and, that October, Lord Duncan smashed the Dutch fleet off Camperdown in Holland.

They were costly victories. In these horrible slogging matches between wooden ships, hard to sink unless they blew up, casualties were appalling and surgeons worked in cramped cockpits without anaesthetics. And everyday conditions were such that in this year of double victory, the Channel fleet had mutinied at Spithead and the North Sea Fleet at the Nore. Callous muddle and malversation of supplies, bad food and bad pay, often in arrears, drove the crews to extremity. Yet their grievances were specific and reasonably expressed. The 'floating' republic hoisted the red or 'bloody' flag, but hauled it down to celebrate the anniversary of the Restoration, and once their grievances had been met, the crews fought with added ferocity: 'Damn my eyes if I understand your lingo. . .,' wrote one mutineer to the Admiralty, 'but in short give us our Due at once and no more at it, till we go in search of the Rascals the Enemies of our Country. Henry Long, on Board His Majesty's Ship *Champion*.'* These mutinies forced the government to pass a Seaman's

* See Christopher Lloyd, *St Vincent and Camperdown*, London, 1963, p. 114. Richard Parker, the principal organizer of the mutiny, who was hung, was originally a village schoolmaster,

Wages Bill and to give rather better treatment to both services. In spite of inept administration, the fleet thus remained what it had to be for the country's survival: 'not only the bulwark of Britain but the terror of the world'.

So the long arm of sea-power reached out into the Mediterranean and the Baltic. For Bonaparte's ambition now gave the British their chance, and they were quick to seize it. Instead of invading Ireland – probably the correct move – Bonaparte preferred the more glamorous East and a threat to India. In 1798 he seized Malta from the Knights, and invaded Egypt. On 1 August Nelson destroyed the French fleet at the battle of the Nile; a greater strategic turning-point than Trafalgar.

The initiative was now with the British: with the occupation of Malta in 1800, they again dominated the Mediterranean, and when, in the following year, the Cape of Good Hope and Ceylon were captured from the Dutch, the British hold on India was strategically secured. They also reasserted their control of another area of vital interest at the expense of the Danes. Following the organization of a so-called League of Armed Neutrality by Russia and the Scandinavian states, Nelson destroyed the Danish fleet in the harbour of Copenhagen itself. Switching from their original appeasement to ruthless aggression, the British were now masters at sea; while Napoleon, who had defeated the second coalition, was master of the continent. The stalemate was recognized by the Treaty of Amiens, ratified by Addington's government, which was set on peace and economy, in 1802.

Pitt had unexpectedly resigned over Ireland. His government had surmounted a financial crisis aggravated by bad harvests, and imposed a novel ten per cent income tax to finance the war. To repress subversion at home while a war for survival was being fought abroad, it had even in 1794 suspended the *Habeas Corpus* Act, and by the Combination Acts of 1799–1800 made the nascent trade unions illegal. Now the strategic danger from Ireland, which had concerned British governments since Tudor times, had again become urgent. Pitt's attempts at introducing a better deal for the Catholics had failed, and, in 1798, with French collaboration, the Catholic Irish, still brooding on memories of the seventeenth century as well as of their own time, had risen in a major revolt. For after the Revolution of 1688, Ireland had become the battle-ground of James II and William III, whose triumph at the Boyne had ensured the protestant ascendancy but had further embittered the Catholic majority. Moreover, during the eighteenth century another,

already twice discharged from the service, and he died disillusioned with his followers. 'Remember,' he wrote, 'never to make yourself the busybody of the lower classes, for they are cowardly, selfish and ungrateful . . . and him whom they have exalted one moment as their Demagogue, the next they will not scruple to exalt upon the gallows.' (p. 116.)

and this time common, grievance against the sort of economic exploitation denounced by Swift had encouraged a demand for more economic and political freedom. And Catholics and dissenting Protestants alike detested the established episcopalian Church of Ireland and its social influence. Henry Grattan, a brilliant Dublin lawyer, had led a campaign to enhance the power of the Irish parliament, and a more radical movement, the 'United Irishmen', had now arisen. Pitt had tried conciliation; but the French war had darkened the scene. Opinion had hardened all round; the Catholic Irish were thought traitors for their contacts with the French, and the Ulster Protestants, appalled at the prospect of a French-supported Catholic Ireland, had rallied to the British. And when, after small French landings in 1796 and 1797, the full-scale rebellion had broken out, they had joined with the British government to put it down.

So in the poverty-stricken and divided country, the old Catholic and 'Orange' feud had revived. To Pitt's mind there was only one remedy; the Union of Ireland and Great Britain under the parliament at Westminster. So in 1801 the two kingdoms were formally united and Irish members entered the imperial parliament at Westminster. But they were still not, as Pitt had intended, representative: bound by his coronation oath, George III refused to give the Catholic majority the vote; only Protestant Irish could be elected. It was thus over the question of Catholic emancipation that Pitt had resigned. The Catholic Irish remained bitterly hostile, more of the landowners became absentees, and the religious grievance would not be rectified until in 1829, against obstinate opposition, Wellington's government passed the Catholic Emancipation Act with unhappy results, at least for English politics.

On the wider European scene, the Peace of Amiens now proved merely a truce. Addington's attempted appeasement gave Napoleon, now First Consul for life, time to mount a more massive threat; and when, in the general panic of 1804, Pitt was recalled to office, a huge French army was already poised for invasion from Flushing to Boulogne. But the accession of Tsar Alexander I gave the diplomats an opening, for he was alarmed at French preponderance in Germany; and when in 1805 Napoleon, already Emperor of the French, proclaimed himself King of Italy, the Austrians joined a third coalition to which Great Britain contributed six and a quarter million pounds. A threat was being mounted against the French in central Europe.

Moreover, that summer, the French admirals failed to secure even temporary command of the Channel. Napoleon cut his losses, and by early September he struck swiftly south east. But though he defeated the Austrians at Ulm and in December routed immense Austro-Russian armies at Austerlitz, the invasion had failed. Nor would the threat recur, for on 21 October, off Cape Trafalgar in south-western Spain, Nelson destroyed the Franco–Spanish fleet and won complete British supremacy of the oceans. For Trafalgar had been not only the crowning example of Nelson's genius, but the 'crushing proof of English naval superiority in tactics, seamanship and gunnery'. The French ships were often better designed, 'but the Revolution had dealt a fatal blow to the personnel of the French navy; the losses of trained and experienced officers through executions and emigration were irreplaceable. Their corps of seamen gunners was disbanded. Such training and experience could not be improvised'.[6]

The island base had been secured; the strategic initiative regained.* But Napoleon was still at the climax of his power on the continent. Following the collapse of the third coalition, he won over Alexander I at Tilsit in 1807; then, to break the British, he turned to economic warfare, a weapon that cut both ways. The British imposed a counter-blockade immensely damaging to the interests of Napoleon's empire, and, with the unprecedented advantage of the early industrial revolution behind them, they extended their already enormous trade across the oceans. The continental allies and satellites grew restive; and, while the British were not seriously threatened by the American War of 1812–14 provoked by the blockade, Napoleon was forced into his greatest and fatal adventure. In 1812 his colossal expedition to Russia broke his empire, already weakened because he had also been forced to invade Spain and Portugal.

Here the British had been able to strike. In 1808 they landed in Portugal and in conjunction with Spanish and Portuguese armies, and with a formidable peasant guerrilla resistance, Wellington's strategy wore down the French invaders. As Wellington wrote, 'I entertain no doubt that from first to last Bonaparte sent 600,000 men into Spain, and I know that not more than 100,000 went out in the shape of an army.... It is true that the result may in part be attributed to the operation of the Allied Armies in the Peninsula; but a great proportion of it must be ascribed to the enmity of the people of Spain.'[7] Along with the gigantic disaster in Russia, the gruelling Spanish campaign from Vimiero in

* Trafalgar was won by new tactics. The British broke through the French line by attacking in column, and after years of warfare, their professional skill was now unsurpassed and taken for granted. When Nelson made his famous signal England 'confides that every man will do his duty', altered to 'expects' since 'confides' was not in the signal-book, Admiral Collingwood remarked testily 'What is Nelson signalling about? We all know what we have to do'. 'Do our duty?' said one seaman, 'of course we will do our duty, I've always done mine, haven't you?' But for the Nelson legend the signal was highly effective; and by pacing the deck in full uniform with stars and ribbons in a close action, this hero of the romantic age, more than did his own. See Michael Lewis, *A Social History of the Navy, 1795–1815*, London, 1960, p. 50 ff, for the best account of the spirit of the navy at the time.

1808, through the defence of Torres Vedras 1809–10, to Salamanca in
1812 and Vitoria in 1813, disintegrated the French land empire, already
being strangled at sea.[8] Soon, after Napoleon had been overwhelmed by
the Russian, Austrian and Prussian armies at Leipzig in 1813, the
British, like their central European and Russian allies, were ready to
invade France itself. After a brilliant defence, Napoleon abdicated; the
decision, confirmed at Waterloo, meant the end of the climax of the
struggle with France, conducted intermittently since the wars against
Louis XIV.

The British emerged as the greatest oceanic and colonial power, as
well as the pioneers of the first Industrial Revolution. But, save for India,
which had long been considered as the most important and profitable
dependency, this second empire was not enthusiastically regarded. The
loss of the American colonies, the appalling casualties in the West Indies
and the expense of a global war had damped the sort of imperialist
enthusiasm shown by Chatham. Australia was still thought fit only for
convicts, and the immense mineral resources and potential agricultural
wealth of Canada were not yet understood. The British even returned
the huge and wealthy East Indies, now Indonesia, to the Dutch. But
strategic naval bases were kept: Malta, Ceylon, Mauritius and the
Cape. And to secure her own survival and her vast overseas trade, Great
Britain would be forced to chart and patrol the oceans of the world;[9]
to create, in short, the nineteenth-century *Pax Britannica*.

In 1807 the British had also confirmed the decision, made in principle
in Parliament at the instance of Fox in 1806, to proceed to the total
prohibition of the Slave Trade to British subjects and British shipping,
the result of a campaign in which the evangelical fervour of Wilberforce
had been allied with the humanitarianism of the Foxite Whigs, though
Wilberforce had remarked of Fox, 'poor fellow, how melancholy his
case! He has not one religious friend or one who knows anything about
it'. This momentous abolition would culminate in 1833, when the Whig
government of Earl Grey would abolish slavery throughout the Empire.

In India, Lord Cornwallis (1786–93), the first Governor-General
under Pitt's India Act, had now developed the paramountcy that the
British had taken over from the decadent Moghul Empire. A thorough
settlement of the land revenue, essential for government, was now set in
train and the bureaucracy better organized. The Governor-General
under the new Act had more extensive if much resented powers towards
the East India Company, and in 1798–1805 Richard Colley Wellesley,
Lord Mornington, by 1799 Marquess Wellesley, launched a policy of
expansion. Napoleon's invasion of Egypt had seemed a menace to India,
and the British were now determined to extirpate all French influence:
on the defensive in Europe, they consolidated an Empire in the East.

And although, after Trafalgar, the strategic domination of the oceans had been secured and with it the control of India, the Franco–Russian alliance concluded at Tilsit now seemed to pose another threat. So in India it was a time not only of conquest but of defensive consolidation; 'the task of conquest was slight', reflected one administrator, 'in comparison with that which awaits us, the preservation of the Empire acquired. . .'.[10] The entire Carnatic had now come under British rule, and Mysore and Hyderabad were 'protected' states. Most decisively, the Mahrattas of central India, the only power capable of withstanding the British, were broken in 1803 at the hard-fought battle of Assaye, the first major success of Arthur Wellesley, later Duke of Wellington, the Governor-General's brother. When the British took over Delhi, the Moghul capital, where the aged Moghul Emperor, Alam Shah, was accorded a formal respect, they had become *de facto* rulers of all India. They now began the most creative and least resented period of their ascendancy.[11] For now, 'under Wellesley's inspiration', the Company had been converted in twenty years 'from a trading organization which held some territory, into a great territorial power which carried on some trade on the side'.[12] His pro-consuls, Malcolm, Elphinstone, Metcalfe, were, like Nelson, men of the romantic age; 'when the cult of the picturesque was at its height, they operated in a landscape of almost excessive picturesqueness. All three were conscious of the living presence of the past, of dying empires and new worlds in the making', and they all respected Indian civilization. Though they were clearing up the wreckage of the Moghul Empire, 'their sense of superiority was neither arrogant nor smug'.[13] It was only when a more impersonal and elaborate bureaucracy, the utilitarian cult of 'improvement' and evangelical Christian missionary zeal, combined to create a deep rift between rulers and ruled, that the estrangement already marked by the Mutiny of 1857, would build up.

So, by 1814, with global naval supremacy unchallenged, it was as an Asian as well as an Atlantic power that Great Britain came to the Congresses convened in Europe by the victorious allies after the Napoleonic wars. Indeed, from 1815 to 1914, their only European war would be with Russia over a supposed threat to Constantinople and the Levant and thus to India.

4

After 1814 the great powers now combined to restore what they thought of as the 'ancient public law of Europe', violated by revolutionary and Napoleonic France. Accepting the inevitable importance of France, they did not attempt to ruin the country, but to restore the old régime as part of an established order. Indeed, their objectives, not much appreciated by Liberal historians who thought democratic nationalism would lead to fraternal peace, were realistic, if soon diversely pursued; and in fact even though the Western and Eastern powers soon ceased to collaborate, the settlement kept the peace for half a century.

But the victors were divided by profound differences of social structure and interest. The autocracies of Potsdam and St Petersburg, with the fluctuating support of the more subtle but effete rulers in Vienna, tried to police Europe by bayonets and cannon. The British, on the other hand, with their relatively liberal outlook, and their oceanic and commercial concerns, followed up their objectives in a different way. They had two constant interests: to secure complete naval supremacy, as they did until the First World War, and to maintain a balance of power on the continent. Only then could they protect their enormous and vulnerable Empire and the trade by which an increasingly industrial country had to live. Viscount Castlereagh, Foreign Secretary in Liverpool's government, was a realist of the school of Pitt; temperamentally suited to a conservative policy and without sympathy or understanding for the liberal and nationalist movements which the Napoleonic Empire had provoked. But the obvious counterpoise to the Eastern and Central European autocracies was a liberal Western Europe; and when, in 1820 there was a revolt against the restored Bourbons in Portugal and Spain, the British government promptly declared at the Congress of Troppau that it could not 'charge itself as a Member of the Alliance with the moral responsibility of administering a general European Police'.[14] Canning, the brilliant extrovert, who succeeded the introspective and suicidal Castlereagh in 1822, then went further.[15] He sensed the danger of the domination of Europe by military autocrats, and that there was no future in imposing an eighteenth-century solution on a nineteenth-century situation; he also understood the importance of nationalism. So he set himself to 'get rid of the Areopagus' of autocratic powers. Canning was therefore determined, as part of maintaining the balance, to maintain good relations with whatever governments controlled the Iberian peninsula, and, following eighteenth-century policy and aware of potential markets with those that were now emancipating themselves from Spain in South America as well. Following President Monroe's declaration in 1823 that the United States would not tolerate further European colonization – in effect interference – in the Americas, in 1824 Canning recognized the independence of Mexico, Colombia and Buenos Aires, making his famous claim to have 'called a new world into existence to redress the balance of the old'.

In Greece, too, sentiment and interest would coincide. In 1824 Byron had died at Missolonghi, a hero of a Greek revolt against the Turks, which had been passionately supported by British philhellenes. The Levant, also economically important, now needed a settlement which would prevent the Russians dismantling the Turkish Empire. Supported at this stage by the French, Canning persuaded Nicholas I to agree to an allied offer of Greek autonomy under Turkish suzerainty; and when the Turkish–Egyptian fleets of Ibrahim Pasha, to whom the Sultan had delegated the congenial task of putting down the revolt, refused the offered armistice, they were destroyed in 1827 by British, French and Russian squadrons under Admiral Codrington at Navarino.

Canning had died before this decision was taken, but the sequel was a triumph for his policy. It secured the limited independence of Greece; won not simply by Russian intervention but by the western powers as well. Prince Otto of Bavaria became the country's first monarch: the Greeks had not secured all their objectives, but they were at last autonomous and their autonomy promoted freer trade in the Levant.

Thus, after the Napoleonic Wars, the British pursued their essential objectives; to maintain their oceanic naval and commercial supremacy, and by recognizing and exploiting the European shifts of policy to maintain the balance of power and so their own continental influence, with an eye on the Levant and India as well as on their interests in the Americas, the Indian Ocean and the Pacific. In a hard world a hard realism had paid off.

5

The outcome of the Napoleonic Wars had been largely determined by the colossal wealth created in Great Britain by the early Industrial Revolution. Hitherto human and animal energy, supplemented by wind or water power, had been the only driving force available: now a new source of energy was found in steady, accurate and indefatigable machinery. First textile manufacturing was mechanized, then the heavy industries based on coal and iron were developed on an unheard-of scale. And in the next stage power became mobile when steam was applied to locomotives running on railroads.

The structure of British society was now transformed. But the process was gradual and came naturally out of a commercial and agricultural prosperity long building up; and it was not, as often supposed, a generally traumatic experience, striking suddenly and strangely at the continuity of British life. The raw factory towns and suburbs that sprawled across the Black Country created a novel and, to conservative eyes, repellent way of life; but the population greatly increased, and on balance the standard of living improved. The main and predictable protest and agitation came not so much from the new factory workers themselves as from pre-industrial artisans, defending their own pride in their craftsmanship and way of life; harking back to seventeenth-century notions of manhood suffrage and to eighteenth-century ideas of rough liberty. Their protest blended with that of middle-class radicals inspired by the egalitarian ideas of the current political upheaval in France.

How it came about that the Industrial Revolution first occurred in Great Britain has been much debated. France, Germany and Russia all had considerable deposits of coal and greater deposits of iron; in 1740, for example, England had come third in the production of cast iron. The English roads and canals were relatively good; but, if communications had been decisive, the first Industrial Revolution might have been expected in the Low Countries or in France. A flourishing commerce had trebled since the Restoration and English banking was relatively well developed;[16] but the lowest rates of interest were still obtainable in Holland and the Dutch were still the main bankers of Europe. France was far the richest country, with the largest potential capital resources, should political, social and economic conditions allow them to be tapped. In spite of the subsequent fame of her inventors, England was then not even technologically or scientifically more advanced than her continental competitors. But probably, in a more open society, the opportunities were better grasped. For England was a relatively free country unhampered by centralized bureaucracy and high taxation, and untouched by the wars that had devastated much of the continent. About a quarter of the people were urban, compared with about a tenth in France; but English agriculture was producing the food and purchasing power which could sustain great industry. It was not out of a depopulated countryside that the Industrial Revolution developed, but out of a rising population and the best agriculture in Europe.

This improvement in agricultural methods and therefore in productivity had been going on intermittently since the price rises and enclosures of Tudor times, and the landowners had not scorned to develop their estates themselves. 'All the well-known capital strokes in husbandry', wrote Arthur Young, 'are traced . . . to gentlemen. From whence came the introduction of the turnip to England but from Tull? Who introduced clover but Sir Richard Weston? Marling in Norfolk is owing to Lord Townshend and Mr Allen. All the county from Holkham to Houghton was a sheep run before the spirit of improvement seized the inhabitants.'[17] The enclosures, culminating in the General Enclosure Act of 1803, had uprooted many small-holding farmers, and England had ceased to have a peasantry in the continental sense, but they had increased the demand for hired and skilled labour. Contrary to the long-received opinion that the countryside was denuded of its people, the population in fact rose where the enclosures were most extensive. 'From 1750 to 1830', writes Professor Landes, 'Britain's agricultural counties doubled their inhabitants. Whether objective evidence of this kind will suffice, however, to do away with what has become something of an article of faith is doubtful'.[18]

It was only during the war in 1795, when the price of wheat doubled and later trebled, that the Speenhamland magistrates had to devise the 'outdoor relief' that 'however detested, probably averted a major agrarian revolt'.[19] It was wartime inflation, not the normal condition of farming, that created hardship.

The background of the Industrial Revolution was thus a thriving agriculture, with vigorous market towns and county capitals: as Young put it in 1770, 'I have proved the nation . . . to possess a vigorous agriculture, flourishing manufacturers, and an extended commerce, in a word to be a great industrial country. It is employment that creates population . . . the increase in employment will be found to raise men like mushrooms.'[20]

On the technological side, the early Industrial Revolution also developed naturally out of the social and geographical background. The cloth industry had remained the staple export until the late seventeenth century, and now, since coal and iron were conveniently juxtaposed, great cotton mills for textiles and blast furnaces for heavy industry would transform the scale of production. The inventors were not the illiterate workmen of popular legend, but craftsmen with a long tradition behind them or minor gentry with an ingenious turn of mind; while the entrepreneurs who exploited their devices were generally the kind of thrusting provincials, often with a Dissenting background, to whom much expanding trade had long been due. They now exerted themselves to make enormous fortunes, and were quickly assimilated into the upper classes to increase the preponderance of a more plutocratic broad-based establishment.

The textile industry was the first to be mechanized, if the inventors themselves on this occasion derived little benefit from their work. As early as 1733 Kay, a weaver and skilled mechanic, had devised a 'flying shuttle', and in 1765 Hargreaves a multiple spinning 'jenny'. Kay was driven from the country by his fellow artisans, and Hargreaves cheated out of most of his profits. Even the inventor Crompton of Bolton, who came of the county gentry in Lancashire, and whose 'mule' (1779), so-called because it was a cross between a spinning jenny and a water frame, was the most decisive invention, had to be granted £5000 by Pitt's government to pay his debts. The most ingenious of them, the Rev. Edmund Cartwright, who devised the power loom (1785), and who came of an old Nottinghamshire family, and had been a fellow of

Magdalen College, Oxford and even Professor of Poetry, had to be compensated with a grant of £10,000 and retired to a farm in Kent.[21] It was not these inventors, but the entrepreneurs and their backers who reaped the profits and went ahead, as they would in nineteenth-century North America in a more spacious context. Sir Richard Arkwright, for example, who exploited the water frame, started life as a barber in Lancashire. Backed by a clockmaker of Warrington and a local publican, he went into partnership with a firm of hosiers in Derby and built the first big cotton mill on the river Derwent. He ended up with a fortune of half a million pounds, for by the 1780s the cotton mills were being geared to steam.

A parallel spate of inventions had now made steam power practicable. In 1709 Darby of Coalbrookdale had hit upon using coke – 'coal coked into cinder' – to make a blast furnace. Then a Scotsman, Henry Cort (also ruined but pensioned by the government) purified pig iron; and John Roebuck, a rich entrepreneur educated at Edinburgh and Leydon, exploited the technique in the Carron ironworks in Scotland which would produce the Carronades decisive both on land and sea in the Napoleonic Wars. Since iron could now stand the pressure of condensed steam, steam power could now be applied to textiles, blast furnaces and armaments.

In 1700, Newcomen, a blacksmith and locksmith of Dartmouth, Devon, had already devised a steam pump to drain mines and supply reservoirs: now James Watt, the son of an architect and grandson of a mathematician,* patented his steam engine, set up by Roebuck at the Carron works in 1769, and known familiarly as *Beelzebub*. Matthew Boulton, a wealthy Birmingham manufacturer of shoe buckles, buttons, and plate, took up Watt's invention with substantial capital behind him: by the 1780s 'fire engines' or 'fire pumps' were in considerable demand. And when in 1781 Watt applied the steam engine to rotative motion it became a source of general power. It was then that Arkwright and the elder Peel took it up. By the turn of the century steam was producing about 10,000 horsepower; by 1815, 210,000. Soon it would be applied to the locomotive. Thus the first and interacting phase of the Industrial Revolution in textiles and heavy industry had begun.[22]

In textile manufactures, the old staple cloth industry was now far outstripped. Massive imports of raw cotton converged on Liverpool from India, the West Indies and the Americas; in the wet Lancashire climate vast quantities of fabric were made so cheaply as to compete even in Indian markets. In cotton alone production rose to £10·5

---

* 'I saw a workman,' wrote a contemporary, 'and expected no more. I found a philosopher.' Watt was a good linguist and well-informed about literature and music: while devising his invention he worked as a surveyor on the Caledonian Canal.

million by 1805; by 1845 it would be £24·3 million. Even through the Napoleonic Wars textile exports boomed, for the cheap British goods flooded markets not only far overseas but, in spite of the blockade, on the continent. And in heavy industry the blast furnaces roared and fumed in the northern fog, pouring out cheap iron, the basis of a technology that would transform the lives of vaster populations in other climates.

In the relatively open English society, where wealth could get a man anywhere, the initiative had been seized not by the state but by the entrepreneurs; even if they exploited the inventors, they have only lately been given the credit that is their due. Outside the world of Parliament, the City, the big landlords and the plutocracy, of the Plantations and of the East, these formidable capitalists and their armies of workpeople gave a new aspect to English society. Their crude and often brutal initiative, coming out of the vigour and freedom of the eighteenth century, would transform Great Britain from a mainly agricultural country to one in which a massive industrial population dependent on great exporting industries would predominate, and make the country the pioneer of new dimensions of productivity.[23] In the distant future, when much British political history, if not British science and literature, has become insignificant, two things at least will be remembered. The British Empire, that brought so many Asian and African peoples into contact with western ideas and technology, and the Industrial Revolution which opened a new era in human history. Its immediate social impact on the island must now be considered.

6

In 1798, in his *Essay on the Principles of Population*, the Rev. Thomas Malthus concluded that since human sexual instincts were 'constant', and unlikely to change without 'an immediate Act of Power by the Being who first arranged the system of the Universe', population must always be controlled by marginal famine. In fact, with the Industrial Revolution, population now broke out of the Malthusian cycle. Factory employment in the towns and better farming, supplemented by poor relief in the country, now created and sustained its own labour force. Here again the long-accepted picture of a half-starved proletariat being exploited by ruthless entrepreneurs is not borne out by the evidence. During the eighteenth century the population had risen from about six to ten million. The statistical evidence after 1800 – now for the first time reasonably clear – depicts a steady though fluctuating improvement in the standard of living. Real wages rose by a quarter between 1800 and 1827, and by forty per cent between 1824 and 1850. Naturally the mass

experience varied: some classes were doing well out of the new industries, others were being ruined, and all were affected by the fluctuation
of the economy. Years of slump and unemployment, as 1815–19 and
1829–32, like those of mid-Victorian recession, meant agitation and riot.
Much of the harrowing literary evidence and the impression of a near
revolutionary populace derives from these years. But as soon as better
times returned, the radical leaders complained that 'you cannot get
them to talk politics when they are employed'. The figures for the consumption of tea and sugar – previously for the well-to-do – indicate a
rising standard of life, and the mass production of cheap consumer
goods, such as earthenware and textiles, would have been totally
impracticable if there had not been a great popular market in England,
as in no other country. And the totally unprecedented population increase during the nineteenth century implies an enormous increase in
the means of subsistence. Nor, whatever their sufferings, did the workers
in the new industries show much desire to return to the conditions of
cottage industry. Pitt's Combination Acts were not meant to repress a
hungry proletariat, but workers trying to maintain a relatively high
wage during a crisis.

The experience of the people differed from region to region, from
industry to industry, and from year to year; and their situations and
interests were so different that one must speak rather of working classes
than of a working class; but to the majority the new conditions brought
both mobility and opportunity. Naturally, there was bitter protest, and
conditions were often appalling, in particular for craftsmen who had
come down in the world. The sundering of families in a strange and
hostile environment, the tyranny and sharp practice of some factory
owners, and the dislike of country-bred people for punctuality and
factory routine, together with the hazards to health and the long hours,
were an affront to the inbred tradition of liberty. But the protest was
much more conservative than revolutionary. The people 'had been
taught so long that the Revolution Settlement of 1688 embodied in the
Constitution of King, Lords and Commons, was the guarantee of
British independence and liberties that the reflex had been set up –
constitution equals liberty'.* So they appealed not so much to French
revolutionary theory as to the rights of free-born Englishmen; they did
not wish to overturn the social order. 'The truth,' wrote Talleyrand in
1792, 'is that the mass of the nation is generally indifferent to those
political discussions that cause so much stir among us.' The typical
British agitators were small artisans, 'tradesmen, shopkeepers and

* See Thompson, *op. cit.*, p. 78. This scholarly and in many ways inspired book, a classic
of its kind, is based mainly on literary evidence; and the conception of a single 'working class'
hardly corresponds to historical reality.

mechanics, asserting seventeenth-century ideas, manhood suffrage, annual parliaments and a rudimentary democracy'; while in France 'a new political man confronted a startled and largely horrified Europe. He was a *Sans Culotte*'.[24] The British protest came mainly from conservative craftsmen threatened by the mass production of the new industries; from handloom weavers, stockingers, cobblers, small tailors. Most of the propagandists were thus not revolutionary intellectuals, but skilled workers with traditions of dissent and radicalism; 'men who, however, poor, could not conceive of themselves as "hands", or a "labour force", men with the dignity of a skill and the mystery of a craft . . . whose values even in adversity, were fixed by an earned independence . . . the ideology of democracy was pre-industrial and its first serious practitioners were artisans'.[25]

After all, English radicalism had always been religious. It had come down from the Lollards and the seventeenth-century sects: Bunyan, not Rousseau, was still its prophet. The Baptists hated sin and 'Satan's Kingdom', and set up the chapel against the 'pub'; but they were not in principle against property; and the Wesleyan Methodists directed their disciplined congregations to religion, not political revolt. Even the radical Tom Paine, whose *Rights of Man* (1792) had a huge circulation and preached a fashionable atheism, did not attack property: he simply wanted to humanize it. Nor were even the Luddite machine wreckers in the 1820s or 'Captain Swing's' gangs in Kent who burnt ricks and terrorized farmers as far away as in Wiltshire and Dorset in the 1830s, militant anarchists, though they sounded like them.* The Luddites smashed carding frames as a threat to extort higher wages, not as often supposed, to destroy machinery as such. And 'Swing's' followers, whatever their methods, were only demanding a living wage, two shillings a day in winter and half-a-crown in summer.

The main pattern of protest was thus traditional, pre-industrial, and seldom revolutionary. But it was now no longer merely negative. The Industrial Revolution itself gave it coherence, and now rudimentary and spontaneous organizations developed from it. When in 1792 Thomas Hardy, the shoemaker, and nine 'well-meaning and industrious men' started the London Corresponding Society, and, following their prosecution, were acquitted by a London jury, they gained an unprecedented popular following. As regional differences diminished and more skilled workers emerged out of the eighteenth century 'lower orders', the working classes became more conscious of their position. Spontaneously but tentatively they began to organize themselves. They

* 'As one of the followers of "King Lud", I am going to inform you that there is six thousand men coming to you in Apral and then we will go and blow Parliament house up and Blow up all afour us us labring peple can't stand it no longer.' E. P. Thompson, *op. cit.*, p. 714.

were not, as often supposed, 'pathetic victims of the Industrial Revolution, waiting helplessly for trade union organization to rescue them', and deserving only 'the enormous condescension of posterity'.[26] In spite of the Combination Acts, not repealed until 1824, many craft unions and 'Friendly Societies' were growing up, a cover name for trade unions. 'What would our trade be,' wrote one stocking weaver in 1812, 'if we did not combine together? See the tailors, shoemakers, bookbinders, gold beaters, printers, bricklayers, coatmakers, hatters, curristes, masons, whitesmiths, none of these trades receive less than 30/- and from that to five guineas, this is all done by combination.'[27] These practical considerations were also supplemented by the far-ranging and Utopian ideas of the self-made philanthropist Robert Owen, who encouraged a more ambitious development of trade unions. His *New View of Society* (1813) insisted that 'the past ages of the world present the history of human irrationality only, and that we are now but advancing towards the dawn of reason and to the period when the mind of man will be born again'. A radical change of environment, a return to the soil, and cooperative labour, he insisted, could redeem the evils of industrial society.

Thus *ad hoc* improvisation among the skilled artisans combined with a wider, if deceptive and impracticable, vision to create the first phase of organization, at its peak in the 1830s. Labourers might commit arson, landowners set man-traps and the yeomanry charge the crowd at Peterloo, while in 1820 the Cato Street conspirators would plot to murder the entire cabinet; but the rioter and the machine wrecker would give way to the trade unionist.

Once new and essentially forward-looking ideas of the rights of man and popular sovereignty had gripped the popular imagination, riots and disturbances tend to acquire a new dimension and assume a stable social and ideological content that they have lacked before . . . industrial society in France and England made an industrial working-class movement and working class political ideas.

Since the time of Wilkes and the Gordon Riots the 'patterns of political protest' had 'changed with the times'.[28]

So, in spite of much suffering and complaint, the first Industrial Revolution did not, as often believed, depress the workpeople into a revolutionary proletariat. And of its lasting benefits there is no doubt. Its hardship provoked sporadic violence and vigorous protest, but seldom doctrines of total revolution or anarchy. And if nothing was done by the authorities to cushion its impact, a paternalistic government would no doubt have hamstrung the enterprise without which it could hardly have taken place. Compared with the physical suffering and loss of political liberty caused by recent state-directed industrialization, the early Industrial Revolution in England was less terrible. There was no widespread famine or deportation, and Malthus's pessimism would not be vindicated in early industrial Great Britain. It was in Ireland in the 1840s that the famine would provide a dreadful 'control' experiment of the results of population increase without great industry to sustain it. The early Industrial Revolution had in fact shown the way out.

While therefore in the nineteenth century many continental countries would experience revolt every generation, England would, at worst, have riots; and the failure of the Chartist movement would provide an ironic backdrop to the continental revolutions of 1848. Here again, only one conclusion can be drawn. The new wealth produced was unevenly shared and a legacy of class hatred would be stored up; but the wealth was shared evenly enough for the majority of the people for the majority of the time to decide, when it came to the crunch, that they had more to gain by working the new system than by overthrowing it. The great non-event of the early and mid-nineteenth century would be the English Revolution.

<h1 style="text-align:center">7</h1>

The vigour of both riot and repression were typical of the age. From the raffish circle of the Prince Regent who, for all his neurotic instability, was often a discriminating patron of the arts, and from the intriguing and eloquent politicians, the high-living, gambling aristocracy and the newly rich,[29] down to the prize fighters, on whom all classes placed their bets, and the poachers, who risked their lives and liberty for a pheasant in battles with gamekeepers armed with shotguns and clubs, there is a great vitality. And British civilization, always many-sided, was now even more versatile. In contrast to the unbridled self-indulgence at the summit of society, there were now many more self-consciously respectable households among the gentry, merchants and professional men. Port-soaked judges who pronounced sentence of hanging or transportation for minor crimes are contemporary with romantic poets; with the extraordinary visions of Blake, breaking out of all the artistic conventions, or with the austerely elegant architecture of the neo-Greek revival. Many aristocrats and squires who hunted or shot all day, gambled and drank most of the night, and laid vast sums on a horse or a card, could still quote Virgil in a parliamentary debate and collect books whose print and binding were unsurpassed. And while a fashion for melodramatic 'subject pictures' now set in, perpetuating the 'academic' rules of composition of the eighteenth century, Turner (1775–1851) and Constable (1776–1837) were original geniuses with a new range;

contributing, for the first time in English history since the Anglo-Saxons, a major influence to European art. Constable, in particular, discarding the academic 'schools' and returning to an older craftsmanship, painted what he saw; the wind, rain and sunshine of the English landscape. He won his first reputation in Paris and profoundly affected the great French painters of the nineteenth century.

The late Georgian age was a time of war, industrial revolution and social strife; it was also singularly rich in 'characters', and in sport, intellect and the arts. At the top, the political world was hard and hectic. Politicians were no longer beheaded, but they were apt to cut their own throats: 'Samuel Whitbread in 1815, Sir Samuel Romilly in 1818, Castlereagh in 1822. . .'. The habit of hard drinking and the fashion for excessive bleeding may 'account for this tendency which prevails no longer among our legislators'.[30] Duelling, now with pistols, was still in fashion; Canning called out Castlereagh to a duel when both were in the cabinet. Speeches were still highly theatrical, though the younger Pitt had set a more sober fashion. When, for example, Canning made his famous pronouncement about the liberation of South America, that he had 'called a new world into existence to redress the balance of the old', his 'voice rose almost to a scream', and the speech was rapturously received. In contrast, the Duke of Wellington was laconic; on occasion devastating. Canning, he remarked, 'had no common sense, these South American States, see what a condition they are in . . . all these powers are nests of Pirates . . . and that is what Canning called calling a new world into existence'.[31] The contrast is representative of the romantic and realist aspects of an age.

Against this background of hard living and often of social brutality, men of serious mind, who would formerly have argued theology, now tried to improve the world. As already observed, Jeremy Bentham's confident eighteenth-century rationalism and indefatigable sense of mission, had won great celebrity. Wilberforce, the leader of the movement to emancipate the slaves, represents the new 'evangelical' Anglicans of the Clapham Sect, who altered the tone of much high society as well as of much middle-class life; and the economists, who, following Adam Smith, tried to rationalize the economic order, and the political theorists who attacked it for callous injustice, all now believed in 'progress'. And in one important field at least their belief had already been justified. Smallpox, the scourge of high and low, which had killed off Queen Mary II, the first Duke of Marlborough's heir, and Louis XV, and as a matter of course cut swathes throughout society high and low, had now been mastered. Edward Jenner (1749–1823) deserves far more credit in world history than he generally gets. Since the early eighteenth century smallpox had been treated by inoculation with a mild dose of the disease, but this procedure was risky and may well have spread it. Jenner, who worked at Berkeley in Gloucester, now observed that the milkmaids who got cowpox were immune from smallpox itself; in 1798 he began to 'vaccinate' with cowpox. By 1808 national vaccine centres were established in London.

In such a vigorous and many-sided society a wide range of literature flourished, some getting its effect by quiet observation and understatement, some by a simple or flamboyant romanticism. Jane Austen (1775–1818), developing the tradition of Richardson, is technically the most skilful of all the English novelists. She can hit off character in a subtle phrase or hint, and she observes society with a kindly, if ironic, insight long ago apparent in Chaucer. Sir Walter Scott, whose characterization now seems tedious, won immense popularity in Great Britain and abroad as the first major novelist to present the past with a serious attempt at authentic detail. The English tradition of genial satire was carried on by Thomas Love Peacock, whose *Nightmare Abbey* (1818) and *Crotchet Castle* made play both with romantic poets and the 'March' of improving 'Mind'. Where Fielding and Smollett had depicted the life of the road and the inn, he recalls the conversation of country house and club. It was the day, too, of the great Quarterly Reviews; the *Edinburgh* (1802), and the *Quarterly* (1809) were both widely influential, their contents more professional than the miscellaneous amenities of the *Gentleman's Magazine*. The literary criticism of Hazlitt and de Quincey has a new depth.

The romantic movement now found its most memorable expression in the poetry of Wordsworth, Coleridge, Shelley, Keats and Byron. Byron was the first English poet to become a major European figure:

a symbol of adventure, liberation, romance and mystery. His extraordinary combination of literary genius, worldly cynicism, theatrical melancholy, aristocratic disdain and political liberalism, together with the rumour not only of a multitude of sexual triumphs but of what used to be called 'nameless' vices, had made him even in his lifetime the object of a perennial fascination which he has retained ever since.[32]

He proclaimed that poets and all those of romantic and introspective sensibility were a law unto themselves, in the realizing of all facets of personality. Byron had immense influence in France, Italy, Germany and Russia.

But Wordsworth (1770–1850) was the greatest of these poets, profoundly original. His *Prelude* is the most powerful autobiographical poem in the language, and his cult of 'emotion recollected in tranquillity' related man to nature in a new way. The scepticism now coming in was assuaged by this contemplative vision of life, and Wordsworth's feeling for nature became a substitute for revealed religion. Here again, is introspection; the individual confronting the universe and by recalling moments of intense vision coming to a deeper understanding of life. Moreover, Wordsworth, though capable of majestic Miltonic rhythms, used simple language with uncanny skill to evoke place, time and personality. This cult of perception and contemplation for its own sake he plainly defined: he wished, he wrote, by a 'selection of language really used by men' to 'achieve a certain colouring of imagination, whereby ordinary things should be presented in an unusual aspect. . .'. This purpose reflects, in poetic idiom, the aim of John Constable when, discarding the conventions of the *picturesque*, he transfigured ordinary landscape and caught the changing face of nature as well as a lifetime of dedicated skill could catch it. While the great world was convulsed with great wars, political conflict and industrial change, by social unrest and popular discontent, these men of genius expressed the liberation of mind and spirit which is the most important aspect of the age.

22

THE MID-VICTORIANS

The mid-Victorians, with immense new wealth and industrial power behind them and a new range of professional knowledge, enriched and broadened out the vigorous civilization of the eighteenth century. Economic enterprise even went along with deliberate improvement when the worst consequences of the Industrial Revolution were tackled by the State, and there was a steady rise in population, which was now shifting from the mainly agricultural south to the industrial north and north west. British engineers constructed a vast network of railroads in the island and beyond, and with the repeal of the Corn Laws and free trade, booming textile and heavy industries created unprecedented prosperity. Although the brisk, high-handed diplomacy of Palmerston was in fact defensive, for the country had far more to lose than to gain in any continental commitment; the riches, confidence and optimism of the mid-Victorians, whose culture marked the climax of a confident and insular Great Britain, was guarded by a navy twice as powerful as any that could challenge it, the guarantee of an oceanic *Pax Britannica*.

In 1832 the Whig government extended the franchise, but the extension was very limited; most members of parliament came from the old kind of background, and the landed interest still remained predominant. But the majority of the ruling classes now accepted the need for the more urgent reforms. The still Hogarthian underworld below the brilliant society depicted by Horace Walpole and below the sedate circles described by Jane Austen, was now gradually cleaned up. The 'low' life still depicted by Dickens in the 1840s was still little less barbarous, but it was receding. Although most working-class supporters of the Reform Bill had soon been alienated, the Catholic emancipation of 1829 had avoided civil war in Ireland, and constitutional Irish government had at least been preserved while, on the continent, there would be mounting revolution and reaction. Within this consensus in politics, parliamentary Royal Commissions now began to find out the facts; and as the work of the Whig governments was carried on in the 1840s by Peel's Tory administration, a new kind of professional civil servant emerged to act on them. The establishment, it seems, had instinctively decided that the Whigs and Peelites could best contain the threat of revolution; the die-hard Tories and extremist radicals were both pushed aside, and the most militant popular discontent would be expressed, ineffectively, out of parliament. The predominant mid-Victorian political bias was Whig and reformist, with only brief Tory minority governments. Within the still very limited circles of the politically enfranchised nation the politics of the 'centre' predominated.

For the mid-Victorian House of Commons was very powerful. It was neither dominated by the Crown, nor by modern mass party discipline. With the Irish votes adding to political instability, it could make and unmake governments. It was now, and not, as once believed, in the eighteenth century, that the Crown became politically a dogeship, and the landowning and moneyed interests a quasi-Venetian oligarchy. In spite of the repeal of the Corn Laws in 1846, most of the landowners continued to prosper; as it turned out, the booming insular economy of the 1850s and 1860s did not need protection, and it was not until the railroads and steamships of the 1870s brought in American and Canadian wheat, that the full consequences of free trade became apparent. In 1867 the share of agriculture in the gross national product was still 15·7%: in 1900 it would be 6·6% and in 1925–34, 3·9%.[1] Following the start gained in the early Industrial Revolution, the Great Exhibition of 1851 marked the apex of Great Britain's role as the workshop of the world. 'A little island with a population half that of France was turning out about two-thirds of the world's coal, more than half its iron and cotton cloth'; and its income per head was far greater than that of France and Germany. In railroads, in shipping, finance and communications, Great Britain was supreme; 'the pace setter and the model' to the world.[2]

This more widely diffused prosperity now took the sting out of violent popular agitation; and the skilled workers drew apart from 'navvies' and 'casual labour' and farm 'hands'. Turning away from the visionary or petty projects of the 1820s and 1830s, they organized a wide range of craft trade unions, now aimed not at revolution but at conserving advantages already won. And the social order was further consolidated – not always advantageously – after Arnold of Rugby in the 1830s had set a new tone in the 'public' schools, which, old and new, assimilated the sons of the *nouveaux riches* into a broader establishment, with a peculiar code which made the upper and middle-class English much more conventional. But the deep-rooted and bitter division in English society which had appeared with the Industrial Revolution was not destroyed; it was covered up, to re-emerge in times of economic adversity and haunt the twentieth century.

With the fleet unchallenged and capital accumulating, trade more than Empire mattered. The Indian market was still the most important and prized; and if, following the gold rush, the small Australian population trebled in the 1850s, an expansive political 'imperialism' was not yet the fashion. The British remained intensely insular, and to the historian the main interest of this vigorous and creative time is still in the island itself.

The predominant convention of 'middle-class' respectability which followed the Hanoverian raffishness of George IV and William IV (1830–7), was mainly due to an Evangelical, Nonconformist and high Anglican reaction to the scepticism and latitudinarian worldliness of the eighteenth century. Victoria (1837–1901) and Albert (1840–61) now made the monarchy respectable: and as the Crown relinquished political power it gained in social influence. Victoria proved to be forceful, conscientious, conventional and representative; Albert, if often regarded as alien and pedantic, was able; the first intellectual to set the tone of the Court since Charles I. The monarchy, sunk to the depths in popular estimation, was now rehabilitated; and though in Victoria's long widowhood and retirement it went into a different kind of eclipse, the queen emerged in the 1890s as a formidable character, the popular and perennial symbol of Victorian Empire.

The penalty for all this affluence was severe. Great Britain became the most urban and proletarianized country in the world, with a population quite out of scale with her previous history and natural resources: from about ten million in 1800 it rose to over twenty-two million in 1850, by the 1950s it would be over fifty million. The island was at once the pioneer and the victim of an industrial process 'new in human experience'.[3] Exporting to live, with a population far outrunning food supply; overcrowded, megalopolitan – the population of London alone greater than that of any Scandinavian state – it would become particularly vulnerable to the fluctuations of world trade and to submarine and air attack.

But to the mid-Victorians, the prospect seemed excellent: they believed in what they saw and they thought it was progress; the more so because the new scientific knowledge appeared to guarantee it, for British scientific genius now had full scope. Darwin transformed the picture of man's place in nature; championed and popularized by T. H. Huxley, the new knowledge attained a pervasive influence, altering the climate of opinion over the whole educated world. So many-sided was the advance of British scientific method that a few famous names must be representative. Following the work of Cavendish and Sir Humphrey Davy, the physicist who said he wanted to 'interrogate nature', Faraday made fundamental discoveries in electro-magnetism, from which the telephone, the cinema, radio and the theory of relativity derive. In medicine, by the 1850s Florence Nightingale began to transform the standard of hospitals and nursing; in the 1860s, Lister devised aseptic surgery. Sir Edwin Chadwick pioneered the sanitation of great cities in a way never attempted anywhere before, and the engineer Brunel designed railroads, bridges and iron ships on a new and magnificent scale. So great a transformation was wrought by these colossal undertakings, unprecedented in history, that the mid-Victorians often seem set entirely on practical objectives.

Yet there was vigorous intellectual enterprise, both in the enrichment of old knowledge and in investigating new subjects, such as archaeology and anthropology, as well as in far-flung exploration. English humour took a new turn, and the 'nonsense' books of Lewis Carroll and Edward Lear have a unique flavour and a queer depth. As will be apparent, the range of Victorian literature is immense.

The age was thus extremely versatile and creative; though in one respect the mid-Victorians have been handicapped in the eyes of posterity. They are the first generation to wear really repellent clothes, and to be recorded accurately by the camera. Why the hideous fashion of deliberately shapeless trousers – a garment hitherto worn in the west only by barbarians – of starched linen with high collars cutting the neck and clumsy double-breasted coats topped by stove-pipe hats, should then have captured the formidable and enterprising *bourgeoisie* of western Europe, while their women plastered their hair with macassar oil and swamped their figures with crinolines and 'bustles', remains a sartorial mystery. Drab broadcloth now superseded the bottle greens, blues and fawns of Regency fashion; no longer, one may suppose, appropriate to the grime of an increasingly urban and industrial civilization. Then, following the Crimean War, beards came in; most of the Victorian celebrities are so disguised that it is hard to discern their characters, for the Victorians were less elegantly bearded than their Tudor and Stuart forebears. Along with the predominantly hideous architecture, furniture and interior decoration, Victorian fashion gives the age a stuffy aspect it does not deserve. In fact, in the long historical perspective, domestic tyranny, sexual hypocrisy, the hard cult of money and the smug cult of respectability, are not the most representative aspects of the time, but the immense energy and enterprise, the practical grasp and range, the independence and versatility. The mid-Victorians had the self-confidence of the last generation of British insular culture, gathering up the inheritance of the whole range of history here surveyed. For the outlook of their descendants would be changed by the influences of empire and its aftermath; by two great wars and a social and technological transformation of the social order by cosmopolitan forces out of scale with previous experience.

2

'It is often said,' writes Disraeli's latest and best biographer, 'that the 1832 Reform Bill gave political power to the "middle class" but on no plausible definition of the middle classes can the proposition be justified as it stands.' On the contrary, the Act of 1832 'continued to perpetuate a representative system based on "interests" rather than a mere counting of heads . . . the majority of counties plus small boroughs still proclaimed the dominance of the landed interest'.[4] The Whig aristocrats are now no longer regarded as liberals ready to bring in democracy. As already emphasized, they were realists who did what was inescapable. The Whig governments of Grey (1830–4) and Melbourne (1835–41), and the Tory administrations of Wellington and Peel (1834) and of Peel alone (1841–6), began to renovate an administration inherited from the eighteenth century and frozen during the Napoleonic Wars. Both parties now accepted the novel Benthamite idea of improvement by legislation. But in principle, the conservative opponents of the extension of the franchise, generally written off as 'blind' reactionaries, had a good case. After 1832 the growing predominance of the House of Commons and the political withdrawal of the monarch began to destroy the old 'balanced' constitution. In the long run a mass electorate was bound to discard it and to go on to attack property, the basis of the old way of life. And universal suffrage would give rise to the virtual if temporary dictatorship of cabinets elected with mass parties behind them, wielding powers far exceeding those of any government hitherto described, and collaborating with the tentacular bureaucracy of the modern social-democratic State. Once it was admitted that government had the right, and indeed the duty, to arrange a 'fairer' distribution of wealth, an increasingly egalitarian and bureaucratic society was predictable. Such a society could have its advantages; certainly it would be radically different from the world inherited by the privileged classes of 1832 and assumed by the individualistic élites and masses of mid-Victorian England. Following two world wars and a vast extension of state power, the old balance of the constitution would cease to exist. The Reform Bill of 1832 was the first step that counts.

Meanwhile immediate facts were faced. The Factory Act of 1833, appointing inspectors and limiting the hours of work to eight for children and twelve for adolescents, does not now seem particularly humane; but it was then a break-through. And, as already recorded, the final abolition of slavery throughout the Empire in 1833 at a cost of twenty million pounds in compensation, is to the credit of Grey's administration, and an event of world significance. Then the Municipal Reform

Act of 1834 abolished archaic corporations. Although many new industrial towns were not included and the Town Councils were elected by closefisted ratepayers, the traditional malversation of funds was diminished; a new instrument of improvement set up. The Poor Law Administration Act of 1834 was bitterly unpopular, but it changed the ramshackle parochial Tudor basis of poor relief, abolished 'outdoor' relief as devised by the Speenhamland magistrates, and grouped the parishes into 'Unions' centralized on the Poor Law Commissions in London. But the new 'Union' workhouses were made deliberately repellent, and it took decades of propaganda to get them humanized. At a grim price, they pushed the 'able-bodied' poor into an expanding labour market.

In 1829 during Wellington's first government, Peel had set up a regular metropolitan police force; and by the Police Act of 1839, decentralized county forces were created, superseding the ineffective local constables inherited from the Elizabethan age. A national register of births, deaths and marriages was compiled, and, in 1843, following Chadwick's *Report on the Sanitary Condition of the Labouring Classes*, a Royal Commission was appointed on the health of towns. By 1848 a Board of Health was set up, supplemented by local boards, and later more fully developed. Such, in essentials, were the relatively limited foundations of much of the bureaucracy of modern times. They were then an original departure.

Against this background of gradual and piecemeal improvement, the famous Victorian political dramas were played out. Nowhere is the versatility and brilliance of the time more apparent than in its statesmen, representative of different facets of society – Lord Grey, who had been a junior colleague of Fox and who hankered for his country house in Northumberland and reluctantly undertook his task of reform; Lord Melbourne, the cynical and charming Whig aristocrat who knew how to manage the young queen and presided, incongruously enough, over the kind of investigations and reforms described; Sir Robert Peel, the grandson of a self-made Lancashire textile manufacturer, but with Eton and Christ Church, Oxford, behind him, whose immense financial and administrative ability is typical of the central Tory tradition. Then, incongruously, there is the Byronic Jewish adventurer and novelist, Disraeli, who became such a rusé and sardonic man of the world, the wittiest character in public life since Charles II; and who, by sheer casual brilliance in debate and ability to deal with problems as they arose, won the leadership of a revived Tory or Conservative party, still based on the interests of the landowners and tenant farmers. And Disraeli at the height of his power appealed to a wider electorate as the impresario of the Empire. Gladstone came of Scottish descent, the son of a well to do Liverpool merchant who had made his fortune from trade with the West Indies, not excluding the slave trade. Like Peel, he had a brilliant career at Eton and Christ Church; he also combined immense financial and administrative ability with an evangelical religious fervour, to be fully expressed when he had worked his way from the Tories, through the Whig administration of Palmerston, out into the radical enthusiasms of the Liberal Party. He became its all too eloquent, tortuous and alarming prophet, at once hated and admired; the first high-minded demagogue in British history to become Prime Minister. He roused great audiences to a moral fervour that the Whig ancestors of the Liberal Party would have found disgusting and tried to introduce moral principles into foreign affairs, often with disastrous results.

Grey, Melbourne and Peel belong to the first half of the century; Disraeli and Gladstone came to their fullest powers in the 1870s and 1880s. It was Palmerston who represented the mid-Victorians. Born to affluence and an Irish peerage which did not exclude him from the House of Commons, this gay aristocrat was said to have neither Grey's aloofness nor Wellington's contempt. A witty and casual early nineteenth-century figure, as Foreign Secretary in the Whig governments in the 1830s, he brought a fresh and alarming wind into the Foreign Office. 'Life,' he wrote of their stuffier drafts, 'is not long enough to correct them and put them into plain English: planting sugar-cane would not be more laborious.'[5] Like Canning, he conducted government with what his biographer calls a certain 'benign casualness' and even flippancy. He was also the first major statesman to know how to handle the Press, which was now much more influential. This last great Whig statesman, a Lord of the Admiralty in 1807, and Prime Minister when he died in 1865, became immensely popular; 'in his later years the personification of England'. His patriotism, his prejudices and his language summarized the opinion of the ordinary man. 'Palmerston distrusted France and Russia; he called Austria "an old woman . . . a European China"; he had a low opinion of Spanish politicians and Italian absolutists, and he considered that all foreigners, at some time or another, might benefit by English advice and English examples. He saw no reason for concealing his opinions.'[6] Defending an enormous Empire, Palmerston again, like Canning, sought to maintain the balance of power as well as liberal principles; and he backed constitutional governments and encouraged liberal movements against the military régimes of Austria and Russia. Though the great continental military powers could call his bluff, as Bismarck did when he took over Schleswig-Holstein from Denmark, Palmerston often made England stand for liberty in Europe and gave a high mid-Victorian moral tone to the pursuit of a defensive political interest.

The decisions of these statesmen, from Grey to Gladstone, often had world-wide repercussions; more is known about them from the mass of their correspondence and despatches than of the statesmen of earlier times; and all have had admirable biographers. Here only their most important policies can be surveyed.[7]

3

These policies and their results now look different from the long-accepted picture. As already observed, the Reform Bill of 1832 was decisive in the long run, but it was very limited and it brought widespread disillusionment. The next major event, the repeal of the Corn Laws in 1846, was not, as often believed, the sudden result of the Irish potato famine that Wellington said had 'put Peel in his damn'd fright': it was part of a long-considered attempt to enhance prosperity by free trade. Peel was not stampeded by the anti-Corn Law League into a hasty *volte-face*. Concerned more with practical expedients than with theory, he had long been convinced – like many of the great landowners – that the ocean gave protection enough, and that repeal would be in the interests of the whole nation as well as of the manufacturers. Since taking office in 1841 to clear up the crisis created by the financially inept Whig government, Peel had reimposed income tax at 7d in the £1; while by the important Bank Act of 1844, which linked the currency more firmly to gold, and by the Companies Act which made registration and regular balance sheets compulsory, he had already increased business confidence. Gladstone, then a rising Tory, was already at the Board of Trade, and tariffs had already been whittled down: the Irish crisis only confirmed Peel's judgement. In spite of Disraeli's effective and unscrupulous attack which eventually won him the leadership of the right-wing Tories, the hounding of Peel from office, and the split in the party which kept it from effective power for twenty years, the dire consequences predicted did not take place. The sequel was free trade and the peak of Victorian affluence, inaugurated by that gigantic show case of glass and iron, the Crystal Palace.

Thus, during the mid-Victorian age, Whig centre-party administrations predominated. Lord John Russell's Whig–Peelite government lasted from 1846 to 1852. Then, following a Tory minority government led by Lord Derby, the Whigs came in again under Lord Aberdeen (1852–5). Then Palmerston succeeded him from 1855 to 1858, and, after another Tory interval under Derby, he formed his second and last administration (1859–65).

These mid-Victorian decades coincided with great prosperity at home, but with major crises on the continent. Though British prestige was at its climax and the navy unchallenged, the limitations of British power on the continent were underlined. The Crimean War of 1854–6 shook the prestige of the army. The Indian Mutiny of 1857–8 remained an affair within the Empire and was swiftly put down. Most important of all, the rise of Prussia in Germany went unchecked.

The Crimean War was not occasioned by an obscure dispute over Russian rights to protect the Orthodox Christian holy places in Jerusalem: it derived from the long Anglo–French policy of maintaining the balance of power in the Levant against Russia in the vacuum left by the Turkish decline, for the British wanted to contain what were considered serious Russian threats to Egypt and even India. The rights claimed in Jerusalem would have given the Russians extensive powers to protect Christian Orthodox minorities in the Balkans and Armenia; and the British, having abandoned Canning's policy of promoting the independence of the Balkan peoples as the best barrier against Russian advance, were reduced to maintaining the power balance by bolstering up the long decadent Turkish Empire.

In the campaign itself Anglo-French strategy proved inept and the tactics muddled. The war also revealed the archaic incompetence of the War Office and the amateurishness of the commanders. But in fact the bloody battles of Alma, Balaclava and Inkerman and the winter siege of Sebastopol achieved their objective, since they at least left the 'Eastern question' where it had been before. It would flare up again in the 1870s, when Disraeli and Salisbury again succeeded in checking Russian expansion, this time by diplomatic means; and when the British secured Cyprus as a base in the Levant.

The Indian Mutiny was more important for its consequences than for the lurid events it occasioned. It was not a nationalist uprising, but made by a minority of the highly-paid Sepoys of the Bengal army in the Ganges valley; and it was swiftly suppressed. But the atrocities committed on both sides recalled the worst days of Clive's India, and the brief emergency became a legend. Hence a slow poison in the relationship of rulers and ruled, long undermined when Macaulay had inevitably geared India to western education rather than to its own rich indigenous cultures, and encouraged a westernized and nationalistic outlook bound in time to put a term to the British Indian Empire.

Meanwhile, as massive shifts of power took place on the continent, the limitations of British insular authority became apparent. In 1859–60 the Italian state was indeed created, with British encouragement and connivance, if the decisive intervention was made by France; but the Prussian domination of Germany was to prove far more momentous. It began in 1864 with the seizure of Schleswig-Holstein from the Danes, when Palmerston had to back down; it continued in the Austro-Prussian war, and it culminated in the Franco-Prussian war of 1870–1. These events proved the prelude to two world wars, the destruction of the *Pax Britannica*, the eclipse of Europe and the dismantling of the European Empires. In 1865 when Palmerston died in office, aged eighty, 'events in Europe had passed beyond the range and interference of Great Britain. The decisions of the next five years belonged to Bismark and the Prussian army commanders'.[8]

By 1866 the last Whig government under Lord John Russell had petered out; but Gladstone, if still in his Whig-Peelite phase, had now emerged as a formidable free trade-orientated Chancellor of the Exchequer. And with the formation of the short-lived Conservative Derby–Disraeli government, the Reform Bill of 1867 extended the franchise to the whole artisan class by plain household suffrage, and added 938,000 votes to an electorate of 1,056,000. More elaborately organized political parties were now to emerge, competing for a more massive vote.

Against this background, the dynamic first Gladstone Liberal government of 1868–74 realized more comprehensive reforms than the Whig and Tory administrations in the 1830s and 1840s. And Disraeli – never a Tory democrat but a realist with an eye for the political main chance – would answer the challenge by combining extensive social improvement at home with a new imperialism abroad. The time of brisk complacent insularity and mid-Victorian consensus politics symbolized by Palmerston was over.

4

The social and economic background to these political events must now be considered. They were all, of course, conditioned by the fluctuations of the economy. From 1830 to 1850, following a time of predominantly falling prices and sporadic set-backs of a basically expanding production, two decades of rising prices and rising incomes set in. During the nineteenth century it is estimated that real national income per head roughly quadrupled: 'in both absolute and *per capita* terms the growth from decade to decade seems to have been positive and continuous over the whole period'.[9] Though the massive shift of population into the towns continued, the old landed interest of the great aristocracy and the richer gentry maintained its power, now often augmented by mining royalties and enormous rents from urban development. For here, as usual, the continuity of English history is remarkable. Lord Derby, for example, the Tory statesman, was descended from the Stanleys who, by deserting Richard III at Bosworth, had placed the Tudors on the throne; Lord John Russell from the first Earl of Bedford who had come to court from Dorset with Philip and Juana of Spain in 1506. Lord Salisbury, who followed Disraeli as Conservative leader, was directly descended from the first Earl, the architect of the Stuart succession. If the dukedoms of Marlborough and Wellington had been earned in great victories of European consequence, other magnates descended from the numerous illegitimates of Charles II, or from the Bentinck and Keppel favourites of William III. For all the push and drive of the new men, the mid-Victorian social order was still overwhelmingly dominated by the aristocracy. And this great landed interest had been bound up for centuries with the substantial squirearchy, often reinforced by fortunes derived from business. The aim of most self-made men was still to become assimilated in the landed establishment.

For the upper-middle classes, moreover, an immense range of opportunity was now opening out in the learned professions as well as in business, while the Anglican church provided comfortable careers to those with social influence and private means, if seldom to those without these advantages. And the universities, never more powerful, were now being linked to the bureaucracy by a new system of examinations. Among the mass of the people, in spite of the often appalling conditions of unskilled urban 'hands' and farm labourers, it now seemed likely that prosperity would swamp the class hatred rife in the earlier decades of the century, and diminish class distinctions in a wider affluence. Smiles's *Self Help*, that bible of the mid-Victorian *bourgeoisie*, appeared, like Darwin's *Origin of Species* and John Stuart Mill's *Essay on Liberty*, in 1859. A most revealing work, it held as an article of faith that men of ability would rise to the level they deserved, thus creating progress and diffusing prosperity.

Such an outlook was natural. In 1801 the national product of the country at current prices was worth about £232 million; by 1851 it was worth £523 million, and twenty years later, £1917 million. Iron production multiplied more than four times between 1832 and 1852; coal production ten times between 1800 and 1870. The railway boom had climaxed in 1847. After the building of the Liverpool to Manchester railway, constructed in 1832, London had been linked to Bristol, Southampton and Manchester; by 1846 there were over 3000 miles of track; by 1850 over 6500, and by 1870 there would be 13,000. The social effect of this infrastructure of great industry was naturally profound; provincials began to travel as a matter of course and a new network of business and communication linked the smoky manufacturing towns and augmented the influence of London and the north. The ancient universities and market towns might deliberately place their railway stations as far away as they could, and conservatives lament the violation of the countryside; but within three decades the tempo of life had been transformed, the regional barriers broken down. The railways were soon employing more men than even the textile industries.

The impact of these fundamental changes on the work people was to sort them out and diminish solidarity. In the earlier decades of the century there had been three main methods of protest. In 1834 Robert Owen, the paternalist reformer who had made his own fortune at New Lanark, had helped to found a Grand National Consolidated Trade Union for the vast majority of the workers who had still not been enfranchised. Along with a Co-operative movement to evade the normal processes of the market, this ambitious organization was designed to transform society. But after giving rise to various strikes it had broken down. At the other end of the scale, were the small Friendly Societies of agricultural labourers, to which the Tolpuddle labourers in Dorset had been affiliated, to their cost. Sentenced to seven years' transportation to Australia, their plight roused nation-wide indignation among the urban workers; they became the 'Martyrs' of trade union tradition and, after two years, they were repatriated.

Much more spectacular but ephemeral, the Chartist movement had now flared up, It occurred mainly among the skilled workers, disillusioned at the continued restriction of the franchise and resentful of a society in which the Devil took the hindmost. They were set more on political than on economic objectives, harking back to those of the Georgian radicals, and demanding manhood suffrage, secret ballots and annual parliaments. Chartism, said Fergus O'Connor, the Irish agitator who exploited and discredited it, appealed to 'fustian jackets, unshorn chins and blistered hands'; and one Wiltshire Chartist stated his characteristic objectives plainly: 'plenty of roast beef, plum pudding and strong beer by working three hours a day'.[10]

The influence of the Chartists waxed and waned with the fluctuations of the economy. They worked through monster petitions and demonstrations to persuade parliament to grant their demands. The 'child of poor harvests and poverty, bad housing, ill-health and unemployment',[11] the movement reached two peaks, in 1837–42 and in 1848. Naturally it got nobody very far: with the prosperity of the mid-century it lost support, and it was superseded by more constructive initiative.

For with the passing of the 'Hungry Forties', the more skilled artisans began to found bigger craft unions, such as the Amalgamated Society of Engineers. The joiners, stonemasons, coal-miners, builders and bricklayers all began to organize themselves into unions – and they would build them up into a power to be reckoned with. Though their position in law remained precarious, sixty years after the passing of the Combination Laws and a generation after their repeal (in 1824), the skilled workers of the country laid the foundation of these societies which were ultimately to do far more than defend a received standard of living against encroachment . . . the trade union movement between 1850 and 1860 was thus the first example of a constructive political achievement carried out almost entirely by working men for working men.[12]

Though well organized, with permanent officials and regular dues, the mid-Victorian trade unions were not yet the massive and bureaucratic unions of modern times. But they superseded the over-ambitious or petty movements of the first stage of working-class solidarity and the unconstructive if spectacular methods of the Chartists. They reflected mid-Victorian respectability and individualism; predominantly liberal-radical rather than socialist.

The gradual but increasing emancipation of women was another important aspect of the time. It owed much to John Stuart Mill, the most influential exponent of mid-Victorian individualism tempered by liberal ideals. And apart from this aspect of his thought, his classic *Essay on Liberty* (1859) obtained extraordinary prestige; indeed, after a long eclipse, it is now again appreciated as the consequences of more dogmatic political theory have become apparent. For Mill stated that 'human goals are many, not all of them commensurable, and in perpetual rivalry with one another'; and, like Burke, he denounced 'ideological conformity and the vivisection of actual human societies into some fixed pattern dictated by our fallible understanding of a largely imaginary past or a wholly imaginary future'.[13] And far from merely 'attempting to inject feeling into the adamantine doctrines of Bentham', he gave the idea of liberty a new Humanist content, restating the old English concern for morality in agnostic terms. Indeed, the *Essay* 'burnt itself into the consciences of each succeeding generation of liberals; whatever else they discarded from mid-Victorian radicalism, they retained the *Essay* – it troubled the consciences of converted Marxists and mellowed the convictions of British socialists'.[14]

Mill, like nearly all his contemporaries, did not realize how precarious was the society he took for granted, for it depended on an exceptional concurrence of prosperity and power; and he was far too hopeful that a rather priggish middle-class élite could 'chide and guide' governments. His religion of humanity, too, now seems curiously arid; but he discerned the dangers of egalitarian mediocrity, bureaucratic power and mass propaganda. He stated that the price paid for persecution of opinion is stagnation; that the precious and only instrument of progress is speculative genius, however odd; and that a civilization that suppresses diversity of thought and variety of taste and conduct must ossify.

His objective was humane and sensible; to enable men to make the best of themselves in a free society, and his vindication of liberty is far from being the fusty and dated political theory of a long-superseded middle class. It remains, even in the present context, one of the most valuable mid-Victorian achievements; a vindication of the importance of personality and a warning against the mounting abuse of power.[15]

5

When the eminent Victorian Walter Bagehot, who had none of the pomposity often attributed to his generation, but a casual, worldly and colloquial brilliance, wrote in 1867 that representative institutions 'let the rulers know' or have 'means to learn what the nation would endure and what it would not endure', he hit upon a reason for the unwritten English constitution's success, a theme apparent in this survey. Bagehot believed in progress; it arose from primitive incoherence through the 'cake of custom' and 'drilling aristocracies' that 'kept the type perfect', up to the 'animated moderation' of government responsive to intelligent opinion.[16] This is the note struck constantly by the confident advocates of the liberal experiment, who regarded their civilization as a proof of advance and, though they sometimes realized that it was insecure, hoped to extend it to the mass of the people – even to the ends of the earth. Where the late Georgian establishment had fought back against what they considered the tides of barbarism and got away with heavy repression, the mid-Victorians set themselves to tame the masses, and believed that compassion and knowledge would in time elevate the entire society. And this belief was natural. As already emphasized, the increasingly predominant and original strain in mid-nineteenth century British thought was scientific; and it had deepened and widened the Benthamite 'March of Mind' inherited from the rationalist eighteenth century.

Appropriately, the decisive influence of Darwin and Huxley had early matured on far-flung voyages. The first had been made in 1831–6, when the Whig governments were undertaking their administrative reforms, and it took Darwin round the world in H.M.S. *Beagle*; outwards by South America and across the Pacific to Australia, back by South Africa. The second had been in H.M.S. *Rattlesnake* in 1846–50, coincident with the repeal of the Corn Laws and its sequel, when Huxley visited Australia, the great Barrier Reef and New Guinea. The voyage of the *Beagle* had first elicited Darwin's genius as a naturalist; and 'in its influence on modern man's outlook upon the world', writes Darwin's editor, 'no voyage since Columbus matches the voyage described in this book'.[17] The voyage of the *Rattlesnake* made Huxley a general biologist, and it gave him his start; on this basis he would become the celebrated exponent of what he termed an '*Active Scepticism* . . . which increasingly thinks to overcome itself and by well-directed research to attain a kind of conditional certainty'.

This had been the method behind *The Origin of Species*, which 'presented a straightforward overwhelming mass of facts attesting the great fact of evolution; summing up and explaining knowledge, Darwinism won the day with surprising speed'.[18] Though it remained for Mendel and De Vries to investigate how the pressure of environment worked on the immense variety of mutations presented to it over a huge span of time, Darwin's principles have never been refuted.

So the mythology of a 'special Creation' in 4004 B C was superseded; a mental revolution today hard to appreciate, but as decisive as that made by Isaac Newton, another English scientist. Many Victorians suffered agonies of 'doubt'; but most of their descendants soon got used to an agnostic outlook strange to that of all the previous generations here surveyed. As Newton had finally destroyed the box-like medieval geocentric cosmos, so now the facts presented by Darwin and Huxley superseded the theological dogmas that still conditioned even many of the ablest minds. The more adaptable theologians and psychologists were now able to reinterpret their experience.

These scientists, with their world-wide influence, were typically mid-Victorian, with the self-reliance and individualism of their time and class. This self-assurance, often based on a secure private income, is apparent in most of the Victorian pioneers, who flung themselves into vast subjects with an enviable gusto. Buckle, for example, whose *History of Civilization in England* first appeared in 1857, the year of the Indian Mutiny, sweeps with superb flair over the entire geographical setting of the world; and Lecky's *The History of The Rise and Influence of Rationalism in Europe* (1865, the year of Palmerston's demise,) paints a colourful and confident panorama of the defeat of ancient superstition. The experience of India and its elaborate and ancient cultures and of far-flung contacts with primitive societies, brought home the relativity of morals and beliefs. Maine's *Ancient Law* and Tylor's *Primitive Culture* are pioneer works in comparative law and anthropology.

The education of élites and would-be élites was thus greatly expanded and enriched. But in popular education the mid-Victorians failed, handicapped by the religious strife between rival denominations unwilling to see the State sponsor anything but their own kind of instruction. And so great was the prestige of Oxford and Cambridge, both strongholds of the Anglican Church, that any secularized education had a hard struggle. The high eighteenth-century culture had been based on an exacting but narrow classical training, extended in the early nineteenth century to include mathematics, but not modern languages, history or geography – still less science. But in 1848, Cambridge set up 'triposes' in natural and moral sciences, supplementing those in mathematics; and in 1850 Oxford created 'honour schools' in history, science and law. Linked with the two ancient universities by closed endowments, even the ancient public schools, Eton and Winchester, Westminster and Harrow, were now subjected to 'reform'. Dr Arnold at Rugby, where he reigned from 1828 to 1841, had brought a new evangelical fervour into education and a closer, if often tenser, relationship between masters and boys.

The oldest foundations, Eton and Winchester, still preserved their esoteric traditions; but his gospel, often distorted, took on in the new public schools. In the 1840s and 1850s they developed a tradition of muscular Anglican Christianity and of the 'stiff upper lip'. So spartan were Marlborough and Cheltenham, Clifton and Wellington, that anyone who had been through them took subsequent hardships in their stride. But, as already observed, this new influence was often Philistine and hidebound, and if it did not much affect the mid-Victorians, it would affect their descendants. As G. M. Young wrote,

the larger and freer upbringing of the earlier Victorians had made them a more receptive and independent audience for literature and science, for philosophic or political controversy; and for this closing of the general intelligence, the replacement of the fresh and vigorous curiosity of the former generation by vaguely social, vaguely moral, vaguely intellectual convention, the public schools must take their share of blame.[19]

And the class bias of education was now more widely emphasised. Even the new University of London, founded in 1828 and expanded in the 1830s, had to face hostility and social prejudice, and the ancient grammar schools now further lost prestige, swamped by the class-conscious 'public' schools. As for the education of the masses, most self-made businessmen, themselves with little education, saw no reason to give the 'lower orders' any 'ideas above their station' or increase their competitive power. In the skilled trades the tradition of apprenticeship was still strong, and there seemed little need for State-sponsored technical education. In 1858 an enquiry into popular education reported that 'among the poorer classes only one child in twenty received any sort of education after the age of thirteen'. It was not until 1868, under Gladstone's first administration, that the problem was tackled on a national scale. And this backwardness would handicap late Victorian England, when American and continental competition became severe. Nor have the consequences even now been eradicated.

Although technologically and scientifically the mid-Victorians had shown genius, they had failed to adapt education to take in and humanize science and technology, or to change the inherited aura of privilege, emphasised as far back as the Restoration, of the great schools and their modern imitators. The Victorian culture of the old universities was formidable and set vigorous standards for élites, and the tradition of liberal reform, which emanated so much from Jowett's Balliol, would affect policy in the governments of 1906–14; but the failure in scientific and popular education could result in narrowness, amateurishness and complacency.

6

The main theme which can be discerned through all this Victorian culture is the conflict between the 'March of Mind', the cult of material progress and experimental science, and the continuing and various aspects of the romantic movement. Some of the most eloquent Victorian writers denounced their age. Carlyle, for example, a Scottish genius much affected by German romantic philosophy, denounced the whole trend of the times with a rhetoric which was curiously pervasive, since it combined the Calvinist sense of sin with a robust cult of heroic individuals wrestling with fate. Carlyle detested industrial civilization and democracy. The showy and eloquent Macaulay's *History of England from the Accession of James* II (1848–61), glorified the Whig interpretation of the English past as leading up to the Victorian climax; but Carlyle's *French Revolution* (1837) and *Letters and Speeches of Oliver Cromwell* (1845) depicted heroic improvisation and heroic failure in a world whose only law is masterful will. This romantic cult of 'heroes' had a wide influence; the more so since conveyed in an original style, at once rhetorical and public, intimate and personal. Both Macaulay and Carlyle had a vast public. They symbolize the contrast between 'progress' and romanticism.

Further, while the scientists were beginning to sap the foundation of conventional religion, the Whig governments in the 1830s had tried to reform the Anglican Church – cutting down the revenue of Canterbury to a mere £15,000 a year from £30,000, and redistributing some of the enormous Church revenues. Naturally the old cry was raised of 'the church in danger'. The Evangelicals had long made a cult of intense personal religion and good works and would inspire much of the far-flung missionary enterprise of the day, in continents unknown to their Anglo-Saxon forerunners; but they were 'Low Church'. Now in 1833, a new Oxford 'Tractarian' movement was initiated by Keble, already a popular hymn writer; it was developed by Pusey and Newman, who

433

reasserted the mystical authority of the Church as an institution and vindicated ritual and ornament. Pugin now designed 'pointed or Christian architecture' to inspire the congregations; and though, by 1845, Newman's critics thought he had given the show away by joining the Catholic Church, ritualistic romanticism had brought back music and colour into the Anglican church. There had been nothing like it since Laud's cult of the 'beauty of holiness'.

From more humanistic assumptions, Matthew Arnold's *Culture and Anarchy* (1869) attacked the more blatant middle-class moneymakers, whom he designated as active 'philistines'; enemies of culture, as against the aristocratic 'barbarians' who were merely innocent of it. Arnold denounced the insularity and ugliness of an age that, as Disraeli put it, had often 'mistaken comfort for civilization'; while Ruskin, whose *Stones of Venice* appeared in 1851–3, made the most eloquent, popular and effective onslaught of them all against the materialism of the time. He had a genius for giving intriguing titles to his books – *The Crown of Wild Olive, Sesame and Lilies, Unto this Last* – and proclaimed that great art must express humane values. He became a prophet not only of aesthetic perception, but of a radical reform of society. William Morris, too, would revolt against the ugliness of industrial civilization, and set much needed new standards for interior decoration among the more sensitive of the *bourgeoisie*. He would advocate a return to craftsmanship and rural life, presenting an idealized vision of the Middle Ages and advocating a sentimental socialism.

The most permanent memorial to this widespread romantic revolt against the predominantly industrial, technological and scientific trend of the time, which marks it off from anything that went before, is architectural. The curiosities of the Gothic revival have been described by Lord Clark, and appreciated by Sir John Betjeman. These churches and public buildings remain agreeably conspicuous when in the right place, if repellent when in the wrong one; the monument to a romantic minority protest, as much representative of its time as the more massive and pervading industrial barbarism.

In an age when the gross were utilitarian and the men of fine spirit were disillusioned, the Gothic Revivalists . . . had one dominating ideal and they converted the materialists to that ideal, as only great enthusiasts can. We may envy their solidly furnished spiritual world, 'blessed are those who have taste', wrote Nietzsche, 'even though it be bad taste'.[20]

Meanwhile, in spite of the achievement of Constable and at a time when the French were creating superb masterpieces, English artists remained insular and conventional. The one original move in painting came through the semi-religious 'Pre-Raphaelite' brotherhood. Break-

434

ing away from the popular and accurate art of Frith, who, within his limitations, painted well, or of Landseer, who, within his, painted badly, these pre-Raphaelite romantics tried to recreate the meticulous art of the Flemish masters and the spiritual force of the Italian 'primitives'. Alembicated and self-conscious, they enjoyed bright colours in an artistic world dominated by dim portraits of aldermen or misty evocations of highland sheep. So they, too, made their protest.

But when the best has been said for mid-Victorian architecture and art, Victorian fiction is in another class. The novel, already highly developed in the eighteenth century and late Georgian times, now shows great vitality. Dickens, whose *Pickwick Papers* appeared in the 1830s, poured out a spate of novels depicting a vast social panorama: he is the English Balzac and much less cynical. He was the first novelist to describe the new industrialized urban civilization, in all its squalor, vigour and variety, and he is essentially urban; an avid observer of a shifting competitive society, with all its frustration, snobbishness and hypocrisy; its cruelty, humour and sentiment. Thackeray, too, is essentially a social observer, but much too detached to share Dickens' passion for social reform; while George Eliot (Mary Ann Evans), whose *Mill on the Floss* was published in 1860, *Silas Marner* in the year after, and *Middlemarch* in 1871, is 'gravely and philosophically in revolt'.[21] She anatomized provincial life and relates her characters to the social problems of a world more homespun than Thackeray's and not so colourful and eccentric as that of Dickens. But the most representative Victorian novelist is Trollope, who in *Barchester Towers* (1857) caught the exact social atmosphere of the Anglican Church in its cathedral cities and parishes, while well able to depict the political and social intrigues of London society. Anyone who wants to know how high political influence was then exercised can do no better than study the tactics of the Duke of Omnium and his creatures. Moreover, the Victorians had a Prime Minister who was also a famous novelist, and whose extraordinary career was punctuated by highly coloured evocations of the life he knew and on which he so cleverly imposed his fantasies. Disraeli's *Vivian Grey* (1826) and *Contarini Fleming* (1831), were followed by *Coningsby* in 1844 and *Sybil* the year after. *Lothair* appeared in 1870, and in the penultimate year of his life the old wizard wrote *Endymion*. These works, in patches preposterous, display a world rather larger than life; and they made their author a substantial amount of money.

The mid-Victorian poets also display the conflict between an inherited romanticism and cult of nature, coming down particularly through Keats and Wordsworth, and the doubt and scepticism created by the new scientific knowledge. Tennyson's *In Memoriam* (1850) is the

435

first memorable poem in the language on the impact of scientific discovery on human life: with his habitual skill, Tennyson re-creates the landscape of his memories, and relates it to the horror of '*Nature red in tooth and claw*'. This must have dawned on many people through the ages; but they had written it off as part of providential order whereby the creation was subordinate to man, or had been too 'red in tooth and claw' themselves to notice it. Now, man was placed right in the middle of it, like the other animals, and Tennyson had to 'trust the larger hope'. Whether or not his solution was convincing, the problem had now been eloquently stated. Further, Tennyson, whose technical skill was superb, had a chameleon-like sensibility to the wide range of moods of the Victorian public, reacting to public events as well as to private experience. No Laureate could have been more representative. Naturally the Queen made him a peer.

Browning, whose *Pippa Passes* appeared in 1841, argues away in verse with a tense, high-wrought, speculative power; and Matthew Arnold carries on the Wordsworthian tradition of introspection related to natural beauty. If, unlike Tennyson, Browning can be robustly optimistic, Arnold is as much worried as any of them about the loss of faith, his poetry haunted by regret for lost certainties. But Arthur Hugh Clough, had his lighter moments and resumed the tattered mantle of Butler's *Hudibras*. He could even write:

> *Thou shalt have one God only; who*
> *Would be at the expense of two?*
> *. . . Thou shalt not kill; but need'st not strive*
> *Officiously to keep alive.*

And perhaps William Johnson, later William Cory, 'who went to Eton as a master in 1845 and left it in somewhat mysterious circumstances in 1872',[22] struck the most representative mid-Victorian note, luxuriating in sentimental regret, as in *Heraclitus*:

> *I wept as I remember'd how often you and I*
> *Have tired the sun with talking and sent him down the sky.*
> *And now that thou art lying, my dear old Carian guest,*
> *A handful of grey ashes, long, long ago at rest,*
> *Still are they pleasant voices, thy nightingales, awake,*
> *For Death, he taketh all away, but them he cannot take.*

With the *fin de siècle*, this prevalent tone of lush melancholy and of the evening shades closing in, would become more pronounced. More representative of the vigour and the defiance of the mid-Victorians, the dying Emily Brontë wrote her last lines:

436

Though earth and man were gone,
And suns and universes cease to be,
And Thou were left alone,
Every existence would exist in Thee.

There is not room for Death,
Nor atom that his might could render void:
Thou – Thou art Being and Breath,
And what Thou art may never be destroyed.

23

CLIMAX OF EMPIRE

'No Caesar or Charlemagne,' remarked Disraeli of the British Empire, 'ever presided over a dominion so peculiar.'[1] No Emperor of Han China, he might have added; no Kublai Khan. It was larger and more diverse than any other; it contained about a quarter of mankind; it was linked by a network of strategic bases, coaling stations and cables, and guarded by the most powerful navy in the world. Formidable as has been the impact of other European empires – Iberian, French and Dutch – the British has had the greatest effect on world history. It largely determined the development of North America, Australasia and South Africa; it affected massive Asian cultures far older than itself, and it determined the future of African and Polynesian peoples confronted with western technology and civilization. Like the Industrial Revolution, its consequences were quite out of proportion to its insular origins.

Though they drew their wealth from world trade, the mid-Victorians had been little concerned with the Empire. Now, running parallel with popular nationalism abroad, the British developed a more self-conscious imperialism: in part perhaps in compensation for their fading industrial supremacy; in part from the conviction, fostered in the post-Arnold public schools, of their moral mission; mainly, of course, for profit. Among all the powers, this vast and vulnerable trading Empire had the most to lose, and the greatest interest in maintaining peace. But by the end of the century there could no longer be a *Pax Britannica*. First, the country became involved in continental alliances; then, in 1914–18 and in 1939–45, in wars which dwarfed even the struggle against Napoleon, much more deeply affected the life of the people, and vastly increased the powers of government, never shaken off.

But though during the mid-nineteenth century the British had not been able to prevent the wars which had now made Germany dominant in Europe – indeed, until 1904 they regarded the French as the main enemy – they were still extremely formidable. Colossal wealth, accumulated since the Industrial Revolution from textile and heavy industries, from half the global tonnage of merchant shipping, and from overseas investments and financial services, still made London the monetary capital of the world. Set back by the depression of the 1870s and outclassed in new industries by the Americans and the Germans, the British still retained a big lead in overall exports and predominant financial power. Hence the mixture of admiration and dislike with which they were widely regarded on the continent. The assets of the Empire were wildly overestimated by those without a 'place in the sun'. In fact free trade with the rest of the world in 1896 amounted to £745 million as against £183 million with the Empire, and British governments reluctantly entered the scramble for Africa to keep rivals out rather than extend what they had. In the year of the Diamond Jubilee of 1897, the African colonies took only 1·2% of British exports, while financially London was always a global not an imperial capital.[2]

Such was the country and Empire, now set, like the other major nation states of Europe, on a collision course towards the Great War of 1914–18; that first bout of mechanized conflict in which they all committed political suicide, began a debasement of international life now taken for granted, and transformed the world power struggle into a confrontation of Eurasian and Atlantic spheres of influences charged with the threat of nuclear annihilation.

2

Against this background the policy of British governments must be considered. With a population which was rising from twenty-two and a half million in the mid-nineteenth century to over fifty million in the mid-twentieth, the country was the most megalopolitan and proletarianized in the world, and with its run-down agriculture it was now dependent on imports for more than half its food. Yet the economy sustained a high standard of living and a constant expectation of betterment. The assumption of inevitable progress was almost universal, and both Liberal and Conservative governments pressed on with the administrative and social improvements first launched in the 1830s and 1840s. Gladstone's first government (1868–74) and Disraeli's second Conservative administration (1874–80) both carried through far-reaching reforms; both parties now had a mass political organization behind them and appealed to a widening electorate. The household suffrage brought in by Disraeli in 1867 was no 'leap in the dark', but designed to maintain a balance between the radical towns and conservative countryside; but the Ballot Act of 1872 and the Rural Franchise Act of 1884 went much further towards full democracy.

The trade unions, too, were now more powerful. Originally craft unions, spontaneously organized to defend wage levels which were the highest in Europe, they were now including the unskilled workers in mass pressure groups of growing influence. Their powers, always greater than those of trades unions on the continent, were now defined and

439

confirmed by both Liberal and Conservative governments. The organized 'working classes' were also reaching out for political power. In 1893 the Independent Labour Party was founded; by 1900 a parliamentary Labour Party with trade union backing, distinct from the Liberal radicals. In 1889 *Fabian Essays*, advocating a gradual and constitutional transition to socialism, gave a lead all the more formidable for not being Marxist and foreign. By 1906 there would be fifty-six Labour members of parliament. Further, in 1889, the dockers were strong enough to win a major strike and the unions were demanding, and beginning to get, an eight-hour day that mid-Victorian employers would never have conceded. This power of mass organized labour was new; and it had coincided with the rise of a bureaucracy selected by examination not by patronage.

As already observed, the typical mid-Victorian élites – and in particular the representative J. S. Mill – had been alarmed at the prospect of mass democracy and bureaucratic state power. Now the Balliol philosopher, T. H. Green, whose complicated *Lectures on the Principles of Political Obligation* were published, after his death, in 1882, was preaching a more positive liberalism. He advocated much more state action to 'hinder hindrances to the good life', which he hoped would be led by everybody, and he set a brisker tone of public morality. He and his influential followers believed that, given a chance, the populace would adopt their own high moral standards, and their views contributed to the foundation of the Welfare State by the pre-war Liberal governments. The Fabian socialists were even more optimistic than the Liberals. They welcomed the new mass society, and an extension of state power that the old Liberal individualists would not have tolerated; advocated state ownership of the means of production, nationalization of coal mines and railways, the redistribution of property by progressive taxation and the destruction of hereditary privilege by death duties. While Marxist doctrines of inevitable class war and proletarian dictatorship, and syndicalist ideas of sudden revolution through a general strike, never took on in Great Britain, the Fabians, in alliance with the trade unions, would contribute to a peaceful social revolution, accelerated by the extension of state power in two world wars. This outcome may be regarded as the usual way in which a changing British establishment survives, substituting a 'meritocracy' for hereditary privilege and bureaucratic 'status' for *laissez-faire* competition. It can also be regarded as the deserved end of the illusions of the Victorian Liberals, lost to their own real interests and set for destruction before the combined forces of big business, independent or nationalized bureaucracy and admass opinion.

Meanwhile, with the accession of Edward VII (1901–10),[3] the plutocratic and imperialist society of late Victorian England took on a new cosmopolitan panache. The generation who went into the First World War with such strange exhilaration had centuries of insular security and wealth behind it; hence the self-confidence and staying power which sustained the struggle, and was still unimpaired in the Second. It is difficult for those who have experienced only the frustrations and austerities of post-imperial Britain to realize the spirited, cheerful and politically brash outlook of the Edwardians of all classes: even the critics were confident of a pacific and prosperous future.

In the vast imperial panorama only the most outstanding features can be surveyed, so far have we travelled from the miniature affairs of Romano–Celtic Britain or Anglo-Saxon, or even Elizabethan England. First the main political events at home; then the vicissitudes and expansion of the Empire and of economic and social change must be considered; then the outstanding achievements of the sciences, now though still little recognized, the most creative aspect of this civilization. The less distinguished contribution of the visual arts will also be touched upon, and the still remarkable quality of the drama and literature. For the writers rooted in late Victorian times had a formidable confidence and range; as in their contrasting ways Thomas Hardy, H. G. Wells and Rudyard Kipling, and while the verse of Masefield has hardly stood the test of time, the memory of Rupert Brooke seems symbolically secure, representing an idealism which would not survive the holocaust to which he and his generation were consigned.

3

The long Whig–Liberal predominance which had culminated under Palmerston, now shifted to a conflict of Liberals and Conservatives, in which on balance the Conservatives would predominate. In 1880 Disraeli's government was ousted by Gladstone's second administration (1880–5). Then Lord Salisbury's Conservative government, though replaced for a year by Gladstone's third, lasted from 1886 to 1892. And after the Liberal Gladstone and Rosebery administrations of 1892–5, the Conservatives regained power for over a decade under Salisbury (1895–1902) and then Balfour, until the landslide Liberal victory in January 1906, when Campbell-Bannerman came in, to be succeeded two years later by Asquith (1908–15).

During the 1870s and 1880s, the European situation remained relatively stable. The main enemy still seemed to be Russia, with France still a potential danger. When in 1877 the Russians defeated the Turks and threatened Constantinople, they were again thought to threaten British communications with India, now more dependent on

Egypt through the Suez Canal. At the Congress of Berlin in 1878 Disraeli's shrewd diplomacy, playing Austria–Hungary against Russia, reprieved the Turkish Empire, winning in effect the second phase of the Crimean War. Following the British wars in the Sudan and South Africa – part of colonial history later described – the mounting hostility of Germany became apparent, added now to the hostility of France. And though the partition of Africa was brought about without a European war, by the turn of the century it was plain that Wilhelmine Germany was challenging the British supremacy in the North Sea, and building a specialized fleet to this end against the all-purpose British navy.

British isolation had never been by choice; nor particularly splendid.* When, in fear of the Germans, Russia made an alliance with the French, the British had already allied themselves to the Japanese, who would take care of the Pacific while they dealt with the west. And though during the Fashoda crisis in the Eastern Sudan, the British and French came near to war, by 1904 they had made a permanent settlement; the British having a free hand in Egypt, the French in Morocco. Hence an informal *entente cordiale*, which led to the French fleet guarding the Mediterranean, and the British the Channel, the North Sea and the Eastern Atlantic. So a Franco–Russian alliance, to which the British were in fact heavily committed, now confronted the German-Austro-Hungarian alliance, which had the unreliable support of the Italians. Such in essentials was the background of power politics which gave rise to the naval armaments race with Germany and to the First World War.

In this increasingly sinister setting, the British continued the work of administrative and social improvement. Gladstone's first administration arranged that the civil service should be recruited by competitive examination; it went a long way to modernize the universities, and removed the religious tests demanded for entry to them. Forster's Act of 1870, long overdue, founded a national system of education; by the 1880s compulsory and, by the 1890s free. Even the law was rationalized: the Judicature Act of 1873, devised by the Lord Chancellor Selborne himself, was 'a piece of tidying up on the largest scale in a field littered with the most venerable survivals from the Middle Ages'.[4] Cardwell, as Secretary for War, abolished the purchase of commissions and improved conditions of recruitment and service. And, contrary to modern experience, these reforms were cheaply brought about, for Gladstone wanted wealth to 'fructify in the pockets of the people'.

* See Christopher Howard, *Splendid Isolation*, London, 1967, *passim*. Salisbury in fact used the phrase only to describe the remoteness of Great Britain from the internal affairs of the Turkish Empire, and to contrast continental conscription with British voluntary enlistment.

Disraeli, in his second administration, also ready to adjust society to inevitable change, tackled problems of housing, health and sanitation that the *laissez-faire* Liberals had left outstanding. The fall of his government was due mainly to the economic depression of the late 1870s. But apart from imperial problems, internal policy in the 1880s and 1890s was distorted by the problem of Ireland, which continued to haunt the British – and the Irish – until after the First World War. Gladstone repeatedly tried to tackle the question and introduce the kind of Home Rule successful in the Dominions. But the attempt failed, blocked by the ancient hostility between the Protestant north and the Catholic south. During the 1870s Irish nationalism had been focused and fanned by Parnell's agitation for Home Rule for the whole island. The Irish invented 'boycotting', and at Westminster Irish members of parliament systematically held up business. In spite of Gladstone's Land Act of 1881, the southern Irish, backed by American and colonial compatriots, remained irreconcilable: the new Viceroy was assassinated in Phoenix Park, Dublin.

Then, as the repeal of the Corn Laws following the Irish famine had wrecked the Tories, Ireland now wrecked the Liberals. When, in 1886, in alliance with Parnell, Gladstone brought in the Home Rule Bill, the Liberal 'Unionists' led by Joseph Chamberlain voted against him. The divided Liberals went down in defeat. In his last administration the aged Gladstone got another Home Rule Bill through the Commons in 1893, but it was defeated in the Lords.

The Conservatives then outbid the Liberals by buying out the land-lords, but the Irish nationalists remained militant. Then, as now, seventeenth-century religious vendettas fanned the conflict, which mounted to a major crisis on the eve of the Great War and inspired the Rebellion of 1916. Where, in the Dominions, there was a cleaner slate and self-government, federation was gradually achieved; in Ireland there would be partition and lasting bitterness reflecting centuries of discord.

Ireland was thus a perennial problem deeply affecting home politics, and the mounting European power struggle was also menacing. But nearly twenty years of Conservative rule proved the Indian summer of the old patrician order. Unlike Disraeli, Lord Salisbury was not much concerned with social improvement, and the 'Tory democrats' led by Lord Randolph Churchill were brushed aside. Joseph Chamberlain, the Liberal 'Unionist', originally a radical municipal reformer, turned his restless energy as Colonial Secretary (1895–1903) to the Empire, which now commanded a new popular enthusiasm as well as the interest of the City. The incomes of the greatest landowners were still immense, often augmented by American and Jewish wealth, and gigantic fortunes were being made in big business. From the Court downwards, wealth was becoming the passport to honours and recognition.

Against the gleam of wealth and the excitements of the Empire, domestic reform now seemed less interesting. In 1888 elected County Councils were set up, taking over the main administrative functions of the Justices of the Peace; in 1891 a Factories Act further limited the working hours of women and children, and in 1894 elected District and Parish Councils were created throughout the country. But it was not until the Balfour Education Act of 1902, planned by Sir Robert Morant, that a big improvement was made in that important field. The County and Borough Councils now financed not only primary but secondary education; new targets were at least set.

After the fall of Balfour's government, the Liberal cabinets of Campbell-Bannerman and Asquith, which both contained men of outstanding ability, including Lloyd George and Winston Churchill, set about much more fundamental improvements which laid the foundation of the Welfare State They also faced mounting external danger and violent political and social controversy, as their more radical Liberalism became apparent. Lloyd George's Merchant Shipping Act improved conditions of service and he established a Port of London Authority to reorganize the docks. Old Age pensions, Unemployment and Health insurance, Labour Exchanges, and a 'Children's Charter', were all devised. There was a Trade Disputes Act, favourable to the trade unions and a Workmen's Compensation Act; for the miners, an eight-hour day. These reforms were not yet adequately co-ordinated, and the legacy of megalopolitan congestion, bad town planning, urban squalor, remained. But these comprehensive measures were a turning point in tackling the problems of mass society.

Further, in view of the mounting tension on the continent, Haldane at the War Office now created the small but efficient expeditionary force which proved decisive in 1914; he also organized the Territorial Army and an Officers' Training Corps; even a General Staff. In face of the German challenge, by 1909 six 'dreadnoughts' were laid down. Fisher, as First Sea Lord, radically reorganized the navy. In 1911 Churchill became First Lord of the Admiralty, and by 1914 the navy had eighteen 'dreadnoughts', giving the margin of superiority which, in spite of tactical defeats, would decide the war at sea.

By the standards of the time, the cost, along with that of the new social services, was immense; in 1909 Lloyd George introduced a 'People's Budget' which set off a major constitutional crisis. Already in 1894, the Liberal Harcourt had introduced 'death duties' and outraged the landed interests. Now Lloyd George in his 'Limehouse' speeches launched an assault on the landowning plutocracy, attacking the dukes with particular virulence, and devising land taxes and a tax on unearned increases in land values. This Finance Bill, which struck at the landed establishment predominant throughout English history, roused fierce opposition. The House of Lords, which had not rejected a Finance Bill for more than two centuries, threw it out. A new note in class hatred was struck, and in the election of 1910 the big Liberal majority was so much reduced that the government depended on the Irish vote. At his accession in April of that year George V (1910–36)[5] was faced with a constitutional crisis between Lords and Commons; and, that autumn, he accepted Asquith's advice to give a secret guarantee to swamp the Lords, if necessary, by creating a vast number of peers. Then, in a second general election, the Liberals and the Conservative-Unionists tied 272–272, with Labour 42, Irish 84. In May 1911, a Parliament Bill was passed, again bitterly opposed in the Lords. Under the threat of a wholesale creation of peers, it was at last accepted. The Lords had suffered decisive constitutional defeat.

The hectic politics of the years before the Great War were further stepped up by the suffragette agitation, by the unprecedented industrial strikes in 1910, and by the dock and railway strikes that followed. Since Victorian times women had gained much legal and social emancipation; now a strident minority demanded the right to vote. They chained themselves to railings, went on hunger strike in prison: one threw herself to her death before the king's horse in the Derby. They physically attacked elderly Liberal politicians. These outrages, though they advertised their 'cause', postponed its success, which had to wait until the Great War had further emancipated women.

But it was over Ireland that political tension reached its climax. The attempt to enact Irish Home Rule had wrecked two Liberal governments; but Asquith now brought in a third Bill to achieve it. By 1913, having twice passed the Commons, it was rejected by the Lords. The Conservative-Unionists stood out in defence of Ulster. Bonar Law, the Conservative leader, backed the protestant extremist, Carson: the nationalist Catholic Irish were equally uncompromising. Civil war now threatened: so violent was the feeling in the army against the coercion of Ulster that high officers threatened to resign their commissions. There was even a movement, at a time of mounting danger on the continent, to hamstring the entire army by the Lords rejecting the Army Annual Act to finance it. In July, 1914, the British were far more concerned with the Buckingham Palace Conference, called in a last attempt at compromise, than with the murder of an Austrian archduke at Sarajevo. Ulster volunteers were gun-running; Southern Irish Sinn Feiners were arming. The central powers' decision to go to war was encouraged by the belief that the British would be paralysed by the Irish crisis.

All these conflicts, constitutional, industrial and Irish, were now dwarfed by the catastrophe of August 4, 1914. The country was launched into the Great War, the inevitable outcome of the power struggle of the European sovereign states, so long looming over the rather hectic prosperity of the early nineteenth century.

4

The Empire which Disraeli had considered so 'peculiar' and which the British were now fighting to defend, was now even more exotic and diverse. The mid-Victorian Liberals had been embarrassed by the 'colonies' and Gladstone had always detested the new 'imperialism'. But in 1897 it could be retrospectively written,

Five-and-twenty years ago the British colonies were regarded, even by experienced statesmen, with a degree of indifference which it is difficult for the present generation to realize. It seemed to be assumed that, sooner or later, each of them would throw off the bond attaching it to the mother country, and that nothing could be gained by maintaining a union of which the value could not be shown in a profit and loss account. A complete change has come over public opinion . . . Imperial federation is in the air.[6]

In the light of the European power struggle which had now culminated in war, it is time to cast back over the development of this vast area.

The colonies of European settlement were now nations in their own right. In 1867 Canada had become a Federation, the first 'Dominion' of the Crown; its capital Ottawa; its institutions British. The French Canadian minority, though swamped by the rapid development of American-style enterprise, retained its own language and its traditional way of life; while the country, united from the east to Vancouver by the Canadian Pacific railroad, now included the vast Hudson's Bay territories of the north.

In Australia, by 1901, another Federal Commonwealth had developed; its capital at Canberra. The early settlements around Botany Bay had spread westwards across the mountains and exploited rich pastures for merino sheep: following the Gold Rush of 1851 to Ballarat in New South Wales, the population had multiplied and the demand for comprehensive government and communications had made Federation inevitable.

In New Zealand, after checkered beginnings, Wellington had been independently founded in 1838; two years afterwards the British Government had intervened in the conflicts between Maoris and settlers, and in the political differences among the settlers themselves. The Maoris had then conditionally surrendered sovereignty by the Treaty of

Waitangi of 1840, and a capital had been established at Auckland in the north. After more hard-fought Maori wars, New Zealand had been united in a Federation, with a parliament in which the Maoris, who retained important areas, were represented. Now, with refrigerated ships, and the development of Australian markets, sheep farming and agriculture were flourishing, and if its economy was over-specialized, the country became a pioneer Welfare State.

In South Africa, Union had also been achieved, but in a much harder way, and with old hatreds unforgotten. In 1836 the more irreconcilable Dutch farmers, exasperated by the emancipation of the slaves within the Empire, had trekked into the interior and founded the Orange Free State and the Transvaal. Rescued from the threat of Zulu massacre by the British, who had themselves suffered initial defeats, the Boers remained intransigent. At Majuba, in the First Boer War, they had even soundly defeated their rescuers and had since maintained an obstinate independence. When colossal wealth had been discovered on the Rand, and a horde of cosmopolitan capitalists and prospectors had descended on the country, the Boers heavily taxed these detested *Uitlanders* and denied them political representation. Further, when Cecil Rhodes, head of the British South Africa Chartered Company, obtained vast concessions to the north, the tide of millionaire enterprise lapped round this archaic and would-be pastoral community. With the Boers controlling the Transvaal, Rhodes's enormous ambitions or even Chamberlain's intent to develop South Africa as a whole, were both impracticable. Hence, in 1895 the premature fiasco of the Jameson Raid, when, with Rhodes' connivance, a *coup* was attempted to bring down the Boer government. Hence, too, the Second Boer War (1899–1902), the greatest of British colonial campaigns; a succession of blunders and defeats only retrieved by better strategy and overwhelming resources, slowly brought to bear. The Treaty of Vereeniging in 1902 was a generous settlement; and by 1910 Union had been contrived, but most of the South African Dutch were never reconciled. The success of Canada, Australia and New Zealand, had not, this time, been brought off.

India was, of course, far the most massive and important strategic and economic area of Empire. This ancient, elaborate, diverse and teeming civilization was still ruled – ultimately by the sword – by a handful of British administrators under the imperial parliament. Since the Mutiny and the construction of swifter communications through the Suez Canal, many of the British, now less cut off from their own country, had become more aloof. In 1877 Victoria had been proclaimed Empress of India, in part in answer to a supposed Russian threat; and the *raj* in all its pomp and oriental grandeur appeared more than ever unassailable.

The imperial splendours of the vice-regal court, the majestic progresses, the laborious migrations of government to Simla in summer, the tiger shoots and the polo, were only the ornaments of an efficient, if sometimes over-bureaucratic, régime. The élite Indian civil service looked after revenue, communications and health; it administered justice and kept an unprecedented peace over the enormous area; while the Indian army not only protected the frontiers but provided an imperial strategic reserve. Strategically, the Indian Empire which now extended to Burma, made the British predominant from the Persian Gulf to the Far East and in the oceans round Australasia. But this régime, so much in the historic Indian tradition, was already being undermined by western ideas. After the India Council Act of 1909, a basically authoritarian government had been confronted with a crop of Indian representatives, extremely articulate but powerless. For the British had created a political framework and sponsored a westernized education which, in spite of the traditional antagonism of Muslims and Hindus, had combined to produce a novel Indian nationalism. British Liberal governments already envisaged an ultimate handing over of authority. Meanwhile, to the surprise of its enemies, the Indian Empire, which retained the support of the more martial peoples of India, remained a bulwark of British power and in 1914–18 would greatly contribute to its victory.

Such had been the fortunes of the old Empire. During the 1880s and 1890s the British had acquired another. The interior of the enormous African continent had long been 'opened up': in 1855 Livingstone had reached the Zambezi; Burton and Speke, in quest of the sources of the Nile, had arrived at the great Lakes Tanganyika and Victoria Nyanza; Baker had discovered Lake Albert. Stanley, after his much-publicized 'rescue' of Livingstone in 1873, had by 1877 traversed the continent through the Congo to the sea. The French and British had long been rivals in Egypt and North Africa. Now, by the 1880s, the European powers were competing to dominate large areas of tropical Africa – a 'scramble' which, mainly through Salisbury's diplomacy, was peacefully, if often haphazardly, decided in Europe itself.

Hitherto vaguely delineated spheres of trade had produced little friction; but when, after 1879 the Belgian monarch, Leopold II, had made a private venture to exploit rich areas of the Congo, the Germans had in 1883–5 annexed parts of South West and East Africa, Togoland and the Cameroons, mainly to step up the competition and embroil the British and French. For the principal rivalry had been between these two great powers in Egypt and the Sudan, as well as in North and West Africa. And in Egypt, as in South Africa, vital imperial interests had been involved, with the protection of the Suez Canal and its hinterland, which now included the Sudan.

Gladstone's second government had been forced, with genuine reluctance, to occupy Egypt. After the bankrupt Egyptian régime had pawned the country to European creditors, a nationalist revolt led by an Egyptian army colonel, Arabi Pasha, had been suppressed; in 1882, the British had bombarded Alexandria and destroyed his army at Tel-el Kebir. And when Mohammed Ahmed, *el Mahdi*, had evicted the Egyptians from the Sudan, the British became further committed. They could neither leave the Upper Nile under hostile control, nor accept a victorious *Jihad* which could set the Arab world ablaze. In 1884 General Gordon had been sent to Khartoum, with the impossible assignment of at once pacifying and evacuating the huge area. Beleaguered in Khartoum, that most glamorous of Victorian paladins had been butchered on the steps of the Governor's Palace by the *Mahdi's* spearmen. Along with the troubles over Ireland, the event had brought down Gladstone's second administration. Then the *Mahdi* had died and the Sudan had come under a formidable *Khalifa* By 1898, an Anglo-Egyptian army under a grimmer paladin, who became Kitchener of Khartoum, and who would just as grimly clear up the war in South Africa, had annexed the country; for good measure razing the *Mahdi's* tomb to the ground and casting the holy man's remains into the Nile. Another vast commitment had been accepted, an Anglo-Egyptian Condominium.

Further, in East Africa and Uganda, the British had taken over large new territories; and now, with the take-over of Bechuanaland and Rhodesia, even Rhodes' project of a Cape to Cairo railroad did not seem impossible. And away on the west coast and in its varied interior, huge areas had also been occupied: in Nigeria, Ashanti and the Gold Coast. Willing or not, in the scramble for Africa, the British had undertaken great new responsibilities.

Such, in broad outline, was the extent of the enormous Empire. It was linked by strategic bases across the world; by Gibraltar, Malta, Cyprus, Aden, Colombo, Singapore, Fiji; in the western hemisphere, by Halifax, Bermuda, the Bahamas, the West Indian bases, by the Falkland Islands in the South Atlantic, and by Esquimault on the Pacific coast of Canada. In 1914 it presented at once deterrent and enticing aspects to Wilhelmine Germany.

5

The British economy, the basis of the Empire and its defence, though even more ostentatiously prosperous than in mid-Victorian times, was

449

now in fact less secure. The 1870s has seen a depression of prices, profits and rates of interest, which did not greatly affect the mass of the people, but which marked the beginnings of decline. It had been international; caused by a cheapening of railway and steamship transport, by the depression of cereal prices following the opening up of the North American prairies, by the expansion of the great industries of the United States and the continent and the consequent over-production. And for Great Britain it marked a recession in the rate of economic growth; as others became more industrialized, the country was ceasing to be the unrivalled workshop of the world, if it remained the financial and mercantile capital. With a population which in England and Wales was 618 to the square mile, where in Germany it was 310 and in France 189; with a diminished agriculture, now so much concentrating on livestock that the import of animal feeding stuffs had doubled, the British were even more urban, dependent on export markets and vulnerable to foreign tariffs. And what was more, Great Britain now conspicuously failed to take the lead or even keep up with the pace-setters.

While, for example, from 1883 to 1910, German and American iron and steel prices fell by 20% and 19%, British prices actually increased by about a third – an odd occurrence in a country with vast resources of capital and skill. It was probably the result of technological obsolescence and of a reservoir of unemployed labour which rendered labour-saving improvements less urgent than in the United States. In contrast to the skilled artisans, a good many unskilled town workmen still often lived on a pittance in a slum. By 1908 German steel production was twice that of Great Britain, and in the new electrical, chemical and light metal industries, the British were being outclassed. They were too much concentrated in the old heavy industries, on coal and on the kind of textiles for which the Empire had long provided an easy market. Overall productivity, which had increased in mid-Victorian times 'by leaps and bounds', was now almost stagnant. The mid-Victorians had been immensely energetic; but their heirs were often easy-going; and eighty per cent of all companies were family firms. There was also a widespread suspicion of 'technical' knowledge, while secondary popular education had long been grossly neglected. Salesmen were often ignorant of foreign languages and of their customer's psychology; too easily out-manœuvred. When, for example, the Brazilians disliked the black wrappings of British needles, the Germans wrapped inferior ones in red paper and captured the market. Much ingenuity was displayed in the new cult of advertising, in particular of patent medicines; but industry failed to make cost-reducing innovations: in a time of stable prices capital tended to be invested in gilt-edged securities or abroad. The British seemed better equipped to sell traditional goods in easy new markets than new goods in competitive old ones. The entrepreneurs seemed less adaptable; while the working classes, afraid of unemployment, resented innovations and tried to share out what work there was. They developed ingenious 'restrictive practices', and constant demarcation disputes and trade union rivalries became taken for granted.

These tendencies were masked by the plutocratic appearance of British society, never more lavish than in the years before the Great War; and by vast lightly taxed revenues drawn from investments about the world. But the industrial attitudes which would contribute to decline are already apparent. The defensive campaign for 'Tariff Reform' – that is, protection – launched by Joseph Chamberlain in 1903, was not successful, but it reflected these changing conditions. Businessmen were no longer asking merely to be allowed to make their fortunes in their own way; they were trying to manipulate the power of the state, and policy would become increasingly and openly influenced by this concern. Elections were now fought much more over economic objectives. And, indeed, Chamberlain himself was a new kind of businessman turned politician; a portent symbolized by the orchid and eye-glass of the 'self-made' Lord Mayor of Birmingham, which contrasted with the Olympian slovenliness of Lord Salisbury or the aloof elegance of Balfour.

Meanwhile, the late Victorian and Edwardian social world was changing fast. People were more mobile: the electric tram, the tube, the motor-bus were superseding horse transport; and sedate victorias and spanking dog-carts giving place to roaring automobiles, still a luxury for the rich. Bicycles had come in during the 1880s; the grim mid-Victorian Sunday became the 'weekend', an English invention. The fashion now took on for cold baths and sea-bathing, golf and lawn tennis; cricket and football drew large crowds of spectators after the popular Press had written them up. For the rich and the well-to-do, fox-hunting and shooting became even more compulsive, and Highland landlords drew bigger revenues from their deer forests than their farmers. Horse-racing and betting united all classes; 'boy scouts' camped in woods and imitated the skills and clothing of the Veldt; indeed their organization became world-wide. Adult explorers, with primitive equipment, ran appalling risks to reach the North and South Poles. Climbers, not content with the Alps, tackled the Himalayas; never had the British cult of sport been more pervasive, followed vicariously by a now mainly urban people, whose physique was so bad that half the volunteers for the army had to be turned down.

In spite of this dismal fact, for most foreigners the representative Englishman was a tall, lean, tweed-clad, pipe-smoking character; reserved, phlegmatic and aloof, whose silences could be heard in several languages. He presented a very different 'image' from the plump, expansive and down-to-earth John Bull of the early eighteenth century; to the gay Cavaliers and ranting fanatics of the seventeenth: the versatile and brilliant Elizabethans, or the sophisticated thugs and chivalrous predators of early Tudor and late medieval times. The common characteristic which had come down since old English times was probably endurance.

6

The late Victorian age also saw a new popular journalism. In the 1880s Alfred and Harold Harmsworth, afterwards Lords Northcliffe and Rothermere, had begun it; obscurely enough with *Tit Bits*. They proceeded to *Answers* and *Comic Cuts*, and in 1896 they launched the *Daily Mail*, which throve on the Sudanese and South African wars. The *Daily Express* appeared in 1900 and, four years later, the *Daily Mirror*. Not since the seventeenth-century Interregnum had such a spate of sensational writing been poured out; it was now concerned, not with religious and constitutional questions, but with matters even nearer to the people's hearts – the new 'jingo' nationalism: sex, crime, scandals in high society and in the City; gambling and sport. And where the seventeenth-century news sheets had reached ten readers, the new popular Press reached hundreds of thousands, exploiting the effects of compulsory mass education. It struck a different note from the sedate journals and quarterlies which had catered for the well-informed, and it depended on advertising. *The Times*, at the height of its influence under the mid-Victorian Delane, was still powerful; but its monopoly was being bypassed. The political power of the new press lords, at its peak during the First World War, was not so great as they thought; they could exploit but not create opinion. But before the advent of radio and television, they had the mass audience to themselves.

These social changes were investigated by a new kind of 'social scientist'; by Graham Wallas, for example, the pioneer sociologist, whose *Human Nature in Politics* (1908) and *The Great Society* (1914) were to be more influential in America than in England. And Trotter's original and devastating analysis, *The Instincts of the Herd in Peace and War*, would be published, appropriately enough, in 1917. But this attempt to apply scientific methods to the examination of society was only a minor aspect of a great sweep of scientific discovery. The achievements of the late Victorian and Edwardian doctors and scientists were outstanding. The great advances in surgery made by Lister have already been recorded; now Sir Ronald Ross discovered that malaria was carried by the mosquito, and in 1904 Bayliss and Starling defined

452

the 'hormones' which controlled internal secretions. Even more far-reaching, the investigations of Sir J. J. Thomson had revealed the existence of the electron; and, by 1911, Rutherford had proved that the atom, far from being the dense irreducible basis of matter, was in fact mainly a void in which positive and negative charges of energy neutralized one another. Here was the first step towards the release of nuclear energy, with its vast and ambivalent consequences. Beside this extraordinary achievement, the political manœuvres of governments are dwarfed. Here, for good and ill, is a more decisive British early twentieth-century contribution to world affairs.

Philosophers, meanwhile, were extricating themselves from the neo-Hegelian metaphysics that had now hypnotized many of them away from the native empirical method. The alembicated prose of F. H. Bradley, with his fine phrases about the 'unearthly ballet of bloodless categories' and his glorification of the existing social order, gave place to the influence of G. E. Moore's *Refutation of Idealism* and *Principia Ethica*, and to the analytical method of the young Bertrand Russell; to that more sober estimate of the philosophical range of mind to be carried further by modern philosophers.

But the late Victorian architects and painters in general have left a painful aesthetic legacy, though their work reflects a peculiar social and intellectual ambience fascinating to the collectors of the subtler nuances of human behaviour. Banks and public buildings were often a hotch-potch of Gothic, Romanesque and pseudo-classical styles; their designers slapping on a bogus Byzantine cupola above an elephantine sham-Palladian façade, or diversifying a neo-Gothic railway station with a sub-Baroque clock tower. Of all the architectural styles of the nineteenth century, late-Victorian imperial is the most oppressive; the more so when new methods of steel construction were available, but, when used, covered up. Sir Edwin Lutyens, an exception to the general rule, designed some memorable and spacious public buildings, and Norman Shaw and Voysey were pioneers in the design of more convenient houses; the latter following the tradition of William Morris and obtaining a gradual but considerable influence.

In music the spirit of the age was expressed by Elgar, whose *Dream of Gerontius* was first produced in 1900 and whose *Land of Hope and Glory* became the blatant anthem of the Empire; while Gilbert and Sullivan had contributed their catchy tunes to the public's entertainment. There was now a cult of folk songs and 'morris' dancing, elicited by Cecil Sharp from sometimes sceptical villagers, only just in time. Vaughan Williams's Edwardian *Sea* and *London Symphonies* were also popular; and by 1908 Delius, who lived abroad and came of German descent, was becoming well known. His achievement is slight but distinguished. The most famous conductor was already Sir Thomas Beecham, who was more cosmopolitan than the others. There was indeed a great upsurge of popular interest in music.

But most of the painters were worse than their mid-Victorian predecessors. The American Sargent's flashy portraits of the rich were much acclaimed, but Whistler, another American, much influenced by Japanese art, had been generally dismissed as a pretentious aesthete; while Sir Alfred Munnings, who could paint horses, was already popular among their owners. Only the early Augustus John, grounded in the great French tradition, brought continental standards into this provincial world.

The playwrights and novelists, on the other hand, were full of vitality and retained a wide public, particularly if they discussed social problems in a *risqué* manner. And since any attack on Victorian convention was so considered, two brilliant Irishmen had it all their own way. Oscar Wilde, whose *The Importance of Being Earnest* won immediate acclaim, was much the better playwright, with a more subtle Hibernian wit; but he did not last, for what were then thought very good reasons. The spectacular disgrace of this aesthete and wit brought writers (and, indeed, artists) into much disrepute; confirming the worst suspicions of Arnold's Philistines. Shaw, on the other hand, was a Philistine himself. He went on battering away until the mid-twentieth century; at once an *enfant terrible* and a grand old man, a combination popular in England if one lives long enough. He was so brilliant that few people realized that his judgement of public affairs was abysmal, and he liberated a vast suburban public from their conventional opinions.

Among the novelists and poets – and he was both – Thomas Hardy (1840–1928) was the greatest writer. He confronted the world-wide religious and philosophical scepticism of the time with old English endurance, its roots in the soil of Wessex and the pagan literature of the Anglo-Saxons. His masterpiece *Tess of the D'Urbervilles* (1891) has an exact and sombre observation of nature and the workings of fate that can compare with the work of the great Russian and French novelists of the nineteenth century. His poems, by which he set much more store than his fiction, range from the panoramic *Dynasts*, which surveys the Napoleonic Wars in a cosmic setting, to subtle evocations of recollected and generally melancholy feeling, made the more memorable by his poignant sense of climate and place.

H. G. Wells, on the other hand, had his roots in late Victorian suburbia and his outlook conditioned by the study of biology. He was by nature an ebullient novelist, avid to depict the nuances of popular character; very funny, very eager. But he made his name as the pioneer of science fiction. When Hardy won independence, he went back to poetry: Wells launched out into a crusade to improve the world. He advocated, rightly enough, a 'Revolt of the Competent', and his influence, now too much discounted, was pervasive. Hardy looked what he was, a small weatherbeaten countryman; Wells, with his cockney accent, twinkling glance and high urgent voice, was typically a Londoner, if rather pampered by cosmopolitan success. With tireless insistence, he pointed out the follies of mankind, the imbecility of power politics and the emptiness of political charades. But these sinister forces had tenacious roots, and Wells's Scientific-Humanist idea of world citizenship has been sadly diminished by the events of the mid-twentieth century.

Meanwhile, Conrad evoked tragedies of character in tropical settings, and E. M. Forster the subtleties of Edwardian social life, extended in his *Passage to India* to Anglo-Indian relationships. The popular novelists Galsworthy and Arnold Bennett were also competent craftsmen when observing the worlds they knew, though they flagged when they went outside them. Of the entertainers and humorists Belloc and Chesterton had an authentic originality and gusto, particularly in their verse, and the Edwardian public greatly enjoyed the work of Anthony Hope (Hawkins), whose *The Prisoner of Zenda* and *Rupert of Hentzau* added the word 'Ruritanian' to the language.

Save for Kipling, who refused the Laureateship, most of the poets of the Edwardian Empire were execrable. The Poet Laureate, Alfred Austin, moved by the relief of Mafeking in 1900, could celebrate:

> *Mafeking's glory with*
> *Kimberley and Ladysmith,*
> *Of our unconquered kith*
> *Prouder and prouder.*

And William Watson, who adjured April to '*laugh her girlish laughter*', discovered that '*the sense of greatness keeps a nation great*'. Only when Robert Bridges was made Poet Laureate in 1913 did the appointment, once held by Tennyson, cease to be farcical.

Yet there were still major poets. Yeats was the best, but his fame belonged to Ireland. Kipling was most subtle and original, particularly in his queer, twisted short stories, with their odd mixture of cruelty and sentiment. He had a sharp psychological insight into how societies hang together, and a genius for animal stories; the most widespread basis of his fame in otherwise unbookish households. He was also vastly creative in verse. He could think himself into the minds of the soldiers of the queen and use their language, and he could evoke exotic landscapes; the heavy scent of tropical flowers in the dusk, the sweat of a column on the march, the smell of leather and dust and gun oil. He could even make machines seem articulate. He was profoundly original, and, with his touch of vulgarity, immensely popular. He cannot, as once believed, be relegated to the limbo of those who outrage the feelings of the hypersensitive. He is formidably authentic and representative of his time.

For the rest, among the minor poets, Masefield struck out a breezy and blasphemous line in describing the life of the people as he saw it, and had a nice feeling for ships and the sea, though subject to sea-sickness himself. Flecker, the best artist in words, created a jewelled, romantic evocation of the Near East and would have achieved more had he not died young. And Rupert Brooke, as already remarked, will probably be remembered, if only because his poetry caught the strange enthusiasm with which his generation entered the shambles of the First World War; to be fought with the new, if still primitive, methods of mechanical slaughter which great industry had put at the disposal of governments with their unprecedented and all-pervasive powers.

EPILOGUE

EPILOGUE:

WORLD WAR AND SOCIAL DEMOCRACY

On 3 August 1914, 'as the lamps were being lit in the summer dusk, Grey, standing in the windows of his room in the Foreign Office overlooking St James's Park, said to a friend "The lamps are going out all over Europe, we shall not see them lit again in our lifetime".'[1] Less famously the Foreign Secretary also observed, 'we shall have labour governments in every country after this'. He had presaged the rise of the masses to political and economic power and a radical transformation of the social order; the overriding themes of the concluding chapter of this survey.

In the preface to this volume it was submitted that in English history 'one realistic and constant theme' could be discerned:

that the undoubted historical success of England, so remarkable in relation to its size, has been a triumph not of any commitment to particular political principle, but rather to the absence of it; to a tradition of pragmatism . . . maintained within a relatively fluid and adaptable social order through the centuries, which has at each critical juncture enabled a new élite to emerge. . . . Hence perhaps the success of the social order which (could) respond to the pressures created by economic and social change . . . so showing itself capable of continuous adaptation without violent extremes.[2]

How far over the last half century can this theme still be discerned? It is too soon for any historian to be certain, but there is evidence that it persists.

The concluding chapter of this survey will therefore be analytic and selective rather than narrative. Instead of recording familiar events which, if adequately described, would destroy the balance of a work on this time-scale, we will enquire how far continuity can still be discerned; and whether the predominant character of England, as here historically displayed, is still constant and relevant to the circumstances of today. With this purpose in mind, representative developments in the political, economic and cultural fields over the half century following the outbreak of the First World War will now be considered.

2

The conflict which would set off the massive and cumulative changes that have come about since the old social order was undermined in 1914 and transform the prospects of Great Britain had long been predictable.

459

As Cruttwell observed in his classic account of the Great War of 1914–18, it was 'a natural result of the policy' that the great states of Europe 'had pursued. In spite of lip service rendered in theory and practice to international law, each had tended, partly sub-consciously, to organize itself on the basis of absolute power, and to worship its own collective image. . . . Moreover, the nineteenth century had identified the nation with the state to a degree hitherto unknown.'[3]

Thus organized and with the new powers of great industry and relatively efficient technology behind them, the great European powers came to head-on collision. Conscript armies were flung into the conflict on a scale unknown even in the Napoleonic wars; the traditions of a common interest among the rulers and of solidarity among élites were abandoned, and the culture that had united European civilization and made it distinctive was trampled down in the pursuit of a total and impracticable victory. The peoples so mobilized were fed into a clumsy but immensely powerful 'war machine', as massed artillery and machine guns confined strategy to trench warfare, and battlefleets manœuvred to destroy each other at ranges at which their targets were barely visible. And now for the first time, the primitive biplanes swooped and twisted in lethal 'dog-fights' in the air. It is not remarkable that the sequel to this colossal abuse of power should have been the erosion of liberty.

For the enhanced authority of the bureaucratic state created by the Great War was its most important consequence, and it had come to stay. When, as in Russia or Germany, the old order collapsed, revolutionary dictatorships seized power; a reversion to a more primitive and brutal but still centralized kind of government. In Great Britain itself the old political and social structure apparently survived; but it was now profoundly shaken, and government would gradually shape and administer an increasingly egalitarian and collectivist society, a process accelerated by the Second World War. The decisive British social revolution did not take place until 1945, with the advent of a third Labour government to power; but as early as 1916 the turning point is apparent. For it was then that 'the state established a hold over its citizens, which though relaxed in peace-time, was never to be removed and which the Second World War was again to increase'.[4] Indeed, when in December of that year Lloyd George, the first really radical demagogue to become Prime Minister, ousted Asquith's traditional and casual régime, he in fact established a virtual dictatorship, and his 'accession to power . . . was more than a change of government. It was a revolution, British style'.* Moreover, although during the twenties the

* Taylor *op. cit.*, p. 73. 'If he wants to be a dictator,' Balfour characteristically observed, 'let him be. If he thinks he can win the war, I'm all for his having a try.' (*ibidem.*)

old economic order had not apparently been greatly modified, in the thirties economic adversity forced governments into much more positive intervention; and during the Second World War the Churchill Coalition wielded even greater social and economic powers than those exercised by Lloyd George's régime. It was more broad-based in the country; it lasted longer; it was more comprehensive and it was better led.

And when, in 1945, the resounding verdict of the electorate, not against Churchill himself but against the MacDonald, Baldwin and Chamberlain governments of the 1930s, had been pronounced, the first Labour administration with a massive majority could use this central-ized power to effect the fundamental changes which established the social–democratic Welfare State; the belated response to the popular demands of the time, and one which has now become accepted in principle by both the great political parties.

But the price has been heavy in terms of traditional liberty. The time-honoured balanced and 'unwritten' constitution of King, Lords and Commons, historically regarded as a safeguard against overriding power from any quarter, has long been superseded. Moreover, in contrast to the United States, where the Supreme Court, as the ultimate interpreter of the constitution, enshrines the principle of the subordin-ation of the legislature to fundamental law, in England there are now no theoretical limits to parliament's power to legislate. For sovereign power now theoretically resides simply in the will of the people, whose decisions at General Elections politicians, pollsters, economists, 'experts' and commentators await, if not with bated breath, with rueful but total submission. A modern Prime Minister, with a big majority and a mass party behind him, has immense internal powers – greater than that of a President of the United States, and limited only by group pressures within the ruling circles and the verdict of the electorate at intervals of five years. For in England the rule whereby the Prime Minister is the leader of the majority in the House of Commons means that Parliament itself can be manipulated by the Government and that, in practice, the legislature is dominated by the executive rather than, as theory would have it, the other way round.

These unprecedented powers have come to be comprehensively employed in the name of national economic interests and social justice. And the cost of the Welfare State, with its unemployment benefits, pensions, state medicine and education, subsidized agriculture and nationalized industries and corporations, as well as the immense cost of defence and of aid to underdeveloped areas of the Commonwealth, has led to direct and indirect taxation far heavier and more regular than that ever imposed by any government in the history here surveyed. This taxation aims strategically at the confiscation of inherited wealth, however acquired, by death duties which halve any substantial fortune and take much more of a great one, in a cumulative attack on private property.

As nineteenth-century Conservatives foresaw, universal adult suffrage has thus had its predictable consequence – a concentration of political administrative and economic power in the hands of a collectivist state. And having taken over many key industries, nationalized mines and railroads, bought itself into private business and set up state-sponsored corporations over vital areas of the economy, modern government has obtained patronage beyond the dreams of eighteenth-century politicians. And this tentacular power is administered by a vast bureaucracy, now recruited on a far broader social basis, so that a great 'meritocracy' or established interest in the system has grown up. Indeed, ability is being assimilated in the old way, the society again showing 'its renowned ability to recruit protesters from below'.[5] The extremes of affluence and poverty are being ironed out; open violence has been avoided, and a gradual but economically thorough social revolution has adjusted the country to the facts of current domestic political and economic power; if at the price of an unprecedented preponderance of a managerial bureaucracy both in government and in industry.

In the light of the English past, such a social adaptation is to be expected; but, as in previous centuries, so novel, pervasive, and some-times arbitrary a power had also provoked a reaction. Though the monarchy has survived, characteristically adapted to the new social order, and prevents political or military adventurers from seizing power and the judiciary from political corruption, since the monarch remains head of the armed forces and appoints the judges; the central-ized Welfare State, like other forms of public power, has come to threaten what would hitherto have been regarded as fundamental personal and regional liberties, and even to undermine the assumption of the rule of law, the admired achievements of England. Hence a widespread malaise and popular resistance, not only from the threatened citadels of the Right, of capitalism and the Law, but from the univer-sities, the Press and the trade unions and the radicals of the Left; indeed, from all those who revolt against a regimented society.

The immense powers of the modern state, first accepted in war, have thus been employed over the last half century, with increasing scope and without violence, to establish a social revolution and the basic social security that public opinion now demands. But these powers now look less necessary, and even harmful to the spontaneity and vigour of a nation notable for these qualities in its past. Reckoning that national characteristics are pretty constant, an historian may perhaps expect a return to freer ways within the essential foundation that the collectivists of the mid-century have secured. The bias of British parliaments has always been pragmatic, not doctrinaire; and the House of Commons still cuts down extremists of both the Right and the Left to size. There is still a long-established parliamentary tradition of dealing with problems in human terms which it is hard for governments and bureaucracy to disregard. Disillusioned with doctrinaire politics, people may even cease to expect the state to hand its citizens affluence and happiness on a plate; and with politics relegated to a less obsessive importance, turn in the old way to the rewards of making the most of their own talents and interests, promoted by a wider range of spontaneous organizations within a now tolerably just society, brought about by what may retrospectively appear emergency powers.

3

Thus the traumatic experience of the First World War, which cut a swathe of death through the whole nation as no conflict had done before, did not, as in Germany and Russia, destroy the traditional fabric of society: the social revolution it began was long masked, and when it came, it was pragmatically achieved by consent; nor did the war at all impair the quality of scientific and technological discovery or of literature.

This slogging struggle of attrition was the first war in which millions of men, most of them conscripts, were committed by a British government to vast continental campaigns. The mass of the people were directly involved. Marlborough and Wellington had been national heroes, lavishly rewarded; but Haig and most of his generals were now widely unpopular, indeed historians have done them less than justice. After the failure at the Dardanelles, due to tactical incompetence in combined operations, they had no alternative but to fight a war of attrition, mobilizing superior allied manpower against the fortress established by the Germans after they had overrun the main industrial regions of France. Above all, they had to prevent a German breakthrough in the west, twice nearly achieved. And as the war was fought for traditional objectives – to prevent a hostile power in command of the continent from occupying the Low Countries, defeating the British Navy and invading or starving out the island base, so it was fought by traditional strategy, if by a more massive military intervention; by vast loans to continental allies, by long-term blockade and by mobilizing extra-European resources by superior sea power.

For though in 1916 Jutland was a tactical reverse, it was a strategic victory; and the British command of the oceans enabled American reinforcements to offset, and far more than offset, the disintegration of

Tsarist Russia and the concentration of German power in the west. As in the eighteenth and nineteenth centuries, this time-honoured oceanic strategy succeeded. Though the struggle involved the masses, and great industry in a new way, in the Great War of 1914–18, the British ran true to type. As in the Napoleonic wars, the tactics of Nelson had been revolutionary. Now the credit, if that is the word, for being the first to develop the tank, the tactical answer to the stalemate of trench warfare, belonged to the British. Better exploited by other states, the primitive invention was destined to restore mobility to warfare. And by 1918, British air power was greater than any other.

The current majority opinion that the Great War was an unnecessary conflict, fought by imbecile means, does not do justice to those concerned, who, within the confines of the possible, displayed the traditional tenacity, endurance and inventiveness in a fight for national survival and ultimate victory. Moreover, contrary to widespread belief, the First World War, in proportion to population and wealth, proved more important for the social changes it began than for the supposedly crippling effect of casualties or expenditure. Though qualitatively, the losses were appalling and affected far wider strata of population than ever before, the proportion of casualties to the size of the armies was in fact lower than in the Napoleonic wars. It is estimated that out of 6,322,427 men in the services from Great Britain and Ireland, 744,702 were killed and 1,693,262 wounded.[6] Atrocious as these figures appear, they are less than the loss from normal peacetime emigration over a similar time. And though the National Debt rose from £650 million in 1914 to £7,435 million in 1919, the destruction of capital assets was not then overwhelming. The dislocation of trade and of the international monetary system in 1929–31 would have much more serious results.

And after the First World War the basic conservatism of most of the British was reaffirmed. While most of the continental monarchies experienced revolutions, the British social and political system survived, and the royal House not only maintained itself but increased in popularity. George v and Queen Mary set standards of strict duty and conventionality not only representative of the predominant establishment but acclaimed by the majority of the people; swiftly disembarrassed of the attractive but temperamental Edward viii, who would only accept the throne on his own terms, and steadfastly carried on by George vi (1936–52), the monarchy would emerge from the Second World War, aloof from politics; and, even more representative and popular under Elizabeth ii, remain the one constitutional link in the Empire turned Commonwealth. Characteristically, the time-honoured order of Peerage and Honours was not abandoned. In spite of the brilliant forays of satirists in the 1920s, and the bitter class feeling and resentment following the immense and justified grievances of the unemployed, who by the early 1930s numbered nearly three millions, most of the British – particularly the English – remained, as they had always been, as averse from overt social as from political revolution.

Thus, though seriously undermined, the old establishment apparently survived the Great War; and, with the fall of Lloyd George in 1922, reverted to the policies of caution and appeasement which had been in fact predominant since the 1890s, and which were natural to a country with so much to lose and dependent on the peaceful conduct of business in a global network of trade and investment.

Here, again, the British ran true to type, as in the civilian reaction at the close of the Marlborough wars and even after Chatham's victories, as well as during the delusive peace advocated by the Whig opposition and attempted under Addington during the pause in the Napoleonic wars. And if now, under the changed circumstances abroad, the foreign policies of Baldwin and Chamberlain were in fact obtuse, provincial, and abysmally misplaced, they were in character and representative. The electorate would then have repudiated any other.

For neither the insular leaders, nor the even more insular public, understood that such traditional calculations were now utterly irrelevant and highly dangerous; and that they were dealing with gangster-revolutionaries who recognized no common interest in negotiation; now, in truth, only war by other means. Yet, being representative, Chamberlain, like Asquith in 1914, at least brought the country united into the Second World War, though a more informed, ruthless, and prescient practice of power politics could perhaps have avoided it. For now again, as in the Napoleonic wars and the Great War, far from disintegrating in class conflict, the insular British held doggedly and confidently together; and in part through their very limitations saved themselves and helped save the civilized world under the greatest leader in their history. For Churchill, whatever current *epigoni* may assert, was a statesman of outstanding genius and world-wide grasp, who combined the gusto and self-confidence of the late Victorian and Edwardian aristocracy with the versatility and drive of his American forebears. And his war cabinet included Attlee and Bevin, men representative of the Liberal–Socialist middle classes and of the trade unions, united in a realistic assessment of the chance of fighting on alone.

As already observed, again the strategy was traditional – the mobilization by sea power of vast extra-European resources in a long war, so that Hitler was forced into the same strategic error as Napoleon. He attacked Russia: after that, and after the miscalculation of the rulers of Japan brought the United States into the war, the victory of the Grand Alliance became inevitable. And though this second and more enormous effort brought about the collapse of Great Britain as a power of the first order, British policy in 1940 had been decisive for the whole conflict, and in character with the course of English history since Elizabethan times.

For though Russian and American manpower and resources clinched the destruction of Hitler's *Reich*, it was the British decision, taken with the full momentum of their history behind them and on a cold calculation of the chances, that made this sequel possible. Moreover, their contribution to the strategy and conduct of the conflict greatly contributed to its success. Today, when the hopes of world order widely entertained after that victory have been largely frustrated, and even the threat of the hydrogen bomb and of bacteriological warfare have failed to stop the habitual but now irrelevant competition of power politics, the colossal achievements of the Second World War have begun to fade. But any objective historian must record how great were these achievements, and the British people's characteristic part in them.

4

When the British swiftly and realistically dismantled their enormous Empire because they had to, they were also acting in character. As Baldwin remarked in 1935 before the second reading of the Government of India Bill whereby, in face of strong opposition, the government in principle conceded a gradual independence, 'we have learnt from experience that we shall preserve our Empire if we succeed in giving the units of it the right amount of liberty in the right way at the right time'.[7]

The colossal Edwardian Empire had emerged from the First World War with even more extensive commitments; in particular through the new 'Mandates' accepted for enemy territory in the oil-rich Middle East. But already by 1931 it was being transformed. Far from disintegrating according to German expectation, the Dominions, India and the Colonial Empire had played a major part in the First World War; and at the Peace Conference the Dominions, as members of the League of Nations, were now represented as sovereign states. In 1931 the Statute of Westminster recognized the accomplished fact of their full independence in a British Commonwealth under the Crown. In spite of the hopes of the 1890s, the nationalism of the Dominions had always rendered imperial federation impracticable and encouraged the assumption of equality: characteristically, the British rulers now settled for what they could. And, at a heavy price, British policy even towards India, though often clumsy and unimaginative, was fairly successful. India had long been regarded as the most important part of the Empire, the basis of British power in both the Near and Far East. Immense new responsibilities had been undertaken in Egypt, the Sudan, Uganda and East

Africa, not so much for commercial advantage as to protect the routes to India; the Boer war itself had been fought in part to retain strategic command of the Indian Ocean.[8] But the British in India, it has been well said, 'were in a false position brought about, through a vast irony, largely through their own virtues – by their capacity to give India a firm basis of material and administrative order'.[9] Confronted by the strident nationalism of the Hindu Congress Party, and by the psychologically alien and singularly effective resistance movement led by Mahatma Gandhi, whose policy of 'non-co-operation' and 'non-resistance' found a following among the mass of peasantry, as well as among the small educated class from which Congress derived, the British made political martyrs of the Congress leaders. The unworkable concept of dyarchy, whereby the provincial governments were given responsibilities subject to an overriding central administration against which there was no appeal, thus served only to exacerbate the nationalist demand for *swaraj*; and even after the India Act of 1935, British India remained under the authority of the parliament at Westminster.

So Congress remained unco-operative. And when, in 1942, under the threat of Japanese invasion, the Cripps mission offered an Indian Federal Union to be created immediately after the war, the dissensions between the Congress leaders, the mounting friction between Muslims and Hindus, and the divergent interests of the Princes, made even this settlement impracticable. So in 1947 the Labour government cut its loss. By the India Independence Act of that year, and at the cost of partition and massacre between the Republic of India and the Dominion of Pakistan, as well as of abandoning apparently firm commitments to the Princes, the British launched the whole sub-continent into political independence.

This hasty, dramatic, dismantling of the most important part of the Empire looked more sudden than it was. Since the 1890s the whole Empire had been over-extended; and under its pomp and grandeur the structure of the Indian *raj* itself had been eroded. In part this recession was due to the waning of British naval and financial world supremacy; in part through a certain failure of will and nerve at the centre, as Liberal and Socialist governments came to power, suspicious of the armed services and proconsular administrators, and representing a democracy indifferent or even hostile to Imperialism.

There remained the administrative structure the British had created; the *lingua franca* of English as a common language and the economic and cultural ties built up over generations. India and Pakistan separated in carnage, but not in such bitterness against the former rulers as in Ireland or South Africa. In the event, Pakistan remained inside the Commonwealth, the Indian Republic in association with it, while the governments and armies retained many British traditions. India never became to the English what Indo-China became to the French and Indonesia to the Dutch; and when Ceylon and Burma became sovereign states – the latter choosing to leave the Commonwealth – here also the transition was made without violence against the former imperial power. But if it is now widely held that nothing became the British better than their abdication of Indian Empire, the decisive fact in world history is that they ever made one; long sustained it and created the administration for most of the sub-continent; not merely that they were realistic enough to get out of it while the going was relatively good.

In Ireland and South Africa, the going had never been good. Deep-rooted nationalisms were inflamed by sectarian hatreds; in Ireland between Catholics and Protestants, in South Africa between Afrikaaner Calvinists, who regarded the Bantu as appointed by God to serve their masters, and the advocates of the imperialism which inspired Rhodes or even Chamberlain. In Ireland, no sooner had the Great War been concluded, than an Irish Republican Army conducted a guerrilla campaign against the police, now reinforced by British 'Black and Tan' auxiliaries. Lloyd George, that master of improvisation, managed to persuade his coalition colleagues to negotiate with Sinn Fein; but the settlement, which established the Irish Free State in 1922, left Ulster still part of the United Kingdom. The partition, politically inevitable, left the perennial problem unresolved. It so rankled among the Southern Irish that they began their independence with civil war against the leaders who had made the compromise. In 1937 the Irish Free State became Eire; it remained neutral during the Second World War, and it refused the use of naval bases to the British in the crucial battle of the Atlantic. Such was the price of long-standing political failure; of a divorce made necessary by centuries of oppression, resistance and incomprehension, going back to Tudor times and exacerbated by religious feuds and strategic necessities. Neither side had ever understood each other; and if, by the mid-twentieth century both now agreed to go their own ways, this relatively hopeful solution had been brought about by an *impasse*. Here again, in the light of history, the outcome was to be expected.

In South Africa the British were again baffled; confronted not, as in the Dominions and India by a situation of their own making in an area long under control, but by an old established multi-racial society, set in its ways long before the brief phase of British domination. It had been hoped, after the Treaty of Vereeniging that South Africa would become another Canada, with Afrikaaners and British comprehended in a Federal Union. But the *Trekboers* had long been more African than

European; a formidable and deeply provincial people practising an inward-looking Calvinism even more self-conscious and extreme than that of the Ulster protestants; obstinately apart as a chosen people from the huge majority of Bantu, Coloureds and Hottentots among whom they had made their settlement.[10]

There was a deep incompatibility between their outlook and that of the Imperial government; and although the Smuts régime supported the rest of the Commonwealth during the Second World War, the Treaty of Vereeniging, in spite of the high hopes of liberal administrators, turned out to have been only a long truce between the Afrikaaner nationalists and the British, who, after the second conflict, were no longer influential enough in South Africa even to hold the Dominion within the Commonwealth.

Another failure was gratuitously incurred. The British sponsors of the settlement of the Jews in Palestine, under the Mandate of the League of Nations after the First World War, were still in command of the Middle East from the great strategic base of India. With the collapse of the Turkish empire, it was believed that, now the Arabs controlled large new territories, they might become reconciled to the settlement of a limited number of western-educated Jews – who after all, it was naïvely argued, were also Semites – and who could create a powerhouse of intellectual and economic enterprise in Palestine. The Middle East might thus become economically more viable, and part of it even perhaps form a British Dominion or an independent federal state. But the sponsors of the plan had reckoned without the mounting nationalism of both Arabs and Jews, and the incompatibility of modern European and traditional Middle Eastern ways of life. Further, the problem was soon exacerbated by the influx of refugees from Hitler's persecutions. In spite of a hopeful start, by 1948 the project ended with the withdrawal of the British, execrated by both sides,; in the first Arab–Israeli war; and in the emergence of the embattled state of Israel.

Apart from the affairs of South Africa, the crucial strategic problem of the African continent had long been Egypt. Here vital imperial interests, now enhanced by the need for Middle Eastern oil, again conflicted with intense nationalism. In spite of formal recognition of Egyptian independence in 1922, the British maintained their strategic bases in the country. And it was as well they did so. In the Second World War the Egyptian base provided the foundation of the decisive North African campaigns, of the first turn of the strategic tide at El Alamein. It was not until 1954 that the British withdrew from the Canal Zone; and it was in Egypt, two years later, that the failure of the Anglo-French adventure at Suez marked the end of an era of colonial power and the appearance of a power vacuum in the Middle and Near East.

In the rest of the vast African continent the problems left by colonialism also proved daunting. Rhodesia has declared unilateral independence: the new East African States have precarious economies, and the independence of Ghana and Nigeria have had discouraging results, though the latter had been considered a show piece of British administration. Apart from the ancient miseries of Ireland, the latest and reluctantly acquired areas of the Empire have thus been the most difficult to handle; and in attempting to reconcile the demands of white and black Africans the former imperial power faces a problem which could disrupt the Commonwealth. But chequered as has been the aftermath of the Empire in Eire, South Africa, the Near East and Colonial Africa, relations with the most important areas of the Commonwealth, including India and Pakistan, have so far been tolerably settled. Even in areas of political failure, economic, scientific and cultural contacts are now more important than any formal political relationship, and they have often been preserved, and sometimes even strengthened, by a realistic policy. The enormous, if disorganized, Commonwealth remains in being, still a considerable influence in world affairs.

Thus it would appear that if, in the swift dismantling of Empire, the British may have shown some failure of nerve and judged complex and alien problems too much in terms of their own now intensely class-conscious politics, they have also shown their usual hard-headed realism in facing the facts of power. Ireland in particular could have become what Algeria would be to France; but even that perennial problem has been shelved and its disruptive influence on domestic politics diminished.

Whether the alternative to Empire may be to merge the British economy and even sovereignty into a European Union, and if this policy would answer the problems created by the strategic, political and economic changes in British power, is anybody's guess. But it is apparent to any historian that such a change would be radical. It would need to be accompanied by strict safeguards of internal autonomy, particularly in the social services and education; and it would make sense, as Churchill always maintained, only in terms of an Atlantic community and of a continuing special relationship with the Commonwealth. The most powerful and probably conclusive arguments in favour of this departure from eight centuries of political insularity are economic and technological: as such, they seem likely to appeal to the pragmatic British establishment as well as to the influential, though not yet representative, minorities who already feel themselves part of a European–Atlantic civilization.

5

With this prospect in mind, the economic situation which has developed over the last half century will now be briefly considered. The social revolution in Great Britain and the dismantling of the Empire has taken place against a background of relative economic decline, though of great scientific and technological inventiveness. The entire panorama surveyed is conditioned by the collapse of the old system of free trade in 1930; by the malaise of international finance, and by the development of new industries at the expense of the old 'heavy' industries and textiles in which Great Britain had long held the lead.

The Great War had finally transferred the centre of industrial and financial power to the United States; and by the Washington Treaty, concluded in 1922, the British accepted parity with America and abandoned the fundamental principle that the Royal Navy should be twice as powerful as any other. Great Britain had made colossal loans to her allies, and since the Russian loans had to be written off, now owed huge sums to the United States. Coal and cotton exports were in deep decline and the failure to compete successfully in new export industries, already observed, now became more serious. For a country so much dependent on imports in which, in the interests of cheap food, agriculture was now further diminished, this imbalance was already menacing. Nor was it helped by the return to the gold standard in 1925, which, while restoring the financial orthodoxy of the City, put up the price of British goods. The country was caught between the need to maintain the cosmopolitan reputation of its banks and insurance companies and the need to maintain employment; following the collapse of the brief post-war boom, employment was sacrificed. Thus the spectres of long-term debt, a balance of payments deficit, and of unemployment were already haunting the economy.

In this precarious situation the American financial collapse of 1929 and the consequent crisis on the continent had severe results, which were only contained by a Coalition and, in effect, Conservative government. Formed ostensibly to maintain the gold standard and the value of the pound, it succeeded, as it was meant to, in limiting the effect of devaluation. The pound did not go the way of the mark; it was stabilized at $3.40 as against $4.86. A temporary advantage was also secured, since British exports were now cheaper; but the abandonment of the gold standard by the rest of the world meant the end of the old free-trading system on which the prosperity of Great Britain had been based, and confined British financial power to a 'sterling' area. Besides this limitation, the erection of tariff barriers and import 'quotas' proved adverse in the long run to a country that lived by international trade. Though, in fact, with a revival of the home market, the worst of the depression was over by the middle of the 1930s, on the eve of the Second World War the economic position of Great Britain was still precarious, though not yet critical.

The Second World War then financially all but ruined the country. It demanded the sale of massive British investments abroad, piled up a far greater foreign debt than had the First, and inflicted crippling damage on shipping and housing, factories and communications. On the eve of victory, 'the legacy of the war seemed almost beyond bearing – £4,198 million of debt, only £1,118 million met by sale of investments and capital assets abroad, her overseas income halved and her exports 40% of the pre-war figure',[11] Great Britain was more than ever dependent on the United States; a situation mitigated, but not altered, by Marshall Aid, and the Organization for European Economic Co-operation.

In 1949, following unrealistic domestic policies, the pound was again devalued, this time to $2.80; and although unemployment was no longer severe and the living standards of the people higher than before, the economy now lurched from one balance of payments crisis to another. The problem was worsened by the renewed need for expenditure on armaments following the post-war tension between the USSR and the West, and by responsibilities still accepted for the remnant of the colonial Empire. To such a pass, in half a century, had come the great Victorian workshop of the world and the plutocratic imperial Great Britain of Edwardian times.

In the Second World War 60,000 civilians had been killed by air attack and over 400,000 men in the armed forces, but again its consequences had not been so terrible in Great Britain as in Russia or Germany. Yet the second conflict had changed the economic position of the industrialized island far more radically than had the first. From one of mastery it had become one of near mendicancy, incongruous when the people had been led to expect an easier way of life. And this when many of the old compulsions and incentives had been systematically removed by government, and when the trade unions, with a background of hard-won rights and memories of chronic unemployment, were unwilling to face the realities of the country's economic position; and if they did, found their authority defied by 'unofficial' strikes.

In the anti-climax of Empire, Great Britain thus appeared to have lost her economic bearings in a way without precedent in her history, hitherto so successful in just this field. An overpopulated social democracy in which most of the population are urban or suburban, the country is now naturally part of a great industrial complex which includes

North Eastern France, the Low Countries and the Rhineland; yet, unlike the continental states, it is dependent for half its food supply on exports which face mounting competition as the industries of the Common Market become better integrated on a continental scale. Once the model of nineteenth-century progress, Great Britain's gross national product has fallen well below that of the leading countries of the world; and though by 1970 the balance of payments was restored, the country was still deeper in debt than ever in its history.

On the other hand, against this economic prospect must be set the inventiveness apparent since the Industrial Revolution and the great scientific contributions of the nineteenth century. The contribution of British physicists to the fundamental research out of which the Americans developed nuclear fission is well known. Further, as in 1914–18, the British had again developed their massive air force and in 1939–45 they invented the jet aircraft which was to transform military and civil aviation. 'Radar', the invention of British scientists, was decisive in defeating the *Luftwaffe* in the Battle of Britain, and the threat of the submarine, the worst danger in the second as in the first conflict, was overcome. Moreover, though the Second World War had so much run down British capital assets, it had pushed industry further away from the old reliance on coal and textiles and forced the development of electrical and chemical industries, of automobile and machine tool manufactures; in all these fields British technicians had shown great inventiveness, not least in that of electronic computers with their immense possibilities in a whole range of industry and communications.

On the humane side of the account, and more important in the long run than most mechanical inventions, the discovery of penicillin by Sir Alexander Fleming in 1927 was developed in 1940 under stress of war by Florey and Chain. It created a revolution in antibiotic medicine which has led to the control of tuberculosis and saved millions more lives than those lost in the two wars. As Lister had first practised modern surgery, now British doctors had pioneered this enormous field, though it was through American resources that the antibiotic drugs were made universally available.

Such are the obvious landmarks in a familiar story; the paradox of the most appalling era of violence in human history conciding with the creation of a welfare state; of constant financial crises and inflation coinciding with a standard of living and leisure among the mass of the people unknown before; and of the invention of atrocious atomic and hydrogen bombs coinciding with immense progress in medical science.

473

6

The political and economic changes of half a century have thus been fundamental and swift; but the change of intellectual climate has been the most profound. The rise of a professionalized scientific outlook was the most original aspect of the nineteenth century. Today, though international power politics, trivial and archaic in relation to the destructive power involved, still defy the biological law that even a belligerent species must adapt themselves to changing reality or perish, the full consequences of the scientific revolution are being more fully if unevenly worked out.

The change in Great Britain, as in the rest of the world, has been reflected in religion, philosophy, morals and the arts; most vividly in literature, where the British, as in science, have always made a great contribution. And it has taken place against a background of a rapid expansion of education, broadcasting, television, paperback books and general mass communication which is slowly creating a far more widespread intellectual awareness among the vast majority of the people; now for the first time part of a mass culture, if of a confused and uneven kind.

For both in the field of religion and philosophy former certainties have vanished. The majority of the nation is no longer actively Christian, and the pale substitute religions provided by metaphysical philosophy have also lost influence. We now observe an increasingly neo-pagan society; sexual freedoms, reprobated in Victorian times, are now taken for granted, and following the economic emancipation of young people, family ties have greatly diminished. Where Darwin and the geologists and archaeologists revealed the depths of prehistoric time, Freud and his successors have revealed the depths of the subconscious mind and made men and women aware of their own motives in a new way. There is now a deeper understanding of the problems of society; yet contrary to the assumptions of Liberal and Socialist reformers, the creative minorities on whom civilization depends are now under attack, if less directly than in totalitarian states. And here is grave danger. As a wise observer has remarked, relating the decline of the civilization of classical antiquity to the current threat to our own, 'the ultimate trouble was that the minority who had once sustained the impetus of civilization was neither humane enough nor intellectually strong enough to reverse the progress of decline. Though no one wished the civilization of antiquity to disappear, it faded out.'[12] But if, today, the creative minorities may be turned into an intellectual proletariat, shorn of the power of leadership by an egalitarian society, and there is a loss of confidence rather similar to that of the declining classical civilization, we have a range of scientific knowledge and technological power quite unknown in antiquity. And while unpractical 'intellectuals' disparage the high civilization whose development has been here surveyed, and to which they owe their own liberties and prestige, scientists and sociologists and professional élites in most walks of life are tired of political slogans and tending to treat social problems in terms of adjustment to the changing facts – indeed of environmental studies and the balance of nature. This new outlook, dramatically fostered by televised pictures of Earth – the common habitat of mankind – in coloured contrast to the desolation of outer space, may well come to supersede the neurotic political obsessions and clichés so disastrously inherited from the nineteenth century and still threatening civilization itself. Moreover, the predominant British realism and common sense – the distrust and indeed ridicule of dogmatic political theories and abstractions – has been shared and developed in a different idiom in the United States. Already a scientific method, unknown to antiquity, has given modern civilization everywhere greater depth, thrusting aside the fear of life, guilt and asceticism that infected the declining European classical culture and the medieval outlook.

In a broad environmental context British historical and social studies are now based on much more elaborate and thorough research. Political history is better related to social and economic themes, to literature and the arts; and with the fading of the political dogmas fashionable in the 1930s, historians are more objectively concerned with what men did and felt rather than interpreting events by retrospective political theory. Hence a salutary realism. Archaeology, in which the British have long been the greatest pioneers and which sets nationalist mythology in a proper perspective, has made spectacular advances – a discipline which combines a cosmopolitan humanism with scientific method. Other broad environmental studies pioneered in the nineteenth century have also expanded and deepened. The current range of geography transcends political prejudice and includes the whole environment of man; and anthropology and comparative sociology, applied to civilized as well as primitive societies, have dispersed much political mythology and provincialism. In most civilized countries it is now widely appreciated that the environment so much polluted and scarified by great industry and urbanization ought to be deliberately conserved, and the rarer animals saved from extinction. All this wider understanding and sympathy must be set against the more desolating consequences of applied science, themselves the result not of scientific method itself, but of the obstinate political refusal to adapt society to it; a refusal which may perhaps be overcome as a more scientific–humane outlook permeates the more politically mature societies, if they remain strong enough not to be overrun by peoples regimented into a more brutal and primitive way of life.

In the arts the shift of patronage from private to public sources has tended to make the debased standards of much Edwardian architecture even more confused. Elephantine blocks decorated by pseudo-Epsteins were put up in the 1920s, and bungaloid ribbon developments have sprawled over the countryside. But, by the mid-century, new designs, mainly pioneered in America and on the continent, were beginning to make better use of the immense potential of modern steel construction and materials; and in the power and style of automobiles, ships and aircraft, British design can more than hold its own.

As might be expected, neither in music nor in painting has the first half of the century produced masters of the first order; but British sculptors, in particular Henry Moore, have won fame, and public enthusiasm for music, encouraged by famous conductors and technically brilliant orchestras, has spread far more widely, aided by radio and television. Thus the new mass communications are having their impact on the arts, as well as making the cult of popular sport even more widespread; a cult which has extended during the first half of the century far beyond the Anglo-Saxon countries in which it chiefly originated, and proved one of their main social influences in the world.

In literature the 1920s saw a brilliant, short-lived efflorescence of writers with a tradition of elegant detachment and privilege behind them. The sophistication of Aldous Huxley, his recondite learning expressed in fastidious prose; the deceptive lucidity of Lytton Strachey; the baroque cadences of Osbert Sitwell's evocation of the past which alternated with devastating and often hilarious satire, are a world away from the pre-war work of Bennett or Galsworthy, or the rumbustious prose of Belloc. Siegfried Sassoon's memoirs evoked the peace of pre-war country-life in contrast to the horrors of the trenches, while Virginia Woolf explored the stream of consciousness in a new way and James Joyce did the same, with more brutally comprehensive scope, in his *Ulysses* (1922) – at once an extraordinary *tour de force* and probably a dead end. D. H. Lawrence, whose best work was written in the 1920s, has been hailed as a great innovator; but to some critics his work now seems forced and self-conscious.

During the late 1930s and the Second World War the more memorable prose writers turned to satire or escapist literature. Where their predecessors in the 1920s were politically to the Left, the best writers were now sceptical of politics; as in the work of the Catholic writers Evelyn Waugh and Grahame Greene, or in the Proustian evocations of Anthony Powell, concerned with nuances of character and conduct within a small upper-class world. But George Orwell's *Animal Farm*

(1945) was the most devastating political satire of its time, followed up with formidable effect by his *1984*. Indeed after the Second World War satire predominated; this time often coming from originally lower middle-class writers disillusioned with the Welfare State and expressed through 'anti-heroes' in a socially confused setting.

But the most radical and representative departure was in poetry. Here the naturalized American T. S. Eliot, whose *Waste Land*, like *Ulysses*, appeared in 1922, devised an elaborately introspective music of ideas. He was a poet of megalopolitan loneliness and disillusionment, and in sheer power of phrase he can compare with the seventeenth-century masters of the school of Donne. Eliot's originality made his influence revolutionary and pervasive. Poetry for Eliot was not so much a communication of simple emotions, but an oblique and symbolic evocation of the poet's own memories; a conversation with himself. And this change from the straightforward pre-war poetry is also apparent in the work of W. H. Auden; a more public poet than Eliot, but just as introspective, his mind conditioned by the new psychology and by megalopolitan life with its gadgets and its machinery. Like Eliot, Auden's power of lyrical phrase puts him in first rank of the poets of his time; while the verse of Sir John Betjeman, in a very different and pre-Eliot idiom, has a singular and original vitality. For he has evoked, for a wide public, aspects of suburban life not expressed before, as well as simpler and traditional emotions, a haunting sense of landscape and of the past. Thus a new predominantly urban experience has been expressed by the most representative of the new poets; while the older and still countrified traditions of Tennyson and Hardy have still been carried on. At the mid-century in literature, as in science, the old vigour of the English has seemed unimpaired, though verse satire might have been more devastating considering the occasions for its deployment.

7

Such, in a necessarily brief and analytic outline, would appear the main political, economic, intellectual and literary developments of the last fifty years. Though an historian's judgement must be tentative, it would seem likely, as one would expect, that in spite of the profound changes recorded, the fundamental character of England is coming through; in particular in the flair for political compromise, for assimilating new men representative of the shifts of power and of range of recruitment, and in the continuing creativeness, long apparent in science and litera-ture. This creativeness is still fostered by great universities and schools which have not only survived the social revolution but are being adapted and expanded to meet it; giving scope for a far wider emergence of élites and an extension of awareness throughout the whole society, with the new force of modern mass communication behind it. For whatever the egalitarian and levelling ideas current, it is an inescapable fact that only by giving ability and creative insight in all fields its scope can such an overpopulated and industrialized society remain viable; and that the price of welfare is adaptability and drive, deployed in what is bound to become a more cosmopolitan setting. In this context it seems not too much to expect that the old realism will be brought out; for in the words of Leopold von Ranke, the greatest historian of the nineteenth century, 'The English intellect is as far removed from the keen dialectics of the French as from the world-embracing ideology of the Germans; it has a narrower horizon; but it knows how to comprehend and to satisfy the requirements of the moment with circumspection and great practical sense.'[13]

NOTES

Part One   Chapter 1   Prehistoric Britain

1   Grahame Clark and Stuart Piggott, *Prehistoric Societies*, London, 1965, p. 140.
2   *Windmill Hill and Avebury: excavations by Alexander Keiller, 1925–39*, Oxford, 1965.
3   Keiller, *op. cit.*, p. 250.
4   Clark and Piggott, *op. cit.*, p. 290.
5   Christopher and Jacquetta Hawkes, *Prehistoric Britain*, London, 1947, p. 73.
6   R. S. Newall, *Stonehenge, Wiltshire*, HM Stationery Office, London, p. 15.
7   Hawkes, *op. cit.*, p. 109.
8   p. 110.
9   *The Geography of Strabo*, trans. H. L. Jones, Loeb, II, p. 247.
10   Stuart Piggott, *The Druids*, in the series 'Ancient Peoples and Places', London, 1968, pp. 105–6, q.v. for the best account.
11   Anne Ross, *Pagan Celtic Britain*, London and New York, 1967, p. 70.
12   *Roman and Native in North Britain*, ed. I. A. Richmond, London 1958; Professor Stuart Piggott, 'Native Economies and the Roman Occupation of North Britain', p. 151.
13   *op. cit.*, p. 25.
14   *op. cit.*, p. 2.

Part One   Chapter 2   Pax Romana

1   *Geography of Strabo*, trans. H. L. Jones, Loeb, I, p. 445.
2   Caesar, *The Gallic War*, trans. H. J. Edwards, Loeb, 1917, vol. IV, p. 205.
3   AD ATT : IV, 6, para 7, quoted T. Rice Holmes, *Ancient Britain and the Invasion of Julius Caesar*, Oxford 1905, p. 329. A work now mainly obsolete, but full of interest and very well written.
4   Caesar, *op. cit.*, IV, p. 219, italics mine.
5   p. 222.
6   Strabo, *op. cit.*, II, p. 254.
7   Dio, *Roman History*, trans. E. Carey, Loeb, 1914, vol. III, p. 383.
8   Richmond, *Roman Britain, op. cit.*, p. 25.
9   *Ad caelum manibus fundentes*, The *Annals* of Tacitus, trans. J. Jackson, Loeb, 1937, vol. IV, p. 155.

479

10   Tacitus, *op. cit.*, p. 159.
11   Dio, *op. cit.*, VIII, p. 85.
12   D. R. Dudley and G. Webster, *The Rebellion of Boudicca and the Roman Conquest,* p. 18.
13   *ibid.*
14   Tacitus, *Agricola*, trans. M. Hutton, Loeb, 1920, p. 209.
15   p. 234.
16   Richmond, *op. cit.*, p. 45.
17   R. G. Collingwood and J. N. L. Myres, *Roman Britain and the English Settlements*, Oxford 1936, pp. 131 ff., for a full account of its construction and purpose.
18   *op. cit.*, p. 132.
19   Ammianus Marcellinus, 335–78 AD, *The Surviving Books*, trans. J. C. Rolfe, 3 vols., Loeb 1956, XXVII, 8, 6–10.
20   B. W. Cunliffe, 'The Excavations at Fishbourne', 1966, *The Antiquaries Journal*, vol. XLVII, 1967, pt. 1. pp. 58–9.
21   J. M. Toynbee, *Art in Roman Britain*, London, 1962.
22   Richmond, *op. cit.*, p. 164.
23   *op. cit.*, p. 162.
24   Claudian, *Panegyric on Stilicho*, ed. M. Platnauer, Loeb, 1922, vol. II, p. 21. Claudian, *c.* 370–420, was born in Egypt, the last and not very good poet of classical Rome.
25   Richmond, *op. cit.*: p. 163.
26   Peter Brown, *Augustine of Hippo*, London, 1967. See pp. 340–52, especially pp. 342 and 349, for Pelagius's influence and setting.
27   M. P. Charlesworth, *The Lost Province, or The Worth of Britain*, Cardiff, 1949, p. 30.

Part One   Chapter 3   Sub-Roman Britain and the Saxon Settlement

1   Claudian, *Panegyric on Stilicho*, *op. cit.*, pp. 155–7.
2   *op. cit.*, p. 21.
3   *History of England*, London, 1926, p. 33.
4   H. R. Loyn, *Anglo-Saxon England and the Norman Conquest*, London, 1962, p. 2.
5   *Gildae de excidio Britanniae: Fragmenta*, ed. H. Williams, *op. cit.*, Introduction, p. viii.
6   Collingwood and Myres, *Roman Britain and the English Settlements*, *op. cit.*, p. 312.
7   Williams, *op. cit.*, p. 44 (author's translation).
8   *The Anglo-Saxon Chronicle*, a revised translation, ed. Dorothy Whitelock with David C. Douglas and Susie E. Tucker, London, 1961, p. 10.
9   '*De stagno in quo balnea sunt Badonis* – the baths of Badon', cited in Williams, *op. cit.*, pp. 62–3.
10   See D. P. Kirby, *Problems of Early West Saxon History*, E. H. R., cccxiv, 1965.

11 Williams, *op. cit.*, pp. 60–1.
12 F. Lot, *Nennius et l'histoire Brittonum*, *op. cit.*, p. 56.
13 *op. cit.*, p. 71.
14 Collingwood and Myres, *op. cit.*, p. 322.
15 See Nora Chadwick, *Celtic Britain*, London, 1963, for a full discussion; also W. P. Ker, *op. cit.*, pp. 66, 336.
16 See also Bede's account in *A History of the English Church and People*, trans. L. Sherley-Price, Penguin, 1955, p. 102.
17 J. B. Bury, *The Life of St Patrick and his Place in History*, London, 1905, p. 264.
18 *A History of England*, London, 1963, p. 48.
19 See my *Western Political Thought*, Methuen (paperback), pp. 145–8.
20 Bede, *op. cit.*, p. 144.
21 *op. cit.*, p. 252.
22 *op. cit.*, 255.
23 Dom David Knowles, *Christian Monasticism*, London, 1969, pp. 31 ff.
24 Sir F. Stenton, *Anglo-Saxon England*, Oxford, 1947, p. 177.

Part One   Chapter 4   The West Saxon Kingdom

1 H. R. Loyn, *Anglo-Saxon England and the Norman Conquest*, London, 1962, *op. cit.*, p. 16, q.v. for the best recent account of its subject with full bibliography.
2 *op. cit.*, p. 19.
3 *op. cit.*, p. 21.
4 *op. cit.*, p. 45.
5 Stenton, *Anglo-Saxon England*, *op. cit.*, p. 389.
6 Loyn, *op. cit.*, p. 199.
7 A-S.C. in *English Historical Documents*, ed. D. Whitelock, London, 1954, I, p. 171.
8 Johannes Brøndsted, *The Vikings*, trans. Estrid Bannister-Good, Penguin, 1960, p. 27. This is the most authentic short account by the Director of the National Museum at Copenhagen, the finest museum of prehistory in the north.
9 *op. cit.*, p. 31.
10 A-S.C. in *E.H.D.*, *op. cit.*, I, p. 166.
11 *op. cit.*, p. 173.
12 *op. cit.*, I, p. 201.
13 *op. cit.*, I, p. 846.
14 A-S.C., *E.H.D.*, *op. cit.*, I, pp. 205–6.
15 *E.H.D.*, *op. cit.*, I, p. 208n.
16 Lynn White, Jr, *Medieval Technology and Social Change*, O.U.P., 1960, pp. 55–6.
17 F. L. A. Attenborough, *The Laws of the Earliest English Kings*, C.U.P., 1922, on which the above account is based.
18 Bede, *op. cit.*, p. 245.

19 R. K. Gordon, *Anglo-Saxon Poetry, Elene*, Everyman, 1949, pp. 234–60.
20 *E.H.D., op. cit.,* I, p. 805.
21 *op. cit.,* I, p. 802.
22 Gordon, *op. cit.,* pp. 317 ff.

Part One   Chapter 5   Anglo-Danish England

 1 Mathew of Westminster, *Flores Historiarum,* ed. H. R. Luard, *Rolls,* 1896, p. 530.
 2 See P. Hunter Blair, *An Introduction to Anglo-Saxon England,* Cambridge, 1956.
 3 Lane Poole, *Domesday Book and Beyond,* Oxford, 1907, pp. 518–19.
 4 Loyn, *op. cit.,* p. 359.
 5 *op. cit.,* p. 361.
 6 *E.H.D., op. cit.,* I, p. 558.
 7 Loyn, *op. cit.,* pp. 103–4.
 8 p. 121.
 9 *E.H.D., op. cit.,* I, p. 553.
10 pp. 549–50.
11 Florence of Worcester, in *E.H.D., op. cit.,* I, p. 291.
12 Loyn, *op. cit.,* p. 258.
13 Cited Whitelock, *The Beginnings of English Society,* Penguin Books, 1952, p. 201.
14 Homilies (forty of them for Saint's Days), *E.H.D.,* I, *op. cit.,* p. 850.
15 *E.H.D., op. cit.,* I, pp. 852–3.
16 pp. 858 ff.
17 Whitelock, *op. cit.,* p. 187.
18 *Vita Edwardi Regis, op. cit.,* p. 12.
19 Barlow, *op. cit. E.H.R.,* 1965.
20 Appendix to *Vita Edwards, op. cit.,* pp. 75 ff.
21 Laurence E. Tanner and A. W. Clapham. *Archaeologia,* 1933, for evidence of the original plan.

Part One   Chapter 6   The Norman Yoke

 1 See V. H. Galbraith, *The Making of Domesday Book,* Oxford, 1961, for the definitive account.
 2 Douglas, *William the Conqueror and the Norman Impact on England,* London, 1964, p. 375.
 3 *E.H.D., op. cit.,* II, p. 224.
 4 J. H. Round, *Feudal England,* London, 1895, pp. 336 ff.
 5 *The Anglo-Saxon Chronicle,* ed. Whitelock and Douglas, *op. cit.,* p. 143 (version D).
 6 William of Poitiers in *E.H.D., op. cit.,* II, p. 226.
 7 *op. cit.,* p. 228.
 8 *op. cit.,* p. 229.

9   C. W. Hollister, 'The Norman Conquest and the Genesis of English Feudalism', *American Historical Review*, lxvi, 1961.

10   See C. W. David, *Robert Curthose, Duke of Normandy*, Harvard, 1920, p. 188, which admirably describes the duke's career.

11   Gaimar, *op. cit.*, lines, 6311–42.

12   Eadmer's *History of Recent Events in England. Historia Novorum in Anglia*, trans. Geoffrey Bosanquet, with a foreword by R. W. Southern, London, 1964, pp. 120–1.

13   William of Malmesbury, *Historia Novella*, ed. K. R. Potter, London, 1955, p. 24.

14   *Ottonis Gesta Frederici Imp:* Lib. I, xvi, S.R.G., p. 30.

15   William of Malmesbury, ed. Potter, *op. cit.*, p. 3.

16   *op. cit.*, p. 44.

17   *E.H.R.*, 1964, lxxx, pp. 305 ff.

18   William of Malmesbury, ed. Potter, *op. cit.*, p. 271.

19   Sayles, *The Medieval Foundations of England, op. cit.*, pp. 173–4.

20   *Dialogus de Scaccario*, written (*c.* 1178) by Thomas FitzNigel, Bishop of London, in *E.H.D., op. cit.*, II, p. 493.

21   Eadmer, *op. cit.*, pp. 149–50.

22   Eadmer, *E.H.D., op. cit.*, II, p. 665.

23   Eadmer's *History of Recent Events in England, op. cit.*, p. 62. The contrasting character of the king and the archbishop are cleverly brought out.

24   *op. cit.*, p. 86.

25   *The Monastic Constitutions of Lanfranc*, ed. Dom David Knowles, 1951.

Part Two   Chapter 7   The Angevin Achievement

1   Henry of Huntingdon, *E.H.D., op. cit.*, II, p. 308.

2   William of Newburgh, *E.H.D.*, II, *op. cit.*, p. 371.

3   *ibid.*, p. 323.

4   *vide* Lane Poole, *Domesday Book to Magna Carta, op. cit.*, p. 336 n.

5   Jordan Fantosme, *Chronicle of the Wars between the English* Scots, 1173–74, trans. by the Rev. J. Stevenson, *Church Histories of England*, vol. IV, pt. 1, London, 1856, lines 1010 ff.

6   Jolliffe, *The Constitutional History of Medieval England*, London, 1937, *op. cit.*, p. 213.

7   Sayles, *op. cit.*, p. 341.

8   Knowles, *op. cit.*, p. 20.

9   *ibid.*

10   Robertson, *op, cit., passim.*

11   Lane Poole, *Domesday Book to Magna Carta, op. cit.*, p. 81.

12   V. H. Galbraith on 'Handwriting', in *Medieval England*, ed. A. Lane Poole, vol. II, pp. 541–58, Oxford (revised ed.), 1958.

13   Quoted by H. Osborn Taylor from *Metalogicus*, in *The Medieval Mind*, London, 1927. vol. II. pp. 157–8.

14   Helen Waddell, *The Wandering Scholars*, London, 1927, p. 129.

15   *op. cit.*, p. 111.

16   Osborn Taylor, *op. cit.*, vol. I, p. 584.

Part Two   Chapter 8   Magna Carta and the Curbing of the Monarchy

1   Cited from the *Itinerarium Richardi I* by M. M. Holbach, *In the Footsteps of Richard Coeur de Lion*, London, n.d., p. 1.
2   *Mathaei Parisisiensis, Historia Anglorum sive, ut vulgo dicitur, Historia Minor*, ed. Sir F. Madden, *Rolls, 1866–9*, vol. II, p. 9.
3   Appleby, *op. cit.*, p. 82.
4   Jolliffe, *op. cit.*, p. 247.
5   M. L. Bazely, *The Extent of the English Forest in the Thirteenth Century*, *Trans. R.H.S.*, 4th series, vol. IV, pp. 144–5.
6   *Political Songs of England from King John to King Edward II*, ed. Thomas Wright, Camden Society, 1839.
7   P. K. Hitti, *History of the Arabs*, London (seventh ed.) 1960. See pp. 633–5 for a corrective to the traditional view.
8   Lane Poole, *op. cit.*, p. 473.
9   Sayles, *Medieval Foundations of England*, *op. cit.*, p. 400.
10 The best analysis is still W. S. McKechnie's *Magna Carta*, Glasgow, 1905. This masterpiece first put the Charter in its proper perspective and its main conclusions have not been superseded. See also J. C. Holt, *Magna Carta*, C.U.P., 1955.
11 McKechnie, *op. cit.*, p. 25.
12 *op. cit.*, p. 265.
13 *op. cit.*, p. 436.
14 Mathew Paris, *op. cit.*, vol. II, p. 159.
15 *op. cit.*, pp. 160–1.
16 Lane Poole, *op. cit.*, p. 276.
17 *Brut y Tywysogion, The Chronicles of the Princes of Wales*, Welsh and English Text, *Rolls*, ed. J. Williams. 1860, p. 61.
18 *op. cit.*, pp. 246–7, q.v. for much Celtic eloquence even in translation.
19 *Giraldi Cambrensis Itinerarium Kambriae et Descriptio Kambriae*, ed. J. F. Dimock, *Rolls*, vol. VI, 1868.
20 Edmund Curtis, *A History of Ireland*, London, 1964, p. 70.
21 Lane Poole, *op. cit.*, p. 316.
22 Dimock, *op. cit.*, vol. V, p. 151.

Part Two   Chapter 9   Thirteenth Century Climax

1   Jolliffe, *op. cit.*, p. 301.
2   *op. cit.*, p. 298.
3   Sir Maurice Powicke, *Henry III and the Lord Edward*, vol. II, Oxford, 1956, p. 342.
4   R. H. C. Davis, *A History of Medieval Europe from Constantine to Saint Louis*, London, 1957. This gives a good short account of the background to Henry III's adventures.
5   *Political Songs*, *op. cit.*, p. 329.
6   Mathew Paris, trans. Giles, *op. cit.*, vol. II, p. 62.
7   *ibid.*

8 Bémont, *op. cit.*, p. 185.
9 Jolliffe, *op. cit.*, p. 296.
10 Bémont, *op. cit.*, p. 230.
11 *History of England, op. cit.*, pp. 175–6.
12 Powicke, *op. cit.*, p. 212.
13 Sayles, *op. cit.*, p. 428.
14 Political Songs, *op. cit.*, pp. 94 ff.
15 M. W. Labarge, *op. cit.*, 1964, p. 277.
16 See M. W. Labarge, *A Baronial Household in the Thirteenth Century*, pp. 82 ff., on which much of the above account is based. Also A. Lane Poole, *Medieval England, op. cit.*, vol. I.
17 *Select Pleas of the Forest*, ed. G. J. Turner, Selden Society, 1901.
18 p. 126.
19 See Maurice Keen, *The Outlaws of Medieval Legend, op. cit.*, for the best short account of the impact of the forest on *Gestes* and ballads.
20 Lane Poole (ed.), *Medieval England, op. cit.*, vol. II, p. 529. See in particular, the comprehensive chapter by Dr A. C. Crombie.
21 Cited Osborn Taylor, *op. cit.*, vol. II, p. 522.
22 *De rerum proprietatibus*, Nuremberg, 1619.

Part Two   Chapter 10   The Edwardian Realm

1 See Sir Maurice Powicke, *Henry III and the Lord Edward, op. cit.*, vol. II, pp. 595 ff., for the best short account on which the above description is based.
2 G. W. S. Barrow, *Robert Bruce and the Community of the Realm of Scotland*, London, 1965, p. 230.
3 Jolliffe, *op. cit.*, p. 336.
4 Johnstone, *op. cit.*, p. 86.
5 *op. cit.*, p. 64.
6 *The Chronicles of the Reigns of Edward I and Edward II (Annales Paulini)*: ed. W. Stubbs, *Rolls*, London, 1882–83, vol. I, p. 262.
7 See the anonymous translation of *Le Brut d'Engleterre* (so-called as it begins with Brutus of Troy's settlement at Topsham, when he overcame the indigenous giants), ed. F. Brie, Early English Text Society, 1906, pt. 1, pp. 252–3, spelling modernized.
8 Feiling, *op. cit.*, p. 179.
9 Brut, *op. cit.*, p. 203.
10 Sir Winston Churchill, *op. cit.*, vol. I, p. 242.
11 A. R. Myers, *England in the Late Middle Ages*, 1307–1536, Penguin, 1952, p. 2.
12 May McKisack, *The Fourteenth Century*, Oxford, 1959, p. 21, q.v. for a modern view of the parliament.
13 *Record of Parliament, op. cit.*, lxxv–vi.
14 Lapsley, *op. cit.*, p. xi.
15 Jolliffe, *op. cit.*, p. 358.

16 P. Elmer, 'The Economic Causes of the Expulsion of the Jews in 1290', *E.H.R.*, May, 1937.
17 Stubbs, *Chronicles of the Reigns of Edward I and Edward II, op. cit.*, pp. 183–92.
18 McKisack, *op. cit.*, p. 292 n.
19 See *E.H.R.*, January, 1947, pp. 33 ff.
20 Fantosme, *op. cit.*, line 251.
21 F. M. Stenton, 'The Road System of Medieval England', *E.H.R.*, November, 1936.
22 J. E. Lloyd, *Wales from the Earliest Times to the Edwardian Conquest*, vol. II, London, 1911, p. 341, q.v. for a spirited account.
23 Andrew Lang, *A History of Scotland*, vol. I, Edinburgh, 1880, p. 221.
24 *Scalachronicon*, p. 57.

Part Two   Chapter 11   The Chivalrous Predators

 1 *Calendar of Venetian and Other Papers*, vol. I, p. 9.
 2 *Chronicles of London*, ed. C. L. Kingsford, Oxford, 1905, p. 96.
 3 McKisack, *op. cit.*, p. 525.
 4 Quoted by McKisack, *op. cit.*, p. 150.
 5 Maurice Keen, *A History of Medieval Europe*, London, 1968, p. 215.
 6 Richard H. Jones, *The Royal Policy of Richard II, Absolutism in the Later Middle Ages*, Oxford, 1968, p. 2.
 7 See Anthony Steel, *Richard II*, London, 1941, for the most comprehensive account.
 8 Froissart, *The Chronicles of England, France and Spain*, Everyman ed., London, 1913, p. 379.
 9 Gervase Mathew, *op. cit.*, p. 152.
10 'Mum the Soothsegger' (Hush, Truth-teller!), ed. M. Day and R. Steele, *E.E.T.S.*, 1936, pp. 262 and 273.
11 *Eulogium Historiarum*, ed. F. S. Haydon, *Rolls* (1858–63), vol. III, p. 378.
12 *Political Poems and Songs* (Edward III and Richard II), ed. Thomas Wright, *Rolls*, 1859, vol. I, p. 369.
13 *Annales Richardi Secundi, Regis Angliae Johannis de Trokelowe*, ed. H. J. Riley, *Rolls*, 1866, p. 240.
14 *op. cit.*, p. 267.
15 *An English Chronicle: Richard II–Henry VI*, ed. J. S. Davies, Camden Soc., 1856, p. 16.
16 Riley, *op. cit.*, p. 281.
17 *ibid.*
18 pp. 284, 286.
19 P. S. Lewis, *Later Medieval France, The Polity*. London, 1968, q.v. for the best account, also highly illuminating for English history.
20 Froissart, *op. cit.*, pp. 379–80.
21 Sir Charles Oman, *The Great Revolt of 1381*, Oxford, 1906. This is still an excellent account.
22 *Anonimal Chronicle of St Mary's York*, printed in Anglo-French in *E.H.R.*,

51, 1898, and translated as Appendix V in Oman, *op. cit.*, pp. 186–213. The full and definitive edition is *The Anonimalle Chronicle 1337–1381*, ed. V. H. Galbraith, Manchester, 1927.

23 Galbraith, *op. cit.*, p. 146.

24 *op. cit.*, p. 193.

25 *Chronicles of London*, ed. Kingsford, *op., cit.*, p. 15.

26 Knighton, *Chronicon*, vol, II *op. cit.*, p. 137 (translation).

27 Galbraith, *op. cit.*, p. 148.

28 Oman, *op. cit.*, p. 13.

29 *E.H.D.*, *op. cit.*, vol. II, pp. 329–30.

30 Brampton, *op. cit.*, p. 19.

31 *Fasciculi Zizaniorum Magistri Johannis Wyclif*, ed. W. W. Shirley, *Rolls*, 1858, Introduction, p. lxv.

32 Knighton, *op. cit.*, p. 152.

33 *Fasciculi, op. cit.*, p. 144.

34 McFarlane, *op. cit.*, p. 93.

35 Quoted by McFarlane, *op. cit.*, p. 133.

36 Edited by F. J. Furnivall, *E.E.T.S.*, 2 vols., nos 119 and 123.

37 Furnivall, *op. cit.*, vol. II, p. 233 (spelling modernized).

38 David Daiches, *A Critical History of English Literature*, London, 1961, vol. I, pp. 89 ff.

39 *The Vision of William concerning Piers the Plowman*, by William Langland or Langley, ed. W. W. Skeat, Oxford, 1906.

40 Chaucer's translation of his *Consolation of Philosophy*, iii, 10, quoted by W. P. Ker, *The Dark Ages*, ed. B. Ifor Evans, Nelson, 1955, p. 109.

41 Gervase Mathew, *The Court of Richard II. op. cit.*, p. 53.

Part Two   Chapter 12   The Erosion of Kingship

1 K. B. McFarlane, *Bulletin of the Institute of Historical Research*, 1945, p. 179.

2 E. F. Jacob, *The Fifteenth Century, 1399–1485*, Oxford, 1961, p. 426.

3 Introduction to the *Governaunce of England* by Sir John Fortescue, London, 1885, p. 15.

4 *The History of Parliament*, ed. Josiah Wedgwood and Anne Holt, London, 1936, vol. 1, p. xxxvi.

5 Wedgwood and Holt, *op. cit.*, p. xlv.

6 Cited by Jacob, *op. cit.*, p. 288.

7 J. H. Wylie, *The Reign of Henry V*, vol. 1, C.U.P., 1914, p. 34. This three-volume biography is the standard work.

8 Jacob, *op. cit.*, p. 31.

9 *Vita Henrici Quinti*, by Tito Livio of Forli, ed. T. Hearne, 1716. For the Tudor version see *The First Life of Henry V*, ed. C. L. Kingsford, Oxford, 1911.

10 Kingsford, *op. cit.*, p. xlv.

11 Wylie, *op. cit.*, vol. I, p. 316.

12 *Political Poems and Songs, op. cit.*, vol. II, p. 23 ff.

13 'Collections of a Yorkist Partisan', in C. L. Kingsford's *English Historical Literature in the Fifteenth Century*, Oxford, 1913, p. 361.

14 Wylie, *op. cit.*, vol. II, p. 479.

15 See C. Hibbert, *Agincourt*, Batsford, 1964, to which the above chapter is indebted.

16 Wylie, *op. cit.*, vol. II, p. 76.

17 p. 167.

18 Kingsford, *op. cit.*, p. 60.

19 *Statutes and Ordinances to be kept in times of werre*: quoted Hibbert, *op. cit.*, from the *Red Book of the Admiralty*.

20 Jacob, *op. cit.*, p. 444.

21 Ed., Sir George Warner, Oxford, 1926.

22 G. M. Trevelyan, *English Social History*, London, 1941, p. 535.

23 *Political Songs, op. cit.*, vol. II, p. 271.

24 J. S. Davies, *The English Chronicle, op. cit.*, pp. 64 and 74.

25 Jacob, *op. cit.*, pp. 283 and 282.

26 J. A. F. Thomson, *The Later Lollards 1414–1520*, Oxford, 1965.

27 *The Cloud of Unknowing and the Book of Privy Counselling*, ed. P. Hodgson, *E.E.T.S.*, 1944, pp. 63 and 119.

28 Introduction to *The Babees Book*, ed. F. J. Furnivall, *E.E.T.S.*, 1864, p. xliv.

29 Furnivall, *ibid.*

30 *Stans Puer in Mensam, The Boy at Table*, 1430, in Furnivall.

31 *A Fifteenth-Century Courtesy Book*, ed. R. W. Chambers, *E.E.T.S.*, Orig. Series, 148, 1941.

32 Spelling modernized.

33 *Medieval England*, Lane Poole, vol. II, ed. Lane Poole.

34 Feiling, p. 326.

Part Three   Chapter 13   The Revival of Royal Government

1 See *De Occupatione Regni Anglie*: The Usurpation of Richard III, by Dominic Mancini, trans. and ed. by C. A. J. Armstrong, Oxford, 1936, p. 133. This is the best contemporary account of Edward IV and Richard III, edited with particularly illuminating and comprehensive notes.

2 J. R. Langer, *The Wars of the Roses*, London, 1965, pp. 20–1.

3 p. 25.

4 Jacob, *The Fifteenth Century, op. cit.*, p. 606.

5 *The Governaunce of England*, ed. C. J. Plummer, Oxford, 1885.

6 *Letters and Papers, Illustrating the Reigns of Richard III and Henry VII*, ed. James Gairdner, *Rolls*, vol. I, p. 12.

7 Sir Thomas More's *History of King Richard the Thirde*, 1543, ed. J. R. Lumby, C.U.P., 1883.

8 Armstrong, *op. cit.*, p. 113.

9 Jacob, *op. cit.*, p. 625.

10 Paul Murray Kendall, *Richard III*, Appendix, 'Who murdered the little princes?', p. 394, London, 1955.

11 *Chronicles of London*, ed. C. L. Kingsford, Oxford, 1905, p. 191.
12 More, *op. cit.*, p. 125.
13 *History of England, op. cit.*, p. 316.
14 *Tudor Royal Proclamations, 1485–1553*, ed. P. L. Hughes and J. F. Larkin, vol. I, Yale, 1964, p. 3.
15 Hughes and Larkin, *op. cit.*, pp. xxix and xxvi.
16 *op. cit.*, p. 32.
17 A. R. Myers, *The Household of Edward IV*, Manchester, 1959.
18 Myers, *op. cit.*, p. 132.
19 *A Relation, or Rather a True Account, of the Island of England about the year 1500*, Trans. C. A. Sneyd, Camden Soc., 1847.
20 Sneyd, *op. cit.*, p. 21.
21 David Daiches, *A Critical History of English Literature*, vol. I, London, 1961, p. 134.
22 Michael Grant, *Cambridge*, London, 1966, p. 60, q.v. for a short and well-illustrated account of Cambridge humanism.
23 Grant, *op. cit.*
24 Henderson, *op. cit.*, Introduction.

Part Three Chapter 14 The Early Tudor State

1 See G. L. Harriss, 'Medieval Government and Statecraft', in *Past and Present*, July 1963, for an increasingly accepted view.
2 *A History of England, op. cit.*, p. 337.
3 British Museum, MSS, Cotton, Titus B.1, fo: 192 ff.
4 G. R. Elton, *The Tudor Revolution in Government*, London, 1953, pp. 300–2.
5 C. H. Williams, *E.H.D., op. cit.*, V, p. 15.
6 Hughes and Larkin, *Tudor Proclamations, op. cit.*, pp. 230 ff.
7 C. H. Williams, *E.H.D., op. cit.*, V, p. 19.
8 J. D. F. Shrewsbury, 'Henry VIII, a medical study', in *Journal of the History of Medicine and Allied Sciences*, vol. III, 1952, pp. 144–85. For a general treatment of the problem, see my *Henry VIII*, London, 1964, pp. 159–61.
9 Hughes and Larkin, *op. cit.*, p. 352.
10 *op. cit.*, p. 356.
11 In *E.H.D.*, V, *op. cit.*, p. 673. *A Supplication for the Beggars, 1528*, by Simon Fish, 1–15, q.v.
12 W. Thomas, *History of Italye*, 1549, p. 77.
13 vide infra, p. 253.
14 See A. G. Dickens, *The English Reformation*, London, 1967, p. 199.
15 See W. C. Richardson, *History of the Court of Augmentations, 1536–54*, Baton Rouge, 1961, for an illuminating account.
16 J. K. McConica, *English Humanists and the Reformation*, Oxford, 1965.
17 *E.H.D., op. cit.*, V, p. 1049–50.
18 *ibid.*, p. 1070.
19 *ibid.*, p. 686.
20 *ibid.*, pp. 619 ff.

21 Hughes and Larkin, *op. cit., p. 122.*
22 C. H. Williams, *E.H.D., op. cit.,* V, pp. 30–1.
23 For a full discussion of the rise in rents see A. G. Dickens, *The English Reformation,* London, *op. cit.,* pp. 213–17.
24 See Denys Hay's edition, Camden Society, LXXIV, 1950, and the same writer's admirable *Polydore Vergil, Renaissance Historian and Man of Letters,* Oxford, 1952.
25 Borde, *op. cit.,* p. 74.
26 Walter Raleigh, *Shakespeare,* London, 1925, p. 2.

Part Three   Chapter 15   Protestant and Catholic Reactions

1 W. K. Jordan, *The Chronicles and Political Papers of Edward VI,* Cornell, 1966, the best edition: pp. xiiff.
2 Trevelyan, *History of England, op. cit.,* p. 318.
3 R. J. Mitchell and M. D. R. Leys, *A History of the English People,* London, 1950, p. 214.
4 H. M. F. Prescott, *Mary Tudor,* New York, 1962, p. 166, q.v.
5 *The Colloquies of Erasmus,* trans. C. R. Thompson, Chicago, 1965, q.v. for the best complete edition of this attractive and many-sided work.
6 *E.H.D., op. cit.,* V, pp. 826 ff.
7 A. G. Dickens, *op. cit.,* p. 302.
8 *Vocacyon of John Bale.* Harleian Misc: VI, pp. 411 ff.
9 A. L. Rowse, *Tudor Cornwall,* London, 1941, p. 14.
10 p. 166.
11 Edith Sitwell, *The Queens and the Hive,* London, 1962, p. 28, q.v. for a brilliant evocation of the atmosphere and drama of the time.
12 Foxe, *op. cit.,* vol. VI, p. 728.
13 F. W. Russell, *Kett's Rebellion in Norfolk, being a History of the Great Civil Commotion,* London, 1859, p. 159.
14 p. 57.
15 Mitchell and Leys, *op. cit.,* p. 194.
16 Richard Hakluyt, *Voyages and Documents,* selected Janet Hampden, Oxford, 1958, p. 11.
17 p. 35.

Part Three   Chapter 16   The Elizabethan Age

1 *The Letters of Queen Elizabeth and King James VI of Scotland,* ed. John Bruce, Camden, 1849, p. 76, q.v. for an authentic close-up. The best modern biography is J. E. Neale's *Queen Elizabeth,* London, 1934.
2 Neale, *Essays, op. cit.,* p. 92.
3 *Memorials of the Rebellion in 1569,* ed. C. Sharp, London, 1841, p. 240.
4 *Nugae Antiquae, op. cit.,* vol. I, p. 9.
5 Ramsey, *Tudor Economic Problems, op. cit.,* pp. 159–61.
6 By I. B. in 'Sorrows Joy, The Cambridge Poems on the Death of Queen

Elizabeth,' 1603; in John Nichols's *The Progresses of James I*, 1828, vol. I, p. 16.

7   'A Short Treatise on Politick Power', *E.H.D., op. cit.*, V. pp. 625–7. It was written at Strasbourg in 1556.

8   W. T. MacCaffrey, 'Place and Patronage in Elizabethan Politics', in *Elizabethan Government and Society, op. cit.*, p. 97.

9   pp. 99 ff.

10 J. E. Neale, *Elizabeth and her Parliaments*, 1559–81, New York, 1958, p. 15.

11 A. L. Rowse, *The England of Elizabeth*, London, 1950, p. 305.

12 Cited by A. L. Rowse, *op. cit.*, p. 121. From J. W. Burgon. *Life and Times of Sir Thomas Gresham*, p. 485.

13 See Ramsey, *op. cit.*, for a good summary of the conditions, pp. 83 ff.

14 A. L. Rowse, *op. cit.*, p. 98, q.v. for the best short account.

15 p. 100.

16 *Britannia*, London, 1607, pp. 176–86, map p. 175. The most attractive translation remains *Britannia*, or a Chorographical Description ... translated into English, with additions and improvements by Edmund Gibson, D. D., 2 vols. London (3rd edition), 1753.

17 *op. cit.*, pp. 346–52.

18 K. R. Andrews, *Elizabethan Privateering, English Privateering during the Spanish War, 1585–1603*, London, 1965, p. 40.

19 Garrett Mattingly, *The Defeat of the Spanish Armada*, London, 1959, p. 226. This classic supersedes previous descriptions and sets the event in a European context.

20 p. 15.

21 Hakluyt, *op. cit.*, p. 367.

22 Quoted by J. H. Elliott on 'The Decline of Spain', in *Crisis in Europe 1560–1660*, ed. Trevor Aston, London, 1965, p. 193.

23 D. B. Quinn, *The Elizabethans and the Irish*, Cornell, 1966, pp. 16–17, on which this account is partly based.

24 Quinn, *op. cit.*, p. 32.

25 A. L. Rowse, *The Expansion of Elizabethan England*. London, 1955, p. 429.

26 Rowse, *op. cit.*, p. 436.

Part Three   Chapter 17   Jacobean England

1   M.P. Pickel, *Charles I as Patron of Poetry and Drama*, London, 1936, p. 1, q.v. for the best account.

2   D. Harris Willson, *James VI and I*, London, 1956, p. 168.

3   John Hacket, *Scrinia Reserata*, A Memorial ... of John Williams D.D., Lord Archbishop of York, London, 1692, p. 39.

4   D. Harris Willson, *op. cit.*, p. 36.

5   Hacket, *op. cit.*, p. 39.

6   *A Selection from the Harleian Miscellany*, London, 1793, A History of the Gunpowder Treason, pp. 250–8 *passim*.

7   C.V.S.P., *op. cit.*, vol. X, item 475

8 Wilson, *op. cit.*, pp. 201–2.
9 Menna Prestwich, *Cranfield*, Oxford, 1965, p. 45, q.v. for a thorough account of these and of subsequent vicissitudes.
10 Ellis, *op. cit.*, vol. III, p. 113.
11 See his illuminating 'Sir Edward Coke – Myth Maker', in *The Intellectual Origins of the English Revolution*, Oxford, 1965, pp. 227 ff.
12 Hill, *op. cit.*, p. 257.
13 *ibidem.*
14 Quoted by Ben McCary, *Indians in Seventeenth Century Virginia*, Williamstown, Va. 1957, pp. 14–15.
15 *Narrative of Virginia*, 1609, reprinted London, Chiswick Press, 1872, p. 1.
16 Ralphe Horner, *A True Discourse of the Present State of Virginia*, London, 1615, p. 2.
17 Smith, *op. cit.*, p. 205.
18 S. E. Morison, *Three Centuries of Harvard*, Harvard, 1965, p. 9.
19 See Victor Harris, *All Coherence Gone*, New York, 1949, for an illuminating account.
20 Christopher Hill, *The Intellectual Origins of the English Revolution*, Oxford, 1965. See in particular chapters III and IV on the influence of Bacon and Ralegh.
21 John Summerson, *Inigo Jones*, Penguin Books, 1966, p. 13.
22 Walter Raleigh, *Shakespeare*, London, 1925, p. 105.
23 *op. cit.*, p. 213.

Part Three   Chapter 18   The Civil Wars and the English Republic

1 Charles Wilson, *England's Apprenticeship 1603–1763*, London, 1965, pp. 109–10.
2 D. Brunton and D. H. Pennington, *Members of the Long Parliament, November 1640–53*, London, 1954, p. 178.
3 Quoted by J. H. Hexter, *The Reign of King Pym*, Harvard, 1941, p. 9.
4 'Social Mobility in England', *Past and Present*, 1966.
5 Lawrence Stone, *The Crisis of the Aristocracy, 1558–1641*, Oxford, 1965, p. 7.
6 C. V. Wedgwood, *The King's Peace*, London, 1958, p. 65, q.v. for the best evocation of the times.
7 Laud's *Works*, Library of Anglo-Catholic Theology, vol. V, Oxford, 1852, p. 349.
8 F. J. Varley, *Cambridge During the Civil War*, Cambridge, 1935, p. 23.
9 Clarendon, *Selections*, ed. G. Huehns, Oxford, 1955, p. 358.
10 See his criticism of Dobb and Hobsbawm in *Crisis in Europe*, ed. Trevor Aston, London, 1963, pp. 59–95.
11 *The King's Servants, The Civil Service of Charles I, 1625–42*, London, 1961, p. 335.
12 A. H. Burne and Peter Young, *The Great Civil War*, London, 1959, p. 234.
13 *Charles I and Cromwell*, London, 1935, pp. 144–5.
14 *State Papers of John Thurloe*, ed. T. Birch, vol. III, London, 1742, p. 445.

15 Charles Wilson, *op. cit.*, p. 63.
16 Mary Coate, *Cornwall in the Civil War*, Oxford, 1960, p. 352.
17 Joseph Frank, *The Levellers*, Harvard, 1940, and William Haller, *Liberty and Reformation in Puritan England*, New York, 1955.
18 Leo F. Solt, *Saints in Arms*, Stanford 1966, q.v,. for the best account which has discredited much tendentious interpretation.
19 Joseph Frank, *The Beginnings of the English Newspaper*, 1620–1660, p. 272.
20 Aubrey's *Brief Lives*, ed. Oliver Lawson Dick, London, 1950, pp. 128–30.
21 Solt, *op. cit.*, p. 28.
22 Robert Burton, *The Anatomy of Melancholy*, vol. III, London, 1923, p. 162.
23 *op. cit.*, p. 438.
24 *op. cit.*, p. 463.
25 Browne, Book III (ed. 1672), p. 208.
26 *op. cit.*, Book IV, p. 238.
27 *op. cit.*, Book VI, p. 377.

Part Four   Chapter 19   The Later Stuarts

1   Thomas Fuller, *The History of the Worthies of England in Church and State*, abridged ed., London, 1684, p. 160.
2   Bishop Burnet, *History of his Life and Times,* ed. T. Stackhouse, Everyman, London, 1906, p. 30.
3   *The Reign of King Pym, op. cit.*, p. 16.
4   *E.H.D., op. cit.*, vol. VIII, 1660–1714, ed. Andrew Browning, London, 1953, p. 4.
5   J. H. Plumb, *The Growth of Political Stability in England*, London, 1967, p. 98.
6   Leopold von Ranke, *History of England*, vol. IV, pp. 364 ff.
7   Selection from the *Harleian Miscellany, op. cit.*, p. 471.
8   L. Pinkham, *William III and the Respectable Revolution*, Harvard, 1954, p. 186.
9   Plumb, *op. cit.*, p. 194.
10 Plumb, *op. cit.*, p. 99.
11 Churchill, *op. cit.*, vol. III, p. 14.
12 J. H. Elliott, *Imperial Spain*, London, 1963, p. 368.
13 Quoted in Wilson, *op. cit.*, p. 208.
14 *op. cit.*, p. 376.
15 *op. cit.*, p. 371.
16 *op. cit.*, p. 234.
17 Ralph Davis, 'English Foreign Trade 1660–1700', *Econ.H.R.*, 2nd series VII (1954), 2. Reprinted E. M. Carus Wilson (ed.), *Essays in Economic History*, vol. II, London, 1962. See also K. Berrill, 'International Trade and the Rate of Economic Growth', *Econ. H.R.*, 1960, p. 358.
18 See my *Hobbes and his Critics*, London, 1951.
19 *Brief Lives, op. cit.*, pp. 5, 83, 205.

Part Four   Chapter 20   Oligarchy and First Empire

1   Lord Hervey's *Memoirs*, ed. and abridged Romney Sedgwick, London, 1952, p. 98.
2   Burnet, *op. cit.*, p. 390.
3   Boswell's *Life of Johnson*, vol. I, Oxford, 1927, p. 30.
4   Plumb, *op. cit.*, p. xv.
5   *op. cit.*, p. 187.
6   Richard Pares, *George III and the Politicians*, Oxford, 1954, p. 176.
7   John B. Owen, *The Rise of the Pelhams*, London, 1957, pp. 38–9.
8   Hervey, *op. cit.*, p. 100.
9   Plumb, *op. cit.*, p. 198.
10 J. H. Plumb, *Sir Robert Walpole*, vol. I, London, 1956. pp. 305, 309, 359.
11 J. B. Owen, *op. cit.*, p. 62.
12 Sir Charles Grant Robertson, *Chatham and the British Empire*, London, 1946, pp. 11 and 19.
13 Owen, *op. cit.*, p. 62.
14 Quoted by Sir Lewis Namier, *The Structure of Politics at the Accession of George III*, London, 1962 (2nd ed.), p. 6.
15 *op. cit.*, pp. 7–8.
16 E. P. Thompson, *The Making of the English Working Class*, Vintage Books, New York, 1966, p. 79.
17 Quoted from Hervey by Plumb, *op. cit.*, p. 88.
18 *History of England, op. cit.*, p. 669.
19 *The Diary of the Late George Bubb Doddington*, Baron of Melcombe Regis, 1749–61, ed. Henry Penruddock Wyndham, 1785, p. 422.
20 Grant Robertson, *op. cit.*, p. 86.
21 Pares, *op. cit.*, p. 64.
22 *op. cit.*, p. 67.
23 Esmond Wright, *Washington and the American Revolution*, London, 1957, p. 51.
24 Elizabeth Longford, *Wellington, the Years of the Sword*, London, 1970, pp. 47–8, q.v. for an admirable retrospect.
25 Philip Woodruff, *The Men who Ruled India*, London (paperback) 1963, vol. I, p. 103, q.v. for the Indian background. See also Sir Percival Spear, *Twilight of the Mughuls*, Cambridge, 1961.
26 See Caroline Robbins, *The Eighteenth Century Commonwealthman*, Harvard, 1958, for the best account.
27 See S. Maccoby, *English Radicalism, 1762–85*, London, 1955.
28 See my *Politics and Opinion in the Nineteenth Century*, London, 1954 and New York, 1964, pp. 51–66, for a short account.
29 David Owen, *English Philanthropy, 1660–1960*, Harvard, 1964, p. 13.
30 *Memoirs and Portraits*, ed. M. Hodgart, London, 1963, p. 10.
31 *op. cit.*, p. 129.
32 *op. cit.*, p. 153.

NOTES

Part Four   Chapter 21   The Napoleonic Wars and the Industrial Revolution

1 See W. W. Rostow, *The Stages of Economic Growth*, London, 1964.
2 *The Age of Improvement*, London, 1959, p. 17.
3 Thompson, *op. cit.*, and George Rudé, *The Crowd in History 1730–1848*, New York, 1965.
4 Pares, *op. cit.*, p. 130.
5 *Vide* Holland Rose, *William Pitt and the Great War, op. cit.*, p. 274.
6 Felix Markham, *Napoleon*, London, 1963, p. 104.
7 *The Conversations of the First Duke of Wellington with George William Chad*, ed. by the Seventh Duke of Wellington, Cambridge, 1956, p. 2.
8 See Elizabeth Longford, *op. cit.*, particularly strong on the geographical setting.
9 See Gerald S. Graham, *Great Britain in the Indian Ocean, A study of Maritime Enterprise, 1810–1850*, Oxford, 1968, for the minor but exacting responsibility discharged in this strategically important area.
10 Michael Edwards, *Glorious Sahibs*, London, 1968, p. 193.
11 Philip Woodruff, *op. cit.*, vol. I, *The Golden Age, 1798–1858*, pp. 183 ff.
12 Edwards, *op. cit.*, p. 232.
13 p. 234.
14 Quoted by E. L. Woodward, *The Age of Reform*, Oxford, 1938, p. 196, q.v. for the best short assessment.
15 H. W. V. Temperley, *The Life of Canning*, ed. 1965. This is still the best account of one of the most original of English statesmen.
16 L. S. Pressnell, *Country Banking in the Industrial Revolution*, and D. M. Joslin, 'London Private Bankers 1720–85', *Econ. H.R.*, 2nd series, vol. VII, no. 2.
17 *A Six Weeks Tour through the Southern Counties of England and Wales*, by the Author of the Farmers' Letters (3rd ed.), London, 1772, p. 3.
18 'Technological Change and Development in Western Europe, 1750–1914', *The Industrial Revolution in Britain*, pp. 274–352, in *The Cambridge Economic History of Europe*, vol. IV, pt. 1, Cambridge, 1965, q.v. for the best short account.
19 Steven Watson, *The Reign of George III*, Oxford, 1960, p. 529.
20 Quoted from Young, *Tour Through the North of England*, in Paul Mantoux, *The Industrial Revolution in the Eighteenth Century*, p. 173. Revised edition with a preface by T. S. Ashton. Methuen paperbacks, London, 1961, p. 345. This is still the most readable and comprehensive survey.
21 Mantoux, *op. cit.*, p. 214. He wrote *Constantia, Almine and Elvira, the Princess of Peace*, and *Sonnets to Eminent Men*.
22 Landes, *op. cit., passim*.
23 Phyllis Deane and W. A. Cole, *British Economic Growth 1688–1959*, Cambridge, 1964, p. 212.
24 See Gwyn Williams, *Artisans and Sans Culottes, Popular Movements in France and Britain during the Industrial Revolution*, London, 1968, pp. 3 and 4.
25 Gwyn Williams, *op. cit.*, p. 144.

26 Thompson, *op. cit.*, p. 12.
27 Quoted *op. cit.*, p. 238.
28 George Rudé, *The Crowd in History, 1730–1848, op. cit.*, New York, 1965, p. 234.
29 *The Creevey Papers*, ed. John Gore, London (paperback), 1963.
30 *Gore, op. cit.*, p. 177.
31 Wellington *Conversations, op. cit.*, p. 12.
32 Robert Blake, *Disraeli*, London, 1966, p. 51, q.v. for a good account of his political influence even on Disraeli's generation.

Part Four   Chapter 22   The Mid-Victorians

1 Deane and Cole, *op. cit.*, p. 298.
2 *C.E.H.E., op. cit.*, vol. VI, pt. 1, p. 353.
3 p. 352.
4 Blake, *op. cit.*, pp. 272–3.
5 H. C. F. Bell, *Lord Palmerston, 1784–1865*, vol. I, London, 1936, p. 261. This American biography is still rewarding.
6 Woodward, *The Age of Reform, 1815–1879, op. cit.*, p. 212.
7 Blake, *op. cit.*; Norman Gash, *Mr Secretary Peel*, London, 1961, and Sir Philip Magnus, *Gladstone, a biography*, London, 1954.
8 Woodward, *op. cit.*, p. 312, q.v. for the best short elucidation of the complicated Schleswig-Holstein question.
9 Deane and Cole, *op. cit.*, p. 282
10 Rudé, *op cit.*, p. 180.
11 *op. cit.*, p. 182.
12 Woodward, *op. cit.*, p. 153.
13 Sir Isaiah Berlin, *Two Concepts of Liberty*, Oxford, 1958, p. 56.
14 Noel Annan in *The English Mind*, ed. H. S. Davies and George Watson, Cambridge, 1964, pp. 219–39 and 235.
15 See J. S. Mill, *On Liberty* and *Considerations on Representative Government*, ed. with an introduction by R. B. McCallum, Oxford, 1948. Also my *Politics and Opinion in the Nineteenth Century*, London, 1954, pp. 194–208, for an attempt to set Mill in his European context.
16 See his *The English Constitution*, 1867 and *Physics and Politics*, London, 1872.
17 See Charles Darwin, *The Voyage of the Beagle*, ed. Leonard Engel, Doubleday Anchor Books, New York, 1962, p. x; T. H. Huxley's Diary of the *Voyage of the Rattlesnake*, ed. Julian Huxley, London, 1935.
18 Engel, *op. cit.*, p. xxii.
19 G. M. Young, *Victorian England, Portrait of an Age*, Oxford (paperback), 1961, p. 158.
20 Kenneth Clark, *The Gothic Revival*, Pelican, London, 1962, p. 206, q.v. for the best account.
21 Young, *op. cit.*, p. 111.
22 Christopher Hollis, *Eton*, London, 1966, p. 276.

Part Four   Chapter 23   Climax of Empire

1   Quoted by James Morris in *Pax Britannica. The Climax of an Empire*. London, 1968, p. 177. This vivid evocation in terms of people and places is an admirable general account of the Empire in 1897.
2   *op. cit.*, pp. 451–2.
3   Sir Philip Magnus, *King Edward the Seventh*, 1964, for the best account.
4   R. C. K. Ensor, *England 1870–1914*, Oxford, 1936, p. 17.
5   See Harold Nicolson, *George V; his Life and Reign*, London, 1952, for an admirable and comprehensive biography.·
6   Sir Herbert Maxwell, *Sixty Years a Queen*, London, 1897. This period piece and its illustrations well recalls the atmosphere of the time.

Epilogue

1   G. M. Trevelyan, *Grey of Fallodon*, p. 266, London, 1937.
2   *vide supra*. p. vii.
3   C. R. M. F. Cruttwell, *A History of the Great War, 1914–18*, Oxford, 1934, pp. 1–2.
4   A. J. P. Taylor, *English History, 1915–1945*, Oxford, 1965, p. 2.
5   A. Marwick, *Britain in the Century of Total War, War, Peace and Social Change*, London, 1968, p. 16.
6   Cruttwell, *op. cit.*, p. 630.
7   Broadcast of 5th February, quoted in G. M. Young, *Stanley Baldwin*, London, 1952, pp. 188–9.
8   R. Robinson and J. Gallagher, with Alice Denny, *Africa and the Victorians, The Official Mind of Empire*, London, 1961, q.v. for the best account.
9   J. C. Beaglehole, 'The British Commonwealth of Nations' in *The New Cambridge Modern History*, vol. XII, 1962, p. 552.
10 For a thorough account of the background see Monica Wilson and Leonard Thompson, (ed.) *The Oxford History of South Africa to 1870*, Oxford, 1968. And for the best short survey C. W. De Kiewiet. *A History of South Africa, Social and Economic*, Oxford, 1951.
11 A. J. P. Taylor, *op. cit.*, p. 599.
12 Sir Llewellyn Woodward, 'Will Civilization Survive?' *Journal of Historical Studies*, London, 1967, q.v. for a realistic appraisal.
13 *A History of England; Principally in the Seventeenth Century*, vol. IV, London, 1875, p. 500.

INDEX

Malplaquet, battle of, 353
Malthus, Rev. Thomas, 409, 413
Mandeville, Geoffrey de, 91
manorial system, 57–8, 69, 73, 188; manor courts, 57, 58, 126
Mantes, siege of, 87
Map, Walter, and Louis VII's remark on Henry II, 104; his *de nugis curialium* on superstitions, 117n.; on Court of Henry II and Marlburian French, 117; background, 117n.
March, Roger Mortimer, Earl of, 163
Marcher Lordships, centres of disaffection, 171–2, 199
Margaret (Queen of Edward I), 157
Margaret (Queen of Henry VI), 206, 221, 231–2
Margaret (Queen of James IV of Scotland), 224
Margaret Maultasche, Duchess of Tyrol, 192
Margaret of Norway, death of, 172
Margaret, Regent of the Netherlands, 227
Margaret of York, Dowager of Burgundy, 226
Maria Theresa, Queen of Hungary, 371–2
Marie de Medici, Queen of France, 315
Marlborough, Celtic drinking cup at, 13, 91; Map on bad French of, 117; John goes fishing there, 120; death of 1st Earl of Salisbury at, described, 297 and n.; mentioned, 37, 91n., 111, 161, 165
Marlborough, John, 1st Duke of, 350, 351, 353, 354, 355, 414, 462
Marlborough, Sarah, Duchess, 354
Marlowe, Christopher, 161, 256, 304, 307–8
Marston Moor, battle of, 312, 324
Marx, Karl, 249, 440
Mary I, Queen, 257, 260–2, 265, 268, 270, 279, 285, 296
Mary II, Queen, 234, 344, 345–6, 348, 352, 414; *see also* William III
Mary (Queen of George V), 464
Mary of Medina (Queen of James II), 345

Mary, Queen of Scots, 259, 274–5 277
Mary Henrietta (daughter of Charles I), 346
Masefield, John, 441, 456
Massachusetts Bay Company, 303
masques, 306, 336, 390
Matilda, Empress, 22, 78, 90–2, 93, 98
Matilda (Queen of William I), 83
Maximilian, Emperor, Henry VIII displays James IV of Scotland's tartan to, 239
mead, considered a rustic drink, 148; mentioned, 284
medicine, Anglo-Saxon, 62; fourteenth century, 213–14, 360; and George III, 376–7, 377n.; eighteenth century advances in, 387–8; and vaccination, 414–15; nineteenth century developments, 419–20; in twentieth century, 452–3, 461, 473
Megalithic religions, 6–7, 8–9, 42
Melbourne, William Lamb, 2nd Viscount, 421, 422, 423
merchant navy, 313, 341, 418, 420, 438, 444, 450, 472, 476
Merchant Adventurers, 282
merchants, their growing importance, 114, 138; protection of, 166; Richard II's forced loans from, 185; importance in cities, 207; during Civil Wars, 318; and charities, 386; in nineteenth century, 413
Meredith ap Theodore, ancestor of Tudors, 223
Methodists, 390, 411
Miesceslas, Duke of Poland, maternal grandfather of Knut, 67
Mile End, Richard II's confrontation with peasants at, 189
Milford Haven, Henry VII's landing at, 223
Mill, J. S., 210, 427, 429–30, 440
Millenary Petition (1603), 296
The Millitarie Instruction for Cavallrie (Cruso), Oliver Cromwell's probable debt to, 32
Milton, John, 22–3, 304, 323, 332, 335–6, 383
Minden, battle of, 374

mining, under Roman occupation, 28, 113; Anglo-Saxon, 70, 114; under Angevins, 113–14; iron, 207, 292, 356, 405, 407, 418, 427, 450; tin, 207, 356; under Henry VII, 230; copper, 283; lead, 356
Minorca, 349, 353, 375
miracle plays, 306–7
missionaries, Celtic, 13, 41–2; Anglo-Saxon, 44, 45–6, 47; Evangelical, 403, 433
monasteries, Anselm and, 97; wealth of, 97, 230, 247–8; discipline in, 97–8; historians in, 98; economic enterprise of, 112; learning in, 98, 99, 247, 266; new foundations, 98; and anti-clericalism, 167, 247; dissolution of, 168, 246–8, 250, 264, 266
Monk, General George, 322, 339, 363
Mons Graupius, 24, 25
Montrose, James Graham, Earl of, 324
Moore, G. E., philosopher, 453
Moore, Henry, 476
Montfort, Simon de, Earl of Leicester, popular support for, 137, 145, 146; death of, at Evesham, 137, 145; opposition to Henry III, 137; 140, 143–5; his victory at Lewes, 140; background, wealth and power of, 143n.; and *Provisions of Oxford*, 144–5; anti-Semitism of, 145, 168; his capture of Henry III at Lewes, 145; alliance with Welsh, 145; poem on, 146
Montfort d'Amauri, 143
More, Sir Thomas, on Richard III, 222, 223; his *Utopia*, 232, 235; defends Universal Church, 243; death, 243; and Tyndale, 249; prose style, 253; humanism, 304
Morris, William, 434, 453
Mount Baden, Celtic victory at, probably near Bath, 37, 38
Mughul Empire, 381, 383, 402, 403
Mulcaster, Richard, schoolmaster, 333
Mun, Thomas, economist, 358
music, in thirteenth century, 148; Henry VIII's enjoyment of, 305; Elizabethan, 305, 310; Jacobean, 305, 310; in Germany, 305; Restoration, 351; eighteenth